AMERICAN GOVERNMENT

American Government:

READINGS AND DOCUMENTS

PETER H. ODEGARD, editor

HARPER & ROW, Publishers

New York, Evanston, and London

Contents

Preface

THIS BOOK contains documents, memoirs and other public papers, court cases, presidential messages, excerpts from books and journals, public speeches, and other significant statements which illuminate and supplement various problems and policies of American government and politics.

This reader was designed at the time of writing *The American Republic: Its Government and Politics,* by Peter H. Odegard and Hans H. Baerwald. Nevertheless, it may be used with other textbooks, or independently of any text.

The Declaration of Independence and the Constitution of the United States are included in full. Many of the other documents and readings have been shortened by omitting paragraphs or sections which are tangential in nature. In making these excisions, however, we have taken care not to sacrifice any essential idea or fact.

Wherever possible, we have included materials which present different points of view on controversial issues.

The purpose of these readings is to give a broader and deeper understanding of the difficult and important problems posed in the course and in the basic text. The readings can also be used profitably in preparing essays or in conducting class or group discussions devoted to these problems.

January, 1964   PETER H. ODEGARD

AMERICAN GOVERNMENT

1

The New Leviathan

1.1. THE CHANGING FUNCTIONS OF GOVERNMENT

One persistent trend in recent history has been the steady expansion of the role of government in nearly every aspect of life. As the author points out in this analysis, the trend is due to a number of factors, over many of which government has had little control. Opposition to the expansion of the State's activities emphasizes the dangers of unlimited governmental power to individual freedom and the stifling effect of overregulation upon a free-enterprise economy.

UNDERLYING THE SLOGANS of the Welfare State are ancient problems which have confronted men and women in all ages. The struggle for freedom has a long history and has taken on different forms in various communities. The fight for liberty has been directed against the crushing weight of tribal custom, the restrictive legalism of priestly class and church, and the tyranny of king or emperor. Today we are only too well aware of the fact that the lamp of freedom, if not altogether extinguished, burns very dimly in many parts of the world. Hundreds of millions of people live in daily fear of the oppressive hand of the police state. . . .

EXTENSION OF GOVERNMENTAL POWERS

In order to achieve perspective on the controversial issues of the Welfare State, it is necessary to refer briefly to the changing functions of the American government.

Despite the individualistic tradition and laissez-faire philosophy

From Asher Achinstein, *The Welfare State* (Washington, D. C.: Library of Congress Legislative Reference Service, June 1950, Public Affairs Bulletin No. 83), pp. 13–40.

1

that dominated the thinking of the United States for a longer period than that of other nations, Americans did not hesitate to approve the expansion of governmental powers. From the early days of the Republic the Federal Government took positive steps to promote the economic development of the country. The protective tariff was enacted to encourage domestic manufacturing; bounties were given to shipowners to promote a merchant marine; and Federal subsidies were granted for the construction of Western railroads in the form of 180 millions of acres of public land. Millions of acres of federally owned lands were also given in aid of education, canal building, and river improvements. To stimulate the settlement of the West the Homestead Act of 1862 and other land acts gave over 200 million acres of public lands free to bona-fide settlers. These grants also had the effect of serving as a species of governmental work relief for those who found it difficult to earn their living in the older sections of the country, or who wanted to strike out on their own.

With the rapid pace of industrialization that took place after the Civil War, government began to assume the functions of regulator of business enterprise, in addition to using funds and public resources to promote business enterprise. The growth of regulation was the response to grievances felt by important segments of the population. When farmers experienced agricultural depression in the 1870s, they turned for relief to state governments to protect them through a series of regulatory laws against the high rates charged by railroads and against discriminatory practices. Finding that state regulation was inadequate to meet the problem, the dissatisfied groups pressed for federal legislation. As a consequence, the Interstate Commerce Commission was established in 1887 to regulate the railroads. When public sentiment reacted against long hours of work of the economically weakest workers and against hazardous working conditions, the states began to adopt protective labor legislation regulating maximum hours for women and children, to require the installation of safety apparatus in factories and mines as well as factory inspection, and to enact workmen's compensation laws against accidents. When business corporations formed pools, combinations, and monopolies, small-business men, farmers, and consumers turned to government to restore competition. The Sherman Anti-Trust Act was passed in 1890, and the Federal Trade Commission and Clayton Acts in 1914. The Federal Government as regulator was manifest in a wide range of industries. Protection of consumer interests is exhibited through the enactment of the Meat Inspection and Pure Food and Drug Laws; of banking, in the establishment of the Federal Reserve Board; of power, in the Federal Power Commission. The depressed state of agriculture in the 1920s led to the creation of such legislation as the Agricultural Credit Act of 1923, the Cooperative Marketing Act of 1926, and the establishment of the Federal Farm Board of 1931.

Following in the wake of our severe economic breakdown after 1929, people everywhere turned to the Federal Government for relief and greater security. Because every section suffered from the depression, there was almost universal demand and support for the use of the powers of the Federal Government to alleviate the situation. Beginning in 1933 the Federal Government vastly increased its responsibilities in the fields of public aid, working conditions, conservation, farming, and housing. It is now seeking to enter more energetically in the fields of education and health. . . .

IMPACT OF SCIENCE AND TECHNOLOGY UPON CHANGING FUNCTIONS OF THE STATE

Why did the increasing powers of the state take place? The answer given by those who see the necessity for further extension of government powers is science and technology. Industrialism not only made possible the rapid growth of population but also brought about the concentration of population in urban centers. A city population became dependent for its livelihood and conditions of work upon factories and upon distant markets for the sale of its products. These firms increased in size with the advantages of large-scale production and the requirements of the machine technology. Corporate enterprises began to dominate increasing areas of economic activity, culminating in the concentration of control by a few firms of the production and prices of their industries. Industrial policies were adopted restricting competition.

In congregating people into cities, the machine was directly and indirectly responsible for overcrowding and for conditions creating the problems of slums. In the absence of adequate municipal regulation of land utilization, housing was constructed which in a generation became known as blighted areas. Factories could belch forth their smoke upon the surrounding dwellings without let or hindrance. Tenements were erected without adequate light and air or decent sanitary facilities. As a result of unregulated site utilization and the lack of zoning and city planning, we have a heritage of miles of slum areas today which many believe cannot be reconstructed without the cooperation of the Federal Government.

Science and technology also require a greater amount of schooling than was necessary in a pre-industrial civilization. The multiplicity of highly diverse occupations called forth by modern machines and appliances requires a broader schooling than the traditional three "R's." Although America has been outstanding in the world for providing free schooling for more than a century, the fact remains that areas of the country which have not benefited from the higher incomes obtained in highly industrialized areas, or from sections rich in raw materials or minerals essential to manufacturing, can afford to spend relatively little for public education. With some children receiving no elementary education at all and a larger number a very substandard education, many persons who are concerned about developiñg an intelligent citizenry are seeking for ways of equalizing educational opportunities. They are convinced that this objective cannot be achieved without federal aid to public education.

Another impact of science and technology has been the decline in the death rate. The improvement of the standard of living which the rapid strides in productivity made possible and the advance in medical knowledge and hygiene have greatly prolonged the average length of life. Industry, however, tends to give preference in employment to younger people. This has augmented the problem of affording security to the aged and their dependents. . . .

THE ISSUES OF FREEDOM VERSUS SECURITY

The issues which divide men and women on the Welfare State originate in the fact that its philosophy and program require the further expansion of the powers of government, especially the Federal Government. Its supporters regard the enactment of federal legislation to increase individual security as a necessary condition for the exercise of freedom. Its opponents look upon the multiplication of centralized controls as producing a decline of liberty and the weakening of the moral fibre of the nation. One group sees in such legislation a widening of individual opportunity, the other group regards it as weakening individual responsibility.

The problem of security versus freedom has its economic as well as political aspects. The upholders of the Welfare State look upon the extension of governmental powers as a necessary condition for the preservation of the free enterprise system; its opponents maintain that strengthening of these tendencies spells the ultimate doom of free enterprise.

Supporters of the Welfare State, as well as those who are against it, avow that they wish to maintain the free enterprise system. Their economic differences arise from different evaluations of the effect of the extension of governmental powers upon the functioning of the economic system. Those who are against greater governmental controls argue that such expansion destroys incentives for investment, fosters an inflexible price system, makes necessary increased taxation and deficit financing, and creates a situation that inhibits technological progress. In short, according to its opponents, the Welfare State not only strengthens the tendencies for restricting freedom of individuals through an expanding government bureaucracy, but it also raises doubts as to the ability of the economy to maintain the rate of economic progress which we have known in the past and which has produced an ever increasing standard of living for the American people. These are some of the problems that must be weighed by those who use the slogans of the Welfare State and kindred labels.

THE INDIVIDUAL AND THE STATE AS VIEWED BY PROPONENTS OF WELFARE STATE

Underlying the views of the proponents of the Welfare State are concepts of the individual and the State which differ from those held by many of its opponents. The doctrine of individualism as self-help is replaced by the view that unless social conditions are devised in which free individuals can thrive, talk about individualism is only an apology for the status quo. It is pointed out that the loudest spokesman for freedom today is Big Business, which desires to maintain its entrenched position in industry and finance. While the demand for freedom originally came from those who sought to change existing institutions, groups interested in maintaining the prevailing situation are seeking to convince others that any attempts to change it are an attack upon freedom. . . .

. . . as soon as one raises the question of maintaining or increasing the freedom of an individual or group, one cannot avoid giving consideration to the question of the effect upon the freedom of others. The question of freedom involves social as well as individual considerations. . . .

In the place of the "negative freedom" in the sense of noninterference by the State, modern social philosophers stress "positive freedom," by which is meant that government must provide the opportunities for every individual to realize the potentialities of which he is possessed. The emphasis upon the idea that freedom is meaningless without the State providing the conditions necessary for self-realization began to appear in the 1870s in the writings of English political philosophers like T. H. Green and F. H. Bradley. Instead of pitting the individual against the State these thinkers argued that individuality can only be achieved through society; self-realization is socially conditioned. . . .

In recent years particular emphasis has been given to the question of economic security. Although science and technology give promise of liberating man from the bondage of insecurity, his mind seems to be preoccupied more than ever with insecurity. Whatever may be the causes of this concern, the fact remains that more and more persons have turned to the State as the agency for the removal of inequalities and the provider of basic securities. In many democratic countries, like the United States, Great Britain, the British self-governing Dominions, and in the Scandinavian countries, political parties have sensed this situation, accepted it, and made it the vehicle of their assumption of power. There has been a vast increase in legislation intending to provide greater security by various devices, including the socialization of certain industries and services, the provision of goods and services based on needs, and the extension of taxation based on ability to pay to finance these new and increasing activities.

According to the political scientist Charles E. Merriam, the function of the State consists in providing security, order, justice, welfare, and freedom. Recognizing that the term welfare is very vague he asks the question: "What is 'welfare' and how shall we know it when we see it?" His reply to this question is likely to be fully endorsed by the exponents of the Welfare State:

The answer is not so difficult if we bear in mind that the state is not the only human association dealing with and promoting human welfare; there is also the family, the church, and a multitude of other associations concerned with welfare in one form and another. They may, and often do, and should indeed, overlap the activities of the political society at times. But the state's interpretation of welfare is set in the constellation of security, order, justice, and freedom in a manner differing from the other societies of which men are a part, just as the state itself is set in a group of other societies as an institution. . . .

The welfare function of the state, old and new, does not consist solely or even principally in the aggregation of a wide variety of special "services" but rather in (1) increasing the productive power of the state, the total national income; (2) establishing minimum standards of living for all, based upon productive possibilities; (3) utilizing the advances made by modern technology, physical and social, in education, medicine, personality adjustment, a broad range of possibilities in the field of invention; and (4) making possible the fullest and highest development of human personality in the framework of social relations.

THE INDIVIDUAL AND THE STATE AS VIEWED BY OPPONENTS OF WELFARE STATE

Opponents of the Welfare State may accept the definition of freedom as the realization of the highest potentialities of the individual but they balk at the idea that we must greatly extend the powers of government to make this possible. They are much more fearful of the power of the State and the dangers to our freedom which such powers would entail. They are fond of quoting the statement of Lord Acton that "power corrupts and absolute power corrupts absolutely." Moreover they stress the virtues of initiative, independence, choice, and responsibility. They look upon government guaranteeing economic securities to all as ushering in the Santa Claus State. They see the impulse toward liberty losing its force and being replaced by the passion for security. . . .

Critics of the Welfare State have frequently remarked that one may have absolute security in prison and absolute equality in the graveyard.

Those who are critical of the extension of government powers argue that the goal of providing economic equality and security means giving increased authority to a governing minority. Men in control of vast government bureaucracies tend to "forget what actual human beings are like, and try to fit men into systems rather than systems to men." Economic freedom is best safeguarded by giving free play to the competitive market. We are much more likely to preserve our liberties through the impersonal character of a competitive price system than through central direction of a government bureau. The market registers the individual choice of millions of individuals, while a method of social organization where the State regulates and controls industry and trade registers the choice of a small group in the higher echelons of a government department. Those who fear the Welfare State look upon the free market as a necessary safeguard of freedom and democracy and therefore seek to keep governmental interference to a minimum. Because they pin their faith upon the free market to preserve our liberties they have a different concept of the State from those who believe that such faith can only have meaning under agrarian pioneer conditions. . . .

It would be unjust to many, if not most, persons who consider themselves opponents of the Welfare State not to mention that they do not subscribe to the extreme view . . . that the essence of the State is coercion. They may readily endorse the view that the function of the State is to promote the general welfare and yet differ from the proponents of the Fair Deal in believing that it is not necessary to extend the powers of the Federal Government. While not questioning that it is the duty of government to take steps to promote the general welfare, they assert that this only poses problems but does not solve them. They may sympathize with the desire to provide against all the contingencies of life by abolishing want and unemployment and developing programs for health, old age, etc., but they believe that they are mindful of certain realities which are overlooked by those who seek to multiply governmental expenditures. They believe that the proponents of the Welfare State are much too optimistic about our technological accomplishments, great as they are, to provide a standard of living which will assure to every family adequate food, clothing, housing, education, health, and a steady job. The power of the State to raise the standard of living is limited by what people produce. How much government can take from national income to carry out policies of redistribution of income without destroying economic incentives is a problem which they believe that the proponents of the Welfare State are inclined to ignore. The latter likewise oversimplify the degree of compulsion which the individual is likely to be subject to because of the extension of the powers of the State. Excluding the more extreme opponents of the Welfare State, the more moderate opposition is likely to agree with the statement that current debate centers around the question of how far must we go in expansion of governmental controls. In this country at least, it is mainly a question of degree of pace in government intervention rather than a real difference in kind.

1.2. THE CASE FOR ANARCHISM

Anarchists, like Emma Goldman, view the State as the greatest foe of social equality and enslaver of the human spirit. Repudiation of the State through revolution and the elimination of all governmental institutions and controls by the direct action of individuals are pictured as necessary prerequisites to the achievement of social harmony and justice.

THE GOAL OF ANARCHISM is the freest possible expression of all the latent powers of the individual. Oscar Wilde defines a perfect personality as "one who develops under perfect conditions, who is not wounded, maimed, or in danger." A perfect personality, then, is only possible in a state of society where man is free to choose the mode of work, the conditions of work, and the freedom to work. One to whom the making of a table, the building of a house, or the tilling of the soil, is what the painting is to the artist and the discovery to the scientist,—the result of inspiration, of intense longing, and deep interest in work as a creative force. That being the ideal of Anarchism, its economic arrangements must consist of voluntary productive and distributive associations, gradually developing into free communism, as the best means of producing with the least waste of human energy. . . .

Such free display of human energy being possible only under complete individual and social freedom, Anarchism directs its forces against the third and greatest foe of all social equality; namely the State, organized authority, or statutory law,—the dominion of human conduct.

Just as religion has fettered the human mind, and as property, or the monopoly of things, has subdued and stifled man's needs, so has the State enslaved his spirit, dictating every phase of conduct. "All government in essence," says Emerson, "is tyranny." It matters not whether it is government by divine right or majority rule. In every instance its aim is the absolute subordination of the individual. . . .

Indeed, the keynote of government is "injustice." With the arrogance and self-sufficiency of the King who could do no wrong, governments ordain, judge, condemn, and punish the most insignificant offenses, while maintaining themselves by the greatest of all offenses, the annihilation of individual liberty. Thus Ouida is right when she maintains that

From Emma Goldman, *Anarchism and Other Essays* (New York: Mother Earth Publishing Assoc., 1910), pp. 61–64, 72–73.

"the State only aims at instilling those qualities in its public by which its demands are obeyed, and its exchequer is filled. Its highest attainment is the reduction of mankind to clockwork. In its atmosphere all those finer and more delicate liberties, which require treatment and spacious expansion, inevitably dry up and perish. The State requires a taxpaying machine in which there is no hitch, an exchequer in which there is never a deficit, and a public, monotonous, obedient, colorless, spiritless, moving humbly like a flock of sheep along a straight high road between two walls."

Yet even a flock of sheep would resist the chicanery of the State, if it were not for the corruptive, tyrannical, and oppressive methods it employs to serve its purposes. Therefore Bakunin repudiates the State as synonymous with the surrender of the liberty of the individual or small minorities,—the destruction of social relationship, the curtailment, or complete denial even, of life itself, for its own aggrandizement. The State is the altar of political freedom and, like the religious altar, it is maintained for the purpose of human sacrifice.

In fact, there is hardly a modern thinker who does not agree that government, organized authority, or the State, is necessary *only* to maintain or protect property and monopoly. It has proven efficient in that function only. . . .

Direct action, having proved effective along economic lines, is equally potent in the environment of the individual. There a hundred forces encroach upon his being, and only persistent resistance to them will finally set him free. Direct action against the authority in the shop, direct action against the authority of the law, direct action against the invasive, meddlesome authority of our moral code, is the logical, consistent method of Anarchism.

Will it not lead to a revolution? Indeed, it will. No real social change has ever come about without a revolution. People are either not familiar with their history, or they have not yet learned that revolution is but thought carried into action.

Anarchism, the great leaven of thought, is today permeating every phase of human endeavor. Science, art, literature, the drama, the effort for economic betterment, in fact every individual and social opposition to the existing disorder of things, is illumined by the spiritual light of Anarchism. It is the philosophy of the sovereignty of the individual. It is the theory of social harmony. It is the great, surging, living truth that is reconstructing the world, and that will usher in the Dawn.

1.3. FASCISM'S EXALTATION OF THE STATE

In this selection, the founder of Italian Fascism extols the alleged virtues of total subservience of the individual to the State. To this once power-

ful Fascist, the State is an organic entity for which power and domination over others are the hallmarks of national vigor and progress.

ANTI-INDIVIDUALISTIC, the Fascist conception of life stresses the importance of the State and accepts the individual only in so far as his interests coincide with those of the State, which stands for the conscience and the universal will of man as a historic entity. It is opposed to classical liberalism which arose as a reaction to absolutism and exhausted its historical function when the State became the expression of the conscience and will of the people. Liberalism denied the State in the name of the individual; Fascism reasserts the rights of the State as expressing the real essence of the individual. And if liberty is to be the attribute of living men and not of abstract dummies invented by individualistic liberalism, then Fascism stands for liberty, and for the only liberty worth having, the liberty of the State and of the individual within the State. The Fascist conception of the State is all-embracing; outside of it no human or spiritual values can exist, much less have value. Thus understood, Fascism is totalitarian, and the Fascist State—a synthesis and a unit inclusive of all values—interprets, develops, and potentiates the whole life of a people.

No individuals or groups (political parties, cultural associations, economic unions, social classes) outside the State. Fascism is therefore opposed to socialism to which unity within the State (which amalgamates classes into a single economic and ethical reality) is unknown, and which sees in history nothing but the class struggle. Fascism is likewise opposed to trade-unionism as a class weapon. But when brought within the orbit of the State, Fascism recognises the real needs which gave rise to socialism and trade-unionism, giving them due weight in the guild or corporative system in which divergent interests are coordinated and harmonised in the unity of the State.

Grouped according to their several interests, individuals form classes; they form trade-unions when organised according to their several economic activities; but first and foremost they form the State, which is no mere matter of numbers, the sum of the individuals forming the majority. Fascism is therefore opposed to that form of democracy which equates a nation to the majority, lowering it to the level of the largest number; but it is the purest form of democracy if the nation be considered—as it should be—from the point of view of quality rather than quantity, as an idea, the mightiest because the most ethical, the most coherent, the truest, expressing itself in a people as the conscience and will of the few, if not, indeed, of one, and tending to express itself in the conscience and the will of the mass, of the whole group ethnically moulded by natural and histor-

From Benito Mussolini, *The Doctrine of Fascism* (Florence, Italy: Vallecchi Editore Firenze, 1935), pp. 13–18.

ical conditions into a nation, advancing, as one conscience and one will, along the selfsame line of development and spiritual formation. Not a race, nor a geographically defined region, but a people, historically perpetuating itself; a multitude unified by an idea and imbued with the will to live, the will to power, self-consciousness, personality.

In so far as it is embodied in a State, this higher personality becomes a nation. It is not the nation which generates the State; that is an antiquated naturalistic concept which afforded a basis for XIXth century publicity in favor of national governments. Rather is it the State which creates the nation, conferring volition and therefore real life on a people made aware of their moral unity. . . . Indeed, it is the State which, as the expression of a universal ethical will, creates the right to national independence.

A nation, as expressed in the State, is a living, ethical entity only in so far as it is progressive. Inactivity is death. Therefore the State is not only Authority which governs and confers legal form and spiritual value on individual wills, but it is also Power which makes its will felt and respected beyond its own frontiers, thus affording practical proof of the universal character of the decisions necessary to ensure its development. This implies organization and expansion, potential if not actual. Thus the State equates itself to the will of man, whose development cannot be checked by obstacles and which, by achieving self-expression, demonstrates its own infinity.

The Fascist State, as a higher and more powerful expression of personality, is a force, but a spiritual one. It sums up all the manifestations of the moral and intellectual life of man. Its functions cannot therefore be limited to those of enforcing order and keeping the peace, as the liberal doctrine had it. It is no mere mechanical device for defining the sphere within which the individual may duly exercise his supposed rights. The Fascist State is an inwardly accepted standard and rule of conduct, a discipline of the whole person; it permeates the will no less than the intellect. It stands for a principle which becomes the central motive of man as a member of civilized society, sinking deep down into his personality; it dwells in the heart of the man of action and of the thinker, of the artist and of the man of science: soul of the soul.

Fascism, in short, is not only a law-giver and a founder of institutions, but an educator and a promoter of spiritual life. It aims at refashioning not only the forms of life but their content—man, his character, and his faith. To achieve this purpose it enforces discipline and uses authority, entering into the soul and ruling with undisputed sway. . . .

The Fascist State expresses the will to exercise power and to command. Here the Roman tradition is embodied in a conception of strength. Imperial power, as understood by the Fascist doctrine, is not only territorial, or military, or commercial; it is also spiritual and ethical. An imperial nation, that is to say a nation which directly or indirectly is a leader of others, can exist without the need of conquering a single square mile of territory. Fascism sees in the imperialistic spirit—i.e. in the tendency of nations to expand—a manifestation of their vitality. In the opposite tendency, which would limit their interests to the fatherland, it sees a symptom of decadence. Peoples who rise or revive are imperialistic; renunciation is characteristic of dying peoples. The Fascist doctrine is that best suited to the tendencies and feelings of a people which, like the Italian, after lying fallow during centuries of foreign servitude, is now reasserting itself in the world.

But imperialism implies discipline, the coordination of efforts, a deep sense of duty and a spirit of self-sacrifice. . . .

Never before have the peoples thirsted for authority, direction, order, as they do now. If each age has its doctrine, then innumerable symptoms indicate that the doctrine of our age is the Fascist.

1.4. DEMOCRATIC GOVERNMENT'S RESPONSE TO CHANGING ECONOMIC CONDITIONS

In this speech during his first campaign for the Presidency, Franklin D. Roosevelt calls for the use of governmental power to control the abuses of private power in the interest of individual freedom and economic security.

I WANT TO SPEAK not of politics but of Government. I want to speak not of parties, but of universal principles. They are not political, except in that larger sense in which a great American once expressed a definition of politics, that nothing in all of human life is foreign to the science of politics. . . .

The issue of Government has always been whether individual men and women will have to serve some system of Government or economics, or whether a system of Government and economics exists to serve individual men and women. This question has persistently dominated the discussion of Government for many generations. On questions relating to these things men have differed, and for time immemorial it is probable that honest men will continue to differ.

The final word belongs to no man; yet we can still believe in change and in progress. Democracy is a quest, a never-ending seeking for better things, and in the seeking for these things and the striving for them, there are many roads to follow. . . .

From an Address by Franklin D. Roosevelt given at the Commonwealth Club, San Francisco, September 23, 1932.

It was in the middle of the nineteenth century that a new force was released and a new dream created. The force was what is called the industrial revolution, the advance of steam and machinery and the rise of the forerunners of the modern industrial plant. The dream was the dream of an economic machine, able to raise the standard of living for everyone; to bring luxury within the reach of the humblest; to annihilate distance by steam power and later by electricity, and to release everyone from the drudgery of the heaviest manual toil. It was to be expected that this would necessarily affect Government. Heretofore, Government had merely been called upon to produce conditions within which people could live happily, labor peacefully, and rest secure. Now it was called upon to aid in the consummation of this new dream. There was, however, a shadow over the dream. To be made real, it required use of the talents of men of tremendous will and trémendous ambition, since by no other force could the problem of financing and engineering and new developments be brought to a consummation.

So manifest were the advantages of the machine age, however, that the United States fearlessly, cheerfully, and, I think, rightly, accepted the bitter with the sweet. It was thought that no price was too high to pay for the advantages which we could draw from a finished industrial system. The history of the last half century is accordingly in large measure a history of a group of financial Titans, whose methods were not scrutinized with too much care, and who were honored in proportion as they produced the results, irrespective of the means they used. The financiers who pushed the railroads to the Pacific were always ruthless, often wasteful, and frequently corrupt; but they did build railroads, and we have them today. It has been estimated that the American investor paid for the American railway system more than three times over in the process; but despite this fact, the net advantage was to the United States. As long as we had free land; as long as population was growing by leaps and bounds; as long as our industrial plants were insufficient to supply our own needs, society chose to give the ambitious man free play and unlimited reward provided only that he produced the economic plant so much desired.

During this period of expansion, there was equal opportunity for all and the business of Government was not to interfere but to assist in the development of industry. This was done at the request of business men themselves. The tariff was originally imposed for the purpose of "fostering our infant industry," a phrase I think the older among you will remember as a political issue not so long ago. The railroads were subsidized, sometimes by grants of money, oftener by grants of land; some of the most valuable oil lands in the United States were granted to assist the financing of the railroad which pushed through the Southwest. A nascent merchant marine was assisted by grants of money, or by mail subsidies, so that our steam shipping might ply the seven seas. Some of my friends tell me that they do not want the Government in business. With this I agree; but I wonder whether they realize the implications of the past. For while it has been American doctrine that the Government must not go into business in competition with private enterprises, still it has been traditional, particularly in Republican administrations, for business urgently to ask the Government to put at private disposal all kinds of Government assistance. . . . Each group has sought protection from the Government for its own special interests, without realizing that the function of Government must be to favor no small group at the expense of its duty to protect the rights of personal freedom and of private property of all its citizens. . . .

A glance at the situation today only too clearly indicates that equality of opportunity as we have known it no longer exists. Our industrial plant is built; the problem just now is whether under existing conditions it is not overbuilt. Our last frontier has long since been reached, and there is practically no more free land. More than half of our people do not live on the farms or on lands and cannot derive a living by cultivating their own property. There is no safety valve in the form of a Western prairie to which those thrown out of work by the Eastern economic machines can go for a new start. We are not able to invite the immigration from Europe to share our endless plenty. We are now providing a drab living for our own people. . . .

Just as freedom to farm has ceased, so also the opportunity in business has narrowed. It still is true that men can start small enterprises, trusting to native shrewdness and ability to keep abreast of competitors; but area after area has been preempted altogether by the great corporations, and even in the fields which still have no great concerns, the small man starts under a handicap. The unfeeling statistics of the past three decades show that the independent business man is running a losing race. Perhaps he is forced to the wall; perhaps he cannot command credit; perhaps he is "squeezed out," in Mr. Wilson's words, by highly organized corporate competitors, as your corner grocery man can tell you. Recently a careful study was made of the concentration of business in the United States. It showed that our economic life was dominated by some six hundred odd corporations who controlled two-thirds of American industry. Ten million small business men divided the other third. More striking still, it appeared that if the process of concentration goes on at the same rate, at the end of another century we shall have all American industry controlled by a dozen corporations, and run by perhaps a hundred men. Put plainly, we are steering a steady course toward economic oligarchy, if we are not there already.

Clearly, all this calls for a re-appraisal of values. A mere builder of more industrial plants, a creator of more railroad systems, an organizer of more corporations, is as likely to be a danger as a help. The day of the great promoter or the financial Titan, to whom we granted anything if only he would build, or develop, is over. Our task now is not discovery or exploitation of natural resources, or necessarily producing more goods. It is the soberer, less dramatic business of administering resources and plants already in hand, of seeking to re-establish foreign markets for our surplus production, of meeting the problem of underconsumption, of adjusting production to consumption, of distributing wealth and products more equitably, of adapting existing economic organizations to the service of the people. The day of enlightened administration has come.

Just as in older times the central Government was first a haven of refuge, and then a threat, so now in a closer economic system the central and ambitious financial unit is no longer a servant of national desire, but a danger. I would draw the parallel one step farther. We did not think because national Government had become a threat in the 18th century that therefore we should abandon the principle of national Government. Nor today should we abandon the principle of strong economic units called corporations, merely because their power is susceptible of easy abuse. In other times we dealt with the problem of an unduly ambitious central Government by modifying it gradually into a constitutional democratic Government. So today we are modifying and controlling our economic units.

As I see it, the task of Government in its relation to business is to assist the development of an economic declaration of rights, an economic constitutional order. This is the common task of statesman and business man. It is the minimum requirement of a more permanently safe order of things. . . .

The Declaration of Independence discusses the problem of Government in terms of a contract. Government is a relation of give and take, a contract, perforce, if we would follow the thinking out of which it grew. Under such a contract, rulers were accorded power, and the people consented to that power on consideration that they be accorded certain rights. The task of statesmanship has always been the re-definition of these rights in terms of a changing and growing social order. New conditions impose new requirements upon Government and those who conduct Government. . . .

I feel that we are coming to a view through the drift of our legislation and our public thinking in the past quarter century that private economic power is, to enlarge an old phrase, a public trust as well. I hold that continued enjoyment of that power by any individual or group must depend upon the fulfillment of that trust. The men who have reached the summit of American business life know this best; happily, many of these urge the binding quality of this greater social contract.

The terms of that contract are as old as the Republic, and as new as the new economic order.

Every man has a right to life; and this means that he has also a right to make a comfortable living. He may by sloth or crime decline to exercise that right; but it may not be denied him. We have no actual famine or dearth; our industrial and agricultural mechanism can produce enough and to spare. Our Government, formal and informal, political and economic, owes to everyone an avenue to possess himself of a portion of that plenty sufficient for his needs, through his own work.

Every man has a right to his own property; which means a right to be assured, to the fullest extent attainable, in the safety of his savings. By no other means can men carry the burdens of those parts of life which, in the nature of things, afford no chance of labor; childhood, sickness, old age. In all thought of property, this right is paramount; all other property rights must yield to it. If, in accord with this principle, we must restrict the operations of the speculator, the manipulator, even the financier, I believe we must accept the restriction as needful, not to hamper individualism but to protect it.

These two requirements must be satisfied, in the main, by the individuals who claim and hold control of the great industrial and financial combinations which dominate so large a part of our industrial life. They have undertaken to be, not business men, but princes of property. I am not prepared to say that the system which produces them is wrong. I am very clear that they must fearlessly and competently assume the responsibility which goes with the power. So many enlightened business men know this that the statement would be little more than a platitude, were it not for an added implication.

This implication is, briefly, that the responsible heads of finance and industry, instead of acting each for himself, must work together to achieve the common end. They must, where necessary, sacrifice this or that private advantage; and in reciprocal self-denial must seek a general advantage. It is here that formal Government—political Government, if you chose—comes in. Whenever in the pursuit of this objective the lone wolf, the unethical competitor, the reckless promoter, the Ishmael or Insull whose hand is against every man's, declines to join in achieving an end recognized as being for the public welfare, and threatens to drag the industry back to a state of anarchy, the Government may properly be asked to apply restraint. Likewise, should the group ever use its collective power contrary to the public welfare, the Government must be swift to enter and protect the public interest.

The Government should assume the function of economic regulation only as a last resort, to be tried only when private initiative, inspired by high responsibility, with such assistance and balance as Government can give, has finally failed. As yet there has been no final failure, because there has been no attempt; and I decline to assume that this Nation is unable to meet the situation.

The final term of the high contract was for liberty and the pursuit of happiness. We have learned a great deal of both in the past century. We know that individual liberty and individual happiness mean nothing unless both are ordered in the sense that one man's meat is not another man's poison. We know that the old "rights of personal competency," the right to read, to think, to speak, to choose and live a mode of life, must be respected at all hazards. We know that liberty to do anything which deprives others of those elemental rights is outside the protection of any compact; and that Government in this regard is the maintenance of a balance, within which every individual may have a place if he will take it; in which every individual may find safety if he wishes it; in which every individual may attain such power as his ability permits, consistent with his assuming the accompanying responsibility.

2

Geopolitics and the American Government

2.1. GEOGRAPHIC FACTORS IN UNIFICATION

Although America had achieved political independence by the end of the eighteenth century, geographic barriers posed major problems for the young nation. As Adams points out in this selection, transportation has been a critical factor in overcoming these barriers.

WITH THE EXCEPTION that half a million people had crossed the Alleghenies and were struggling with difficulties all their own, in an isolation like that of Jutes or Angles in the fifth century, America, so far as concerned physical problems, had changed little in fifty years. The old landmarks remained nearly where they stood before. The same bad roads and difficult rivers, connecting the same small towns, stretched into the same forests in 1800 as when the armies of Braddock and Amherst pierced the western and northern wilderness, except that these roads extended a few miles farther from the seacoast. Nature was rather man's master than his servant, and the five million Americans struggling with the untamed continent seemed hardly more competent to their task than the beavers and buffalo which had for countless generations made bridges and roads of their own.

Even by water, along the seaboard, communication was as slow and almost as irregular as in colonial times. The wars in Europe caused a sudden and great increase in American shipping employed in foreign commerce, without yet leading to general improvement in navigation. The ordinary sea-going vessel carried a freight of about two hundred and fifty

From Henry Adams, *History of the United States of America during the Administration of Thomas Jefferson* (New York: Charles Scribner's Sons, 1889), pp. 5–8.

tons; the largest merchant ships hardly reached four hundred tons. . . . Elaborately rigged as ships or brigs, the small merchant craft required large crews and were slow sailers; but the voyage to Europe was comparatively more comfortable and more regular than the voyage from New York to Albany, or through Long Island Sound to Providence. No regular packet plied between New York and Albany. Passengers waited till a sloop was advertised to sail; they provided their own bedding and supplies; and within the nineteenth century Captain Elias Bunker won much fame by building the sloop "Experiment," of one hundred and ten tons, to start regularly on a fixed day for Albany, for the convenience of passengers only, supplying beds, wine, and provisions for the voyage of one hundred and fifty miles. A week on the North River or on the Sound was an experience not at all unknown to travellers.

While little improvement has been made in water-travel, every increase of distance added to the difficulties of the westward journey. The settler who after buying wagon and horses hauled his family and goods across the mountains, might buy or build a broad flat-bottomed ark, to float with him and his fortunes down the Ohio, in constant peril of upsetting or of being sunk; but only light boats with strong oars could mount the stream, or boats forced against the current by laboriously poling in shallow water. If he carried his tobacco and wheat down the Mississippi to the Spanish port of New Orleans, and sold it, he might return to his home in Kentucky or Ohio by a long and dangerous journey on horseback through the Indian country from Natchez to Nashville, or he might take ship to Philadelphia, if a ship were about to sail, and again cross the Alleghenies. Compared with river travel, the sea was commonly an easy and safe highway. Nearly all the rivers which penetrated the interior were unsure, liable to be made dangerous by freshets, and both dangerous and impassable by drought; yet such as they were, these streams made the main paths of traffic. Through the mountainous gorges of the Susquehanna the produce of western New York first found an outlet; the Cuyahoga and Muskingum were the first highway from the Lakes to the Ohio; the Ohio itself, with its great tributaries the Cumberland and the Tennessee, marked the lines of western migration; and every stream which could at high water float a boat was thought likely to become a path for commerce. . . . The experience of mankind proved trade to be dependent on water communications, and as yet Americans did not dream that the experience of mankind was useless to them.

If America was to be developed along the lines of water communication alone, by such means as were known to Europe, Nature had decided that the experiment of a single republican government must meet extreme difficulties. The valley of the Ohio had no more to do with that of the Hudson, the Susquehanna, the Potomac, the Roanoke, and the Santee, than the valley of the Danube with that of the Rhone, the Po, or the Elbe. Close communication by land could alone hold the great geographical divisions together either in interest or in fear. The union of New England with New York and Pennsylvania was not an easy task even as a problem of geography, and with an ocean highway; but the union of New England with the Carolinas, and of the seacoast with the interior, promised to be a hopeless undertaking. Physical contact alone could make one country of these isolated empires, but to the patriotic American of 1800, struggling for the continued existence of an embryo nation, with machinery so inadequate, the idea of ever bringing the Mississippi River, either by land or water, into close contact with New England, must have seemed wild.

2.2. AN EARLY VIEW OF SECTIONALISM IN AMERICA

This report by an English author after a two-year visit to America in the 1830s combines some trenchant observations about the realities of sectional conflict with respect and affection for the American people. She finds "generous patriotism" the cure for the folly of sectional prejudice.

IT IS THE PRACTICE at Washington to pay the Members of Congress, not only a per diem allowance, but their travelling expenses; at so much per twenty miles. Two Members of Congress from Missouri made charges widely different in amount. Complaints were made that the Members were not confined to a mail route, and that the country had to pay for any digressions the honourable gentlemen might be in the humour to make. Upon this, a Member observed that, so far from wishing to confine the congressional travellers to a mail route, he would, if possible, prescribe the condition that they should travel, both in coming and going, through every State of the Union. Any money thus expended, would be, he considered, a cheap price to pay for the conquest of prejudices and dispersion of unfriendly feelings, which would be the consequence of the rambles he proposed.

The Members of Congress from the north like to revert to the day when there were only two universities, Harvard and Yale, to which all the youth of the Union repaired for education. The southern members love to boast of the increase of colleges, so that every State will soon be educating its own youth. The northern men miss the sweet sounds of acknowledgment which used to meet their ears, as often as past days were

From Harriet Martineau, *Society in America*, I. (New York: Saunders & Otley, 1837), pp. 135–138.

referred to—the grateful mention of the New England retreats where the years of preparation for active life were spent. The southern men are mortified at the supposition that everything intellectual must come out of New England. When they boast that Virginia has produced almost all their Presidents, they are met by the boast that New England has furnished almost all the school-masters, professors, and clergy of the country. While the north is still fostering a reverence for the Union, the south loses no opportunity of enlarging lovingly on the virtue of passionate attachment to one's native state.

There is much nature and much reason in all this. It is true that there is advantage in the youth of the whole country being brought together within college walls, at the age when warm friendships are formed. They can hardly quarrel very desperately in Congress, after having striven, and loved, and learned together, in their bright early days. The cadets at West Point spoke warmly to me of this. They told me that when a youth is coming from afar, the youths who have arrived from an opposite point of the compass prepare to look cold upon him and quiz him, and receive him frigidly enough; but the second Sunday seldom comes round before they wonder at him and themselves, and acknowledge that he might almost have been born in their own State. On the other hand, it is true that it would be an absurdity and a hardship to the dwellers in the south and west to have no means of educating their youth at home; but to be obliged to send them a thousand miles in pursuit of necessary learning. It is also true that medical colleges should abound; that peculiar diseases, incident to climate and locality, may be studied on the spot. In this, as in many other cases, some good must be sacrificed for the attainment of a greater good.

The question is, need sectional prejudices increase under the new arrangements? Are there no means of counteracting this great evil, except the ancient methods? Is West Point the last spot whereon common interests may rally, and whence state jealousies may be excluded?

I should be sorry if the answer were unfavorable; for this Sectional Prejudice, carried beyond the point of due political vigilance, is folly,—childish folly. Events prove it to be so. Deadly political enemies meet at Washington, and snarl and declaim at one another with mighty fierceness. They find themselves, some sunny day, lying on the grass under the shade of a tree, at the country-house of an acquaintance; they rise up cordial friends. They have actually discussed the question of questions, the American System and Nullification; and yet they rise up cordial friends. Again; a Boston gentleman and his lady travel for health through the south and west. They hear abuse of their State and city in abundance by the roadside; but their hearts are touched by the hospitality and friendliness they meet under every roof. Again; the planter carries his family to a Rhode Island bathing place, for the hot season: and there he finds some to whom he can open his heart about his domestic troubles, caused by slavery; he gains their sympathy, and carries away their esteem. The sectional hatred, if not an abstraction, is founded mainly on abstractions, and gives way at once when the parties are confronted. Does it not deserve to be called childish folly?

Yet "hatred" is not too strong a term for his sectional prejudice. Many a time in America have I been conscious of that pang and shudder which are felt only in the presence of hatred. I question whether the enmity between the British and the Americans, at the most exasperating crisis of the war, could ever have been more intense than some that I have seen flashing in the eyes, and heard from the lips, of Americans against fellow-citizens in distant sections of their country. I have scarcely known whether to laugh or to mourn when I have been told that the New England people are all pedlars or canting priests; that the people of the south are all heathens; and those of the west all barbarians. Nay, I was even told in New York that the Rhode Island people were all heathens, and the New Jersey folks no better. Some Baltimore ladies told me that the Philadelphia ladies say that no Baltimore lady knows how to put on a bonnet: but that the Philadelphians have something worse the matter with them than that; for that they do not know how to be hospitable to strangers. Without stopping to settle which is the gravest of these heavy charges, I am anxious to bear my testimony against the correctness of either. I saw some pretty bonnets, most becomingly worn, at Baltimore; and I can speak confidently to the hospitality of Philadelphia.

Trifling as some instances appear of the manifestation of this puerile spirit, it sometimes, it always, issues in results which are no trifle; —always, because the spirit of jealousy is a deadly curse to him who is possessed by it, whether it be founded on fact, or no. It cannot co-exist with a generous patriotism, one essential requisite of which is an enlarged faith in fellow-citizens. All republicans are patriotic, more or less frequently and loftily. If every American will look into himself at the moment he is glowing with patriotism, he will find his sectional prejudices melted away and gone, for the season. The Americans feel this in their travels abroad, when their country is attacked. They yearn towards the remotest dwellers in their country as if they were the nearest and dearest. Would they could always feel thus at home, and in the absence of provocation!

2.3. A CLASSIC COMMENTARY ON SECTIONALISM

Geographic influences upon social life and political institutions are not easily measured. In the following selection a renowned historian probes the impact of "the American physical map" on the history of American

politics. He believes America to be a federation of sections rather than
of states, and he stresses the consistency of sectional differences with
national unity.

. . . AMERICAN SECTIONALISM has been very inadequately dealt with by
our historians. Impressed by the artificial political boundary lines of states,
they have almost entirely given their attention either to national or to
state history, or to the broad division of North and South, overlooking
the fact that there are several natural, economic, and social sections that
are fundamental in American historical development. As population extended itself, it flowed into various physiographic provinces, some of them
comparable in size and resources, not only to the greater nations of
Europe, but even to some of the great empires that have from time to
time been formed by combinations of these nations. The American
physical map may be regarded as a map of potential nations and empires,
each to be conquered and colonized, each to rise through stages of development, each to achieve a certain social and industrial unity, each to
possess certain fundamental assumptions, certain psychological traits, and
each to interact with the others, and in combination to form that United
States, the explanation of the development of which is the task of the
historian.

. . . The influence of New England upon the political history of
the Middle West, and through it upon the nation, has been profound. Its
effect in forming the social and moral ideas of the central region of the
republic can hardly be overstated. But we really know but little about this
colonization compared with the detailed information which historical investigators have given us about the location of the homes of the Pilgrims.
We cannot even state with approximate correctness the periods when the
various Western states received their largest numbers of New England
settlers. Nor has the replacement of this New England stock in the parent
region by immigration been adequately studied. We shall not understand
the New England of today until we have a fuller account of the industrial,
social, political, and religious effect of this transformation of New England
by replacement of its labor population and by the revolution in its industrial life, with the accompaniments of social stratification, loss of homo-
geneity, and changed ideals in respect to democracy.

Not to dwell too long upon this region, let us turn for a moment
to indicate a few of the problems that arise when the South is considered
from this same point of view. The term South as a sectional designation
is misleading. Through a long period of our history the "Solid South" did

From Frederick Jackson Turner, *The Significance of Sections in American
History* (New York: Holt, Rinehart and Winston, Inc., 1932; copyright renewed in 1960 by Dorothy T. Main), pp. 8–15, 50–51, 318–326, 334–339.

not exist. We must bear in mind, not only the differences between the various states of the Southern seaboard, but also the more fundamental differences between the upcountry (the Piedmont region) and the Atlantic Plains. The interior of the South needs treatment as a unit. State historians of Virginia and the Carolinas, for example, recognize the fundamental contrasts in physiography, colonization, stock, and economic and social characteristics, between the lowlands and the uplands in their respective states. But as yet no one has attacked the problem of the settlement, development, and influence of the Piedmont Plains as a whole. This peninsula, as we may conceive it, thrust down through the Great Valley from Pennsylvania, between the mountains and the seaboard, the land that received the German, Scotch-Irish, and poorer white English settlers, developed, in the second half of the eighteenth century, an independent social, economic, and political character. It was a region of free labor upon small farms. It was devoted to cereals rather than to the great staple crops of the seaboard.

. . . It struggled for just representation in the legislatures, and for adequate local self-government. The domestic history of the South is for many years the history of a contest between these eastern and western sections. When the cotton belt, with slavery as its labor element, spread across this Piedmont area, the region became assimilated to the seaboard. The small farmers, raising crops by the labor of their own families, were compelled either to adjust themselves to the plantation economy, or to migrate. . . . A migration of small farmers from the Piedmont across the Ohio and into the Gulf region followed. Many had moral and religious objections to slavery; many were unable to change their agricultural habits to meet the new conditions; many lacked the necessary capital for a slave plantation and preferred to accept the price of their lands offered by the planters, and to migrate to the public lands where they could continue their old industrial and social type of society. . . .

. . . the whole industrial and social history of the South has been obscured by the emphasis placed on the political aspects of the slavery struggle. We need a history of the plantation in its various areas and at different periods. Such a study would give us the key to Southern history. The rise and fall of cotton values, the price of slaves, the agrarian history of the South, the relation of its political demands to these conditions, the distribution of rival political parties in the region—these and similar topics would come into prominence if the historian should select for treatment the Southern provinces of the Atlantic Plains, the Piedmont, and the Gulf Plains, their interaction, and the shifting center of political power between them.

It is unnecessary to point out that similar advantages would come from attempts to explain the evolution of the social structure of the Lake and Prairie Plains, the Great Plains, the Pacific Coast, etc. We should study the contact of whites and Indians, the history of the occupation of the public lands in these provinces; the movement into them of settlers from other sections; the industrial transformations of the provinces from primitive farming up to the complex economic conditions of today; the development and influence of railroad systems; the rise of cities; the rise of peculiar views of life in the respective sections. . . .

The problems of interprovincial relations need study also. The whole history of American politics needs to be interpreted in the terms of a contest between these economic and social sections. Periods when it seemed that there was no great issue dividing political parties will be found to abound in evidences—in the legislation of Congress, for example —that intense political struggles actually went on between the separate sections, combining and rearranging their forces as occasion showed the need. It is only when we get below the surface of national politics to consider the sectional party groupings that we are able to discover the lines on which new party issues are forming and the significance of the utterances of the leaders of these rival sections. Again and again, we shall find the party candidates anxious to conciliate the conflicting interests of the different sections and attempting to "straddle" upon vital problems, which nevertheless continue to force themselves to the front. The outcome is determined by the combination of these rival sections for and against the proposition. . . .

The economic rivalries and industrial interrelations of the different sections of the country also are continuous factors in our history, and are more familiar to business men and to railroad managers than they are, as a rule, to the historian.

The significance of the section in American history is that it is the faint image of a European nation and that we need to reexamine our history in the light of this fact. Our politics and our society have been shaped by sectional complexity and interplay not unlike what goes on between European nations. The greater sections are the result of the joint influence of (1) the geologists' physiographic provinces and (2) the colonizing stocks that entered them.

The result is found in popular speech in which New England, the Middle States, the South, the Middle West, etc., are as common names as Massachusetts or Wisconsin. The Census divisions are more definite and official designations. Of course, the boundary lines are not definite and fixed. Neither are those of European nations. These larger sections have taken their characteristic and peculiar attitudes in American civilization in general.

We have furnished to Europe the example of a continental federation of sections over an area equal to Europe itself, and by substituting discussion and concession and compromised legislation for force, we have shown the possibility of international political parties, international legislative bodies, and international peace. Our party system and our variety in regional geography have helped to preserve the American peace. By having our combination of sections represented in a national legislative body, by possessing what may be called a League of Sections, comparable to a League of Nations, if it included political parties and a legislative body, we have enabled these minority sections to defend their interests and yet avoid the use of force.

The thing to be avoided, if the lessons of history are followed, is the insistence upon the particular interests and ideals of the section in which we live, without sympathetic comprehension of the ideals, the interests, and the rights of other sections. We must shape our national action to the fact of a vast and varied Union of unlike sections.

. . . the explanation of our lack of sympathy with the methods and the fundamental assumptions of continental Europe lies in large measure in the different course which the sections of the Union ran as compared with the nations of Europe. We substituted the system of a sectional union and legislative adjustment, for the settlement by the sword. We learned how to discuss, how to concede, and how to adjust differences, how to combine a loyalty to parties which ran across sectional lines, with loyalty to local interests. Like an elastic band, the common national feeling and party ties draw sections together, but at the same time yield in some measure to sectional interests when these are gravely threatened.

We in America are in reality a federation of sections rather than of states. State sovereignty was never influential except as a constitutional shield for the section. In political matters the states act in groups rather than as individual members of the Union. They act in sections and are responsive to the respective interests and ideals of these sections. They have their sectional leaders, who, in Congress and in party conventions, voice the attitude of the section and confer and compromise their differences, or form sectional combinations to achieve a national policy and position. Party policy and congressional legislation emerge from a process of sectional contests and sectional bargainings. Legislation is almost never the result of purely national or purely sectional considerations. It is the result of sectional adjustments to meet national needs. For the most part, such adjustments take place in the formative stages of bills, in the committee rooms, and in the process of framing the measures by amendments. It is in these stages that the bill is most easily affected by sectional interests. . . .

But even final votes in the Congress of the United States, both in the Senate and the House, upon important matters are . . . far less frequently by parties than is ordinarily supposed. If we proceed a step further and, instead of taking account of congressional majorities by totals and reckoning the votes by party affiliation, we arrange those votes by sections and place the result on a map of the United States, we shall be astonished at how much is concealed by the mere alphabetical or party record. Under the drawing pen, as vote after vote by congressional districts is recorded on the map, they gradually arrange themselves to show the outlines of contending sections. The areas of great geographic provinces are revealed by the map of votes.

Although political sectionalism is still a term of reproach, implying unfairness and a disregard of national interests, the section reproved is seldom conscious that its action is adverse to the common good. We are so large and diversified a nation that it is almost impossible to see the situation except through sectional spectacles. The section either conceives of itself as an aggrieved and oppressed minority, suffering from the injustice of the other sections of the nation, or it thinks of its own culture, its economic policies, and well-being as best for all the nation. It thinks, in other words, of the nation in terms of itself. "I love thy rocks and rills, thy woods and templed hills," runs our American anthem. It was written by a New Englander and its scene is that of New England, not of the snow-capped mountains, the far stretches of Great Plains, or Arid America. We think sectionally and do not fully understand one another.

Underneath the party sectionalism there is, of course, a sectionalism of material interests—of business, manufacturing, mining, agriculture, transportation. . . .

What is the logic of all this? Does it mean the ultimate political organization of the different groups of states into sectional units for representation and administration—the formal recognition of a new federation, a replacement of the feeble states by powerful sections, each with its special economic interest? Does it mean that in the last analysis men shape their political action according to their material advantage?

This last question is not radically different from the question of the interpretation of history in general. No single factor is determinative. Men are not absolutely dictated to by climate, geography, soils, or economic interests. The influence of the stock from which they sprang, the inherited ideals, the spiritual factors, often triumph over the material interests. There is also the influence of personality. Men do follow leaders, and sometimes into paths inconsistent with the section's material interests. But in the long run the statesman must speak the language of his people on fundamentals, both of interests and ideals. Not seldom the ideals grow out of the interests. It is the statesman's duty and his great opportunity to lift his section to a higher and broader, a more far-seeing, conception of its interests as a part of the Union, to induce his section to accept the compromises and adjustments which he arranges with the leaders of other sections in the spirit of reconciliation of interests in the nation as a whole. He must be at once the section's spokesman, its negotiator, and its enlightened guide, loyal to the nation as a whole.

At the same time that we realize the danger of provincialism and sectional selfishness, we must also recognize that the sections serve as restraints upon a deadly uniformity. They are breakwaters against overwhelming surges of national emotion. They are fields for experiment in the growth of different types of society, political institutions, and ideals. They constitute an impelling force for progress along the diagonal of contending varieties; they issue a challenge to each section to prove the virtue of its own culture; and they cross-fertilize each other. They promote that reasonable competition and cooperation which is the way of a richer life. A national vision must take account of the existence of these varied sections; otherwise the national vision will be only a sectional mirage.

As the case stands, sections still, as in the past, reflect the distances and the differences of the American continent. Improvements in communication, such as the automobile, the telephone, radio, and moving pictures, have diminished localism rather than sectionalism. Class conflict and sectional conflict often coincide. . . .

But in countless ways the power of the section is conditioned largely upon its moderation. Every section is in unstable equilibrium; public opinion is often closely divided and responds to national ideals.

For, underneath all, there is a common historical inheritance, a common set of institutions, a common law, and a common language. There is an American spirit. There are American ideals. We are members of one body, though it is a varied body. It is inconceivable that we should follow the evil path of Europe and place our reliance upon triumphant force. We shall not become cynical, and convinced that sections, like European nations, must dominate their neighbors and strike first and hardest. However profound the economic changes, we shall not give up our American ideals and our hopes for man, which had their origin in our own pioneering experience, in favor of any mechanical solution offered by doctrinaires educated in Old World grievances. Rather, we shall find strength to build from our past a nobler structure, in which each section will find its place as a fit room in a worthy house. We shall courageously maintain the American system expressed by nation-wide parties, acting under sectional and class compromises. . . .

2.4. THE ROLE OF REGIONALISM

This 1935 report discusses the consequences for national policy of the rise of regional consciousness. It focuses on the problems of coordination and planning in the development of comprehensive regional programs and discusses devices for the sharing of authority and responsibility by the national and state governments.

. . . THROUGHOUT OUR HISTORY the role of the States in the Federal system and the interplay of forces between them and the National Government, have been fundamental factors. This is true not only of the States, but of groups of States. From this fact has arisen a recognition of "sectionalism," whose importance has been demonstrated by the historian F. J. Turner. There have sometimes been efforts to suppress sectionalism by ignoring it; it has been viewed as a policy of selfishness and intransigence. Recently, however, it has been recognized as a factor of value and importance in the encouragement of a more varied and a richer life for the Nation, whereby the peculiar characteristics, resources, and contributions of the major sections of the country, and within each of its constituent parts, could be protected from invasion and suppression by ill-considered and hasty national policies. The very stimulation of the self-consciousness of the section may recruit a wider leadership for civic affairs, and a richer culture. Thus within the past two decades a regional approach to American life and its problems and opportunities can be found in the social studies, geography, literature, the drama, painting, architecture, history, and civic education. Controversies arise as to the true interpretation of the place of a region within the Nation and of the policies which it should follow. With the reduction in immigration, the closing of the great westward movement into unsettled country, the increasing influence of the historical societies, the growth of regional expression in literature and the arts, it is possible that the increasing ease of communication and economic interdependence of the Nation will be accompanied by a regional consciousness arising from more settled and self-conscious local communities. Nor should we ignore the possibility that this very economic interdependence may rest upon a more carefully conceived analysis of local needs and possibilities achieved through city, rural, and State planning. Such a development will increase, rather than suppress, local civic consciousness. City planners assert that the processes whereby local zoning ordinances are created invariably lead many citizens, for the first time, to see their local communities as a whole when they come to consider the relationship of their own house, factory or store to the zoning plan and the relation of the zoning plan to the functions, needs, and opportunities of the city. Similarly the analysis of the role of the local community within the State from which it receives its legal authority, and of the natural resources or other area from which it derives its raw materials and in which it finds its markets and its recreational areas will inevitably have a similar civic educative effect.

To say this is but to point the way to ultimate issues, and not to answer them. What, for example, are the exact boundaries of these re-

From U.S. National Resources Committee, *Regional Factors in National Planning and Development* (Washington, D.C.: U.S. Government Printing Office, 1935), pp. 8–9, 197, 199.

gions of which historians, artists, novelists speak? Will they eventually absorb both from the Federal Government and the States political functions that will lead to, as one writer terms it, a "United Regions of America"? Should such regions seek specialization based upon their peculiarities of resources and form an organic whole as a nation, or should they seek autonomous self-containment? These questions point to very fundamental issues affecting the way of life and the ultimate ideals of the American people. It will appear cowardly and evasive to many not to attempt an immediate answer.

There is, however, a case for proposing to clear a way for relating such fundamental questions, at present explored by only a few people, to the ordinary every day problems that press upon us all. It is good that they should be raised, and it would be a valuable thing to see those engaged in formulating the policies of Government on all levels—National, State, and local—reexamine their problems and policies in the light of such long-range considerations. The process of planning, from this point of view, is not only important for immediate purposes of Government policy in the narrower sense, but is an aspect of civic education. Whatever facilitates such a self-analysis on the part of the citizen of the resources about him, of the kind of life he wishes to create from them, of the loyalties which he serves, will enhance, in the long run, the quality of his citizenship and of his Government. We cannot predict what answers he may be giving to these questions a century hence; we can, and should, make clear to him that they must be faced if he is to realize the best of the opportunities that America possesses.

The growth or decline of a regional consciousness cannot be predicted with exactness. The contributing influences are subtle, varied, and fluctuating. They include: The relation of people to and their use of resources; the changes in knowledge and techniques which shift the value and importance of resources and occupations; changes in communication which redirect the relationship of one community to another; the rivalry of cities in seeking to attach wider areas to their spheres of influence, and the strategy of competing economic interests; the stimulation of regional consciousness by the historian, the artist, the novelist and poet, the architect, and the educator; and the channeling of political action and careers by the political system with its parties and leaders. These are only some of the influences which vary in their relative importance from time to time and from place to place. We have seen such influences reflected in problems so urgent that they force experiments in political organization and administration. We cannot foresee what precise form such pressure to express regional needs will take. A more conscious effort should be made to reflect these needs, and the ideas developed within the region as to how those needs should be met, in formulating and executing national policies. To say this is only to reiterate a doctrine fundamental in American development and inherent in Federal systems.

This is the ultimate basis for encouraging in the field the advance planning of national policies in such a way as will reflect emerging regional policies also, and provide better integrated and more economical means for executing them through all the levels of government. That there will continue to be sharp conflicts over the policies, we have no doubt; such conflicts exist now, and have always been present throughout our history. But they are the more serious and harmful because there has been lacking a careful and sympathetic exploration in advance of the fundamental factors, physical as well as constitutional, present in a major problem that involves more than one State, and both the State and the National Governments. We have, therefore, emphasized here the need for obtaining a comprehensive view of the development of and coordination of governments in a region, rather than the details of organization and procedure which may be modified as experience teaches.

But we would emphasize strongly that if the National Government is to participate in any such effort to develop comprehensive regional programs as a part of its own task of formulating national policy, it must be eager to coordinate the activities of its own agencies. Good administration requires not only a nice articulation of the constitutional powers of the National Government with those of the States; it equally requires a similar care in coordinating the work of one bureau with another within departments and between departments. . . .

If it be objected that any procedure which provides such coordination between the National and State Governments in their activities in a given region adds further complexity to an already complex government, there is this to be remembered: A Federal system of government necessarily is complex; if one desires a Federal system of distributed powers, he must pay the price. That price is the establishing of means whereby the different parts, established to reflect politically the varying desires and interests of the constituent corporate members of the Federal Union, may cooperate with one another and with the whole in exercising their powers in such a way as to solve their problems. One does not, presumably, establish governments in order that they may be either simple or complex; one establishes them to help him solve his problems.

But this too should be remembered. Under any circumstances some sharing of authority and responsibility between the levels of government exists. Some efforts are now made to obtain integration in the exercise of these powers. Within the past few months, such efforts have been extended by Congress into the field, for example, of social insurance. The practical question is not, therefore, one of avoiding complexity, but of facilitating in every way possible the most effective functioning of a system which is by definition, being Federal, complex.

Nor should we forget the very heavy responsibility which is placed, in our Government, upon the President and his colleagues in the formulating of administrative policy. While one may say that he is exercising Federal power alone, the fact is that every exercise of such power has its impact at local points somewhere in the area of the United States. The stream dredged for interstate commerce by Federal authority and with Federal expenditure and agencies will vitally affect local communities; and the same point is true for a commodity program for potatoes or cotton, or the location of a Federal forest, park, or wildlife refuge. How, then, can the President and his advisers be enabled best to visualize this local impact of a Federal program? Reports indicating the future commitments of all the agencies concerned, and indicating priorities in construction, operation, and expenditure are as necessary for him as the data supplied by the Bureau of the Budget. This knowledge, indeed, underlies the budget; upon such information decisions for expenditures should be based.

If it be objected that no clear cut delineation of regions exists or that if any does exist and is discoverable it will soon be obsolete because of social changes, it may be pointed out that this makes all the more important the continuous adjustment of the boundaries of any planning region to these social changes. The centers described in its previous section of the report should, indeed, be the first point at which shifts of this kind are noted and appraised. The selection of the centers and the extent of area with which they should be related should be based upon an analysis of the planning problems similar to that already undertaken in earlier investigations by the National Resources Committee and many other agencies, the grouping of problems by regions evidenced by these factors, and by consultation with staffs of Federal agencies responsible for dealing with these problems and the State officials. The objective to be emphasized is not the protection of the vested interests of a bureau or a unit of government, but an effort to see as a whole the problems which confront what appears to be an organic area with some self-consciousness of needs and desires peculiar to it, and the attempt to work out an equally comprehensive view of the way in which these problems can best be attacked through the cooperation of all the authorities.

In the course of this search, through the analysis of planning problems, for any natural grouping or clustering of problems by area, it is possible that there may appear, for several Federal agencies, important advantages in attempting a coincidence of departmental districting. This possibility should be kept in mind in decentralizing planning procedure. We recognize, indeed, that the determination of the proper assignment of work within a bureau by districts may have no relevance for regional considerations other than convenience in office procedure, and that any arbitrary plan of establishing Federal districts without regard to the function performed by the bureau would be wasteful and undesirable. On the other hand, the more effective development of policies by bureaus whose work should be coordinated in the field operations and therefore in the preliminary preparation of policy as well, would clearly be assisted if there were a coincidence of field units with the problem areas. A more logical grouping of districts would stimulate a parallel coordination of functions among the local governments affected by common problem areas.

. . . there is no single form of organization to be recommended for general adoption for the development program of a region. The kind of organization should be determined by (1) the functions which it is to perform, (2) the extent of the area over which it is to operate, and (3) the distribution of the constitutional authority from which it must derive its own authority to execute the functions assigned to it. While as a general rule the creation of new units is to be avoided to prevent duplication of governments with their resulting increased overhead administrative costs and complexity of spending and operating units, the objective of government, it may be repeated, is to solve the problems assigned to it.

. . . in developing a regional program some projects may include several interdependent factors such as stream pollution, flood prevention, prevention of soil erosion, reforestation, and other closely interwoven functions, so concentrated in an area that the task of construction and operation should be assigned to a single unit which will either be entirely responsible for the major portion of construction and operation, or at least for scheduling and coordinating the activities of several Federal and State agencies in the area. Here the experience of the Tennessee Valley Authority illustrates the place for employing a Federal public authority cooperating with Federal services as well as State services.

Where the project is interstate in extent, but largely local in benefits, as illustrated by the Lake Champlain Bridge, and where the apportionment of constitutional power permits or requires, the interstate authority seems to us more satisfactory. This is particularly true where the costs can be liquidated by the charges made to the users.

It is possible that a third type of public corporate authority might be created under the joint ownership of both the National Government and those States concerned in regional projects affecting the owners. There are certain areas in which the developments which should be undertaken lie within a twilight zone between clear-cut national powers and State powers, yet in which the problem requires carefully articulated cooperation of all. This is true of a river system in which the Federal power over navigation for purposes of interstate commerce and State power over stream pollution and local planning require comprehensive exercise, and involve also joint cooperation in reforestation, the prevention of soil erosion, and land-use planning.

We would stress the fact, however, that much more informal

arrangements than the creation of new agencies may be adequate. It may be possible, through the agency of the regional planning commission and its encouragement, to implement certain proposals through the cooperation of two States, as New York and New Jersey cooperate in the administration of the Palisades Interstate Park. . . .

If any new Federal or Federal-interstate authorities should be established in different regions, they should be given some responsible relationship to the department or agency at Washington which has the major responsibility for formulating the national policy relating to the function which the regional authority performs. This relationship should not be aimed at limiting the discretion conferred upon the operating authority by law, but should be designed to insure the consideration of the total national program relating to that particular function, and the part which each regional project plays in that national program.

2.5. THE IMPORTANCE OF PRESERVING OUR NATURAL RESOURCES

The constantly increasing rate of consumption of raw materials in the mid-twentieth century has awakened Americans to our problem of dwindling natural resources. This study calls for the "resources of ingenuity" in order to alleviate threatened shortages of basic materials.

THE QUESTION, "Has the United States of America the material means to sustain its civilization?" would never have occurred to the men who brought this Nation into greatness as the twentieth century dawned. But with the twentieth century now half gone by, the question presses and the honest answers are not glib.

. . . . . .

This Report, *Resources for Freedom,* has as its central task an examination of the adequacy of materials, chiefly industrial materials, to meet the needs of the free world in the years ahead. Even a casual assessment of these years would show many causes for concern. In area after area the same pattern seems discernible: soaring demands, shrinking resources, the consequent pressure toward rising real costs, the risk of wartime shortages, the ultimate threat of an arrest or decline in the standard of living we cherish and hope to help others to attain. If such a threat is to be averted, it will not be by inaction. After successive years of think-

From Report of President's Materials Policy Commission, *Resources for Freedom: A Report to the President,* I. (Washington, D.C.: U.S. Government Printing Office, 1952), pp. 1, 4–6, 169.

ing about unemployment, reemployment, full employment, about factory production, inflation and deflation, and hundreds of other matters in the structure of economic life, the United States must now give new and deep consideration to the fundamental upon which all employment, all daily activity, eventually rests; the contents of the earth and its physical environment.

. . . the United States problem today is precisely the reverse of the problem to which all our tradition has accustomed us. A hundred years ago resources seemed limitless and the struggle upward from meager conditions of life was the struggle to create the means and methods of getting these materials into use. In this struggle we have succeeded so well that today, in thinking of expansion programs, full employment, new plants, or the design of a radical new turbine blade, too many of us blankly forget to look back to the mine, the land, the forest: the sources upon which we absolutely depend. So well have we built our high-output factories, so efficiently have we opened the lines of distribution to our remotest consumers that our sources are weakening under the constantly increasing strain of demand. As a Nation, we have always been more interested in sawmills than seedlings. We have put much more engineering thought into the layout of factories to cut up metals than into mining processes to produce them. We think about materials resources last, not first.

THE CONVERGING FORCES

Today, throughout the industrial world, but centering inevitably in the heavily industrialized United States, the resulting materials problem bears down with considerable severity. The nature of the problem can perhaps be successfully oversimplified by saying that the consumption of almost all materials is expanding at compound rates and is thus pressing harder and harder against resources which, whatever else they may be doing, are not similarly expanding. . . .

The intensity of the problem arises from the convergence of powerful historical forces which need to be examined. The first lies in the profound shift in the basic materials position of the United States—the worsening relationship between our requirements and our means of satisfying them. A second is to be found in the difficulties encountered by other high-consuming nations, primarily in Western Europe, which stem from the serious depletion of their own resources coupled with the weakening or severing of ties with their colonies. A third lies in the rising ambitions of the resource-rich but less developed nations, especially of former colonial status. . . .

. . . In the first 50 years of the twentieth century, United States population doubled. National output in this same time reached five times the 1900 level. The per capita national income for Americans rose from roughly $325 in 1900, to $530 in 1925 and $864 in 1950 (in 1939 dollars).

It took a considerably expanding flow of raw materials to support this growth, but not in the same high proportion. The value of the materials stream (in constant dollars) rose only half as much as the national output; services were beginning to become a larger proportion of the goods and services that made up this output, and more value was being added to materials by successively higher fabrication as time went on. It was for such reasons as these that relatively smaller materials values could sustain the more rapidly growing total output.

Even more striking than the increase in the total size of this stream were the shifts in its composition. Our total consumption of agricultural products of all sorts, including food, increased 2¼ times; fishery and wildlife products rose little more, and our total use of forest products actually declined 1 percent. But our consumption of minerals, including fuels, rose to six times 1900 totals. By 1950—in comparison with the year 1900—we were using from the earth:

> Two and one-half times more bituminous coal.
> Three times more copper.
> Three and one-half times more iron ore.
> Four times more zinc.
> Twenty-six times more natural gas.
> Thirty times more crude oil.

Indeed, there is scarcely a metal or a mineral fuel of which the quantity used in the United States since the outbreak of the First World War did not exceed the total used throughout the world in all the centuries preceding.

The minerals increase is compounded partly out of the needs that rise with growing populations, partly out of a per capita consumption which has increased threefold in the same time, and is still growing. Fundamentally it reflects the increasing mechanization of modern society. As a result of the turret lathe and tractor, the automobile and airplane, the submarine and tank, the electric washing machine and vacuum cleaner, we have been drawing down our most exhaustible resources even faster than the resources that can, in theory at any rate, be renewed. A ton of ore removed from the earth is a ton gone forever; each barrel of oil used up means one less remaining. This mounting strain upon resources that cannot be replaced has become the most challenging aspect of our present-day economy.

But "renewable" resources have also felt the strain. Ninety percent of our virgin timber stand in the commercial forest area has been cut, and thus far we have done a poor job of growing replacement crops. At present we are using up our inventory of saw-timber at a rate 40 percent faster than its annual growth rate. Millions of acres have been taken out of forest growth; other millions have gone to brush and inferior trees. Upon our agricultural land we have imposed a heavy burden of depletion; we have opened it, exploited it heavily, abandoned much of it after its fertility had been drained, and moved on to repeat the process elsewhere. Partly because of soil erosion, even water, once regarded as a "free commodity" of virtually unlimited supply, has become a problem in areas where once it was plentiful.

. . . The plain fact seems to be that we have skimmed the cream of our resources as we now understand them; there must not be, at this decisive point in history, too long a pause before our understanding catches up with our needs. . . .

Growth of demand is at the core of the materials problem we face; it is the probability of continued growth, even more than the incursions of past growth and two world wars, that present us now with our long-range problem. It is mainly our unwillingness to stand still, to accept the status of a "mature economy," that challenges the adequacy of our resources.

In contrast to other industrial nations, we have been able in the past to satisfy the bulk of our materials demand from our own domestic resources, with much to spare for export. Accordingly the United States has used up its resources considerably faster than the rest of the free world. With less than 10 percent of the free world's population and 8 percent of its land area, the United States consumes close to half the free world volume of materials.

One thing seems certain about the materials problem: it will persist. Its forms will alter; its severities may be controlled, and partial solutions will brightly present themselves—but the forces that brought the problem into being will increase rather than diminish. The central fact seems unalterable: as industrial civilizations grow in complexity they compound the demands made upon materials. This Commission does not accept the view that the world's increasing population pressures are catastrophic; it believes the reason Malthusian doom is so overdue is that Malthusian calculations have never given sufficient weight to the extraordinary ingenuity of mankind in extricating himself from situations before they become wholly and finally intolerable.

This Commission began its report with an expression of faith—faith in growth, in enterprise, in the future of freedom. It tends it with a reaffirmation: the materials problem may never be solved but it can be compensated. We will accomplish this, however, only if we recognize that as physical resources decline, the resources of ingenuity must rise up to serve mankind in their stead. . . . Greater and greater drafts of ingenuity will be called for in the future, to compensate for the slow failure of what used to be supplied us, more or less to our needs, by "nature." . . .

In this and other volumes of its Report, the Commission has attempted to outline the main features of the materials problem as seen from mid-century, and to find realistic answers to some of the questions it poses. The Commission believes that the policies and programs it has recommended will, if promptly and vigorously administered, do much to alleviate threatened shortages and to stimulate economic growth and promote free world security.

At the same time, the Commission is well aware that no single study by a temporary group can deal adequately with an immensely complicated situation cutting across the entire economy, persisting indefinitely, and changing from year to year. It was for this reason that, earlier in the Report, the Commission stated: "A task of such scope and complexity cannot be completed in one attempt. . . . The most important conclusion this Commission presents is . . . that the job must be carried on, cooperatively by Government and private citizens, not periodically at widely spaced intervals, but day by day and year by year."

2.6. GOVERNMENT'S ROLE IN RESOURCE DEVELOPMENT

The author maintains that economic abundance has been a key factor in the achievement of democracy in America. He further contends that a policy of assisting the people to gain access to wealth had been consistently followed by our government, through appropriately changing means as the nation has evolved.

. . . AMERICANS have always been especially prone to regard all things as resulting from the free choice of a free will. Probably no people have so little determinism in their philosophy, and as individuals we have regarded our economic status, our matrimonial happiness, and even our eternal salvation as things of our own making. Why should we not then regard our political felicity, likewise, as a virtue which is also virtue's reward? . . .

By viewing democracy simply as a question of political morality, we have blinded ourselves to the fact that, in every country, the system of government is a by-product of the general conditions of life, including, of course, the economic conditions, and that democracy, like any other system, is appropriate for countries where these conditions are suited to it and inappropriate for others with unsuitable conditions, or at

From David M. Potter, *People of Plenty: Economic Abundance and the American Character* (Chicago: The University of Chicago Press, 1954).

least that it is vastly more appropriate for some than for others. Viewed in these terms, there is a strong case for believing that democracy is clearly most appropriate for countries which enjoy an economic surplus and least appropriate for countries where there is an economic insufficiency. In short, economic abundance is conducive to political democracy.

At first glance this proposition may seem abjectly deterministic and may seem to imply that our democracy, like our climate, is a mere matter of luck, involving no merit. But it does not necessarily mean that we enjoy democracy without achieving it; rather, it means that we have achieved it less by sheer ideological devotion to the democratic principle than by the creation of economic conditions in which democracy will grow. In doing this, we have, of course, enjoyed the advantage of un-equaled natural resources, but, as I have already sought to show, abund-ant physical endowments do not automatically or invariably produce an economic surplus for the area which possesses them. For instance, New England, poorly endowed by nature, became, in the nineteenth century, one of the richest regions of the United States, while the Cotton South, richly endowed, committed itself to a slave-labor system, a one-crop system, and an economy restricted to producing raw materials, which, in the end, left it the poorest part of the nation. . . .

But, though this view does not, in a deterministic sense, deny man credit for democratic accomplishments, it does argue that he should distinguish very carefully the things for which credit is claimed. A nation may properly be proud that it has developed the economic means which enable it to afford a full-fledged democracy or that it has utilized demo-cratic practices to create the economic base on which a democracy can be further broadened. But it cannot, with any validity, attribute its democ-racy to sheer moral and ideological virtue. . . .

In all societies of economic insufficiency, which is the only kind that existed up to about two centuries ago, certain social conditions have been fixed and inevitable. The vast majority of the people were inescapably destined to heavy toil and bare subsistence, and the economic surplus in excess of such bare subsistence was not sufficient to give leisure and abundance to more than a tiny minority. In these circumstances, certainly the society could not afford either the economic or the emotional costs of conducting a great social steeplechase for the purpose of selecting a handful of winners to occupy the few enviable positions. It was much sounder public policy to assign these positions by an arbitrary system of status and at the same time to assign to the great bulk of the people the burdens which most of them were destined to bear regardless of what regime was in power. Under a system of subordination transmitted by heredity, social competition, with its attendant loss of energy through friction, was avoided; the status-bound individual often gained a sense of contentment with his lot and even of dignity within his narrow sphere, and all that he sacrificed for this psychological advantage was a statistically negligible chance for advancement. Moreover in a relatively static and relatively simple society such as that of Tudor or Stuart England, the problems of government were not very intricate, and the only qualities required in the local ruling class were integrity and a willingness to accept responsibility. These qualities could usually be found and could readily be transmitted even in a squirearchy of low intellectual attainments, and therefore there was no need to recruit widely for leadership, as a society must do when it requires intelligence, specialized skill, and adaptability in its administration.

A country with inadequate wealth, therefore, could not safely promise its citizens more than security of status—at a low level in the social hierarchy and with a meager living. But this promise is, in its denial of equality, by definition, undemocratic. A democracy, by contrast, setting equality as its goal, must promise opportunity, for the goal of equality becomes a mockery unless there is some means of attaining it. But in promising opportunity, the democracy is constantly arousing expectations which it lacks the current means to fulfil and is betting on its ability to procure the necessary means by the very act of stimulating people to demand them and go after them. It is constantly educating large numbers of people without waiting to see whether jobs requiring education are available for all of them; it does this in the expectation that the supply will create a demand and that a society constantly rising in the level of its education will constantly generate new posts in which educated people are needed. Also, democracy is forever encouraging individuals to determine their own goals and set their own courses toward these goals, even though only a small proportion can attain complete success; the time and effort of many may be wasted in the pursuit, but the advantage to society of having the maximum number of people developing their maximum potentialities of intellect and personality is thought to justify the social cost.

All this is very well and works admirably if the country following these practices has the necessary physical resources and human resourcefulness to raise the standard of living, to create new occupational opportunities, and to find outlets for the abilities of an ever increasing class of trained men. But it must have this endowment to begin with, or it is certain to suffer intensely from the social waste that results from giving training which cannot be utilized and from the psychological damage that results when a competition has an excess of participants and a paucity of rewards. In short, to succeed as a democracy, a country must enjoy an economic surplus to begin with or must contrive to attain one. . . .

Not only has the presence of . . . more than enough rewards for those who strive, made the maintenance of a democratic system possible in America; it has also given a characteristic tone to American equalitarianism as distinguished from the equalitarianism of the Old World. Essentially, the difference is that Europe has always conceived of redistribution of wealth as necessitating the expropriation of some and the corresponding aggrandizement of others; but America has conceived of it primarily in terms of giving to some without taking from others. Hence, Europe cannot think of altering the relationship between the various levels of society without assuming a class struggle; but America has altered and can alter these relationships without necessarily treating one class as the victim or even, in an ultimate sense, the antagonist of another. The European mind often assumes implicitly that the volume of wealth is fixed; that most of the potential wealth has already been converted into actual wealth; that this actual wealth is already in the hands of owners; and, therefore, that the only way for one person or group to secure more is to wrest it from some other person or group, leaving that person or group with less. . . .

Our practice, indeed, has been to overlap problems—to bypass them—rather than to solve them. For instance, in the 1880s and 1890s there seemed to be three major public problems—the problem of a shrinking bullion supply; the problem of the control of an entire industry by a small group of monopolists, like John D. Rockefeller and his associates in the oil industry; and the problem of regulation of the railroads, which enjoyed a natural monopoly of transportation. Reformers struggled with all three of these problems, and various political solutions were proposed: the adoption of a bimetallic currency to relieve the bullion stringency, the enactment of an anti-trust law to curb Mr. Rockefeller, and the adoption of an Interstate Commerce Act to protect the shipper vis-à-vis the railroads. But in each case technological change interposed to relieve the acuteness of the problem or even to make it obsolete: the discovery of new gold supplies in the Klondike and of new methods of recovering gold reversed the process of shrinkage in the bullion supply; the discovery of the vast new deposits of oil in Texas and elsewhere undermined the dominance of Rockefeller in the oil industry as no legislative prohibtion was ever able to do; and the introduction of trucks moving over a network of national highways ended the natural monopoly of transportation by the railroads before Congress ceased the long quest for a legislative solution.

There is a widespread belief in the United States that the basic policy of our government underwent a sudden change about twenty years ago, with the advent of the New Deal. According to this belief, the American Republic has been a thoroughgoing laissez faire state during its first century and a half—a state where government scrupulously refrained from intervention in the economic sphere, and private enterprise alone shaped the country's economic progress. Then, it is supposed, an abrupt reversal of policy took place, and, turning our backs upon the principles that had guided us to our earlier economic triumphs, we embraced a paternalistic program of governmental regulation and control which started us on the road to the welfare state. . . .

Without denying that a major transformation occurred, we need to be aware of the strands of continuity, as well as of the shifts and new departures in our history. If we are to appreciate the links with the past, we must recognize that laissez faire was not the unique principle of policy in our eighteenth- and nineteenth-century development but that one of the key principles was certainly the constant endeavor of government to make the economic abundance of the nation accessible to the public. The tactics by which this was done changed as the form of abundance itself changed, but the basic purpose—to keep our population in contact with the sources of wealth—has remained steadily in the ascendant throughout our history.

In the early nineteenth century the major form in which abundance presented itself was the fertility of unsettled land. For a people of whom 90 percent followed agricultural pursuits, access to abundance meant opportunity to settle the new lands. The government responded by a series of land laws, beginning with the Ordinance of 1785 and extending far past the Homestead Act of 1862, which made land progressively easier for settlers to attain, until at last they could acquire title to 160 acres absolutely free. Over the years, while this was happening, some eminently public spirited men like John Quincy Adams contended for a program that would have conserved the assets of the public domain by distributing it gradually and on a basis that would yield revenue to the Treasury; but all such proposals were defeated, and quick settlement was stimulated even by legislation which encouraged squatters to occupy the land before it had been opened to public entry. Widespread access to wealth was preferred over the public capitalization of a great economic asset.

Relatively early, however, it became clear that access to soil did not mean access to wealth unless it was accompanied by access to market. Fertile soil remained a mere potentiality when its products could not reach the consumer. The market was the source of wealth to which access was needed, and again government responded by providing the internal improvements which would give such access. Sometimes the federal government did this, as, for instance, by the construction of the Cumberland Pike; sometimes the state governments took the initiative, as New York did with the digging of the Erie Canal; and sometimes government did not execute the project itself but encouraged private interests to do so by offering such tangible inducements as direct financial support, use of the public credit, and use of the power of eminent domain. Even in so great a project as the building of the first transcontinental railroad, the government virtually furnished all the funds, and, though the ownership was private, a congressman from New York could truthfully point out that the government in fact had built the railroads.

Later still, the wealth to which access was needed appeared increasingly in forms that could not be handled by the individual acting as a solitary operator. Iron resources, coal resources, petroleum resources, water-power resources, and other physical assets promised to raise the standard of living; but the only means of access to their value was through large-scale concentration of capital and labor. Again, government responded by facilitating the means of access: it made easy the process of concentration by sanctioning the wide use of the practice of incorporation; it assured the new corporations, through judicial interpretation of the Fourteenth Amendment, that they would enjoy the fullest legal security and even advantage; by the tariffs of the Civil War and post-Civil War periods, it guaranteed the corporations control of the American market. In return they did what was expected of them: they converted potential wealth into usable wealth, wastefully, selfishly, and ruthlessly in many cases, but quickly—and results were the primary thing demanded of them.

By the third decade of the twentieth century, the form in which wealth appeared had again altered drastically. No longer did it consist in natural resources of soil or subsoil, requiring to be put into operation. Access to wealth was now dependent upon the continued movement of the production lines rather than upon the throwing open of untrapped resources. In these circumstances, the operation of the business cycle, manifesting itself in the great Depression, seemed to block access to wealth as completely as the barriers of physical distance had blocked it a century earlier. In both cases, though the overt circumstances seemed wholly dissimilar, Americans found consolation in the same basic and comforting conviction—that abundance was there, and the problem was not to create it or to get along without it but simply to find how to get at it. And in both cases government responded with steps to provide access. If access depended upon the creation of purchasing power, government under the New Deal was ready to create it by spending, lending, priming the pump, and enacting minimum-wage laws; if it depended upon the capacity of workers to bargain collectively, government was ready to confer that capacity by law; if it depended upon securing industry against some of the hazards of competition, government offered a National Industrial Recovery Act to remove these hazards.

Writers on public questions often assume that in our early history we had a basic commitment to individualism and that we have recently abandoned this traditional principle just for the sake of security. But what we really were committed to was realizing on the potentialities of our unmatched assets and raising our standard of living. Because the standard of living involves comfort and material things, a basic concern with it is commonly regarded as ignoble; yet, as I have already suggested, it is only because we have attained a relatively high standard of living that we can afford to own and operate a democratic system. But, whether noble or not, our commitment to abundance was primary, and individualism was sanctioned as the very best means of fulfilling the possibilities of abundance. When it ceased to be the best means, we modified it with a readiness alarming to people who had supposed that it was the individualism itself which was basic. We did this because a great many people had never regarded it, at bottom, as more than a means to an end. The politics of our democracy was a politics of abundance rather than a politics of individualism, a politics of increasing our wealth quickly rather than of dividing it precisely, a politics which smiled both on those who valued abundance as a means to safeguard freedom and on those who valued freedom as an aid in securing abundance. . . .

But, though Americans have caused freedom and abundance to converge, the two are not by nature prone to convergence, and for the world at large they have not been closely linked. Consequently, when America, out of her abundance, preaches the gospel of democracy to countries which see no means of attaining abundance, the message does not carry the meaning which it is meant to convey. No other part of American activity has been so consistently and so completely a failure as our attempt to export democracy. At this point, the duality between abundance and freedom in the American democratic formula ceases to be abstract and becomes painfully concrete, for it is the lack of understanding of what we have to offer to the rest of the world that has vitiated our efforts to fulfil a national mission which we undertook with real dedication and for which we have made real sacrifices.

3

We the People

3.1. WHAT IS AN AMERICAN?

For more than a century America was a golden door of freedom for millions of immigrants. How a "new race" of Americans was to emerge from this was seen very early by St. John Crèvecoeur, himself an immigrant.

I WISH I could be acquainted with the feelings and thoughts which must agitate the heart and present themselves to the mind of an enlightened Englishman, when he first lands on this continent. He must greatly rejoice that he lived at a time to see this fair country discovered and settled; he must necessarily feel a share of national pride, when he views the chain of settlements which embellishes these extended shores. When he says to himself, this is the work of my countrymen, who, when convulsed by factions, afflicted by a variety of miseries and wants, restless and impatient, took refuge here. They brought along with them their national genius, to which they principally owe what liberty they enjoy, and what substance they possess. Here he sees the industry of his native country displayed in a new manner, and traces in their works the embrios of all the arts, sciences, and ingenuity which flourish in Europe. Here he beholds fair cities, substantial villages, extensive fields, an immense country filled with decent houses, good roads, orchards, meadows, and bridges, where an hundred years ago all was wild, woody and uncultivated! What a train of pleasing ideas this fair spectacle must suggest; it is a prospect which must inspire a good citizen with the most heartfelt pleasure. The difficulty consists in the manner of viewing so extensive a scene. He is arrived on a new continent; a modern society offers itself to his contemplation, different from what he had hitherto seen. It is not composed, as in Europe, of great lords who possess every thing, and of a herd of peo-

From J. Hector St. John Crèvecoeur, *Letters from an American Farmer* (New York: Duffield & Co., 1904; originally: 1782).

45

ple who have nothing. Here are no aristocratical families, no courts, no kings, no bishops, no ecclesiastical dominion, no invisible power giving to few a very visible one; no great manufacturers employing thousands, no great refinements of luxury. The rich and the poor are not so far removed from each other as they are in Europe. Some few towns excepted, we are all tillers of the earth, from Nova Scotia to West Florida. We are a people of cultivators, scattered over an immense territory, communicating with each other by means of good roads and navigable rivers, united by the silken bands of mild government, all respecting the laws, without dreading their power, because they are equitable. We are all animated with the spirit of an industry which is unfettered and unrestrained, because each person works for himself. If he travels through our rural districts he views not the hostile castle, and the haughty mansion, contrasted with the clay-built hut and miserable cabin, where cattle and men help to keep each other warm, and dwell in meanness, smoke, and indigence. A pleasing uniformity of decent competence appears throughout our habitations. The meanest of our log-houses is a dry and comfortable habitation. . . . Here man is free as he ought to be; nor is this pleasing equality so transitory as many others are. Many ages will not see the shores of our great lakes replenished with inland nations; nor the unknown bounds of North America entirely peopled. Who can tell how far it extends? Who can tell the millions of men whom it will feed and contain? for no European foot has as yet travelled half the extent of this mighty continent!

The next wish of this traveller will be to know whence came all these people? They are a mixture of English, Scotch, Irish, French, Dutch, Germans, and Swedes. From this promiscuous breed, that race now called Americans have arisen. . . .

In this great American asylum, the poor of Europe have by some means met together, and in consequence of various causes; to what purpose should they ask one another what countrymen they are? Alas, two thirds of them had no country. Can a wretch who wanders about, who works and starves, whose life is a continual scene of sore affliction or pinching penury; can that man call England or any other kingdom his country? A country that had no bread for him, whose fields procured him no harvest, who met with nothing but the frowns of the rich, the severity of the laws, with jails and punishments; who owned not a single foot of the extensive surface of this planet? No! urged by a variety of motives, here they came. Everything has tended to regenerate them; new laws, a new mode of living, a new social system; here they are become men: in Europe they were as so many useless plants, wanting vegitative mould, and refreshing showers; they withered, and were mowed down by want, hunger, and war; but now by the power of transplantation, like all other plants they have taken root and flourished! Formerly they were not numbered in any civil lists of their country, except in those of the poor; here they rank as citizens. By what invisible power has this surprising meta-morphosis been performed? By that of the laws and that of their industry. The laws, the indulgent laws, protect them as they arrive, stamping on them the symbol of adoption; they receive ample rewards for their labours; these accumulated rewards procure them lands; those lands confer on them the title of freemen, and to that title every benefit is affixed which men can possibly require. This is the great operation daily performed by our laws. From whence proceed these laws? From our government. Whence the government? It is derived from the original genius and strong desire of the people ratified and confirmed by the crown. This is the great chain which links us all, this is the picture which every province exhibits. . . .

What attachment can a poor European immigrant have for a country where he had nothing? The knowledge of the language, the love of a few kindred as poor as himself, were the only cords that tied him: his country is now that which gives him land, bread, protection, and consequence: *Ubi panis ibi patria,* is the motto of all emigrants. What then is the American, this new man? He is either an European, or the descendant of an European, hence that strange mixture of blood, which you will find in no other country. . . . He becomes an American by being received in the broad lap of our great *Alma Mater.* Here individuals of all nations are melted into a new race of men, whose labours and posterity will one day cause great changes in the world. Americans are the western pilgrims, who are carrying along with them that great mass of arts, sciences, vigour, and industry which began long since in the east; they will finish the great circle. The Americans were once scattered all over Europe; here they are incorporated into one of the finest systems of population which has ever appeared, and which will hereafter become distinct by the power of the different climates they inhabit. . . . From involuntary idleness, servile dependence, penury, and useless labour, he has passed to toils of a very different nature, rewarded by ample subsistence.—This is an American.

3.2. PRESIDENT WILSON'S OPPOSITION TO ARBITRARY RESTRAINT ON IMMIGRATION

Spurred by the fear of new mass waves of immigration brought on by World War I, Congress sought in 1914 to impose literacy tests as prerequisites to the admission of immigrants. President Wilson's veto message castigated the bill for seeking to close America's gates of asylum.

To the House of Representatives:
It is with unaffected regret that I find myself constrained by clear

conviction to return this bill (H. R. 6060, "An act to regulate the immigration of aliens to and the residence of aliens in the United States") without my signature. Not only do I feel it to be a very serious matter to exercise the power of veto in any case, because it involves opposing the single judgment of the President to the judgment of a majority of both the Houses of the Congress, a step which no man who realizes his own liability to error can take without great hesitation, but also because this particular bill is in so many important respects admirable, well conceived, and desirable. Its enactment into law would undoubtedly enhance the efficiency and improve the methods of handling the important branch of the public service to which it relates. But candor and a sense of duty with regard to the responsibility so clearly imposed upon me by the Constitution in matters of legislation leave me no choice but to dissent.

In two particulars of vital consequence this bill embodies a radical departure from the traditional and long-established policy of this country, a policy in which our people have conceived the very character of their Government to be expressed, the very mission and spirit of the Nation in respect of its relations to the peoples of the world outside their borders. It seeks to all but close entirely the gates of asylum which have always been open to those who could find nowhere else the right and opportunity of constitutional agitation for what they conceived to be the natural and inalienable rights of men; and it excludes those to whom the opportunities of elementary education have been denied, without regard to their character, their purposes, or their natural capacity.

Restrictions like these, adopted earlier in our history as a Nation, would very materially have altered the course and cooled the humane ardors of our politics. The right of political asylum has brought to this country many a man of noble character and elevated purpose who was marked as an outlaw in his own less fortunate land, and who has yet become an ornament to our citizenship and to our public councils. The children and the compatriots of these illustrious Americans must stand amazed to see the representatives of their Nation now resolved, in the fullness of our national strength and at the maturity of our great institutions, to risk turning such men back from our shores without test of quality or purpose. It is difficult for me to believe that the full effect of this feature of the bill was realized when it was framed and adopted, and it is impossible for me to assent to it in the form in which it is here cast.

The literacy test and the tests and restrictions which accompany it constitute an even more radical change in the policy of the Nation. Hitherto we have generously kept our doors open to all who were not unfitted by reason of disease or incapacity for self-support or such personal records and antecedents as were likely to make them a menace to

From President Woodrow Wilson's Veto of Immigration Bill (*The Congressional Record*, Vol. 52, Pt. 3, January 28, 1915), pp. 2481–2482.

our peace and order or to the wholesome and essential relationships of life. In this bill it is proposed to turn away from tests of character and of quality and impose tests which exclude and restrict; for the new tests here embodied are not tests of quality or of character or of personal fitness, but tests of opportunity. Those who come seeking opportunity are not to be admitted unless they have already had one of the chief of the opportunities they seek, the opportunity of education. The object of such provisions is restriction, not selection.

. . . Let the platforms of parties speak out upon this policy and the people pronounce their wish. The matter is too fundamental to be settled otherwise.

I have no pride of opinion in this question. I am not foolish enough to profess to know the wishes and ideals of America better than the body of her chosen representatives know them. I only want instruction direct from those whose fortunes, with ours and all men's, are involved.

3.3. PRESIDENT TRUMAN'S CRITIQUE OF THE QUOTA SYSTEM

The conflict between Congress and the President over our immigration policy emerged once more in 1952, when Congress passed the McCarran-Walter Immigration Bill. President Truman denounced the bill vigorously for its failure to shake off "the dead weight of past mistakes," especially its retention of discriminatory provisions based on race and nationality. The bill became law nonetheless when Congress overrode the President's veto.

To the House of Representatives:

I return herewith, without my approval, H. R. 5678, the proposed Immigration and Nationality Act.

H. R. 5678 is an omnibus bill which would revise and codify all of our laws relating to immigration, naturalization, and nationality.

A general revision and modernization of these laws unquestionably is needed and long overdue, particularly with respect to immigration. But this bill would not provide us with an immigration policy adequate for the present world situation. Indeed, the bill, taking all its provisions together, would be a step backward and not a step forward. In view of the

From President Harry S Truman's Veto of the Immigration Bill of 1952, in *Whom Shall We Welcome?* (Washington, D.C.: U.S. Government Printing Office, 1953).

crying need for reform in the field of immigration, I deeply regret that I am unable to approve H. R. 5678.

. . . What we do in the field of immigration and naturalization is vital to the continued growth and internal development of the United States—to the economic and social strength of our country—which is the core of the defense of the free world. Our immigration policy is equally, if not more, important to the conduct of our foreign relations and to our responsibilities of moral leadership in the struggle for world peace.

In one respect, this bill recognizes the great international significance of our immigration and naturalization policy, and takes a step to improve existing laws. All racial bars to naturalization would be removed, and at least some minimum immigration quota would be afforded to each of the free nations of Asia. . . .

But now this most desirable provision comes before me embedded in a mass of legislation which would perpetuate injustices of long standing against many other nations of the world, hamper the efforts we are making to rally the men of the east and west alike to the cause of freedom, and intensify the repressive and inhumane aspects of our immigration procedures. The price is too high and, in good conscience, I cannot agree to pay it. . . .

In addition to removing racial bars to naturalization, the bill would permit American women citizens to bring their alien husbands to this country as nonquota immigrants, and enable alien husbands of resident women aliens to come in under the quota in a preferred status. These provisions would be a step toward preserving the integrity of the family under our immigration laws, and are clearly desirable.

The bill would also relieve transportation companies of some of the unjustified burdens and penalities now imposed upon them. In particular, it would put an end to the archaic requirement that ·carriers pay the expenses of aliens detained at the port of entry, even though such aliens have arrived with proper travel documents.

But these few improvements are heavily outweighed by other provisions of the bill which retain existing defects in our laws, and add many undesirable new features.

The bill would continue, practically without change, the national origins quota system, which was enacted into law in 1924, and put into effect in 1929. This quota system—always based upon assumptions at variance with our American ideals—is long since out of date and more than ever unrealistic in the face of present world conditions. . . .

The over-all quota limitation, under the law of 1924, restricted annual immigration to approximately 150,000. This was about one-seventh of 1 percent of our total population in 1920. Taking into account the growth in population since 1920, the law now allows us but one-tenth of 1 percent of our total population. And since the largest national quotas are only partly used, the number actually coming in has been in the neighborhood of one-fifteenth of 1 percent. This is far less than we must have in the years ahead to keep up with the growing needs of our Nation for manpower to maintain the strength and vigor of our economy.

The greatest vice of the present quota system, however, is that it discriminates, deliberately and intentionally, against many of the peoples of the world. The purpose behind it was to cut down and virtually eliminate immigration to this country from Southern and Eastern Europe. A theory was invented to rationalize this objective. The theory was that in order to be readily assimilable, European immigrants should be admitted in proportion to the number of persons of their respective national stocks already here as shown by the census of 1920. Since Americans of English, Irish, and German descent were most numerous, immigrants of those three nationalities got the lion's share—more than two-thirds—of the total quota. The remaining third was divided up among all the other nations given quotas. . . .

The idea behind this discriminatory policy was, to put it baldly, that Americans with English or Irish names were better people and better citizens than Americans with Italian or Greek or Polish names. It was thought that people of West European origin made better citizens than Rumanians or Yugoslavs or Ukrainians or Hungarians or Balts or Austrians. Such a concept is utterly unworthy of our traditions and our ideals. It violates the great political doctrine of the Declaration of Independence that "all men are created equal." It denies the humanitarian creed inscribed beneath the Statue of Liberty proclaiming to all nations, "Give me your tired, your poor, your huddled masses yearning to breathe free."

It repudiates our basic religious concepts, our belief in the brotherhood of man, and in the words of St. Paul that "there is neither Jew nor Greek, there is neither bond nor free, . . . for ye are all one in Christ Jesus."

The basis of this quota system was false and unworthy in 1924. It is even worse now. . . . It is incredible to me that, in this year of 1952, we should again be enacting into law such a slur on the patriotism, the capacity, and the decency of a large part of our citizenry.

The time to shake off this dead weight of past mistakes is now. The time to develop a decent policy of immigration—a fitting instrument for our foreign policy and a true reflection of the ideals we stand for, at home and abroad—is now. In my earlier message on immigration, I tried to explain to the Congress that the situation we face in immigration is an emergency—that it must be met promptly. I have pointed out that in the last few years, we have blazed a new trail in immigration, through our displaced persons program. Through the combined efforts to the Government and private agencies, working together not to keep people out, but to bring qualified people in, we summoned our resources of good will and human feeling to meet the task. In this program we have found better techniques to meet the immigration problems of the 1950s.

None of this fruitful experience of the last 3 years is reflected in this bill before me. None of the crying human needs of this time of trouble is recognized in this bill. But it is not too late. The Congress can remedy these defects, and it can adopt legislation to meet the most critical problems before adjournment.

3.4. ARGUMENT FOR A "CLOSED DOOR" IMMIGRATION POLICY

This testimony presents the arguments for a restrictive immigration policy by the United States. Mr. Wilmeth maintains that only those races and nationalities which have made a positive contribution to our way of life should be allowed admission as immigrants.

. . . WE BEG to submit that we consider the quotas established in the present immigration law ample and sufficient for all needs of our economic and social conditions and our general American economy. We submit that it would be a useless thing to liberalize quotas or to enact special legislation such as H. R. 7376 to admit 300,000 immigrants over and above the quota system because of overpopulation or charitable considerations.

In our judgment, it is a poor policy to enact special legislation authorizing nonquota visas for a large number of people to be admitted as immigrants, and we would consider such action by Congress as a deliberate attempt to break down immigration barriers and to open the doors to immigrants whose services are not needed for the welfare or well-being of the United States. We are strictly opposed to the proposition of relieving overpopulated countries such as Italy, for instance, and call attention to your honorable committee to the fact that we have in the United States overpopulated areas and cities of our own where people live in crowded tenements and many of them in poverty. It is a well-known fact that Italy is an overpopulated country not from infiltration of refugees and escapees but by its own prolific people.

We submit further that there should be no increase over the McCarran-Walter bill quotas for Italy, Japan, Russia, and the Asiatic countries. All of these nations now have a quota and some of them con-

From Statement of James L. Wilmeth before the President's Commission on Immigration and Naturalization (October 1, 1952).

tributed nothing whatsoever to the colonization of America and the establishment of our Government and its free institutions and liberties.

We believe that the quotas in the present immigration law recently passed by Congress are fair and just, and that with the selective system of immigration the United States will receive all of the new blood from the old countries it needs. Certainly we do not wish to admit by special legislation a flood of immigrants who will be in competition with our own working people and whose services are not now urgently needed, and will be much less needed after the Korean conflict is over and peace fully restored. The American people are likely to find themselves in the position of having a horde of foreigners here in this country when peace comes who will have no jobs and will be a burden to the taxpayer by reason of their being on relief rolls.

We have seen the bad effects of unrestricted immigration. We know that there are many people in many lands who want to come to our shores, and we know that some of our overzealous people including certain Senators and Representatives are pleading for their admission on the grounds of present immigration laws being unfair and unjust. We take no stock in any such arguments and consider them to be only excuses for legislation which will break down immigration barriers and admit aliens, including refugees and escapees whose presence could become a menace to our own people. Of course, these aliens want to come to America and their appeal is something in the nature of asserting a right, but we submit that our own country should be the judge as to eligibility and who may be admitted as an immigrant, and that the present good immigration law establishes in no uncertain terms just who may come and under what conditions. . . .

We are having trouble here in the United States by reason of the infiltration of communism. We are bidding for more trouble if we liberalize our immigration laws, throw down the bars and let everyone who wants to be admitted come in. We tried that system and had to abandon it. A striking example of how such liberties are abused arose from the Chinese situation prior to the turn of the century when, through the promiscuous and unregulated immigration of Chinese people and their settling together in large cities like San Francisco and New York, they became a menace to our American civilization and, as a result, Chinese exclusion laws had to be enacted. We want no repetition of such conditions.

Further, our order has been active in the suppression of communism. The McCarran-Walter bill is positive in its control and regulation of the admission of Communist followers. . . .

We submit to your honorable Commission that humanitarian considerations should have no place in immigration legislation. To be sure, we are sympathetic with those who are in trouble, which is usually of their own making and not of ours. The United States has never received any substantial consideration on humanitarian grounds but it is constantly extending its benefits to those who are in trouble, but the American people should hesitate before adopting any law which will admit people on the grounds of sympathy rather than merit. What we are pleading for is confining our humanitarian efforts to those people who are embraced within the present statute without the enactment of a special law by Congress. . . . It is time for the patriotic people who want to preserve our institutions and our American way of life to advise your Commission in no uncertain terms that they will bitterly oppose any such legislation. It is entirely too liberal. It will admit people who would be unworthy of American citizenship and would go a long way toward the destruction and tearing down of all immigration restriction barriers. We want to go on record now with your Commission at this hearing as opposing such liberality in dealing with the important question which affects the American citizenship.

We offer the following suggestions and submit that they are not the views of isolationism but of patriotic American citizens who want to preserve the American way of life:

1. The quota system should not be disturbed. It is selective and will bring in a good class of citizens.

2. Contrary to statements, we submit that aliens who are admitted upon considerations of humanitarianism, or refugees or escapees will contribute but little to the United States either socially or politically or economically.

3. The services of immigrants over and above present quotas are not now needed in American industry.

4. It is a well-known fact that escapees and refugees, or many of them, come from nations which would not receive them back if deported because of violation of our laws.

5. To tear down the immigration bars and admit a flood of immigrants over and above the quotas established in the present law would work a hardship upon our taxpayers and American working people by reason of competition.

6. We suggest that the administration of the immigration system should be placed under the Immigration and Naturalization Service of the Department of Justice. This suggestion does not include the work now performed by the State Department.

Our country fortunately is not bound by law, certainly not by equity or charitable considerations, or by the public good to attempt through legislation to relieve overpopulation in any nation. We are unalterably opposed to any legislation of this kind.

The CHAIRMAN. Thank you very much, Mr. Wilmeth.

3.5. A PLEA FOR ABANDONMENT OF THE NATIONAL ORIGINS SYSTEM

The President's Commission on Immigration and Naturalization made a comprehensive study of the principles, operations, and implications of our recent policies on immigration. In a forthright report the Commission challenged the validity of the assumptions that led to the establishment of the national origins system in the Immigration Act of 1924. Despite the Commission's plea, our immigration laws continue basically unchanged.

IN REVIEWING the history of debates on the problem of immigration, the Commission was impressed by the fact that those opposing immigration appear to have been influenced in this view by a pessimistic outlook regarding the future economic growth of the United States. The nation was barely founded before a Congressman rose to say on the floor of the House of Representatives in 1797 that while a liberal immigration policy was satisfactory when the country was new and unsettled, now that the United States had reached maturity and was fully populated, further immigration should be stopped.

However, such views have continued throughout our history. In 1921, the Immigration Committee of the House of Representatives again recommended complete termination of all immigration. By the 1920s there was widespread fear that the country could not profitably absorb immigration in the volume received before World War I. The territorial frontier was gone. The country was "filled up" in the sense that good agricultural land was almost fully occupied and under cultivation. The economy was rapidly becoming industrialized, a "mature" economy was emerging, and therefore, it was argued, immigration had to be drastically curtailed.

With the 1921 Quota Act, originally designed for a 1-year emergency, there began a wholly new departure in American law: a limitation on the number of immigrants that could be admitted into the United States. The Immigration Act of 1924 not only carried into permanent law the concept of a limitation on numbers, but also initiated the formula of selection on the basis of race and nationality. The Immigration and Nationality Act of 1952 continued and strengthened the same principles. . . .

Our economy has expanded by leaps and bounds. Our gross

From Report of the President's Commission on Immigration and Naturalization, in *Whom Shall We Welcome?* (Washington, D.C.: U.S. Government Printing Office, 1953).

national product in 1924 of $140 billion (in 1951 dollars) grew to $329 billion in 1951; foreign exports of goods expanded from 6½ billion (1951 dollars) in 1924 to $15 billion in 1951; manufacturing production increased by 140 percent, and agricultural output by 51 percent between 1924 and 1951. Our farmers had an average per capita income from farming of only $302 in 1924 (in terms of 1951 purchasing power), which rose to $760 per capita in 1951. These are but a few examples of growth since the 1920s, and of the dynamic nature of our economy.

This economic expansion required an expanding labor force. The demands were met, as in the past, partly through natural growth and partly from migration. The labor force increased from 41.2 million in 1920 to 66 million in 1951. When the normal sources of European immigration were substantially cut off by our legislation of the 1920s, our industries had to seek other sources of labor. This they found in three ways: (1) by enormous migration from our own rural areas in the United States; (2) by increased immigration from Puerto Rico, the West Indies, and the nonquota countries of the Western Hemisphere; and (3) by special legislation providing for temporary immigration from neighboring countries.

During World War II, and after, many hundreds of thousands of workers were drawn from the farms to man the factories and other establishments of our urban centers. Since 1940 over one and a half million southern Negroes moved to the cities of the North and West to fill the manpower shortages. The Negro population of the North and West more than doubled through this migration. But this was not enough. This source of manpower had to be supplemented by some 200,000 Puerto Ricans, and other West Indians. Quite aside from the movements of native white people in the United States, there were nearly 2 million total migrants who moved into the northern and western States from these internal sources in the decade 1940–50, and the movement continues unabated.

During the same period there was a net foreign immigration of one and a half million people that went chiefly to the industrial areas of the country. Thus, the total migration to the North and West from the South and from abroad during the forties was at least as large as the net immigration in the decade 1890–1900, the third largest decade of European immigration in our history. In other words, the northern cities continued to need immigrants but had to get them mainly from elsewhere than Europe.

But even this was not enough to meet the demands of our growing economy. Congress also found it necessary to enact special immigration legislation admitting certain groups of immigrants temporarily to meet the manpower shortage, both in agricultural and nonagricultural employment.

As a result of acute labor shortages in agriculture during World

War II, special programs for recruitment of seasonal and temporary workers from Western Hemisphere countries were undertaken by intergovernmental agreements. Large numbers of aliens were involved in these programs, both during the war and after. The greatest number of Mexican farm workers legally in the United States for this purpose at any one time during World War II was 67,860 around August 1, 1944. As many as 21,000 Jamaicans and 6,000 Bahamans, as well as small numbers of Canadians and other North Americans, entered the United States under similar programs from time to time during this period. After the war, and under a law enacted in 1948, this recruitment of immigrant agricultural workers was continued on a peacetime basis. During the year 1951, some 191,000 Mexican nationals were admitted temporarily for agricultural work. Even this movement of immigrants, authorized by Congress, is overshadowed by the illegal entry each year of over half a million Mexican "wetbacks." . . .

During the war a manpower gap also appeared in the nonagricultral occupations. A total of 135,283 Mexican nationals worked on railroads in the United States from May 1943 to August 1945. More might have been used, but the Mexican government imposed a maximum ceiling of 75,000 who could be permitted in this country at any particular time. During the fiscal year 1951 some 10,000 Canadian woodsmen were permitted entry into Maine, Vermont, New Hampshire, and New York to fill a need for manpower not otherwise available. . . .

In the light of this experience under the restrictive limitations on immigration under the laws in effect since 1924, the Commission finds that immigration continues to be what it has always been in our history, a source of necessary manpower. Despite the efforts to change this situation by shutting off immigration from its customary sources, the American economy still continues to demand some form of immigration to meet the manpower demands of a growing and vigorous nation. . . .

The United States is the only major English-speaking country in the world which has written discrimination into its national immigration laws. Great Britain, Canada, Australia, and New Zealand, the other great English-speaking countries, all of them immigrant-receiving countries, have neither a national origins system nor an inflexible quota limitation.

The national origins system is also unique among the laws of English-speaking nations in the candor of its purpose. The legislative history, the statements by its sponsors and the nature of its operation, all point to the fact that the 1924 national origins system was designed and intended to discriminate on the basis of national origin, race, color, and (in effect) religion. It was designed to favor immigrants from Northern and Western Europe and to discriminate against those from Southern and Eastern Europe, and against Orientals.

Three groups were set up in the 1924 national origins law:

(1) the people of the Western Hemisphere who were granted non-quota status and permitted to enter the United States without regard to any numerical limitation; (2) Orientals, who were completely excluded; and (3) Europeans and others from the rest of the world, for whom some 154,000 quota numbers were allocated for distribution on the basis of place of birth. . . .

The 1952 act intentionally perpetuates the national origins system, principally to preserve what the committee stated was the "sociological and cultural balance in the population of the United States." This is merely a gentle way of saying that its purpose was to continue racial and national discrimination.

That racial and national discrimination is the essence of the Immigration and Nationality Act of 1952 is shown in several other ways. For the first time in American history a subquota is created for immigrants born in the colonies or dependent areas of the Western Hemisphere. This substantially reduces immigration of Negroes from the Caribbean areas. For example, it shrinks immigration from Jamaica, from an average of 1,000 annually to a statutory maximum of 100 annually.

A second indication of the intentionally discriminatory character of the act of 1952 is the fact that although the law repeals the Japanese Exclusion Act and sets up a minimum quota for Japanese, it establishes a racial quota under which Orientals are to be charged to the "Asia-Pacific Triangle" on the basis not of place of birth—as is true in all other cases—but of their own racial background.

This is the national origins system. Until 1921 the United States followed its great tradition of regarding all peoples as being equal and of examining the intrinsic worth of immigrants in terms of their prospective individual contributions to the American scene. In 1921, in 1924, and even more emphatically in 1952, our immigration laws abandoned our traditional faith in the individual human being.

4

Democracy in America

4.1. JOHN ADAMS' VIEWS ON THE CONSTITUTION

How shall the machinery of government be organized so as to take advantage of man's best qualities and thwart those qualities which lead to faction, selfishness, corruption, and civil strife? This was a major concern of the man who was to become our second President.

MARCHAMONT NEDHAM lays it down as a fundamental principle and an undeniable rule, "that the people, (that is, such as shall be successively chosen to represent the people,) are the best keepers of their own liberties, and that for many reasons. First, because they never think of usurping over other men's rights, but mind which way to preserve their own."

The proposition of our author . . . should be reversed, and it should have been said, that they mind so much their own, that they never think enough of others. . . .

Would Mr. Nedham be responsible that, if all were to be decided by a vote of the majority, the eight or nine millions who have no property, would not think of usurping over the rights of the one or two millions who have? Property is surely a right of mankind as really as liberty. Perhaps, at first, prejudice, habit, shame or fear, principle or religion, would restrain the poor from attacking the rich, and the idle from usurping on the industrious; but the time would not be long before courage and enterprise would come, and pretexts be invented by degrees, to

From John Adams, *Works,* Vol. VI (Boston: Little, Brown and Co., 1851).

countenance the majority in dividing all the property among them, or at least, in sharing it equally with its present possessors. Debts would be abolished first; taxes laid heavy on the rich, and not at all on the others; and at last a downright equal division of every thing be demanded, and voted. What would be the consequence of this? The idle, the vicious, the intemperate, would rush into the utmost extravagance of debauchery, sell and spend all their share, and then demand a new division of those who purchased from them. The moment the idea is admitted into society, that property is not as sacred as the laws of God, and that there is not a force of law and public justice to protect it, anarchy and tyranny commence. If "THOU SHALT NOT COVET," and "THOU SHALT NOT STEAL," were not commandments of Heaven, they must be made inviolable precepts in every society, before it can be civilized or made free.

. . . Of all possible forms of government, a sovereignty in one assembly, successively chosen by the people, is perhaps the best calculated to facilitate the gratification of self-love, and the pursuit of the private interest of a few individuals; a few eminent conspicuous characters will be continued in their seats in the sovereign assembly, from one election to another, whatever changes are made in the seats around them; by superior art, address, and opulence, by more splendid birth, reputations, and connections, they will be able to intrigue with the people and their leaders, out of doors, until they worm out most of their opposers, and introduce their friends; to this end, they will bestow all offices, contracts, privileges in commerce, and other emoluments, on the latter and their connections, and throw every vexation and disappointment in the way of the former, until they establish such a system of hopes and fears throughout the state, as shall enable them to carry a majority in every fresh election of the house. . . .

It may sound oddly to say that the majority is a faction; but it is, nevertheless, literally just. If the majority are partial in their own favor, if they refuse or deny a perfect equality to every member of the minority, they are a faction; and as a popular assembly, collective or representative, cannot act, or will, but by a vote, the first step they take, if they are not unanimous, occasions a division into majority and minority, that is, into two parties, and the moment the former is unjust it is a faction. . . .

It is pretended by some, that a sovereignty in a single assembly, annually elected, is the only one in which there is any responsibility for the exercise of power. In the mixed government we contend for, the ministers, at least of the executive power, are responsible for every instance of the exercise of it; and if they dispose of a single commission by corruption, they are responsible to a house of representatives, who may, by impeachment, make them responsible before a senate, where they may be accused, tried, condemned, and punished by independent judges. But in a single sovereign assembly, each member, at the end of his year, is only responsible to his constituents; and the majority of members who have been of one party, and carried all before them, are to be responsible only to their constituents, not to the constituents of the minority who have been overborne, injured, and plundered. . . .

It is agreed that the people are the best keepers of their own liberties, and the only keepers who can be always trusted; and, therefore, the people's fair, full, and honest consent, to every law, by their representatives, must be made an essential part of the constitution; but it is denied that they are the best keepers, or any keepers at all, of their own liberties, when they hold collectively, or by representation, the executive and judicial power, or the whole and uncontrolled legislative; on the contrary, the experience of all ages has proved, that they instantly give away their liberties into the hand of grandees, or kings, idols of their own creation. The management of the executive and judicial powers together always corrupts them, and throws the whole power into the hands of the most profligate and abandoned among themselves. The honest men are generally nearly equally divided in sentiment, and, therefore, the vicious and unprincipled, by joining one party, carry the majority; and the vicious and unprincipled always follow the most profligate leader, him who bribes the highest, and sets all decency and shame at defiance. It becomes more profitable, and reputable too, except with a very few, to be a party man than a public-spirited one.

It is agreed that "the end of all government is the good and ease of the people, in a secure enjoyment of their rights, without oppression"; but it must be remembered, that the rich are *people* as well as the poor; that they have rights as well as others; that they have as clear and as *sacred* a right to their large property as others have to theirs which is smaller; that oppression to them is as possible and as wicked as to others; that stealing, robbing, cheating, are the same crimes and sins, whether committed against them or others. The rich, therefore, ought to have an effectual barrier in the constitution against being robbed, plundered, and murdered, as well as the poor; and this can never be without an independent senate. The poor should have a bulwark against the same dangers and oppressions; and this can never be without a house of representatives of the people. But neither the rich nor the poor can be defended by their respective guardians in the constitution, without an executive power, vested with a negative, equal to either, to hold the balance even between them, and decide when they cannot agree. . . . "Powerful and crafty underminers" have nowhere such rare sport as in a simple democracy or single popular assembly. Nowhere, not in the completest despotism, does human nature show itself so completely depraved, so nearly approaching an equal mixture of brutality and devilism, as in the last stages of such a democracy, and in the beginning of that despotism that always succeeds it.

4.2. WHAT IS A REPUBLICAN FORM OF GOVERNMENT?

The classic commentary on the American Constitution is the series of essays by Alexander Hamilton, John Jay, and James Madison which have been named The Federalist Papers. *In this brief selection Madison defines the essential qualities of a republic as a representative form of democracy.*

IF WE RESORT for a criterion to the different principles on which different forms of government are established, we may define a republic to be, or at least may bestow that name on, a government which derives all its powers directly or indirectly from the great body of the people, and is administered by persons holding their offices during pleasure, for a limited period, or during a good behaviour. It is *essential* to such a government that it be derived from the great body of the society, not from an inconsiderable proportion, or a favoured class of it; otherwise a handful of tyrannical nobles, exercising their oppressions by a delegation of their powers, might aspire to the rank of republicans, and claim for their government the honourable title of republic. It is *sufficient* for such a government that the persons administering it be appointed, either directly or indirectly, by the people; and that they hold their appointments by either of the tenures just specified; otherwise every government in the United States, as well as every other popular government that has been or can be well organised or well executed, would be degraded from the republican character. According to the constitution of every State in the Union, some one or other of the officers of government are appointed indirectly only by the people. According to most of them, the chief magistrate himself is so appointed. And according to one, this mode of appointment is extended to one of the co-ordinate branches of the legislature. According to all the constitutions, also, the tenure of the highest offices is extended to a definite period, and in many instances, both within the legislative and executive departments, to a period of years. According to the provisions of most of the constitutions, again, as well as according to the most respectable and received opinions on the subject, the members of the judiciary department are to retain their offices by the firm tenure of good behavior. . . .

From James Madison, *The Federalist, No. 39* [1788].

4.3. DEMOCRACY OF THE TOWN MEETING

Participation by citizens in the processes of government has always been a major factor in democracy. In this selection the author extols the New England town meeting as a form of democracy. The spirit of the town meeting, he points out, is the basis of all political life in the United States.

OUT OF THE innumerable places which one might visit in America, there are none which would better reward such careful observation, or which are more full of interest for the comparative historian, than the rural towns and mountain villages of New England; that part of English America which is oldest in civilization (though not in actual date of settlement), and which, while most completely English in blood and in traditions, is at the same time most completely American in so far as it has most distinctly illustrated and most successively represented those political ideas which have given to American history its chief significance in the general work of civilization. . . .

The settlement of New England by the Puritans occupies a peculiar position in the annals of colonization, and without understanding this we cannot properly appreciate the character of the purely democratic society which I have sought to describe. As a general rule colonies have been founded, either by governments or by private enterprise, for political or commercial reasons. The aim has been—on the part of governments—to annoy some rival power, or to get rid of criminals, or to open some new avenue of trade, or—on the part of the people—to escape from straitened circumstances at home, or to find a refuge from religious persecution. In the settlement of New England none of these motives were operative except the last, and that only to a slight extent. The Puritans who fled from Nottinghamshire to Holland in 1608, and twelve years afterwards crossed the ocean in the *Mayflower,* may be said to have been driven from England by persecution. But this was not the case with the Puritans who between 1630 and 1650 went from Lincolnshire, Norfolk and Suffolk, and from Dorset and Devonshire, and founded the colonies of Massachusetts and Connecticut. These men left their homes at a time when Puritanism was waxing powerful and could not be assailed with impunity. They belonged to the upper and middle classes of the society of that day, outside of the peerage. Mr. Freeman has pointed out the importance of the change by which, after the Norman Conquest, the Old-English nobility or *thegnhood* was pushed down into "a secondary place in the political and social scale." . . . The proximate effect was that "the ancient lords of the soil, thus thrust down into the second rank, formed that great body of free-

From John Fiske, *American Political Ideas* (New York: Harper & Row, 1902; originally: 1884), pp. 18, 27–32.

holders, the stout gentry and yeomanry of England, who were for so many ages the strength of the land." It was from this ancient thegnhood that the Puritan settlers of New England were mainly descended.

. . . Immediately on their arrival in New England, the settlers proceeded to form for themselves a government as purely democratic as any that has ever been seen in the world. Instead of scattering about over the country, the requirements of education and of public worship, as well as of defence against Indian attacks, obliged them to form small village communities. As these villages multiplied, the surface of the country came to be laid out in small districts (usually from six to ten miles in length and breadth) called *townships*. Each township contained its village together with the woodlands surrounding. In later days two or more villages have often grown up within the limits of the same township and the road from one village to another is sometimes bordered with homesteads and cultivated fields throughout nearly its whole length. In the neighbourhood of Boston villages and small towns crowd closely together for twenty miles in every direction; and all these will no doubt by and by grow together into a vast and complicated city, in somewhat the same way that London has grown.

From the outset the government of the township was vested in the TOWN-MEETING,—an institution which in its present form is said to be peculiar to New England, but which, as we shall see, has close analogies with local self-governing bodies in other ages and countries. Once in each year—usually in the month of March—a meeting is held, at which every adult male residing within the limits of the township is expected to be present, and is at liberty to address the meeting or to vote upon any question that may come up. . . .

I have described the Town-meeting as it exists in the states where it first grew up and has since chiefly flourished. But something very like the "town-meeting principle" lies at the bottom of all the political life of the United States. To maintain vitality in the centre without sacrificing it in the parts; to preserve tranquillity in the mutual relations of forty powerful states, while keeping the people everywhere as far as possible in direct contact with the government; such is the political problem which the American Union exists for the purpose of solving; and of this great truth every American citizen is supposed to have some glimmering, however crude.

4.4   THE IDEALLY BEST FORM
OF GOVERNMENT

The framers of the United States Constitution were not enamored of "democracy," by which they meant government directly by the people, as in ancient Athens. As noted earlier, they preferred to call the new government they were establishing a republic. The most vigorous defense of republican or representative government as the best form of government is by John Stuart Mill, an English utilitarian of the late nineteenth century.

THERE IS NO DIFFICULTY in showing that the ideally best form of government is that in which the sovereignty, or supreme controlling power in the last resort, is vested in the entire aggregate of the community, every citizen not only having a voice in the exercise of that ultimate sovereignty, but being, at least occasionally, called on to take an actual part in the government by the personal discharge of some public function, local or general.

To test this proposition, it has to be examined in reference to the two branches into which . . . the inquiry into the goodness of a government conveniently divides itself, namely, how far it promotes the good management of the affairs of society by means of the existing faculties, moral, intellectual, and active, of its various members, and what is its effect in improving or deteriorating those faculties.

The ideally best form of government, it is scarcely necessary to say, does not mean one which is practicable or eligible in all states of civilization, but the one which, in the circumstances in which it is practicable and eligible, is attended with the greatest amount of beneficial consequences, immediate and prospective. A completely popular government is the only polity which can make out any claim to this character. It is pre-eminent in both the departments between which the excellence of a political Constitution is divided. It is both more favorable to present good government, and promotes a better and higher form of national character than any other polity whatsoever. . . .

Its superiority in reference to present well-being rests upon two principles, of as universal truth and applicability as any general propositions which can be laid down respecting human affairs. The first is, that the rights and interests of every or any person are only secure from being disregarded when the person interested is himself able, and habitually disposed to stand up for them. The second is, that the general prosperity attains a greater height, and is more widely diffused, in proportion to the amount and variety of the personal energies enlisted in promoting it.

Putting these two propositions into a shape more special to their present application—human beings are only secure from evil at the hands of others in proportion as they have the power of being, and are self-*protecting;* and they only achieve a high degree of success in their struggle

From John Stuart Mill, *Considerations on Representative Government* (New York: Holt, Rinehart and Winston, Inc., 1875), pp. 64–66, 68, 69, 80.

with Nature in proportion as they are self-*dependent*, relying on what they themselves can do, either separately or in concert, rather than on what others do for them.

The former proposition—that each is the only safe guardian of his own rights and interests—is one of those elementary maxims of prudence which every person capable of conducting his own affairs implicitly acts upon wherever he himself is interested. Many, indeed, have a great dislike to it as a political doctrine, and are fond of holding it up to obloquy as a doctrine of universal selfishness. To which we may answer, that whenever it ceases to be true that mankind, as a rule, prefer themselves to others, and those nearest them to those more remote, from that moment Communism is not only practicable, but the only defensible form of society, and will, when that time arrives, be assuredly carried into effect. For my own part, not believing in universal selfishness, I have no difficulty in admitting that Communism would even now be practicable among the *élite* of mankind, and may become so among the rest. But as this opinion is any thing but popular with those defenders of existing institutions who find fault with the doctrine of the general predominance of self-interest, I am inclined to think they do in reality believe that most men consider themselves before other people. It is not, however, necessary to affirm even thus much in order to support the claim of all to participate in the sovereign power. We need not suppose that when power resides in an exclusive class, that class will knowingly and deliberately sacrifice the other classes to themselves: it suffices that, in the absence of its natural defenders, the interest of the excluded is always in danger of being overlooked; and, when looked at, is seen with very different eyes from those of the persons whom it directly concerns. . . .

It must be acknowledged that the benefits of freedom, so far as they have hitherto been enjoyed, were obtained by the extension of its privileges to a part only of the community, and that a government in which they are extended impartially to all is a desideratum still unrealized. But, though every approach to this has an independent value, and in many cases more than an approach could not, in the existing state of general improvement, be made, the participation of all in these benefits is the ideally perfect conception of free government. In proportion as any, no matter who, are excluded from it, the interests of the excluded are left without the guaranty accorded to the rest, and they themselves have less scope and encouragement than they might otherwise have to that exertion of their energies for the good of themselves and of the community to which the general prosperity is always proportioned. . . .

From these accumulated considerations, it is evident that the only government which can fully satisfy all the exigencies of the social state is one in which the whole people participate; that any participation, even in the smallest public function, is useful; that the participation should every where be as great as the general degree of improvement of the community will allow; and that nothing less can be ultimately desirable than the admission of all to a share in the sovereign power of the state. But since all can not, in a community exceeding a single small town, participate personally in any but some very minor portions of the public business, it follows that the ideal type of a perfect government must be representative.

4.5. THE CHALLENGE OF COMMUNISM TO DEMOCRACY

Although contemporary Communists refer to their governments as "people's democracies," they give a special meaning to the term. As one can see in the following selection by the triumphant leader of the Russian Revolution, Communist ideology flatly denies the basic tenets of representative democracy.

IN THE USUAL debates about the State . . . it is constantly forgotten that the destruction of the State involves also the destruction of democracy; that the "withering away" of the State also means the "withering away" of democracy. At first sight such a statement seems exceedingly strange and incomprehensible. Indeed, perhaps some one or other may begin to fear lest we be expecting the advent of such an order of society in which the principle of majority rule will not be respected—for is not a democracy just the recognition of this principle?

No, democracy is not identical with majority rule. No, democracy is a *State* which recognizes the subjection of the minority to the majority, that is, an organization for the systematic use of *violence* by one class against the other, by one part of the population against another. . . .

In capitalist society, under the conditions most favorable to its development, we have a more or less complete democracy in the form of a democratic republic. But this democracy is always bound by the narrow framework of capitalist exploitation, and consequently always remains, in reality, a democracy only for the minority, only for the possessing classes, only for the rich. Freedom in capitalist society always remains more or less the same as it was in the ancient Greek republics, that is, freedom for the slave owners. The modern wage-slaves, in virtue of the conditions of capitalist exploitation, remain to such an extent crushed by want and poverty that they "cannot be bothered with democracy," have

From Nikolai Lenin, *The State and Revolution* (New York: Vanguard Press, 1926; originally: 1917), pp. 187, 191, 192–195.

"no time for politics"; that, in the ordinary peaceful course of events, the majority of the population is debarred from participating in public political life. . . .

Democracy for an insignificant minority, democracy for the rich —that is the democracy of capitalist society. If we look more closely into the mechanism of capitalist democracy, everywhere—in the so-called "petty" details of the suffrage (the residential qualification, the exclusion of women, etc.), in the technique of the representative institutions, in the actual obstacles to the right of meeting (public buildings are not for the "poor"), in the purely capitalist organization of the daily press, etc., etc.— on all sides we shall see restrictions upon restrictions of democracy. These restrictions, exceptions, exclusions, obstacles for the poor, seem slight —especially in the eyes of one who has himself never known want, and has never lived in close contact with the oppressed classes in their hard life, and nine-tenths, if not ninety-nine hundredths, of the bourgeois publicists and politicians are of this class! But in their sum these restrictions exclude and thrust out the poor from politics and from an active share in democracy. Marx splendidly grasped the *essence* of capitalist democracy, when, in his analysis of the experience of the Commune, he said that the oppressed are allowed, once every few years to decide which particular representatives of the oppressing class are to represent and repress them in Parliament!

But from this capitalist democracy—inevitably narrow, stealthily thrusting aside the poor, and therefore, to its core, hypocritical and treacherous—progress does not march along a simple, smooth and direct path to "greater and greater democracy," as the Liberal professors and the lower middle class opportunists would have us believe. No, progressive development—that is, towards Communism—marches through the dictatorship of the proletariat; and cannot do otherwise, for there is no one else who can *break the resistance* of the exploiting capitalists, and no other way of doing it.

And the dictatorship of the proletariat—that is, the organization of the advance-guard of the oppressed as the ruling class, for the purpose of crushing the oppressors—cannot produce merely an expansion of democracy. *Together* with an immense expansion of democracy—for the first time becoming democracy for the poor, democracy for the people, and not democracy for the rich folk—the dictatorship of the proletariat will produce a series of restrictions of liberty in the case of the oppressors, exploiters and capitalists. We must crush them in order to free humanity from wage-slavery; their resistance must be broken by force. It is clear that where there is suppression there must also be violence, and there cannot be liberty or democracy.

Engels expressed this splendidly in his letter to Bebel when he said, as the reader will remember, that "the proletariat needs the State, not in the interests of liberty, but for the purpose of crushing its opponents; and, when one will be able to speak of freedom, the State will have ceased to exist."

Democracy for the vast majority of the nation, and the suppression by force—that is, the exclusion from democracy—of the exploiters and oppressors of the nation; this is the modification of democracy which we shall see during the *transition* from capitalism to Communism.

Only in Communist society, when the resistance of the capitalists has finally been broken, when the capitalists have disappeared, when there are no longer any classes (that is, when there is no difference between the members of society in respect of their social means of production) *only then* "does the State disappear *and one can speak of freedom.*" Only then will be possible and will be realized a really full democracy, a democracy without any exceptions. And only then will democracy itself begin to wither away in virtue of the simple fact that, freed from capitalist slavery, from the innumerable horrors, savagery, absurdities and infamies of capitalist exploitation, people will gradually *become accustomed* to the observation of the elementary rules of social life, known for centuries, repeated for thousands of years in all sermons. They will become accustomed to their observance without force, without constraint, without subjection, without the *special apparatus* for compulsion which is called the State.

The expression "the State withers away," is very well chosen, for it indicates the gradual and elemental nature of the process. Only habit can, and undoubtedly will, have such an effect: for we see around us millions of times how readily people get accustomed to observe the necessary rules of life in common, if there is no exploitation, if there is nothing that causes indignation, that calls forth protest and revolt and has to be suppressed.

Thus, in capitalist society, we have a democracy that is curtailed, wretched, false; a democracy only for the rich, for the minority. The dictatorship of the proletariat, the period of transition to Communism, will, for the first time, produce a democracy for the people, for the majority, side by side with the necessary suppression of the minority constituted by the exploiters. Communism alone is capable of giving a really complete democracy, and the fuller it is the more quickly will it become unnecessary and wither away of itself. In other words, under capitalism we have a State in the proper sense of the word: that is, a special instrument for the suppression of one class by another, and of the majority by the minority at that. Naturally, for the successful discharge of such a task as the systematic suppression by the minority of exploiters of the majority of exploited, the greatest ferocity and savagery of suppression is required, and seas of blood are needed, through which humanity has to direct its path, in a condition of slavery, serfdom and wage labor.

Again, during the *transition* from capitalism to Communism, suppression is *still* necessary; but in this case it is suppression of the minority of exploiters by the majority of exploited. A special instrument, a special machine for suppression—that is, the "State"—is necessary, but this is now a transitional State, no longer a State in the ordinary sense of the term. For the suppression of the minority of exploiters, by the majority of those who were *but yesterday* wage slaves, is a matter comparatively so easy, simple and natural that it will cost far less bloodshed than the suppression of the risings of the slaves, serfs or wage laborers, and will cost the human race far less. And it is compatible with the diffusion of democracy over such an overwhelming majority of the nation that the need for any *special machinery* for *suppression* will gradually cease to exist. The exploiters are unable, of course, to suppress the people without a most complex machine for performing this duty; but *the people* can suppress the exploiters even with a very simple "machine"—almost without any "machine" at all, without any special apparatus—by the simple *organization of the armed masses* (such as the Councils of Workers' and Soldiers' Deputies, we may remark, anticipating a little).

Finally, only under Communism will the State become quite unnecessary, for there will be *no one* to suppress—"no one" in the sense of a *class,* in the sense of a systematic struggle with a definite section of the population. We are not utopians, and we do not in the least deny the possibility and inevitability of excesses by *individual persons,* and equally the need to suppress such excesses. But, in the first place, for this no special machine, no special instrument of repression is needed. This will be done by the armed nation itself, as simply and as readily as any crowd of civilized people, even in modern society, parts a pair of combatants or does not allow a woman to be outraged. And, secondly, we know that the fundamental social cause of excesses which violate the rules of social life is the exploitation of the masses, their want and their poverty. With the removal of this chief cause, excesses will inevitably begin to "wither away." We do not know how quickly and in what stages, but we know that they will be withering away. With their withering away, the State will also wither away.

5

Government by the People

5.1. THE NEED TO CONTROL FACTION

Among the potential evils of government, none is more dangerous than faction, according to Madison. In this selection he explains the meaning of faction and endorses republican government as the best means of controlling its effects. The Federalist, No. 10, *is a basic document in the history of American political thought.*

AMONG the numerous advantages promised by a well constructed Union, none deserves to be more accurately developed than its tendency to break and control the violence of faction. . . .

By a faction, I understand a number of citizens, whether amounting to a majority or minority of the whole, who are united and actuated by some common impulse of passion, or of interest, adverse to the rights of other citizens, or to the permanent and aggregate interests of the community.

There are two methods of curing the mischiefs of faction. The one, by removing its causes; the other, by controlling its effects.

There are again two methods of removing the causes of faction: The one, by destroying the liberty which is essential to its existence; the other, by giving to every citizen the same opinions, the same passions, and the same interests.

It could never be more truly said, that of the first remedy, that it was worse than the disease. Liberty is to faction what air is to fire, an aliment, without which it instantly expires. But it could not be a less folly to abolish liberty, which is essential to political life because it nourishes faction, than it would be to wish the annihilation of air, which is essential to animal life, because it imparts to fire its destructive agency.

From James Madison, *The Federalist, No. 10* [1788].

The second expedient is as impracticable, as the first would be unwise. As long as the reason of man continues fallible, and he is at liberty to exercise it, different opinions will be formed. As long as the connection subsists between his reason and his self-love, his opinions and his passions will have a reciprocal influence on each other; and the former will be objects to which the latter will attach themselves. The diversity in the faculties of men, from which the rights of property originate, is not less an insuperable obstacle to an uniformity of interests. The protection of those faculties is the first object of government. From the protection of different and unequal faculties of acquiring property, the possession of different degrees and kinds of property immediately results; and from the influence of these on the sentiments and views of the respective proprietors, ensues a division of the society into different interests and parties.

. . . the most common and durable source of factions has been the various and unequal distribution of property. Those who hold, and those who are without property, have ever formed distinct interests in society. Those who are creditors, and those who are debtors, fall under a like discrimination. A landed interest, a manufacturing interest, a mercantile interest, a moneyed interest, with many lesser interests, grow up of necessity in civilized nations, and divide them into different classes, actuated by different sentiments and views. The regulation of these various and interfering interests forms the principal task of modern legislation, and involves the spirit of party and faction in the necessary and ordinary operations of government. . . .

It is in vain to say, that enlightened statesmen will be able to adjust these clashing interests, and render them all subservient to the public good. Enlightened statesmen will not always be at the helm: nor, in many cases, can such an adjustment be made at all, without taking into view indirect and remote considerations, which will rarely prevail over the immediate interest ·which one party may find in disregarding the rights of another, or the good of the whole.

The inference to which we are brought is, that the *causes* of faction cannot be removed; and that relief is only to be sought in the means of controlling its *effects*. . . .

By what means is this object attainable? Evidently by one of two only. Either the existence of the same passion or interest in a majority, at the same time must be prevented; or the majority, having such coexistent passion or interest, must be rendered, by their number and local situation, unable to concert and carry into effect schemes of oppression. If the impulse and the opportunity be suffered to coincide, we well know, that neither moral nor religious motives can be relied on as an adequate control. They are not found to be such on the injustice and violence of individuals, and lose their efficacy in proportion to the number combined together; that is, in proportion as their efficacy becomes needful.

From this view of the subject, it may be concluded, that a pure democracy, by which I mean a society consisting of a small number of citizens, who assemble and administer the government in person, can admit of no cure from the mischiefs of faction. A common passion or interest will, in almost every case, be felt by a majority of the whole; a communication and concert, results from the form of government itself; and there is nothing to check the inducements to sacrifice the weaker party, or an obnoxious individual. Hence it is, that such democracies have ever been spectacles of turbulence and contention; have ever been found incompatible with personal security, or the rights of property; and have, in general, been as short in their lives, as they have been violent in their deaths. . . .

A republic, by which I mean a government in which the scheme of representation takes place, opens a different prospect, and promises the cure for which we are seeking. Let us examine the points in which it varies from pure democracy, and we shall comprehend both the nature of the cure and the efficacy which it must derive from the union.

The two great points of difference, between a democracy and a republic, are, first, the delegation of the government, in the latter, to a small number of citizens elected by the rest; secondly, the greater number of citizens, and greater sphere of country, over which the latter may be extended.

The effect of the first difference is, on the one hand, to refine and enlarge the public views, by passing them through the medium of a chosen body of citizens, whose wisdom may best discern the true interest of their country, and whose patriotism and love of justice, will be least likely to sacrifice it to temporary or partial considerations. Under such a regulation, it may well happen, that the public voice, pronounced by the representatives of the people, will be more consonant to the public good, than if pronounced by the people themselves, convened for the purpose. On the other hand, the effect may be inverted. Men of factious tempers, of local prejudices, or of sinister designs, may by intrigue, by corruption, or by other means, first obtain the suffrages, and then betray the interests of the people. The question resulting is, whether small or extensive republics are most favourable to the election of proper guardians of the public weal; and it is clearly decided in favour of the latter by two obvious considerations.

In the first place, it is to be remarked, that however small the republic may be, the representatives must be raised to a certain number, in order to guard against the cabals of a few; and that however large it may be, they must be limited to a certain number, in order to guard against the confusion of a multitude. Hence, the number of representatives in the two cases not being in proportion to that of the constituents, and being proportionally greatest in the small republic, it follows that if the proportion of fit characters be not less in the large than in the small republic, the former will present a greater option, and consequently a greater probability of a fit choice. . . .

The other point of difference is, the greater number of citizens, and extent of territory, which may be brought within the compass of republican, than of democratic government; and it is this circumstance principally which renders factious combinations less to be dreaded in the former, than in the latter. The smaller the society, the fewer probably will be the distinct parties and interests composing it; the fewer the distinct parties and interests, the more frequently will a majority be found of the same party; and the smaller the number of individuals composing a majority, and the smaller the compass within which they are placed, the more easily will they concert and execute their plans of oppression. Extend the sphere, and you take in a greater variety of parties and interests; you make it less probable that a majority of the whole will have a common motive to invade the rights of other citizens; or if such a common motive exists, it will be more difficult for all who feel it to discover their own strength, and to act in unison with each other. Besides other impediments, it may be remarked, that where there is a consciousness of unjust or dishonourable purposes, communication is always checked by distrust, in proportion to the number whose concurrence is necessary.

Hence, it clearly appears, that the same advantage, which a republic has over a democracy, in controlling the effects of faction, is enjoyed by a large over a small republic—is enjoyed by the union over the states composing it. . . .

5.2. THE DEBATES AT THE CONSTITUTIONAL CONVENTION

From the notes kept by delegates to the Constitutional Convention the student may learn of the great and often bitter differences which had to be resolved before the Constitution was approved.

MR. HAMILTON.—. . . I see great difficulty of drawing forth a good representation. What, for example, will be the inducements for gentlemen of fortune and abilities to leave their houses and business to attend annually and long? It cannot be the wages; for these, I presume, must be small. Will not the power, therefore, be thrown into the hands of the

From Max Farrand, ed., *Records of the Federal Convention* (New Haven: Yale University Press, 1937).

demagogue or middling politician, who, for the sake of a small stipend and the hopes of advancement, will offer himself as a candidate, and the real men of weight and influence, by remaining at home, add strength to the state governments? . . . The people are turbulent and changing; they seldom judge or determine right. Give therefore to the first class a distinct, permanent share in the government. They will check the unsteadiness of the second, and as they cannot receive any advantage by a change, they therefore will ever maintain good government. Can a democratic assembly, who annually revolve in the mass of the people, be supposed steadily to pursue the public good? Nothing but a permanent body can check the imprudence of democracy. Their turbulent and uncontrouling disposition requires checks. The senate of New-York, although chosen for four years, we have found to be inefficient. Will, on the Virginia plan, a continuance of seven years do it? It is admitted that you cannot have a good executive upon a democratic plan. See the excellency of the British executive—He is placed above temptation —He can have no distinct interests from the public welfare. Nothing short of such an executive can be efficient. . . .

Let one body of the legislature be constituted during good behaviour or life.

Let one executive be appointed who dares execute his powers.

It may be asked is this a republican system? It is strictly so, as long as they remain elective.

And let me observe, that an executive is less dangerous to the liberties of the people when in office during life, than for seven years. . . . Let electors be appointed in each of the states to elect the executive [Yates's notes indicate that here Hamilton presented a paper, obviously recording his plan for the federal "legislature"] to consist of. two branches—and I would give them the unlimited power of passing *all laws* without exception. The assembly to be elected for three years by the people in districts—the senate to be elected by electors to be chosen for that purpose by the people, and to remain in office during life. The executive to have the power of negativing all laws—to make war or peace, with the advice of the senate—to make treaties with their advice, but to have the sole direction of all military operations, and to send ambassadors and appoint all military officers. . . .

I confess that this plan and that from Virginia are very remote from the idea of the people. Perhaps the Jersey plan is nearest their expectation. But the people are gradually ripening in their opinions of government—they begin to be tired of an excess of democracy—and what even is the Virginia plan, but *pork still, with a little change of the sauce.*

Mr. Sherman. Govt. is instituted for those who live under it. It ought therefore to be so constituted as not to be dangerous to their liberties. The more permanency it has the worse if it be a bad Govt. Frequent elections are necessary to preserve the good behavior of rulers. They also tend to give permanency to the Government, by preserving that good behavior, because it ensures their reelection. In Connecticut elections have been very frequent, yet great stability & uniformity both as to persons & measures have been experienced from its original establishmt. to the present time; a period of more than 130 years. He wished to have provision made for steadiness & wisdom in the system to be adopted; but he thought six or four years would be sufficient. He shd. be content with either.

. . . . . .

"Art IV. Sect. 1.[1] taken up."

Mr. Govr. Morris moved to strike out the last member of the section beginning with the words "qualifications of Electors," in order that some other provision might be substituted which wd. restrain the right of suffrage to freeholders.

. . . It was difficult to form any uniform rule of qualifications for all the States. Unnecessary innovations he thought too should be avoided. It would be very hard & disagreeable for the same persons, at the same time, to vote for representatives in the State Legislature and to be excluded from a vote for those in the Natl. Legislature.

Mr. Govr. Morris. Such a hardship would be neither great nor novel. The people are accustomed to it and not dissatisfied with it, in several of the States. In some the qualifications are different for the choice of the Govr. & Representatives; In others for different Houses of the Legislature. Another objection agst. the clause as it stands is that it makes the qualifications of the Natl. Legislature depend on the will of the States, which he thought not proper. . . .

Mr. Elseworth. How shall the freehold be defined? Ought not every man who pays a tax to vote for the representative who is to levy & dispose of his money? Shall the wealthy merchants and manufacturers, who will bear a full share of the public burdens be not allowed a voice in the imposition of them . . .

Mr. Govr. Morris. He had long learned not to be the dupe of words. The sound of Aristocracy therefore, had no effect on him. It was the thing, not the name, to which he was opposed, and one of his principal objections to the Constitution as it is now before us, is that it threatens this Country with an Aristocracy. The aristocracy will grow out of the House of Representatives. Give the votes to people who have

---

[1] Article IV, Sect 1. "The members of the House of Representatives shall be chosen every second year, by the people of the several States comprehended within this Union. The qualifications of the electors shall be the same, from time to time, as those of the electors in the several States, of the most numerous branch of their own legislatures."

no property, and they will sell them to the rich who will be able to buy them. We should not confine our attention to the present moment. The time is not distant when this Country will abound with mechanics & manufacturers who will receive their bread from their employers. Will such men be the secure & faithful Guardians of liberty? Will they be the impregnable barrier agst. aristocracy? . . .

Col. Mason. We all feel so strongly the remains of ancient prejudices, and view things too much through a British Medium. A Freehold is the qualification in England, & hence it is imagined to be the only proper one. The true idea in his opinion was that every man having evidence of attachment to & permanent common interest with the Society ought to share in all its rights & privileges. Was this qualification restrained to freeholders? Does no other kind of property but land evidence a common interest in the proprietor? does nothing besides property mark a permanent attachment. Ought the merchant, the monied man, the parent of a number of children whose fortunes are to be pursued in their own Country, to be viewed as suspicious characters, and unworthy to be trusted with the common rights of their fellow Citizens?

5.3. THE CONCEPT OF THE CONCURRENT MAJORITY

A decade before the outbreak of the Civil War, the leading Southern statesman argued that some means had to be found to reconcile the conflicting interests dividing the nation. This should be accomplished, he held, by accommodating policy to the majority interests of communities and not simply to the majority interests of numbers of individuals.

IT RESULTS, from what has been said, that there are two different modes in which the sense of the community may be taken; one, simply by the right of suffrage, unaided; the other, by the right through a proper organism. Each collects the sense of the majority. But one regards numbers only, and considers the whole community as a unit, having but one common interest throughout; and collects the sense of the greater number of the whole, as that of the community. The other, on the contrary, regards interests as well as numbers;—considering the community as made up of different and conflicting interests, as far as the action of the government is concerned; and takes the sense of each, through its majority or appropriate organ, and the united sense of all, as the sense of the entire community. The former of these I shall call the numerical, or

From John C. Calhoun, *A Disquisition on Government,* 1853 (New York: Political Science Classics, 1947), pp. 28–29.

absolute majority; and the latter, the concurrent, or constitutional majority. I call it the constitutional majority, because it is an essential element in every constitutional government,—be its form what it may. So great is the difference, politically speaking, between the two majorities, that they cannot be confounded, without leading to great and fatal errors; and yet the distinction between them has been so entirely overlooked, that when the term *majority* is used in political discussions, it is applied exclusively to designate the numerical,—as if there were no other. Until this distinction is recognized, and better understood, there will continue to be great liability to error in properly constructing constitutional governments, especially of the popular form, and of preserving them when properly constructed. Until then, the latter will have a strong tendency to slide, first, into the government of the numerical majority, and, finally, into absolute government of some other form. . . .

5.4. RECENT VIEWS OF THE RIGHT TO VOTE

The lengthy and arduous process by which the right to vote has been extended through enforcement of the Fourteenth and Fifteenth Amendments is examined carefully in this comprehensive report.

AT THE TIME the Constitution became effective, the prevailing views upon the subject of suffrage were these: (1) the sovereign power was in the hands of the electorate, to be exercised through their representatives; (2) the electorate did not include all of the people; (3) the determination of which people should be included in the electorate was to be made by each of the several states for itself, and for the national government; (4) direct participation of the electorate in the selection of the personnel of the national government was limited to the lower house of Congress; (5) the actual conduct of elections of the members of the national legislative body was left to the several states, but a latent and limited power paramount to supersede such methods was reluctantly conferred upon the Congress; and (6) explicit methods—affording prominence to the several States—were detailed for the selection of the President. Because the organization of the National Government did not supplant determinative State power over matters pertaining to suffrage, it is essential to study the schemes of selection of the electorate reflected by State laws and constitutions in order to understand the development of suffrage in the United States.

A characteristic of the essentially empirical American system

From U.S. Commission on Civil Rights, *Report* (Washington, D.C.: U.S. Government Printing Office, 1959).

is that there is no single theory of suffrage. If the electoral franchise is regarded as a *privilege*, considerations of the status of the individual in the political community, "the good of the state," and political expediency assume dominant proportions in selection of the criteria for voter qualification. If it is regarded as a *right*, whether by natural law or as an attribute of citizenship, ethical considerations founded upon the equal moral worth of all men in a free society raise suffrage to the plane of an essential means for the development of individual character. . . .

It is the development of racial exclusions that is of primary importance to this phase of the Commission's study. The principal racial group affected is, of course, the Negro. . . .

The development of suffrage in the United States to the time of the Civil War makes clear that the principle of universal suffrage was never practiced during that period. As the Commission on Civil Rights is specifically charged with the duty of investigating alleged denial of the right to vote, the Commission has recognized the importance of considering the nature, development, and extent of these rights before evaluating any possible interference. . . .

. . . Under Johnson's plan, the freed Negroes would not vote because the existing antebellum laws of the affected States excluded Negroes from the polls. This was most offensive to the Radical Republican leaders, particularly Senator Charles Sumner, Representative Thaddeus Stevens, and Chief Justice Salmon P. Chase, who were committed to Negro enfranchisement. . . .

To the Radical Republicans, the denial of Negro suffrage and the enactment of the "Black Codes" was proof enough that the South could not be treated with Johnson's brand of benevolence. It was their view, not Johnson's, that finally prevailed. Then Congress passed the first Civil Rights Act, which anticipated the Fourteenth Amendment in declaring all persons born in the United States, excluding Indians not taxed, to be citizens of the United States.

On June 13, 1866, Congress proposed the Fourteenth Amendment.

1. All persons born or naturalized in the United States and subject to the jurisdiction thereof, are citizens of the United States and of the State wherein they reside. No state shall make or enforce any law which shall abridge the privileges or immunities of citizens of the United States; nor shall any State deprive any person of life, liberty, or property, without due process of law; nor deny to any person within its jurisdiction the equal protection of the laws.

Of the Southern States, Tennessee alone ratified the proposed amendment and was readmitted on July 24, 1866. The other ten ex-Confederate States rejected the offer to be readmitted upon ratification of the Amendment.

In December 1866, Senator James G. Blaine of Maine demanded Negro suffrage clauses in all the Southern constitutions, and three months later Congress passed an act that according to its title was designed to "provide for a more efficient government of the Rebel States." The act declared that no government then existed in the ten ex-Confederate States; this had the effect of overturning the governments set up under the administration plan. The act divided the South into five military divisions and required of each State, before it could be declared entitled to representation in Congress, (1) that Negroes be admitted to suffrage when elections for delegates to the constitutional conventions were held; (2) that the new constitutions provide permanently for Negro voting, and (3) that the Fourteenth Amendment be ratified.

An act passed on March 23, 1867, designated who might vote for delegates to the conventions and moved to enfranchise the Negroes by simply not excluding them—although excluding certain white Southerners. Reconstruction, conducted under military rule, was now begun. . . .

The Southern white man's answer was the Ku Klux Klan, founded in Pulaski, Tennessee, and commanded by General Nathan Bedford Forrest. Although always ready with the whip and the bucket of tar and feathers, the Klan was most active at election time. In some desperation, Congress passed enforcement acts that included a prohibition against wearing masks on a public highway for the purpose of preventing citizens from voting. The Klan movement declined, not so much as a result of the new laws as through the withdrawal of moderate men of influence who could not stomach its bloody violence.

Meanwhile, the Fourteenth Amendment was ratified on July 28, 1868. Section 1 of the Fifteenth Amendment, ratified on March 30, 1870, declared:

The right of citizens of the United States to vote shall not be denied or abridged by the United States or by any State on account of race, color, or previous condition of servitude.

Having adopted constitutions consistent with the Fifteenth Amendment, the former Confederate States undergoing reconstruction were all readmitted to the Union by 1870.

In 1877, Reconstruction ended with the withdrawal of Federal troops, and control of the South was returned to its own white leaders. . . .

Fraud, accomplished in part with controlled Negro votes, prompted moves toward systematic disfranchisement of Negroes. But probably the greatest motivating force was the threat posed to the solidarity and dominance of the Democratic Party by the Southern Farmers Alliance. This agrarian protest movement, which sprang up to challenge the business-minded conservatives during the farm depression of the 1870s and 1880s was everywhere identified with, and in many places merged with, the Populist Party. . . .

The Negro, it appeared, might soon hold the balance of power in Southern politics. White factions, though bitterly at odds with each other, began to close ranks against him. It was not Emancipation or Reconstruction but this move to preserve white political dominance that also brought the beginnings of mass compulsory segregation called Jim Crow. . . .

Thus the South became a one-party region. Since the turn of the century the Democratic Party has dominated all State government and, except for a few localities (principally in Virginia, North Carolina and Tennessee), local government as well. With rare exceptions, the only genuine contests for public office have been in the nominating primaries of the Democratic Party, where victory is tantamount to election. Republican candidacies have been perfunctory or non-existent.

To be eligible to vote at a direct primary, a person must be a qualified voter under the laws of the State but another qualification, party membership, was always added in the South and in a majority of other States as well on the logical premise that only members of a party should take part in the selection of party nominees. The Southern laws, however, had some distinctive features. In most of these states, the administration of the direct primary was delegated, by statute, to the individual party, making the party responsible for holding its own primary including the determination of who was eligible to vote. Leaders of the Democratic Party determined that Negroes could not be Democrats and automatically excluded them in some States. A Democratic primary for whites only was finally given the popular name, white primary. . . .

Article I, section 2 [of the Constitution], provides that electors for Members of Congress shall have qualifications requisite for electors of the most numerous branch of the State legislature. This is the basic source of every State's power to determine which of its citizens may vote. By prescribing and administering voting qualifications, the States effectively determine who may vote in a national election. But this does not mean that the right is derived from the States. For the Supreme Court has ruled that the right to vote for Members of Congress is a right derived from and secured by the Constitution of the United States.

The elective rights guaranteed by the Fourteenth Amendment afford protection only against deprivations by States, and those guaranteed by the Fifteenth Amendment only against deprivations by the United States and the States. The right to vote for Members of Congress, on the other hand, is secured against the actions of individuals as well as States. . . .

Nowhere has article I, section 2, been more useful than in connection with problems of discrimination in primary elections. One of these problems was the so-called white primary, which for years in the South had been effectively employed as a method of depriving Negroes of an opportunity to vote. . . .

Inspiration for the first legislative prescription of the "white primary" apparently came from the inconclusive decision of the Supreme Court in *Newberry* v. *United States*. The Court declared that a primary is no part of an election, and hence that the part of the Federal Corrupt Practices Act intended to limit the expenditures of a senatorial candidate in a primary was unconstitutional.

Soon after this decision, the Texas Legislature enacted a law barring Negroes from the polls in any Democratic primary in the State. This law was invalidated by the Supreme Court in *Nixon* v. *Herndon* as a violation of the equal protection of the laws. The attempt to vest the same power of discrimination in the State executive committee of the party failed because the committee received its authority to act from the legislature and hence was an agent of the State.

But in *Grovey* v. *Townsend,* in 1935, the Court upheld the exclusion of a Negro voter from the Democratic primary under a resolution of the State Democratic convention. Here the Court declared that to deny a vote in a primary was a mere refusal of party membership in a private organization, with which "the State need have no concern." The action by the State Democratic convention was considered not to be State action.

The great turning point came in 1941 in the *Classic* case. Here the Court held that section 4 of article I of the Constitution authorizes Congress to regulate primaries as well as general elections where the primary is by law an integral part of the procedure of choice [of a representative in Congress], or where in fact the primary effectively controls the choice. That qualified citizens and inhabitants of a State have a constitutional right to choose Congressmen was underscored by the Court in the following language:

Obviously included within the right to choose, secured by the Constitution, is the right of qualified voters within a State to cast their ballots and have them counted at congressional elections. . . . And since the constitutional command is without restriction or limitation, the right, unlike those guaranteed by the Fourteenth and Fifteenth Amendments, is secured against the action of individuals as well as of States. . . .

Where the State law has made the primary an integral part of the procedure of choice, or where in fact the primary effectively controls the choice, the right of the elector to have his ballot counted at the primary is likewise included in the right protected by article I, section 2.

And this right of participation is protected just as is the right to vote at the election. . . .

Then in 1944 in *Smith* v. *Allwright*, the "white primary" was outlawed as violative of the Fifteenth Amendment. The Court declared that the constitutional right to be free from racial discrimination in voting "is not to be nullified by a State through casting its electoral process in a form which permits a private organization to practice racial discrimination in the election." Declaring that "it may now be taken as a postulate that the right to vote in . . . a primary . . . without discrimination by the State . . . is a right secured by the Constitution," the Court went on to hold that, since by State law the primary was made an integral part of the State election machinery, the action of the party in excluding Negroes was action by the State and consequently in violation of the Fifteenth Amendment. Thus the controlling issue here as in the *Grovey* case was whether the Negro had been barred from the primary by State action. The Court held that he had, and consequently *Grovey* v. *Townsend* was overruled. . . .

South Carolina promptly repealed all statutory and constitutional laws relating to primaries, and the Democratic primary was thereafter conducted under rules prescribed by the Democratic Party. This bold attempt to circumvent the *Allwright* decision was struck down by the United States district court in *Elmore* v. *Rice*.

Elmore had been denied the right to vote in the Democratic primary under rules promulgated by the Democratic convention, which limited the right to vote in the primary to white persons. Both the district court and the court of appeals ruled that the party and the primary were still used as instruments of the State in the electoral process, despite the repeal of all laws relating to primaries. . . .

Still unyielding, the Democratic Party authorities of South Carolina sought to evade the *Elmore* decision by vesting control of primaries in clubs from which Negroes were barred, and by requiring of one who desired to vote in the primaries an oath, which was particularly objectionable to Negroes, stipulating among other things that he believed in the social and educational separation of the races. This effort failed in both the district court and the court of appeals on the strength of the principle enunciated in the *Elmore* case. . . .

To summarize, the preceding cases taken as a whole substantiate the proposition that actions taken by clubs, groups, or organizations cannot be considered private actions when they control the choice of public officials and the right of qualified citizens to participate freely in the exercise of their franchise. . . .

To understand fully the import of the Fourteenth Amendment in the area of voting, it is necessary to know its precise coverage

THE CONCEPT OF CITIZENSHIP

1. Persons are citizens of the United States who, if subject to the jurisdiction of the United States, are born in the United States or born abroad of American parentage; or who become citizens by qualifying for it in accordance with naturalization statutes; or whose citizenship is thrust upon them, such as members of certain Indian tribes and inhabitants of certain dependencies of the United States.

2. The Fourteenth Amendment recognizes and establishes a distinction between U.S. citizenship and State citizenship. For a citizen of the United States to be a citizen of a State he must reside in that State with a fixed intent to remain resident. Birth or naturalization in the United States does not alone confer State citizenship.

3. While national citizenship was not created by the Fourteenth Amendment, it was therein made "paramount" to State citizenship.

4. National citizenship is not a qualification for voting in the absence of State constitutional or statutory requirements, so that a person could be a citizen of a State, thereby complying with residential voting requirements, yet not be a citizen of the United States.

PRIVILEGES AND IMMUNITIES

1. The privileges-and-immunities clause is the only provision of the first section of the Fourteenth Amendment confined exclusively to citizens rather than persons generally.

2. As a source of power to protect the franchise, the privileges-and-immunities clause has been rendered ineffective by interpretation. The courts have held that it only forbids a State to discriminate against citizens of other States in favor of its own. The clause has not been applied to voting controversies between a State and its citizens. In short, it does not convert the rights of the citizens of each State, as of the date when the Fourteenth Amendment was adopted, into privileges and immunities of U.S. citizenship.

EQUAL PROTECTION OF THE LAWS

1. The prohibition against denial of equal protection of the laws refers exclusively to State action. This means that no agency or instrumentality of the State nor any person exerting State power may deny equal protection to any person within the jurisdiction of the State. This refers both to discriminatory legislation in favor of particular individuals as against others in like condition, and to the way a law is administered.

2. Unlike the privileges-and-immunities clause, the equal-protec-

tion clause provides a guaranty to any person within the jurisdiction of a State. It is not limited to citizens of the United States or of a State.

3. The equal-protection clause applies to all persons—individual, corporate, or otherwise—within the jurisdiction of a State. The restriction of "within the jurisdiction" in relation to individual persons has never required judicial construction, since article 4, section 2, of the U.S. Constitution has always entitled citizens of each State to the privileges and immunities of citizens in the several States.

4. The clause does not require that identical treatment be accorded all persons without recognizing differences in relevant circumstances. It requires only that equal laws shall apply to all under like circumstances in the enjoyment of personal and civil rights, in acquisition and enjoyment of property, and in access to the courts. It is intended to prevent undue favor, individual or class privilege, and hostile discrimination or oppression.

5. It was not intended to interfere with a State's power, sometimes called police power, to prescribe regulations dealing with health, morals, education, peace, or to legislate for the purpose of increasing the industry, health, and prosperity of the state. This type of regulation may impose greater burdens upon some than on others, but it is designed to promote the general good rather than impose unequal or unnecessary restrictions upon any person. If these differences operate alike on all persons and property under the same circumstances and conditions, they do not violate the equal-protection clause. . . .

THE FIFTEENTH AMENDMENT

While the Fifteenth Amendment is precise in protecting the franchise, the scope of its protection is limited.

First, it does not directly confer the right of suffrage upon anyone, but rather affords to citizens the constitutional right of "exemption from discrimination in the exercise of the elective franchise on account of race, color, or previous condition of servitude."

Second, it recognizes (a) that the right of suffrage is not a necessary attribute of national citizenship, (b) that voting qualifications are determined by States, and (c) that only exemption from discrimination comes from the United States.

Third, its limitations apply only to action of a State or the United States and not to individual action, even though such action might result in denying to an individual his right of suffrage because of race, color, or previous condition of servitude.

Fourth, even where there is action by a State that prevents a citizen, black or white, from voting, there is no violation of the Fifteenth

Amendment unless the action is taken because of the voter's race, color, or previous condition of servitude.

Fifth, while initially it seems to have been assumed that Congress did not intend the legislation it enacted pursuant to this amendment to apply to State and local elections, it now is applied to elections for State as well as for Federal offices.

6

The American Political Parties

6.1. WASHINGTON ON PARTIES

In addition to his famous warning against "foreign entanglements," our first President also cautioned against what seemed to him the harmful effects of political parties. He concludes that "the Spirit of Party" is inherent in human nature but that it is "not to be encouraged."

ALL OBSTRUCTIONS to the execution of the Laws, all combinations and associations, under whatever plausible character, with the real design to direct, control, counteract, or awe the regular deliberation and action of the constituted authorities, are destructive of this fundamental principle, and of fatal tendency.—They serve to organize faction, to give it an artificial and extraordinary force—to put in the place of the delegated will of the Nation, the will of a party;—often a small but artful and enterprizing minority of the community;—and, according to the alternate triumphs of different parties, to make the public administration the mirror of the ill-concerted and incongruous projects of faction, rather than the organ of consistent and wholesome plans digested by common councils, and modified by mutual interests.—However combinations or associations of the above description may now and then answer popular ends, they are likely, in the course of time and things, to become potent engines, by which cunning, ambitious, and unprincipled men will be enabled to subvert the Power of the People and to usurp for themselves the reins of Government; destroying afterwards the very engines, which have lifted them to unjust dominion.—

I have already intimated to you the danger of Parties in the State, with particular reference to the founding of them on Geographical

From George Washington, "Farewell Address," September 17, 1796, *Writings of George Washington*, P. L. Ford, ed. (New York: G. P. Putnam's Sons), Vol. XIII.

discriminations.—Let me now take a more comprehensive view, and warn you in the most solemn manner against the baneful effects of the Spirit of Party, generally.

This Spirit, unfortunately, is inseparable from our nature, having its root in the strongest passions of the human mind.—It exists under different shapes in all Governments, more or less stifled, controuled, or repressed; but, in those of the popular form, it is seen in its greatest rankness, and is truly their worst enemy.—

The alternate domination of one faction over another, sharpened by the spirit of revenge natural to party dissension, which in different ages and countries has perpetrated the most horrid enormities, is itself a frightful despotism.—But this leads at length to a more formal and permanent despotism.—The disorders and miseries, which result, gradually incline the minds of men to seek security and repose in the absolute power of an Individual: and sooner or later the chief of some prevailing faction, more able or more fortunate than his competitors, turns this disposition to the purposes of his own elevation, on the ruins of Public Liberty.

It serves always to distract the Public Councils, and enfeeble the Public administration.—It agitates the community with ill-founded jealousies and false alarms, kindles the animosity of one part against another, foments occasionally riot and insurrection.—It opens the doors to foreign influence and corruption, which find a facilitated access to the Government itself through the channels of party passions. Thus the policy and the will of one country, are subjected to the policy and will of another.

There is an opinion that parties in free countries are useful checks upon the Administration of the Government, and serve to keep alive the Spirit of Liberty.—This within certain limits is probably true—and in Governments of a Monarchical cast, Patriotism may look with indulgence, if not with favour, upon the spirit of party.—But in those of the popular character, in Governments purely elective, it is a spirit not to be encouraged.—From their natural tendency, it is certain there will always be enough of that spirit for every salutary purpose,—and there being constant danger of excess, the effort ought to be, by force of public opinion, to mitigate and assuage it.—A fire not to be quenched; it demands a uniform vigilance to prevent its bursting into a flame, lest instead of warming, it should consume.

6.2. DIFFERENCES BETWEEN THE POLITICAL PARTIES

Viscount Bryce, British Ambassador and scholar, came to the United States some forty years after the famous French observer, Alexis de

Tocqueville, as much to study American Institutions as to represent his country in Washington. In this revised version of his famous work, he offers his comments on the problem that has always fascinated Europeans —the differences and similarities between our two political parties.

THERE ARE now two great and several minor parties in the United States. The great parties are the Republicans and the Democrats. What are their principles, their distinctive tenets, their tendencies? Which of them is for tariff reform, for the further extension of civil service reform, for a spirited foreign policy, for the regulation of railroads and telegraphs by legislation, for changes in the currency, for any other of the twenty issues which one hears discussed in the country as seriously involving its welfare?

This is what a European is always asking of intelligent Republicans and intelligent Democrats. He is always asking because he never gets an answer. The replies leave him in deeper perplexity. After some months the truth begins to dawn upon him. Neither party has, as a party, anything definite to say on these issues; neither party has any clean-cut principles, any distinctive tenets. Both have traditions. Both claim to have tendencies. Both have certainly war cries, organizations, interests, enlisted in their support. But those interests are in the main the interests of getting or keeping the patronage of the government. Distinctive tenets and policies, points of political doctrine and points of political practice, have all but vanished. They have not been thrown away, but have been stripped away by Time and the progress of events, fulfilling some policies, blotting out others. All has been lost, except office or the hope of it.

Parties go on contending because their members have formed habits of joint action, and have contracted hatreds and prejudices, and also because the leaders find their advantage in using these habits and playing on these prejudices. The American parties now continue to exist, because they have existed. The mill has been constructed, and its machinery goes on turning, even when there is no grist to grind.

Yet one cannot say that there is to-day no difference between the two great parties. There is a difference of spirit or sentiment perceptible even by a stranger when, after having mixed for some time with members of the one he begins to mix with those of the other, and doubtless more patent to a native American. . . . The intellectual view of a Democrat of the better sort has been not quite the same as that of his Republican compeer. Each of course thinks meanly of the other; but while the Democrat has generally deemed the Republican "dangerous" (*i.e.* likely to undermine the Constitution), the Republican was more apt to think the Democrat (at least in the North) low toned or reckless.

From James Bryce, *American Commonwealth* (New York: The Macmillan Company, 1914; originally: 1893), pp. 21, 24, 28–29.

. . . But these statements, generally true of Democrats and Republicans from the time of the Civil War till near the end of the century, have latterly been less applicable. There is still a contrast between the larger and more radical wing of the Democratic party and the older school of Republicans, but the conservative section of the Democrats differ very little from the conservative Republicans; and there are radical Republicans whose views are shared by plenty of Democrats. This approximation seems to indicate that the time for a reconstruction of parties is approaching; but party organizations are strong things, and often interfere with the course of natural evolution.

It cannot be charged on the American parties that they have drawn towards one another by forsaking their old principles. It is time that has changed the circumstances of the country, and made those old principles inapplicable. An eminent journalist remarked to me in 1908 that the two great parties were like two bottles. Each bore a label denoting the kind of liquor it contained, but each was empty. This at any rate may be said, that the parties may seem to have erred rather by having clung too long to out-worn issues, and by neglecting to discover and work out new principles capable of solving the problems which now perplex the country. In a country so full of change and movement as America new questions are always coming up, and must be answered. New troubles surround a government, and a way must be found to escape from them; new diseases attack the nation, and have to be cured. The duty of a great party is to face these, to find answers and remedies, applying to the facts of the hour the doctrines it has lived by, so far as they are still applicable, and when they have ceased to be applicable, thinking out new doctrines comformable to the main principles and tendencies which it represents. This is a work to be accomplished by its ruling minds, while the habit of party loyalty to the leaders powerfully serves to diffuse through the mass of followers the conclusions of the leaders and the reasonings they have employed.

6.3. DIFFERENCES BETWEEN REPUBLICANS AND DEMOCRATS

In recent years American scholars have been concerned with political sociology and demography as factors affecting political behavior. Professor McDonald examines some aspects of this comparatively new approach to the study of American politics.

. . . ELEVEN PARTY bases have been studied with special reference to the parties of the United States. These bases are: age, sex, income, race, ethnic or national origins, religion, section, class, education, urban-rural and union membership. Between any two or more political parties there may be as many base differences as there are mathematical ways of combining the eleven. . . .

Studies are unanimous in showing that a greater proportion of young and new voters support Democratic candidates than support Republican candidates. This tendency even withstood the Eisenhower landslide in 1952. . . . Whatever the explanation, youth's preference for Democratic candidates seems to be well demonstrated in recent studies. It is not possible to tell how old this tendency is since studies are recent. Nor is the level of significance established. It simply means that if all Democratic voters are compared with all Republican voters, youth will constitute a higher proportion of the total Democratic votes and thus occupy a more important place in the base of that party. We know little more than that. . . .

Studies show that the more education a person has the more likely he is to support Republican candidates. In the 1948 election the Michigan study showed that persons with some college education voted over three to one for Dewey, whereas persons with only grade-school education voted two to one for Truman. . . . The difference in party preference is often said to be really a difference in income level. For the West, at least, education seems independent. That is, regardless of income, people who go to college are more likely to come from Republican homes and to associate with Republicans. It follows that the Republican base contains a higher percentage of better educated people.

All studies confirm the general proposition that there is a relation between income level and party adherence. According to the Michigan study of 1948 the income level of $3,000–4,000 seems to be the dividing line. Of those below this level there is a predominance of Democrats and above a greater proportion of Republicans. Those with incomes of $1,000–3,000 voted two to one for Truman. Over $5,000 they voted two to one for Dewey. . . .

What is known of the religious base of political parties in the United States? Lazarsfeld in reporting on the 1940 Erie County study finds that religion, the Catholic-Protestant axis, was as important as socioeconomic status in placing Catholics behind Democratic candidates and Protestants behind Republicans. He found that as early as May 1940 (before the conventions), 60 percent of the Protestants and only 23 percent of the Catholics intended to vote Republican. On what he calls SES level (Socio-Economic Status) religion was found to be important. That is to say, rich, upper-class Catholics were significantly more disposed to vote for Democratic candidates. The Elmira study found that

From Neal McDonald, *The Study of Political Parties.* © Copyright 1955 by Random House, Inc. (pp. 39–46, 50–51). Reprinted by permission.

Catholics voted Republican less than half as often as Democratic. Berelson and his associates concluded that in Elmira religious affiliation and ethnic difference are together the strongest influences on the vote. They found in Elmira that Catholics reaching a SES comparable to Protestants did not basically modify their Democratic loyalty. The Michigan study of the 1948 election reported that Catholics voted two to one for Truman, whereas the Protestant vote divided about equally. It found that 54 percent of Democrats were Protestant, whereas 73 percent of Republicans were Protestant: that 32 percent of Democrats were Catholic, as compared with 20 percent of Republicans who were Catholic. These findings were substantially confirmed by the 1952 study. . . .

There is a close relationship between labor-union membership and support for Democratic candidates. Harris reports that union members split 60-40 for Stevenson as compared with 68-32 for Eisenhower in the population at large. Union members' families gave a slight edge to Eisenhower—55-45. In an election characterized by great group shifts to Eisenhower, Harris found union members remarkably loyal to the Democratic candidate. The 1948 Michigan study revealed that Union members in its sample voted 56 percent for Truman, 13 percent for Dewey, and that 27 percent did not vote. . . .

In Elmira in 1948 it was found that although the union members who registered their party affiliation were about evenly split as between Democratic and Republican preferences, in actual voting union members were consistently more Democratic than Republican. It was also found that the stronger a person's union attachment, the stronger his Democratic attachment. These studies show that even where the general climate of preference compels people to register Republican, as in Elmira, the actual vote of union members is more likely to be Democratic than is that of persons who are not union members. . . .

It should be noted that in discussing the ethnic bases of parties most attention has been paid to the Democrats. This is because the Democratic Party seems to have a more varied base and probably greater ethnic instability. It should be kept in mind that the foundations of both parties contain all significant classifications of the population. The base of no party is made up 100 percent of one ethnic group, nor does 100 percent of any ethnic group steadily support either party. But of 100 typical Republican votes there would be more north Europeans, except Irish, and among 100 typical Democratic votes there would be more eastern and southern Europeans and Irish. The Irish component in the Democratic base may be developing instability. Thus the change in the position of Germans from an earlier firmness in the Republican base may be countered by a shift in the Irish from their former firm position in the Democratic base. It is interesting to speculate on how, if at all, this will modify the influence of either ethnic group.

From the earliest times there has been a big city component of the Democratic Party. The pre-Civil War coalition of southern and western rural with northern middle Atlantic cities was a famous election-winning combination. It was upset by the Civil War and Reconstruction and Post-Reconstruction attempts to re-establish it were in turn upset by Bryan and the agrarians capturing control of the Democratic party name. But as Lubell so clearly shows, by the 1920s the forces of protest in urban areas began to range themselves in support of Democratic candidates. While the Republicanism of the country seemed to increase beginning in 1920 and continuing through the election of 1928, the Democratic vote in twelve great metropolitan areas increased until it became a majority in 1928. By 1936 virtually every city gave Roosevelt a large plurality. Despite the third-term issue, this urban vote tended to stay put in the 1940 election and in varying degrees in the elections that have followed. Even Philadelphia, almost the last hold-out among the great cities, seems to have moved over into the Democratic base. . . . Harris in interpreting this trend suggests that the rural southerner shares something of an underprivileged status with the northern urban dweller and thus both are attracted to the Democratic party. . . .

The most durable sectional component of either party is the South in the Democratic Party. Historically, the Republican Party's nearest counterpart has been the northeastern states. A third great region is the West, which is not firmly fixed in either party. . . .

The enduring interests which are associated with each party remain largely unchanged, but the important thing is the other interests or factors that they must team up with in order to win an election. The fundamental problem of the Democrats in these terms is to combine the more rural tobacco and cotton interests of the South with the lower-income metropolitan populations of the North. The combination that the Republicans have to effect is that between the well-to-do urban voters of the North and the bulk of all rural small-town inhabitants. Given these bases, each party, by candidates, by platforms, and by campaigning, go after the decisive middle-class urban vote, especially in great metropolitan centers for presidential elections and in congressional districts of mixed interests for congressional elections. . . .

If section is distinguished from urban-rural cleavage it would seem that at the present time the only very pronounced sectional basic component in the major parties is the South in the Democratic base. Not only would 100 typical Democratic votes contain many more from the South than would the 100 typical Republican votes, but no other single section would contribute so many votes to the Republican 100 as the South would contribute to the Democrats.

For the most part, race as a component of party bases is largely confined to the Negro-white split. There is a cleavage in a few south-western states involving Indians, natives, and Mexicans. But the numbers are few and integration is not overwhelmingly a problem of racial difference. From the time of the Civil War and Negro enfranchisement until the present, Negroes as a group have apparently changed from being an important Republican component to being an equally important Democratic component. The revolt of Negroes against the Republicans came as Negroes joined other northern urban minorities in steadily increasing their Democratic preferences throughout the 1920s. Gradually the Negro vote in the South became increasingly Democratic. According to the Michigan study of 1948 nearly two out of three Negroes did not vote (this figure includes a very low Negro vote in the South), but of those who did vote nearly two voted Democratic for every one who voted Republican. In Northern metropolitan areas Negro turnout was high. Harris, in reporting on Northern Negroes in the 1952 election, characteries them as dedicated and single-minded and as being on the way to becoming one of the indispensable elements in the Democratic party. . . . On the basis of the studies cited, other preliminary and less comprehensive studies that they support, and observation of how professional politicians plan electoral battles, the following seem pretty well agreed to: For every 100 votes cast for the national ticket of each major political party in the United States, the Democratic 100 votes will include more young persons, more Catholics, more urban residents, more labor-union members, more southerners, more low-income persons, more Negroes, more Jews and recent immigrants in general, more lower-class and more poorly educated persons, than would every 100 Republican votes. The 100 Republican votes would contain more older persons, Protestant, rural and small-town residents, professional and managerial persons, northerners, wealthy, whites, English, Scotch, German and Scandinavians, upper class and well educated. In any given election there will be changes in the percentages. But over a period of time the indicated preponderant characteristics in each 100 votes will persist, or tend to persist. Having said this, however, two further things should be said. The political significance of these indicated patterns cannot be taken for granted. Secondly, the quantification in all of these matters is extremely crude. It is even hard to measure the same thing in the same way between elections. The continuity between the Michigan studies of 1948 and 1952 and the Erie County and Elmira studies represents a step in a necessary direction. Finally there has been such a strong tendency to emphasize that there are more steady Republican than Democratic adherents among the wealthy and more Catholics among the Democratic supporters that little attention has been given to the rich Democrats and the Catholic Republicans. Yet this would seem to be an important point at which to examine the party tie. The studies that suggest, as the 1952 Michigan study does, that a strong active Democrat is likely to be less influenced politically by his Church than is a weak or generally indifferent Democrat, indicate a fruitful area for further study. This suggests that party itself may, in addition to being a reflector, be an influencing force.

6.4. DIFFERENCES WITHIN AND BETWEEN PARTIES

McClosky and his confreres report that there are in fact important ideological differences between the Republican and Democratic parties, and that the differences are greater between the leaders of the two parties than between their followers.

AMERICAN political parties are often regarded as "brokerage" organizations, weak in principle, devoid of ideology, and inclined to differ chiefly over unimportant questions. In contrast to the "ideological" parties of Europe—which supposedly appeal to their followers through sharply defined, coherent, and logically related doctrines—the American parties are thought to fit their convictions to the changing demands of the political contest. According to this view, each set of American party leaders is satisfied to play Tweedledee to the other's Tweedledum.

Although these "conclusions" are mainly derived from *a priori* analysis or from casual observations of "anecdotal" data (little systematic effort having been made so far to verify or refute them), they are often taken as confirmed—largely, one imagines, because they are compatible with certain conspicuous features of American politics. Among these features is the entrenchment of a two-party system which, by affording both parties a genuine opportunity to win elections, tempts them to appeal to as many diverse elements in the electorate as are needed to put together a majority. Since both parties want to attract support from the centrist and moderate segments of the electorate, their views on basic issues will, it is thought, tend to converge. Like giant business enterprises competing for the same market, they will be led to offer commodities that are in many respects identical. It is one thing for a small party in a multiparty system to preserve its ideological purity, quite another for a mass party in a two-party system to do so. The one has little hope of becoming a majority, and can most easily survive by remaining identified with the narrow audience from which it draws its chief supporters; the other can succeed only by accommodating the conflicting claims of many diverse groups—only, in short, by blunting ideological distinctions.

From Herbert McClosky, Paul J. Hoffmann, and Rosemary O'Hara, "Issue Conflict and Consensus Among Party Leaders and Followers," *The American Political Science Review,* LIV, No. 2 (June, 1960), pp. 406–407, 410–411, 413–422.

Constraints against enlarging intellectual differences also spring from the loosely confederated nature of the American party system, and from each national party's need to adjust its policies to the competing interests of the locality, the state, and the nation. Many party units are more concerned with local than with national elections, and prefer not to be handicapped by clear-cut national programs. Every ambitious politician, moreover, hopes to achieve a *modus vivendi* tailored to the particular and often idiosyncratic complex of forces prevailing in his constituency, an objective rarely compatible with doctrinal purity. Often, too, local politics are largely non-partisan or are partisan in ways that scarcely affect the great national issues around which ideologies might be expected to form. The development and enforcement of a sharply delineated ideology is also hindered by the absence in either party of a firmly established, authoritative, and continuing organizational center empowered to decide questions of doctrine and discipline. Party affiliation is loosely defined, responsibility is weak or non-existent, and organs for indoctrinating or communicating with party members are at best rudimentary.

Cultural and historical differences may also contribute to the weaker ideological emphasis among American, as compared with European, parties. Many of the great historical cleavages that have divided European nations for centuries—monarchism *vs.* republicanism; clericalism *vs.* anti-clericalism; democracy *vs.* autocracy, etc.—have never taken root in this country. Apart from the slavery (and subsequently the race) issue, the United States has not experienced the intense class or caste conflict often found abroad, and contests of the capitalism *vs.* socialism variety have never achieved an important role in American politics. In addition, never having known a titled nobility, we have largely been freed from the conflicts found elsewhere between the classes of inherited and acquired privilege.

Consider, too, the progress made in the United States toward neutralizing the forces which ordinarily lead to sharp social, and hence intellectual and political, differentiation. The class and status structure of American society has attained a rate of mobility equalling or exceeding that of any other long established society. Popular education, and other facilities for the creation of common attitudes, have been developed on a scale unequalled elsewhere. Improvements in transportation and communication, and rapid shifts in population and industry have weakened even sectionalism as a source of political cleavage. Rural-urban differences continue to exist, of course, but they too have been diminishing in force and have become less salient for American politics than the differences prevailing, for example, between a French peasant proprietor and a Parisian *boulevardier*. In short, a great many Americans have been subjected in their public lives to identical stimuli—a condition unlikely to generate strong, competing ideologies.

The research reported here was designed not to refute these observations but to test the accuracy of the claim that they are sufficient to prevent differences in outlook from taking root in the American party system. We believed that the homogenizing tendencies referred to are strongly offset by contrary influences, and that voters are preponderantly led to support the party whose opinions they share. We further thought that the competition for office, though giving rise to similarities between the parties, also impels them to diverge from each other in order to sharpen their respective appeals. For this and other reasons, we expected to find that the leaders of the two parties, instead of ignoring differences alleged to exist within the electorate, would differ on issues more sharply than their followers would. We believed further that even in a brokerage system the parties would serve as independent reference groups, developing norms, values, and self-images to which their supporters could readily respond. Their influence, we felt, would frequently exceed that of ethnic, occupational, residential and other reference groups. In sum, we proceeded on the belief that the parties are not simply spokesmen for other interest groups, but are in their own right agencies for formulating, transmitting, and anchoring political opinions, that they attract adherents who in general share those opinions, and that through a feedback process of mutual reinforcement between the organization and its typical supporters, the parties develop integrated and stable political tendencies. Other hypotheses will be specified as we present and analyze our findings. . . .

No more conclusive findings emerge from our study of party issues than those growing out of the comparisons between the two sets of party leaders. Despite the brokerage tendency of the American parties, their active members are obviously separated by large and important differences. The differences, moreover, conform with the popular image in which the Democratic party is seen as the more "progressive" or "radical," the Republican as the more "moderate" or "conservative" of the two. In addition, the disagreements are remarkably consistent, a function not of chance but of systematic points of view, whereby the responses to any one of the issues could reasonably have been predicted from knowledge of the responses to the other issues. . . .

V. O. Key, among others, has observed that the Republican party is especially responsive to the "financial and manufacturing community," reflecting the view that government should intervene as little as possible to burden or restrain prevailing business interests. The validity of this observation is evident throughout all our data, and is most clearly seen in the responses to the issues listed under Government Regulation of the Economy, Equalitarianism and Human Welfare, Tax Policy. Democratic leaders are far more eager than Republican leaders to strengthen enforcement of antimonopoly laws and to increase regulation of public utilities and business. Indeed, the solidarity of Republican opposition to the regulation of business is rather overwhelming: 84 percent want to decrease such regulation and fewer than .01 percent say they want to increase it. Although the Democrats, on balance, also feel that government controls on business should not be expanded further, the differences between the two samples on this issue are nevertheless substantial.

The two sets of leaders are also far apart on the farm issue, the Democrats preferring slightly to increase farm supports, the Republicans wanting strongly to reduce them. The Republican ratio score of .20 on this issue is among the lowest in the entire set of scores. The magnitude of these scores somewhat surprised us, for while opposition to agricultural subsidies is consistent with Republican dislike for state intervention, we had expected the leaders to conform more closely to the familiar image of the Republican as the more "rural" of the two parties. It appears, however, that the party's connection with business is far more compelling than its association with agriculture. The Republican desire to reduce government expenditures and to promote independence from "government handouts" prevails on the farm question as it does on other issues, while the Democratic preference for a more regulated economy in which government intervenes to reduce economic risk and to stabilize prosperity is equally evident on the other side. Party attitudes on this issue appear to be determined as much by ideological tendencies as by deliberate calculation of the political advantages to be gained by favoring or opposing subsidies to farmers. Comparison of our findings with Turner's earlier data on farm votes in Congress suggests, in addition, that the sharp party difference on the farm issue is neither a recent development nor a mere product of the personal philosophy of the present Secretary of Agriculture.

Having implied that agricultural policies partly result from principle, we must note that on three other issues in this category (trade unions, credit, and tariffs), principle seems to be overweighed by old-fashioned economic considerations. In spite of their distaste for government interference in economic affairs, the Republicans almost unanimously favor greater regulation of trade unions and they are more strongly disposed than the Democrats toward government intervention to restrict credit and to raise tariffs. Of course, party cleavages over the credit and tariff issues have a long history, which may by now have endowed them with ideological force beyond immediate economic considerations. The preponderant Democratic preference for greater regulation of trade unions is doubtless a response to recent "exposures" of corrupt labor practices, though it may also signify that the party's perspective toward the trade unions is shifting somewhat.

The closer Republican identification with business, free enterprise, and economic conservatism in general, and the friendlier Democratic attitude toward labor and toward government regulation of the economy, are easily observed in the data from other parts of our questionnaire. Republican leaders score very much higher than Democratic leaders on, for example, such scales as economic conservatism, independence of government, and business attitudes. . . .

The self-images and reference group identifications of the two parties also should be noted in this connection. For example, many more Democratic than Republican leaders call themselves liberal and state that they would be most likely to take advice from liberal reform organizations, the Farmers' Union, and (as we have seen) from the trade unions; only a small number consider themselves conservative or would seek advice from conservative reform organizations, the National Association of Manufacturers, or the Farm Bureau Federation. The Republicans have in almost all instances the reverse identifications. . . . The Democrats are also significantly more inclined than the Republicans to consider Catholics, Jews, and the foreign born as having "too little power." While self-descriptions and reference group identifications often correspond poorly with actual beliefs—among the general population they scarcely correspond at all, in fact—we are dealing, in the case of the leaders, with a politically informed and highly articulate set of people who have little difficulty connecting the beliefs they hold and the groups that promote or obstruct those beliefs.

Our fourth category, Tax Policy, divides the parties almost as severely as do the other categories. . . .

. . . the differences between the parties on the tax issues follow the patterns previously observed and that tax policy is for the Democrats a device for redistributing income and promoting social equality. Neither party, however, is keen about raising taxes for *any* group: even the Democrats have little enthusiasm for new taxes on upper income groups or on business and corporate enterprises. The Republican leaders are overwhelmingly opposed to increased taxes for *any* group, rich *or* poor. . . . But while they are far more eager than the Democratic leaders to cut taxes on corporate and private wealth, they are less willing to reduce taxes on the lower income groups. These differences, it should be remarked, are not primarily a function of differences in the income of the two samples. Although there are more people with high incomes among the Republican leaders, the disproportion between the two samples is not nearly great enough to account for the dissimilarities in their tax views.

Of the five categories considered, Foreign Policy shows the smallest average difference, but even on these issue the divergence between Democratic and Republican leader attitudes is significant. Except for defense spending the Democrats turn out to be more internationalist than the Republicans, as evidenced in their greater commitment to the United Nations and to American participation in international military alliances like NATO. Twice as many Democrats as Republicans want the United

States to rely more heavily upon such organizations, while many more Republicans want to reduce our international involvements. Both parties are predominantly in favor of cutting back foreign aid—a somewhat surprising finding in light of Democratic public pronouncements on this subject—but more Republicans feel strongly on the subject. Our data thus furnish little support for the claim that the parties hold the same views on foreign policy or that their seeming differences are merely a response to the demands of political competition.

Nevertheless, it would be incorrect to conclude that one party believes in internationalism and the other in isolationism. . . .

The pattern of Republican responses on both the issue and scale items signifies, however, that the leaders of that party generally accept the degree of "internationalism" now in effect, but shrink from extending it further. Consider too, the similarities in the leaders' scores on defense spending, for despite their greater leaning toward isolationism, the Republicans are no more inclined than the Democrats to leave the country defenseless. . . .

So far we have addressed ourselves to the differences between Democratic and Republican *leaders*. . . . the two sets of party *followers* may also be compared. . . . All the issues on which the followers significantly disagree are of the "bread and butter" variety, the more symbolic issues being so remotely experienced and so vaguely grasped that rank and file voters are often unable to identify them with either party. Policies affecting farm prices, business regulation, taxes, or minimum wages, by contrast, are quickly felt by the groups to whom they are addressed and are therefore more capable of arousing partisan identifications. It should also be noted that while the average differences are small for all five categories, they are smallest of all for foreign policy—the most removed and least well understood group of issues in the entire array.

Democratic and Republican followers were also compared on a number of scales and reference group questions. The results, while generally consistent with the differences between the leaders, show the followers to be far more united than their leaders on these measures as well. Even on business attitudes, independence of government, and economic conservatism, the differences are small and barely significant. No differences were found on such scales as tolerance, faith in democracy, procedural rights, conservatism-liberalism (classical), the California F scale and isolationism. The average Democrat is slightly more willing than the average Republican to label himself a liberal or to seek advice from liberal organizations; the contrary is true when it comes to adopting conservative identifications. Only in the differential trust they express toward business and labor are the two sets of followers widely separated. . . .

Why, however, are the leaders so much more sharply divided

than their followers? The reasons are not hard to understand and are consistent with several of the hypotheses that underlay the present study.

(1) Consider, to begin with, that the leaders come from the more articulate segments of society and, on the average, are politically more aware than their followers and far better informed about issues. For them, political issues and opinions are the everyday currency of party competition, not esoteric matters that surpass understanding. With their greater awareness and responsibility, and their greater need to defend their party's stands, they have more interest in developing a consistent set of attitudes—perhaps even an ideology. The followers of each party, often ignorant of the issues and their consequences, find it difficult to distinguish their beliefs from those of the opposition and have little reason to be concerned with the consistency of their attitudes. Furthermore, the American parties make only a feeble effort to educate the rank and file politically, and since no central source exists for the authoritative pronouncement of party policy, the followers often do not know what their leaders believe or on what issues the parties chiefly divide. In short, if we mean by ideology a coherent body of informed social doctrine, it is possessed mainly by the articulate leadership, rarely by the masses.

(2) Differences in the degree of partisan involvement parallel the differences in knowledge and have similar consequences. The leaders, of course, have more party spirit than the followers and, as the election studies make plain, the stronger the partisanship, the larger the differences on issues. The leaders are more highly motivated not only to belong to a party appropriate to their beliefs, but to accept its doctrines and to learn how it differs from the opposition party. Since politics is more salient for leaders than for followers, they develop a greater stake in the outcome of the political contest and are more eager to discover the intellectual grounds by which they hope to make victory possible. Through a process of circular reinforcement, those for whom politics is most important are likely to become the most zealous participants, succeeding to the posts that deal in the formation of opinion. Ideology serves the instrumental purpose, in addition, of justifying the heavy investment that party leaders make in political activity. While politics offers many rewards, it also makes great demands on the time, money, and energies of its practitioners—sacrifices which they can more easily justify if they believe they are serving worthwhile social goals. The followers, in contrast, are intellectually far less involved, have less personal stake in the outcome of the competition, have little need to be concerned with the "correctness" of their views on public questions, and have even less reason to learn in precisely what ways their opinions differ from their opponents'. . . .

(3) Part of the explanation for the greater consensus among followers than leaders resides in the nature and size of the two types of

groups. Whereas the leader groups are comparatively small and selective, each of the follower groups number in the millions and, by their very size and unwieldiness, are predisposed to duplicate the characteristics of the population as a whole. Even if the Republicans draw disproportionately from the business-managerial classes and the Democrats from the trade union movement, neither interest group has enough influence to shape distinctively the aggregrate opinions of so large a mass of supporters. Size also affects the nature and frequency of interaction within the two types of groups. Because they comprise a smaller, more selectively chosen, organized, and articulate élite, the leaders are apt to associate with people of their own political persuasion more frequently and consistently than the followers do. They are not only less cross-pressured than the rank and file but they are also subjected to strong party group efforts to induce them to conform. Because their political values are continually renewed through frequent communication with people of like opinions, and because they acquire intense reference group identifications, they develop an extraordinary ability to resist the force of the opposition's arguments. While the followers, too, are thrown together and shielded to some extent, they are likely to mingle more freely with people of hostile political persuasions, to receive fewer partisan communications, and to hold views that are only intermittently and inconsistently reinforced. Since, by comparison with the leaders, they possess little interest or information about politics, they can more easily embrace "deviant" attitudes without discomfort and without challenge from their associates. Nor are they likely to be strongly rewarded for troubling to have "correct" opinions. The followers, in short, are less often and less effectively indoctrinated than their leaders. . . .

(4) Political competition itself operates to divide the leaders more than the followers. If the parties are impelled to present a common face to the electorate, they are also strongly influenced to distinguish themselves from each other. For one thing, they have a more heightened sense of the "national interest" than the followers do, even if they do not all conceive it in the same way. For another, they hope to improve their chances at the polls by offering the electorate a recognizable and attractive commodity. In addition, they seek emotional gratification in the heightened sense of brotherhood brought on by the struggle against an "out-group" whose claim to office seems always, somehow, to border upon usurpation. As with many ingroup-outgroup distinctions, the participants search for moral grounds to justify their antagonisms toward each other, and ideologies help to furnish such grounds. Among the followers, on the other hand, these needs exist, if at all, in much weaker form.

7

Conventions and Elections

7.1. A CRITICAL VIEW OF THE CONVENTION SYSTEM

Of the Europeans who came to observe the political process in America, Ostrogorski was perhaps the most depressed by what he thought he saw. His acid appraisal of the convention system for nominating candidates for the Presidency contained grains of sharp insight well worth pondering in our own time.

AT LAST, after a session of several days, the end is reached; the convention adjourns *sine die*. All is over. As you step out of the building you inhale with relief the gentle breeze which tempers the scorching heat of July; you come to yourself; you recover your sensibility, which has been blunted by the incessant uproar, and your faculty of judgment, which has been held in abeyance amid the pandemonium in which day after day has been passed. You collect your impressions, and you realize what a colossal travesty of popular institutions you have just been witnessing. A greedy crowd of office-holders, or of office-seekers, disguised as delegates of the people, on the pretence of holding the grand council of the party, indulged in, or were the victims of, intrigues and manœuvres, the object of which was the chief magistracy of the greatest Republic of the two hemispheres,—the succession to the Washingtons and the Jeffersons. With an elaborate respect for forms extending to the smallest details of procedure, they pretended to deliberate, and then passed resolutions settled by a handful of wire-pullers in the obscurity of committees and private caucuses; they proclaimed as the creed of the party appealing to

From M. Ostrogorski, *Democracy and the Organization of Political Parties* (New York: The Macmillan Company, 1902), pp. 278–279.

its piety, a collection of hollow, vague phrases, strung together by a few experts in the art of using meaningless language, and adopted still more precipitately without examination and without conviction; with their hand upon their heart, they adjured the assembly to support aspirants in whose success they had not the faintest belief; they voted in public for candidates whom they were scheming to defeat. Cut off from their conscience by selfish calculations and from their judgment by the tumultuous crowd of spectators, which alone made all attempt at deliberation an impossibility, they submitted without resistance to the pressure of the galleries masquerading as popular opinion, and made up of a *claque* and of a raving mob which, under ordinary circumstances, could only be formed by the inmates of all the lunatic asylums of the country who had made their escape at the same time. Here this mob discharges a great political function; it supplies the "enthusiasm" which is the primary element of the convention, which does duty for discussion and controls all its movements. Produced to order of the astute managers, "enthusiasm" is served out to the delegates as a strong drink, to gain completer mastery over their will. But in the fit of intoxication they yield to the most sudden impulses, dart in the most unexpected directions, and it is blind chance which has the last word. The name of the candidate for the Presidency of the Republic issues from the votes of the convention like a number from a lottery. And all the followers of the party, from the Atlantic to the Pacific, are bound, on pain of apostasy, to vote for the product of that lottery. Yet, when you carry your thoughts back from the scene which you have just witnessed and review the line of Presidents, you find that if they have not all been great men—far from it—they were all honourable men; and you cannot help repeating the American saying: "God takes care of drunkards, of little children, and of the United States!"

7.2. THE EVIL OF INVISIBLE GOVERNMENT

Criticism of the instruments of politics has by no means been confined to politics at the national level. In this selection Elihu Root, a former Secretary of State and distinguished lawyer, pleads with the delegates to New York's Constitutional Convention of 1915 to put an end to the "invisible government" of political bosses and the patronage system they control.

. . . MR. CHAIRMAN, there never was a reform in administration in this world which did not have to make its way against the strong feeling of

From Elihu Root, "Address in New York Constitutional Convention of 1915," in *Addresses on Government and Citizenship* (Cambridge: Harvard University Press, 1916), pp. 200–204.

good, honest men, concerned in existing methods of administration, and who saw nothing wrong. Never! It is no impeachment to a man's honesty, his integrity, that he thinks the methods that he is familiar with and in which he is engaged are all right. But you cannot make any improvements in this world without overriding the satisfaction that men have in the things as they are, and of which they are a contented and successful part. . . .

The governments of our cities: why, twenty years ago, when James Bryce wrote his *American Commonwealth,* the government of American cities was a byword and a shame for Americans all over the world. Heaven be thanked, the government of our cities has now gone far toward redeeming itself and us from that disgrace, and the government of American cities today is in the main far superior to the government of American states. I challenge contradiction to that statement. How has it been reached? How have our cities been lifted up from the low grade of incompetency and corruption on which they stood when the *American Commonwealth* was written? It has been done by applying the principles of this bill to city government, by giving power to the men elected by the people to do the things for which they were elected. But I say it is quite plain that that is not all. . . .

. . . I treat this subject in my own mind not as a personal question to any man. I am talking about the system. From the days of Fenton, and Conkling, and Arthur, and Cornell, and Platt, from the days of David B. Hill, down to the present time, the government of the state has presented two different lines of activity, one of the constitutional and statutory officers of the state, and the other of the party leaders,—they call them party bosses. They call the system—I do not coin the phrase, I adopt it because it carries its own meaning—the system they call "invisible government." For I do not remember how many years, Mr. Conkling was the supreme ruler in this state; the governor did not count, the legislatures did not count; comptrollers and secretaries of state and what not, did not count. It was what Mr. Conkling said; and in a great outburst of public rage he was pulled down.

Then Mr. Platt ruled the state; for nigh upon twenty years he ruled. It was not the governor; it was not the legislature; it was not any elected officers; it was Mr. Platt. And the capitol was not here; it was at 49 Broadway; with Mr. Platt and his lieutenants. . . . The ruler of the state during the greater part of the forty years of my acquaintance with the state government has not been any man authorized by the constitution or by the law; and, sir, there is throughout the length and breadth of this state a deep and sullen and long-continued resentment at being governed thus by men not of the people's choosing. The party leader is elected by no one, accountable to one, bound by no oath of office, removable by no one. . . .

How is it accomplished? How is it done? Mr. Chairman, it is done by the use of patronage, and the patronage that my friends on the other side of this question have been arguing and pleading for in this convention, is the power to continue that invisible government against that authorized by the people. Everywhere, sir, that these two systems of government co-exist, there is a conflict day by day, and year by year, between two principles of appointment to office, two radically opposed principles. The elected officer or the appointed officer, the lawful officer who is to be held responsible for the administration of his office, desires to get men into the different positions of his office who will do their work in a way that is creditable to him and his administration. Whether it be a president appointing a judge, or a governor appointing a superintendent of public works, whatever it may be, the officer wants to make a success, and he wants to get the man selected upon the ground of his ability to do the work.

How is it about the boss? What does the boss have to do? He has to urge the appointment of a man whose appointment will consolidate his power and preserve the organization. The invisible government proceeds to build up and maintain its power by a reversal of the fundamental principle of good government, which is that men should be selected to perform the duties of the office; and to substitute the idea that men should be appointed to office for the preservation and enhancement of power of the political leader. The one, the true one, looks upon appointment to office with a view to the service that can be given to the public. The other, the false one, looks upon appointment to office with a view to what can be gotten out of it.

. . . Both parties are alike; all parties are alike. The system extends through all. . . . when we refuse to make one governor elected by the people the real chief executive, we make inevitable the setting up of a chief executive not selected by the people, not acting for the people's interest, but for the selfish interest of the few who control the party, whichever party it may be.

Think for a moment of what this patronage system means. How many of you are there who would be willing to do to your private client, or customer, or any private trust, or to a friend or neighbor, what you see being done to the state of New York every year of your lives in the taking of money out of her treasury without service?

7.3. A PROPOSAL TO ABOLISH
THE ELECTORAL COLLEGE

Henry Cabot Lodge, then United States Senator, proposed in 1950 that the Constitution be amended to eliminate the Electoral College as a device for choosing the President and Vice-President. Under the Lodge Plan, electoral votes in Presidential elections would be counted in proportion to the popular votes received.

MR. LODGE: Mr. President, I desire to make a presentation concerning Senate Joint Resolution 2, which proposes an amendment to the Constitution of the United States, abolishing the electoral college and providing for the counting of the electoral vote for President and Vice President in proportion to the popular vote. . . .

Let me say now that it does three things, principally:

First, it abolishes entirely the office of Presidential elector. The electoral vote per State, which is equal to the total number of Representatives and Senators, is retained, but purely as an automatic counting device.

Second, it eliminates any possibility that an election may be thrown into the House of Representatives—a possibility which, as Senators know, was a very real one in connection with the 1948 election.

Third, it does away with the so-called unit-rule system of counting electoral votes. Under the existing system, the candidate receiving a plurality of the popular vote in any given State is credited with all the electoral votes of that State, regardless of how infinitesimal the plurality. Under the proposed system, the electoral votes in each State are automatically divided among the candidates in direct proportion to the popular vote.

The electoral votes which each candidate receives, therefore, represent his proportional strength in the State. These votes are then taken and added to the electoral votes received in all the other States. The candidate having the greatest number of electoral votes wins the Presidency. Votes for Vice President are counted in precisely the same manner. . . .

The indictment that can be drawn up against the present procedure is an impressive one. In general, there are three principal counts in this indictment:

First. The evils arising from the retention of the "dummy" office of president elector.

Second. The method of selecting a President when no candidate commands a majority of electoral votes.

Third. The defects and dangers which derive from the so-called unit-rule method of crediting all of a State's electoral votes to the plurality candidate.

An analysis of each of these three broad counts of the indictment follows:

From Senator Henry Cabot Lodge, in *The Congressional Record,* 81st Congress, 2d Session, Vol. 96, Part 1 (January 25, 1950).

. . . it is most important to note that the individual elector is only morally bound to vote for candidates of his party for President and Vice President. He is not legally bound. In fact, recent State and Federal decisions make it very doubtful, indeed, whether a State can constitutionally impose a legal obligation on an elector to cast his vote for his party's candidate, It is possible, therefore, for individual members of the electoral college to cast their votes for whomsoever they please, utterly ignoring the mandate of the people and disregarding, if they so choose, their own pledges. Indeed, there have been several examples in the past of what I call the free-wheeling elector. In the 1948 elections a Tennessee elector, running on both the Democrat and Dixiecrat slates, cast his vote for the Dixiecrat candidate despite the fact that the State turned in a substantial plurality for the Democratic candidate. . . .

The second count in the indictment against the present method of electing the President concerns the constitutional provision which designates the House of Representatives as the final umpire of presidential elections in which no candidate receives a majority of the electoral votes.

A candidate, in order to win the election, must secure a majority of the whole number of electors, which at present means 266 votes. In case no person receives an electoral majority for President, the House of Representatives, voting by State units, elects the President from those receiving the three highest totals of electoral votes. A majority of the State votes—in other words, 25—is required to settle the issue. . . .

This particular aspect of our election machinery has found very few, if any defenders. The chief criticism, of course, is the inequity that results from giving to all States, without regard to differences in population, equal power in electing the President. This procedure, it may be noted, entirely abrogates the basic principle upon which our whole approach to Presidential elections is predicated, namely, that each State's relative voting power shall be measured in terms both of the State as a unit, represented by the two electoral votes for the two Senators, and the State in terms of relative population, represented by the number of electoral votes for the number of Representatives. This means, simply, that each State has the same number of electoral votes as it has votes in Congress. But when an election is thrown into the House of Representatives, this principle is wholly disregarded and each State stands on an equal basis with every other State. . . .

Serious as is this possibility that the House of Representatives may completely thwart the popular will, a still more dangerous evil lurks behind the provision that the House shall umpire deadlocked presidential elections. It is entirely possible that the House itself might become deadlocked, with the result that Inauguration Day might come and go without a duly elected President.

Political analysts have demonstrated how the 1948 elections illustrate the possibility of this danger. A change of less than six tenths of the votes from Mr. Truman in two States would have thrown the election into the House. A careful analysis of the 48 State delegations in the House have revealed that neither the Republicans nor the Democrats would have been able to command the constitutional majority of 25 States necessary to elect. At the outset of the Eighty-first Congress, 21 delegations had a Democratic majority, 20 delegations had a Republican majority, 3 were evenly divided, and 4 delegations represented States which were carried by the Dixiecrat candidate. That brings it very close to home, Mr. President. On the first ballot, consequently, the result would have been: For Mr. Truman, 21; for Mr. Dewey, 20; for Mr. Thurmond, 4. Assuming that the delegations from the 4 States carried by Mr. Thurmond had held fast, even the shift of the 3 evenly divided delegations either to Mr. Truman or to Mr. Dewey would not have commanded the requisite constitutional majority of 25. There is something to think about. It would have left Mr. Thurmond as the arbiter of the whole situation.

The procedure contained in the constitutional amendment proposed in Senate Joint Resolution 2 makes this danger an impossibility. The successful candidates for President and Vice President need not obtain a majority of electoral votes; the person, to quote the language of the amendment, "having the greatest number of electoral votes for President shall be President. If two or more persons shall have an equal and the highest number of such votes," the amendment continues, "then the one for whom the greatest number of popular votes were cast shall be President." There can be no deadlocked decisions, and the universally condemned procedure of casting Congress in the role of final umpire is wholly eliminated. . . .

The defects, unhealthy practices, and potential evils of the unit-rule or general ticket procedure for counting electoral votes are many and varied. Only those of particular importance will be outlined here.

In effect, literally millions of American voters are disfranchised in every presidential election because of the unit-rule system.

This contention is more than a figure of speech. It is an actuality. The 1948 elections furnish an excellent example of this point.

Mr. Dewey received in the 16 States which he carried a total of 8,600,000 votes. These 16 States gave him a total of 189 electoral votes. But in the 32 States which Mr. Dewey failed to carry he had a total of 13,300,000 votes. This great mass of popular votes for Mr. Dewey gave him not one single electoral vote and, therefore, counted for naught. They were of no more effect than if they had not been cast at all. . . .

The term "minority President" is frequently used with two different meanings. It may refer to a President who is elected without a majority of the popular vote, but nevertheless with more popular votes than any of his opponents. This has happened in almost half—14—of the 32 elections for President between 1824 and 1948, inclusive.

It may also refer to a President who was elected despite the fact that he had fewer popular votes than his leading opponent. This has happened three times in our history—Adams in 1824, Hayes in 1876, and Harrison in 1888. It is in this latter meaning of the term "minority President" that we discuss the phrase here.

Such a result as this is directly attributable to three characteristics of our election procedure: (a) The unit-rule method of counting electoral votes; (b) the distribution of electoral votes to States on the basis of the number of votes each State has in Congress; and (c) the fact that all save two of each State's electoral votes are awarded on the basis of population, rather than voting strength. . . . The so-called doubtful or pivotal States monopolize the attention of the candidates and the campaign-fund spenders during the canvass for popular votes, while other areas not regarded as doubtful are generally ignored. . . .

Another charge which can be leveled against the unit-rule system is that it perpetuates so-called solid or one-party States.

Voting statistics show a high correlation between the degree of closeness of the State-wide popular vote and the amount of popular participation. In the doubtful State there is a strong incentive for the voter to vote; in States where the outcome on a State-wide basis is a foregone conclusion, there is little incentive for the voter, regardless of his political inclinations, to take the trouble to register his preference. . . .

The Brookings Institution, referring to Senate Joint Resolution 2, summarized this whole problem in these words—record of hearings, page 15:

Sure States will no longer be neglected as they are at present both in nominations and campaigns because a substantial minority vote in these States will result in electoral votes for the candidate of their party. Voters opposed to the dominant party in their respective States will be encouraged to work and vote for their candidate because their work and votes may actually affect the results. Their votes will be cast and counted for the candidates of their choice and not thrown away as under the present system. . . .

The fact that pressure groups do hold a balance of power in States where the contest between the two major parties is close—and I call attention to the situation in New York State in the 1948 election, where Henry Wallace's party certainly exercised very great power—is an evil of the unit-rule system that has far-reaching but understandable effects. It causes both of the major parties to give undue attention to the demands and programs of relatively unimportant groups or factions. Because of the strategic position which these groups may occupy, even though in the over-all national scene the particular group may not be numerically important, they may be the vital pivot upon which a large block of electoral votes will turn. Hence, the major parties feel it necessary to make large concessions and enter strong bids for their support. . . .

7.4. DEBATE OVER ELECTORAL COLLEGE REFORM

In the debate which followed Senator Lodge's proposal, the Senators argued vigorously over whether elimination of the practice of allocating all the electoral votes of a state to a single candidate would encourage the growth of splinter parties, disrupt the federal system, and necessitate national supervision of all elections. In this selection Senator Ferguson of Michigan leads the attack and Senator Langer of North Dakota proposes an alternative.

MR. FERGUSON: Senate Joint Resolution 2 provides that in recording a State's electoral votes, they shall be credited to respective candidates in proportion to their popular votes in each State, and then totaled for each candidate for the Nation as a whole.

This is the most revolutionary and the most controversial of the changes proposed by Senate Joint Resolution 2. As sponsors of the resolution freely admit, this proportionate division of electoral votes will work decided changes in voting habits, in the make-up of the poltical party system as we know it in this country, and upon the conduct of Presidential election campaigns.

Under the present system, commonly called the unit rule, the candidate receiving the most votes in each State receives the whole of the State's electoral vote. Further, he has to get an absolute majority of all electoral votes in the Nation and more than any other candidate to win the Presidency.

Senate Joint Resolution 2 proposes to abolish this system, and in its place to divide up the electoral votes in each State in the proportions indicated by the popular vote. A radical candidate who had no hope of election in one or a group of States under the present system could add up all his electoral votes in all 48 States, under Senate Joint Resolution 2, and make a strong showing. He would not need a majority to win. A plurality—merely one vote more than the next highest candidate—would be enough under Senate Joint Resolution 2. Then, if there were three

From Senator Homer Ferguson, in *The Congressional Record,* 81st Congress, 2d Session, Vol. 96, Part 1 (January 30 and February 1, 1950).

or four candidates in the field, a radical candidate with 30 percent of the vote could become the Chief Executive. . . .

If proportional sharing of the vote in the solid South offers an incentive for Republicans to make progress there, why would not the chance for electoral votes on a sharing basis offer incentives to minority groups all over the country, since the Republican Party is nothing more nor less than a minority party in the South.

When sponsors of the resolution wish to appeal to Republicans, they cite the chance for them to get electoral votes in the South. But when critics point out that the same incentive is held out to minority groups elsewhere and everywhere, the sponsors pooh-pooh the idea. They can hardly have it both ways.

I firmly believe the proportionate sharing of electoral votes is a direct encouragement to the growth of multiple parties. As I have discussed this possibility in another connection, such a prospect carries grave implications. It would mean an end to the two-party system which has been so instrumental in preserving political stability and responsible government. In its place would come splinter factions and multiple parties which have plagued and retarded respresentative government wherever they have appeared. . . .

Mr. Kefauver: The Senator has asked why we in the South think this proposal would strengthen the two-party system and would not lead to the formation of third parties or splinter parties in the South.

Our idea is that under the system here proposed, if put into effect, both political parties, instead of conceding or marking off the electoral votes of the South, would fight for and work for votes in the South just as they do in the pivotal States, and therefore the problems of the South and of States in a similar situation would receive more consideration by the platform writers and policy makers of the two major political parties. Likewise, the voters of the South and of other sections of the country would find better representation and a stronger voice in the programs and policies of the two major political parties, and consequently would stay with those two major parties. . . .

Mr. Ferguson: Mr. President, I answer the Senator by saying that what he has just stated is a speculation which has been disproved by actual fact. The actual fact is that in 1948 when the South disagreed with the Democratic Party, some of the Southern States bolted the Democratic Party at the convention. Did they come over to the Republican Party? Oh, no, Mr. President. Instead, they formed their own party, a splinter party, the Dixiecrat Party, There is the fact; that is what happened. . . .

Mr. Kefauver: I should like to call the Senator's attention to the fact that in most of the States, the governors and other State officials are elected on a plurality basis. Yet we have seen less development of so-called splinter parties or third parties or minority parties in the States of the Union than we have in the Federal Government under the electoral-college system. This leads the junior Senator from Tennessee to the conclusion that the people of the Nation believe in, appreciate the value of, and wish to sustain the two-party system, and are not going to support multiple parties, as have the French people. That is evidenced by the fact that throughout the United States there have been so few splinter parties in State elections.

However, if we drop a system whereby all sections of the country are considered by the two major political parties, then we shall have a strengthening, not a deterioration, of the two-party system.

Mr. Ferguson: Mr. President, I cannot agree that that is the reason why the State elections have not led to the formation of splinter parties. I think a State is dominated by what occurs in the national scene. In each of the States the important election is the presidential election; it overshadows all other elections. The presidential election is very definitely the largest, most important election. Therefore, the parties line up behind the candidates for Senator and Representatives and the presidential candidate. That is what keeps the States from developing splinter parties, whereas the adoption of the proposed plurality counting method would have the opposite effect.

If southerners open the door to minority parties, they will not be able to confine party allegiance to the two major parties and to the Dixiecrat Party. Throughout the Nation today there are threats to our political system as a result of other parties which wish to take over. Splinter parties are already on the horizon. . . .

Sponsors of the resolution make much of the disfranchisement of voters under the present system. They speak of votes being lost, or counted for the opposition. But, under their resolution, a plurality winner may have only 40 percent or less of the electoral votes. What of the defeated majority, with 60 percent of the votes? Are their votes not lost, too, or considered as counted for the minority winners? As a matter of fact, I cannot become excited over the argument of lost votes. It seems to me to be only an appeal for popular support for the resolution, an appeal without real substance in reason and logic. In every election where there can be but a single winner, all votes cast for the losing candidates can be said to be lost. Sponsors of the resolution would merely transfer the lost votes so-called from the State to the national level. In truth, no votes are lost when validly cast in an election. They are counted toward whatever the final decision is, whether it be the unit of an electoral majority or the plurality of electoral votes, and if found insufficient to win, they have simply exhausted their power as votes. . . .

Third parties, given the incentive of a chance to elect a President, will maintain their identity by putting up full slates for Congress.

It is this which in the end will give us bloc government. Minorities, given a voice, will not be satisfied when their voice is canceled out or lost, as it would be under the proposed scheme. Their dissatisfaction will mount further, if a plurality winner receives only 40 percent of the total electoral vote. They will then demand full proportional representation in the Congress and on Government boards and commissions, just as the two major parties do now, because they are too strong to be ignored. We have certain laws now providing that the two major parties shall have representation on commissions and boards. If such a thing becomes possible under the law, and if it occurs, as it seems indicated it will, the demand will be that other minorities, and lesser minorities, have such representation. It is at this stage that proportional representation, as in France and other parts of Europe, is likely to flower from Senate Joint Resolution 2. And wherever proportional representation, so-called, is at work, government has been plagued, confused, and weakened. The existing system of counting electoral votes has avoided that. It has preserved the two-party system, by which Government has been held stable and responsible.

I see also in abandonment of the unit rule for recording electoral votes a decided weakening of the principle which created and held together the Federal Union, namely, the preservation of the independence of the States. . . .

This weakening of the States gives rise also to serious question of whether complete Federal control of elections might not legally and logically follow. Have those who believe in States' rights considered this question? For instance, if a candidate is to receive credit, by constitutional provision, for the proportion of popular votes cast for him, as provided by Senate Joint Resolution 2, could he not demand that in order to receive complete credit nationally, a State should be required to place his name on the ballot? The States now jealously guard their prerogative to control the ballot. But how can they maintain this position after they have accepted the idea that a candidate with popular votes is entitled to a share of electoral votes?

Mr. Lodge: I should like to ask the Senator five or six questions.

Mr. Ferguson: I shall be glad to have the Senator ask them.

Mr. Lodge: The Senator does not think, does he, that it is a bad thing to have a President elected by a plurality?

Mr. Ferguson: I do think it is a bad thing.

Mr. Lodge: Does the Senator think it was bad that Abraham Lincoln was elected, although he received only 39 percent of the popular vote?

Mr. Ferguson: I think it is better for a candidate to receive a majority.

Mr. Lodge: Does the Senator think it was a bad thing that 12

Presidents in our history, including Wilson, Cleveland, Harrison, Garfield, and Truman, were elected by a plurality of the popular vote?

Mr. Ferguson: I still think it was a bad thing. I think it would have been much better if they had received a majority. As the Senator has said, Abraham Lincoln was elected with only 39 percent of the popular vote. The Senator can see how a third, fourth, or fifth party can put up a candidate and elect a President when only 25 percent of the people want him as President and 75 percent do not want him.

Mr. Lodge: If 25 percent of the American people want to be Socialists, 25 percent want to be Democrats, 25 percent want to be Republicans, and 25 percent want to be Communists, does the Senator think there is any law or any constitutional amendment that can stop them from taking those positions if they desire to do so?

Mr. Ferguson: No; but I hope we can guard against exploitation by a determined, compact minority. Where there is a two-party system, and those in one party range in their political views from one extreme to the other, and those in the other party, which is the majority party, we will say, also represent a wide range of thought, it is much better to have people working in the party, follow the platform of the party, so that there can be party responsibility, than it is to have them broken down into various splinters and have them become independent, and, therefore, have no party responsibility whatever. I say that if the desire is to increase the Socialist vote in America, or to have the Socialist Party become a strong party, or if the desire is to have the Communists become a strong party, and not be trying to infiltrate into the other parties, the kind of proportional representation proposed by the joint resolution would bring about such a condition. . . .

Mr. Langer: Mr. President, I ask unanimous consent to be allowed to modify my substitute. . . . I am offering the substitute because I am conscientiously and firmly convinced that the American people ought to have the right to vote for President and Vice President of the United States by direct vote. Senate Joint Resolution 2 does not so provide. It merely abolishes the electoral college, as such, in name, but as a matter of fact the people themselves still would not be voting directly for President and Vice-President.

Mr. President, we elect our school boards, we elect the mayors of our towns, by direct vote of the people. We elect the Governors of the States, the Members of the House of Representatives, and United States Senators, by direct vote of the people, and I know of no reason why we should not elect the President of the United States by direct vote of the people.

The pending measure, Senate Joint Resolution 2, does not eliminate political games. A group of Republicans a few months before election could still get together in a smoke-filled room and nominate some man whom the people of the country did not want. A few days later the Democrats could meet and nominate another man of the same character. Then the big business interests, which had nominated those two men, neither of whom was desired by the rank and file of the people of America, would proceed to campaign for the men they had nominated. The only choice the people would have would be to vote for one or the other.

Under my substitute any man or woman who desired to run as a candidate for President of the United States could do so. There could be a direct primary in June, and whoever was the high candidate in the Republican Party or in the Democratic Party would be the nominee of the party, just as is done in the case of governors at the present time. Then in the month of November the two men chosen by the rank and file of the people would be the two candidates, with the result that the people would have nominated in a primary election the Democrat or the Republican they would choose to be President.

Mr. President, that is not the only provision of the substitute. It provides also that an independent group, if they could get one-half of 1 percent of all the people who voted in the last presidential election, could nominate a man to run independently.

I ask, Mr. President, is it not true that in the last election, and in the election 4 years before that, those in America who were opposed to war had absolutely no chance to vote for a candidate who shared that opposition? Some may say there was no interest in the question, but I remember that when Burton K. Wheeler spoke in Los Angeles, 108,000 people attended the meeting where he spoke. It was a meeting called by those who were opposed to the United States entering World War II.

7.5. A RECENT ANALYSIS OF THE CONVENTION SYSTEM

Although the authors admit that the party convention system grew without plan, they insist that it performs democratically and well in selecting candidates, presenting them to the electorate, and educating the populace about issues facing the nation. Better organization of convention committees and more frequent meetings are suggested as aids in these tasks.

NATIONAL PARTY conventions entered the American scene during Andrew

From Paul David, Ralph Goldman, and Richard Bain, *The Politics of National Party Conventions* (Washington, D.C.: Brookings Institution, 1960), pp. 1–3, 495–496.

Jackson's first term as President. Uncertain and held irregularly at first, within a few decades they had developed the main features that have characterized them ever since. In a world of constant political change, they are among the oldest important political institutions to be found in any country.

Taken together as an interacting political system, the conventions of the two major parties provide widespread representation and make critical political decisions for the entire electorate. This high mission, however, is in strong contrast to the popular conception of them. It is also compromised by many aspects of their composition and institutional behavior.

Among political scientists, opinion on the technical effectiveness of the conventions is mixed. They have been described, for instance, as "unwieldy, unrepresentative, and less than responsible." They have been regarded also as a serious obstacle to the establishment of responsible party government, because of the undue control exercised by the assembled party bosses. On the other hand, some scholars consider the conventions highly useful, because they provide the valuable service of testing the skill of competing politicians and developing party leadership. A study of the present kind must necessarily devote attention to the practical question implied in such appraisals: are the conventions nothing more than meetings of party bosses hidden behind a noisy political circus, or can they be treated seriously as representative assemblies competent to decide the party's leadership and principles? . . .

Whether the conventions are "truly representative" institutions, worthy of respect in a democratic society, is a question—or tangle of questions—that may generate more heated theoretical argument than practical wisdom. Confusion on this subject stems from several characteristics of party politics and of the conventions themselves.

First, there is the fact that state party organizations are far more autonomous than state governments. They are united in a national party by rules and customs far less definitely federal than those that unite the states in a national government. Accordingly, a national party convention takes on some of the characteristics of an international conference of delegations from sovereign nations, some of which may be democracies, others autocracies of one sort or another. In one delegation to a party convention each member may have a direct relationship to a specific constituency of party voters; in another the members collectively may owe allegiance to a state committee or convention that is remote from the voters and little subject to their control. But each of these delegations represents its state party in one way or another, and the variation among them does not necessarily prevent the assembly as a whole from retaining its representative nature. . . .

As legal entities, the conventions have been very nearly unrecognized in federal law until recently. Political parties are not mentioned in the federal Constitution, and only rarely and indirectly in federal statutes. The Supreme Court, however, had occasion in 1952 to refer to "a state political party, affiliated with a national party through acceptance of the national call to send state delegates to the national convention"; the Court upheld the authority of a state party committee to require would-be presidential electors to sign a pledge of support for the national party's candidates, still to be selected. Recent proposals to establish a federal Presidential Primaries Commission seem to have been drafted on the assumption that the party convention is a type of representative institution. The establishment of such a commission would indirectly subject major features of the conventions to prescriptions of federal law.

The argument over what the conventions ought to be has undoubtedly been complicated by a basic uncertainty: is nomination by a party organization proper at all? The most critical aspects of the nominating process arise from the fact that the alternatives of choice must be discovered as a part of the process. It is the function of the nominating process to reduce to finality the alternatives that can be made the subject of an election. The difference between the nominating process and the election process is nonetheless often misunderstood, because of a hasty assumption that the nominating procedures of the two major parties are limited to only two opposing possibilities—candidates will be chosen by a small inner circle of bosses unless they are determined in a national primary where all voters may take part.

Actually the party conventions occupy a middle ground. They can draw heavily on the voters for guidance, which they obtain formally in state primaries and informally by many kinds of grass-roots contact. They can also perform a service that is practicable only in a general parley—that of solving the problems of compromise, of combining first and second choices into some result that the whole party will support, thus maintaining party unity and avoiding disruption into splinter parties. This service of compromise is one of the essential differences between a major-party nomination and a general election, and one that makes it futile to judge the representative character of the nomination by the standards appropriate to an election. . . .

Recent studies of voting have found that many voters review their party preferences most actively at the time of the conventions, with the object of deciding for whom they will vote in the forthcoming election. The conventions have the effect of projecting an image of the parties in their collective, corporate identity. They provide a setting within which the major-party leaders and the eventual candidates can be subjected to an intense form of public scrutiny. All these aspects have been amplified by television broadcasting. In 1952, for example, the conventions repeatedly attracted television audiences larger than most of those that would view the speeches and rallies in the later campaign.

Political strategists of both parties have thus been compelled to recognize that the campaign begins at the convention, not afterwards, and that it should therefore be conducted as a major segment of the campaign. Pressures mount for broad participation by local political leaders from all over the country who can be energized and sent home to work enthusiastically in the campaign. Pressures also mount to show the convention in the guise of a happy family gathering, keeping the less attractive forms of conflict off stage, in the relative privacy of the committees. . . .

Granting this, a specific four-point program for dealing with some of the problems might consist of the following steps.

1. *More effective scheduling and execution of preparatory work in advance of the conventions.* . . .

2. *Changing the structure of the national committee and convention committees to make them more representative.* . . . If this kind of change were placed in effect, more business could be entrusted to the national committee and other committees meeting in advance of the conventions, with less danger that recommendations would only have to be reversed by the convention as a whole.

3. *Providing an executive committee of heads of delegations, modeled somewhat on the standard operating procedures of large international conferences, to secure a more effective control of convention time and operations.*

On the face of it, an executive committee to secure a tighter control over what happens on the floor may seem undemocratic. But, in a meeting as large as a party convention, unrestrained freedom of the members to offer motions and speak from the floor is physically impossible. Some control is necessary to allow any business to be transacted, and in present practice the control, by the time the convention is doing business, is in the hands of one man—the permanent chairman, customarily the party leader in the House of Representatives. In view of the frequent differences in point of view between the congressional and the presidential wings of the party, it seems fair to suggest that a system of control by a committee clearly representing the whole presidential constituency would often be likely to satisfy the desires of the majority more closely than the control exercised in recent years by the party leader in Congress and the associates with whom such a leader inevitably surrounds himself.

4. *More frequent meetings of the conventions, with biennial meetings as a first step.* Conventions in the mid-term years would provide a means for focusing national attention upon the parties and their current status at the beginning of each contest for control of Congress.

7.6. MORALITY IN POLITICAL CAMPAIGNING

Incitement of religious prejudice was a commonplace campaign technique in the Presidential election of 1928 when a Catholic, Al Smith, was nominated for President for the first time in history. In this talk before the 1960 campaign went into high gear, the late Senator Kefauver warns the people against the professional hatemongers.

MR. KEFAUVER: In every national election the claim is made that the Nation is at a crossroads. This claim is not altogether untrue, because, when examined carefully, each of our national elections has taken place in the shadow of one or more important issues.

It is not the purpose of my remarks today to enumerate the many important issues facing the American people when they go to the polls in November 1960.

Nor is it my purpose to dwell on the fact that the rest of the world—both Communist and free—always watches our elections with much interest. It will watch more carefully than usual this time, because the hope for freedom on every continent hangs on the survival of a strong American democracy. We can no longer afford the luxury of indifference to the people who watch us. Our lives may well depend on their reactions.

If we allow this present contest to descend to the low level of some past elections, we cannot help but lower ourselves in the eyes of those upon whose help and friendship we depend and also give aid and comfort to those who boast that they will "bury" us.

But, more important in my view is the harm which a hatemongering election will do to us as a nation.

Hate begets hate; passion begets passion. Not only will a smear campaign damage the image of our country, it will also damage the soul and the conscience of our Nation.

Therefore, I would like to join those who have raised their voices to warn against the professional hatemongers and poison-pen pamphleteers who will come into this election as they have in others.

It is not enough to dissociate oneself from scurrilous propaganda put out on one's behalf, but a candidate has the responsibility to take active measures against it.

The purpose of a political campaign is to make clear the parties' stands on major problems and to demonstrate the candidates' abilities to

From Senator Estes Kefauver, in *The Congressional Record*, 86th Congress, Special Session, Vol. 106 (August 30, 1960).

deal on critical questions. The American people can make an intelligent decision this year only if the issues are presented to them honestly.

If the American people succeed, it will be despite the efforts of some strong forces to deflect them. There will be organizations and publications—like the Ku Klux Klan, the falsely named committee for constitutional government, and a magazine called Human Events, to mention just three—that will peddle messages of suspicion and falsehood, that will attempt to rally prejudice in place of reason. . . .

Certainly there can be no doubt that the political conscience of America is non-partisan. The National Committee on Fair Campaign Practices is led by a courageous Republican, Charles P. Taft of Cincinnati, who has worked hard and effectively to secure the observance of fair campaign practices codes. My Democratic colleague from Tennessee [Mr. Gore], has labored long and hard in this field. A Republican and a Democrat, the senior Senator from Wisconsin [Mr. Wiley] and the senior Senator from Rhode Island [Mr. Green], made the presentations before the Internal Revenue Commission which led to a denial of tax exemptions for the political propaganda for Edward Rumely's committee for constitutional government. . . .

. . . in 1928, we went through . . . a dirty campaign, and one in which the vilified candidate lost. There is certainly grave doubt that Al Smith would have won in 1928 even if there had been no scurrilous attack upon him because of his religion—it was probably not a Democratic year in any event. But this detracts not one whit from the fact that part of his defeat was directly due to a campaign calculated to stir up religious hatreds. . . .

The question now is whether the ghost of 1928 has been laid to rest.

All indications are that it has not—that it is riding high, at least in some places.

The country is being flooded once again with false and libelous anti-Catholic materials. Some of it is obscene. Most of it is unsigned.

There is every likelihood that this hate campaign will get worse before it gets better. There is no telling what type of disgusting trash may be shoved under the doors or put in the mailboxes of millions of decent Americans.

Mr. Gore: Mr. President, will the Senator yield?

Mr. Kefauver: I am happy to yield to my distinguished colleague from Tennessee.

Mr. Gore: Does not the Senator believe that, regrettable though this type of activity is, it may be better for the electorate that it has started so soon? Starting so soon, the American people will have ample opportunity to measure it and reject it.

Mr. Kefauver: Yes; I agree with my colleague that it is regrettable that there must be distortion and smear literature and misrepresentations. I commend the many outstanding statesmen and public servants, both Democrats and Republicans, for denouncing it. I thank my colleague. He is right that, with the smear campaign having started early, and with the American people analyzing and weighing it over a period of time, its effect will certainly be diminished and, in many cases, completely demolished.

However, there is every present indication that we can expect an increasing flow of different types of smear literature and unsigned political documents. I believe that immediately before the election we may anticipate new types. Therefore, I think it is well that the American people be forewarned as to what to expect and what might happen, so that they can be on the lookout for it. . . .

The American people themselves must be informed on the activities of hate peddlers. . . .

They must become suspicious of all unsigned political literature, especially leaflets and pamphlets containing stories that are too pat or too inflammatory. . . .

They should be informed that there are both Federal and State laws against corrupt campaign practices and unsigned literature.

They should know that there is a national committee on fair campaign practices which is ready, willing, and able to help cut down on the evil effects of hate peddling.

8

Strengthening The Party System

8.1. A PROPOSAL FOR IMPROVING OUR PARTIES

In this report a group of distinguished political science professors analyze the ills of the American political party system and suggest some basic cures. They decry, in particular, the alleged lack of party responsibility and they favor steps to widen participation of the citizenry in political parties and to strengthen party discipline from the local to the national level.

THROUGHOUT this report political parties are treated as indispensable instruments of government. That is to say, we proceed on the proposition that *popular government in a nation of more than 150 million people requires political parties which provide the electorate with a proper range of choice between alternatives of action.* The party system thus serves as the main device for bringing into continuing relationship those ideas about liberty, majority rule and leadership which Americans are largely taking for granted. . . .

Moreover, in contrast with any other political organization today in existence, the major parties even now are forced to consider public policy at least broadly enough to make it likely for them to win elections. If public esteem of the parties is much less high than it might be, the depressed state of their reputation has resulted in the main from their past indifference to broadly conceived public policy. This indifference has fixed

From the Committee on Political Parties, American Political Science Association, *Toward a More Responsible Two-Party System* (New York: Holt, Rinehart and Winston, Inc., 1950).

123

in the popular mind the idea of spoils, patronage and plunder. It is hence not astonishing when one hears a chosen representative assert for the public ear that in his state "people put principles above party." Much of the agitation for nonpartisanship—despite the impossibility of nonpartisan organization on a national level—is rooted in the same attitudes. . . .

An effective party system requires, first, that the parties are able to bring forth programs to which they commit themselves and, second, that the parties possess sufficient internal cohesion to carry out these programs. In such a system, the party program becomes the work program of the party, so recognized by the party leaders in and out of the government, by the party body as a whole, and by the public. This condition is unattainable unless party institutions have been created through which agreement can be reached about the general position of the party. . . .

In spite of the fact that the two-party system is part of the American political tradition, it cannot be said that the role of the opposition party is well understood. This is unfortunate because democratic government is greatly influenced by the character of the opposition party. The measures proposed elsewhere in our report to help the party in power to clarify its policies are equally applicable to the opposition.

The opposition most conducive to responsible government is an organized party opposition, produced by the organic operation of the two-party system. When there are two parties identifiable by the kinds of action they propose, the voters have an actual choice. On the other hand, the sort of opposition presented by a coalition that cuts across party lines, as a regular thing, tends to deprive the public of a meaningful alternative. When such coalitions are formed after the elections are over, the public usually finds it difficult to understand the new situation and to reconcile it with the purpose of the ballot. Moreover, on that basis it is next to impossible to hold either party responsible for its political record. This is a serious source of public discontent. . . .

By themselves, the interest groups cannot attempt to define public policy democratically. Coherent public policies do not emerge as the mathematical result of the claims of all of the pressure groups. The integration of the interest groups into the political system is a function of the parties. Any tendency in the direction of a strengthened party system encourages the interest groups to align themselves with one or the other of the major parties. Such a tendency is already at work. One of the noteworthy features of contemporary American politics is the fact that not a few interest groups have found it impossible to remain neutral towards both parties. To illustrate, the entry of organized labor upon the political scene has in turn impelled antagonistic special interests to coalesce in closer political alignments. . . .

As for party cohesion in Congress, the parties have done little to build up the kind of unity within the congressional party that is now so widely desired. Traditionally congressional candidates are treated as if they were the orphans of the political system, with no truly adequate party mechanism available for the conduct of their campaigns. Enjoying remarkably little national or local party support, congressional candidates have mostly been left to cope with political hazards of their occupation on their own account. *A basis for party cohesion in Congress will be established as soon as the parties interest themselves sufficiently in their congressional candidates to set up strong and active campaign organizations in the constituencies.* Discipline is less a matter of what the parties do to their congressional candidates than what the parties do for them. . . .

Party responsibility to the public, enforced in elections, implies that there be more than one party, for the public can hold a party responsible only if it has a choice. Again, unless the parties identify themselves with programs, the public is unable to make an intelligent choice between them. The public can understand the general management of the government only in terms of policies. When the parties lack the capacity to define their action in terms of policies, they turn irresponsible because the electoral choice between the parties becomes devoid of meaning. . . .

. . . *Party responsibility includes also the responsibility of party leaders to the party membership, as enforced in primaries, caucuses and conventions.* To this end the internal processes of the parties must be democratic, the party members must have an opportunity to participate in intraparty business, and the leaders must be accountable to the party. Responsibility demands that the parties concern themselves with the development of good relations between the leaders and the members. Only thus can the parties act as intermediaries between the government and the people. Strengthening the parties involves, therefore, the improvement of the internal democratic processes by which the leaders of the party are kept in contact with the members. . . .

The political developments of our time place a heavy emphasis on national issues as the basis of party programs. As a result, the party membership is coming to look to the national party leaders for a larger role in intraparty affairs. There is some evidence of growing general agreement within the membership of each party, strong enough to form a basis of party unity, provided the parties maintain close contact with their own supporters.

In particular, *national party leaders have a legitimate interest in the nomination of congressional candidates,* though normally they try hard to avoid the appearance of any intervention. Depending on the circumstances, this interest can be expressed quite sufficiently by seeking a chance to discuss the nomination with the party membership in the congressional district. On the other hand, it should not be assumed that state and local party leaders usually have an interest in congressional nominations antagonistic to the interest of the national leaders in maintaining the general party policy. As a matter of fact, congressional nominations are not considered great prizes by the local party organization as generally as one might think. It is neglect of congressional nominations and elections more than any other factor that weakens party unity in Congress. It should be added, however, that what is said here about intraparty relations with respect to congressional nominations applies also to other party nominations.

The existing party system is inadequately prepared to meet the demands now being made upon it chiefly because its central institutions are not well organized to deal with national questions.

. . . *The two parties are organized on a federal basis,* probably as a natural result of our federal type of government. In Charles E. Merriam's words, "The American party system has its roots in the states. Its regulation and control is conducted almost wholly, although not entirely, by the states acting separately." This means that *the national and state party organizations are largely independent of one another,* each operating within its own sphere, *without appreciable common approach to problems of party policy and strategy. . . .*

On that score, the party system is weighted much more heavily toward the state-local side than is true today of the federal system of government in the United States. The gap produces serious disabilities in government. It needs to be closed, . . .

. . . In part because of the centrifugal drives that run through the party system, *party organization does not vest leadership of the party as a whole in either a single person or a committee.* The President, by virtue of his conspicuous position and his real as well as symbolic role in public opinion, is commonly considered the leader of his party. If he has a vigorous personality and the disposition to press his views on party policy and strategy, he may become the actual leader during his presidential term. But even the President has no official position within the party organization and his leadership is often resented and opposed. The presidential nominee of the defeated party is generally recognized as the "titular leader" of his party, yet the very title implies a lack of authority. . . .

. . . The vagueness of formal leadership that prevails at the top has its counterpart in the vagueness of formal membership at the bottom. *No understandings or rules or criteria exist with respect to membership in a party. . . .*

We have summarized the main problems that arise in the present-day operation of the American two-party system. We now turn to an indication of the direction in which remedies might be sought. This is best done by setting forth specific proposals for creating a more suitable national party structure. . . .

. . . It has already been said earlier that the National Convention is unwieldy, unrepresentative and less than responsible in mandate and action. The abuse resulting from an undemocratic system of representation was, in fact, recognized by many Republicans almost from the beginning of the Republican party, and has been corrected for that party to a considerable extent. The Democratic party also recognized the need for improvement at the Convention in 1936, and a new rule of apportionment became effective in 1944. But in either case the existing formula falls distinctly short of true representation of the party's grass-roots strength in the individual states. . . .

As a practical matter the National Convention, in spite of its shortcomings, has become one of the traditional party agencies. *We assume its continuation as the principal representative and deliberative organ of the party.* With certain modifications, the convention can quite satisfactorily attend to its customary functions. These are to nominate presidential candidates (or, should the presidential primary be established on a national scale, to declare the results); to adopt or approve the party platform; to adopt rules and regulations governing the party; and in general to act as the supreme organ of the party.

But in the interest of greater effectiveness *the convention should meet at least biennially* instead of only quadrennially as at present, *with easy provision for special meetings. It also should cease to be a delegate convention of unwieldly size.* Much better results could be attained with a convention of not more than 500–600 members, composed mostly of delegates elected directly by the party voters on a more representative basis (300–350 members), a substantial number of ex-officio members (the National Committee, state party chairman, congressional leaders— probably about 150 altogether), and a selected group of prominent party leaders outside the party organizations (probably 25). . . .

. . . The National Committee is another traditional party agency, primarily concerned with the success of the presidential campaign. Although it is nominally chosen by the National Convention and the agent of that body, state legislation and party practice have modified this concept. Both have introduced various methods of selection (by state committee, by state convention, by the party voters at the primary, by the delegations to the National Convention) which have in substance, if not in form, replaced selection by the National Convention. . . .

. . . One of the most serious problems in the present scheme of party organization is that of securing a proper measure of common understanding and harmony of action between the national, congressional, and state organizations of the same party.

A solution requires, first, that some means be found for obtaining such cohesion within the congressional organization itself. As one aspect a sufficient degree of joint House and Senate organization is needed, instead of the present separate and independent party organizations for each house. A solution requires secondly, that there be better machinery for White House liaison with the congressional organization on general legislative policy. It is necessary to provide appropriate consultation between the President and the leaders of his own party in Congress to avoid the danger of putting the President in the role of the exclusive leader in respect to legislation; and to cultivate the idea that the party in power itself, rather than particular individuals at either end of Pennsylvania Avenue, is responsible for its record of legislative and executive action. Thus it will be easier to develop harmony and understanding, instead of jealousy and suspicion, between the President and Congress.

Such a Party Council should consider and settle the larger problems of party management, within limits prescribed by the National Convention; propose a preliminary draft of the party platform to the National Convention; interpret the platform in relation to current problems; choose for the National Convention the group of party leaders outside the party organizations; consider and make recommendations to appropriate party organs in respect to congressional candidates; and make recommendations to the National Convention, the National Committee or other appropriate party organs with respect to conspicuous departures from general party decisions by state or local party organizations. . . .

Although both bodies have on several occasions exercised these powers, *consideration should be given to the development of additional means of dealing with rebellious and disloyal state organizations.* Authoritative pronouncements by the Party Council and public appeal to the party membership affected may be such means. Use of party funds to replace the disloyal leadership of the state organization may be another. Still another might be appointment of temporary state officers, perhaps by the Party Council. One thing is entirely clear. It is contrary to the basic concept of our two-party system, destructive of party responsibility and disruptive of the party as a whole to permit organized disloyalty to continue. . . .

Members of Congress commonly claim the right to determine the party position on matters of legislation, especially after the off-year elections. The National Committee sometimes attempts to interpret the platform, but finds its authority sharply challenged. The President can make such attempts with more success for the majority party, although certainly not with ease. For the minority party there is no one with the President's standing or power. This is one of the serious gaps in the party machinery, which would best be filled by the proposed Party Council. *As a body representing the various parts of the party structure, the Party Council should be able to give authoritative and reasonably acceptable interpretations of the platform.* Perhaps it could occasionally even make more specific or reformulate the party principles in their application to current situations.

8.2. IMPROVING OUR PARTIES:
A CONTRARY VIEW

The Report of the Committee on Political Parties did not meet with universal approval even among political scientists. Professor Turner disputes the Committee's conclusion that we have no political party responsibility in America, and charges that adoption of the Committee's recommendations would increase the number of one-party areas.

BECAUSE of the influence which the report will have on students of the party system, it is unfortunate that there was no minority report to indicate disagreement or doubt within the Committee. Readers may conclude that the recommendations should be accepted with the same trust as the recommendations of a group of physicians who have agreed on the diagnosis of a disease. The Committee's reference to "the results of scientific analysis that have come from the research activity of a great number of specialists" suggests that such an analogy was considered. . . .

But the report can be no more than a starting point, for its value is limited by errors in two broad aspects, as follows:

I. The Committee has underestimated present party responsibility.

II. Some reforms which the Committee proposes will accentuate present defects in our party system. . . .

There are two questions involved in criticism of the present responsibility of parties: 1. Do the parties present clear alternatives to the voters, so that there is reality in the choice on election day? 2. Once the voters have made a choice between alternatives, are policies which received the support of the majority carried into effect?

1. *Do the parties present clear alternatives to the voters?* The Committee believes that the answer is "No." In discussing platforms, the report maintains that "alternatives between the parties are defined so badly that it is often difficult to determine what the election has decided even in broadest terms." In what appears to be a comment on Congress, the report states that "the sort of opposition presented by a coalition that cuts across party lines, *as a regular thing,* tends to deprive the public of a meaningful alternative. . . . Moreover, on that basis it is next to impossible to hold either party responsible for its political record."

From Julius Turner, "Responsible Parties: A Dissent from the Floor," in *The American Political Science Review,* Vol. 45 (March, 1951).

Contrary to the Committee's conclusions, platforms do reveal party differences on national issues affecting many groups. Analysis of the platforms of 1948, for example, reveals collisions in ideology and differences in emphasis which could hardly escape a serious reader. Democrats advocated repeal of the Taft-Hartley act; Republicans commended themselves for having passed it. Republicans advocated "prudent conservation of resources" in foreign aid programs; Democrats boasted that "generous sums have been provided." Republicans promised another reduction in taxes, especially to provide an incentive to new industry; Democrats advocated a reduction, when possible, for low-income groups only. Republicans advocated either voluntary cooperation, or state and local control of public policies; Democrats pointed to a long list of federal legislation enacted by their party.

On many other points, to be sure, the promises, claims, or criticisms of one party were not met squarely by the other. For example, Democratic criticism of tariff, immigration, anti-inflation, housing and "thought control" legislative action in the Republican 80th Congress was met by Republican emphasis on the more popular aspects of the same legislation. Republican criticism of "the tragic lack of foresight and general inadequacy of the Executive" was countered by specific Democratic reference to acts and recommendations of the President deemed valuable in the campaign, such as the Truman doctrine, the recognition of Israel, and the President's civil rights program.

Greater differences in party platforms than those mentioned above would impose a burden which politicians in a republican system could not be expected to bear. If the platforms were to point out clearly all differences between parties, then each party would be forced to reveal not only its assets but also its liabilities. In such a utopian situation, Democrats might be expected to admit that expanded welfare programs require increased taxation or debt, and Republicans would frankly state that an increase in the proportion of Protestant immigrants to the United States necessarily cuts down the proportion of Catholics and Jews admitted. Such political naivete is not characteristic even in countries with highly disciplined parties, and would not be countenanced by American politicians, however reformed.

The shortcomings of present platforms lie, in other words, not in their failure to present reasonable alternatives, but in a popular belief that platforms have little meaning for the voter. Public belief that platforms rarely reveal party differences probably springs from public ignorance of each platform's contents. . . .

The Committee has erred to a greater extent in its discussion of Congress than in its analysis of platforms. Contrary to popular impression, the parties usually maintain their ranks on congressional votes, including those of headline significance, with sufficient solidarity so that voters may distinguish between two points of view. In eight modern sessions, for example, party behavior could be scientifically distinguished on 407 of the 455 roll calls recorded in the House of Representatives. . . .

On a national scale, there is little reason for the voter to be unable to distinguish between the parties in Congress. In states and congressional districts, however, the voter may have more difficulty. The national parties as a whole show significant lines of disàgreement, but some individual congressmen confuse the voters by support for the policies of the other party. The problem, however, does not affect many districts. Of 4,658 members of the House in eleven selected modern sessions, only 181, or less than four percent (about sixteen congressmen each year), voted with the opposing party more often than with their own. The proportion was slightly higher in the Senate, where smaller numbers promote independence. Of the 847 Senators in nine sessions, 63, or 7.4 percent (seven Senators a year), bolted their parties on a majority of the votes. . . .

In the South, where most modern insurgency occurs, the problem of voting alternatives is another matter. In most southern districts the parties never present a practical alternative in the general election, since Republican candidates have no chance of election. While the behavior of Southerners rarely corrupts Democratic discipline to the extent that the national parties cannot be distinguished, there is an obvious need for party reform in the South and in all one-party areas. . . .

2. *Is the program which received the support of a majority of voters put into effect?* If it is assumed that a majority of the voters favored the Democratic platform and President Truman's campaign speeches in 1948, then obviously the program desired by the majority has not been carried out in full. Since 1948 we have seen the Democrats fail to repeal the Taft-Hartley Act and to enact federal aid to education and civil rights legislation. On the other hand, the Democrats succeeded in carrying out a large part of their program, including extension of the Marshall plan, European armament legislation, changes in the reciprocal trade agreements act, expansion and increases in social security, an increase in the minimum wage, the middle income housing bill, and aid to farmers through crop insurance, rural electrification, irrigation and reclamation.

There is some reason for doubt, however, as to whether all parts of the Truman program actually received the support of a majority of voters. It would be a fortunate coincidence if the Democratic platform should happen to include no proposals opposed by a majority. Such a coincidence is made more unlikely by the fact that the planners of platforms and presidential campaigns do not direct their appeal to all voters on an equal basis. The peculiarities of our Electoral College force presidential candidates to place great weight on votes received in large, marginal states, whose voters may not necessarily agree with the rest of the country. Members of Congress may, therefore, furnish a better index of public opinion than the President, although congressmen, too, are unrepresentative to the extent that districts are gerrymandered and voters are uninformed.

In short, the program supported by the majority is not put into effect in entirety, if it is assumed that the national platform and the speeches of the victorious presidential candidate represent that program. Confusion is created, however, by the fact that the President, his party in Congress, and the National Convention all represent different electorates. . . .

A review of the responsibility of parties at present indicates that the need for reform is not great. Most voters, if they had the information, could distinguish between alternatives offered by parties and candidates. Most of the majority program is carried into effect. Moderate reforms can be utilized to make up for such defects as exist. It remains to be seen whether the Committee reforms would be "moderate," and whether these reforms would have any harmful effect.

. . : Undesirable results would follow from the implementation of the report of the Committee on Political Parties, for the Committee would give weapons to the dominant groups in each party by means of which 1) the number of one-party areas in the United States would be increased, and 2) the self-destructive tendencies of the minority party would be accentuated. . . .

The Committee's proposals for restrictions on the party program and membership may well prevent the Republicans, as issues change or accidents occur, from welcoming new ideas and new blood into the party. Since 1932 the minority has been attempting, with little success, to formulate a program which will receive the support of a majority of the voters. As long as the same groups within the party continue to dominate its appeal to the electorate, it is unlikely to win more than occasional skirmishes. The party is in great need of insurgents. The Committee might consequently devote its attention to the promotion of insurgency within the party rather than to reforms which will cement present groups in power.

The Committee supports several proposals of great value, such as . . . reform of representation in National Conventions to conform with state populations. These proposals would give the President, Congress, and the national convention more similar constituencies, and would help to decrease uncertainties in the interpretation of the popular mandate in elections. Electoral College reform . . . would encourage each party to compete in areas monopolized by the other. Other excellent suggestions are made for the consultation of all party groups in the formulation of policy, for democratic control of party leadership, and for abolition of various forms of non-partisan and bi-partisan primaries. These reforms are needed, and would not lead to one-party monopoly. Those proposals, however, which would give greater power to dominant groups in either party should be rejected.

8.3. HOW TO BECOME A STATESMAN

A classic account of the old-time political boss is William L. Riordan's Plunkitt of Tammany Hall. *The book, published originally at the turn of the century, records a "series of very plain talks on very practical politics, delivered by Senator George Washington Plunkitt, the Tammany philosopher, from his rostrum—the New York County Court House Bootblack Stand." What is said in this brief excerpt on "How To Become A Statesman" is not bad advice, even today.*

THERE'S thousands of young men in this city who will go to the polls for the first time next November. Among them will be many who have watched the careers of successful men in politics, and who are longin' to make names and fortunes for themselves at the same game. It is to these youths that I want to give advice. First, let me say that I am in a position to give what the courts call expert testimony on the subject. I don't think you can easily find a better example than I am of success in politics. After forty years' experience at the game I am—well, I'm George Washington Plunkitt. Everybody knows what figure I cut in the greatest organization on earth, and if you hear people say that I've laid away a million or so since I was a butcher's boy in Washington Market, don't come to me for an indignant denial. I'm pretty comfortable, thank you.

Now, havin' qualified as an expert, as the lawyers say, I am goin' to give advice free to the young men who are goin' to cast their first votes, and who are lookin' forward to political glory and lots of cash. Some young men think they can learn how to be successful in politics from books, and they cram their heads with all sorts of college rot. They couldn't make a bigger mistake. Now, understand me, I ain't sayin' nothin' against colleges. I guess they'll have to exist as long as there's bookworms, and I suppose they do some good in a certain way, but they don't count in politics. In fact, a young man who has gone through the college course is handicapped at the outset. He may succeed in politics, but the chances are 100 to 1 against him.

Another mistake: some young men think that the best way to prepare for the political game is to practice speakin' and becomin' orators.

From William L. Riordan, ed., *Plunkitt of Tammany Hall* (New York: E. P. Dutton & Co., 1963), pp. 7–10.

That's all wrong. We've got some orators in Tammany Hall, but they're chiefly ornamental. You never heard of Charlie Murphy delivering a speech, did you? Or Richard Croker, or John Kelly, or any other man who has been a real power in the organization? Look at the thirty-six district leaders of Tammany Hall today. How many of them travel on their tongues? Maybe one or two, and they don't count when business is doin' at Tammany Hall. The men who rule have practiced keepin' their tongues still, not exercisin' them. So you want to drop the orator idea unless you mean to go into politics just to perform the skyrocket act.

Now, I've told you what not to do; I guess I can explain best what to do to succeed in politics by tellin' you what I did. After goin' through the apprenticeship of the business while I was a boy by workin' around the district headquarters and hustlin' about the polls on election day, I set out when I cast my first vote to win fame and money in New York City politics. Did I offer my services to the district leader as a stump-speaker? Not much. The woods are always full of speakers. Did I get up a book on municipal government and show it to the leader? I wasn't such a fool. What I did was to get some marketable goods before goin' to the leaders. What do I mean by marketable goods? Let me tell you: I had a cousin, a young man who didn't take any particular interest in politics. I went to him and said: "Tommy, I'm goin' to be a politician, and I want to get a followin'; can I count on you?" He said: "Sure, George." That's how I started in business. I got a marketable commodity —one vote. Then I went to the district leader and told him I could command two votes on election day, Tommy's and my own. He smiled on me and told me to go ahead. If I had offered him a speech or a bookful of learnin', he would have said, "Oh, forget it!"

That was beginnin' business in a small way, wasn't it? But that is the only way to become a real lastin' statesman. I soon branched out. Two young men in the flat next to mine were school friends. I went to them, just as I went to Tommy, and they agreed to stand by me. Then I had a followin' of three voters and I began to get a bit chesty. Whenever I dropped into district headquarters, everybody shook hands with me, and the leader one day honored me by lightin' a match for my cigar. And so it went on like a snowball rollin' down a hill. I worked the flat-house that I lived in from the basement to the top floor, and I got about a dozen young men to follow me. Then I tackled the next house and so on down the block and around the corner. Before long I had sixty men back of me, and formed the George Washington Plunkitt Association.

What did the district leader say then when I called at headquarters? I didn't have to call at headquarters. He came after me and said: "George, what do you want? If you don't see what you want, ask for it. Wouldn't you like to have a job or two in the departments for your friends?" I said: "I'll think it over; I haven't yet decided what the

George Washington Plunkitt Association will do in the next campaign." You ought to have seen how I was courted and petted by the leaders of the rival organizations. I had marketable goods and there was bids for them from all sides, and I was a risin' man in politics. As time went on, and my association grew, I thought I would like to go to the Assembly. I just had to hint at what I wanted, and three different organizations offered me the nomination. Afterwards, I went to the Board of Aldermen, then to the State Senate, then became leader of the district, and so on up till I became a statesman.

That is the way and the only way to make a lastin' success in politics. If you are goin' to cast your first vote next November and want to go into politics, do as I did. Get a followin', if it's only one man, and then go to the district leader and say: "I want to join the organization. I've got one man who'll follow me through thick and thin." The leader won't laugh at your one-man followin'. He'll shake your hand warmly, offer to propose you for membership in his club, take you down to the corner for a drink and ask you to call again. But go to him and say: "I took first prize at college in Aristotle; I can recite all Shakespeare forwards and backwards; there ain't nothin' in science that ain't as familiar to me as blockades on the elevated roads and I'm the real thing in the way of silver-tongued orators." What will he answer? He'll probably say: "I guess you are not to blame for your misfortunes, but we have no use for you here."

8.4. FINANCING PRESIDENTIAL CAMPAIGNS

The conduct of election campaigns in the United States is a costly business. A Presidential Commission has reported that "expenditures on behalf of all candidates for all public offices in the United States probably reached $165 to $175 millions in 1960." If political parties and/or candidates come to depend for their funds upon a small number of individuals or interest groups, the democratic process may well be corrupted at its source. To study the problem of campaign finance, President Kennedy appointed an Advisory Commission under the chairmanship of Alexander Heard, now President of Vanderbilt University. A summary of the Commission's report follows.

. . . PRESIDENTIAL CAMPAIGNS and elections over the decades have served

---

From the Report of The President's Commission on Campaign Costs, *Financing Presidential Campaigns* (Washington, D.C.: U.S. Government Printing Office, April, 1962).

as shining emblems of effective democracy, opening new doors of hope to people seeking freedom all around the world.

In 1960, approximately 150 foreign correspondents covered each of the 2 presidential nominating conventions. . . . These observers saw a presidential campaign molded by the long heritage of American political life, a heritage consistently embracing two important elements: (1) a profound belief in widespread citizen participation; and (2) an equally deep belief in voluntary action—a belief that politics should be animated by the voluntary efforts of individuals, groups, and organizations rather than by government.

Many problems have been encountered in the long story of presidential campaigns, campaigns varying from that of 1860 when Abraham Lincoln never left Springfield nor made a single speech, to that of 1960 when John F. Kennedy made 360 speeches while traveling 44,000 miles in 43 States, and Richard M. Nixon gave 212 speeches and journeyed 65,000 miles through 50 States.

No problem, however, has become more troublesome than that of providing adequate financial support for campaigns.

A chronic difficulty in maintaining adequate support has long been the lurking suspicion that contributing to political parties is somehow a shoddy business. This is unfortunate. . . . This Commission hopes the American people will come to regard contributions to parties with the same sense of obligation they display toward contributions to education and charitable institutions.

. . . . . .

The rocketing costs of presidential campaigns, and the recurring difficulties parties encounter in meeting these costs, require us to seek new methods and incentives for financing our political parties.

We agree with President Kennedy, former President Eisenhower, and other leaders of both parties that the existing system of presidential campaign finance poses serious problems. It is not desirable to have candidates for high office, especially for President and Vice President, dependent on individuals or organizations with special interests who are willing to make large contributions in the form of cash or campaign services. As President Kennedy has stated, "it is not healthy for the democratic process—or for the ethical standards in our government—to keep our national candidates in (the present) condition of dependence."

Many of the existing legal regulations of campaign finance have become a mockery. They are not realistic in light of today's campaign requirements. As a consequence, many provisions of the law are evaded or avoided, a condition contributing to the unfavorable climate that has surrounded fund-raising efforts.

In this climate, the political parties have found it increasingly difficult to meet satisfactorily the "great financial burdens" of presidential campaigns noted by the President. Further, the parties have lacked the continuity of leadership and the staff necessary for efficient fund raising and campaigning.

Mindful of these problems, we have sought to find ways that (1) Presidential candidates and the political parties supporting them can be helped in raising funds; (2) public confidence in the ways these campaigns are financed can be increased; (3) public respect for the system of legal regulation can be instilled; and (4) Presidential campaign costs can be reduced.

. . . We have had the benefit of hundreds of suggestions from experienced individuals and organizations who are knowledgeable about financing political activities. We have considered these suggestions in the light of three basic beliefs shared by all members of the Commission: (1) In a strongly organized and effectively functioning two-party system; (2) in widespread participation by citizens in the political system through the political party of their choice; and (3) in the desirability of voluntary, private action wherever such effort will suffice to meet the common needs of the society.

While our recommendations are directed toward problems of presidential and vice presidential campaign finance, in accordance with our charge, our recommendations carry implications for campaigning for other offices. . . .

We recommend:

1. That individuals and private organizations—including corporations, labor unions, farm organizations, civic societies, and other appropriate groups—be encouraged to take part in and to make expenditures for voluntary *bipartisan* political activities, and where an individual or organization is subject to taxation, that the reasonable costs of such activities be declared a deductible expense for tax purposes.

2. That for an experimental period extending over two presidential campaigns political contributors be given a credit against their Federal income tax of 50 percent of contributions, up to a maximum of $10 in credits per year. Contributors be permitted, alternatively, to claim the full amount of their contributions as a deduction from taxable income up to a maximum of $1,000 per tax return per year. The only contributions eligible for these benefits be ones made to the national committee of a party, and to a State political committee designated by such a national committee (provided that no more than one committee per State be designated by a national committee).

3. That an effective system of public disclosure be adopted which requires that the principal sources and uses of money in presidential campaigns be reported to a Registry of Election Finance. That toward this end periodic reports be submitted by all political parties, committees, and other campaign groups receiving or disbursing as much as $2,500

per year, any part of which aided a presidential or vice presidential candidate for nomination or election. That such reports shows total income and outgo, and itemize contributions that aggregate $250 or more from one source (including purchases of tickets to dinners or other fund-raising events), expenditures of $100 or over and transfers of funds and debts.

That candidates for nomination or election to those offices be required to submit similar reports. That any individual or family (husband, wife, and dependent children) contributing to the above committees as much as $5,000 in the aggregate in a single year, or spending and contributing a combined total of that much on behalf of such a candidate or candidates, shall also submit reports of such disbursements. That similar reports of both direct or indirect expenditures be required of individuals and groups taking part or spending money in bipartisan political activities as urged in our first recommendation, if such expenditures total $5,000 or more in a year. That the present meaningless ceilings on individual contributions and on total expenditures by political committees be abolished.

4. That the present equal treatment of corporations and labor unions by Section 610, Title 18, *United States Code,* that prohibits direct, partisan campaign contributions and expenditures, be maintained and strictly enforced.

5. That all other statutes regulating the financing of political parties and candidates be vigorously enforced.

6. That the political parties take full advantage of opportunities to modernize and increase the effectiveness of their fund-raising practices.

7. That research to increase campaign efficiency and help reduce campaign waste be encouraged among individuals and organizations, public and private.

8. That the Congress provide funds to pay the reasonable and necessary costs of preparing and installing in office new administrations during the "transition" period between the election and inauguration of a new President.

9. That a further temporary suspension of section 315 of the Federal Communications Act be enacted to permit broadcasters to make their facilities available on an equal basis to the nominees of the major political parties for President and Vice President without the legal compulsion of doing likewise for minor party candidates for those offices.

10. That a nonpartisan White House Conference on Campaign Finance be called by the President of the United States to launch broad solicitation programs by all parties following the adoption of measures to stimulate such giving, such a conference to include representatives designated by the important political parties, as well as representatives from various sectors of political life and the communications media, and

to lay the groundwork for further continuing efforts to encourage voluntary, private action in meeting campaign costs.

11. That the several States consider measures similar to those recommended in this report along with others that would help to reduce the costs of campaigning and make it easier for the parties and candidates to meet them, and that the Post Office Department make its change-of-address files available to the parties as well as to election boards as a way of assisting in local registration drives.

12. That, after a trial period with the measures here proposed, the President should provide for another nonpartisan evaluation of presidential campaign finance, and that, if the objectives sought by our proposals have not been realized, study be given to additional measures to achieve them, especially a "matching incentive" system to stimulate party solicitation.

OTHER PROPOSALS EXAMINED

We have considered many proposed courses of action that do not appear among our recommendations. The reasons for our rejection of most of them are clear from the ones we chose. We list below some others of special interest or prominence. The necessary brevity of our comments about them does not reflect the interesting features of many of these proposals, nor the careful consideration given to them.

1. *Shortening the length of campaigns.* This is often suggested as a way of reducing costs. Under prevailing conditions, the present duration is needed if the necessary organizational work is to be accomplished. Shorter campaigns would substantially handicap a candidate not already in office or not well known across the Nation.

2. *Collection boxes in supermarkets.* An imaginative proposal was made by F. P. Kilpatrik of the Brookings Institution for placing collection boxes at supermarket checkout counters during presidential campaigns. Evaluations of the proposal by technically qualified persons indicate it is worthy of further exploration. Perhaps this is a project for an organization growing out of the White House Conference on Campaign Finance proposed in Recommendation No. 10.

3. *Public financing of the national conventions.* The costs of the presidential nominating conventions are now met chiefly through tax-deductible corporate contributions and are not a financial burden on the parties. Cities vie with each other to attract the conventions and citizens' groups pledge large sums—$400,000 in both Los Angeles and Chicago in 1960—to help meet the bills.

4. *Tax assignment plan.* This proposal would authorize a taxpayer to assign a portion of his Federal income tax payment (e.g., one-half of 1 percent) to the State political committee of his choice.

5. *Tax deductibility of campaign expenditures made from personal funds by presidential and vice presidential candidates.* This would favor wealthy candidates more than others.

6. *Compulsory registration and voting.* These would reduce campaign costs. Matters of registration and voting, controlled by the States, fall outside our purview.

7. *Nationwide poll tax.* The proceeds of this tax would be used to finance campaigns. We do not approve of a poll tax as a prerequisite for voting.

8. *Extension of franking privilege and similar services to candidates.* For administrative reasons, a direct subsidy for the purchase of stamps would appear preferable to extending use of franked envelopes. Proposals to put Government aircraft, office space, sleeping quarters, the Government Printing Office, and other facilities at the disposal of the candidates were foregone in favor of measures to increase the popular financial support of campaigns.

8.5. STUDYING VOTING BEHAVIOR

An early example of scientific method in the study of voting behavior is The People's Choice *by Paul F. Lazarsfeld and Associates. The following selection from the Introduction to that now-famous book describes the scope and method of the so-called panel technique for the investigation of causal factors affecting the individual voter's decision.*

THIS IS a report on modern American political behavior—specifically on the formation of votes during a presidential campaign . . . What the people do in the course of this campaign represents the reactions reviewed and analyzed in these pages.

We are interested here in all those conditions which determine the political behavior of people. Briefly, our problem is this: to discover how and why people decided to vote as they did. What were the major influences upon them during the campaign of 1940? We believe we know some of the answers; we are sure we do not know them all. Similar studies of a series of major elections, especially in comparison with one another, will confirm the valid findings of this report, correct its deficiencies, and in general clarify and complete existing knowledge of the determinants of political opinion in a modern democracy.

There are several ways to analyze elections. Until relatively recently, official vote records constituted the only available material on elections.

From Paul F. Lazarsfeld and Associates, *The People's Choice* (New York: Columbia University Press, 1944), pp. 1–7.

They were useful for the study of the geographical distribution of the political temper of the people and not much else. Then a group of political scientists centering around the University of Chicago introduced what might be called the ecological analysis of voting. By examining vote records for small units of a city or state for which a considerable number of background (census) data were available, they were able to isolate to some extent the effects upon the vote of such factors as religion and nationality and gross economic status. Although they worked under the handicap of dealing with voters in the large—e.g., not everyone living in a predominantly Irish district was an Irishman—nevertheless they increased our understanding of some major determinants of political decision.

Then came the public opinion polls and they advanced our knowledge by relating political opinion to the characteristics of the individual voter and by revealing vote intentions before the election itself. They made much more precise the study of certain determinants of the vote and, to some extent, they made possible the study of the development of the vote during a political campaign.

But it was at this very point that further progress was needed. The full effect of a campaign cannot be investigated through a sequence of polls conducted with different people. They show only majority tendencies which are actually the residual result of various sorts of changes —to or from indecision and from one party to the other. They conceal minor changes which cancel out one another and even major changes if they are countered by opposing trends. And most of all, they do not show *who* is changing. They do not follow the vagaries of the individual voter along the path to his vote, to discover the relative effect of various influential factors upon his final vote.

In short, never before has the development of a person's vote been traced throughout a political campaign, from his pre-convention attitudes through his reactions to the barrage of propaganda which constitutes the campaign proper to his actual vote on Election Day. Only by such an investigation can we establish more closely the roles of the several influences upon vote (and other political attitudes), from both predispositions and stimuli. This study, designed to yield such answers, used the so-called panel technique as the next step forward in opinion research: *repeated interviewing of the same people.*

A NEW RESEARCH METHOD

Let us briefly examine the technical plan of the investigation. . . .
The survey was done in Erie County, Ohio, located on Lake Erie between Cleveland and Toledo. This county was chosen because it was small enough to permit close supervision of the interviewers, because

it was relatively free from sectional peculiarities, because it was not dominated by any large urban center although it did furnish an opportunity to compare rural political opinion with opinion in a small urban center, and because for forty years—in every presidential election in the twentieth century—it had deviated very little from the national voting trends. . . .

In May, 1940, every fourth house in Erie County was visited by a member of the staff of from twelve to fifteen specially trained local interviewers, chiefly women. In this way, approximately 3,000 persons were chosen to represent as closely as possible the population of the county as a whole. This group—the poll—resembled the county in age, sex, residence, education, telephone and car ownership, and nativity.

From this poll, four groups of 600 persons each were selected by stratified sampling. Each group was closely matched to the others and constituted, in effect, a miniature sample of the whole poll and of the county itself. Of these four groups of 600, three were reinterviewed only once each—one in July, one in August, and one in October. They were used as "control groups" to test the effect that repeated interviewing might have on the panel. At the same time they provided a larger sample (1,200 respondents) on a variety of important questions asked at the control points. The fourth group—the panel—was interviewed once each month from May to November.

Interviews were spaced about a month apart to fit best the natural course of campaign events. The first two interviews were made in May and June, prior to the Republican Convention—the original poll and the first recall on the panel members. The third interview came in July, between the two conventions, and the fourth in August, after both conventions. Two more calls were made between the conventions and Election Day, the second as close to the eve of the election as possible. The seventh and last interview was made in November, shortly after the election.

Thus, the 600 people of the panel were kept under continual observation from May until November, 1940. Whenever a person changed his vote intention in any way, from one interview to the next, detailed information was gathered on why he had changed. The respondents were also interviewed regularly on their exposure to campaign propaganda in all the media of communication—the press, radio, personal contacts, and others. In addition, the repeated interviews made it possible to secure voluminous information about each respondent's personal characteristics, social philosophy, political history, personality traits, relationships with other people, opinions on issues related to the election—in short, information on anything which might contribute to our knowledge of the formation of his political preferences.

• • • • • •

In summary, then, the panel was devised as a more effective

method of getting at the important questions. What is the effect of social status upon vote? How are people influenced by the party conventions and the nominations? What role does formal propaganda play? How about the press and the radio? What of the influence of family and friends? Where do issues come in, and how? Why do some people settle their vote early and some late? In short, how do votes develop? Why do people vote as they do? By inference and by direct accounts of the respondents, we shall try to show what influences operated between May and November to determine the ballots cast on November 5, 1940.

Before pushing on to the findings themselves, let us summarize briefly the major contributions of the panel technique.

(1) We can determine who the changers are during the campaign and can study their characteristics. . . .

(2) We can accumulate information pertaining to the whole campaign from one interview to the next. For example, we are able to distinguish people according to whether they were exposed to predominantly Republican or predominantly Democratic propaganda, on the basis of indices constructed from their answers at different times. . . .

(3) When a respondent changes his vote intention between two interviews, we catch his opinion in a process of flux. It obviously tells us little to ask a man who has voted Republican all his life why he favors the present Republican candidate. If, however, a respondent intended to vote Democratic last month and this month intends to vote Republican, the reasons for his change enable us to gauge the effectiveness of the propaganda and other influences to which he was subjected. . . .

(4) Repeated interviews also permit us to trace the effects of propaganda statistically. For example, we can study the people who are undecided at one interview but who have an opinion at the next. Anything such people did or thought at the time of the first interview, then, precedes the time of their decision. By studying such data, we can infer what made the respondents decide as they did. This kind of information is quite different from that found in the usual public opinion surveys, which provide data related to opinion at the same point in time. There we cannot tell what is cause and what is effect, but the repeated interview technique allows us to establish a time sequence and therefore greatly facilitates causal analysis. . . .

8.6. BEHAVIORAL RESEARCH IN POLITICAL SCIENCE

The study of American politics has been greatly enriched in recent years by the research of a somewhat new breed of political scientists calling themselves behavioralists. Much of our recent understanding of voting behavior, decision making, legislative, administrative, and even judicial behavior we owe to these political behavioralists. In the following excerpt from his longer essay on "The Current Meaning of Behavioralism in Political Science," Professor David Easton outlines some of the major components of this exciting approach to the study of government and politics.

. . . MOST STUDENTS of politics, even those unwilling to accept classification as behavioralists, would probably agree about the general nature of its assumptions and objectives, although strong differences might well arise concerning the precise emphasis to be given to any one of these.

What is the nature of these assumptions and objectives, the intellectual foundation stones on which this movement has been constructed? No single way of characterizing them is satisfactory to everyone, but the following itemized list provides a tolerably accurate and reasonably exhaustive account of them.

(1) Regularities: There are discoverable uniformities in political behavior. These can be expressed in generalizations or theories with explanatory and predictive value.

(2) Verification: The validity of such generalizations must be testable, in principle, by reference to relevant behavior.

(3) Techniques: Means for acquiring and interpreting data cannot be taken for granted. They are problematic and need to be examined self-consciously, refined, and validated so that rigorous means can be found for observing, recording, and analyzing behavior.

(4) Quantification: Precision in the recording of data and the statement of findings require measurement and quantification, not for their own sake, but only where possible, relevant, and meaningful in the light of other objectives.

(5) Values: Ethical evaluation and empirical explanation involve two different kinds of propositions that, for the sake of clarity, should be kept analytically distinct. However, a student of political behavior is not prohibited from asserting propositions of either kind separately or in combination as long as he does not mistake one for the other.

(6) Systematization: Research ought to be systematic; that is to say, theory and research are to be seen as closely intertwined parts of a coherent and orderly body of knowledge. Research untutored by theory may prove trivial, and theory unsupportable by data, futile.

(7) Pure science: The application of knowledge is as much a part of the scientific enterprise as theoretical understanding. But the

From David Easton, "The Current Meaning of Behavioralism in Political Science," in James C. Charlesworth, *The Limits of Behavioralism in Political Science* (Philadelphia: The American Academy of Political and Social Science, October, 1962).

understanding and explanation of political behavior logically precede and provide the basis for efforts to utilize political knowledge in the solution or urgent practical problems of society.

(8) Integration: Because the social sciences deal with the whole human situation, political research can ignore the findings of other disciplines only at the peril of weakening the validity and undermining the generality of its own results. Recognition of this interrelationship will help to bring political science back to its status of earlier centuries and return it to the main fold of the social sciences.

The list probably includes all the major tenets of the behavioral credo and represents the major differences between the behavioral and traditional modes of research. . . .

. . . . . .

Behavioral research thus stands for a new departure in social research as a whole; it is the most recent development in a long line of changing approaches to the understanding of society. It means more than scientific techniques, more than rigor. This alone would indeed mean *rigor mortis* as its critics from the traditional point of view, both classical and institutional, have been so quick and correct to point out. The behavioral approach testifies to the coming of age of theory in the social sciences as a whole, wedded, however, to a commitment to the assumptions and methods of empirical science. Unlike the great traditional theories of past political thought, new theory tends to be analytic, not substantive, general rather than particular, and explanatory rather than ethical. That portion of political research which shares these commitments to both the new theory and the technical means of analysis and verification thereby links political science to broader behavioral tendencies in the social sciences and, hence, its description as political behavior. This is the full meaning and significance of the behavioral approach in political science today.

8.7. WHO SPEAKS FOR THE PARTY?

In the continuing dialogue concerning the American party system, Dean Stephen K. Bailey offers an exceptionally succinct analysis and prescription.

OBVIOUSLY, this question cannot be handled without first asking such prior questions as "where" and "when." When we speak of the national party, are we speaking of the in-party? The out-party? The party in the Senate? The party in the House? The party as represented by its national

From Stephen K. Bailey, *The Condition of Our National Political Parties* (Santa Barbara, Calif.: Center for the Study of Democratic Institutions, 1959).

committee? The party in quadrennial convention? All of these? Only some of these? And at what point in time?

Let us start with a presidential election year and a national convention. "Conventions," as Richard Rovere has written, ". . . are exercises in definition." The choice for the Presidency personifies the majority decision of the national convention, and in this respect the winning nominee speaks with special authority as a symbol of what the party stands for at that moment. The image may be particularly clear when an incumbent is renominated, since he usually has had a commanding influence over the drafting of the party platform. In any case, what the candidate decides to emphasize from (or outside of) the platform creates a more powerful image of party policy than the platform itself. From the moment of nomination until election, the presidential candidate is usually the undisputed voice of the party. This does not mean that the voice will necessarily be clear, but no other is likely to be clearer.

There is a circumstance, however, in which even this last generalization needs qualification. Special problems arise when an incumbent President and a new presidential nominee are of the same party. In 1952, for example, with Adlai Stevenson as the Democratic nominee but with Harry S Truman still in the White House, a series of delicate issues developed over campaign strategy, organization and policy. President Truman wanted Stevenson to retain Frank McKinney as chairman of the Democratic National Committee. Stevenson, however, exercised his influence to see to it that the Committee selected Stephen Mitchell. Once appointed, Mitchell set up office, as expected, in the Democratic National Committee headquarters in Washington. But Stevenson was still Governor of Illinois. The question immediately arose, was Wilson Wyatt, as Stevenson's personal campaign manager, to give orders to Stephen Mitchell, the chairman of the National Committee? Chaos could have resulted if the answer to this had been no. Then, because of deteriorating relations between Springfield and the White House, Stephen Mitchell took pains to stress that President Truman was still the head of the party, that the Springfield headquarters was to be considered the Springfield office of the Democratic National Committee, and that one of the Committee's channels of authority would still run to the White House.

. . . . . .

THE PRESIDENT AS PARTY SPOKESMAN

. . . . .

The extent to which a President can create the image of a reasonably united party, depends, of course, on his capacity to make his own policy pronouncement dominant in the party. This is not always automatic,

especially if the President is successfully blocked by powerful leaders of
his own party in the Congress or is running out the last two years of his
last term. But, even then, the power of his voice generally reduces the
voice of self- or group-appointed party spokesmen to a subordinate level.

THE PROBLEM OF THE "OUT-PARTY"

If the in-party has problems in creating a clear party image, the
task is many times more difficult for the out-party. No real answer has
yet been found to the question of who speaks for the party when it does
not control the White House, or when no presidential campaign is in
progress. . . .

The contention that the leaders of the out-party in Congress have
the responsibility and the right to speak for their party has been staunchly
defended by those leaders. But, in the years since World War II, intra-
mural struggles between national committee chairmen and spokesmen
on the one hand, and congressional leaders and staff on the other, have
been staples in out-party politics, regardless of which party was "out." . . .

Obvious problems arise in having the congressional leaders speak
for the out-party. Congress itself is bifurcated, and its power, as we have
said, tends to gravitate into the hands of men who are not necessarily responsive to the party majorities . . . There are no party policy or steering committees in the House worthy of the name, and those in the Senate
lack power and representativeness.

The result is that there are a large number of Democratic and
Republican party memebers who may have no effective voice in the Congress (to say nothing of the White House) but who still feel that they
should have a hand in determining their party's national policies. The
national committee tends to represent the interests of members of the
out-party who feel un- or underrepresented in the Congress. In addition,
it may be said that the out-party's national committee is the official representative of the party's *executive wing*.

. . . . . .

THE DEMOCRATIC ADVISORY COUNCIL

The absence of any fully accepted out-party national spokesman
has led each party sporadically over the years to try to fill the vacuum.
More than a generation ago, the Republicans established an Advisory
Committee on Policies and Platform to help focus ideas and power prior
to the 1920 convention. The Committee performed its function and died.
Similar groups have been formed from time to time.

Perhaps the most noteworthy out-party voice in recent years has
been the Democratic Advisory Council of the Democratic Natonal Com-

mittee. Established by a resolution of the Executive Committee of the Democratic National Committee on November 27, 1956, the Council exists to provide "a collective voice for the Democratic Party, representing on a year-round basis the millions of Democrats who may or may not be represented in either House of the Congress." The official congressional leaders of the party have refused membership on the Council, but many of the party's national figures . . . belong, as do the members of the Executive Committee of the Democratic National Comittee. The Council is helped in its deliberations by advisory committees of distinguished party intellectuals on such matters as foreign policy, domestic economic policy, labor policy, urban problems, science and technology, and party organization.*

The Democratic Advisory Council is [was] a significant development. At the moment, it is sufficient to note that although it has given the out-party a firmer voice and a clearer public philosophy than was available before, it has no effective power base in the party, it is not the only voice and image the out-party has, and the party portrait it paints can easily be distorted or obscured by the record of the party in Congress.

PARTY FINANCE AND PARTY COHERENCE

The problem of the out-party in developing a recognizable philosophy and coherent political program is further complicated by the disorganized state of its finances . . . Money-raising for national and congressional campaigns is such a jungle, and so choked with the vines of subterfuge to get around the Hatch Act and other unrealistic laws, that efforts to develop coherent national organizations are seriously impeded.

It is an axiom of congressional campaigning, for example, that little direct financial help can be expected either from Washington (campaign committees on Capitol Hill or the national committees) or from state committees . . . Since the party as party (no matter how defined) has not been a sure source of financial help to the man campaigning for a seat in the Senate or House, what obligation does he owe to it, or to programs endorsed by it?

And there is a further obligation. Some support for congressional candidates may come in the form of what Senator Benton used to call "emotional money"—money given by friends and admirers, with no strings attached. But much of it comes from constituent interests, or powerful national interests, expecting, if not favors, at least sympathetic understanding and ready access . . .

Attempts by the national committees to raise money "for the party" have gone largely into the staggering costs of presidential campaigns, past or present. And even when, as in the case of the Republican

---

* Editor's note: the Democratic Advisory Council no longer exists.

National Finance Committee, a consolidated drive has been carried out for the benefit of the campaign committees of Congress as well as for the national committee, no attempt has been made to develop any national party criteria for allocating the funds . . .

It is probable that the first national committee to develop a mass financial base sufficient to allow a spillover from presidential to legislative campaigns will have made the most important political break-through of the century. But this is still in the future, and will involve legal revision as well as monetary success.

These, then, are our national parties: unified for presidential contests, otherwise divided in power and lacking in definition; sporadically financed through various channels, subterfuges, and individual candidacies; peculiarly confused as out-parties; weak vehicles for executive-legislative cooperation as in-parties. They have performed valued services of reconciliation and compromise in our history—services which should not be underestimated. But the problem today is how to transcend these services in order to provide the government with sustained and responsible national power. How should our national party system be modified in order to make the parties effective instruments of our national purposes and needs?

. . . . . .

In suggesting new directions for our national party system, . . . the British parliamentary model is ruled out. But it is not ruled out simply because its wholesale adoption here is unthinkable. It is ruled out because it has shortcomings which do not warrant emulation. The relative independence of the legislature in the American system of government is, within limits, a powerful asset. At its best, it assures continuing social criticism and review of the bureaucracy without which big government might easily become lethargic and unresponsive or officious and dangerous.

What we are after is a national two-party system that will continue to have room for diversity and compromise but will nevertheless bring about more coherent and responsible programming by the executive and legislative branches and more coherent and responsible criticism of policy and administration. . . .

This neither presumes nor suggests ideological or highly disciplined parties, although it does presume differences in the ideological propensities of each party and also presumes that party members who vote consistently against their own party's majority will not be favored with positions of party power inside or outside the Congress.

Various changes in state primary laws, in methods of choosing national convention delegates and national committee members, and in grass-roots political organization could have a profound influence on national party behavior. But, in my opinion, changes of this sort will come about rapidly only if prior attention is given to the following political reforms (some of which are already under way):

One: To create mass-based, long-range, and (in part) tax-supported national party financing . . .

Two: To expand two-party competition into all congressional districts and states;

Three: To create, by formal action of the two national conventions, permanent advisory councils and staffs to both national committees;

Four: To provide social and office facilities for each national party along the Mall, between the White House and Capitol Hill, to serve as symbolic and practical links between the executive and legislative branches of government, as well as between the party and its membership across the country;

Five: To provide, by constitutional amendment, for the simultaneous election every four years of the President, the House of Representatives, and half the members of the United States Senate—all Senators to serve for eight years.

Six: To establish or strengthen party policy committees in the House and Senate to guide congressional business; hold reasonably frequent party caucuses; nominate members for committee assignments, who would then be elected in the caucuses; and receive, hold joint hearings, and report on all general presidential messages;

Seven: To find a mathematical formula for computing congressional seniority which will give added weight to those legislators who come from competitive two-party districts and states;

Eight: To repeal the Twenty-second Amendment;

Nine: To develop machinery for keeping an active roster of talented people for the important executive posts in the national government.

9

Constitutionalism and Democracy

9.1. AN OUTCRY AGAINST PERSECUTION

*History tells us it is not unusual for nonconformists victimized by perse-
cution in one time or place to become persecutors of nonconformists in
another. The Puritan Church of New England, which had sought religious
freedom in America, tried to enforce its orthodox dogma against dissenters. Roger Williams, himself a minister, was an outspoken critic of
such practices.*

FIRST: That the blood of so many hundred thousand souls of protestants
and papists, spilt in the wars of present and former ages, for their respective consciences, is not required nor accepted by Jesus Christ the
Prince of Peace.

Secondly. Pregnant scriptures and arguments are throughout the
work proposed against the doctrine of persecution for cause of conscience.

Thirdly. Satisfactory answers are given to scriptures and objections produced by Mr. Calvin, Beza, Mr. Cotton, and the ministers of the
New English churches, and others former and later, tending to prove the
doctrine of persecution for cause of conscience.

Fourthly. The doctrine of persecution for cause of conscience, is
proved guilty of all the blood of the souls crying for vengeance under
the altar.

Fifthly. All civil states, with their officers of justice, in their respective constitutions and administrations, are proved essentially civil, and

From Roger Williams, *The Bloudy Tenent of Persecution*, 1644.

151

therefore not judges, governors, or defenders of the spiritual, or Christian, state and worship.

Sixthly. It is the will and command of God that, since the coming of his Son the Lord Jesus, a permission of the most Paganish, Jewish, Turkish, or anti-christian consciences and worships be granted to all men in all nations and countries: and they are only to be fought against with that sword which is only, in soul matters, able to conquer: to wit, the sword of God's Spirit, the word of God.

Seventhly. The state of the land of Israel, the kings and people thereof, in peace and war, is proved figurative and ceremonial, and no pattern nor precedent for any kingdom or civil state in the world to follow.

Eighthly. God requireth not an uniformity of religion to be enacted and enforced in any civil state; which enforced uniformity, sooner or later, is the greatest occasion of civil war, ravishing of conscience, persecution of Christ Jesus in his servants, and of the hypocrisy and destruction of millions of souls.

Ninthly. In holding an enforced uniformity of religion in a civil state, we must necessarily disclaim our desires and hopes of the Jews' conversion to Christ.

Tenthly. An enforced uniformity of religion throughout a nation or civil state, confounds the civil and religious, denies the principles of Christianity and civility, and that Jesus Christ is come in the flesh.

Eleventhly. The permission of other consciences and worships than a state professeth, only can, according to God, procure a firm and lasting peace; good assurance being taken, according to the wisdom of the civil state, for uniformity of civil obedience from all sorts.

Twelfthly. Lastly, true civility and Christianity may both flourish in a state or kingdom, notwithstanding the permission of divers and contrary consciences, either of Jews or Gentile. . . .

While I plead the cause of truth and innocency against the bloody doctrine of persecution for cause of conscience, I judge it not unfit to give alarm to myself, and to [all] men, to prepare to be persecuted or hunted for cause of conscience.

Whether thou standest charged with ten or but two talents, if thou huntest any for cause of conscience, how canst thou say thou followest the Lamb of God, who so abhorred that practice?

If Paul, if Jesus Christ, were present here at London, and the question were proposed, what religion would they approve of—the papists, prelatists, Presbyterians, Independents, &c., would each say, Of mine, Of mine? . . .

Oh! how likely is the jealous Jehovah, the consuming fire, to end these present slaughters of the holy witnesses in a greater slaughter! Rev. v.

Six years preaching of so much truth of Christ as that time afforded in K. Edward's days, kindles the flames of Q. Mary's bloody persecutions.

Who can now but expect that after so many scores of years preaching and professing of more truth, and amongst so many great contentions amongst the very best of protestants, a fiery furnace should be heat, and who sees not now the fires kindling?

I confess I have little hopes, till those flames are over, that this discourse against the doctrine of persecution for cause of conscience should pass current, I say not amongst the wolves and lions, but even amongst the sheep of Christ themselves. Yet, . . . I have not hid within my breast my soul's belief. And, although sleeping on the bed either of the pleasures or profits of sin, thinkest thou thy conscience bound to smite at him that dares to waken thee? . . .

. . . And however in civil things we may be servants unto men, yet in divine and spiritual things the poorest peasant must disdain the service of the highest prince. Be ye not the servants of men, 1 Cor. vii. (23). . . .

In vain have English parliaments permitted English bibles in the poorest English houses, and the simplest man or woman to search the scriptures, if yet against their souls persuasion from the scripture, they should be forced, as if they lived in Spain or Rome itself without the sight of a bible, to believe as the church believes.

Fourthly. Having tried, we must hold fast, 1 Thes. v. (21), upon the loss of a crown, Rev. iii. (11); we must not let go for all the fleabitings of the present afflictions, &c. Having bought truth dear, we must not sell it cheap, not the least grain of it for the whole world; no, not for the saving of souls, though our own most precious; least of all for the bitter sweetening of a little vanishing pleasure;—For a little puff of credit and reputation from the changeable breath of uncertain sons of men: for the broken bags of riches on eagles' wings: for a dream of these—any or all of these, which on our death-bed vanish and leave tormenting stings behind them. Oh! how much better is it from the love of truth, from the love of the Father of lights from whence it comes, from the love of the Son of God, who is the way and the truth, to say as he, John xviii. 37: For this end was I born, and for this end came I into the world, that I might bear witness to the truth. . . .

9.2. IN PRAISE OF INDIVIDUALISM

Advocates of constitutionalism, like this leader of the American Revolution, stress the importance of limiting state authority over individuals. In this selection, written before the Declaration of Independence, Adams reminds the British Parliament that the American colonists are entitled to all the constitutional rights of Englishmen.

THE NATURAL LIBERTY of Men by entering into society is abridg'd or restrained so far only as is necessary for the Great end of Society the best good of the whole—

In the state of nature, every man is under God, Judge and sole Judge, of his own rights and the injuries done him: By entering into society, he agrees to an Arbiter or indifferent Judge between him and his neighbours; but he no more renounces his original right, than by taking a cause out of the ordinary course of law, and leaving the decision to Referees or indifferent Arbitrations. . . .

"The natural liberty of man is to be free from any superior power on earth, and not to be under the will or legislative authority of man; but only to have the law of nature for his rule."—

In short it is the greatest absurdity to suppose it in the power of one or any number of men at the entering into society, to renounce their essential natural rights, or the means of preserving those rights when the great end of civil government from the very nature of its institution is for the support, protection and defence of those very rights: the principal of which as is before observed, is life liberty and property. If men through fear, fraud or mistake, should *in terms* renounce and give up any essential natural right, the eternal law of reason and the great end of society, would absolutely vacate such renunciation; the right to freedom being *the gift* of God Almighty, it is not in the power of Man to alienate this gift, . . .—

A Common Wealth or state is a body politick or civil society of men, united together to promote their mutual safety and prosperity, by means of their union.

The *absolute Rights* of Englishmen, and all freemen in or out of Civil society, are principally, *personal security personal liberty* and *private property.*

All Persons born in the British American Colonies are by the laws of God and nature, and by the Common law of England, *exclusive of all charters from the Crown,* well Entitled, and by the Acts of the British Parliament are declared to be entitled to all the natural essential, inherent & inseparable Rights Liberties and Privileges of Subjects born in Great Britain, or within the Realm. Among those Rights are the following; which no men or body of men, consistently with their own rights as men and

From Samuel Adams, "The Rights of the Colonists," in *The Writings of Samuel Adams,* Harry Alonzo Cushing, ed. (New York: G. P. Putnam's Sons, 1906), pp. 350–359.

citizens or members of society, can for themselves give up, or take away from others.

First, "The first fundamental positive law of all Commonwealths or States, is the establishing the legislative power; as the first fundamental *natural* law also, which is to govern even the legislative power itself, is the preservation of the Society."

Secondly, The Legislative has no right to absolute arbitrary power over the lives and fortunes of the people: Nor can mortals assume a prerogative, not only too high for men, but for Angels; and therefore reserved for the exercise of the *Deity* alone.—

"The Legislative cannot Justly *assume* to itself a power to rule by extempore arbitrary decrees; but it is bound to see that Justice is dispensed, and that the rights of the subjects be decided, by promulgated, standing and known laws, and authorized *independent Judges";* that is independent as far as possible of Prince or People. *"There shall be one rule of Justice for rich and poor; for the favorite in Court, and the Countryman at the Plough."*

Thirdly, The Supreme power cannot Justly take from any man, any part of his property without his consent, in person or by his Representative.—

These are some of the first principles of natural law & Justice, and the great Barriers of all free states, and of the British Constitution in particular. It is utterly irreconcileable to these principles, and to many other fundamental maxims of the common law, common sense and reason, that a British house of commons, should have a right, at pleasure, to give and grant the property of the Colonists. That these Colonists are well entitled to all the essential rights, liberties and privileges of men and freemen, born in Britain, is manifest, not only from the Colony charter, in general, but acts of the British Parliament. . . .

9.3. ON THE NATURAL RIGHTS OF THE AMERICAN COLONISTS

James Otis addressed himself to the same general problem of constitutionalism as did Samuel Adams. However, in this passage, we find emphasized the right of representation in the legislative body.

A PLANTATION or colony, is a settlement of subjects, in a *territory disjoined* or remote from the mother country, and may be made by private

From James Otis, "The Rights of the British Colonies," 1764.

adventurers or the public; but in both cases the Colonists are entitled to as *ample* rights, liberties, and privileges as the subjects of the mother country are, and in some respects *to more*. . . .

. . . the first principles of law and justice [are] the great barriers of a free state, and of the British constitution in particular. I ask, I want no more—Now let it be shown how 'tis reconcilable with principles, or to many other fundamental maxims of the British constitution, as well as the natural and civil rights, which by the law of their country, all British subjects are entitled to, as their best inheritance and birth-right, that all the northern colonies, who are without one representative in the house of Commons, should be taxed by the British parliament. . . .

I can see no reason to doubt, but that the imposition of taxes, whether on trade, or on land, or houses, or ships, on real or personal, fixed or floating property, in the colonies, is absolutely irreconcilable with the rights of the Colonists, as British subjects, and as men. I say men, for in a state of nature, no man can take my property from me, without my consent: If he does, he deprives me of my liberty, and makes me a slave. If such a proceeding is a breach of the law of nature, no law of society can make it just—The very act of taxing, exercised over those who are not represented, appears to me to be depriving them of one of their most essential rights, as freemen; and if continued, seems to be in effect an entire disfranchisement of every civil right. For what one civil right is worth a rush, after a man's property is subject to be taken from him at pleasure, without his consent. If a man is not his *own assessor* in person, or by deputy, his liberty is gone, or lays entirely at the mercy of others. . . .

The power of parliament is uncontrollable, but by themselves, and we must obey. They only can repeal their own acts. There would be an end of all government, if one or a number of subjects or subordinate provinces should take upon them so far to judge of the justice of an act of parliament, as to refuse obedience to it. If there was nothing else to restrain such a step, prudence ought to do it, for forcibly resisting the parliament and the King's law, is high treason. Therefore let the parliament lay what burthens they please on us, we must, it is our duty to submit and patiently bear them, till they will be pleased to relieve us. And 'tis to be presumed, the wisdom and justice of that august assembly, always will afford us relief by repealing such acts, as through mistake, or other human infirmities, have been suffered to pass, if they can be convinced that their proceedings are not constitutional, or not for the common good. . . .

No representation of the Colonies in parliament alone, would however be equivalent to a subordinate legislative among themselves; nor so well answer the ends of increasing their prosperity and the commerce of Great Britain. It would be impossible for the parliament to judge so well, of their abilities to bear taxes, impositions on trade, and other duties and burthens, or of the local laws that might be really needful, as a legislative here.

9.4. A STEP TOWARD INDEPENDENCE

The Resolutions of the Stamp Act Congress are often asserted to be the source of the slogan: "No taxation without representation." Section IV, for example, suggests the growing desire of the colonists not to be taxed at all by the mother country.

THE MEMBERS of this Congress, sincerely devoted, with the warmest sentiments of affection and duty to his Majesty's person and government, inviolably attached to the present happy establishment of the Protestant succession, and with minds deeply impressed by a sense of the present and impending misfortunes of the British colonies on this continent; having considered as maturely as time will permit, the circumstances of the said colonies, esteem it our indispensible duty to make the following declarations of our humble opinion, respecting the most essential rights and liberties of the colonists, and of the grievances under which they labour, by reason of several late acts of parliament.

I. That his Majesty's subjects in these colonies, owe the same allegiance to the crown of Great Britain, that is owing from his subjects born within the realm, and all due subordination to that august body the parliament of Great-Britain.

II. That his Majesty's liege subjects in these colonies, are intitled to all the inherent rights and liberties of his natural born subjects, within the kingdom of Great-Britain.

III. That it is inseparably essential to the freedom of a people, and the undoubted right of Englishmen, that no Taxes be imposed on them but with their own consent, given personally, or by their representatives.

IV. That the people of these colonies are not, and, from their local circumstances, cannot be, represented in the House of Commons in Great-Britain.

V. That the only representatives of the people of these colonies are persons chosen therein by themselves, and that no taxes ever have been, or can be constitutionally imposed on them, but by their respective legislatures.

VI. That all supplies to the crown being free gifts of the people,

From the Resolutions of the Stamp Act Congress, 1765.

it is unreasonable and inconsistent with the principles and spirit of the British constitution, for the people of Great-Britain to grant to his Majesty the property of the colonists.

VII. That trial by jury, is the inherent and invaluable right of every British subject in these colonies.

VIII. That . . . [the Stamp Act] . . . , by imposing taxes on the inhabitants of these colonies, and the said act, and several other acts, by extending the jurisdiction of the courts of admiralty beyond its ancient limits, have a manifest tendency to subvert the rights and liberties of the colonists.

IX. That the duties imposed by several late acts of parliament, from the peculiar circumstances of these colonies, will be extremely burthensome and grievous; and from the scarcity of specie, the payment of them absolutely impracticable.

X. That as the profits of the trade of these colonies utimately center in Great-Britain, to pay for the manufactures which they are obliged to take from thence, they eventually contribute very largely to all supplies granted there to the crown.

XI. That the restrictions imposed by several late acts of parliament on the trade of these colonies, will render them unable to purchase the manufactures of Great-Britain.

XII. That the increase, prosperity and happiness of these colonies, depend on the full and free enjoyments of their rights and liberties, and an intercourse with Great-Britain mutually affectionate and advantageous.

XIII. That it is the right of the British subjects in these colonies to petition the king, or either house of parliament. Lastly, that it is the indispensible duty of these colonies, to the best of sovereigns, to the mother country, and to themselves, to endeavour by a loyal and dutiful address to his Majesty, and humble applications to both houses of parliament, to procure the repeal of the act for granting and applying certain stamp duties, of all clauses of any other acts of parliament, whereby the jurisdiction of the admiralty is extended as aforesaid, and of the other late acts for the restriction of American commerce.

9.5. THE DECLARATION OF INDEPENDENCE, 1776

This inspiring document, written by Thomas Jefferson, embodies the dignity and fervor of the American belief in democracy. As an indictment of arbitrary power and a testament to the equality of all mankind, its message to the world is timeless.

WHEN IN THE COURSE of human events, it becomes necessary for one people to dissolve the political bands which have connected them with another, and to assume among the Powers of the earth, the separate and equal station to which the Laws of Nature and of Nature's God entitle them, a decent respect to the opinions of mankind requires that they should declare the causes which impel them to the separation.

We hold these truths to be self-evident, that all men are created equal, that they are endowed by their Creator with certain unalienable Rights, that among these are Life, Liberty and the pursuit of Happiness. That to secure these rights, Governments are instituted among Men, deriving their just powers from the consent of the governed, That whenever any Form of Government becomes destructive of these ends, it is the Right of the People to alter or to abolish it, and to institute new Government, laying its foundation on such principles and organizing its powers in such form, as to them shall seem most likely to effect their Safety and Happiness. Prudence, indeed, will dictate that Governments long established should not be changed for light and transient causes; and accordingly all experience hath shown, that mankind are more disposed to suffer, while evils are sufferable, than to right themselves by abolishing the forms to which they are accustomed. But when a long train of abuses and usurpations, pursuing invariably the same Object evinces a design to reduce them under absolute Despotism, it is their right, it is their duty, to throw off such Government, and to provide new Guards for their future security.— Such has been the patient sufferance of these Colonies; and such is now the necessity which constrains them to alter their former Systems of Government. The history of the present King of Great Britain is a history of repeated injuries and usurpations, all having in direct object the establishment of an absolute Tyranny over these States. To prove this, let Facts be submitted to a candid world.

He has refused his Assent to Laws, the most wholesome and necessary for the public good.

He has forbidden his Governors to pass Laws of immediate and pressing importance, unless suspended in their operation till his Assent should be obtained; and when so suspended, he has utterly neglected to attend to them.

He has refused to pass other Laws for the accommodaton of large districts of people, unless those people would relinquish the right of Representation in the Legislature, a right inestimable to them and formidable to tyrants only.

He has called together legislative bodies at places unusual, uncomfortable, and distant from the depository of their Public Records, for the sole purpose of fatiguing them into compliance with his measures.

He has dissolved Representative Houses repeatedly, for opposing with manly firmness his invasions on the rights of the people.

He has refused for a long time, after such dissolutions, to cause others to be elected; whereby the Legislative Powers, incapable of Annihilation, have returned to the People at large for their exercise; the State remaining in the mean time exposed to all the dangers of invasion from without, and convulsions within.

He has endeavoured to prevent the population of these States; for that purpose obstructing the Laws of Naturalization of Foreigners; refusing to pass others to encourage their migration hither, and raising the conditions of new Appropriations of Lands.

He has obstructed the Administration of Justice, by refusing his Assent to Laws for establishing Judiciary Powers.

He has made Judges dependent on his Will alone, for the tenure of their offices, and the amount and payment of their salaries.

He has erected a multitude of New Offices, and sent hither swarms of Officers to harass our People, and eat out their substance.

He has kept among us, in times of peace, Standing Armies without the Consent of our legislature.

He has affected to render the Military independent of and superior to the Civil Power.

He has combined with others to subject us to a jurisdiction foreign to our constitution, and unacknowledged by our laws giving his Assent to their acts of pretended legislation:

For quartering large bodies of armed troops among us:

For protecting them, by a mock Trial, from Punishment for any Murders which they should commit on the Inhabitants of these States:

For cutting off our Trade with all parts of the world:

For imposing taxes on us without our Consent:

For depriving us in many cases, of the benefits of Trial by jury:

For transporting us beyond Seas to be tried for pretended offences:

For abolishing the free System of English Laws in a neighboring Province, establishing therein an Arbitrary government, and enlarging its Boundaries so as to render it at once an example and fit instrument for introducing the same absolute rule into these Colonies:

For taking away our Charters, abolishing our most valuable Laws, and altering fundamentally the Forms of our Governments:

For suspending our own Legislature, and declaring themselves invested with Power to legislate for us in all cases whatsoever.

He has abdicated Government here, by declaring us out of his Protection and waging War against us.

He has plundered our seas, ravaged our Coasts, burnt our towns, and destroyed the lives of our people.

He is at this time transporting large armies of foreign mercenaries to compleat the works of death, desolation and tyranny, already begun with circumstances of Cruelty & perfidy scarcely paralleled in the most barbarous ages, and totally unworthy the Head of a civilized nation.

He has constrained our fellow Citizens taken Captive on the high Seas to bear Arms against their Country, to become the executioners of their friends and Brethren, or to fall themselves by their Hands.

He has excited domestic insurrections amongst us, and has endeavoured to bring on the inhabitants of our frontiers, the merciless Indian Savages, whose known rule of warfare, is an undistinguished destruction of all ages, sexes and conditions.

In every stage of these Oppressions We have Petitioned for Redress in the most humble terms: Our repeated Petitions have been answered only by repeated injury. A Prince, whose character is thus marked by every act which may define a Tyrant, is unfit to be the ruler of a free People.

Nor have We been wanting in attention to our British brethren. We have warned them from time to time of attempts by their legislature to extend an unwarrantable jurisdiction over us. We have reminded them of the circumstances of our emigration and settlement here. We have appealed to their native justice and magnanimity, and we have conjured them by the ties of our common kindred to disavow these usurpations, which, would inevitably interrupt our connections and correspondence. They too have been deaf to the voice of justice and of consanguinity. We must, therefore, acquiesce in the necessity, which denounces our Separation, and hold them, as we hold the rest of mankind, Enemies in War, in Peace, Friends.

We, therefore, the Representatives of the united States of America, in General Congress, Assembled, appealing to the Supreme Judge of the world for the rectitude of our intentions, do, in the Name, and by Authority of the good People of these Colonies, solemnly publish and declare, That these United Colonies are, and of Right ought to be Free and Independent States; that they are Absolved from all Allegiance to the British Crown, and that all political connection between them and the State of Great Britain, is and ought to be totally dissolved; and that as Free and Independent States, they have full Power to levy War, conclude Peace, contract Alliances, establish Commerce, and to do all other Acts and Things which Independent States may of right do. And for the support of this Declaration, with a firm reliance on the Protection of Divine Providence, we mutually pledge to each other our Lives, our Fortunes and our sacred Honor.

10

Framing the Constitution

10.1. WEAKNESSES OF THE ARTICLES OF CONFEDERATION

Between the time independence was won and the new Constitution was adopted, the former colonies were joined together in a weak league under the Articles of Confederation. In this selection from The Federalist *Papers, Hamilton speaks out bitterly against the havoc allegedly wrought through disunity. His solution calls for a new and powerful federal union.*

WE MAY INDEED, with propriety, be said to have reached almost the last stage of national humiliation. There is scarcely anything that can wound the pride, or degrade the character, of an independent people, which we do not experience. Are there engagements, to the performance of which we are held by every tie respectable among men? These are the subjects of constant and unblushing violation. Do we owe debts to foreigners, and to our own citizens, contracted in a time of imminent peril, for the preservation of our political existence? These remain without any proper or satisfactory provision for their discharge. Have we valuable territories and important posts in the possession of a foreign power, which, by express stipulations, ought long since to have been surrendered? These are still retained, to the prejudice of our interest not less than of our rights. Are we in a condition to resent, or to repel the aggression? We have neither troops, nor treasury, nor government. Are we even in a condition to remonstrate with dignity. The just imputations on our own faith, in respect to the same treaty, ought first to be removed. Are we entitled, by nature and compact, to a free participation in the navigation of the Mississippi?

From Alexander Hamilton, *The Federalist, No. 15* [1788].

Spain excludes us from it. Is public credit an indispensable resource in time of public danger? We seem to have abandoned its cause as desperate and irretrievable. Is commerce of importance to national wealth? Ours is at the lowest point of declension. Is respectability in the eyes of foreign powers, a safeguard against foreign encroachments? The imbecility of our government even forbids them to treat with us: Our ambassadors abroad are the mere pageants of mimic sovereignty. Is a violent and unnatural decrease in the value of land, a symptom of national distress? The price of improved land, in most parts of the country, is much lower than can be accounted for by the quantity of waste land at market, and can only be fully explained by that want of private and public confidence, which are so alarmingly prevalent among all ranks, and which have a direct tendency to depreciate property of every kind. Is private credit the friend and patron of industry? That most useful kind which relates to borrowing and lending, is reduced within the narrowest limits, and this still more from an opinion of insecurity than from a scarcity of money. To shorten an enumeration of particulars which can afford neither pleasure nor instruction, it may in general be demanded, what indication is there of national disorder, poverty, and insignificance, that could befall a community so peculiarly blessed with natural advantages as we are, which does not form a part of the dark catalogue of our public misfortunes?

This is the melancholy situation to which we have been brought by those very maxims and counsels, which would now deter us from adopting the proposed constitution; . . .

The great, and radical vice, in the construction of the existing confederation, is in the principle of LEGISLATION for STATES or GOVERNMENTS, in their CORPORATE or COLLECTIVE CAPACITIES, and as contradistinguished from the INDIVIDUALS of whom they consist. . . .

The consequence of this is, that, though in theory, their resolutions concerning those objects, are laws, constitutionally binding on the members of the union, yet, in practice, they are mere recommendations, which the states observe or disregard at their option. . . .

There is nothing absurd or impracticable, in the idea of a league or alliance between independent nations, for certain defined purposes precisely stated in a treaty; regulating all the details of time, place, circumstance, and quantity; leaving nothing to future discretion; and depending for its execution on the good faith of the parties. Compacts of this kind exist among all civilized nations, subject to the usual vicissitudes of peace and war; of observance and non-observance, as the interests or passions of the contracting powers dictate. . . .

If the particular states in this country are disposed to stand in a similar relation to each other, and to drop the project of a general DISCRETIONARY SUPERINTENDENCE, the scheme would indeed be perni-

cious, and would entail upon us all the mischiefs which have been enumerated under the first head; but it would have the merit of being, at least,
consistent and practicable. Abandoning all views towards a confederate
government, this would bring us to a simple alliance, offensive and defensive; and would place us in a situation to be alternately friends and
enemies of each other, as our mutual jealousies and rivalships, nourished
by the intrigues of foreign nations, should prescribe to us.

But if we are unwilling to be placed in this perilous situation; if
we still adhere to the design of a national government, or, which is the
same thing, of a superintending power, under the direction of a common
council, we must resolve to incorporate into our plan those ingredients
which may be considered as forming the characteristic difference between
a league and a government; we must extend the authority of the union
to the persons of the citizens—the only proper objects of government. . . .

In our case, the concurrence of thirteen distinct sovereign wills is
requisite under the confederation, to the complete execution of every important measure, that proceeds from the union. It has happened, as was
to have been foreseen. The measures of the union have not been executed;
the delinquencies of the states have, step by step, matured themselves to
an extreme, which has at length arrested all the wheels of the national
government, and brought them to an awful stand. Congress at this time
scarcely possess the means of keeping up the forms of administration, till
the states can have time to agree upon a more substantial substitute for
the present shadow of a federal government. Things did not come to this
desperate extremity at once. The causes which have been specified, pro-
ducd at first only unequal and disproportionate degrees of compliance
with the requisitions of the union. The greater deficiences of some states
furnished the pretext of example, and the temptation of interest to the
complying, or at least delinquent states. Why should we do more in proportion than those who are embarked with us in the same political voyage? Why should we consent to bear more than our proper share of the
common burthen? These were suggestions which human selfishness could
not withstand, and which even speculative men, who looked forward to
remote consequences, could not without hesitation combat. Each state,
yielding to the persuasive voice of immediate interest or convenience,
has successively withdrawn its support, till the frail and tottering edifice
seems ready to fall upon our heads and to crush us beneath its ruins.

10.2. CONFLICTING PROPOSALS
FOR REPRESENTATION

*The Constitution of the United States has often been labeled a "bundle
of compromises." The acute conflict between large and small states, as*

*embodied in the divergent proposals for representation of the Virginia
and New Jersey Plans, could have delayed unification of the new nation
if the principle of compromise had not prevailed. Edmund Randolph of
Virginia was the spokesman for representation based on population,
whereas William Paterson of New Jersey favored representation based
on statehood.*

MR. RANDOLPH then opened the main business:—

He expressed his regret, that it should fall to him, rather than
those who were of longer standing in life and political experience, to open
the great subject of their mission. But as the Convention had originated
from Virginia, and his colleagues supposed that some proposition was expected from them, they had imposed this task on him.

He then commented on the difficulty of the crisis, and the necessity of preventing the fulfilment of the prophecies of the American down-
fall. . . .

He then proceeded to the remedy; the basis of which he said must
be the republican principle.

He proposed, as comfortable to his ideas, the following resolutions, which he explained one by one.

1. "Resolved, that the Articles of Confederation ought to be so
corrected and enlarged as to accomplish the objects proposed by their
institution; namely, 'common defence, security of liberty, and general welfare.'

2. "Resolved, therefore, that the rights of suffrage in the National Legislature ought to be proportioned to the quotas of contribution,
or to the number of free inhabitants, as the one or the other rule may
seem best in different cases.

3. "Resolved, that the National Legislature ought to consist of
two branches.

4. "Resolved, that the members of the first branch of the National Legislature ought to be elected by the people of the several States
every _____ for the term of _____; to be of the age of _____
years at least; to receive liberal stipends by which they may be compensated for the devotion of their time to the public service; to be ineligible
to any office established by a particular State, or under the authority of
the United States, except those peculiarly belonging to the functions of
the first branch, during the term of service, and for the space of _____
after its expiration; to be incapable of re-election for the space of _____
after the expiration of their term of service, and to be subject to recall.

5. "Resolved, that the members of the second branch of the

From the Virginia Plan and the New Jersey Plan, *Journal of the Constitutional Convention of 1787* (edited 1819).

National Legislature ought to be elected by those of the first, out of a proper number of persons nominated by the individual Legislatures, to be of the age of _____ years at least; to hold their offices for a term sufficient to ensure their independency; to receive liberal stipends, by which they may be compensated for the devotion of their time to the public service; and to be ineligible to any office established by a particular State, or under the authority of the United States, except those peculiarly belonging to the functions of the second branch, during the term of service; and for the space of _____ after the expiration thereof.

6. "Resolved, that each branch ought to possess the right of originating acts; that the National Legislature ought to be empowered to enjoy the legislative rights vested in Congress by the Confederaton, and moreover to legislate in all cases to which the separate States are incompetent, or in which the harmony of the United States may be interrupted by the exercise of individual legislation; to negative all laws passed by the several States contravening, in the opinion of the National Legislature, the Articles of Union, or any treaty subsisting under the authority of the Union; and to call forth the force of the Union against any member of the Union failing to fulfil its duty under the Articles thereof. . . .

In Convention.—Mr. Paterson laid before the Convention the plan which he said several of the Deputations wished to be substituted in place of that proposed by Mr. Randolph. After some little discussion of the most proper mode of giving it a fair deliberation, it was agreed, that it should be referred to a Committee of the Whole; and that, in order to place the two plans in due comparison, the other should be recommitted. At the earnest request of Mr. Lansing and some other gentlemen, it was also agreed that the Convention should not go into Committee of the Whole on the subject till to-morrow; by which delay the friends of the plan proposed by Mr. Paterson would be better prepared to explain and support it, and all would have an opportunity of taking copies.

The propositions from New Jersey, moved by Mr. Paterson, were in the words following:

1. Resolved, that the Articles of Confederation ought to be so revised, corrected, and enlarged, as to render the Federal Constitution adequate to the exigencies of government, and the preservation of the Union.

2. Resolved, that, in addition to the powers vested in the United States in Congress, by the present existing Articles of Confederation, they be authorized to pass acts for raising a revenue, by levying a duty or duties on all goods or merchandises of foreign growth or manufacture, imported into any part of the United States; by stamps on paper, vellum or parchment; and by a postage on all letters or packages passing through the general post-office; to be applied to such Federal purposes as they shall deem proper and expedient; to make rules and regulations for the collection

thereof; and the same, from time to time, to alter and amend in such manner as they shall think proper; to pass acts for the regulation of trade and commerce, as well with foreign nations as with each other; provided that all punishments, fines, forfeitures and penalties, to be incurred for contravening such acts, rules, and regulations, shall be adjudged by the common law Judiciaries of the State in which any offence contrary to the true intent and meaning of such acts, rules, and regulations, shall have been committed or perpetrated, with liberty of commencing in the first instance all suits and prosecutions for that purpose in the Superior common law Judiciary in such state; subject, nevertheless, for the correction of all errors, both in law and fact, in rendering judgment, to an appeal to the Judiciary of the United States.

3. Resolved, that whenever requisitions shall be necessary, instead of the rule for making requisitions mentioned in the Articles of Confederation, the United States in Congress be authorized to make such requisitions in proportion to the whole number of white and other free citizens and inhabitants, of every age, sex, and condition, including those bound to servitude for a term of years, and three fifths of all other persons not comprehended in the foregoing description, except Indians not paying taxes; that, if such requisitions be not complied with, in the time specified therein, to direct the collection thereof in the non-complying States; and for that purpose to devise and pass acts directing and authorizing the same; provided, that none of the powers hereby vested in the United States in Congress, shall be exercised without the consent of at least _____ States; and in that proportion, if the number of confederated States should hereafter be increased or diminished.

10.3. RATIFICATION OF THE CONSTITUTION

The new proposed Constitution did not meet with immediate approval by all the states. Strong opposition developed in key states, such as New York, Virginia, and Massachusetts. This selection shows how one state, Massachusetts, ratified the Constitution but recommended basic alterations and additions, several of which were later incorporated into the Bill of Rights.

THE CONVENTION, having impartially discussed and fully considered the Constitution for the United States of America, reported to Congress by the Convention of delegates from the United States of America, and submitted to us by a resolution of the General Court of the said common-

---

From the Massachusetts Act of Ratification, 1788.

wealth, passed the twenty-fifth day of October last past; and acknowledging, with grateful hearts, the goodness of the Supreme Ruler of the universe in affording the people of the United States, in the course of his providence, an opportunity, deliberately and peaceably, without fraud or surprise, of entering into an explicit and solemn compact with each other, by assenting to and ratifying a new Constitution, in order to form a more perfect union, establish justice, insure domestic tranquillity, provide for the common defence, promote the general welfare, and secure the blessings of liberty to themselves and their posterity, DO, in the name and in behalf of the people of the commonwealth of Massachusetts, assent to and ratify the said Constitution for the United States of America.

And, as it is the opinion of this Convention, that certain amendments and alterations in the said Constitution would remove the fears and quiet the apprehensions of many of the good people of the commonwealth, and more effectually guard against an undue administration of the federal government, the Convention do therefore recommend that the following alterations and provisions be introduced into the said Constitution:

First. That it be explicitly declared, that all powers not expressly delegated by the aforesaid Constitution are reserved to the several states, to be by them exercised.

Secondly. That there shall be one representative to every thirty thousand persons, according to the census mentioned in the Constitution, until the whole number of representatives amount to two hundred. . . .

. . . . . .

Sixthly. That no person shall be tried for any crime, by which he may incur an infamous punishment, or loss of life, until he be first indicted by a grand jury, except in such cases as may arise in the government and regulation of the land and naval forces.

Seventhly. The Supreme Judicial Federal Court shall have no jurisdiction of causes between citizens of different states, unless the matter in dispute, whether it concern the realty or personalty, be of the value of three thousand dollars at the least; nor shall the federal judicial powers extend to any action between citizens of different states, where the matter in dispute, whether it concern the realty or personalty, is not of the value of fifteen hundred dollars at the least.

Eighthly. In civil actions between citizens of different states, every issue of fact, arising in actions at common law, shall be tried by a jury, if the parties, or either of them, request it.

Ninthly. Congress shall at no time consent that any person holding an office of trust or profit, under the United States, shall accept of a title of nobility or any other title or office, from any king, prince, or foreign state.

And the Convention do, in the name and in the behalf of the people of this commonwealth, enjoin it upon their representatives in Congress, at all times, until the alterations and provisions aforesaid have been considered, agreeably to the 5th article of the said Constitution, to exert all their influence, and use all reasonable and legal methods, to obtain a ratification of the said alterations and provisions, in such manner as is provided in the said article.

10.4. COMMENTARY ON THE MOTIVES OF THE FOUNDING FATHERS

The idea that factors other than altruistic ones played an important role in the formulation and ratification of the Constitution came into public debate in 1913. Historian Charles A. Beard, in analyzing the backgrounds of the framers and ratifiers, theorized that economic factors probably played the dominant role. Professor McDonald has subjected the Beard thesis to an intense scrutiny.

EARLY IN 1913 there emerged . . . a work that was destined to become a classic. In that year Charles A. Beard, then a young professor of politics at Columbia University, published his *An Economic Interpretation of the Constitution of the United States,* a brilliant, challenging, and provocative study that has towered over everything else written on the subject, before or since. No other work on the making or the nature of the Constitution has been so much debated, so widely known, and ultimately so widely accepted.

The central points in the thesis advanced by Professor Beard were these: "Large and important groups of economic interests were adversely affected by the system of government under the Articles of Confederation, namely, those of public securities, shipping and manufacturing, money at interest; in short, capital as opposed to land." After failing to safeguard their rights, "particularly those of the public creditors," through the regular legal channels, these groups called a convention in the hope of obtaining "the adoption of a revolutionary programme." In other words, the movement for the Constitution originated with and was pushed through by "a small and active group of men immediately interested through their personal possessions in the outcome of their labors. . . . The propertyless masses were . . . excluded at the outset from participation (through representatives) in the work of framing the Constitution. The members of

From Forrest McDonald, *We the People: The Economic Origins of the Constitution* (Chicago: The University of Chicago Press, 1958).

the Philadelphia Convention which drafted the Constitution were, with a few exceptions, immediately, directly, and personally interested in, and derived economic advantage from, the establishment of the new system." . . .

It was perhaps inevitable, in view of the immaturity of American historiography at the time Beard wrote, and the fact that his work was a piece of pioneering, that he should have based his case on an ingenious polarization of facts, assumption, and inductive and deductive reasoning. Furthermore, while a substantial body of *theory* of economic interpretation of history had been developed long before Beard's time, no systematic methodology had yet been formulated by American historians for applying such theory to the analysis of specific historical phenomena. Thus to implement and substantiate his pioneering thesis Beard had to pioneer also in the matter of methodology. If his book is to be fruitfully examined, it is therefore necessary at the outset to analyze it in terms of these components: the facts presented, the assumptions made, the logic employed, and the methodology applied. . . .

From his analysis of the Philadelphia Convention, Beard concluded that the Constitution was essentially "an economic document drawn with superb skill" by a "consolidated economic group . . . whose property interests were immediately at stake"; that these interests "knew no state boundaries but were truly national in their scope."

From a thorough reconsideration of the Philadelphia Convention, however, the following facts emerge. Fully a fourth of the delegates in the convention had voted in their state legislatures for paper-money and or debtor-relief laws. These were the very kinds of laws which, according to Beard's thesis, the delegates had convened to prevent. Another fourth of the delegates had important economic interests that were adversely affected, directly and immediately, by the Constitution they helped write. The most common and by far the most important property holdings of the delegates were not, as Beard has asserted, mercantile, manufacturing, and public security investments, but agricultural property. Finally, it is abundantly evident that the delegates, once inside the Convention, behaved as anything but a consolidated economic group.

In the light of these and other facts presented in the foregoing chapters, it is impossible to justify Beard's interpretation of the Constitution as "an economic document" drawn by a "consolidated economic group whose property interests were immediately at stake."

Beard asserted that the ultimate test of the validity of an economic interpretation of the Constitution would rest upon a comparative analysis of the economic interests of all the persons voting for and all the persons voting against ratification. He made an analysis of the economic interests of some of the leaders in the movement for ratification and concluded that "in the ratification, it became manifest that the line of cleavage for and against the Constitution was between substantial personalty interests on the one hand and the small farming and debtor interests on the other."

For the purpose of analyzing this proposition it is necessary to employ Beard's own definitions of interest groups. In the paragraphs that follow, as in the foregoing chapters, the term "men of personalty interests" is used to mean those groups which Beard himself had in mind when he used the term, namely money, public securities, manufacturing and shipping, and western lands held for speculation.

From a thorough reconsideration of the contests over ratification the following facts emerge.

1. In three states (Delaware, New Jersey, and Georgia) the decisions of the ratifying conventions were unanimous, and it is therefore impossible to compare the interests of contending parties. . . .

2. In two states in which the decision was contested (Virginia and North Carolina) the great majority of the delegates on both sides of the question were farmers. . . .

3. In four states (Connecticut, Maryland, South Carolina, and New Hampshire) agrarian interests were dominant, but large minorities of delegates had personality interests. . . .

4. In four states (Massachusetts, Pennsylvania, New York, and Rhode Island) men having personalty interests were in a majority in the ratifying conventions. . . .

Beard's thesis—that the line of cleavage as regards the Constitution was between substantial personalty interests on the one hand and small farming and debtor interests on the other—is entirely incompatible with the facts.

Beard was less certain of the foregoing point, however, than he was of this next one:

Inasmuch as so many leaders in the movement for ratification were large security holders, and inasmuch as securities constituted such a large proportion of personalty, this economic interest must have formed a very considerable dynamic element, if not the preponderating element, in bringing about the adoption of the new system. . . . Some holders of public securities are found among the opponents of the Constitution, but they are not numerous. . . .

. . . This assertion is incompatible with the facts. The facts are these:

1. In three states (Delaware, New Jersey, and Georgia) there were no votes against the Constitution in the ratifying conventions, and hence no comparisons can be made. . . .

2. In two states (New Hampshire and North Carolina) the numbers of security holders among the delegates were very small. . . .

3. In three states (Rhode Island, Maryland, and Virginia) where there were contests and considerable numbers of security holders, the advocates and the opponents of ratification included approximately the same percentages of security holders: . . . The facts relative to these three states clearly contradict Beard's thesis.

4. In two states (Massachusetts and Connecticut) the advocates of ratification included a considerably larger percentage of holders of securities than did the opponents. . . .

In the light of the foregoing facts it is abundantly evident that there are no more grounds for considering the holding of public securities the dynamic element in the ratification than for considering this economic interest the dynamic element in the opposition. There were, indeed, some holders of public securities among the opponents of the Constitution and, contrary to Beard's assertion, they were as numerous as the security holders among the supporters of the Constitution.

On all counts, then, Beard's thesis is entirely incompatible with the facts. Beard's essential error was in attempting to formulate a single set of generalizations that would apply to all the states. Any such effort is necessarily futile, for the various interest groups operated under different conditions in the several states, and their attitudes toward the Constitution varied with the internal conditions in their states. . . .

Among the more important groups that were affected favorably there were numerous conflicts. The interests of manufacturers were opposed to those of importing merchants and of land speculators. The interests of public security holders were divided: the interests of those favorably affected by ratification coincided with those of manufacturers but conflicted with those of land speculators and purchasers of confiscated property. The interests of wheat merchants and wheat farmers also conflicted with those of many land speculators, and so on.

It is therefore not even theoretically possible to devise a single set of alignments on the issue of ratification that would explain the contest as one in which economic self-interest was the principal motivating force.

11

The Living Constitution

11.1. THE CONSTITUTION OF THE UNITED STATES OF AMERICA

Thirty-nine members of the Constitutional Convention signed this document on September 17, 1787. After ratification by nine states it became the Constitution of the United States, one of the oldest written constitutions in the world.

(Literal Print)

[*Preamble*]
We the People of the United States, in Order to form a more perfect Union, establish Justice, insure domestic Tranquility, provide for the common defence, promote the general Welfare, and secure the Blessings of Liberty to ourselves and our Posterity, do ordain and establish this Constitution for the United States of America.

ARTICLE 1

Section 1
[*Legislative Powers*]
All legislative Powers herein granted shall be vested in a Congress of the United States, which shall consist of a Senate and a House of Representatives.

Section 2
[*House of Representatives, How Constituted, Power of Impeachment*]
The House of Representatives shall be composed of Members

173

chosen every second Year by the People of the several States, and the Electors in each State shall have [the] Qualifications requisite for Electors of the most numerous Branch of the State Legislature.

No Person shall be a Representative who shall not have attained to the Age of twenty five Years, and been seven Years a Citizen of the United States, and who shall not when elected, be an Inhabitant of that State in which he shall be chosen.

Representatives and *direct Taxes shall be apportioned* [1] among the several States which may be included within this Union, according to their respective Numbers, *which shall be determined by adding to the whole Number of free Persons, including those bound to Service for a Term of Years, and excluding Indians not taxed, three fifths of all other Persons.* [2] The actual Enumeration shall be made within three Years after the first Meeting of the Congress of the United States, and within every subsequent Term of ten Years, in such Manner as they shall by Law direct. The Number of Representatives shall not exceed one for every thirty Thousand, but each State shall have at Least one Representative; *and until such enumeration shall be made, the State of New Hampshire shall be entitled to chuse three, Massachusetts eight, Rhode-Island and Providence Plantations one, Connecticut five, New York six, New Jersey four, Pennsylvania eight, Delaware one, Maryland six, Virginia ten, North Carolina five, South Carolina five, and Georgia three.* [3]

When vacancies happen in the Representation from any State, the Executive Authority thereof shall issue Writs of Election to fill such Vacancies.

The House of Representatives shall chuse their Speaker and other Officers; and shall have the sole Power of Impeachment.

Section 3
[The Senate, How Constituted, Impeachment Trials]
The Senate of the United States shall be composed of Two Senators from each State, *chosen by the Legislature thereof,* [4] for six Years; and each Senator shall have one Vote.

Immediately after they shall be assembled in Consequence of the first Election, they shall be divided as equally as may be into three Classes. The Seats of the Senators of the first Class shall be vacated at the Expiration of the second Year, of the second Class at the Expiration of the fourth Year, and of the third Class at the Expiration of the sixth Year, so that one third may be chosen every second Year; *and if Vacancies happen by Resignation, or otherwise, during the Recess of the Legislature*

---

[1] Modified by Sixteenth Amendment.
[2] Modified by Fourteenth Amendment.
[3] Temporary provision.
[4] Modified by Seventeenth Amendment.

of any State, the Executive thereof may make temporary Appointments until the next Meeting of the Legislature, which shall then fill such Vacancies.[5]

No Person shall be a Senator who shall not have attained to the Age of thirty Years, and been nine Years a Citizen of the United States, and who shall not, when elected, be an Inhabitant of that State for which he shall be chosen.

The Vice President of the United States shall be President of the Senate, but shall have no Vote, unless they be equally divided.

The Senate shall chuse their other Officers, and also a President pro tempore, in the Absence of the Vice President, or when he shall exercise the Office of President of the United States.

The Senate shall have the sole power to try all Impeachments. When sitting for that Purpose, they shall be on Oath or Affirmation. When the President of the United States [is tried] the Chief Justice shall preside: And no Person shall be convicted without the Concurrence of two thirds of the Members present.

Judgment in Cases of Impeachment shall not extend further than to removal from Office, and disqualification to hold and enjoy any Office of honor, Trust or Profit under the United States: but the Party convicted shall nevertheless be liable and subject to Indictment, Trial, Judgment and Punishment, according to Law.

Section 4
[Election of Senators and Representatives]

The Times, Places and Manner of holding Elections for Senators and Representatives, shall be prescribed in each State by the Legislature thereof; but the Congress may at any time by Law make or alter such Regulations, except as to the Places of chusing Senators.

The Congress shall assemble at least once in every Year, and such Meeting shall be on the first Monday in December, unless they shall by Law appoint a different Day.[6]

Section 5
[Quorum, Journals, Meetings, Adjournments]

Each House shall be the Judge of the Elections, Returns and Qualifications of its own Members, and a Majority of each shall constitute a Quorum to do Business; but a smaller Number may adjourn from day to day, and may be authorized to compel the Attendance of absent Members, in such Manner, and under such Penalties as each House may provide.

Each House may determine the Rules of its Proceedings, punish

---

[5] *Ibid.*
[6] Modified by Twentieth Amendment.

its Members for disorderly Behaviour, and, with the Concurrence of two thirds, expel a Member.

Each House shall keep a Journal of its Proceedings, and from time to time publish the same, excepting such Parts as may in their Judgment require Secrecy; and the Yeas and Nays of the Members of either House on any question shall, at the Desire of one fifth of those Present, be entered on the Journal.

Neither House, during the Session of Congress, shall, without the Consent of the other, adjourn for more than three days, nor to any other Place than that in which the two Houses shall be sitting.

Section 6
[Compensation, Privileges, Disabilities]

The Senators and Representatives shall receive a Compensation for their Services, to be ascertained by Law, and paid out of the Treasury of the United States. They shall in all Cases, except Treason, Felony and Breach of the Peace, be privileged from Arrest during their Attendance at the Session of their respective Houses, and in going to and returning from the same; and for any Speech or Debate in either House, they shall not be questioned in any other Place.

No Senator or Representative shall, during the Time for which he was elected, be appointed to any civil Office under the Authority of the United States, which shall have been created, or the Emoluments whereof shall have been encreased during such time; and no Person holding any Office under the United States, shall be a Member of either House during his Continuance in Office.

Section 7
[Procedure in Passing Bills and Resolutions]

All Bills for raising Revenue shall originate in the House of Representatives; but the Senate may propose or concur with Amendments as on other Bills.

Every Bill which shall have passed the House of Representatives and the Senate, shall, before it become a Law, be presented to the President of the United States; If he approve he shall sign it, but if not he shall return it, with his Objections to that House in which it shall have originated, who shall enter the Objections at large on their Journal, and proceed to reconsider it. If after such Reconsideration two thirds of that House shall agree to pass the Bill, it shall be sent, together with the Objections, to the other House, by which it shall likewise be reconsidered, and if approved by two thirds of that House, it shall become a Law. But in all such Cases the Votes of both Houses shall be determined by yeas and Nays, and the Names of the Persons voting for and against the Bill shall be entered on the Journal of each House respectively. If any Bill shall not be returned by the President within ten Days (Sundays excepted) after it shall have been presented to him, the Same shall be a Law, in like Manner as if he had signed it, unless the Congress by their Adjournment prevent its Return, in which Case it shall not be a Law.

Every Order, Resolution, or Vote to which the Concurrence of the Senate and House of Representatives may be necessary (except on a question of Adjournment) shall be presented to the President of the United States; and before the Same shall take Effect, shall be approved by him, or being disapproved by him, shall be repassed by two thirds of the Senate and House of Representatives, according to the Rules and Limitations prescribed in the Case of a Bill.

Section 8
[Powers of Congress]

The Congress shall have the Power To lay and collect Taxes, Duties, Imposts and Excises, to pay the Debts and provide for the common Defence and general Welfare of the United States; but all Duties, Imposts and Excises shall be uniform throughout the United States;

To borrow Money on the credit of the United States;

To regulate Commerce with foreign Nations and among the several States, and with the Indian Tribes;

To establish an uniform Rule of Naturalization, and uniform Laws on the subject of Bankruptcies throughout the United States;

To Coin Money, regulate the Value thereof, and of foreign Coin, and fix the Standard of Weights and Measures;

To provide for the Punishment of counterfeiting the Securities and current Coin of the United States;

To establish Post Offices and post Roads;

To promote the Progress of Science and useful Arts, by securing for limited Times to Authors and Inventors the exclusive Right to their respective Writings and Discoveries;

To constitute Tribunals inferior to the supreme Court;

To define and punish Piracies and Felonies committed on the high Seas, and Offences against the Law of Nations;

To declare War, grant Letters of Marque and Reprisal, and make Rules concerning Captures on Land and Water;

To raise and support Armies, but no Appropriation of Money to that Use shall be for a longer Term than two Years;

To provide and maintain a Navy;

To make Rules for the Government and Regulation of the land and naval Forces;

To provide for calling forth the Militia to execute the Laws of the Union, suppress Insurrections and repel Invasions;

To provide for organizing, arming, and disciplining, the Militia, and for governing such Part of them as may be employed in the Service of the United States, reserving to the States respectively, the Appointment of the Officers, and the Authority of training the Militia according to the discipline prescribed by Congress;

To exercise exclusive Legislation in all Cases whatsoever, over such District (not exceeding ten Miles square) as may, by Cession of particular States, and the Acceptance of Congress, become the Seat of the Government of the United States, and to exercise like Authority over all Places purchased by the Consent of the Legislature of the State in which the Same shall be, for the Erection of Forts, Magazines, Arsenals, dock- *clause* Yards, and other needful Buildings;—And

To make all Laws which shall be <u>necessary and proper</u> for carrying into Execution the foregoing Powers, and all other Powers vested by this Constitution in the Government of the United States, or in any Department or Officer thereof. *Elastic clause*

Section 9
[Limitations upon Powers of Congress]

The Migration or Importation of such Persons as any of the States now existing shall think proper to admit, shall not be prohibited by the Congress prior to the Year one thousand eight hundred and eight,[7] but a Tax or duty may be imposed on such Importation, not exceeding ten dollars for each Person.

The Privilege of the Writ of Habeas Corpus shall not be suspended, unless when in Cases of Rebellion or Invasion the public Safety may require it.

No Bill of Attainder or ex post facto Law shall be passed.

No Capitation, or other direct, Tax shall be laid, unless in Proportion to the Census or Enumeration herein before directed to be taken.[8]

No Tax or Duty shall be laid on Articles exported from any State.

No Preference shall be given by any Regulation of Commerce or Revenue to the Ports of one State over those of another; nor shall Vessels bound to, or from, one State, be obliged to enter, clear, or pay Duties in another.

No Money shall be drawn from the Treasury, but in Consequence of Appropriations made by Law; and a regular Statement and Account of the Receipts and Expenditures of all public Money shall be published from time to time.

No Title of Nobility shall be granted by the United States: And no Person holding any Office of Profit or Trust under them, shall, without the Consent of the Congress, accept of any present, Emolument.

[7] Temporary provision.
[8] Modified by Sixteenth Amendment.

Office, or Title, of any kind whatever, from any King, Prince, or foreign State.

Section 10
[Restrictions upon Powers of States]

No State shall enter into any Treaty, Alliance, or Confederation; grant Letters of Marque and Reprisal; coin Money; emit Bills of Credit; make any Thing but gold and silver Coin a Tender in Payment of Debts; pass any Bill of Attainder, ex post facto Law, or Law impairing the Obligation of Contracts, or grant any Title of Nobility.

No State shall, without the Consent of [the] Congress, lay any Imposts or Duties on Imports or Exports, except what may be absolutely necessary for executing its inspection Laws: and the net Produce of all Duties and Imposts, laid by any State on Imports or Exports, shall be for the Use of the Treasury of the United States; and all such Laws shall be subject to the Revision and Controul of [the] Congress.

No State shall, without the Consent of Congress, lay any Duty of Tonnage, keep Troops, or Ships of War in time of Peace, enter into any Agreement or Compact with another State, or with a foreign Power, or engage in War, unless actually invaded, or in such imminent Danger as will not admit of delay.

ARTICLE 2

Section 1
[Executive Power, Election, Qualifications of the President]

The executive Power shall be vested in a President of the United States of America. *He shall hold his Office during the Term of four Years, and, together with the Vice President, chosen for the same Term, be elected, as follows.*[9]

Each State shall appoint, in such Manner as the Legislature thereof may direct, a Number of Electors, equal to the whole Number of Senators and Representatives to which the State may be entitled in the Congress: but no Senator or Representative, or Person holding an Office of Trust or Profit under the United States, shall be appointed an Elector.

The Electors shall meet in their respective States, and vote by Ballot for two Persons, of whom one at least shall not be an Inhabitant of the same State with themselves. And they shall make a List of all the Persons voted for, and of the Number of Votes for each; which List they shall sign and certify, and transmit sealed to the Seat of the Government of the United States, directed to the President of the Senate. The President of the Senate shall, in the Presence of the Senate and House of

---

[9] Number of terms limited to two by Twenty-second Amendment.

Representatives, open all the Certificates, and the Votes shall then be counted. The Person having the greatest Number of Votes shall be the President, if such Number be a Majority of the whole Number of Electors appointed; and if there be more than one who have such Majority, and have an equal Number of Votes, then the House of Representatives shall immediately chuse by Ballot one of them for President; and if no Person have a Majority, then from the five highest on the List the said House shall in like Manner chuse the President. But in chusing the President, the Votes shall be taken by States, the Representation from each State having one Vote; A quorum for this Purpose shall consist of a Member or Members from two thirds of the States, and a Majority of all the States shall be necessary to a Choice. In every Case, after the Choice of the President, the Person having the greatest Number of Votes of the Electors shall be the Vice President. But if there should remain two or more who have equal Votes, the Senate shall chuse from them by Ballot the Vice President.[10]

The Congress may determine the Time of chusing the Electors, and the Day on which they shall give their Votes; which Day shall be the same throughout the United States.

No Person except a natural born Citizen, or a Citizen of the United States, at the time of the Adoption of this Constitution, shall be eligible to the Office of President; neither shall any Person be eligible to that Office who shall not have attained to the Age of thirty five Years, and been fourteen Years a Resident within the United States.

In Case of the Removal of the President from Office, or of his Death, Resignation, or Inability to discharge the Powers and Duties of the said Office, the Same shall devolve on the Vice President, and the Congress may by Law provide for the Case of Removal, Death, Resignation or Inability, both of the President and Vice President, declaring what Officer shall then act as President, and such Officer shall act accordingly, until the Disability be removed, or a President shall be elected.

The President shall, at stated Times, receive for his Services, a Compensation, which shall neither be encreased nor diminished during the Period for which he shall have been elected, and he shall not receive within that Period any other Emolument from the United States, or any of them.

Before he enter on the Execution of his Office, he shall take the following Oath or Affirmation:—"I do solemnly swear (or affirm) that I will faithfully execute the Office of President of the United States, and will to the best of my Ability, preserve, protect and defend the Constitution of the United States."

---

[10] Modified by Twelfth and Twentieth Amendments.

Section 2
[Powers of the President]

The President shall be Commander in Chief of the Army and Navy of the United States, and of the Militia of the several States, when called into the actual Service of the United States; he may require the Opinion, in writing, of the principal Officer in each of the executive Departments, upon any subject relating to the Duties of their respective Offices, and he shall have Power to grant Reprieves and Pardons for Offences against the United States, except in Cases of Impeachment.

He shall have Power, by and with the Advice and Consent of the Senate, to make Treaties, provided two thirds of the Senators present concur; and he shall nominate, and by and with the Advice and Consent of the Senate, shall appoint Ambassadors, other public Ministers and Consuls, Judges of the supreme Court, and all other Officers of the United States, whose Appointments are not herein otherwise provided for, and which shall be established by Law: but the Congress may by Law vest the Appointment of such inferior Officers, as they think proper in the President alone, in the Courts of Law, or in the Heads of Departments.

The President shall have Power to fill up all Vacancies that may happen during the Recess of the Senate, by granting Commissions which shall expire at the End of their next Session.

Section 3
[Powers and Duties of the President]

He shall from time to time give to the Congress Information of the State of the Union, and recommend to their Consideration such Measures as he shall judge necessary and expedient; he may, on extraordinary Occasions, convene both Houses, or either of them, and in Case of Disagreement between them, with Respect to the Time of Adjournment, he may adjourn them to such Time as he shall think proper; he shall receive Ambassadors and other public Ministers; he shall take Care that the Laws be faithfully executed, and shall Commission all the Officers of the United States.

Section 4
[Impeachment]

The President, Vice President and all civil Officers of the United States, shall be removed from Office on Impeachment for, and Conviction of, Treason, Bribery, or other high Crimes and Misdemeanors.

ARTICLE 3
Section 1
[Judicial Power, Tenure of Office]

The judicial Power of the United States, shall be vested in one supreme Court, and in such inferior Courts as the Congress may from time to time ordain and establish. The Judges, both of the supreme and inferior Courts, shall hold their Offices during good Behaviour, and shall, at stated Times, receive for their Services, a Compensation, which shall not be diminished during their Continuance in Office.

Section 2

[*Jurisdiction*]

The judicial Power shall extend to all Cases, in Law and Equity, arising under this Constitution, the Laws of the United States, and Treaties made, or which shall be made, under their Authority;—to all Cases affecting Ambassadors, other public Ministers and Consuls;—to all Cases of admiralty and maritime Jurisdiction;—to Controversies to which the United States shall be a Party;—to Controversies between two or more States;—*between a State and Citizens of another State;*—between Citizens of different States,—between Citizens of the same State claiming Lands under Grants of different States, *and between a State,* or the Citizens thereof, *and foreign* States, *Citizens or Subjects.*[11]

In all Cases affecting Ambassadors, other public Ministers and Consuls, and those in which a State shall be Party, the supreme Court shall have original Jurisdiction. In all the other Cases before mentioned, the supreme Court shall have appellate Jurisdiction, both as to Law and Fact, with such Exceptions, and under such Regulations as the Congress shall make.

The Trial of all Crimes, except in Cases of Impeachment, shall be by Jury; and such Trial shall be held in the State where the said Crimes shall have been committed; but when not committed within any State, the Trial shall be at such Place or Places as the Congress may by Law have directed.

Section 3

[*Treason, Proof and Punishment*]

Treason against the United States, shall consist only in levying War against them, or in adhering to their Enemies, giving them Aid and Comfort. No Person shall be convicted of Treason unless on the Testimony of two Witnesses to the same overt Act, or on Confession in open Court.

The Congress shall have Power to declare the Punishment of Treason, but no Attainder of Treason shall work Corruption of Blood, or Forfeiture except during the Life of the Person attainted.

---

[11] Modified by Eleventh Amendment.

ARTICLE 4

Section 1

[Faith and Credit among States]

Full Faith and Credit shall be given in each State to the public Acts, Records, and judicial Proceedings of every other State. And the Congress may by general Laws prescribe the Manner in which such Acts, Records and Proceedings shall be proved, and the Effect thereof.

Section 2

[Privileges and Immunities, Fugitives]

The Citizens of each State shall be entitled to all Privileges and Immunities of Citizens in the several States.

A Person charged in any State with Treason, Felony, or other Crime, who shall flee from Justice, and be found in another State, shall on Demand of the executive Authority of the State from which he fled, be delivered up, to be removed to the State having Jurisdiction of the Crime.

No Person held to Service or Labour in one State, under the Laws thereof, escaping into another, shall, in Consequence of any Law or Regulation therein, be discharged from such Service or Labour, but shall be delivered up on Claim of the Party to whom such Service or Labour may be due.[12]

Section 3

[Admission of New States]

New States may be admitted by the Congress into this Union; but no new State shall be formed or erected within the Jurisdiction of any other State; nor any State be formed by the Junction of two or more States, or Parts of States, without the Consent of the Legislatures of the States concerned as well as of the Congress.

The Congress shall have Power to dispose of and make all needful Rules and Regulations respecting the Territory or other Property belonging to the United States; and nothing in this Constitution shall be so construed as to Prejudice any Claims of the United States, or of any particular State.

Section 4

[Guarantee of Republican Government]

The United States shall guarantee to every State in this Union a Republican Form of Government, and shall protect each of them against

---

[12] Repealed by the Thirteenth Amendment.

Invasion; and on Application of the Legislature, or of the Executive (when the Legislature cannot be convened) against domestic Violence.

ARTICLE 5

[Amendment of the Constitution]

The Congress, whenever two thirds of both Houses shall deem it necessary, shall propose Amendments to this Constitution, or, on the Application of the Legislatures of two thirds of the several States, shall call a Convention for proposing Amendments, which, in either Case, shall be valid to all Intents and Purposes, as Part of this Constitution, when ratified by the Legislatures of three fourths of the several States, or by Conventions in three fourths thereof, as the one or the other Mode of Ratification may be proposed by the Congress; Provided *that no Amendment which may be made prior to the Year One thousand eight hundred and eight shall in any Manner affect the first and fourth Clauses in the Ninth Section of the first Article,*[13] and that no State, without its Consent, shall be deprived of its equal Suffrage in the Senate.

ARTICLE 6

[Debts, Supremacy, Oath]

All Debts contracted and Engagements entered into, before the Adoption of this Constitution, shall be as valid against the United States under this Constitution, as under the Confederation.

This Constitution, and the Laws of the United States which shall be made in Pursuance thereof; and all Treaties made, or which shall be made, under the Authority of the United States, shall be the supreme Law of the Land; and the Judges in every State shall be bound thereby, any Thing in the Constitution or Laws of any State to the Contrary notwithstanding.

The Senators and Representatives before mentioned, and the Members of the several State Legislatures, and all executive and judicial Officers, both of the United States and of the several States, shall be bound by Oath or Affirmation, to support this Constitution; but no religious Test shall ever be required as a Qualification to any Office or public Trust under the United States.

ARTICLE 7

[Ratification and Establishment]

The Ratification of the Conventions of nine States, shall be suf-

---

[13] Temporary provision.

ficient for the Establishment of this Constitution between the States so ratifying the Same.[14]

done in Convention by the Unanimous Consent of the States present the Seventeenth Day of September in the Year of our Lord one thousand seven hundred and Eighty seven and of the Independence of the United States of America the Twelfth In witness whereof We have hereunto subscribed our Names.

GEORGE WASHINGTON—President
and deputy from Virginia

New Hampshire
{ JOHN LANGDON
NICHOLAS GILMAN

Massachusetts
{ NATHANIEL GORHAM
RUFUS KING

Connecticut
{ WM SAML JOHNSON
ROGER SHERMAN

New York
ALEXANDER HAMILTON

New Jersey
{ WIL: LIVINGSTON
DAVID BREARLEY
WM PATERSON
JONA: DAYTON

Pennsylvania
{ B FRANKLIN
THOMAS MIFFLIN
ROBT MORRIS
GEO. CLYMER
THOS. FITZSIMONS
JARED INGERSOLL
JAMES WILSON
GOUV MORRIS

Delaware
{ GEO. READ
GUNNING BEDFORD jun
JOHN DICKINSON
RICHARD BASSETT
JACO: BROOM

[14] The Constitution was submitted on September 17, 1787, by the Constitutional Convention, was ratified by the conventions of several states at various dates up to May 29, 1790, and became effective on March 4, 1789.

Maryland	JAMES McHENRY
	DAN OF ST THOS. JENIFER
	DANL CARROLL

| Virginia | JOHN BLAIR— |
| | JAMES MADISON JR. |

North Carolina	WM BLOUNT
	RICHD DOBBS SPAIGHT.
	HU WILLIAMSON

South Carolina	J. RUTLEDGE
	CHARLES COTESWORTH PINCKNEY
	CHARLES PINCKNEY
	PIERCE BUTLER

| Georgia | WILLIAM FEW |
| | ABR BALDWIN |

Amendments to the Constitution

[The first ten amendments were proposed by Congress on September 25, 1789; ratified and adoption certified on December 15, 1791.]

AMENDMENT I

[Freedom of Religion, of Speech, and of the Press]

Congress shall make no law respecting an establishment of religion, or prohibiting the free exercise thereof; or abridging the freedom of speech, or of the press; or the right of the people peaceably to assemble, and to petition the Government for a redress of grievances.

AMENDMENT II

[Right to Keep and Bear Arms]

A well regulated Militia being necessary to the security of a free State, the right of the people to keep and bear Arms, shall not be infringed.

AMENDMENT III

[Quartering of Soldiers]

No Soldier shall, in time of peace be quartered in any house, without the consent of the Owner, nor in time of war, but in a manner to be prescribed by law.

AMENDMENT IV

[Security from Unwarrantable Search and Seizure]

The right of the people to be secure in their persons, houses, papers, and effects, against unreasonable searches and seizures, shall not be violated, and no Warrants shall issue, but upon probable cause, supported by Oath or affirmation, and particularly describing the place to be searched, and the persons or things to be seized.

AMENDMENT V

[Rights of Accused in Criminal Proceedings]

No person shall be held to answer for a capital, or otherwise infamous crime, unless on a presentment or indictment of a Grand Jury, except in cases arising in the land or naval forces, or in the Militia, when in actual service in time of War or public danger; nor shall any person be subject for the same offense to be twice put in jeopardy of life or limb; nor shall be compelled in any criminal case to be a witness against himself, nor be deprived of life, liberty, or property, without due process of law; nor shall private property be taken for public use, without just compensation.

AMENDMENT VI

[Right to Speedy Trial, Witnesses, etc.]

In all criminal prosecutions, the accused shall enjoy the right to a speedy and public trial, by an impartial jury of the State and district wherein the crime shall have been committed, which district shall have been previously ascertained by law, and to be informed of the nature and cause of the accusation; to be confronted with the witnesses against him; to have compulsory process for obtaining witnesses in his favor, and to have the Assistance of Counsel for his defence.

AMENDMENT VII

[Trial by Jury in Civil Cases]

In Suits at common law, where the value in controversy shall exceed twenty dollars, the right of trial by jury shall be preserved, and no fact tried by a jury, shall be otherwise reexamined in any Court of the United States, than according to the rules of the common law.

AMENDMENT VIII

[Bails, Fines, Punishments]

Excessive bail shall not be required, nor excessive fines imposed, nor cruel and unusual punishments inflicted.

AMENDMENT IX

[Reservation of Rights of the People]

The enumeration in the Constitution, of certain rights, shall not be construed to deny or disparage others retained by the people.

AMENDMENT X

[Powers Reserved to States or People]

The powers not delegated to the United States by the Constitution, nor prohibited by it to the States, are reserved to the States respectively, or to the people.

AMENDMENT XI

[Proposed by Congress on March 4, 1794; declared ratified on January 8, 1798.]

[Restriction of Judicial Power]

The Judicial power of the United States shall not be construed to extend to any suit in law or equity, commenced or prosecuted against one of the United States by Ctizens of another State, or by Citizens or Subjects of any Foreign State.

AMENDMENT XII

[Proposed by Congress on December 9, 1803; declared ratified on September 25, 1804.]

[Election of President and Vice-President]

The Electors shall meet in their respective states, and vote by ballot for President and Vice-President, one of whom, at least, shall not be an inhabitant of the same state with themselves; they shall name in their ballots the person voted for as President, and in distinct ballots the person voted for as Vice-President and they shall make distinct lists of all persons voted for as President, and of all persons voted for as Vice-President, and of the number of votes for each, which lists they shall sign and certify, and transmit sealed to the seat of the government of the United States, directed to the President of the Senate;—The President of the Senate shall, in the presence of the Senate and House of Representatives, open all the certificates and the votes shall then be counted;—The person having the greatest number of votes for President, shall be the President, if such number be a majority of the whole number of Electors appointed; and if no person have such majority, then from the persons having the highest numbers not exceeding three on the list of those voted for as President, the House of Representatives shall choose immediately, by ballot, the President. But in choosing the President, the votes shall be taken by states, the representation from each state having one vote; a quorum for this purpose shall consist of a member or members from two-thirds of the states, and a majority of all the states shall be necessary to a choice. *And if the House of Representatives shall not choose a President whenever the right of choice shall devolve upon them, before the fourth day of March next following, then the Vice-President shall act as President,*[15] as in the case of the death or other constitutional disability of the President.—The person having the greatest number of votes as Vice-President, shall be the Vice-President, if such number be a majority of the whole number of Electors appointed, and if no person have a majority, then from the two highest numbers on the list, the Senate shall choose the Vice-President; a quorum for the purpose shall consist of two-thirds of the whole number of Senators, and a majority of the whole number shall be necessary to a choice. But no person constitutionally ineligible to the office of President shall be eligible to that of Vice-President of the United States.

AMENDMENT XIII

[Proposed by Congress on January 31, 1865; declared ratified on December 18, 1865.]

Section 1
[Abolition of Slavery]
Neither slavery nor involuntary servitude, except as a punishment for crime whereof the party shall have been duly convicted, shall exist within the United States, or any place subject to their jurisdiction.

Section 2
[Power to Enforce This Article]
Congress shall have power to enforce this article by appropriate legislation.

AMENDMENT XIV

[Proposed by Congress on June 13, 1866; declared ratified on July 28, 1868.]

Section 1
[Citizenship Rights Not to Be Abridged by States]
All persons born or naturalized in the United States, and subject to the jurisdiction thereof, are citizens of the United States and of the

---

[15] Modified by Twentieth Amendment.

State wherein they reside. No State shall make or enforce any law which shall abridge the privileges or immunities of citizens of the United States; nor shall any State deprive any person of life, liberty, or property, without due process of law; nor deny to any person within its jurisdiction the equal protection of the laws.

Section 2
[Apportionment of Representatives in Congress]

Representatives shall be apportioned among the several States according to their respective numbers, counting the whole number of persons in each State, excluding Indians not taxed. But when the right to vote at any election for the choice of electors for President and Vice-President of the United States, Representatives in Congress, the Executive and Judicial officers of a State, or the members of the Legislature thereof, is denied to any of the male inhabitants of such State, being twenty-one years of age, and citizens of the United States, or in any way abridged, except for participation in rebellion, or other crime, the basis of representation therein shall be reduced in the proportion which the number of such male citizens shall bear to the whole number of male citizens twenty-one years of age in such State.

Section 3
[Persons Disqualified from Holding Office]

No person shall be a Senator or Representative in Congress, or elector of President and Vice-President, or hold any office, civil or military, under the United States, or under any State, who, having previously taken an oath, as a member of Congress, or as an officer of the United States, or as a member of any State legislature, or as an executive or judicial officer of any State, to support the Constitution of the United States, shall have engaged in insurrection or rebellion against the same, or given aid or comfort to the enemies thereof. But Congress may by a vote of two-thirds of each House, remove such disability.

Section 4
[What Public Debts Are Valid]

The validity of the public debt of the United States, authorized by law, including debts incurred for payment of pensions and bounties for services in suppressing insurrection or rebellion, shall not be questioned. But neither the United States nor any State shall assume or pay any debt or obligation incurred in aid of insurrection or rebellion against the United States, or any claim for the loss or emancipation of any slave; but all such debts, obligations and claims shall be held illegal and void.

Section 5
[Power to Enforce This Article]
The Congress shall have power to enforce, by appropriate legislation, the provisions of this article.

AMENDMENT XV

[Proposed by Congress on February 26, 1869; declared ratified on March 30, 1870.]

Section 1
[Negro Suffrage]
The right of citizens of the United States to vote shall not be denied or abridged by the United States or by any State on account of race, color, or previous condition of servitude.

Section 2
[Power to Enforce This Article]
The Congress shall have power to enforce this article by appropriate legislation.

AMENDMENT XVI

[Proposed by Congress on July 12, 1909; declared ratified on February 25, 1913.]
[Authorizing Income Taxes]
The Congress shall have power to lay and collect taxes on incomes, from whatever source derived, without apportionment among the several States, and without regard to any census or enumeration.

AMENDMENT XVII

[Proposed by Congress on May 13, 1912; declared ratified on May 31, 1913.]
[Popular Election of Senators]
The Senate of the United States shall be composed of two Senators from each State, elected by the people thereof, for six years; and each Senator shall have one vote. The electors in each State shall have the qualifications requisite for electors of the most numerous branch of the State legislatures.

When vacancies happen in the representation of any State in the Senate, the executive authority of such State shall issue writs of election to fill such vacancies: *Provided,* That the legislature of any State may empower the executive thereof to make temporary appointments until the people fill the vacancies by election as the legislature may direct.

This amendment shall not be so construed as to affect the election or term of any Senator chosen before it becomes valid as part of the Constitution.

AMENDMENT XVIII

[Proposed by Congress on December 18, 1917; declared ratified on January 29, 1919.]

Section 1
[*National Liquor Prohibition*]
After one year from the ratification of this article the manu-facture, sale, or transportation of intoxicating liquors within, the importa-tion thereof into, or the exportation thereof from the United States and all territory subject to the jurisdiction thereof for beverage purposes is hereby prohibited.[16]

Section 2
[*Power to Enforce This Article*]
The Congress and the several States shall have concurrent power to enforce this article by appropriate legislation.

Section 3
[*Ratification within Seven Years*]
This article shall be inoperative unless it shall have been ratified as an amendment to the Constitution by the legislatures of the several States, as provided in the Constitution, within seven years from the date of the submission hereof to the States by the Congress.

AMENDMENT XIX

[Proposed by Congress on June 4, 1919; declared ratified on August 26, 1920.]
[*Woman Suffrage*]
The right of citizens of the United States to vote shall not be denied or abridged by the United States or by any State on account of sex.

Congress shall have power to enforce this article by appropriate legislation.

AMENDMENT XX

[Proposed by Congress on March 2, 1932; declared ratified on February 6, 1933.]

---

[16] Repealed by Twenty-first Amendment.

Section 1
[Terms of Office]

The terms of the President and Vice President shall end at noon on the 20th day of January, and the terms of Senators and Representatives at noon on the 3rd day of January, of the years in which such terms would have ended if this article had not been ratified; and the terms of their successors shall then begin.

Section 2
[Time of Convening Congress]

The Congress shall assemble at least once in every year, and such meeting shall begin at noon on the 3rd day of January, unless they shall by law appoint a different day.

Section 3
[Death of President Elect]

If, at the time fixed for the beginning of the term of the President, the President elect shall have died, the Vice President elect shall become President. If a President shall not have been chosen before the time fixed for the beginning of his term, or if the President elect shall have failed to qualify, then the Vice President elect shall act as President until a President shall have qualified; and the Congress may by law provide for the case wherein neither a President elect nor a Vice President elect shall have qualified, declaring who shall then act as President, or the manner in which one who is to act shall be selected, and such person shall act accordingly until a President or Vice President shall have qualified.

Section 4
[Election of the President]

The Congress may by law provide for the case of the death of any of the persons from whom the House of Representatives may choose a President whenever the right of choice shall have devolved upon them, and for the case of the death of any of the persons from whom the Senate may choose a Vice President whenever the right of choice shall have devolved upon them.

Section 5

Sections 1 and 2 shall take effect on the 15th day of October following the ratification of this article.

Section 6
This article shall be inoperative unless it shall have been ratified as an amendment to the Constitution by the legislatures of three-fourths of the several States within seven years from the date of its submission.

AMENDMENT XXI
[Proposed by Congress on February 20, 1933; declared ratified on December 5, 1933.]

Section 1
[National Liquor Prohibition Repealed]
The eighteenth article of amendment to the Constitution of the United States is hereby repealed.

Section 2
[Transportation of Liquor into "Dry" States]
The transportation or importation into any States, Territory, or possession of the United States for delivery or use therein of intoxicating liquors, in violation of the laws thereof, is hereby prohibited.

Section 3
This article shall be inoperative unless it shall have been ratified as an amendment to the Constitution by conventions in the several States, as provided in the Constitution, within seven years from the date of the submission hereof to the States by the Congress.

AMENDMENT XXII
[Proposed by Congress on March 21, 1947; declared ratified on February 26, 1951.]

Section 1
[Tenure of President Limited]
No person shall be elected to the office of the President more than twice, and no person who has held the office of President, or acted as President for more than two years of a term to which some other person was elected President shall be elected to the office of the President more than once. But this Article shall not apply to any person holding the office of President when this Article was proposed by the Congress, and shall not prevent any person who may be holding the office of President,

or acting as President, during the term within which this Article becomes operative from holding the office of President, or acting as President during the remainder of such term.

Section 2

This Article shall be inoperative unless it shall have been ratified as an amendment to the Constitution by the legislatures of three-fourths of the several States within seven years from the date of its submission to the States by the Congress.

AMENDMENT XXIII

[Proposed by Congress on June 17, 1960; declared ratified on March 25, 1961.]

Section 1
[District of Columbia Suffrage in Presidential Elections]

The District constituting the seat of Government of the United States shall appoint in such manner as the Congress may direct:

A number of electors of President and Vice President equal to the whole number of Senators and Representatives in Congress to which the District would be entitled if it were a State, but in no event more than the least populous State; they shall be in addition to those appointed by the States, but they shall be considered, for the purposes of the election of President and Vice President, to be electors appointed by a State; and they shall meet in the District and perform such duties as provided by the twelfth article of amendment.

Section 2

The Congress shall have power to enforce this article by appropriate legislation.

AMENDMENT XXIV

[Proposed by Congress on August 27, 1962; declared ratified on January 23, 1964].

Section 1
[Bars Poll Tax in Federal Elections]

The right of citizens of the United States to vote in any primary or other election for President or Vice President, for electors for President or Vice President, or for Senator or Representative in Congress, shall not be denied or abridged by the United States or any State by reason of failure to pay any poll tax or other tax.

Section 2
The Congress shall have power to enforce this article by appropriate legislation.

11.2. SECOND THOUGHTS ON THE CONSTITUTION

Following ratification of the Constitution, there were still misgivings among some prominent citizens. In this letter to Madison, we see Jefferson's concern: "What right have we to bind future generations to this form of government?"

DEAR SIR,—I sit down to write to you without knowing by what occasion I shall send my letter. I do it, because a subject comes into my head, which I would wish to develop a little more than is practicable in the hurry of the moment of making up general despatches.

The question, whether one generation of men has a right to bind another, seems never to have been stated either on this or our side of the water. Yet it is a question of such consequences as not only to merit decision, but place also among the fundamental principles of every government. The course of reflection in which we are immersed here, on the elementary principles of society, has presented this question to my mind; and that no such obligation can be transmitted, I think very capable of proof. I set out on this ground, which I suppose to be self-evident, that the *earth belongs in usufruct to the living;* that the dead have neither powers nor rights over it. . . .

What is true of every member of the society, individually, is true of them all collectively; since the rights of the whole can be no more than the sum of the rights of the individuals. To keep our ideas clear when applying them to a multitude, let us suppose a whole generation of men to be born on the same day, to attain mature age on the same day, and to die on the same day, leaving a succeeding generation in the moment of attaining their mature age, all together. Let the ripe age be supposed of twenty-one years, and their period of life thirty-four years more, that being the average term given by the bills of mortality to persons of twenty-one years of age. Each successive generation would, in this way, come and go off the stage at a fixed moment, as individuals do now. Then I say, the earth belongs to each of these generations during its course, fully and

From Letter of Thomas Jefferson in Paris to James Madison, September 6, 1789.

in its own right. The second generation receives it clear of the debts and incumbrances of the first, the third of the second, and so on. For if the first could charge it with a debt, then the earth would belong to the dead and not to the living generation. Then, no generation can contract debts greater than may be paid during the course of its own existence. . . .

. . . . . .

What is true of generations succeeding one another at fixed epochs, as has been supposed for clearer conception, is true for those renewed daily, as in the actual course of nature. As a majority of the contracting generation will continue in being thirty-four years, and a new majority will then come into possession, the former may extend their engagements to that term, and no longer. The conclusion then, is, that neither the representatives of a nation, nor the whole nation itself assembled, can validly engage debts beyond what they may pay in their own time, that is to say, within thirty-four years of the date of the engagement.

On similar ground it may be proved, that no society can make a perpetual constitution, or even a perpetual law. The earth belongs always to the living generation; they may manage it, then, and what proceeds from it, as they please, during their usufruct. They are masters, too, of their own persons and consequently may govern them as they please. But persons and property make the sum of the objects of government. The constitution and the laws of their predecessors are extinguished then, in their natural course, with those whose will gave them being. This could preserve that being, till it ceased to be itself, and no longer. . . .

. . . . . .

I am always, with great and sincere esteem, dear Sir, your affectionate friend and servant.

11.3. THE CONSTITUTION AS A FLEXIBLE DOCUMENT

One of the keys to whether the new Constitution would endure was the interpretation to which it would be subjected by the courts. In one of the most famous of the U.S. Supreme Court's decisions, Chief Justice John Marshall formulates and applies the doctrine of "implied powers" as a means of enhancing national power and constitutional flexibility.

IN THE CASE now to be determined, the defendant, a sovereign state, denies the obligation of a law enacted by the legislature of the Union, and

From *McCulloch* v. *Maryland,* 4 Wheaton 316 (1819).

the plaintiff, on his part, contests the validity of an act which has been passed by the legislature of that state. The constitution of our country, in its most interesting and vital parts, is to be considered; the conflicting powers of the government of the Union and of its members, as marked in that constitution, are to be discussed; and an opinion given, which may essentially influence the great operatjons of the government. No tribunal can approach such a question without a deep sense of its importance, and of the awful responsibility involved in its decision. But it must be decided peacefully, or remain a source of hostile legislation, perhaps of hostility of a still more serious nature; and if it is to be so decided, by this tribunal alone can the decision be made. On the Supreme Court of the United States has the constitution of our country devolved this important duty.

The first question made in the cause is, has Congress power to incorporate a bank? . . .

In discussing this question, the counsel for the state of Maryland have deemed it of some importance, in the construction of the constitution, to consider that instrument not as emanating from the people, but as the act of sovereign and independent states. The powers of the general government, it has been said, are delegated by the states, who alone are truly sovereign; and must be exercised in subordination to the states, who alone possess supreme dominion.

It would be difficult to sustain this proposition. The convention which framed the constitution was indeed elected by the state legislatures. But the instrument, when it came from their hands, was a mere proposal, without obligation, or pretensions to it. It was reported to the then existing Congress of the United States, with a request that it might 'be submitted to a convention of delegates, chosen in each state by the people thereof, under the recommendation of its legislature, for their assent and ratification.' This mode of proceeding was adopted; and by the convention, by Congress, and by the state legislatures, the instrument was submitted to the people. They acted upon it in the only manner in which they can act safely, effectively, and wisely, on such a subject, by assembling in convention. . . .

From these conventions the constitution derives its whole authority. The government proceeds directly from the people; is 'ordained and established' in the name of the people; and is declared to be ordained, 'in order to form a more perfect union, establish justice, insure domestic tranquility, and secure the blessings of liberty to themselves and to their posterity.' The assent of the states, in their sovereign capacity, is implied in calling a convention, and thus submitting that instrument to the people. But the people were at perfect liberty to accept or reject it; and their act was final. It required not the affirmance, and could not be negatived, by the state governments. The constitution, when thus adopted, was of complete obligation, and bound the state sovereignties. . . .

The government of the Union, then (whatever may be the influence of this fact on the case), is, emphatically, and truly, a government of the people. In form and in substance it emanates from them. Its powers are granted by them, and are to be exercised directly on them, and for their benefit.

This government is acknowledged by all to be one of enumerated powers. The principle, that it can exercise only the powers granted to it, would seem too apparent to have required to be enforced by all those arguments which its enlightened friends, while it was pending before the people, found it necessary to urge. That principle is now universally admitted. . . .

If any one proposition could command the universal assent of mankind, we might expect it would be this—that the government of the Union, though limited in its powers, is supreme within its sphere of action. This would seem to result necessarily from its nature. It is the government of all; its powers are delegated by all; it represents all, and acts for all. . . .

But this question is not left to mere reason; the people have, in express terms, decided it by saying, 'this constitution, and the laws of the United States, which shall be made in pursuance thereof,' 'shall be the supreme law of the land,' and by requiring that the members of the state legislatures, and the officers of the executive and judicial departments of the states shall take the oath of fidelity to it. . . .

Among the enumerated powers, we do not find that of establishing a bank or creating a corporation. But there is no phrase in the instrument which, like the articles of confederation, excludes incidental or implied powers; and which requires that everything granted shall be expressly and minutely described. Even the 10th amendment, which was framed for the purpose of quieting the excessive jealousies which had been excited, omits the word 'expressly,' and declares only that the powers 'not delegated to the United States, nor prohibited to the states, are reserved to the states or to the people'; thus leaving the question, whether the particular power which may become the subject of contest has been delegated to the one government, or prohibited to the other, to depend on a fair construction of the whole instrument. The men who drew and adopted this amendment had experienced the embarrassments resulting from the insertion of this word in the articles of confederation, and probably omitted it to avoid those embarrassments. A constitution, to contain an accurate detail of all the subdivisions of which its great powers will admit, and of all the means by which they may be carried into execution, would partake of a prolixity of a legal code, and could scarcely be embraced by the human mind. It would probably never be understood by the public. Its nature, therefore, requires that only its great outlines should be marked, its important objects designated, and the minor ingredients which compose those objects be deduced from the nature of the objects themselves. . . . In considering this question, then, we must never forget that it is a constitution we are expounding.

Although, among the enumerated powers of government, we do not find the word 'bank' or 'incorporation,' we find the great powers to lay and collect taxes; to borrow money; to regulate commerce; to declare and conduct a war; and to raise and support armies and navies. The sword and the purse, all the external relations, and no inconsiderable portion of the industry of the nation, are entrusted to its government. It can never be pretended that these vast powers draw after them others of inferior importance, merely because they are inferior. Such an idea can never be advanced. But it may with great reason be contended, that a government, entrusted with such ample powers, on the due execution of which the happiness and prosperity of the nation so vitally depends, must also be entrusted with ample means for their execution. The power being given, it is the interest of the nation to facilitate its execution. It can never be their interest, and cannot be presumed to have been their intention, to clog and embarrass its execution by withholding the most appropriate means. . . . It is, then, the subject of fair inquiry, how far such means may be employed. It is not denied that the powers given to the government imply the ordinary means of execution. . . . But it is denied that the government has its choice of means; or, that it may employ the most convenient means, if, to employ them, it be necessary to erect a corporation. . . .

But the argument on which most reliance is placed, is drawn from the peculiar language of this clause. Congress is not empowered by it to make all laws, which may have relation to the powers conferred on the government, but such only as may be 'necessary and proper' for carrying them into execution. The word 'necessary' is considered as controlling the whole sentence, and as limiting the right to pass laws for the execution of the granted powers, to such as are indispensable, and without which the power would be nugatory. That it excludes the choice of means, and leaves to Congress, in each case, that only which is most direct and simple.

Is it true that this is the sense in which the word 'necessary' is always used? Does it always import an absolute physical necessity, so strong that one thing, to which another may be termed necessary, cannot exist without that other? We think it does not. . . . It must have been the intention of those who gave these powers, to insure, as far as human prudence could insure, their beneficial execution. This could not be done by confining the choice of means of such narrow limits as not to leave it in the power of Congress to adopt any which might be appropriate, and which were conducive to the end. This provision is made in a constitution intended to endure for ages to come, and, consequently, to be adapted to the various crises of human affairs. To have prescribed the means by which government should, in all future time, execute its powers, would have been to change, entirely, the character of the instrument, and give it the properties of a legal code. It would have been an unwise attempt to provide, by immutable rules, for exigencies which, if foreseen at all, must have been seen dimly, and which can be best provided for as they occur. To have declared that the best means shall not be used, but those alone without which the powers given would be nugatory, would have been to deprive the legislature of the capacity to avail itself of experience, to exercise its reason, and to accommodate its legislation to circumstances. . . .

But the argument which most conclusively demonstrates the error of the construction contended for by the counsel for the state of Maryland, is founded on the intention of the convention, as manifested in the whole clause. . . .

. . . Its terms purport to enlarge, not to diminish the powers vested in the government. It purports to be an additional power, not a restriction on those already granted. . . .

The result of the most careful and attentive consideration bestowed upon this clause is, that if it does not enlarge, it cannot be construed to restrain the powers of Congress, or to impair the right of the legislature to exercise its best judgment in the selection of measures to carry into execution the constitutional powers of the government. If no other motive for its insertion can be suggested, a sufficient one is found in the desire to remove all doubts respecting the right to legislate on that vast mass of incidental powers which must be involved in the constitution, if that instrument be not a splendid bauble.

We admit, as all must admit, that the powers of the government are limited, and that its limits are not to be transcended. But we think the sound construction of the constitution must allow to the national legislature that discretion, with respect to the means by which the powers it confers are to be carried into execution, which will enable that body to perform the high duties assigned to it, in the manner most beneficial to the people. Let the end be legitimate, let it be within the scope of the constitution, and all means which are appropriate, which are plainly adapted to that end, which are not prohibited, but consist with the letter and spirit of the constitution, are constitutional. . . .

11.4. THE POLICY ROLE OF THE JUDICIARY

The Supreme Court, as well as Congress and the President, has played a major role in adapting the powers of government to changing national the Federal system through its construction of the commerce clause of circumstances. In this decision the Court helps to mold the contours of the Constitution.

MR. CHIEF JUSTICE WAITE delivered the opinion of the court.

Congress has power "to regulate commerce with foreign nations and among the several States" (Const. art. 1, sect. 8, par. 3); and "to establish post-offices and post-roads" (id., par. 7). The Constitution of the United States and the laws made in pursuance thereof are the supreme law of the land. Art. 6, par. 2. A law of Congress made in pursuance of the Constitution suspends or overrides all State statutes with which it is in conflict.

Since the case of *Gibbons* v. *Ogden* (9 Wheat. 1), it has never been doubted that commercial intercourse is an element of commerce which comes within the regulating power of Congress. Post-offices and post-roads are established to facilitate the transmission of intelligence. Both commerce and the postal service are placed within the power of Congress, because, being national in their operation, they should be under the protecting care of the national government.

The powers thus granted are not confined to the instrumentalities of commerce, or the postal service known or in use when the Constitution was adopted, but they keep pace with the progress of the country, and adapt themselves to the new developments of time and circumstances. They extend from the horse with its rider to the stage-coach, from the sailing-vessel to the steamboat, from the coach and the steamboat to the railroad, and from the railroad to the telegraph, as these new agencies are successively brought into use to meet the demands of increasing population and wealth. They were intended for the government of the business to which they relate, at all times and under all circumstances. As they were intrusted to the general government for the good of the nation, it is not only the right, but the duty, of Congress to see to it that intercourse among the States and the transmission of intelligence are not obstructed or unnecessarily encumbered by State legislation.

The electric telegraph marks an epoch in the progress of time. In a little more than a quarter of a century it has changed the habits of business, and become one of the necessities of commerce. It is indispensable as a means of inter-communication. but especially is it so in commercial transactions. The statistics of the business before the recent reduction in rates show that more than eighty per cent of all the messages sent by telegraph related to commerce. Goods are sold and money paid upon

From *Pensacola Telegraph Company* v. *Western Union Telegraph Company*, 96 U.S. 1 (1877).

telegraphic orders. Contracts are made by telegraphic correspondence, cargoes secured, and the movement of ships directed. The telegraphic announcement of the markets abroad regulates prices at home, and a prudent merchant rarely enters upon an important transaction without using the telegraph freely to secure information.

It is not only important to the people, but to the government. By means of it the heads of the departments in Washington are kept in close communication with all their various agencies at home and abroad, and can know at almost any hour, by inquiry, what is transpiring anywhere that affects the interest they have in charge. Under such circumstances, it cannot for a moment be doubted that this powerful agency of commerce and inter-communication comes within the controlling power of Congress, certainly as against hostile State legislation. In fact, from the beginning, it seems to have been assumed that Congress might aid in developing the system; for the first telegraph line of any considerable extent ever erected was built between Washington and Baltimore, only a little more than thirty years ago, with money appropriated by Congress for that purpose (5 Stat. 618); . . . The present case is satisfied, if we find that Congress has power, by appropriate legislation, to prevent the States from placing obstructions in the way of its usefulness.

The government of the United States, within the scope of its powers, operates upon every foot of territory under its jurisdiction. It legislates for the whole nation, and is not embarrassed by State lines. Its peculiar duty is to protect one part of the country from encroachments by another upon the national rights which belong to all.

The State of Florida has attempted to confer upon a single corporation the exclusive right of transmitting intelligence by telegraph over a certain portion of its territory. This embraces the two westernmost counties of the State, and extends from Alabama to the Gulf. . . . Within it is situated an important seaport, at which business centres, and with which those engaged in commercial pursuits have occasion more or less to communicate. The United States have there also the necessary machinery of the national government. They have a navy-yard, forts, custom-houses, courts, post-offices, and the appropriate officers for the enforcement of the laws. The legislation of Florida, if sustained, excludes all commercial intercourse by telegraph between the citizens of the other States and those residing upon this territory, except by the employment of this corporation. The United States cannot communicate with their own officers by telegraph except in the same way. The State, therefore, clearly has attempted to regulate commercial intercourse between its citizens and those of other States, and to control the transmission of all telegraphic correspondence within its own jurisdiction.

It is unnecesary to decide how far this might have been done if Congress had not acted upon the same subject, for it has acted. The statute of July 24, 1866, in effect, amounts to a prohibition of all State monopolies in this particular. It substantially declares, in the interest of commerce and the convenient transmission of intelligence from place to place by the government of the United States and its citizens, that the erection of telegraph lines shall, so far as State interference is concerned, be free to all who will submit to the conditions imposed by Congress. . . .

The State law in question, so far as it confers exclusive rights upon the Pensacola Company, is certainly in conflict with this legislation of Congress. To that extent it is, therefore, inoperative as against a corporation of another State entitled to the privileges of the act of Congress. Such being the case, the charter of the Pensacola Company does not exclude the Western Union Company from the occupancy of the right of way of the Pensacola and Louisville Railroad Company under the arrangement made for that purpose.

11.5. THE CONSTITUTION AS A LIVING DOCUMENT

The fears Jefferson expressed in his letter to Madison about the Constitution have not been borne out in practice. Professor McBain attributes the success of the Constitution as a framework of government to its growth and development through custom and legislative interpretation.

STATE CONSTITUTIONS in the United States have developed—have in other words kept approximate pace with changes in our economic and social life and in our political thinking—chiefly by the process of periodic general revision and by the further process of piecemeal amendment. Not so our national constitution. It has never been generally revised. . . . But it *has* developed. It has been altered and enlarged by several different methods. These can be merely illustrated at this point. Some of them will be discussed more fully later.

The constitution has developed by the growth of customs and especially the customs or practises of political parties. There are a number of well-known examples of this. The constitution decrees that the President shall be chosen by groups of electors in the several states. Thus did the Fathers think to exalt this office above debasing partisan antagonisms. But political parties early decreed otherwise. Candidates are nominated by parties and the electors chosen thereafter merely rubber-stamp these nominations. The form remains; the substance has long since passed into limbo. Tradition, not the constitution, prescribes that a President may

From Howard Lee McBain, *The Living Constitution* (New York: The Macmillan Company, 1927), *passim*, pp. 25–31. Courtesy of AFL-CIO.

not be reelected for a third term. The President's Cabinet, which varies in influence from President to President, is unknown to the fundamental law. The constitution ordains that the President shall "nominate and, by and with the advice and consent of the Senate, shall appoint" officers. The President has never taken the advice of the Senate in the matter of appointments; but party practise ordains that, as to federal officers in the several states, the President shall not only take but also follow the advice of the senator or senators of his own party, if any, from the state in which the appointment is to be made. The senator, not the President, makes the nomination. The constitution is silent as to the power of removal; but from the beginning the President has exercised this power on an extensive scale.

The constitution makes the President the chief executive of the nation. In political practise candidates for this high office stand before the people upon a program consisting largely of legislative proposals; and a President seeking reelection is held to account far more usually upon his legislative than upon his executive record. This is perhaps the most significant of all the "customs of the constitution" that have been wrought upon it by the impious hands of political parties.

. . . The constitution does not require that congressmen shall be residents of the districts of their election; but party practise does so require. . . .

These, then, are some of the customs or conventions of the American constitution, by which this or that provision has been added, expanded, contracted, perverted, or even wholly nullified. They "constitute," as is obvious, a not unimportant part of our constitutional system.

The constitution has also developed by act of Congress or by the action of one or the other house of Congress. Thus the provision of the constitution relating to the counting of the votes of presidential electors in the presence of the Senate and the House is, as one expositor has put it with unintended humor, "pregnant with omissions." Congress has supplied these omissions by an elaborate and rather slovenly law enacted in 1886, ten years after the Tilden-Hayes controversy first disclosed this deficiency of the fundamental law. Again the constitution makes each house the judge of the "qualifications" of its own members; and although the constitution itself prescribes the qualifications, the houses have on occasion exercised the power both of adding to and subtracting from these qualifications. In 1900 the House refused to seat a duly elected member from Utah, who, being a Mormon, had too many wives. In one or two instances the Senate has seated persons who, being a little short of the prescribed age of thirty, were not, as it were, constitutionally adult for the Senate. Repeatedly, moreover, committees of both houses, and especially of the Senate, exercise inquisitorial power over witnesses that is of dubious constitutionality. But this opens a large question, mixed of law, of the rights of witnesses, and of the rights of the public, which cannot be entered here.

In a much more important way, however, than anything yet mentioned has the constitution been developed by Congress. We usually speak of the huge development of our constitution by judicial interpretation. Everything, right or wrong, is laid on the doorstep of the courts, and especially of the Supreme Court. But the courts have nothing to interpret, nothing to develop, until Congress or the state legislatures have acted. Legislative interpretation, legislative development, of the constitution comes first. And nobody can assess the complete effect of the system. It is impossible to say how many laws are enacted by Congress and the state legislatures in the disguised hope and belief that they will be declared unconstitutional by the courts. No one knows how many proposed laws fail of enactment because of genuine conviction that they would be declared void if enacted. On the face of the result, however, we owe our vast expansion of federal powers, particularly under the elastic commerce clause, primarily to Congress. The courts have merely followed where Congress has led; they have merely permited what Congress has prescribed.

Nor is this all. Whatever limitations have been imposed by the courts on attempted exertions of power by Congress are as nothing compared with the limitations that Congress has by inaction imposed upon itself. There is probably an immense realm of regulatory power which Congress might with the sanction of the courts constitutionally occupy, but which, wisely or unwisely, Congress has as yet not seen fit to occupy. Action by Congress in the years ahead will unquestionably prove this.

In a very real sense, therefore, may it be said that the constitution has been developed by act of Congress. . . .

Nearly all the laws of Congress by which the physiognomy of the constitution has been materially or even slightly altered have been contested before the courts. In the body of these laws there is usually no mention of the constitution, although in the process of enacting them there is commonly high, and sometimes very able, debate upon points of constitutionality. But when these laws reach the courts the judges in their written opinions discuss at great length the meaning of the words and phrases of the constitution. Now the record of Congress that is of chief importance is the law itself. This is printed in the statute books and is thus completely severed from the record of the investigations, the reports, the debates, that may have attended upon its enactment. The record of the court is of course its judgment of the validity or invalidity of the law as applied to a particular set of facts. But this record is closely coupled with the arguments employed and the reasons advanced for the conclusion reached. The opinion and the judgment are printed together in the volumes of the reports of cases decided. Though legally speaking the opinion and the judgment are separable, they are in fact part and parcel of a single pronouncement by the court. And thus they appear. The record, therefore, is filled with declarations that this or that word or phrase or clause of the constitution means or does not mean thus and so. Moreover, the court has the last word upon the subject. Its declaration of meaning is final, unless it is changed by some subsequent declaration made by the court itself.

It is because of this nature of their records and this finality of their adjudications that we think and speak of the courts, and especially of the United States Supreme Court, as being the principal agency by which our written constitution has been and is being developed. As expounders of the constitution their role has truly been of great significance in the unfolding of our institutional life.

"A word," says Mr. Justice Holmes, "is the skin of an idea." As applied to the words of a living constitution the expression is peculiarly apt; for living skin is elastic, expansible, and is constantly being renewed. The constitution of the United States contains only about six thousand words; but millions of words have been written by the courts in elucidation of the ideas these few words encase.

12

Separation of Powers

12.1. SEPARATION OF POWERS IN THE CONSTITUTION

Here Madison explores the question of just how separate and independent the three great branches of government can be.

TO WHAT EXPEDIENT, then, shall we finally resort, for maintaining in practice the necessary partition of power among the several departments, as laid down in the Constitution? The only answer that can be given is, that as all these exterior provisions are found to be inadequate, the defect must be supplied, by so contriving the interior structure of the government as that its several constituent parts may, by their mutual relations, be the means of keeping each other in their proper places. Without presuming to undertake a full development of this important idea, I will hazard a few general observations, which may perhaps place it in a clearer light, and enable us to form a more correct judgment of the principles and structure of the government planned by the convention.

In order to lay a due foundation for that separate and distinct exercise of the different powers of government, which to a certain extent is admitted on all hands to be essential to the preservation of liberty, it is evident that each department should have a will of its own; and consequently should be so constituted that the members of each should have as little agency as possible in the appointment of the members of the others. Were this principle rigorously adhered to, it would require that all the appointments for the supreme executive, legislative, and judiciary magistracies should be drawn from the same fountain of authority, the people, through channels having no communication whatever with one another. Perhaps such a plan of constructing the several departments

From Alexander Hamilton, James Madison, and John Jay, *The Federalist, No. 51* [1788].

would be less difficult in practice than it may in contemplation appear. Some difficulties, however, and some additional expense would attend the execution of it. Some deviations, therefore, from the principle must be admitted. In the constitution of the judiciary department in particular, it might be inexpedient to insist rigorously on the principle: first, because peculiar qualifications being essential in the members, the primary consideration ought to be to select that mode of choice which best secures these qualifications; secondly, because the permanent tenure by which the appointments are held in that department must soon destroy all sense of dependence on the authority conferring them.

It is equally evident, that the members of each department should be as little dependent as possible on those of the others, for the emoluments annexed to their offices. Were the executive magistrate, or the judges, not independent of the legislature in this particular, their independence in every other would be merely nominal.

But the great security against a gradual concentration of the several powers in the same department, consists in giving to those who administer each department the necessary constitutional means and personal motives to resist encroachments of the others. The provision for defence must in this, as in all other cases, be made commensurate to the danger of attack. Ambition must be made to counteract ambition. The interest of the man must be connected with the constitutional rights of the place. It may be a reflection on human nature that such devices should be necessary to control the abuses of government. But what is government itself but the greatest of all reflections on human nature? If men were angels, no government would be necessary. If angels were to govern men, neither external nor internal controls on government would be necessary. In framing a government which is to be administered by men over men, the great difficulty lies in this: you must first enable the government to control the governed; and in the next place oblige it to control itself. A dependence on the people is, no doubt, the primary control on the government; but experience has taught mankind the necessity of auxiliary precautions.

This policy of supplying, by opposite and rival interests, the defect of better motives, might be traced through the whole system of human affairs, private as well as public. We see it particularly displayed in all the subordinate distributions of power, where the constant aim is to divide and arrange the several offices in such a manner as that each may be a check on the other—that the private interest of every individual may be a sentinel over the public rights. These inventions of prudence cannot be less requisite in the distribution of the supreme powers of the State.

But it is not possible to give to each department an equal power of self-defence. In republican government, the legislative authority necessarily predominates. The remedy for this inconveniency is to divide the legislature into different branches; and to render them, by different modes of election and different principles of action, as little connected with each other as the nature of their common functions and their common dependence on the society will admit. It may even be necessary to guard against dangerous encroachments by still further precautions. As the weight of the legislative authority requires that it should be thus divided, the weakness of the executive may require, on the other hand, that it should be fortified. An absolute negative on the legislature appears, at first, to be the natural defence with which the executive magistrate should be armed. But perhaps it would be neither altogether safe nor alone sufficient. On ordinary occasions it might not be exerted with the requisite firmness, and on extraordinary occasions it might be perfidiously abused. May not this defect of an absolute negative be supplied by some qualified connection between this weaker department and the weaker branch of the stronger department, by which the latter may be led to support the constitutional rights of the former, without being too much detached from the rights of its own department?

If the principles on which these observations are founded be just, as I persuade myself they are, and they be applied as a criterion to the several State constitutions, and to the federal Constitution, it will be found that if the latter does not perfectly correspond with them, the former are infinitely less able to bear such a test.

12.2. TOWARD A RESPONSIBLE CABINET

Many who decry our principle of separation of powers as unnecessary, outmoded, or ineffective have looked to aspects of the British cabinet system as their model for reform. It was the opinion of President Taft, among others, that the right to question cabinet members during debates in the legislature would contribute to the enactment of beneficial legislation without destroying the independence of either the executive or the legislative branches.

To the Senate and House of Representatives:
This is the third of a series of messages in which I have brought to the attention of the Congress the important transactions of the Government in each of its departments during the last year and have discussed needed reforms.

I recommended the adoption of legislation which shall make it

From a Message of President William Howard Taft to Congress, in *The Congressional Record*, Vol. 49, Part 1, pp. 895–896.

the duty of heads of departments—the members of the President's Cabinet —at convenient times to attend the session of the House and the Senate, which shall provide seats for them in each House, and give them the opportunity to take part in all discussions and to answer questions of which they have had due notice. The rigid holding apart of the executive and the legislative branches of this Government has not worked for the great advantage of either. There has been much lost motion in the machinery, due to the lack of cooperation and interchange of views face to face between the representatives of the Executive and the Members of the two legislative branches of the Government. It was never intended that they should be separated in the sense of not being in constant effective touch and relationship to each other. The legislative and the executive each performs its own appropriate function, but these functions must be coordinated. Time and time again debates have arisen in each House upon issues which the information of a particular department head would have enabled him, if present, to end at once by a simple explanation or statement. Time and time again a forceful and earnest presentation of facts and arguments by the representative of the Executive whose duty it is to enforce the law would have brought about a useful reform by amendment, which in the absence of such a statement has failed of passage. I do not think I am mistaken in saying that the presence of the members of the Cabinet on the floor of each House would greatly contribute to the enactment of beneficial legislation. Nor would this in any degree deprive either the legislative or the executive of the independence which separation of the two branches has been intended to promote. It would only facilitate their cooperation in the public interest.

On the other hand, I am sure that the necessity and duty imposed upon department heads of appearing in each House and in answer to searching questions, of rendering upon their feet an account of what they have done, or what has been done by the administration, will spur each member of the Cabinet to closer attention to the details of this department, to greater familiarity with its needs, and to greater care to avoid the just criticism which the answers brought out in questions put and discussions arising between the Members of either House and the members of the Cabinet may properly evoke.

Objection is made that the members of the administration having no vote could exercise no power on the floor of the House, and could not assume that attitude of authority and control which the English parliamentary Government have and which enables them to meet the responsibilities the English system thrusts upon them. I agree that in certain respects it would be more satisfactory if members of the Cabinet could at the same time be Members of both Houses, with voting power, but this is impossible under our system; and while a lack of this feature may detract from the influence of the department chiefs, it will not prevent the good results which I have described above both in the matter of legislation and in the matter of administration. The enactment of such a law would be quite within the power of Congress without constitutional amendment, and it has such possibilities of usefulness that we might well make the experiment, and if we are disappointed the misstep can be easily retraced by a repeal of the enabling legislation.

This is not a new proposition. In the House of Representatives, in the Thirty-eighth Congress, the proposition was referred to a select committee of seven Members. The committee made an extensive report and urged the adoption of the reform. The report showed that our history had not been without illustration of the necessity and the examples of the practice by pointing out that in early days Secretaries were repeatedly called in to the presence of either House for consultation, advice, and information.

12.3 A PROPOSAL FOR A CONGRESSIONAL "QUESTION HOUR"

Laws embodying President Taft's suggestions have been proposed in Congress from time to time but none has come close to enactment. The late Senator Kefauver, for example, when a member of the House, was unable to have such a bill reported out of the Rules Committee chaired by Representative Cannon. Here Kefauver pleads for a hearing on the bill to require heads of executive departments and agencies to appear for questioning in the House.

I AM SERVING my third term. I am frank to confess that there are many departments of the Government with which I am very poorly acquainted. Certainly I do not have time or the means under our present system to know as much about the workings of the bureaus as I should. These bureaus, mind you, were established by us and it is our duty to acquire more knowledge of what they are doing and to become better versed with their problems.

I have an idea that even a well-versed Member like the distinguished gentleman from Missouri would secure much valuable information, particularly on international relations, from reports by the Secretary of State, the Administrator of Foreign Economic Administration, and other officials who have charge of the direction of our international affairs.

The principal arguments advanced against the proposal by the

From a Speech by Representative Estes Kefauver, in *The Congressional Record*, 78th Congress, 2d Session (March 29, 1944).

gentleman from Missouri [Mr. Cannon] and my reply to them are as follows:

I. Argument: The difference between the English and the American systems makes parallels between the two inapplicable.

Reply: The fact that the American Cabinet is responsible to the President rather than directly to Congress makes it all the more important that Congress as a whole should have ways and means to inform itself as to whether its intentions are in fact carried out. It is also all the more important that it have opportunities the better to understand the operations of the Executive. When Cabinet members—as in the British system—are also members of Parliament, such opportunities are normal and frequent, and interchange of ideas is consequently natural. In the American system such interchange of ideas is as fully desirable as under the British system, but special procedures must be set up in order to secure such interchange.

II. Argument: The United States already has measures permitting Congress to inquire of and investigate the Executive. These measures are the resolution of inquiry, the standing committees, press conferences of the President, personal contact, Government reports.

Reply: Each of these measures, while appropriate and effective within limits, suffers from certain defects. The resolution of inquiry is somewhat cumbersome and relatively little used. Where it is used it seldom, if ever, is reported favorably by the appropriate committee. If it were frequently used it would provide a much greater burden upon the time of Congress than the question hour now proposed, inasmuch as presumably each resolution would have to be debated by the House as a whole before it would be passed.

Questioning by committees is the most effective of the devices at the present time. Nevertheless, but few Members relatively are present at committee hearings, and the time of Members does not allow them to follow the hearings of committees other than their own in any detail. The committees are most suited to lengthy and detailed investigations, whereas the question hour in the House as a whole should, and would, furnish a far better opportunity for questions and declarations concerning general policy and for focusing attention upon some particular event.

The suggestion that Congress should abdicate its investigatory function to reporters of the press is a strange one. This argument also suggests that Congress should overlook the opportunity to gain back some of its own lost prestige through the publicity which would attend its proceedings.

Personal contact is excellent as far as it goes. However, it is not a substitute for a responsible public declaration of policy.

Government reports also are excellent for a comprehensive view of an agency's work. These views are uniformly favorable rather than critical. However, questions which would be asked would, to a considerable extent, deal with problems of the kind which the reports would not, and often could not, include.

H. R. 327 is designed not to supersede existing channels but to add to them one which would have peculiar advantages of its own. It would promote not only the securing of information but the betterment of understanding. Such understanding is characteristic of person-to-person contacts of this type.

III. Argument: The proposal violates separation of powers insofar as it would force the Executive to attend to the wishes of the legislative branch.

Reply: In the first place, separation of powers under our Constitution was from the very outset intentionally and profoundly modified by the constitutional system of checks and balances. Controls of the executive by the legislative branch were provided for under the constitution, in connection with appropriations, investigations, impeachments, and approval of appointments. Moreover, that it is a bad thing for the executive branch to attend upon the wishes of the legislative branch would not find very many supporters. This argument smacks of a bureaucratic origin.

IV. Argument: The proposal would result in a bitter partisan fight and would increase the dissension between the executive and the legislative.

Reply: This argument assumes that Congress would not behave responsibly. In fact the whole development of the argument seems to imply that the Rules and other committees and the individual Members of the House would operate after the fashion of a Roman holiday. The selection of questions to be asked and the control of the time of the House by responsible leaders and committees, as well as the good sense of the overwhelming majority of the Members, could and would establish a tradition of responsible behavior which would befit the occasion.

V. Argument: The interest in and publicity attendant upon the question hour would crowd the House and fill the newspapers.

Reply: This is an argument in favor of the measure and not against it. It would go far toward creating a feeling on the part of the American public that Congress really mattered and would at long last result in publicizing congressional activity more on a par with the Executive. . . .

A procedure would be inaugurated, if this resolution were passed, which would establish the importance of Congress in the public mind. At present executive administrators hold press conferences. These press conferences are given more play in the newspapers and over the radio than action taken by Congress on important measures. If the plans and proposals for the administration of laws are brought out on the floor of the House, pursuant to questions from Members, the important news would arise from what was said on the floor and not what was said at some press conference.

This procedure would be beneficial to the Cabinet members and heads of the departments. In the first place, the President in making appointments would have to take into consideration that they would be called upon to appear on the floor of the House. The President's administration would be judged to a considerable extent by the impression these administrators made. He would be doubly sure that he secured outstanding men as heads of the executive agencies of the Government. The procedure would enable the administrators to obtain the people's views as expressed directly by the people's representatives. The administrators would consider more deliberately their decisions if they knew they would be called upon to give an account of what they were doing before the House. There could be no ghost writing. These men would have to know their departments and be able to give facts.

It frequently happens that rumors or unjust criticism are spread about executive officers. If this criticism comes from a Member of the House, the executive officer has no opportunity to answer except through the newspapers. Under this procedure he would be given an opportunity of appearing and explaining his side of the controversy.

In a complex society such as we have today, it is necessary to concentrate great and far-reaching power in the Executive. This condition will continue regardless of the administration in power. One of the great values of having Cabinet members and administrative agents report in person to the Members of the House is that such appearances would necessitate clear definitions of policy on the part of the Executive. Some Cabinet members and heads of agencies do not know what the President's policy is on certain particular matters under their jurisdiction. This is no reflection on the present administration as the same condition has always existed. Before an administrator appeared at a question period, he would naturally call upon the Chief Executive to clearly define the policy of the administration in regard to the matter about which he would be questioned. Also, many questions of policy which should be decided by the administrator himself remain undetermined. Faced with the invitation of making a personal report to Congress, the administrator would be running a great risk if he did not settle those undetermined matters of policy affecting his department before submitting himself to the House Members for interrogation. . . .

To sum up—if Congress wants to hold its authority, if the House wants to keep pace with the executive departments, if the House wants to meet the expectations of the people of this country, we must improve our machinery. I think this plan is worth trying. I think it would work to the benefit of Congress, the departments, and the people. If it does not, the committees do not have to issue any invitations and, furthermore, if we do not like the way the system works, we can repeal the rule. Let us at least give it a trial.

12.4. LIMITS TO THE DELEGATION OF POWER

In this decision of the early New Deal era, the Supreme Court justices deal a powerful blow to President Roosevelt's program for meeting the economic crisis of the 1930s. The Court rules that Congress has delegated lawmaking powers to the President in the National Industrial Recovery Act and that the legislature has thereby violated the separation of powers principle of the Constitution.

MR. CHIEF JUSTICE HUGHES delivered the opinion of the Court, saying in part:

Petitioners . . . were convicted in the district court of the United States for the eastern district of New York on eighteen counts of an indictment charging violations of what is known as the "Live Poultry Code," and on an additional count for conspiracy to commit such violations. . . .

The "Live Poultry Code" was promulgated under §3 of the National Industrial Recovery Act. That section . . . authorizes the President to approve "codes of fair competition." . . .

The "Live Poultry Code" was approved by the President on April 13, 1934. . . . The code is established as "a code for fair competition for the live poultry industry of the metropolitan area in and about the City of New York." . . .

The seventh article, containing "trade practice provisions," prohibits various practices which are said to constitute "unfair methods of competition." . . .

The President approved the code by an executive order. . . .

. . . . . .

The Constitution provides that "all legislative powers herein granted shall be vested in a Congress of the United States, which shall consist of a Senate and House of Representatives," Art. 1, section 1. And the Congress is authorized "to make all laws which shall be necessary and proper for carrying into execution" its general power, Art. 1, section 8, clause 18. The Congress is not permitted to abdicate or to transfer to others the essential legislative functions with which it is thus vested.

We have repeatedly recognized the necessity of adapting legislation to complex conditions involving a host of details with which the national legislature cannot deal directly. We pointed out in the Panama Refining Co. case that the Constitution has never been regarded as deny-

From *Schechter* v. *United States*, 295 U.S. 495 (1935).

ing to Congress the necessary resources of flexibility and practicality, which will enable it to perform its function in laying down policies and establishing standards, while leaving to selected instrumentalities the making of subordinate rules within prescribed limits and the determination of facts to which the policy as declared by the legislature is to apply.

But we said that the constant recognition of the necessity and validity of such provisions, and the wide range of administrative authority which has been developed by means of them, cannot be allowed to obscure the limitations of the authority to delegate, if our constitutional system is to be maintained.

Accordingly, we look to the statute to see whether Congress has overstepped these limitations, whether Congress in authorizing "Codes of Fair Competition" has established the standards of legal obligation, thus performing its essential legislative function, or, by the failure to enact such standards, has attempted to transfer that function to others. . . .

What is meant by "fair competition" as the term is used in the act? Does it refer to a category established in the law, and is the authority to make codes limited accordingly?

Or is it used as a convenient designation for whatever set of laws the formulators of a code for a particular trade or industry may propose and the President may approve (subject to certain restrictions), or the President may himself prescribe, as being wise and beneficent provisions for the government of the trade or industry in order to accomplish the broad purposes of rehabilitation, correction and expansion which are stated in the first section of title I?

The act does not define "fair competition." "Unfair competition" as known to common law is a limited concept, primarily, and strictly, it relates to the palming off of one's goods as those of a rival trader. . . .

The President is authorized to impose such conditions "for the protection of consumers, competitors, employees and others, and in furtherance of the public interest, and may provide such exception to and exemptions from the provisions of such code as the President in his discretion deems necessary to effectuate the policy herein declared." . . .

The government urges that the code will "consist of rules of competition deemed fair for each industry by representative members of that industry, by the persons most vitally concerned and most familiar with its problems." . . .

But would it be seriously contended that Congress could delegate its legislative authority to trade or industrial associations or groups so as to empower them to enact the laws they deem to be wise and beneficent for the rehabilitation and expansion of their trade or industries?

Could trade or industrial associations or groups be constituted legislative bodies for that purpose because such associations or groups are familiar with the problems of their enterprises?

And could an effort of that sort be made valid by such a preface of generalities as to permissible aims as we find in §1 of title I? The answer is obvious. Such a delegation of legislative power is unknown to our law and is utterly inconsistent with the constitutional prerogatives and duties of Congress. . . .

To summarize and conclude . . . §3 of the Recovery Act is without precedent. It supplies no standards for any trade, industry or activity. It does not undertake to prescribe rules of conduct to be applied to particular states of fact determined by appropriate administrative procedure.

Instead of prescribing rules of conduct, it authorizes the making of codes to prescribe them. For that legislative undertaking, §3 sets up no standards, aside from the statement of the general aims of rehabilitation, correction and expansion described in §1.

In view of the scope of that broad declaration, and of the nature of the few restrictions that are imposed, the discretion of the President in approving or prescribing codes, and thus enacting laws for the government of trade and industry throughout the country, is virtually unfettered.

We think that the code-making authority thus conferred is an unconstitutional delegation of legislative power.

13

Congress and the National Will

13.1. LIMITS ON THE MAJORITY

These excerpts from The Federalist Papers *focus on the structure and powers of the House of Representatives and the Senate. The framers of the Constitution saw the Senate functioning as a necessary check on popular passions and factions which might control the House.*

NOTWITHSTANDING the equal authority which will subsist between the two houses on all legislative subjects, except the originating of money bills, it cannot be doubted that the House, composed of the greater number of members, when supported by the more powerful States, and speaking the known and determined sense of a majority of the people, will have no small advantage in a question depending on the comparative firmness of the two houses.

This advantage must be increased by the consciousness, felt by the same side, of being supported in its demands by right, by reason, and by the Constitution; and the consciousness, on the opposite side, of contending against the force of all these solemn considerations.

. . . [I]n all legislative assemblies the greater the number composing them may be, the fewer will be the men who will in fact direct their proceedings. In the first place, the more numerous an assembly may be, of whatever characters composed, the greater is known to be the ascendancy of passion over reason. In the next place, the larger the number, the greater will be the proportion of members of limited information and of weak capacities. Now, it is precisely on characters of this description that the eloquence and address of the few are known to act with all their force. In the ancient republics, where the whole body of

---

From Alexander Hamilton, James Madison, and John Jay, *The Federalist, Nos. 58 and 62* [1788].

the people assembled in person, a single orator, or an artful statesman, was generally seen to rule with as complete a sway as if a sceptre had been placed in his single hand. On the same principle, the more multitudinous a representative assembly may be rendered, the more it will partake of the infirmities incident to collective meetings of the people. Ignorance will be the dupe of cunning, and passion the slave of sophistry and declamation. The people can never err more than in supposing that by multiplying their representatives beyond a certain limit, they strengthen the barrier against the government of a few. Experience will forever admonish them that, on the contrary, *after securing a sufficient number for the purposes of safety, of local information, and of diffusive sympathy with the whole society,* they will counteract their own views by every addition to their representatives. The countenance of the government may become more democratic, but the soul that animates it will be more oligarchic. The machine will be enlarged, but the fewer, and often the more secret, will be the springs by which its motions are directed.

· · · · · ·

Having examined the constitution of the House of Representatives, and answered such of the objections against it as seemed to merit notice, I enter next on the examination of the Senate. . . . The equality of representation in the Senate is another point, which, being evidently the result of compromise between the opposite pretensions of the large and small States, does not call for much discussion. If indeed it be right, that among a people thoroughly incorporated into one nation, every district ought to have a *proportional* share in the government, and that among independent and sovereign States, bound together by a simple league, the parties, however unequal in size, ought to have an *equal* share in the common councils, it does not appear to be without some reason that in a compound republic, partaking both of the national and federal character, the government ought to be founded on a mixture of the principles of proportional and equal representation. But it is superfluous to try, by the standard of theory, a part of the Constitution which is allowed on all hands to be the result, not of a theory, but "of a spirit of amity, and that mutual deference and concession which the peculiarity of our political situation rendered indispensable." A common government, with powers equal to its objects, is called for by the voice, and still more loudly by the political situation, of America. A government founded on principles more consonant to the wishes of the larger States is not likely to be obtained from the smaller States. The only option, then, for the former, lies between the proposed government and a government still more objectionable. Under this alternative, the advice of prudence must be to embrace the lesser evil; and, instead of indulging a fruitless anticipation of the possible mischiefs which may ensue, to contemplate rather the advantageous consequences which may qualify the sacrifice. . . .

. . . It is a misfortune incident to republican government, though in a less degree than to other governments, that those who administer it may forget their obligations to their constituents, and prove unfaithful to their important trust. In this point of view, a senate, as a second branch of the legislative assembly, distinct from, and dividing the power with, a first, must be in all cases a salutary check on the government. It doubles the security to the people, by requiring the concurrence of two distinct bodies in schemes of usurpation or perfidy, where the ambition or corruption of one would otherwise be sufficient. This is a precaution founded on such clear principles, and now so well understood in the United States, that it would be more than superfluous to enlarge it. I will barely remark, that as the improbability of sinister combinations will be in proportion to the dissimilarity in the genius of the two bodies, it must be politic to distinguish them from each other by every circumstance which will consist with a due harmony in all proper measures, and with the genuine principles of republican government.

. . . The necessity of a senate is not less indicated by the propensity of all single and numerous assemblies to yield to the impulse of sudden and violent passions, and to be seduced by factious leaders into intemperate and pernicious resolutions. Examples on this subject might be cited without number; and from proceedings within the United States, as well as from the history of other nations. But a position that will not be contradicted need not be proved. All that need be remarked is, that a body which is to correct this infirmity ought itself to be free from it, and consequently ought to be less numerous. It ought, moreover, to possess great firmness, and consequently ought to hold its authority by a tenure of considerable duration.

13.2. THE RULES COMMITTEE CONTROVERSY

The House Rules Committee has been flayed by critics as an instrument by which a small minority can keep the majority will from being served by Congress. The following remarks of Representative Gerald Flynn presage the alterations in the size of the Committee made at the beginning of the 87th Congress.

MR. FLYNN: Mr. Speaker, as we draw near to the close of this legislative session it becomes crystal clear to many of us here and to many citizens throughout the country that the rules of this House under which we operate have defects—defects that are working against the best interest of the people of the United States.

From *The Congressional Record*, 86th Congress, 2d Session, Vol. 106, No. 143 (August 26, 1960).

. . . It is only fitting and proper that this body should have a Rules Committee, a Rules Committee designed to direct the orderly flow of legislation onto this floor in order that consideration can be given to all bills coming before it offered by Members of this body. It is no different than the traffic cop that the police force has stationed at a busy corner downtown. It is the function of the traffic cop not to confiscate the car that you ride in, not to set up a blockade so you cannot go through, but to direct the traffic so that you and the others may pass in an orderly manner and reach your destination. That is the true function of the Rules Committee.

Under our rules we have made it possible for the members of that committee to usurp or to take unto themselves certain power, absolute power, that it never was the intention of this body to convey, powers that are too great for any one committee to have, because these men are able not only to stifle legislation introduced into this House or into the Senate, but they have the power of life and death over this legislation.

Let us look at this committee as presently set up.

These are 12 men; fine men individually, men of honor and integrity, men of great ability and leaders in this great House. Most of them are men with many years of service. But if six of these men refuse to pass out a bill that comes to their committee, it stays there indefinitely and dies there. Thereby they have the power of life and death over the bill and, like the traffic cop on the corner, they not only can direct the flow of legislation, but they can kill it just as if the traffic cop confiscated the car in which you were riding.

They say that the number of bills they hold up runs only to 7 to 10 percent of the bills that are referred to them. But what bills fall into this area? I will tell you what bills fall into this area. They are bills affecting the people, affecting the little people; they are the bills that are beneficial to people who do not have the money to hire a lobbyist, who do not have the money to hire somebody to come up here and represent them. Those bills are held in this committee and this is against the best interests of the people of this country. . . .

This is the greatest deliberative body in the world and this committee is denying the Members of this body an opportunity to debate, to discuss, to pass and vote upon a bill which is in the interests of the people of the United States, all the people of this great country. And if the rules of this House permit this, then the rules should be changed.

13.3. PROS AND CONS OF THE FILIBUSTER

Most people agree that majority rule is one of the principal components of democratic government. But is the public interest served if a majority by Senators Talmadge of Georgia and Javits of New York over filibuster-stifles minority interests? This question is at the base of the arguments ing in the Senate.

VIEWS OF SENATOR HERMAN TALMADGE

Any proposal for further limiting debate in the United States Senate is a matter of grave consequence which, by its very nature, demands that it not be acted upon capriciously or without the benefit of thorough study and full consideration of all its ramifications.

It is out of that deep conviction that I insisted upon comprehensive hearings on the eight resolutions which sought that end, that I have given long and careful study to the transcript of testimony taken at those hearings and to all related materials, and that I herewith set forth in the most earnest terms at my command the compelling reasons why Senate rule XXII must be upheld as written. . . .

Historically, freedom of debate in the Senate is not a party or sectional device. It has served the whole country and both political parties well at one time or another. History records the fact time and again that the benefits of free debate far outweigh the few instances where the privilege to speak thoroughly may have been abused—and only the most partisan would not admit there have been some abuses.

Any further concession on the part of proponents of free debate will have the disastrous eventual result of majority cloture. Then the process of erosion will turn to the seniority system and other long established and heretofore unchallenged procedures and precedents. . . .

Even a cursory study of constitutional history and an examination of contemporary documents penned at the time of the drafting of the Constitution and its approval by the States show beyond any doubt that the creation of the Senate, as a continuing council of States wherein each has an equal voice, was the price of forming the General Government.

At the formation of this Government the Constitutonal Convention stood for the protection of private economic interests; a stronger central authority; a stabilized monetary policy; orderly legal processes; and for a republican form of government as opposed to an unlimited democracy.

The whole motivating spirit of the Convention—not expressed but clearly understood—was to make the Nation safe from the tyranny of unchecked majorities. The intention is unmistakable as one may deduce from James Madison's own notes and also from the papers of most of the delegates. . . .

It is argued by the opponents of free debate that the Senate of

From U.S. Congress, Senate, *Report of the Committee on Rules and Administration,* 85th Congress, 2d Session (Senate Report No. 1509), 1958.

the United States is the only place in the world where the gag rule does not prevail.

My answer to that is: "So what?"

The patriots who established this Government were free men and did not elect to surrender their new and hard-won liberties nor to copy the governments of foreign lands where freedom either did not exist or came and went with the political tide. . . .

The Senate cannot legitimately be compared in any terms with either State senates or with the assemblies of foreign nations.

One reason given by those advocating that the Senate of the United States surrender its freedom of debate is that the House of Commons of the British Parliament has done so.

What they either forget or choose deliberately to ignore is that much of the difficulty experienced by Great Britain as a nation and as a world power has stemmed directly from the loss of freedom of debate in the House of Commons and a steady diminution in the power of the House of Lords. . . .

All of the great injustices of history have been committed in the name of unchecked and unbridled "majority rule." The late Senator James A. Reed of Missouri, in one of the most forceful speeches ever delivered before the Senate, observed with great truth:

The majority crucified Jesus Christ.

The majority burned the Christians at the stake.

The majority drove the Jews into exile and to the ghetto.

The majority established slavery.

The majority chained to stakes and surrounded with circles of flame martyrs through all the ages of the world's history.

The majority jeered when Columbus said the world was round.

The majority threw him into a dungeon for having discovered a new world.

The majority said that Galileo must recant or that Galileo must go to prison.

The majority cut off the ears of John Pym because he dared advocate the liberty of the press.

. . . . . .

Now is no time to forget the lessons of history.

Before tearing down a chamber that has served the United States and its people well, Senators should search for truth by asking themselves:

Are we so blind as not to realize that if free debate perishes in the Senate our leaders in the future will be rising like jacks-in-the-box to move the previous question?

Do we not know that this evil thing will become the weapon of the majority party or coalition to be resorted to habitually in stifling all opposition?

Do we not know that when such an event comes to pass minority thought and opinion will lie prostrate and defenseless against the tyrannical abuses of any transient majority that might for the moment occupy the seats of the Senate?

Have we forgotten that everyone, at one time or another, belongs to a minority?

Have we lost sight of the unchanging truth that unbridled majority sway without proper restraint is mob rule?

Are our memories so short that we have forgotten the maxim that free government destroying dissenting opinion, thereby destroys itself?

Have we forgotten that in such circumstances dictatorship of one form or another steps into the vacuum thus created to wrest all rights from the people, minorities and majorities alike?

The alternative to unlimited debate is gag rule, which was aptly defined by the late Senator Reed as "the last resort of the legislative scoundrel."

The issue at stake here is far more fundamental than any mere question of legislation. It is as basic as our freedom itself. Gag rule, and its stepchild, censorship, are abhorrent to and incompatible with our American heritage.

The Senate has proved itself worthy of the rules by which it now operates.

Common sense and the Nation's survival dictate that our time-honored procedures should not be subjected to whimsical tampering on the slightest provocation.

It is essential to our interests as a nation that we keep vital and inviolate our system of checks and balances.

VIEWS OF SENATOR JACOB JAVITS

I do not believe that the present rule XXII serves the purpose of deliberation within the Senate or of education of the public generally. No one questions those two objectives. What I do question is a delegation of the power and responsibility of the majority to a determined minority, which has been and can be again and again an arbitrary block to action, contrary to the will of the majority of this body and of the people to whom they are responsible. Indeed, it seems to me prophetic that this report is filed at an hour of basic crisis in the defense of our country when the weapons which challenge us are precisely so mortally dangerous because of the speed at which they may be effectively used to destroy us. In such a time—and there is nothing temporary about this new frame of reference—there is a justifiable demand for making our organs of decision conform to the challenge. How appropriate, then, to consider now a rule of debate which can and has paralyzed decision in the Senate and which can be used by a determined minority to paralyze it on any subject—not alone civil rights. Rule XXII as now written was archaic long before the first Russian earth satellite was launched and is even more so now. . . .

Rule XXII as it now reads provides that 2 calendar days after presentation to the Senate of a written motion for cloture signed by 16 Senators, cloture may be imposed by affirmative vote of two-thirds of the Senators "duly chosen and sworn" (i. e., 64). If such cloture motion be adopted each Senator is thereafter limited to a total of 1 hour's time in debate on the pending matter. The rule further provides that even this difficult cloture may *not* be imposed on any motion or resolution to change any of the standing rules of the Senate including rule XXII itself. (This further restriction is probably beyond the power of the Senate to adopt, as the advisory opinion of Vice President Nixon, January 4, 1957, concluded.)

Rule XXII prevents the imposition of cloture unless 64 Senators *appear* and *vote* in favor of a cloture motion. . . .

The ability to carry on a filibuster can affect the kind of legislation passed by the Senate even though no actual filibuster is undertaken. The incidence of a filibuster or the certain knowledge that a filibuster would be organized has made the majority come to terms before. The mere threat that a filibuster of great length would be undertaken against some proposal or unless amendment to a bill was accepted has in effect resulted in the majority of the Senate acquiescing in changes in legislation which otherwise they would probably not have considered wise or desirable. . . .

On the one hand, without question the southern Senators on the civil-rights issue had accomplished a great deal, from their point of view. Senator Russell of Georgia summed up this matter for the opposition in retrospect on August 30, 1957, when he said in the Senate:

When it is considered that there were only 18 out of 96 Senators, all of us suspect because we were from the South, who were willing to wage an all-out fight on this bill, I think that I can, in all modesty, say for myself and my associates that the legislative history of the Senate does not reveal as great a victory from so small a group as the one we attained.

At the same time, Senator Russell admitted that the use of the filibuster was often discussed by the southern bloc, but that it was generally decided to avoid it. This decision was not universally accepted. Senator Thurmond established a record of speaking for over 24 hours—a feat which turned out to be completely unrelated to effective opposition to the final version of the bill. It did, however, serve to emphasize, if it were necessary, that rule XXII contains a coercive power that could not be underestimated. . . .

If the men who conceived our Constitution had thought we

needed the concurrence of the majority of two Houses, the assent of the President, and in addition the forbearance of 33 Senators to make law, I assume they would have said so. If this additional check on governmental action is necessary, let us amend the Constitution. The standing rules of the Senate were not drafted in Philadelphia in 1787. The American people neither concurred in them nor agreed to be bound by them—nor did the States. In each Congress, as adopted or acquiesced in, and, to the extent they are constitutional, they bind our Senate procedure so long as they remain unchanged, but they are not the supreme law. They are not the bulwark of free speech and States rights; nor are they immutable.

In my study I have given close attention to the arguments put forward by many of those opposed to any change in rule XXII and who appeared before our subcommittee. Some of these are superficial and based upon an erroneous conception of our Government. However, there are impressive lines of reasoning employed in defense of the present wording of rule XXII, and much of this, too, was brought out during the hearings. . . .

On the first question, one may, of course, argue that the existence of rule XXII by which any substantial group of Senators can conduct a filibuster so as to act as a veto, constitutes a "power" which may be exercised on behalf of the States represented by the filibustering Senators; but it is the power neither of persuasion nor of public education. It is an arbitrary power unsanctioned by the Constitution and indeed in direct conflict with its spirit. . . .

There was a great question of the proper balance of State representation in the Congress of 1787. A study of the debates of the Constitutional Convention shows very clearly that the decision to establish 2 Houses, one to be based on a reference to population, and the other to have 2 Senators from each State regardless of size or population, was the compromise between the delegates from big States and the delegates from the small States. This was the only basis on which the small States would agree to join the Federal Union. This was the great compromise that gave the small States an equal measure of legislative power with the more populous States in this body.

As far as the big States are concerned, according to Madison and others devoted to the principle of proportional representation, they had given enough and more than enough when they finally agreed that each State should have two votes in the Senate. No one then dreamed that in the future Senators would want to upset this balance and add an additional check by a small minority of one-third upon the power of a majority of the Senate as so constituted. This, of course, was long prior to the time when John C. Calhoun developed his theory of concurrent majorities under which legislation favored by a majority in the country as a whole or in the Congress would be subject to the veto of a majority of each and every sectional interest in the country. . . .

Permitting a Senator or a group of Senators to talk for hours and days on any conceivable subject or on no subject in order to consume time and prevent the Senate from voting, affords no dignity to the Senate and adds nothing to its deliberative function. Reading recipes for "pot licker," "fried oysters," quoting from Aesop's Fables, and otherwise talking in utter irrelevancies does nothing to enhance the Senate's standing as a great deliberative body.

Senators have a right—and freely exercise it—to express their views on any question before the Senate or before the country. Without doubt it would be a violation of the letter and the spirit of the Constitution to deny or even seriously abridge the right of debate. But, it is also a most flagrant violation of the spirit of the Constitution to clothe this body with forms of procedure by which it may be blocked in the exercise of the legislative powers, and thereby suspended of every other function except that of speaking. The Senate has a duty to debate, but it is likewise a constitutional duty of a majority of this body to act, and with some reasonable expedition. We are obligated not only to pass laws, but also to pass them in time to meet the public need and the general welfare of the country.

13.4. LOBBYING BEFORE CONGRESS

In this selection, the author of Congress Makes a Law *discusses with members of the House Committee on Lobbying Activities his views on how lobbies influence Congress. He sees effective lobbying as "a reflection of interests shared by shifting coalitions."*

THE FIRST real move in the direction of full-employment legislation came in 1944 from an outside pressure group—the National Farmers' Union. Russell Smith of the National Farmers Union wrote a so-called full employment amendment to the pending Kilgore reconversion bill in the summer of 1944. This amendment, although never passed, was circulated around town by James Patton, president of the National Farmers' Union, and was picked up with enthusiasm by Senator James E. Murray, of Montana, who was at that time chairman of the War Contracts Subcommittee of the Senate Committee on Military Affairs.

After the 1944 fall election, one of Senator Murray's staff as-

From U.S. Congress, House, *Hearings Before the House Select Committee on Lobbying Activities,* 81st Congress, 2d Session, 1950 (Statement of Professor Stephen K. Bailey, March 27, 1950).

sistants, Mr. Bertram M. Gross, who was on loan from the Navy Department, was given the task of drafting a full-employment bill, using the Farmers' Union amendment as a point of departure. Gross immediately formed a drafting committee headed by himself, but including agency economists from the Budget Bureau, OPA, the Labor Department, the Department of Agriculture, the Social Security Board, and the War Manpower Commission. Russell Smith of the National Farmers' Union was also invited to attend the drafting sessions.

I should like to emphasize right here that the executive agency personnel who worked on bill drafting were invited by a legislative staff representative of a Senate subcommittee. The initiative, in other words, came from the Congress, not from the agencies. I emphasize this fact because a great deal of the soliciting of agency and private interest group aid behind or against the bill throughout its storming history came from Members of Congress and their staff assistants. How complicated this enterprise became can perhaps be illustrated by the fact that during the House fight, Congressman George Outland asked representatives of a number of supporting liberal and labor organizations to call upon their local chapters and membership throughout the country to write to President Truman, asking him to do everything he could do to persuade Democratic members on the House Committee on Expenditures to report out soon and favorably on the full-employment bill. This type of quadruple play from Congress to pressure groups to the President and back to Congress may be unusual, but I have reason to believe that double and triple plays initiated by, or with assists by, Members of Congress are not at all unusual. . . .

The staff solicited outside pressure-group support by aiding in the formulation and guidance of a so-called "continuations group," spearheaded by the Union for Democratic Action, but consisting of representatives of nearly 50 liberal and labor organizations. The most important of these organizations were the American Federation of Labor; Americans United for World Government; Brotherhood of Maintenance of Way Employees; Brotherhood of Railway Trainmen; Businessmen of America, Inc.; the CIO; the Council for Social Action of the Congregational Christian Churches; the Independent Citizens Committee of the Arts, Sciences, and Professions; the National Association for the Advancement of Colored People; . . .

The Senate staff carried on other types of activities in lining up pressure support. One of the most interesting techniques was a letter program. The staff built up a list of 1,500 names of "public-opinion formers" in the United States. The organizations and individuals canvassed included representatives of business, labor, agriculture, public organizations including religious, health, education and research, minority, welfare, public education, and civic groups, international and peace organizations, women's groups, veterans' organizations, local government officials, columnists and editors, and experts in the social sciences. The staff, over the signature of Senator Wagner, sent letters to these 1,500 individuals asking for comments and criticisms on the proposed bill. The design, of course, was among other things to build public interest and pressure support for S. 380.

Finally, the staff made a particular effort to split the opposition: that is, to line up representatives, particularly from business, agriculture, and veterans, who would oppose the conservative stands taken by various spokesmen for these key pressure confederations.

On the opposition side of the picture, the vast majority of the members of the House Committee on Expenditures, including the chairman, were bitterly opposed to the bill as introduced. The House committee, however, had no staff of its own and the members tended, consequently, to look to outside pressure groups for staff services. For instance, Congressman Will Whittington, who was the key man in writing the bill for House and conference consideration, solicited bill drafts from the United States Chamber of Commerce, the Committee for Economic Development, Dr. George Terborgh of the Machinery and Allied Products Institute, as well as from Mr. Fred Vinson, who was then Secretary of the Treasury. . . .

In the chapter in my book called Conservative Pressures, I have described in some detail the anti-full employment bill activities of organizations like the National Association of Manufacturers, the United States Chamber of Commerce, including its State and local affiliates, the Committee for Constitutional Government, and the American Farm Bureau Federation. Most of these groups conducted standard lobbying operations: preparing literature against the bill; conducting public opinion campaigns; testifying before congressional committees; writing and wiring individual Congressmen; and approaching Congressmen directly.

The one thing I should like to point out here is the close connection—or parallelism of ideas—which exists between the opinion leaders in big business and the opinion centers in agriculture. It seems to me significant that the National Association of Manufacturers sends editorial material all ready to go to print to 7,500 rural weekly newspapers and that it maintains a service called *Farm and Industry*—a release which it sends to 35,000 farm leaders.

When I studied the press clippings on the full-employment bill, I counted 72 editorial comments in 50 small-town dailies and weeklies. Of these 72 editorial comments, all except 5 were hostile to the original bill. I think it is interesting to note some of the following "coincidences": On February 20, 1945, without credit line, editorials attacking the bill appeared in the Zanesville (Ohio) Times Recorder and the Cheyenne (Wyo.) State Tribune. These editorials were identical. On September 7,

1945, the Clarksburg (W. Va.) Exponent published an editorial against the bill. On September 10, 1945, the identical editorial appeared in the Lima (Ohio) News. On September 7, 1945, identical editorials quoting anti-full-employment bill material prepared by the Committee for Constitutional Government appeared in the Macon (Ga.) Telegraph and the Cumberland (Md.) Times.

Since the editors and publishers of small-town and rural papers are generally important members of the local community and since Congressmen pay a good deal of attention to the home-town press, editorial decisions to select for publication hand-outs from the national opinion machines of big business have considerable significance.

Mr. Brown. Mr. Chairman, I happen to be a newspaperman. You mention a number of newspapers opposed to this bill and I notice that you mentioned the Farm Journal. It seems to me you have gone out of your way to mention the Farm Journal in connection with the Pew family. Is it your opinion the newspapers of the country and these editorial writers and publishers just swallow whatever is sent to them by any organization?

Mr. Bailey. No, sir.

Mr. Brown. Is it not true that editorials and articles and every kind of a press release you can imagine was sent out in favor of this bill to these same newspapers?

Mr. Bailey. Well, the groups who were in favor of the bill as originally introduced, whether it was a question of not having the money or the machinery by which to do this, were not able to get out to the rural press. . . .

. . . The only thing I would like to suggest, sir, is perhaps it would be interesting to the public to know where that material came from. I think it is important for the public to know where the opinions of the newspaper carriers have their origin.

I have no objection at all, certainly, to anyone publishing what he wants to and what he believes, and I am not accusing these editors of knuckling under to anybody. They make their selection among materials.

Mr. O'Hara. If there are editorials in favor of the legislation, are they identical? Where did they come from?

Mr. Bailey. Sir, I checked through the material pretty carefully in the press and I found no example of identical editorials where there were not by-lines on the side of the proponents of this particular bill. . . .

As far as my conclusions are concerned, and I have obviously hit only some of the highlights, they lead me to the conclusion that lobbying can be understood only as the reflection of interests shared by shifting coalitions made up by Members of Congress, outside pressures, and executive agencies. Because of training, background, or the recognition of important power factors in their own constituencies, legislators frequently turn for assistance to those groups or individuals in and out of the Government who are in a position to render service in a common cause. Agency and outside pressure groups return the compliment.

If this is a correct assumption, then it seems to me that your problem is the enormously complicated one of analyzing the interrelationships among private group interests, Members of Congress, and agency personnel. If lobbying were simply a one-way track, the problem could be solved in a hurry simply by putting the finger of responsibility upon individual Members of Congress who knuckle under to the importunities of outside pressures. But what is more natural than for a Congressman coming from a peanut-growing district to get together with a peanut lobbyist and a bureaucrat concerned with peanuts in the Department of Agriculture, to work out answers to the peanut problem. The initiative may come from the Congressman, from the agency, or from the lobbyist. The point of initiation is irrelevant. The fact of cooperation is not irrelevant.

13.5. A CRITIQUE OF GROUP THEORIES OF POLITICS

The following selection from Professor Schattschneider's recent book,
The Semi-Sovereign People, *offers an analysis of so-called pressure politics that avoids the brash dogmatism of both extreme critics and protagonists of this phenomenon. Schattschneider is a veteran observer of what has been called the group basis of politics.*

IT IS EXTREMELY unlikely that the vogue of group theories of politics would have attained its present status if its basic assumptions had not been first established by some concept of economic determinism. The economic interpretation of politics has always appealed to those political philosophers who have sought a single prime mover, a sort of philosopher's stone of political science around which to organize their ideas. The search for a single, ultimate cause has something to do with the attempt to explain *everything* about politics in terms of group concepts. The logic of economic determinism is to *identify the origins of conflict and to assume the conclusion.* This kind of thought has some of the earmarks of an illusion. The somnambulatory quality of thinking in this field appears also in the tendency of research to deal only with successful pressure campaigns or the willingness of scholars to be satisfied with having placed pressure groups on the scene of the crime without following through to

From Elmer E. Schattschneider. *The Semi-Sovereign People* (New York: Holt, Rinehart and Winston, Inc., 1960), pp. 36–43.

see if the effect can really be attributed to the cause. What makes this kind of thinking remarkable is the fact that in political contests there are as many failures as there are successes. Where in the literature of pressure politics are the failures?

Students of special-interest politics need a more sophisticated set of intellectual tools than they have developed thus far. The theoretical problem involved in the search for a single cause is that all power relations in a democracy are reciprocal. Trying to find the original cause is like trying to find the first wave of the ocean.

Can we really assume that we know all that is to be known about a conflict if we understand its *origins?* Everything we know about politics suggests that a conflict is likely to change profoundly as it becomes political. . . . It is extremely difficult to predict the outcome of a fight by watching its beginning because we do not even know who else is going to get into the conflict. The logical consequence of the exclusive emphasis on the determinism of the private origins of conflict is to assign zero value to the political process.

The very expression "pressure politics" invites us to misconceive the role of special-interest groups in politics. The word "pressure" implies the use of some kind of force, a form of intimidation, something other than reason and information, to induce public authorities to act against their own best judgment. . . .

It is hard to imagine a more effective way of saying that Congress has no mind or force of its own or that Congress is unable to invoke new forces that might alter the equation.

. . . . . .

Moreover, the notion of "pressure" distorts the image of the power relations involved. *Private conflicts are taken into the public arena precisely because someone wants to make certain the power ratio among the private interests most immediately involved shall not prevail.* To treat a conflict as a mere test of the strength of the private interests is to leave out the most significant factors. This is so true that it might indeed be said that the only way to preserve private power ratios is to keep conflicts out of the public arena. . . .

. . . The assumption is that conflict is monopolized narrowly by the parties immediately concerned. There is no room for a majority when conflict is defined so narrowly. It is a great deficiency of the group theory that it has found no place in the political system for the majority. The force of the majority is of an entirely different order of magnitude, something not to be measured by pressure-group standards.

Instead of attempting to exterminate all political forms, organizations, and alignments that do not qualify as pressure groups, would it not be better to attempt to make a synthesis, covering the whole political system and finding a place for all kinds of political life?

One possible synthesis of pressure politics and party politics might be produced by *describing politics as the socialization of conflict.* That is to say, the political process is a sequence: conflicts are initiated by highly motivated, high-tension groups so directly and immediately involved that it is difficult for them to see the justice of competing claims. As long as the conflicts of these groups remain *private* (carried on in terms of economic competition, reciprocal denial of goods and services, private negotiations, and bargaining, struggles for corporate control or competition for membership), no political proces is initiated. Conflicts become political only when an attempt is made to involve the wider public. Pressure politics might be described as a stage in the socialization of conflict. This analysis makes pressure politics an integral part of all politics, including party politics.

One of the characteristic points of origin of pressure politics is a breakdown of the business community. The flight to government is perpetual. Something like this is likely to happen wherever there is a point of contact between competing power systems. It is the *losers in intrabusiness conflict who seek redress from public authority. The dominant business interests resist appeals to the government.* The role of the government as the patron of the defeated private interest sheds light on its function as the critic of private power relations.

Since the contestants in private conflicts are apt to be unequal in strength, it follows that *the most powerful special interests want private settlements* because they are able to dictate the outcome as long as the conflict remains private. Therefore, it is the weak, not the strong, who appeal to public authority for relief. It is the weak who want to socialize conflict, i.e.; to involve more and more people in the conflict until the balance of forces is changed. . . . It is the function of public authority to *modify private power relations by enlarging the scope of the conflict.* Nothing could be more mistaken than to suppose that public authority merely registers the dominance of the strong over the weak. The mere existence of public order has already ruled out a great variety of forms of private pressure. Nothing could be more confusing than to suppose that the refugees from the business community who come to Congress for relief and protection *force* Congress to do their bidding.

. . . . . .

It is probably a mistake to assume that pressure politics is the typical or even the most important relation between government and business. The pressure group is by no means the perfect instrument of the business community. . . . The most elementary considerations of strategy call for the business community to develop some kind of common policy more broadly based than any special-interest group is likely to be.

. . . . . .

The attempt to mobilize a united front of the whole business community does not resemble the classical concept of pressure politics. . . . The search is for a broad base of political mobilization grounded on the strategic need for political organization on a wider scale than is possible in the case of the historical pressure group. Once the business community begins to think in terms of a larger scale of political organization the Republican party looms large in business politics.

. . . . . .

The Republican party has played a major role in *the political organization of the business community,* a far greater role than many students of politics seem to have realized. The influence of business in the Republican party is great, but it is never absolute because business is remarkably dependent on the party. The business community is too small, it arouses too much antagonism, and its aims are too narrow to win the support of a popular majority. The political education of business is a function of the Republican party that can never be done so well by anyone else.

. . . The success of special interests in Congress is due less to the "pressure" exerted by these groups than it is due to the fact that Republican members of Congress are committed in advance to a general probusiness attitude. The notion that business groups coerce Republican congressmen into voting for their bills underestimates the whole Republican posture in American politics.

. . . The fact that business has not become hopelessly divided and that it has retained great influence in American politics has been due chiefly to the over-all mediating role played by the Republican party. There has never been a pressure group or a combination of pressure groups capable of performing this function.

14

The Grand Inquest

14.1. INVESTIGATION AS AN ADJUNCT OF LEGISLATION

How extensive is the power of Congress to conduct investigations? In this decision in McGrain v. Daugherty *in 1927, the Supreme Court sanctions broad use of the investigatory power as a necessary aid in obtaining information the legislature needs to pass laws.*

MR. JUSTICE VAN DEVANTER delivered the opinion of the court. . . .

. . . . . .

We are of opinion that the power of inquiry—with process to enforce it—is an essential and appropriate auxiliary to the legislative function. It was so regarded and employed in American legislatures before the Constitution was framed and ratified. Both houses of Congress took this view of it early in their history—the House of Representatives with the approving votes of Mr. Madison and other members whose service in the convention which framed the Constitution gives special significance to their action—and both houses have employed the power accordingly up to the present time. The acts of 1798 and 1857, judged by their comprehensive terms, were intended to recognize the existence of this power in both houses and to enable them to employ it "more effectually" than before. So, when their practice in the matter is appraised according to the circumstances in which it was begun and to those in which it has been continued, it falls nothing short of a practical construction, long continued, of the constitutional provisions respecting their powers, and therefore should be taken as fixing the meaning of those provisions, if otherwise doubtful.

We are further of opinion that the provisions are not of doubtful

From *McGrain* v. *Daugherty*, 273 U.S. 135 (1927).

236

meaning, but, as was held by this court in the cases we have reviewed, are intended to be effectively exercised, and therefore to carry with them such auxiliary powers as are necesary and appropriate to that end. . . .

A legislative body cannot legislate wisely or effectively in the absence of information respecting the conditions which the legislation is intended to affect or change; and where the legislative body does not itself possess the requisite information—which not infrequently is true—recourse must be had to others who do possess it. Experience has taught that mere requests for such information often are unavailing, and also that information which is volunteered is not always accurate or complete; so some means of compulsion are essential to obtain what is needed. All this was true before and when the Constitution was framed and adopted. In that period the power of inquiry—with enforcing process—was regarded and employed as a necessary and appropriae attribute of the power to legislate—indeed, was treated as inhering in it. Thus there is ample warrant for thinking, as we do, that the constitutional provisions which commit the legislative function to the two houses are intended to include this attribute to the end that the function may be effectively exercised.

The contention is earnestly made on behalf of the witness that this power of inquiry, if sustained, may be abusively and oppressively exerted. If this be so, it affords no ground for denying the power. The same contention might be directed against the power to legislate, and of course would be unavailing. We must assume, for present purposes, that neither house will be disposed to exert the power beyond its proper bounds, or without due regard to the rights of witnesses. But if, contrary to this assumption, controlling limitations or restrictions are disregarded, the decisions in *Kilbourn* v. *Thompson* and *Marshall* v. *Gordon* point to admissible measures of relief. And it is a necessary deduction from the decisions in *Kilbourn* v. *Thompson* and *In re Chapman* that a witness rightfully may refuse to answer where the bounds of the power are exceeded or the questions are not pertinent to the matter under inquiry.

. . . . . .

It is quite true that the resolution directing the investigation does not in terms avow that it is intended to be in aid of legislation; but it does show that the subject to be investigated was the administration of the Department of Justice—whether its functions were being properly discharged or were being neglected or misdirected, and particularly whether the Attorney General and his assistants were performing or neglecting their duties in respect of the institution and prosecution of proceedings to punish crimes and enforce appropriate remedies against the wrongdoers—specific instances of alleged neglect being recited. Plainly the subject was one on which legislation could be had and would be materially aided by the information which the investigation was calculated to elicit. This becomes manifest when it is reflected that the functions of the Department of Justice, the powers and duties of the Attorney General and the duties of his assistants, are all subject to regulation by congressional legislation, and that the department is maintained and its activities are carried on under such appropriations as in the judgment of Congress are needed from year to year.

. . . . . .

We conclude that the investigation was ordered for a legitimate object; that the witness wrongfully refused to appear and testify before the committee and was lawfully attached; that the Senate is entitled to have him give testimony pertinent to the inquiry, either at its bar or before the committee; and that the district court erred in discharging him from custody under the attachment.

14.2. A CRITIQUE OF LEGISLATIVE INVESTIGATIONS

Bitter charges against congressional "star-chamber" techniques have focused attention in recent years on the problems of congressional investigations. Here a prominent lawyer criticizes the techniques and consequences of the late Senator McCarthy's investigations, among others, and calls for able, fair-minded, and responsible leadership of investigating committees.

THE ISSUES and abuses that we have discussed in this chapter, underlined by the tensions and emotions awakened by controversial investigations and investigators, have now led to a veritable flood of proposals for "codes of fair practices" to govern Congressional investigative procedures. During the . . . Eighty-third Congress, bills and resolutions embodying such codes were introduced by Senator Estes Kefauver of Tennessee (for himself and eighteen other Democratic Senators), Senators Paul Douglas of Illinois and Prescott Bush of Connecticut, and by Representatives Javits, Keating, and Celler of New York, Scott of Pennsylvania, and Frelinghuysen of New Jersey. Numerous private organizations and individuals have also engaged in code-drafting, and in New York State the Legislature during its 1954 session enacted a statutory code to govern the procedures of its investigative committees and commissions.

Some of these proposed codes are more extensive and drastic

From Telford Taylor, *Grand Inquest* (New York: Simon and Schuster, Inc., 1955), *passim*, pp. 252–262.

than others, but there is a high degree of similarity among them. Nearly all provide that witnesses shall have the right of counsel, and some go on to specify that the attorney may raise procedural or substantive objections, ask his client questions to bring out favorable evidence, and generally conduct himself more or less like a lawyer in a courtroom.

Very commonly, too, these codes provide for notice to the witness in advance of his appearance, specifying with reasonable precision the matters about which he is to be questioned. The witness is authorized to make a statement of his own in addition to answering questions, and is to be furnished with, or given access to, a copy of his testimony at its conclusion.

Beyond these provisions, however, the differences among the proposals are much greater. Some of them give individuals who have been unfavorably mentioned the right to appear and reply, to call witnesses in their own behalf, and to cross-examine hostile witnesses. Usually, however, the extent to which these rights may be availed of is limited in some way, so that investigations will not become uncontrollable or so protracted as to destroy their usefulness. The proposals with respect to visual publicity show little agreement, but it is most commonly prescribed that during the testimony the witness cannot be photographed or put on television if he objects.

In addition to protection for witnesses, the codes usually contain rules governing the initiation of investigations, issuances of subpoenas, executive sessions, and reports. "One-man committees" are frequently prohibited, with the requirement that members representing both major political parties must be present at hearings. The main purpose of all of these is to guard against an irresponsible monopoly of the committee's powers by the chairman, and they are plainly stimulated by the uninhibited methods of Senator McCarthy, Congressman Velde, and other chairmen who have treated their committees as their private property.

But the respect in which the proposed codes vary most widely is that of how they are to be enforced. This question is of primary importance, particularly from the standpoint of witnesses, who will be chiefly interested in knowing what they can do and what relief they can obtain if the rules are broken. . . .

. . . the fact is that these proposals cannot all be tied in a single bundle. Some of them are simple and easily enforceable, such as the witness' right to the effective assistance of counsel, to reasonable notice of the time and subjects of his appearance, to make a statement, and to have access to the record of his testimony. . . . There is, it seems to me, no reason why these should not be enacted into statutory law as absolute requirements of investigative procedure, so that Congress' power to punish recalcitrant witnesses would be conditioned on its observance of these elemental rules of fairness.

But when we turn to propositions for giving persons under investigation the right to call witnesses in their own behalf and to cross-examine hostile witnesses, we must guard against encumbering the investigative power and destroying its flexibility and efficacy. Courts are concerned with individual rights and liabilities, and their procedures are governed accordingly. Legislative committees have broader functions which require looser procedural standards; the informing function will wither if unduly circumscribed. A committee investigating social, economic or political problems cannot be required to weigh every disputed question of fact as if it were a judicial tribunal. I do not believe that it is feasible or practical to lay down rigid requirements with respect to the summoning and cross-examination of witnesses without undermining the investigative process itself.

There is another and equally serious objection. The only method of law enforcement that is consonant with our constitutional democracy is judicial enforcement. The more investigating committees are hedged about with legal restrictions on their procedures, therefore, the more the courts would be called upon to perform a supervisory function. Increasingly, the committees would appear to be inferior tribunals. subject to appellate review by the courts.

But this is not the relationship envisaged by the Constitution, or embodied in our governmental traditions. . . .

The elected members of legislative bodies are politicians, whose duty it is to take into account the most varied and often conflicting views and pressures in the processes of election and legislation. Judges, in contrast, are under a solemn obligation to be non-political, and to exclude extraneous pressures from the field of decision. It is a total incompatibility, not of person but of function, that renders futile and unwise any effort to assimiliate an investigative committee to a court. . . .

In fact, one of the dangers of these far-reaching proposals for reform of investigative procedures is that, in the event of their adoption, the public would conclude that committee hearings had been turned into real trials, in the course of which guilt or innocence might be determined. It would, I believe, be far more useful for Congress to reaffirm that investigations are *not* trials, and to adopt as legally mandatory a few simple and basic reforms. . . . Some others—such as the right of an individual accused before a committee to call and cross-examine witnesses—might be tried out as voluntary, non-mandatory committee practices. . . . Fundamentally, the problem of Congressional investigations is a political rather than a legal problem, and must be dealt with by political means. It is a reflection of the cold civil war, and so long as Congressmen and Senators so gauge the temper of the country that they are unwilling to put a curb on the inquisitions, there is little enough that can be accomplished by new regulations and statutes. But there are, I believe, two things that Congress might do—both simple and neither experimental—that would bring worthwhile improvements over the present situation.

These two propositions relate to starting investigations in the first instance, and to stopping them when they overlap their authority and assert powers of inquiry which they do not rightfully possess. They relate, in short, to *initiation* and to *challenge*. For it is clear that it has become far too easy—especially in the Senate—to set in motion an investigation backed by the power of subpoena. And it is equally plain that present procedures make it far too risky a business to test the power of a Congressional committee to make an inquiry, because the probable penalty for an unfounded challenge, even if based on honest mistake, is a jail sentence. In each case, something can and should be done about it. . . .

. . . by whom and how was Senator McCarthy's recent investigation of the Army Signal Corps laboratories at Fort Monmouth initiated and authorized? The Senate itself never considered the matter, nor so far as has been learned, did the other members of the Government Operations Committee or its Subcommittee on Investigations. There was no responsible opinion among government officials, civil or miltary, that a Congressional investigation at Fort Monmouth was necessary or desirable. The entire affair was the brainchild of Senator McCarthy and one or two members of his staff.

That, however, was all that was required to launch the inquiry, because: (1) Congress, in the Legislative Reorganization Act of 1946, had given the Government Operations Committee, like all standing Senate committees, permanent and general power of subpoena, which can be used in support of the very broad range of subjects within the purview of each committee; and (2) the members of the Government Operations Committee, like many of our legislators, displayed small sense of responsibility in the use of Congress' investigative power, and allowed Senator McCarthy to take off on a frolic of his own without paying sufficient attention to the matter. . . .

I believe, accordingly, that a first, simple, and highly desirable step in the rehabilitation of Congressional investigations would be to repeal the provision of the Legislative Reorganization Act which gives permanent subpoena power to all the standing committees of the Senate, and return to the requirements that had proved their value for over 150 years before 1946. Of course, this is no sure preventive of unnecessary or misdirected investigations, for the House and Senate are themselves quite capable of error in this regard. Only last year the House launched the second investigation of tax-exempt foundations in as many sessions, which proved not only shockingly duplicative and wasteful, but so incredibly misconducted as to disgrace a debating society at a reformatory for wayward and backward children. In both Houses of Congress a rebirth of restraint, common sense, and courage is necessary to check investigative excesses. Repeal of the Senate committees' permanent subpoena power might be hoped to trigger a renaissance of legislative decorum.

My second suggestion concerns the method by which the investigative power is to be enforced and, when unlawfully exercised, how it is to be checked. . . .

For the benefit of both committees and witnesses, . . . there should be a better method—speedier and more effective for the committee and less hazardous for the witness—to test and enforce investigative power. And such a method can be successfully developed along the lines of the New York statute that Judge Daly applied in 1855—that is, enforcement of the committee's process by court order. It is a procedure well-suited to obtain for the committee the information to which it is entitled, and it permits the witness to resist queries that he believes to be unauthorized and test the committee's power without incurring the risk of prosecution.

This means of enforcement is widely and successfully used in many comparable situations. Congress early resorted to it for the benefit of administrative agencies (which generally have no contempt power), to enable them to compel testimony by applying for a court order, disobedience to which is punished by the court as a contempt. This is now a standard form of judicial proceeding in connection with administrative agencies, which has been upheld and applied by the courts in many cases. It is entirely adaptable to legislative committee investigations, and in fact has twice been authorized for joint investigating committees of the two Houses of Congress.

Utilization of this procedure today, in place of criminal prosecution, would give investigating committees speedy and direct compulsory process, and would relieve witnesses of the grave and unnecessary hazards which now attend the testing of legal questions. The over-all result, in Representative Kenneth Keating's words, would be "salutary for everyone concerned."

14.3. SCOPE OF THE INVESTIGATORY POWER

What limitations are there on Congress' investigative power? In this landmark decision, the Court administers a verbal spanking to the House Committee on Un-American Activities for its conduct of a loyalty investigation. The Watkins *decision also exhorts Congress to be more explicit in stating the purpose of its investigations and the powers of its committees.*

MR. CHIEF JUSTICE WARREN delivered the opinion of the Court.

This is a review . . . of a conviction . . . for "contempt of Congress." The misdemeanor is alleged to have been committed during a hearing before a congressional investigating committee. It is not the case of a truculent or contumacious witness who refuses to answer all questions or who, by boisterous or discourteous conduct, disturbs the decorum of the committee room. Petitioner was prosecuted for refusing to make certain disclosures which he asserted to be beyond the authority of the committee to demand. The controversy thus rests upon fundamental principles of the power of the Congress and the limitations upon that power. We approach the questions presented with conscious awareness of the far-reaching ramifications that can follow from a decision of this nature. . . .

The character of petitioner's testimony on these matters can perhaps best be summarized by the Government's own appraisal in its brief:

A more complete and candid statement of his past political associations and activities (treating the Communist Party for present purposes as a mere political party) can hardly be imagined. Petitioner certainly was not attempting to conceal or withhold from the Committee his own past political associations, predilections, and preferences. Furthermore, petitioner told the Committee that he was entirely willing to identify for the Committee, and answer any questions it might have concerning, "those persons whom I knew to be members of the Communist Party," provided that, "to [his] best knowledge and belief," they still were members of the Party. . . .

The Subcommittee, too, was apparently satisfied with petitioner's disclosures. After some further discussion elaborating on the statement, counsel for the Committee turned to another aspect of Rumsey's testimony. Rumsey had identified a group of persons whom he had known as members of the Communist Party, and counsel began to read this list of names to petitioner. Petitioner stated that he did not know several of the persons. Of those whom he did know, he refused to tell whether he knew them to have been members of the Communist Party. He explained to the Subcommittee why he took such a position:

I am not going to plead the fifth amendment, but I refuse to answer certain questions that I believe are outside the proper scope of your committee's activities. I will answer any questions which this committee puts to me about myself. I will also answer questions about those persons whom I knew to be members of the Communist Party and whom I believe still are. I will not, however, answer any questions with respect to others with whom I associated in the past. . . .

We start with several basic premises on which there is general agreement. The power of the Congress to conduct investigations is inherent in the legislative process. That power is broad. It encompasses inquiries

From *Watkins* v. *United States,* 354 U.S. 178 (1957).

concerning the administration of existing laws as well as proposed or possibly needed statutes. It concludes surveys of defects in our social, economic or political system for the purpose of enabling the Congress to remedy them. It comprehends probes into departments of the Federal Government to expose corruption, inefficiency or waste. But broad as is this power of inquiry, it is not unlimited. There is no general authority to expose the private affairs of individuals without justification in terms of the functions of the Congress. This was freely conceded by the Solicitor General in his argument of this case. Nor is the Congress a law enforcement or trial agency. These are functions of the executive and judicial departments of government. No inquiry is an end in itself; it must be related to and in furtherance of a legitimate task of the Congress. Investigations conducted solely for the personal aggrandizement of the investigators or to "punish" those investigated are indefensible.

It is unquestionably the duty of all citizens to cooperate with the Congress in its efforts to obtain the facts needed for intelligent legislative action. It is their unremitting obligation to respond to subpoenas, to respect the dignity of the Congress and its committees and to testify fully with respect to matters within the province of proper investigation. This, of course, assumes that the constitutional rights of witnesses will be respected by the Congress as they are in a court of justice. The Bill of Rights is applicable to investigations as to all forms of governmental action. Witnesses cannot be compelled to give evidence against themselves. They cannot be subjected to unreasonable search and seizure. Nor can the First Amendment freedoms of speech, press, religion, or political belief and association be abridged. . . .

In the decade following World War II, there appeared a new kind of congressional inquiry unknown in prior periods of American history. Principally this was the result of the various investigations into the threat of subversion of the United States Government, but other subjects of congressional interest also contributed to the changed scene. This new phase of legislative inquiry involved a broad-scale intrusion into the lives and affairs of private citizens. It brought before the courts novel questions of the appropriate limits of congressional inquiry. Prior cases, like Kilbourn, McGrain and Sinclair, had defined the scope of investigative power in terms of the inherent limitations of the sources of that power. In the more recent cases, the emphasis shifted to problems of accommodating the interest of the Government with the rights and privileges of individuals. The central theme was the application of the Bill of Rights as a restraint upon the assertion of governmental power in this form. . . .

Abuses of the investigative process may imperceptibly lead to abridgment of protected freedoms. The mere summoning of a witness and compelling him to testify, against his will, about his beliefs, expressions or associations is a measure of governmental interference. And when those forced revelations concern matters that are unorthodox, unpopular, or even hateful to the general public, the reaction in the life of the witness may be disastrous. This effect is even more harsh when it is past beliefs, expressions or associations that are disclosed and judged by current standards rather than those contemporary with the matters exposed. Nor does the witness alone suffer the consequences. Those who are identified by witnesses and thereby placed in the same glare of publicity are equally subject to public stigma, scorn and obloquy. . . .

Petitioner has earnestly suggested that the difficult questions of protecting these rights from infringement by legislative inquiries can be surmounted in this case because there was no public purpose served in his interrogation. His conclusion is based upon the thesis that the Subcommittee was engaged in a program of exposure for the sake of exposure. The sole purpose of the inquiry, he contends, was to bring down upon himself and others the violence of public reaction because of their past beliefs, expressions and associations. In support of this argument, petitioner has marshalled an impressive array of evidence that some Congressmen have believed that such was their duty, or part of it.

We have no doubt that there is no congressional power to expose for the sake of exposure. The public is, of course, entitled to be informed concerning the workings of its government. That cannot be inflated into a general power to expose where the predominant result can only be an invasion of the private rights of individuals. But a solution to our problem is not to be found in testing the motives of committee members for this purpose. Such is not our function. Their motives alone would not vitiate an investigation which had been instituted by a House of Congress if that assembly's legislative purpose is being served. . . .

An essential premise in this situation is that the House or Senate shall have instructed the committee members on what they are to do with the power delegated to them. It is the responsibility of the Congress, in the first instance, to insure that compulsory process is used only in furtherance of a legislative purpose. That requires that the instructions to an investigating committee spell out that group's jurisdiction and purpose with sufficient particularity. Those instructions are embodied in the authorizing resolution. . . .

The Committee on Un-American Activities, as a whole or by subcommittee, is authorized to make from time to time investigations of (i) the extent, character, and objects of un-American propaganda activities in the United states, (ii) the diffusion within the United States of subversive and un-American propaganda that is instigated from foreign countries or of a domestic origin and attacks the principle of the form of government as guaranteed by our Constitution, and (iii) all other questions in relation thereto that would aid Congress in any necessary remedial legislation.

It would be difficult to imagine a less explicit authorizing resolution. Who can define the meaning of "un-American"? What is that single, solitary "principle of the form of government as guaranteed by our Constitution"? There is no need to dwell upon the language, however. At one time, perhaps, the resolution might have been read narrowly to confine the Committee to the subject of propaganda. The events that have transpired in the fifteen years before the interrogation of petitioner make such a construction impossible at this date.

The members of the Committee have clearly demonstrated that they did not feel themselves restricted in any way to propaganda in the narrow sense of the word. Unquestionably the Committee conceived of its task in the grand view of its name. Un-American activities were its target, no matter how or where manifested. Notwithstanding the broad purview of the Committee's experience, the House of Representatives repeatedly approved its continuation. Five times it extended the life of the special committee. Then it made the group a standing committee of the House. A year later, the Committee's charter was embodied in the Legislative Reorganization Act. On five occasions, at the beginning of sessions of Congress, it has made the authorizing resolution part of the rules of the House. On innumerable occasions, it has passed appropriation bills to allow the Committee to continue its efforts.

Combining the language of the resolution with the construction it has been given, it is evident that the preliminary control of the Committee exercised by the House of Representatives is slight or non-existent. No one could reasonably deduce from the charter the kind of investigation that the Committee was directed to make. . . .

The Government contends that the public interest at the core of the investigations of the Un-American Activities Committee is the need by the Congress to be informed of efforts to overthrow the Government by force and violence so that adequate legislative safeguards can be erected. From this core, however, the Committee can radiate outward infinitely to any topic thought to be related in some way to armed insurrection. The outer reaches of this domain are known only by the content of "un-American activities." Remoteness of subject can be aggravated by a probe for a depth of detail even farther removed from any basis of legislative action. A third dimension is added when the investigators turn their attention to the past to collect minutiae on remote topics, on the hypothesis that the past may reflect upon the present. . . .

The appropriate statute . . . provides:

Every person who having been summoned as a witness by the authority of either House of Congress to give testimony or to produce papers upon any matter under inquiry before either House, or any joint committee established by a joint or concurrent resolution of the two Houses of Congress, or any committee of either House of Congress, willfully makes default, or who, having appeared, refuses to answer any question pertinent to the question under inquiry, shall be deemed guilty of a misdemeanor, punishable by a fine of not more than $1,000 nor less than $100 and imprisonment in a common jail for not less than one month nor more than twelve months.

In fulfillment of their obligation under this statute, the courts must accord to the defendants every right which is guaranteed to defendants in all other criminal cases. Among these is the right to have available, through a sufficiently precise statute, information revealing the standard of criminality before the commission of the alleged offense. Applied to persons prosecuted under § 192, this raises a special problem in that the statute defines the crime as a refusal to answer "any question pertinent to the question under inquiry." Part of the standard of criminality, therefore, is the pertinency of the questions propounded to the witness.

The problem attains proportion when viewed from the standpoint of the witness who appears before a congressional committee. He must decide at the time the questions are propounded whether or not to answer . . . the witness acts at his peril. He is . . . bound rightly to construe the statute. . . . An erroneous determination on his part, even if made in the utmost good faith, does not exculpate him if the court should later rule that the questions were pertinent to the question under inquiry.

It is obvious that a person compelled to make this choice is entitled to have knowledge of the subject to which the interrogation is deemed pertinent. That knowledge must be available with the same degree of explicitness and clarity that the Due Process Clause requires in the expression of any element of a criminal offense. The "vice of vagueness" must be avoided here as in all other crimes. . . .

The Government believes that the topic of inquiry before the Subcommittee concerned Communist infiltration in labor. In his introductory remarks, the Chairman made reference to a bill, then pending before the Committee, which would have penalized labor unions controlled or dominated by persons who were, or had been, members of a "Communist-action" organization, as defined in the Internal Security Act of 1950. The Subcommittee, it is contended, might have been endeavoring to determine the extent of such a problem.

This view is corroborated somewhat by the witnesses who preceded and followed petitioner before the Subcommittee. Looking at the entire hearings, however, there is strong reason to doubt that the subject revolved about labor matters. The published transcript is entitled: Investigation of Communist Activities in the Chicago Area, and six of the nine witnesses had no connection with labor at all. . . .

. . . The conclusions we have reached in this case will not prevent the Congress, through its committees, from obtaining any information it needs for the proper fulfillment of its role in our scheme of government.

The legislature is free to determine the kinds of data that should be collected. It is only those investigations that are conducted by use of compulsory process that give rise to a need to protect the rights of individuals against illegal encroachment. That protection can be readily achieved through procedures which prevent the separation of power from responsibility and which provide the constitutional requisites of fairness for witnesses. A measure of added care on the part of the House and the Senate in authorizing the use of compulsory process and by their committees in exercising that power would suffice. That is a small price to pay if it serves to uphold the principles of limited, constitutional government without constricting the power of the Congress to inform itself.

The judgment of the Court of Appeals is reversed, and the case is remanded to the District Court with instructions to dismiss the indictment.

14.4. A MORE RECENT JUDICIAL VIEW

Two years after the Watkins *decision, the Supreme Court was again called upon to construe the legality of questioning of witnesses by the House Committee on Un-American Activities. In this 5–4 decision, the justices uphold the Committee's actions and reject the claim that Congress has violated the petitioner's First Amendment rights.*

MR. JUSTICE HARLAN delivered the opinion of the Court.

Once more the Court is required to resolve the conflicting constitutional claims of congressional power and of an individual's right to resist its exercise. The congressional power in question concerns the internal process of Congress in moving within its legislative domain; it involves the utilization of its committees to secure "testimony needed to enable it efficiently to exercise a legislative function belonging to it under the Constitution." . . .

The congressional power of inquiry, its range and scope, and an individual's duty in relation to it, must be viewed in proper perspective. . . . The power and the right of resistance to it are to be judged in the concrete, not on the basis of abstractions. In the present case congressional efforts to learn the extent of a nationwide, indeed worldwide, problem have brought one of its investigating committees into the field of education. Of course, broadly viewed, inquiries cannot be made into the teaching that is pursued in any of our educational institutions. When academic teaching-freedom and its corollary learning-freedom, so essential to the well-being of the Nation, are claimed, this Court will always be on the

From *Barenblatt v. United States*, 360 U.S. 109 (1959).

alert against intrusion by Congress into this constitutionally protected domain. But this does not mean that the Congress is precluded from interrogating a witness merely because he is a teacher. An educational institution is not a constitutional sanctuary from inquiry into matters that may otherwise be within the constitutional legislative domain merely for the reason that inquiry is made of someone within its walls. . . .

Pursuant to a subpoena, and accompanied by counsel, petitioner on June 28, 1954, appeared as a witness before this congressional Subcommittee. After answering a few preliminary questions and testifying that he had been a graduate student and teaching fellow at the University of Michigan from 1947 to 1950 and an instructor in psychology at Vassar College from 1950 to shortly before his appearance before the Subcommittee, petitioner objected generally to the right of the Subcommittee to inquire into his "political" and "religious" beliefs or any "other personal and private affairs" or "associational activities," upon grounds set forth in a previously prepared memorandum which he was allowed to file with the Subcommittee. Thereafter petitioner specifically declined to answer each of the following five questions:

> Are you now a member of the Communist Party? (Count One.)
> Have you ever been a member of the Communist Party? (Count Two.)
> Now, you have stated that you knew Francis Crowley. Did you know Francis Crowley as a member of the Communist Party? (Count Three.)
> Were you ever a member of the Haldane Club of the Communist Party while at the University of Michigan? (Count Four.)
> Were you a member while a student of the University of Michigan Council of Arts, Sciences, and Professions? (Count Five.)

In each instance the grounds of refusal were those set forth in the prepared statement. Petitioner expressly disclaimed reliance upon "the Fifth Amendment."

Following receipt of the Subcommittee's report of these occurrences the House duly certified the matter to the District of Columbia United States Attorney for contempt proceedings. An indictment in five Counts, each embracing one of petitioner's several refusals to answer, ensued. With the consent of both sides the case was tried to the court without a jury, and upon conviction under all Counts a general sentence of six months' imprisonment and a fine of $250 was imposed. . . .

Petitioner's various contentions resolve themselves into three propositions: First, the compelling of testimony by the Subcommittee was neither legislatively authorized nor constitutionally permissible because of the vagueness of Rule XI of the House of Representatives, Eighty-third Congress, the charter of authority of the parent Committee. Second, petitioner was not adequately apprised of the pertinency of the Subcommittee's questions to the subject matter of the inquiry. Third, the questions petitioner refused to answer infringed rights protected by the First Amendment.

At the outset it should be noted that Rule XI authorized this Subcommittee to compel testimony within the framework of the investigative authority conferred on the Un-American Activities Committee. . . . In light of his prepared memorandum of constitutional objections there can be no doubt that this petitioner was well aware of the Subcommittee's authority and purpose to question him as it did. . . . In addition the other sources of this information . . . leave no room for a "pertinency" objection on this record. . . .

The precise constitutional issue confronting us is whether the Subcommittee's inquiry into petitioner's past or present membership in the Communist Party transgressed the provisions of the First Amendment, which of course reach and limit congressional investigations.

The Court's past cases establish sure guides to decision. Undeniably, the First Amendment in some circumstances protects an individual from being compelled to disclose his associational relationships. However, the protections of the First Amendment, unlike a proper claim of the privilege against self-incrimination under the Fifth Amendment, do not afford a witness the right to resist inquiry in all circumstances. Where First Amendment rights are asserted to bar governmental interrogation, resolution of the issue always involves a balancing by the courts of the competing private and public interests at stake in the particular circumstances shown. These principles were recognized in the *Watkins* case, where, in speaking of the First Amendment in relation to congressional inquiries, we said . . . : "It is manifest that despite the adverse effects which follow upon compelled disclosure of private matters, not all such inquiries are barred. . . . The critical element is the existence of, and the weight to be ascribed to, the interest of the Congress in demanding disclosures from an unwilling witness." . . .

The first question is whether this investigation was related to a valid legislative purpose, for Congress may not constitutionally require an individual to disclose his political relationships or other private affairs except in relation to such a purpose. See *Watkins* v. *United States, supra,* at 198.

That Congress has wide power to legislate in the field of Communist activity in this Country, and to conduct appropriate investigations in aid thereof, is hardly debatable. The existence of such power has never been questioned by this Court, and it is sufficient to say, without particularization, that Congress has enacted or considered in this field a wide range of legislative measures, not a few of which have stemmed from recommendations of the very Committee whose actions have been drawn in question here. In the last analysis this power rests on the right of self-preservation, "the ultimate value of any society." . . . Justification for its exercise in turn rests on the long and widely accepted view that the tenets of the Communist Party include the ultimate overthrow of the Government of the United States by force and violence, a view which has been given formal expression by the Congress. . . .

. . . The constitutional legislative power of Congress in this instance is beyond question.

Finally, the record is barren of other factors which in themselves might sometimes lead to the conclusion that the individual interests at stake were not subordinate to those of the state. There is no indication in this record that the Subcommittee was attempting to pillory witnesses. Nor did petitioner's appearance as a witness follow from indiscriminate dragnet procedures, lacking in probable cause for belief that he possessed information which might be helpful to the Subcommittee." And the relevancy of the questions put to him by the Subcommittee is not open to doubt.

We conclude that the balance between the individual and the governmental interests here at stake must be struck in favor of the latter, and that therefore the provisions of the First Amendment have not been offended.

We hold that petitioner's conviction for contempt of Congress discloses no infirmity, and that the judgment of the Court of Appeals must be *Affirmed.*

15

The President of the United States

15.1. THE SCOPE OF THE PRESIDENT'S EXECUTIVE POWER

What does Article II of the Constitution mean when it says, "The executive Power shall be vested in a President of the United States"? Writing in 1793, Alexander Hamilton maintains that this language confers broad and comprehensive powers on the President, beyond those specifically conferred.

THE SECOND ARTICLE of the Constitution of the United States, section first, establishes this general proposition, that "the EXECUTIVE POWER shall be vested in a President of the United States of America."

The same article, in a succeeding section, proceeds to delineate particular cases of executive power. It declares, among other things, that the president shall be commander in chief of the army and navy of the United States, and of the militia of the several states, when called into the actual service of the United States; that he shall have power, by and with the advice and consent of the senate, to make treaties; that it shall be his duty to receive ambassadors and other public ministers, *and to take care that the laws be faithfully executed.*

It would not consist with the rules of sound construction, to consider this enumeration of particular authorities as derogating from the more comprehensive grant in the general clause, further than as it may be coupled with express restrictions or limitations; as in regard to the co-operation of the senate in the appointment of officers, and the making of treaties; which are plainly qualifications of the general executive powers

From John C. Hamilton, *The Works of Alexander Hamilton* (New York: Trow, 1851), pp. 80–81.

of appointing officers and making treaties. The difficulty of a complete enumeration of all the cases of executive authority, would naturally dictate the use of general terms, and would render it improbable that a specification of certain particulars was designed as a substitute for those terms, when antecedently used. The different mode of expression employed in the constitution, in regard to the two powers, the legislative and the executive, serves to confirm this inference. In the article which gives the legislative powers of the government, the expressions are, "All legislative powers herein granted shall be vested in a congress of the United States." In that which grants the executive power, the expressions are, *"The executive power* shall be vested in a President of the United States."

The enumeration ought therefore to be considered, as intended merely to specify the principal articles implied in the definition of executive power; leaving the rest to flow from the general grant of that power, interpreted in conformity with other parts of the Constitution, and with the principles of free government.

The general doctrine of our Constitution then is, that the *executive power* of the nation is vested in the President; subject only to the *exceptions* and *qualifications,* which are expressed in the instrument.

15.2.   ARE GREAT MEN CHOSEN PRESIDENT?

The Constitution, custom, and practice have made of the American President a unique political figure. James Bryce, at one time Great Britain's Ambassador to the United States and a perceptive student of politics, explains in this classic statement why he thinks the United States has elected fewer great men to highest office than have European nations.

EUROPEANS often ask, and Americans do not always explain, how it happens that this great office, the greatest in the world, unless we except the Papacy, to which any man can rise by his own merits, is not more frequently filled by great and striking men? In America, which is beyond all other countries the country of a "career open to talents," a country, moreover, in which political life is unusually keen and political ambition widely diffused, it might be expected that the highest place would always be won by a man of brilliant gifts. But since the heroes of the Revolution died out with Jefferson and Adams and Madison some sixty years ago, no person except General Grant has reached the chair whose name would have been remembered had he not been President, and no President except Abraham Lincoln has displayed rare or striking qualities in the chair. Who now knows or cares to know anything about the personality

From James Bryce, *The American Commonwealth* (New York: The Macmillan Co., 1888), pp. 77–84.

of James K. Polk or Franklin Pierce? The only thing remarkable about them is that being so commonplace they should have climbed so high.

Several reasons may be suggested for the fact, which Americans are themselves the first to admit.

One is that the proportion of first-rate ability drawn into politics is smaller in America than in most European countries. This is a phenomenon whose causes must be elucidated later: in the meantime it is enough to say that in France and Italy, where half-revolutionary conditions have made public life exciting and accessible; in Germany, where an admirably-organized civil service cultivates and develops state-craft with unusual success; in England, where many persons of wealth and leisure seek to enter the political arena, while burning questions touch the interests of all classes and make men eager observers of the combatants, the total quantity of talent devoted to parliamentary or administrative work is far larger, relatively to the population, than in America, where much of the best ability, both for thought and for action, for planning and for executing, rushes into a field which is comparatively narrow in Europe, the business of developing the material resources of the country.

Another is that the methods and habits of Congress, and indeed of political life generally, seem to give fewer opportunities for personal distinction, fewer modes in which a man may commend himself to his countrymen by eminent capacity in thought, in speech, or in administration, than is the case in the free countries of Europe.

A third reason is that eminent men make more enemies, and give those enemies more assailable points, than obscure men do. They are therefore in so far less desirable candidates. . . .

The safe candidate may not draw in quite so many votes from the moderate men of the other side as the brilliant one would, but he will not lose nearly so many from his own ranks. Even those who admit his mediocrity will vote straight when the moment for voting comes. Besides, the ordinary American voter does not object to mediocrity. He has a lower conception of the qualities requisite to make a statesman than those who direct public opinion in Europe have. He likes his candidate to be sensible, vigorous, and, above all, what he calls "magnetic," and does not value, because he sees no need for, originality or profundity, a fine culture or a wide knowledge. . . .

It must also be remembered that the merits of a President are one thing and those of a candidate another thing. . . . It will be a misfortune to the party, as well as to the country, if the candidate elected should prove a bad President. But it is a greater misfortune to the party that it should be beaten in the impending election, for the evil of losing national patronage will have come four years sooner. "B" (so reason the leaders), "who is one of our possible candidates, may be an abler man than A, who is the other. But we have a better chance of winning with A than with B, while X, the candidate of our opponents, is anyhow no better than A. We must therefore run A." This reasoning is all the more forcible because the previous career of the possible candidates has generally made it easier to say who will succeed as a candidate than who will succeed as a President; and because the wire-pullers with whom the choice rests are better judges of the former question than of the latter.

After all, too, and this is a point much less obvious to Europeans than to Americans, a President need not be a man of brilliant intellectual gifts. . . . His main duties are to be prompt and firm in securing the due execution of the laws and maintaining the public peace, careful and upright in the choice of the executive officials of the country. . . . Four-fifths of his work is the same in kind as that which devolves on the chairman of a commercial .company or the manager of a railway, the work of choosing good subordinates, seeing that they attend to their business, and taking a sound practical view of such administrative questions as require his decision. Firmness, common sense, and most of all, honesty, an honesty above all suspicion of personal interest, are the qualities which the country chiefly needs in its chief magistrate.

So far we have been considering personal merits. But in the selection of a candidate many considerations have to be regarded besides personal merits, whether they be the merits of a candidate, or of a possible President. The chief of these considerations is the amount of support which can be secured from different States or from different regions, or, as the Americans say "sections," of the Union. State feeling and sectional feeling are powerful factors in a presidential election. . . .

A large State casts a heavier vote in the election; and every State is of course more likely to be carried by one of its own children than by a stranger, because his fellow-citizens, while they feel honoured by the choice, gain also a substantial advantage, having a better prospect of such favours as the administration can bestow. Hence, . . . a man from a large State is preferable as a candidate. . . . The problem is further complicated by the fact that some States are already safe for one or other party, while others are doubtful. The North-western and New England States are most of them certain to go Republican: the Southern States are (at present) all of them certain to go Democratic. It is more important to gratify a doubtful State than one you have got already; and hence, . . . a candidate from a doubtful State, such as New York or Indiana, is to be preferred. . . .

Although several Presidents have survived their departure from office by many years, only one, John Quincy Adams, has played a part in politics after quitting the White House. It may be that the ex-President has not been a great leader before his accession to office; it may be that he does not care to exert himself after he has held and dropped the great prize, and found (one may safely add) how little of a prize it is. Something, however, must also be ascribed to other features of the political system of the country. It is often hard to find a vacancy in the representation of a given State through which to re-enter Congress; it is disagreeable to recur to the arts by which seats are secured. Past greatness is rather an encumbrance than a help to resuming a political career. Exalted power, on which the unsleeping eye of hostile critics was fixed, has probably disclosed all a President's weaknesses, and has either forced him to make enemies by disobliging adherents, or exposed him to censure for subservience to party interests. He is regarded as having had his day; he belongs already to the past, and unless, like Grant, he is endeared to the people by the memory of some splendid service, he soon sinks into the crowd or avoids neglect by retirement. Possibly he may deserve to be forgotten; but more frequently he is a man of sufficient ability and character to make the experience he has gained valuable to the country, could it be retained in a place where he might turn it to account. They managed things better at Rome in the days of the republic, gathering into their Senate all the fame and experience, all the wisdom and skill, of those who had ruled and fought as consuls and praetors at home and abroad.

"What shall we do with our ex-Presidents?" is a question often put in America, but never yet answered. The position of a past chief magistrate is not a happy one. He has been a species of sovereign at home. He is received—General Grant was—with almost royal honours abroad. His private income may be insufficient to enable him to live in ease, yet he cannot without loss of dignity, the country's dignity as well as his own, go back to practice at the bar or become partner in a mercantile firm. If he tries to enter the Senate, it may happen that there is no seat vacant for his own State, or that the majority in the State legislature is against him. It has been suggested that he might be given a seat in that chamber as an extra member; but to this plan there is the objection that it would give to the State from which he comes a third senator, and thus put other States at a disadvantage. In any case, however, it would seem only right to bestow such a pension as would relieve him from the necessity of re-entering business or a profession.

We may now answer the question from which we started. Great men are not chosen Presidents, firstly, because great men are rare in politics; secondly, because the method of choice does not bring them to the top; thirdly, because they are not, in quiet times, absolutely needed. I may observe that the Presidents, regarded historically, fall into three periods, the second inferior to the first, the third rather better than the second.

Down till the election of Andrew Jackson in 1828, all the Presidents had been statesmen in the European sense of the word, men of education, of administrative experience, of a certain largeness of view and dignity of character. All except the first two had served in the great office of secretary of state; all were well known to the nation from the part they had played. In the second period, from Jackson till the outbreak of the Civil War in 1861, the Presidents were either mere politicians, such as Van Buren, Polk, or Buchanan, or else successful soldiers, such as Harrison or Taylor, whom their party found useful as figure-heads. They were intellectual pigmies beside the real leaders of that generation—Clay, Calhoun, and Webster. A new series begins with Lincoln in 1861. He and General Grant his successor, who cover sixteen years between them, belong to the history of the world. The other less distinguished Presidents of this period contrast favourably with the Polks and Pierces of the days before the war, but they are not, like the early Presidents, the first men of the country. If we compare the eighteen Presidents who have been elected to office since 1789 with the nineteen English prime ministers of the same hundred years, there are but six of the latter, and at least eight of the former whom history calls personally insignificant, while only Washington, Jefferson, Lincoln, and Grant can claim to belong to a front rank represented in the English list by seven or possibly eight names. It would seem that the natural selection of the English parliamentary system, even as modified by the aristocratic habits of that country, has more tendency to bring the highest gifts to the highest place than the more artificial selection of America.

15.3. PRESIDENTIAL CONFLICT WITH CONGRESS

Woodrow Wilson's examination as a young political scientist of the office to which he was later elected leads him to conclude that the powers of Congress have become predominant in the national government. Having "virtually taken into its own hands all the substantial powers of government," Congress, he argued, had brought about the decline of the President's prestige and power.

IT IS NOTEWORTHY that Mr. Adams, possibly because he had himself been President, describes the executive as constituting only *"in some degree"* a check upon Congress, though he puts no such limitation upon the other balances of the system. Independently of experience, however, it might reasonably have been expected that the prerogatives of the President would have been one of the most effectual restraints upon the power of Congress.

From Woodrow Wilson, *Congressional Government* (Boston: Houghton Mifflin Co., 1885), pp. 41–45.

He was constituted one of the three great coordinate branches of the government; his functions were made of the highest dignity; his privileges many and substantial—so great, indeed, that it has pleased the fancy of some writers to parade them as exceeding those of the British crown; and there can be little doubt that, had the presidential chair always been filled by men of commanding character, of acknowledged ability, and of thorough political training, it would have continued to be a seat of the highest authority and consideration, the true centre of the federal structure, the real throne of administration, and the frequent source of policies. Washington and his Cabinet commanded the ear of Congress, and gave shape to its deliberations; Adams, though often crossed and thwarted, gave character to the government; and Jefferson, as President no less than as Secretary of State, was the real leader of his party. But the prestige of the presidential office has declined with the character of the Presidents. And the character of the Presidents has declined as the perfection of selfish party tactics has advanced.

It was inevitable that it should be so. After independence of choice on the part of the presidential electors had given place to the choice of presidential candidates by party conventions, it became absolutely necessary, in the eyes of politicians, and more and more necessary as time went on, to make expediency and availability the only rules of selection. . . . When the presidential candidate came to be chosen, it was recognized as imperatively necessary that he should have as short a political record as possible, and that he should wear a clean and irreproachable insignificance. . . . A decisive career which gives a man a well-understood place in public estimation constitutes a positive disability for the presidency; because candidacy must precede election, and the shoals of candidacy can be passed only by a light boat which carries little freight and can be turned readily about to suit the intricacies of the passage.

I am disposed to think, however, that the decline in the character of the Presidents is not the cause, but only the accompanying manifestation, of the declining prestige of the presidential office. That high office has fallen from its first estate of dignity because its power has waned; and its power has waned because the power of Congress has become predominant. The early Presidents were, as I have said, men of such a stamp that they would under any circumstances have made their influence felt; but their opportunities were exceptional. What with quarreling and fighting with England, buying Louisiana and Florida, building dykes to keep out the flood of the French Revolution, and extricating the country from ceaseless broils with the South American Republics, the government was, as has been pointed out, constantly busy, during the first quarter century of its existence, with the adjustment of foreign relations; and with foreign relations, of course, the Presidents had everything to do, since theirs was the office of negotiation.

Moreover, as regards home policy also those times were not like ours. Congress was somewhat awkward' in exercising its untried powers, and its machinery was new, and without that fine adjustment which has since made it perfect of its kind. Not having as yet learned the art of governing itself to the best advantage, and being without that facility of legislation which it afterwards acquired, the Legislature was glad to get guidance and suggestions of policy from the Executive.

But this state of things did not last long. Congress was very quick and apt in learning what it could do and in getting into thoroughly good trim to do it. It very early divided itself into standing committees which it equipped with very comprehensive and thorough-going privileges of legislative initiative and control, and set itself through these to administer the government. Congress is (to adopt Mr. Bagehot's description of Parliament) "nothing less than a big meeting of more or less idle people. In proportion as you give it power it will inquire into everything, settle everything, meddle in everything. In an ordinary despotism the powers of the despot are limited by his bodily capacity, and by the calls of pleasure; he is but one man; there are but twelve hours in his day, and he is not disposed to employ more than a small part in dull business: he keeps the rest for the court, or the harem, or for society." But Congress "is a despot who has unlimited time,—who has unlimited vanity,— who has, or believes he has, unlimited comprehension,—whose pleasure is in action, whose life is work." Accordingly it has entered more and more into the details of administration, until it has virtually taken into its own hands all the substantial powers of government. It does not domineer over the President himself, but it makes the Secretaries its humble servants. Not that it would hesitate, upon occasion, to deal directly with the chief magistrate himself; but it has few calls to do so, because our latter-day Presidents live by proxy; they are the executive in theory, but the Secretaries are the executive in fact. At the very first session of Congress steps were taken towards parceling out executive work amongst several departments, according to a then sufficiently thorough division of labor; and if the President of the day was not able to direct administrative details, of course the President of today is infinitely less able to do so, and must content himself with such general supervision as he may find time to exercise. He is in all every-day concerns shielded by the responsibility of his subordinates.

15.4. WILSON'S REAPPRAISAL OF THE PRESIDENT'S ROLE

In the twenty-three years that elapsed between Congressional Government *and* Constitutional Government in the United States, *Woodrow Wilson's views about the powers and prestige of the President changed considerably. Perhaps in recognition of Theodore Roosevelt's achievements as President during part of this period, Wilson asserts that a forceful personality who has "boldly accepted the role of leader" can make of his office what he chooses.*

AS LEGAL executive, his constitutional aspect, the President cannot be thought of alone. He cannot execute laws. Their actual daily execution must be taken care of by the several executive departments and by the now innumerable body of federal officials throughout the country. In respect of the strictly executive duties of his office the President may be said to administer the presidency in conjunction with the members of his cabinet, like the chairman of a commission. He is even of necessity much less active in the actual carrying out of the law than are his colleagues and advisers. It is therefore becoming more and more true, as the business of the government becomes more and more complex and extended, that the President is becoming more and more a political and less and less an executive officer. His executive powers are in commission, while his political powers more and more centre and accumulate upon him and are in their very nature personal and inalienable.

Only the larger sort of executive questions are brought to him. Departments which run with easy routine and whose transactions bring few questions of general policy to the surface may proceed with their business for months and even years together without demanding his attention; and no department is in any sense under his direct charge. Cabinet meetings do not discuss detail: they are concerned only with the larger matters of policy or expediency which important business is constantly disclosing. There are no more hours in the President's day than in another man's. If he is indeed the executive, he must act almost entirely by delegation, and is in the hands of his colleagues. He is likely to be praised if things go well, and blamed if they go wrong; but his only real control is of the persons to whom he deputes the performance of executive duties. It is through no fault or neglect of his that the duties apparently assigned to him by the Constitution have come to be his less conspicuous, less important duties, and that duties apparently not assigned to him at all chiefly occupy his time and energy. The one set of duties it has proved practically impossible for him to perform; the other it has proved impossible for him to escape.

He cannot escape being the leader of his party except by incapacity and lack of personal force, because he is at once the choice of the

From Woodrow Wilson, *Constitutional Government in the United States* (New York: Columbia University Press, 1908), pp. 66–69, 72–73.

party and of the nation. He is the party nominee, and the only party nominee for whom the whole nation votes. Members of the House and Senate are representatives of localities, are voted for only by sections of voters, or by local bodies of electors like the members of the state legislatures. There is no national party choice except that of President. No one else represents the people as a whole, . . . and inasmuch as his strictly executive duties are in fact subordinated, so far at any rate as all detail is concerned, the President represents not so much the party's governing efficiency as its controlling ideals and principles. He is not so much part of its organization as its vital link of connection with the thinking nation. He can dominate his party by being spokesman for the real sentiment and purpose of the country, by giving direction to opinion, by giving the country at once the information and the statements of policy which will enable it to form its judgments alike of parties and of men.

For he is also the political leader of the nation, or has it in his choice to be. The nation as a whole has chosen him, and is conscious that it has no other political spokesman. His is the only national voice in affairs. Let him once win the admiration and confidence of the country, and no other single force can withstand him, no combination of forces will easily overpower him. His position takes the imagination of the country. He is the representative of no constituency, but of the whole people. When he speaks in his true character, he speaks for no special interest. If he rightly interpret the national thought and boldly insist upon it, he is irresistible; and the country never feels the zest of action so much as when its President is of such insight and calibre. Its instinct is for unified action, and it craves a single leader. It is for this reason that it will often prefer to choose a man rather than a party. A President whom it trusts can not only lead it, but form it to his own views.

. . . The President may also, if he will, stand within the party counsels and use the advantage of his power and personal force to control its actual programs. He may be both the leader of his party and the leader of the nation, or he may be one or the other. If he lead the nation, his party can hardly resist him. His office is anything he has the sagacity and force to make it. . . .

The political powers of the President are not quite so obvious in their scope and character when we consider his relations with Congress as when we consider his relations to his party and to the nation. They need, therefore, a somewhat more critical examination. Leadership in government naturally belongs to its executive officers, who are daily in contact with practical conditions and exigencies and whose reputations alike for good judgment and for fidelity are at stake much more than are those of the members of the legislative body at every turn of the law's application. The law-making part of the government ought certainly to be very hospitable to the suggestions of the planning and acting part of it.

Those Presidents who have felt themselves bound to adhere to the strict literary theory of the Constitution have scrupulously refrained from attempting to determine either the subjects or the character of legislation, except so far as they were obliged to decide for themselves, after Congress had acted, whether they should acquiesce in it or not. And yet the Constitution explicitly authorizes the President to recommend to Congress "such measures as he shall deem necessary and expedient," and it is not necessary to the integrity of even the literary theory of the Constitution to insist that such recommendations should be merely perfunctory. Certainly General Washington did not so regard them, and he stood much nearer the Whig theory than we do. A President's messages to Congress have no more weight or authority than their intrinsic reasonableness and importance give them: but that is their only constitutional limitation. The Constitution certainly does not forbid the President to back them up, as General Washington did, with such personal force and influence as he may possess. Some of our Presidents have felt the need, which unquestionably exists in our system, for some spokesman of the nation as a whole, in matters of legislation no less than in other matters, and have tried to supply Congress with the leadership of suggestion, backed by argument and by iteration and by every legitimate appeal to public opinion. Cabinet officers are shut out from Congress; the President himself has, by custom, no access to its floor; many long-established barriers of precedent, though not of law, hinder him from exercising any direct influence upon its deliberations; and yet he is undoubtedly the only spokesman of the whole people. They have again and again, as often as they were afforded the opportunity, manifested their satisfaction when he has boldly accepted the rôle of leader, to which the peculiar origin and character of his authority entitle him. The Constitution bids him speak, and times of stress and change must more and more thrust upon him the attitude of originator of policies.

15.5. THE PRESIDENT AS STATESMAN

The President's responsibility for the conduct of foreign affairs offers him great opportunity for leadership. In this excerpt from the revision of his earlier book, Wilson cites our war with Spain in 1898 as an explanation for the renewed importance of the President.

MUCH the most important change to be noticed is the result of the war with Spain upon the lodgment and exercise of power within our federal system: the greatly increased power and opportunity for constructive states-

From Woodrow Wilson, *Congressional Government* (Boston: Houghton Mifflin Co., 1913), pp. xi–xii.

manship given the President, by the plunge into international politics and
into the administration of distant dependencies, which has been that war's
most striking and momentous consequence. When foreign affairs play a
prominent part in the politics and policy of a nation, its Executive must
of necessity be its guide: must utter every initial judgment, take every
first step of action, supply the information upon which it is to act, suggest
and in large measure control its conduct. The President of the United
States is now, as of course, at the front of affairs, as no president, except
Lincoln, has been since the first quarter of the nineteenth century, when
the foreign relations of the new nation had first to be adjusted. There
is no trouble now about getting the President's speeches printed and read,
every word. Upon his choice, his character, his experience hang some of
the most weighty issues of the future. The government of dependencies
must be largely in his hands. Interesting things may come out of the
singular change.

16

The Presidency: Policy and Administration

16.1. A THEORY OF LIMITED PRESIDENTIAL POWER

According to President Taft, the Constitution confers no "undefined residuum" of power on the President. Disagreeing with Theodore Roosevelt's broad conception of executive power, Taft argues that the President is limited to those narrow and specific exercises of power granted him by the Constitution and acts of Congress. Even where broad powers might have beneficial results in an emergency, the possibility of arbitrary action must be avoided at all costs.

THE TRUE view of the Executive functions is, as I conceive it, that the President can exercise no power which cannot be fairly and reasonably traced to some specific grant of power or justly implied and included within such express grant as proper and necessary to its exercise. Such specific grant must be either in the Federal Constitution or in an act of Congress passed in pursuance thereof. There is no undefined residuum of power which he can exercise because it seems to him to be in the public interest, and there is nothing in the Neagle case and its definition of a law of the United States, or in other precedents, warranting such an inference. The grants of Executive power are necessarily in general terms in order not to embarrass the Executive within the field of action plainly marked for him, but his jurisdiction must be justified and vindicated by affirmative constitutional or statutory provision, or it does not exist. There have not been wanting, however, eminent men in high public

From William Howard Taft, *Our Chief Magistrate* (New York: Columbia University Press, 1916), pp. 139–144.

office holding a different view and who have insisted upon the necessity for an undefined residuum of Executive power in the public interest. They have not been confined to the present generation. We may learn this from the complaint of a Virginia statesman, Abel P. Upshur, a strict constructionist of the old school, who succeeded Daniel Webster as Secretary of State under President Tyler. He was aroused by Story's commentaries on the Constitution to write a monograph answering and criticizing them, and in the course of this he comments as follows on the Executive power under the Constitution:

The most defective part of the Constitution beyond all question, is that which related to the Executive Department. It is impossible to read that instrument, without being struck with the loose and unguarded terms in which the powers and duties of the President are pointed out. So far as the legislature is concerned, the limitations of the Constitution, are, perhaps, as precise and strict as they could safely have been made; but in regard to the Executive, the Convention appears to have studiously selected such loose and general expressions, as would enable the President, by implication and construction either to neglect his duties or to enlarge his powers. *We have heard it gravely asserted in Congress that whatever power is neither legislative nor judiciary, is of course executive, and, as such, belongs to the President under the Constitution.* How far a majority of that body would have sustained a doctrine so monstrous, and so utterly at war with the whole genius of our government, it is impossible to say, but this, at least, we know, that it met with no rebuke from those who supported the particular act of Executive power, in defense of which it was urged. Be this as it may, it is a reproach to the Constitution that the Executive trust is so ill-defined, as to leave any plausible pretense even to the insane zeal of party devotion, for attributing to the President of the United States the powers of a despot; powers which are wholly unknown in any limited monarchy in the world.

The view that he takes as a result of the loose language defining the Executive powers seems exaggerated. But one most agree with him in his condemnation of the view of the Executive power which he says was advanced in Congress. In recent years there has been put forward a similar view by executive officials and to some extent acted on. Men who are not such strict constructionists of the Constitution as Mr. Upshur may well feel real concern if such views are to receive the general acquiescence. Mr. Garfield, when Secretary of the Interior, under Mr. Roosevelt, in his final report to Congress in reference to the power of the Executive over the public domain, said:

Full power under the Constitution was vested in the Executive Branch of the Government and the extent to which that power may be exercised is governed wholly by the discretion of the Executive unless any specific act has been prohibited either by the Constitution or by legislation.

In pursuance of this principle, Mr. Garfield, under an act for the reclamation of arid land by irrigation, which authorized him to make contracts for irrigation works and incur liability equal to the amount on deposit in the Reclamation Fund, made contracts with associations of settlers by which it was agreed that if these settlers would advance money and work, they might receive certificates from the government engineers of the labor and money furnished by them, and that such certificates might be received in the future in the discharge of their legal obligations to the government for water rent and other things under the statute. It became necessary for the succeeding administration to pass on the validity of these government certificates. They were held by Attorney-General Wickersham to be illegal, on the ground that no authority existed for their issuance. He relied on the Floyd acceptances in 7th Wallace, in which recovery was sought in the Court of Claims on commercial paper in the form of acceptances signed by Mr. Floyd when Secretary of War and delivered to certain contractors. The Court held that they were void because the Secretary of War had no statutory authority to issue them. Mr. Justice Miller, in deciding the case, said:

The answer which at once suggests itself to one familiar with the structure of our government, in which all power is delegated, and is defined by law, constitutional or statutory, is, that to one or both of these sources we must resort in every instance. We have no officers in this government, from the President down to the most subordinate agent, who does not hold office under the law, with prescribed duties and limited authority. And while some of these, as the President, the Legislature, and the Judiciary, exercise powers in some sense left to the more general definitions necessarily incident to fundamental law found in the Constitution, the larger portion of them are the creation of statutory law, with duties and powers prescribed and limited by that law.   .

In the light of this view of the Supreme Court it is interesting to compare the language of Mr. Roosevelt in his "Notes for a Possible Autobiography" on the subject of "Executive Powers," in which he says:

The most important factor in getting the right spirit in my Administration, next to insistence upon courage, honesty, and a genuine democracy of desire to serve the plain people, was my insistence upon the theory that the executive power was limited only by specific restrictions and prohibitions appearing in the Constitution or imposed by Congress under its constitutional powers. My view was that every Executive officer and above all every Executive officer in high position was a steward of the people bound actively and affirmatively to do all he could for the people and not to content himself with the negative merit of keeping his talents undamaged in a napkin. I declined to adopt this view that what was imperatively necessary for the Nation could not be done by the President, unless he could find some specific authorization to do it. My belief was that it was not only his right but his duty to do anything that the needs of the Nation demanded unless such action was forbidden by the Constitution or by the laws. Under this interpretation of executive power I did and caused to be done many things not previously done by the President and the heads of the departments. I did not usurp power but I did greatly broaden the use of executive power. In other words, I acted for the common well being of all our people whenever and in whatever measure was necessary, unless prevented by direct constitutional or legislative prohibition.

I may add that Mr. Roosevelt, by way of illustrating his meaning as to the differing usefulness of Presidents, divides the Presidents into two classes, and designates them as "Lincoln Presidents" and "Buchanan Presidents." In order more fully to illustrate his division of Presidents on their merits, he places himself in the Lincoln class of Presidents, and me in the Buchanan class. The identification of Mr. Roosevelt with Mr. Lincoln might otherwise have escaped notice, because there are many differences between the two, presumably superficial, which would give the impartial student of history a different impression. It suggests a story which a friend of mine told of his little daughter Mary. As he came walking home after a business day, she ran out from the house to greet him, all aglow with the importance of what she wished to tell him. She said, "Papa, I am the best scholar in the class." The father's heart throbbed with pleasure as he inquired, "Why, Mary, you surprise me. When did the teacher tell you? This afternoon?" "Oh, no," Mary's reply was, "the teacher didn't tell me—I just noticed it myself."

My judgment is that the view of Mr. Garfield and Mr. Roosevelt, ascribing an undefined residuum of power to the President is an unsafe doctrine and that it might lead under emergencies to results of an arbitrary character, doing irremediable injustice to private right. The mainspring of such a view is that the Executive is charged with responsibility for the welfare of all the people in a general way, that he is to play the part of a Universal Providence and set all things right, and that anything that in his judgment will help the people he ought to do, unless he is expressly forbidden not to do it. The wide field of action that this would give to the Executive one can hardly limit. . . .

16.2. A COMPREHENSIVE ANALYSIS OF THE PRESIDENCY

Although past Presidents have disagreed with one another on the scope and power of the President's office in our political system, the fact remains that the American people expect and demand a great deal of the modern President. Professor Rossiter here catalogs and analyzes the President's complex tasks. He reminds us that the "thousand-man job" of the Presidency must in the final analysis be performed by a single human individual under our Constitution.

THIS PRESENTATION must begin with a careful accounting of those tasks we call upon the President to perform, for if there is any one thing about him that strikes the eye immediately, it is the staggering burden he bears for all of us. Those who cherish Gilbert and Sullivan will remember Pooh-Bah, the "particularly haughty and exclusive person" in *The Mikado* who filled the offices of "First Lord of the Treasury, Lord Chief Justice, Commander-in-Chief, Lord High Admiral, Master of the Buck-hounds, Groom of the Back Stairs, Archbishop of Titipu, and Lord Mayor, both acting and elect." We chuckle at the fictitious Pooh-Bah; we can only wonder at the real one that history has made of the American President. He has at least three jobs for every one of Pooh-Bah's, and they are not performed with the flick of a lacquered fan. At the risk of being perhaps too analytical, let me review the functions of the modern President. These, as I interpret them, are the major roles he plays in the sprawling drama of American government.

First, the President is Chief of State. He remains today, as he has always been, the ceremonial head of the government of the United States, and he must take part with real or apparent enthusiasm in a range of activities that would keep him running and posing from sunrise to bedtime if he were not protected by a cold-blooded staff. Some of these activities are solemn or even priestly in nature; others, through no fault of his own, are flirtations with vulgarity. The long catalogue of public duties that the Queen discharges in England, the President of the Republic in France, and the Governor-General in Canada is the President's responsibility in this country, and the catalogue is even longer because he is not a king, or even the agent of one, and is therefore expected to go through some rather undignified paces by a people who think of him as a combination of scoutmaster, Delphic oracle, hero of the silver screen, and father of the multitudes.

As figurehead rather than working head of our government, he greets distinguished visitors from all parts of the world, lays wreaths on the tomb of the Unknown Soldier and before the statue of Lincoln, makes proclamations of thanksgiving and commemoration, bestows medals on flustered pilots, holds state dinners for the diplomatic corps and the Supreme Court, lights the nation's Christmas tree, buys the first poppy from the Veterans of Foreign Wars, gives the first crisp banknote to the

From *The American Presidency* © 1956, by Clinton Rossiter, pp. 16–17, 19–20, 22–25, 28–32, 34–43. Reprinted by permission of Harcourt, Brace & World, Inc.

Red Cross, throws out the first ball for the Senators (the harmless ones out at Griffith Stadium), rolls the first egg for the Easter Bunny, and in the course of any month greets a fantastic procession of firemen, athletes, veterans, Boy Scouts, Campfire Girls, boosters, hog callers, exchange students, and heroic school children. The annual United Fund Drive could not possibly get under way without a five-minute telecast from the White House; Sunday is not Sunday if the President and his lady skip church; a public-works project is not public until the President presses a silver key in Washington and explodes a charge of dynamite in Fort Peck or Hanford or the Tennessee Valley. . . .

The framers of the Constitution took a momentous step when they fused the dignity of a king and the power of a prime minister in one elective office. And, if they did nothing else, they gave us a "father image" that should satisfy even the most demanding political Freudians.

The second of the President's roles is that of Chief Executive. He reigns, but he also rules; he symbolizes the people, but also runs their government. . . .

Both the Constitution and Congress have recognized his authority to supervise the day-to-day activities of the executive branch, strained and restrained though this supervision may often be in practice. From the Constitution, explicitly or implicitly, he receives the twin powers of appointment and removal, as well as the primary duty, which no law or plan or circumstance can ever take away from him, to "take care that the laws be faithfully executed." He alone may appoint, with the advice and consent of the Senate, the several thousand top officials who run the government; he alone may remove, with varying degrees of abruptness, those who are not executing the laws faithfully—or, in the case of all those Secretaries and generals and attorneys directly under his command, not executing them in a manner consistent with his own policies.

It is the power of removal—the "gun behind the door"—that makes it possible for the President to bend his "team" to his will. More to the point, this power is the symbol and final sanction of his position as Chief Executive, and no official in the administration, not even the most nonpartisan chairman of the most independent regulatory commission, is entirely immune to a fatal attack of presidential displeasure. A member of the Federal Trade Commission or Interstate Commerce Commission is protected by statute and judicial decision against the kind of arbitrary removal the President may visit upon a Secretary of the Army or Director of the Budget, but if he has stepped out of line in a way for all the world to see—if, to take a crude example, he has been drunk on the job for weeks on end—then he cannot hope to stand up to the man who has been commanded by the Constitution to see to the faithful execution of the laws of the United States. . . .

The President's third major function is one he could not escape if he wished, and several Presidents have wished it mightily. The Constitution designates him specifically as "Commander-in-Chief of the Army and Navy of the United States, and of the militia of the several States when called into the actual service of the United States." In peace and war he is the supreme commander of the armed forces, the living guarantee of the American belief in "the supremacy of the civil over military authority."

In time of peace he raises, trains, supervises, and deploys the forces that Congress is willing to maintain, and he has a great deal to say about the size and make-up of these forces. With the aid of the Secretary of Defense, the Secretaries of the three services, the Joint Chiefs of Staff, and the members of the National Security Council—every one of these men his personal choice—he looks constantly to the state of the nation's defenses. He is never for one day allowed to forget that he will be held accountable by people, Congress, and history for the nation's readiness to meet an enemy assault. . . .

. . . most citizens agreed with Mr. Truman's brisk assertion in 1950 that it was for the President to decide whether the H-bomb should be built. Congress might have refused to grant funds for such an undertaking, but this would not have stopped the President from pushing ahead as best he could with the other resources at his command. And, as the same doughty man demonstrated in 1945, it is for the President to decide in time of war when and where and how the H-bomb or A-bomb or any other bomb should be dropped.

But this, the power of command, is only a fraction of the vast responsibility the modern President draws from the Commander in Chief clause. The framers of the Constitution, to be sure, took a narrow view of the authority they had granted. "It would amount," Hamilton wrote offhandedly in *The Federalist,* "to nothing more than the supreme command and direction of the military and naval forces, as first General and Admiral of the Confederacy." This view of presidential power as something purely military foundered on the hard facts of the first of our modern wars. Faced by an overriding necessity for harsh, even dictatorial action, Lincoln used the Commander in Chief clause, at first gingerly, in the end boldly, to justify an unprecedented series of measures that cut deeply into the accepted liberties of the people and the routine pattern of government. Wilson added another cubit to the stature of the wartime Presidency by demanding that Congress give him those powers over the economy about which there was any constitutional doubt, and Franklin Roosevelt, who had read about Lincoln and lived with Wilson, carried the wartime Presidency to breath-taking heights of authority over the American economy and social order. The creation and staffing of a whole array of emergency boards and offices, the seizure and operation of more than sixty strike-bound or strike-threatened plants and industries, and the forced evacuation of 70,000 American citizens of Japanese descent from the West Coast are three startling and prophetic examples of what a President can do as Commander in Chief to stiffen the home front in support of the fighting forces. It is important to recall that Congress came to Roosevelt's aid in each of these series of actions by passing laws empowering him to do what he had done already or by fixing penalties for violating the orders of his subordinates. Congress, too, likes to win wars, and Congressmen are more likely to needle the President for inactivity and timidity than to accuse him of acting too swiftly and arbitrarily.

Now that total war, which ignores the old line between battlefield and home front, has been compounded by the absolute weapon, which mocks every rule we have ever tried to honor, we may expect the President to be nothing short of a "constitutional dictator" in the event of war. The next wartime President, who may well be our last, will have the right, of which Lincoln spoke with feeling, to take "any measure which may best subdue the enemy," and he alone will be the judge of what is "best" for the survival of the republic. We have placed a shocking amount of military power in the President's keeping, but where else, we may ask, could it possibly have been placed?

Next, the President is Chief Diplomat. Although authority in the field of foreign relations is shared constitutionally among three organs— President, Congress, and, for two special purposes, the Senate—his position is paramount, if not indeed dominant. . . .

In recent years, the role of Chief Diplomat has become the most important and exacting of all those we call upon the President to play. Indeed, when one thinks of the hours of "prayerful consideration" President Eisenhower devoted each week to briefing sessions with the Dulles brothers, conferences with the National Security Council, lunches with Senators Fulbright and Wiley, chats with Nehru or Macmillan or Diefenbaker or whoever else might be in town, explanatory and inspirational speeches to the nation, and lonely wrestling bouts with appointments and reports and messages to Congress—not to mention his correspondence with Khrushchev, Zhukov, and Bulganin—it is a wonder that he had a moment's time for any of his other duties.

The President's duties are not all purely executive in nature. He is also intimately associated, by Constitution and custom, with the legislative process, and we may therefore consider him to be the Chief Legislator. Congress has a wealth of strong and talented men, but the complexity of the problems they are asked to solve by a people who assume that all problems are solvable has made *external* leadership a requisite of effective operation. The President alone is in a political, constitutional, and practical position to provide such leadership, and he is therefore expected within the limits of constitutional and political propriety, to guide Congress in much of its lawmaking activity. Indeed, since Congress is no longer organized to guide itself, not even under such tough-minded leaders as Senator Johnson and Speaker Rayburn, the refusal or inability of the President to point out the way results in weak or, at best, stalemated government. . . .

Upon many of our most celebrated laws the presidential imprint is clearly stamped. Each of these was drafted in the President's offices, introduced and supported by his friends, defended in committee by his aides, voted through by a party over which every form of discipline and persuasion was exerted, and then made law by his signature. The signature, of course, was affixed with several dozen fountain pens, which were then passed out among the beaming friends and aides. Among the "ploys and gambits" the President may have used in the process were the White House breakfast with his chief lieutenants, or perhaps with his chief obstructionists; the fireside chat with his constituents, some of whom were also constituents of the obstructionists; the press conference, in which he proclaimed his astonishment at the way Congress was dragging its feet; the dangled patronage or favor, which brought a wavering or even hostile Senator to his side; and the threat of a veto, which he brandished like the Gorgon's head to frighten the mavericks into removing objectionable amendments to the bill he had first sent over.

Even the President who lacks a congressional majority must go through the motions of leadership. The Republicans in the Eightieth Congress always waited politely for Mr. Truman's proposals on labor, taxes, inflation, civil rights, and education, however scant the regard they intended to pay them. The Democrats, if we may believe the protests of Speaker Rayburn and Senator Johnson, were impatient to hear President Eisenhower's proposals and to feel the lash of his leadership. In any case, the chief responsibility for bridging the constitutional gulf between executive and legislature now rests irrevocably with the President. His tasks as leader of Congress are difficult and delicate, yet he must bend to them steadily or be judged a failure. The President who will not give his best thoughts to guiding Congress, more so the President who is temperamentally or politically unfitted to "get along with Congress," is now rightly considered a national liability.

Chief of State, Chief Executive, Commander in Chief, Chief Diplomat, Chief Legislator—these functions make up the strictly constitutional burden of the President. As Mr. Truman himself allowed in several of his folksy sermons on the Presidency, they form an aggregate of power that would have made Caesar or Genghis Khan or Napoleon bite his nails with envy. Yet even these are not the whole weight of presidential responsibility. I count at least five additional functions that have been piled on top of the original load.

The first of these is the President's role as Chief of Party, one that he has played by popular demand and to a mixed reception ever since the administration of Thomas Jefferson. However sincere Washington's abhorrence of "factions" may have been, his own administration and policies spawned our first two parties, and their arrival upon the scene altered the character of the Presidency radically. No matter how fondly or how often we may long for a President who is above the heat of political strife, we must acknowledge resolutely his right and duty to be the leader of his party. He is at once the least political and most political of all heads of government.

The value of this function has been attested by all our first-rate Presidents. Jackson, Lincoln, Wilson, and the two Roosevelts were especially skillful party leaders. By playing the politician with unashamed zest the first of these gave his epic administration a unique sense of cohesion, the second rallied doubting Republican leaders and their followings to the cause of the Union, and the other three achieved genuine triumphs as catalysts of congressional action. That elegant amateur, Dwight D. Eisenhower, played the role with devotion if not exactly zest. It would have astonished George Washington, but it cannot even ruffle us, to learn that the President devoted breakfast and most of the morning of June 20, 1955—a day otherwise given over to solemn celebration of the tenth birthday of the United Nations—to mending a few fences with Republican leaders of California. He was demonstrating only what close observers of the Presidency know well: that its incumbent must devote an hour or two of every working day to the profession of Chief Democrat or Chief Republican. The President dictates the selection of the national chairman and other top party officials, reminds his partisans in Congress that the legislative record must be bright if victory is to crown their joint efforts, delivers "fight talks" to the endless procession of professionals who call upon him, and, through the careful distribution of the loaves and fishes of federal patronage, keeps the party a going concern. The loaves and fishes are not so plentiful as they were in the days of Jackson and Lincoln, but the President is still a wholesale distributor of "jobs for the boys." . . .

Yet he is, at the same time if not in the same breath, the Voice of the People, the leading formulator and expounder of public opinion in the United States. While he acts as political leader of some, he serves as moral spokesman for all. . . .

The President is the American people's one authentic trumpet, and he has no higher duty than to give a clear and certain sound. "Words at great moments of history are deeds," Clement Attlee said of Winston Churchill on the day the latter stepped down in 1945. The strong and imaginative President can make with his own words the kind of history that Churchill made in 1940 and 1941. When the events of 1933 are all but forgotten, we shall still recall Roosevelt's words, "The only thing we have to fear is fear itself."

In the memorable case of *In re Neagle* (1890), which still makes good reading for those who like a touch of horse opera in their constitutional law, Justice Samuel Miller spoke with feeling of the "peace of the United States"—a happy condition, it would appear, of domestic tranquillity and national prosperity that is often broken by violent men and forces and just as often restored by the President. Perhaps the least known of his functions is the mandate he holds from the Constitution and the laws, but even more positively from the people of the United States, to act as Protector of the Peace. The emergencies that can disturb the peace of the United States seem to grow thicker and more vexing every year, and hardly a week now goes by that the President is not called upon to take forceful steps in behalf of a section or city or group or enterprise that has been hit hard and suddenly by disaster. Generally, it is for state and local authorities to deal with social and natural calamities, but in the face of a riot in Detroit or floods in New England or a tornado in Missouri or a railroad strike in Chicago or a panic in Wall Street, the people turn almost instinctively to the White House and its occupant for aid and comfort. . . .

. . . he remains constitutionally, we might even say extraconstitutionally, empowered to respond to an atomic attack by declaring straight-out martial law through all the land. This, be it noted for future reference, is exactly what President Eisenhower pretended to do in the simulated hydrogen-bomb attack of June 1955. One of the remarkable events of that three-day test of our readiness for atomic war was the startled discovery by Mr. Eisenhower and his staff that "the inherent powers of the Presidency," something about which Republicans usually maintain uneasy silence, would be the nation's chief crutch in the aftermath of the ultimate disaster. This fact, and thus his status as Protector of the Peace, had already been recognized by a group of Senators who called on Mr. Eisenhower to "assume personal responsibility" for creating an adequate program of civil defense, something he shortly proceeded to do within the limits of his budget and our expectations.

There is at least one area of American life, the economy, in which the people of this country are no longer content to let disaster fall upon them unopposed. They now expect their government, under the direct leadership of the President, to prevent a depression or panic and not simply to wait until one has developed before putting it to rout. Thus the President has a new function, which is still taking shape, that of Manager of Prosperity. . . .

The very notion of the President as Manager of Prosperity strikes many people as an economic and political heresy, especially those who still swear allegiance to the tattered doctrine of the self-healing economy. Most of us, however, now accept the idea of a federal government openly engaged in preventing runaway booms and plunging busts. We need only think of Mr. Eisenhower's creditable performance in the slack days of 1954—or, for that matter, of his uninspired performance in the harder days of 1958-1959—to recognize the central position of the Presidency in this new kind of government. Lest there be any doubt how the President himself felt about the new dimension of government responsibility, let me quote from his message to Congress accompanying the Economic Report for 1953:

The demands of modern life and the unsettled status of the world require a more important role for government than it played in earlier and quieter times. . . .

Government must use its vast power to help maintain employment and purchasing power as well as to maintain reasonably stable prices.

Government must be alert and sensitive to economic developments, including is own myriad activities. It must be prepared to take preventive as well as remedial action; and it must be ready to cope with new situations that may arise. This is not a start-and-stop responsibility, but a continuous one.

The arsenal of weapons at the disposal of Government for maintaining economic stability is formidable. It includes credit controls administered by the Federal Reserve System; the debt-management policies of the Treasury; authority of the President to vary the terms of mortgages carrying Federal insurance; flexibility in administration of the budget; agricultural supports; modification of the tax structure; and public works. We shall not hesitate to use any or all of these weapons as the situation may require.

And this from a Republican President dedicated to the glories of free enterprise! Thus far have we and the Presidency moved in a generation of welfare and warfare.

In order to grasp the full import of the last of the President's roles, we must take him as Chief Diplomat, Commander in Chief, and Chief of State, then thrust him onto a far wider stage, there to perform before a much more numerous and more critical audience. For the modern President is, whether we or our friends abroad like it or not, marked out for duty as a World Leader. The President has a much larger constituency than the American electorate: his words and deeds in behalf of our own survival as a free nation have a direct bearing upon the freedom and stability of at least several score other countries. . . .

This role is not much more than a decade old, although there was a short rehearsal of it in late 1918 and the first few months of 1919.

Whether it will continue to grow in the years of tension ahead depends, of course, on just how high the tension remains. It does seem probable that the President will have no choice but to act consciously for and speak openly to the nations with whom we are associated in defense of freedom—to act as Truman did in the North Korean aggression of June 1950, to speak as Eisenhower did in his proposal for an international atomic-energy pool delivered to the Assembly of the United Nations in December 1953, to act and speak together as Eisenhower did in the Berlin crisis of 1959. If the British Prime Minister often seemed to be the most influential figure in the Atlantic coalition during the first part of that nerve-racking year, this could be ascribed to the reluctance of the President rather than to any decline in the stature of the Presidency. Whoever the incumbent of our first office may be, its stature in the world grows mightier with every passing year. For some time to come the President of the United States will also be the "President of the West." . . .

At the same time, several of these functions are plainly in competition, even in conflict, with one another, and not just in terms of their demands on the President's time and energy. The roles of Voice of the People and Chief of Party cannot both be played with equal fervor, as Mr. Truman proved on several occasions that had best be forgotten, while to act as Chief Diplomat but to think as Chief of Party, as he was apparently persuaded to do in the Palestine crisis of 1948, can throw our foreign relations into indelicate confusion. Mr. Eisenhower certainly had his periods in which, despite perfect health, he reigned too much and thus ruled too little, and one can think of several competent Presidents —Cleveland and Taft and Hoover, to name three out of the last hundred years—who tried much too hard to be faithful Chief Executives. . . .

Yet if it has become a thousand-man job in the budget and in the minds of students of public administration, it remains a one-man job in the Constitution and in the minds of the people—a truth of which we were dramatically reminded when the President fell ill in September 1955. Since it is a one-man job, the one man who holds it can never escape making the final decisions in each of the many areas in which the American people and their Constitution hold him responsible.

16.3. THE BRICKER AMENDMENT

One of the principal proposals in recent years to limit the President's powers was the constitutional amendment drafted by former Senator Bricker of Ohio. The amendment failed, but the arguments for and against restricting the President's power to make treaties and executive agreements remain cogent in the problems of Presidential leadership and discretion today.

TEXT OF THE PROPOSED BRICKER AMENDMENT

S. J. Res. 1 (84th Cong. 1st Sess.)—A joint resolution proposing an amendment to the Constitution of the United States, relating to the legal effect of certain treaties and other international agreements.

Resolved by the Senate and House of Representatives of the United States of America in Congress assembled (two-thirds of each House concurring therein), That the following article is proposed as an amendment to the Constitution of the United States, which shall be valid to all intents and purposes as part of the Constitution when ratified by the legislatures of three-fourths of the several States:

SEC. 1. A provision of a treaty or other international agreement which conflicts with this Constitution, or which is not made in pursuance thereof, shall not be the supreme law of the land nor be of any force or effect.

SEC. 2. A treaty or other international agreement shall become effective as internal law in the United States only through legislation valid in the absence of international agreement.

SEC. 3. On the question of advising and consenting to the ratification of a treaty, the vote shall be determined by the yeas and nays, and the names of the persons voting for and against shall be entered on the Journal of the Senate.

SEC. 4. This article shall be inoperative unless it shall have been ratified as an amendment to the Constitution by the legislatures of three-fourths of the several States within seven years from the date of its submission.

PRO BY JOHN W. BRICKER

From the very beginning proponents of a treaty-control amendment have been striving to achieve in the simplest and most effective language these two ends:

1. A treaty or other international agreement which conflicts with the Constitution shall not be of any force or effect; and,

2. A treaty or other international agreement shall not become effective as internal law except through valid and appropriate legislation.

Now, the opponents of this amendment say that it would tie the hands of the President. That is true in one sense, but untrue in the impression intended to be conveyed. The President's hands are tied by the Constitution, particularly by the wise restraints of the Bill of Rights. My amendment would also tie the President's hands, but only to the extent that he could not make international agreements in conflict with the Constitution nor make one-man laws for the people of the United

---

From The Senate Judiciary Subcommittee Hearings: Pro—John W. Bricker, April 27, 1955; Con—John Foster Dulles, May 2, 1955.

States by executive agreement. Why shouldn't the President's hands be tied to that extent? Why should the President have power to make treaties and other international agreements which conflict with the Constitution of the United States? What domestic laws should the President have power to make by international agreements not approved by either House of Congress? I have never heard a convincing answer to these questions. . . .

This amendment is no radical innovation. Nor is it a grab for legislative power at the expense of Executive power. For more than a century, four well-recognized limitations on the power to make international agreements were thought to exist. Until fairly recent times, American Presidents, courts, Members of Congress, and eminent constitutional lawyers believed that these four safeguards were part of the Constitution. And I want to enumerate them:

1. Treaties and other international agreements cannot authorize what the Constitution expressly forbids. . . .

2. International agreements cannot be used to barter away the sovereignty and independence of the United States. . . .

3. The scope of the treaty power is limited to problems of genuine international concern which cannot be adjusted or regulated except by negotiation and contract between sovereign nations. . . .

4. Treaties cannot be used to take powers from the States and give them to the Federal Government. . . .

The prime legal issue raised by the amendment is simply this: Can a treaty or other international agreement override the Constitution? Of course, the founders of our Republic never dreamed that that could happen. If the treatymaking power is unlimited, then as Jefferson observed, 'we have no Constitution.' Nevertheless, no specific provision in the Constitution makes it supreme over conflicting treaties. Moreover, the records of the Constitutional Convention of 1787 reveal no discussion whatever on the question, 'Can a treaty or other international agreement override the Constitution?'

The Constitution says that three kinds of law are supreme. Article VI, paragraph 2, describes as the supreme law of the land:

1. The Constitution of the United States;

2. Laws of the United States made in pursuance of the Constitution; and

3. Treaties made, or which shall be made under the authority of the United States.

I emphasize in '2' that laws of the Congress must be in pursuance of the Constitution and that treaties under '3' are made under the authority of the United States.

Then article VI goes on to provide that this supreme law of the land—all three kinds—shall bind the judges in every State: 'any Thing in the Constitution or Laws of any State to the Contrary notwithstanding.'

Article VI, therefore, does not deal with the problem of relative supremacy as between the Constitution and treaties. Acts of Congress were subordinated to the Constitution by the requirement that they be made 'in pursuance thereof.' That phrase could not be used in connection with treaties without invalidating treaties made prior to the adoption of the Constitution. No provision of the Constitution was more fully discussed in the Convention nor the subject of more drafts than what finally emerged as paragraph 2 of article VI. All of the discussion, however, concerned what kinds of law should be binding on the States and how respect for such law should be secured. The nature and extent of the treaty power were left to implication.

I have already mentioned the implied limitations on the treaty power which were developed in the last century and respected until 1920. Then came the famous case of *Missouri* v. *Holland*. That case opened up the loophole which S.J. Res. 1 is designed to plug.

In *United States* v. *Pink,* the Supreme Court said that an executive agreement became, like a treaty, 'the supreme law of the land.'

After the *Holland,* the *Curtiss-Wright,* and the *Pink* cases were decided, experts in the field of international and constitutional law began to reappraise the treatymaking power. Among those who made such reappraisal was Mr. John Foster Dulles. Addressing a regional meeting of the American Bar Association in Louisville, Ky., on April 11, 1952, Mr. Dulles said:

The treatymaking power is an extraordinary power, liable to abuse. Treaties make international law and also they make domestic law. Under our Constitution, treaties become the supreme law of the land. They are, indeed, more supreme than ordinary laws for congressional laws are invalid if they do not conform to the Constitution, whereas treaty law can override the Constitution. Treaties, for example, can take powers away from the Congress and give them to the President; they can take powers from the States and give them to the Federal Government or to some international body, and they can cut across the rights given the people by their constitutional Bill of Rights.

That is the classic statement on the danger of treaty law. No other statement describes so well the dangers which confront us today. . . .

A number of world government enthusiasts advance the reactionary theory that the United Nations Charter should be amended, if necessary by interpretation rather than by formal amendment.

That the U.N. Charter can be amended without Senate approval is based on the wholly false premise that the United Nations Charter is a world constitution. The United Nations Charter is a treaty. The Senate advised and consented to its ratification in 1945. I shall never stop insisting that the United Nations Charter and all other treaties to which the

United States is, or may become a party, are contracts rather than constitutional documents. That was the sense in which the Founding Fathers used the word 'treaty' in the Constitution.

I have no objection to any person becoming a protagonist of any change that he wants to in the Constitution of the United States if it goes before the American people, as this amendment will, by approval of two-thirds of the Senate and the House, and through ratification of three-fourths of the States of the Union. But I do not want it done by informal amendment of the United Nations Charter.

The end result is the same—the United States would cease to be a sovereign, independent nation. When independence is destroyed, our liberties are destroyed at the same time. That is one of the most important reasons why we need a constitutional amendment safeguarding the power to make treaties and executive agreements.

CON BY JOHN FOSTER DULLES

The Resolution has two substantive sections. Section 1 says (a) that 'A provision of a treaty or other international agreement which conflicts with the Constitution . . . shall not be the supreme law of the land nor be of any force or effect' and (b) that the same is true if the treaty or international agreement is not made in pursuance of the Constitution.

Section 2 would do away with the present provision that treaties are law of the land and require (a) that treaties or other international agreements 'shall become effective as internal law only through legislation' and (b) that the legislation must be legislation which would be 'valid in the absence of international agreement.'

The portion of section 1 which deals with the supremacy of the Constitution is urged on the ground that the Constitution does not now indicate the relative supremacy of the Constitution itself and treaties made under the authority of the United States. It is suggested that recent developments in the field of international relations and recent judicial decisions make it desirable that the Constitution itself make it clear that if there is a conflict between a treaty or executive agreement and the Constitution, the Constitution will prevail.

Many feel that the decisions of the United States Supreme Court now adequately and authoritatively establish a proper balance between treaties and the Constitution and make it clear that the Constitution cannot be violated by treaties or executive agreements. Nevertheless, as President Eisenhower has said, there does exist within the country a certain fear that treaties, or even executive agreements, might supersede the Constitution. Therefore, the President has said that he would find it acceptable to have a constitutional amendment reaffirming that any provision of a treaty or international agreement which conflicts with the

Constitution should not be of any force or effect. I fully concur in this position.

Section 1 of the proposed amendment goes, however, considerably beyond this. It says that treaties or international agreements are of no effect unless made in pursuance of the Constitution.

Our Constitution now distinguishes between Federal laws and national treaties. Federal laws must be made in pursuance of the Constitution. But treaties are only required to be made under the authority of the U. S. There are different theories to explain that difference.

One theory is that the present language was designed merely to preserve treaties which had been concluded prior to coming into force of the Constitution which, therefore, could not have been made pursuant to it. One example is the Treaty of Peace of 1783 between the United States and Great Britain, which gave this Nation its independence. Thus it may be that the effect of this portion of the proposed constitutional amendment is merely to invalidate treaties made before the adoption of the Constitution in 1788.

However, there is another theory, which is that suggested in the Migratory Bird case of *Missouri* v. *Holland*. It was there indicated that the phrase 'in pursuance of the Constitution' was used relative to statutory law, for the reason that the executive branch of the Nation was limited to the exercise of expressly delegated powers; but that different language was used in relation to treaties because, in the field of foreign affairs, the President and the Senate were to act for the Nation as a whole.

If this interpretation is accepted, the result of applying the 'pursuant to' clause to treaties might be to invalidate that large part of our existing treaty structure which is applicable to States and to create, for the future, the very situation of impotence which the Constitution was designed to end.

As President Eisenhower pointed out on April 27 last: 'The Constitution had as one of its principal reasons for coming into being the conduct of the foreign affairs of the United States as a single unit, not as 48 States.'

Section 2 of the proposed joint resolution reads: 'A treaty or other international agreement shall become effective as internal law in the United States only through legislation valid in the absence of international agreement.'

This is a revolutionary provision. Under our federal system of government, certain legislative powers are vested in the Federal Government and other legislative powers are vested in the States. However, our Constitution does not project this division of power into our international relations. There the Nation is one. The States are forbidden to make treaties, and the President and the Senate, acting by a two-thirds vote, speak for the Nation as a whole.

In the Senate, the States are represented on a basis of sovereign equality, designed to enable them to preserve what the Federalist Papers called their residual sovereignty. Thus 17 of the 48 States can prevent any treaty from exercising the powers reserved to the States.

The proposed amendment undoes that constitutional concept of the Nation acting as a unit in relation to foreign affairs. It would make it impossible, in the absence of legislation by the Congress and by the 48 States, to conclude and make effective many traditional types of treaties. These would include the treaties of friendship, commerce, and navigation, which secure numerous and substantial benefits for our citizens abroad in return for a promise of the same treatment for foreign nationals in this country. They would include treaties on extradition, narcotics control, the right to inherit property, and the right to collect debts. . . .

By applying not only to treaties but to other international agreements, section 2 would infringe the President's powers as Commander in Chief and in the conduct of our foreign relations. It speaks of agreements in terms of their being 'effective as internal law.' This phrase has no settled meaning. It might be construed to mean affecting the determination of issues in judicial or administrative proceedings.

In this sense most international agreements have some effect which our courts will recognize.

The executive branch of the Government, in carrying on the Nation's business with foreign countries, negotiates and concludes numerous agreements and other arrangements that do not reach the dignity of treaties. Among these are military armistices and recognitions of foreign governments. All of these have legal effects which our courts recognize. If the proposed section 2 is to end that, then the President would be unable properly to conduct foreign relations. The President's powers in this respect would be shared by the Congress; it would become deeply involved in the impossible task of trying itself to manage the current conduct of foreign affairs, and the traditional balance of powers between the executive and legislative branches of government would be impaired.

17

The Federal Bureaucracy

17.1. A PROFILE OF THE FEDERAL CIVIL SERVICE

Professor Kaufman examines the reasons for vast increases in scope and size of the Federal bureaucracy since the days of George Washington's administration. He traces also the factors that led to overthrow of the "spoils system" and establishment of the independent and nonpartisan Civil Service Commission to direct government employment.

YOU WOULD NOT EXPECT a country such as ours was at the start to have a very large civil service. Indeed, even if the ratio of federal employees to total population in those days had been what it is today (our 2,300,000 civil servants constitute 1.4 percent of our 160 million people), there would have been about 49,000 on the payrolls. As a matter of fact, however, the Federal Government Service then numbered in the hundreds rather than in the thousands; there were about 350 people in it at the start of Washington's administration, and only about 2,100 as late as 1801. The public service has increased in size far more rapidly than the general population.

It was not a steady, orderly growth; it occurred in spasms of expansion and contraction, in fits and starts. It started modestly enough. As late as 1861, the year of the start of the Civil War, the total civil service consisted of 49,000 employees (less than two-tenths of one percent of the population, which had meanwhile risen to 31 million), and it

From Herbert Kaufman, "The Growth of the Federal Personnel System," in *The Federal Government Service: Its Character, Prestige, and Problems* (New York: The American Assembly, Columbia University, 1954), pp. 15–18, 32–36.

comprised only 208,000 at the turn of the century (while the population reached 76 million, so that the ratio was still less than three-tenths of one percent). In the Twentieth Century, however, federal employment increased more rapidly—it had reached 435,000 when World War I broke out; 515,000 in 1923; 572,000 in 1933; and 920,000 in 1939, when it constituted seven-tenths of one percent of the population of 130 million.

Then the number of civil servants shot upwards under the impact of World War II; by war's end in 1945, it stood at three and three-quarter million. The figure declined with the cessation of combat, but government employment was never again to fall back to the pre-World War II levels. Even in June of 1950, the month of the North Korean invasion of South Korea, it was almost two million. The Korean War brought it back up to more than 2,600,000, and only the end of action there has allowed the number of government personnel to slip back to the present figure of 2,300,000. It seems to have settled at about this level for the time being.

Perhaps the most striking thing in this brief historical sketch is the fact that three-quarters—1,781,078 out of 2,327,297—of the positions in the Federal Government service today were established and filled in the last 20 years!

Why has this happened? Clearly, the increase in population, though a factor, is by no means sufficient to explain it.

For the answer, we have only to look at some of the younger agencies of government. The Federal Communications Commission, for example. The Civil Aeronautics Board. The Civil Aeronautics Administration. The National Advisory Committee for Aeronautics. The Atomic Energy Commission. All of these—and the list is not exhaustive—were forced into existence by technological change.

Take the Department of Defense. The Veterans Administration. The Selective Service System. The War Claims Commission. The Foreign Operations Administration. The Central Intelligence Agency. The Office of Defense Mobilization. The expansion of the State Department. The Renegotiation Board. The Federal Civil Defense Administration. These were imposed on us by the conduct of war, the consequences of war, the threat of war, the "cold war."

Look at the Federal Deposit Insurance Corporation. The Department of Health, Education, and Welfare. The Housing and Home Finance Agency. The Reconstruction Finance Corporation. The National Labor Relations Board. The Farmers Home Administration. The Rural Electrification Administration. These, and many other units in the oldline departments, were brought into being by the depression.

These are the reasons the civil service grew so large so suddenly. . . . The reasons for the recent increase in the civil service are even more apparent if you look at the way government workers are divided among the agencies of the Federal Government. In March, 1954, half of them (1,162,232, to be exact) worked for the Department of Defense. This does not include uniformed personnel; it includes only civilians who man the shipyards of the Navy, the arsenals and ordnance plants and factories of the Army and Air Force, and who see that soldiers, sailors, airmen, and marines get their paychecks, that the proper allotments are sent to their dependents, that their records are kept up to date, and a thousand and one other things.

Another 20 percent worked for the Post Office; that department employs half a million people. Their work needs no explanation.

An additional eight percent (128,825 people) were in the employ of the Veterans Administration. They run hospitals for disabled veterans. They operate a huge insurance system. They help veterans get through school, get started in business, get established in homes.

Pause here for a moment. We have just accounted for more than three-quarters of all federal personnel—for 78 percent of them—and for most of the growth in recent years. Before World War II, the Veterans Administration was one-sixth its present size (there are 13 million veterans of that war, millions more from the Korean War, thousands more completing their terms of military service every year, and a GI Bill of Rights that did not exist before 1944 to be administered). Before World War II —in 1939, for example—we had 187,000 men in our Regular Army; our Navy consisted of about 151,000 officers and men; there was no separate Air Force. Today, we have 3,500,000 men under arms and on active duty in all three branches of the armed forces, not counting the reserves and National Guard, and they are much more elaborately equipped and require much more to sustain them in the field than would have been the case for an equal number of men a generation ago. Even the Post Office almost doubled its work force in the last 20 years (from 270,000 to over 500,000). In these three organizations work all but 22 percent of the federal civil servants, and all three increased enormously in size almost overnight.

What do the other 22 percent do? Everything else the United States Government does. There are 85,000 in the Treasury Department who print our paper money and stamps, mint our coins, collect taxes and customs, man the Coast Guard, control narcotics, and handle the records on United States Government Bonds. About 70,000 work in the Department of Agriculture, providing technical advice and service and financial assistance to the nation's farmers, managing 180 million acres of national forests, operating crop insurance programs, promoting soil conservation, and conducting research. In the Commerce Department, 42,000 perform the work of the Civil Aeronautics Administration, the Coast and Geodetic Survey, the Census Bureau, the Bureau of Standards, the Weather Bureau, and the Patent Office.

The Department of the Interior employs 52,000 to revitalize land that is now unproductive (the Bureau of Reclamation's job), to run a vast system of national parks (the Park Service), to administer grazing permits on the public domain (the Grazing Service), and generally to manage the remainder of the public domain (the Bureau of Land Management). It takes 36,000 in the Department of Health, Education, and Welfare to run the recently expanded social security system, the Public Health Service, and the Food and Drug Administration, to name a few of its components. There are 29,000 in the Department of Justice enforcing federal law, including the famed FBI. That much-maligned child of scorn, the State Department, has 20,000 employees maintaining posts in every corner of the world. These seven departments, together, have about 334,000 civil servants—about 15 percent of the total.

Ten agencies, in sum, employ about 93 percent of all those on the federal civilian payrolls. The remaining seven percent staff a total of 45 agencies—the Bureau of the Budget, the Department of Labor, the Panama Canal Zone Government, the Export-Import Bank, the General Services Administration, the Interstate Commerce Commission, the Federal Reserve System, the Securities and Exchange Commission, the Panama Canal Company, the United States Information Agency, and three dozen others. If all of them were eliminated tomorrow, the impact on the size of the bureaucracy would be slight. . . .

A great many things were blamed on the spoils system during the fight to overthrow it. Every evidence of dishonesty. Every display of incompetence. Every suggestion of inefficiency. Everything low and mean and degrading that ever occurred in the government service was blamed on the spoils system. Indeed, one merit system enthusiast, looking back to the days of spoils, even charged that the spoils system encouraged prostitution:

Some young women in despair, losing hope at the loss of their jobs, went wrong on the town, for Washington like other cities big and little had its red light district . . .

It is said that young women suddenly deprived of their positions under the spoils system were sometimes driven by extremity to those notorious resorts.

Oh! the pity of it. Strangers in a strange city unexpectedly turned out of office, their salary then too small to permit of savings, without funds or friends, the amiable madam's [sic] of the oldest trade in the world hospitally [sic] extended a welcome to these unfortunate recruits, and the folks back home unknowingly continued to enjoy the wages of sin of an erring daughter whom of course they still thought a Government employee.

It was not really necessary to resort to near-hysterical accusations to discredit spoils. The disadvantages of this means of staffing government agencies were profound and obvious enough not to require artistic heightening. In the long run, the government service tended to deteriorate under these conditions. Spoils may have democratized politics; it threatened to degenerate administration as it continued completely unchecked. The government, it is true, continued to do its job under spoils—but at what cost? For how long could it have continued to do so after the rise of specialization? How well was it working?

The spoils system put a premium on the creation of extra jobs —both to provide additional political currency and also to lighten the workload so that loyal political partisans would have time for their assigned political tasks.

It resulted in the employment of many individuals who were not qualified to perform the duties for which they were hired.

It tempted government officials to use their official positions for personal gain, for they had generally only four years in which to reap the harvest for which they had labored long and hard in the political vineyards.

It meant that a good deal of energy went into the orientation and basic training of a new work force every four years.

It reduced the President to the level of petty job broker, and diverted his strength and attention from important matters of state to the dispensation of hundreds of posts under the greatest pressure. The President gained bargaining leverage, but at the price of his health and vigor, his peace of mind, and the dignity and decorum of his high office. The Executive Mansion was besieged. The Chief Executive could not escape to protect either the nation's welfare or his own sanity.

All these concomitants of spoils were clearly visible even to the most dispassionate observer. They moved men of conscience and goodwill to strive for reform.

The reformers adopted a simple but drastic formula to correct the defects of the civil service system. Since they ascribed the defects almost entirely to politically motivated appointments and removals, they proposed to take these powers out of the hands of the politicians. They planned to vest the control of these personnel actions in a relatively independent non-political body that would administer examinations to screen applicants for vacancies, and that would act to prevent dismissal for purely political reasons. The politicians were accused of corrupting the public service; the reformers' remedy was to isolate the public service from their machinations. . . .

The provisions of the Civil Service Act of 1883 reflect the reformers conviction that power to make appointments had to be transferred in large part, if not entirely, from political officers to a nonpolitical agency as they believed it had been in England. . . .

What the law did, in effect, was to substitute the Commission for

Congressional and party officials in providing appointment advice to the President and his department heads. The politicians had determined who would be in the public service on the basis of the political contributions made by the applicants; the Commission would now make the same determination, but on the basis of fitness for office evaluated by examination. . . .

The assumption imbedded in the Civil Service Act—indeed, in the philosophy of civil service reform—is that the civil service is a "neutral instrument," without policy preferences of its own (taken as a body) and without any inclination to attempt to impose any policy on the country. For the civil service reformers, the civil service was like a hammer or a saw; it would do nothing at all by itself, but it would serve any purpose, wise or unwise, good or bad, to which any user put it. That is why the reformers concentrated all their efforts on the ability of government personnel to do their jobs; they were anxious to make the best tool possible available to whoever occupied the highest seats in the American governmental system. They conceived of policy and administration as distinct and separate, though related, activities, and they wanted to restrict partisanship to the policy-makers in order to provide a superlative mechanism by which the voters' mandates could be carried out. They perfected the instrument; let the people put it to what use they would. . . .

17.2. THE CURSE OF CIVIL SERVICE REFORM

An eloquent if somewhat overdrawn defense of the spoils system by an old-time Tammany boss is this speech on "The Curse of Civil Service Reform," by the late George Washington Plunkitt. The account of Mr. Flaherty, the red-haired, blue-eyed son of Tammany driven to desert his country by a civil service examination, is almost more than the loyal heart of Plunkitt can sustain.

THIS CIVIL SERVICE law is the biggest fraud of the age. It is the curse of the nation. . . . First this great and glorious country was built up by political parties; second parties can't hold together if their workers don't get the offices when they win; third, if the parties go to pieces, the government they built up must go to pieces, too; fourth, then there'll be h——— to pay.

Could anything be clearer than that? Say, honest now; can you answer that argument? Of course you won't deny that the government was built up by the great parties. That's history, and you can't go back

From William L. Riordan, ed., *Plunkitt of Tammany Hall* (New York: E. P. Dutton & Co., 1963), pp. 19, 24–29.

of the returns. As to my second proposition, you can't deny that either. When parties can't get offices, they'll bust. They ain't far from the bustin' point now, with all this civil service business keepin' most of the good things from them. How are you goin' to keep up patriotism if this thing goes on? You can't do it. Let me tell you that patriotism has been dying out fast for the last twenty years. Before then when a party won, its workers got everything in sight. That was somethin' to make a man patriotic. Now, when a party wins and its men come forward and ask for their reward, the reply is, "Nothin' doin', unless you can answer a list of questions about Egyptian mummies and how many years it will take for a bird to wear out a mass of iron as big as the earth by steppin' on it once in a century?"

I have studied politics and men for forty-five years, and I see how things are driftin'. Sad indeed is the change that has come over the young men, even in my district, where I try to keep up the fire of patriotism by gettin' a lot of jobs for my constituents, whether Tammany is in or out. The boys and men don't get excited any more when they see a United States flag or hear the "Star Spangled Banner! They don't care no more for firecrackers on the Fourth of July. And why should they? What is there in it for them? They know that no matter how hard they work for their country in a campaign, the jobs will go to fellows who can tell about the mummies and the bird steppin' on the iron. Are you surprised then that the young men of the country are beginning to look oddly on the flag and don't care to put up a nickel for firecrackers?

Say, let me tell of one case. After the battle of San Juan Hill, the Americans found a dead man with a light complexion, red hair and blue eyes. They could see he wasn't a Spaniard, although he had on a Spanish uniform. Several officers looked him over, and then a private of the Seventy-first Regiment saw him and yelled, "Good Lord, that's Flaherty." That man grew up in my district and he was once the most patriotic American boy on the West Side. He couldn't see a flag without yellin' himself hoarse.

Now, how did he come to be lying dead with a Spanish uniform on? I found out all about it, and I'll vouch for the story. Well, in the municipal campaign of 1897, that young man, chockful of patriotism, worked day and night for the Tammany ticket. Tammany won, and the young man determined to devote his life to the service of the city. He picked out a place that would suit him, and sent in his application to the head of department. He got a reply that he must take a civil service examination to get the place. He didn't know what these examinations were, so he went, all light-hearted, to the Civil Service Board. He read the questions about the mummies, the bird on the iron, and all the other fool questions—and he left that office an enemy of the country that he had loved so well. The mummies and the bird blasted his patriotism. He went to Cuba, enlisted in the Spanish army at the breakin' out of the war, and died fightin' his country.

That is but one victim of the infamous civil service. If that young man had not run up against the civil [service] examination, but had been allowed to serve his country as he wished, he would be in a good office today, drawin' a good salary. Ah, how many young men have had their patriotism blasted in the same way!

Now, what is goin' to happen when civil service crushes out patriotism? Only one thing can happen—the republic will go to pieces. Then a czar or a sultan will turn up, which brings me to the fourthly of my argument; that is, there will be h———— to pay. And that ain't no lie.

17.3. MYTHS ABOUT GOVERNMENT EMPLOYMENT

Criticism of the Federal service is often based upon misconceptions about government employment. Seven of the more common myths are dealt with by the United States Civil Service Commission in this selection designed to present an accurate image of the system.

1. *All government employees are clerks.*

Government employees work in almost as many different kinds of jobs as employees in private industry. You can hardly call these clerks—chemists in the Food and Drug Administration and the Department of Agriculture, rangers in the Forest Service, physicists in the Army and Navy, doctors and nurses in the Veterans' Administration. Electrician, lawyer, bricklayer, economist, blacksmith, librarian, typesetter, engineer—all these and hundreds of other kinds of positions are found in the government service.

2. *Most government employees work in Washington.*

Only about a tenth of the employees of the government are in jobs in Washington, D. C. The remainder work in other parts of the United States and in other parts of the world. There are more than twice as many people working for the Postal Service alone, in towns and cities throughout the country, as there are working in Washington for all the executive agencies.

3. *Government employees can't be fired.*

Many people think that a government job is a lifetime job. For

---

From *Working for the U. S. A.* (Washington, D.C.: U.S. Civil Service Commission, 1957), pp. 12–13.

an employee who is efficient and trustworthy it can be a lifetime job, but figures prove that many government employees are dismissed every year. During a recent year, more than 21,000 were discharged from their positions for inefficiency, misconduct or delinquency, or for other serious causes.

4. *The best way to get a government job is to write your congressman.*

The best way to apply for a government job is to find out what examinations are open and then file an application with the United States Civil Service Commission or one of its offices. Ninety-one percent of all positions in agencies of the government in the continental United States are in the "competitive service"; they are filled by competitive examination, or by promoting or transferring employees already in the competitive service, or by reemploying persons who have left the service and wish to return to it.

5. *Civil-service examinations are always written tests.*

In the majority of examinations, civil-service examiners rate applicants on the experience and training they have listed on their application forms. The examiners check up on these claims by writing to former employers and fellow workers of the applicants. The announcement of an examination tells whether it consists of, or includes, a written test.

6. *The Civil Service Commission does all the hiring.*

The only people hired by the Civil Service Commission are those who work in the Commission's own offices. The employees of other agencies are hired, in each case, by officials of those agencies. For every job to be filled, the appointing officer has the legal right to choose one person from among the three whose names are at the top of the list of eligibles. The Civil Service Commission sends him the names of the top three people on the appropriate list. The appointing officer does the hiring.

7. *The more employees a supervisor has, the higher his salary.*

The number of employees supervised is one thing considered in deciding what salary or grade a supervisor should have, but only one. A supervisor who has under him a small group of employees who do difficult and complex work is paid a higher salary than a person who supervises a large group of employees who do simple, routine work.

17.4. RESPONSIBILITIES OF THE CAREER SERVICE

The change from one administration to another involves an extensive turnover of policy makers in the higher echelons. The normal functions of career civil servants continue, however, along with responsibility for adapting to the new administration's policies. This article stresses the responsi-

*bilities and opportunities of the career civil servant for improving the
governmental process.*

NEXT JANUARY 20, a new President of the United States will take office.
Regardless of whether he is a Republican or a Democrat, new men and
women in the Cabinet offices and the other key executive positions of the
Government departments and agencies will assume responsibility for administering the Federal programs which have been authorized by thousands of separate laws. These will be new players stepping into roles they
have not played before—roles of tremendous and almost frightening importance to the welfare of 180 million Americans. . . .

An important factor in a smooth transition from one national
administration to another is advanced preparation by the career staff. This
fact has been clearly demonstrated by the experience of past changes in
administration. Regrettably, until 1952, there has been very little transition
planning, although some steps in the direction of such planning were
undertaken in 1948.

Federal career officials, and personnel officers in particular, must
recognize and accept a dual responsibility: first, to prepare the agencies
and the personnel of the agencies to respond to the programs and policies
of the new administration, and second, to prepare to assist the new political officials to come to full effectiveness in their new roles as quickly
as possible. . . .

During a transition in administration, career civil servants represent the ongoing force of the Government. Nothing comes to a full halt,
and neither program nor staff operations can be shut down, even if such
action seems desirable. This state of affairs has come about gradually as
a result of changes in the structure of our society. Through most of the
19th century we were largely an agricultural nation, with a Federal Government whose primary functions were maintaining law and order on the
frontier and conducting foreign relations in a world where our geography
furnished great protection. Little of moment was apt to happen between
election day and inauguration day 4 months later. Today we are a highly
industrialized society. Economic, technological, and political developments
have caused significant changes in the role of government, and heightened
a thousand-fold the interdependence of men and their government. Now
events often outrun plans made yesterday, and much can and does happen
between the first week in November and the third week in January. . . .

Career officials must be concerned during the coming months
with doing everything they can to make the transition smooth and fast.

From Roger W. Jones, Chairman, United States Civil Service Commission,
"Career Service Can Set Scene," in *Civil Service Journal,* July–September,
1960, pp. 26–30.

The tempo, complexity, and perils of our time make it imperative that the Government change hands with practically no lost motion. More specifically, the fact that we serve a representative form of government requires us to respond effectively and willingly to the policies of the new administration. Just as we must take for granted integrity of person and purpose in the new administration, so must all of us in the career service use our technical competence and administrative know-how to demonstrate that the incoming political executives and the general public can take for granted the ability and the essentially nonpartisan character of career people in the civil service. Ours is a responsibility to use our power in such a way as to counteract the fears of some that political leaders may become the "captives of the entrenched bureaucracy." . . .

The career service must not allow itself to arrive at the transition without making a real effort to gain an undertanding of the commitments and thought processes of the new executive leadership. The party platform takes on a new dimension after the election: the interpretation, and the emphasis given certain parts by the President-elect must receive full consideration in charting the probable future course of the new administration. It would be highly desirable if the study of party platforms and the views of candidates and other leaders of both parties could be carried on by a small staff in each agency, with the results made available to all agency officials. (A very useful device, in 1952 and again in 1956, was the preparation by some Government offices of compendiums in which such information was collected and indexed by subject matter and program area.) Then as soon as the new head of his agency is designated, the career executive should acquaint himself with that individual's background and views, particularly as they relate to his agency's programs, in order to be best prepared to assist in carrying out new policies.

Such a study of party platforms, policies, and views of new agency heads is not improper in any respect; it is a responsibility that a career executive has in our form of government. As a civil servant, he must never forget that however well qualified an expert he may be in his job, and however well motivated, he is not elected to it by any vote. Neither is he the direct delegate of the President in most instances. His chain of command leads clearly to the President, but the higher links in the chain are there. Career executives who believe that representative democracy is the right form of government for this country cannot, in good conscience, do anything other than help political executives carry out policy as enunciated by the President and his principal officers. . . .

After the new administration takes office and its policies become clear, each career executive should examine his emotional and intellectual commitments to the programs in which he is involved. If he finds that he cannot in all honesty give his support to the new administration and cannot help carry out faithfully its policies respecting his programs, he should have the courage to seek other employment—perhaps in another Government program which can use his stature and status and in which old commitments on policy and program will not work against his success. . . .

It seems to me that there are four factors that will be of great importance to the new political executive. Career officials, before the new administration comes in, should be planning how they will go about acquainting the new political executive with his resources and limitations in these areas:

1. *Personnel.*

The men and women of the career service, from administrative assistant secretaries and bureau chiefs to the newest stenographer, are the most important resources the new political executive will have. The personnel officer will have the primary responsibility for informing him concerning the career service. He must explain the organization to the new executive, and he must help the staff to become acquainted with the new political executive and his plans and views. One method that might be helpful in carrying out this responsibility is to provide an inventory of personnel showing their location, numbers, special abilities, and occupations. Factual statements on the background of career management officials should be furnished. . . .

2. *Budget*

The new political executive will have to operate for over 5 months with appropriations enacted in the previous administration on the basis of previous programs and commitments. In addition, he will either have to defend a budget for the next fiscal year which was prepared before he took office, or he will have to propose an alternative budget very quickly. Participating actively in the budget process is one of the quickest ways a new political executive can learn about his agency. Career officials should encourage him to take a deep interest in the budget, and should keep in mind in presenting their budgets that this can be one of the most meaningful experiences for the new executive.

3. *Laws, rules, and precedents*

In the Federal Government, laws, rules, regulations, precedents, traditions, and key court decisions underlie and largely control (along with money) the major outlines of Federal programs. While familiarity makes an orderly framework out of this for the career executive, it will be largely an unknown and forbidding jungle to the new administrator. Early understanding of the outlines can be of enormous help in smoothing the path of new administration.

Operating within this framework is so customary for career officials that we often are not aware of why we do not do certain things, or why we do other things in a particular fashion. One of the reasons for misunderstanding between career officials and their political superiors is sometimes the career man's lack of ability to express clearly and understandably the concepts, attitudes, and values underlying our operations. Would it not be worthwhile, in preparation for a change, to try to articulate the basic principles and goals of our programs? If there is ambiguity, as there is in most programs, can we state clearly the conflicting values leading to the ambiguity? Can we state in understandable terms the factors that have shaped our programs, such as court decisions, Attorney General's opinions, congressional views, group views, and the impact of other agencies? . . .

4. *Legislative, organizations, and public relationships*

The personnel officer, and all other career officials, must develop and maintain a sensitivity to changes in emphasis in the programs of the new administration. Because the career official knows the history and background of the agency, has the files, and "knows where the bodies are buried," he is in the best position to help the new political executives avoid the pitfalls in the unfamiliar terrain, such as legislative issues that are certain to arise, the historical attitudes of the Congress, and its committees, and the senior members of those committees. New political officers often are badly trapped by their assumption that party lines are always sharply drawn in committees. They often do not know what the program commitments of the committees are. Career staff officials do know. The political officer must also know, or be taught, the attitudes and activities of various groups which are interested in his agency—the national and sectional interests and special-interest groups—and how these are reflected in the Congress. . . .

The new political executive must understand the expectations of the public as to conduct. Practices which are completely acceptable in nonpublic employment may be unacceptable in public officials. Many a promising and capable political executive has learned this too late. He should, of course, be informed of the conflict-of-interest laws, but even more important is the getting across of the general concept that he will operate in a goldfish bowl. His business and how he does it is public business, in the conduct of which appearances as well as realities are important. He can never forget the maxim that public office is a public trust. . . .

There is another responsibility of the career official which is shared with the political executive: the maintenance of the integrity of the career service. It is clear that a competent, effective, responsible career service is a prerequisite to representative government in the modern age. Career officials must insist on, and defend, selection and retention of personnel on the basis of merit without regard to politics, race, religion, or creed. While job security is not an end in itself, during transitional periods any threat to job security not based on efficiency or program needs is a threat to the integrity to the merit system.

The personnel system of the Federal Government has two qualities which are of prime importance in a transition: It fosters a highly competent, stable, and efficient work force through the application of merit principles, and it is flexible enough to respond to changes in public policy. . . .

17.5. IMPROVING ADMINISTRATIVE MANAGEMENT

A fundamental problem of democracy is the effective implementation of public policy by the bureaucracy. The President's Committee on Administrative Management in 1937 reported on the pressing need for efficiency in the executive branch. This selection summarizes the five major suggestions of the Committee for enhancing administrative management. Many of the comments remain relevant to the problems of bureaucracy today.

THE EFFICIENCY of government rests upon two factors: the consent of the governed and good management. In a democracy consent may be achieved readily, though not without some effort, as it is the cornerstone of the constitution. Efficient management in a democracy is a factor of peculiar significance.

Administrative efficiency is not merely a matter of paper clips, time clocks, and standardized economies of motion. These are but minor gadgets. Real efficiency goes much deeper down. It must be built into the structure of a government just as it is built into a piece of machinery.

Fortunately the foundations of effective management in public affairs, no less than in private, are well known. They have emerged universally wherever men have worked together for some common purpose, whether through the state, the church, the private association, or the commercial enterprise. They have been written into constitutions, charters, and articles of incorporation, and exist as habits of work in the daily life of all organized peoples. Stated in simple terms these canons of efficiency require the establishment of a responsible and effective chief executive as the center of energy, direction, and administrative management; the systematic organization of all activities in the hands of a qualified personnel under the direction of the chief executive; and to aid him in this, the establishment of appropriate managerial and staff agencies. There must also be provision for planning, a complete fiscal system, and means for holding the Executive accountable for his program.

Taken together, these principles, drawn from the experience of mankind in carrying on large-scale enterprises, may be considered as the

From *Report with Special Studies* (Washington, D.C.: The President's Committee on Administrative Management, 1937), pp. 2–53.

first requirement of good management. They comprehend the subject matter of administrative management as it is dealt with in this report. Administrative management concerns itself in a democracy with the executive and his duties, with managerial and staff aides, with organization, with personnel, and with the fiscal system because these are the indispensable means of making good the popular will in a people's government.

In the light of these canons of efficiency, what must be said of the Government of the United States today? Speaking in the broadest terms at this point, and in detail later on, we find in the American Government at the present time that the effectiveness of the Chief Executive is limited and restricted, in spite of the clear intent of the Constitution to the contrary; that the work of the Executive Branch is badly organized; that the managerial agencies are weak and out of date; that the public services does not include its share of men and women of outstanding capacity and character; and that the fiscal and auditing systems are inadequate. These weaknesses are found at the center of our Government and involve the office of the Chief Executive itself.

While in general principle our organization of the Presidency challenges the admiration of the world, yet in equipment for administrative management our Executive Office is not fully abreast of the trend of our American times, either in business or in government. Where, for example, can there be found an executive in any way comparable upon whom so much petty work is thrown? Or who is forced to see so many persons on unrelated matters and to make so many decisions on the basis of what may be, because of the very press of work, incomplete information? How is it humanly possible to know fully the affairs and problems of over 100 separate major agencies, to say nothing of being responsible for their general direction and coordination?

These facts have been known for many years and are so well appreciated that it is not necessary for us to prove again that the President's administrative equipment is far less developed than his responsibilities, and that a major task before the American Government is to remedy this dangerous situation. What we need is not a new principle, but a modernizing of our managerial equipment. . . .

On the basis of this experience and our examination of the Executive Branch we conclude that the following steps should now be taken:

1. To deal with the greatly increased duties of executive management falling upon the President the White House staff should be expanded.

2. The managerial agencies of the Government, particularly those dealing with the budget, efficiency research, personnel, and planning, should be greatly strengthened and developed as arms of the Chief Executive.

3. The merit system should be extended upward, outward, and

downward to cover all non-policy-determining posts, and the civil service system should be reorganized and opportunities established for a career system attractive to the best talent of the Nation.

4. The whole Executive Branch of the Government should be overhauled and the present 100 agencies reorganized under a few large departments in which every executive activity would find its place.

5. The fiscal system should be extensively revised in the light of the best governmental and private practice, particularly with reference to financial records, audit, and accountability of the Executive to the Congress. . . .

In proceeding to the reorganization of the Government it is important to keep prominently before us the ends of reorganization. Too close a view of machinery must not cut off from sight the true purpose of efficient management. Economy is not the only objective, though reorganization is the first step to savings; the elimination of duplication and contradictory policies is not the only objective, though this will follow; a simple and symmetrical organization is not the only objective, though the new organization will be simple and symmetrical; higher salaries and better jobs are not the only objectives, though these are necessary; better business methods and fiscal controls are not the only objectives, though these too are demanded. There is but one grand purpose, namely, to make democracy work today in our National Government; that is, to make our Government an up-to-date, efficient, and effective instrument for carrying out the will of the Nation. It is for this purpose that the Government needs thoroughly modern tools of management.

As a people we congratulate ourselves justly on our skill as managers—in the home, on the farm, in business big and little—and we properly expect that management in government shall be of the best American model. We do not always get these results, and we must modestly say "we count not ourselves to have attained", but there is a steady purpose in America to press forward until the practices of our governmental administration are as high as the purpose and standards of our people. We know that bad management may spoil good purposes, and that without good management democracy itself cannot achieve its highest goals. . . .

These changes taken together will give to the Executive agencies of fiscal management, personnel management, and planning management. Under the plans proposed these three arms of management are knit together in the White House, under the immediate direction of the President.

The drastic reduction in the number of departments, commissions, boards, authorities, agencies, and activities from over 100 to 12 will have many implications. It will take us back to the Constitution in that it ties in the wandering independencies and abolishes the irresponsible and headless "fourth branch" of the Government which has grown up unnoticed. It will reestablish a single Executive Branch, with the President as its responsible head, as provided by the Constitution. Moreover, it will make it humanly possible for a President to do his job, and to coordinate the activities for which he is constitutionally, legally, and popularly responsible, by greatly lessening the contacts and detail which now engulf him. It will make of the Government a businesslike organization for effective and efficient service, and, finally, will render the whole Government more easily understood and controllable by the people, and thus a more faithful servant of the people.

At the same time, sharper lines of accountability to the Congress are traced, and forms of decentralization, both geographical and departmental, outlined.

Your Committee fully appreciates that there is no magic in management alone. Management is a servant, not a master—a means, not an end, a tool in the hands and for the purposes of the Nation. Public service is the service of the common good in peace or war and will be judged by this standard. Not merely lower unit costs but higher human happiness and values are the supreme ends of our national life, and by these terms this and every other system must finally be tested. Good management will promote in the fullest measure the conservation and utilization of our national resources, and spell this out plainly in social justice, security, order, liberty, prosperity, in material benefits, and in higher values of life. The adjustments and arrangements we suggest have no other purpose or justification than better public service for our people through better administrative management.

It may be said that there is danger that management itself will grow too great and forget where it came from or what it is for—in the old and recurring insolence of office. But in the judgment of your Committee, based upon broad observation of the bewildering sweep of recent events here and elsewhere, the really imminent danger now is that our democracy and perhaps others may be led by false or mistaken guides to place their trust in weak and faltering inaction, which in the bitter end runs to futility and defeat. In the late war, democracies showed vast strength and tenacity in times of strain that racked every fiber of the ship of state. And now we face and will master the critical tasks of reorganization and readjustment of many tangled parts of our national life on many new frontiers. The injustice and oppression intertwined with solid good in our American system will not always yield without a firm display of our national constitutional powers. Our national will must be expressed not merely in a brief, exultant moment of electoral decision, but in persistent, determined, competent day-by-day administration of what the Nation has decided to do.

Honesty and courage alone are not enough for victory, either in peace or in war. Intelligence, vision, fairness, firmness, and flexibility are required in an assembled, competent, strong organization of democracy.

To falter at this point is fatal. A weak administration can neither advance nor retreat successfully—it can merely muddle. Those who waiver at the sight of needed power are false friends of modern democracy. Strong executive leadership is essential to democratic government today. Our choice is not between power and no power, but between responsible but capable popular government and irresponsible autocracy.

The forward march of American democracy at this point of our history depends more upon effective management than upon any other single factor. The times demand better governmental organization, staffed with more competent public servants, more free to do their best, and coordinated by an Executive accountable to the Congress and fully equipped with modern tools of management. Thus the President will have effective managerial authority over the Executive Branch commensuate with his responsibility under the Constitution of the United States.

17.6. CURRENT PROBLEMS IN REGULATORY ADMINISTRATION

This selection indicates some of the fundamental problems involved in regulatory administration. Delay and bias in decision making, low quality of political personnel, and failure to coordinate policy are among the criticisms Dean Landis included in the analysis which he prepared for President-elect John F. Kennedy.

THE FEDERAL COMMUNICATIONS COMMISSION presents a somewhat extraordinary spectacle. Despite considerable technical excellence on the part of its staff, the Commission has drifted, vacillated and stalled in almost every major area. It seems incapable of policy planning, of disposing within a reasonable period of time the business before it, of fashioning procedures that are effective to deal with its problems. The available evidence indicates that it, more than any other agency, has been susceptible to *ex parte* presentations, and that it has been subservient, far too subservient, to the subcommittees on communications of the Congress and their members. A strong suspicion also exists that far too great an influence is exercised over the Commission by the networks.

The quality of its top personnel is, of course, primarily responsible for these defects. The members of the Commission do not appear to be overworked in the sense that the Commission's docket is bulging with

From James M. Landis, *Report on Regulatory Agencies to the President-Elect* (Washington, D.C., 86th Congress, 2d Session, Senate Committee on the Judiciary, December, 1960), pp. 53–54, 66–68, 70–71, 74–77.

cases calling for disposition. Nevertheless disposition lags. Only 32 cases, all dealing with broadcasting licenses, were decided by the Commission during fiscal 1959, other than cases dismissed or in which the examiner's report became final. Commission action following the examiner's report in 9 of these cases took from 6 to 12 months and in 10 cases from one year to two years. In broadcast license cases no criteria for decision have evolved. True, criteria of various different kinds are articulated but they are patently not the grounds motivating decision. No firm decisional policy has evolved from these case-by-case dispositions. Instead the anonymous opinion writers for the Commission pick from a collection of standards those that will support whatever decision the Commission chooses to make.

Observers of the procedures employed by the Commission agree that the issues litigated are unreal and a mass of useless evidence, expensive to prepare, is required to be adduced. The uselessness of much of this evidence derives from several causes. The first is that programming proposed by applicants is of high-sounding moral and ethical content in order to establish that their operation of a radio and television station would be in the "public interest". The actual programming bears no reasonable similitude to the programming proposed. The Commission knows this but ignores these differentiations at the time when renewal of licenses of the station is before them. Nevertheless, it continues with its Alice-in-Wonderland procedures. Also because of the varying standards that the Commission employs, a vast amount of unrealistic testimony is adduced to support each of these standards, incumbering the record with useless data.

On major policy matters, the Commission seems incapable of reaching conclusions. The UHF debacle has been plainly apparent for some 5 to 6 years. Nothing of any substantial consequence has yet been accomplished by the Commission to relieve the situation, although they are now purporting to make available additional VHF channels in one and two V-channel markets.

The procedures employed by the Commission in adjudicatory matters as well as in purely exploratory matters seem primarily at fault for these deficiencies. Leadership in the effort to solve problems seems too frequently to be left to commercial interests rather than taken by the Commission itself. No patent solution for this situation exists other than the incubation of vigor and courage in the Commission by giving it strong and competent leadership, and thereby evolving sensible procedures for the disposition of its business. . . .

The prime key to the improvement of the administrative process is the selection of qualified personnel. Good men can make poor laws workable; poor men will wreak havoc with good laws.

As long as the selection of men for key administrative posts is based upon political reward rather than competency, little else that is done will really matter. Thus, the real issues are two: (1) are these posts sufficiently attractive to draw good men, and (2) how can these men be found?

Good men are primarily attracted by the challenge inherent in a job. Salary is a secondary consideration, provided only that it is high enough to enable them to meet reasonable standards of living comparable to their positions in the society. Our universities have known and, indeed, traded on these facts. Tenure is another consideration of more importance than salary, for with tenure goes independence and the opportunity for long-range planning.

Basic challenges have been missing in the last decade. Good men cannot be attracted to agencies if they see that the colleagues with whom they are called upon to work, the staffs that they must utilize, are not measurable by standards they believe to be appropriate. Such a condition implies a lack of concern or a lack of understanding of the regulatory process by the President, either or both of which are destructive of the very thing that could hold an appeal. The appeal of a job can also be destroyed if the President, through design or neglect, permits his prejudices in behalf of political associates or friends to dictate the deposition of individual items of business. No truly good man can submit to such interference. Finally, the job's relationship to the general program of the Administration must be clear and that clarity of relationship with the help of the President constantly maintained. These are the essential ingredients of the concept of challenge. They are also essential lures for the enlistment of talent.

Compensation is a consideration. Present salaries for top administrative personnel are in the neighborhood of $20,000 per year. This is a reasonable salary for the present level of the cost of living. Increasing it by $2500 or even $5000 would not appreciably affect the situation. But there are two things that could make these positions more attractive at a very reasonable cost. The first is the grant of a moderate entertainment allowance to the administrator. Like an ambassador he needs to maintain a certain prestige with the industry. He should be able to entertain rather than be required to suffer entertainment. At conferences, which he not infrequently is required to call, luncheon breaks should provide something better than service from a government cafeteria. The second matter is an adequate retirement allowance. For unexplained reasons the retirement allowance for executive employees is considerably less than the allowances available to legislators. As an alleged servant of the Congress, the independent Commissioner or his counterpart could be enfolded within the legislative scheme. This fringe benefit could well make a difference. . . .

Tenure is of importance. A term of five or seven years is too short . . . longer tenures would mean opportunities for longer-scale planning, freedom from worry as to re-appointment, and generally the concept of devotion to a career rather than that of a stepping stone to further political or professional advancement. Turnover would probably be reduced as is true of the members of the Federal Reserve Board whose tenures are fourteen years. Expertise would have a better chance to develop and the sense of security would inculcate the spirit of independence. Life tenure is, perhaps, too dangerous in these areas of dynamic activity but certainly a ten year term is not too much to suggest. . . .

Industry orientation of agency members is a common criticism, frequently expressed in terms that the regulatees have become the regulators. Of course, if this type of orientation characterizes an individual prior to his appointment, there is little that can be done about it. But the real problem relates to those who are originally oriented towards the public interest but who gradually and honestly begin to view that interest more in terms of the private interest. This is particularly likely to occur in agencies which in addition to there regulatory functions have promotional functions. It was manifested in the innate reaction of the Civil Aeronautics Board to the non-scheduled airlines and to the newer all-cargo air carriers. The Civil Aeronautics Board to date has not considered the provision of subsidy to these all-cargo air carriers. This is not a plea that it should urge the provision of such subsidy, but some rationalization for the grant of subsidy to local service carriers and its denial to the all-cargo air carriers should be made, since there is an obvious national interest in expanding the development of this branch of our transportation system. The Interstate Commerce Commission has frequently been characterized as railroad-minded, the Federal Communication Commission as dominated by the networks, while the actions of the Federal Power Commission speak for themselves.

This tendency toward industry orientation is subtle and difficult to deal with. It arises primarily from the fact that of necessity contacts with the industry are frequent and generally productive of intelligent ideas. Contacts with the public, however, are rare and generally unproductive of anything except complaint. For example, the public that our security legislation is designed to protect is the "investor", but the investor rarely appears and when he does he is too rarely an investor and too frequently a speculator who deserves exactly what happened to him.

Irrespective of the absence of social contacts and the acceptance of undue hospitality, it is the daily machine-gun-like impact on both agency and its staff of industry representation that makes for industry orientation on the part of many honest and capable agency members as well as agency staffs. . . .

Coordination of agency policy is meaningless in the absence of the internal development of policy by the individual agencies. The lack of such development in recent years has been commented upon and, in previous sections methods have been suggested as how that deficiency could be cured, namely the evolution of new procedures, the strengthening of planning divisions and the relief of agency members themselves from the multitudinous and frequently minor duties that they are required to perform.

In various areas, however, agency policies must be coordinated and welded into an integrated whole. Certain areas such as transportation, communication and energy are obvious areas where such coordination is essential. . . .

Plans and blueprints for mechanisms such as a Department of Transportation have been in existence for years and new ones are being devised. None have as yet received substantial Congressional or Executive support. The blueprints, even the best of them, are unrealistic, beautiful in design but lacking in the appreciation of those earthy factors that are embedded in our regulatory transportation structure. Most of them entail the concept of some person in the nature of a czar sitting astride the whole transportation structure and exercising through subordinate bodies many of the functions now vested in the regulatory agencies. Others conceive of splitting away the adjudicatory functions but consolidating other functions in an executive department. It may be that we can eventually attain some such goal but the means of reaching it or an equally satisfactory goal must still be developed. . . .

If we would build towards the goal of coordinating our transportation system and its problems, we should do this carefully and on the basis of accumulating experience not merely as to problems but as to mechanisms to deal with these problems. A beginning along this line was made in 1953 by the creation in the Department of Commerce of an Undersecretary of Transportation. Although valuable work has been done in this office, that mechanism is probably not sufficient for the task. The reason is not necessarily the men who hold that office. It is the nature of the office itself. An office capable of doing such a task cannot be subordinate to the Secretary of Commerce, for its responsibilities are vaster and more important than all the other functions vested in the Department of Commerce. An arrangement of this nature makes achievement of these goals impossible. Such subordination destroys the very element of prestige necessary if leadership in this area is to evolve. It removes the fashioning of transportation policy one and even two steps from the President and, in so doing, permits the intrusion into that field of personages of lesser consequence weakening the sense of an authoritative approach to the problem.

The evolution of a national transportation policy must have a close and intimate relationship to the President. . . . Development of the coordinating function could be placed in the Executive Office of the President. It should not be vested in a White House assistant because such coordinating activity needs protection from trivia, from personality conflicts and even from poltics, as well as the objectivity of approach that can be given the coordinating authority by vesting it in an office already constituted to perform staff and not personal functions for the President. The office would need no regulatory powers. It does need the constant personal support of the President and through him the President's Cabinet and the Bureau of the Budget. Given these, a coordination of policy can be effected by such an office among the various regulatory agencies, implemented where necessary by executive order. And, as experience demonstrates, coordination and consolidation of functions among them can be effected by the wise use of the President's power under the Reorganization Act.

18

The Supreme Court

18.1. THE SUPREME COURT AND JUDICIAL REVIEW

The power of judicial review, which is not specifically provided for in the Constitution, was first asserted by Chief Justice John Marshall in the landmark decision of Marbury v. Madison. A judicial appointee of President Adams, William Marbury, sought a writ of mandamus to compel President Jefferson's secretary of state, James Madison, to deliver his commission of appointment. That part of the Judiciary Act of 1789 providing for the issuance of writs of mandamus was found to be contrary to Article III of the Constitution and, therefore, void.

OPINION OF THE COURT. [Delivered by Chief Justice Marshall.]
   At the last term on the affidavits then read and filed with the clerk, a rule was granted in this case, requiring the secretary of state to show cause why a mandamus should not issue, directing him to deliver to William Marbury his commission as a justice of the peace for the county of Washington, in the District of Columbia. . . .
   The first object of inquiry is, 1st. Has the applicant a right to the commission he demands? . . . Mr. Marbury, then, since his commission was signed by the President and sealed by the Secretary of State, was appointed; and as the law creating the office gave the officer a right to hold for five years, independent of the executive, the appointment was not revocable, but vested in the officer legal rights, which are protected by the laws of his country. To withhold his commission, therefore, is an act deemed by the court not warranted by law, but violative of a vested legal right.

From *Marbury* v. *Madison,* 1 Cranch 137 (1803).

This brings us to the second inquiry, which is, 2d. If he has a right, and that right has been violated, do the laws of his country afford him a remedy? . . .

It is then the opinion of the court,

1st. That by signing the commission of Mr. Marbury, the President of the United States appointed him a justice of peace for the county of Washington, in the District of Columbia; and that the seal of the United States, affixed thereto by the Secretary of State, is conclusive testimony of the verity of the signature, and of the completion of the appointment; and that the appointment conferred on him a legal right to the office for the space of five years.

2dly. That, having this legal title to the office, he has a consequent right to the commission; a refusal to deliver which is a plain violation of that right, for which the laws of his country afford him a remedy. . . .

This, then, is a plain case for a mandamus, either to deliver the commission, or a copy of it from the record; and it only remains to be inquired,

Whether it can issue from this court.

The act to establish the judicial courts of the United States authorizes the Supreme Court "to issue writs of mandamus in cases warranted by the principles and usages of law, to any courts appointed, or persons holding office, under the authority of the United States."

The secretary of state, being a person holding an office under the authority of the United States, is precisely within the letter of the description, and if this court is not authorized to issue a writ of mandamus to such an officer, it must be because the law is unconstitutional, and therefore absolutely incapable of conferring the authority, and assigning the duties which its words purport to confer and assign.

The constitution vests the whole judicial power of the United States in one Supreme Court, and such inferior courts as congress shall, from time to time, ordain and establish. This power is expressly extended to all cases arising under the laws of the United States; and, consequently, in some form, may be exercised over the present case; because the right claimed is given by a law of the United States.

In the distribution of this power it is declared that "the Supreme Court shall have original jurisdiction in all cases affecting ambassadors, other public ministers and consuls, and those in which a state shall be a party. In all other cases, the Supreme Court shall have appellate jurisdiction." . . .

When an instrument organizing fundamentally a judicial system, divides it into one supreme, and so many inferior courts as the legislature may ordain and establish; then enumerates its powers, and proceeds so far to distribute them, as to define the jurisdiction of the Supreme

Court by declaring the cases in which it shall take original jurisdiction, and that in others it shall take appellate jurisdiction; the plain import of the words seems to be, that in one class of cases its jurisdiction is original, and not appellate; in the other it is appellate, and not original. . . .

It is the essential criterion of appellate jurisdiction, that it revises and corrects the proceedings in a cause already instituted, and does not create that cause. Although, therefore, a mandamus may be directed to courts, yet to issue such a writ to an officer for the delivery of a paper, is in effect the same as to sustain an original action for that paper, and, therefore, seems not to belong to appellate but to original jurisdiction. . . .

The authority, therefore, given to the Supreme Court, by the act establishing the judicial courts of the United States, to issue writs of mandamus to public officers, appears not to be warranted by the constitution; and it becomes necessary to inquire whether a jurisdiction so conferred can be exercised.

The question, whether an act, repugnant to the constitution, can become the law of the land, is a queston deeply interesting to the United States; but, happily, not of an intricacy proportioned to its interest. It seems only necessary to recognize certain principles, supposed to have been long and well established, to decide it.

That the people have an original right to establish, for their future government, such principles as, in their opinion, shall most conduce to their own happiness is the basis on which the whole American fabric has been erected. The exercise of the original right is a very great exertion; nor can it, nor ought it, to be frequently repeated. The principles, therefore, so established, are deemed fundamental. And as the authority from which they proceed is supreme, and can seldom act, they are designed to be permanent.

This original and supreme will organizes the government, and assigns to different departments their respective powers. It may either stop here, or establish certain limits not to be transcended by those departments.

The government of the United States is of the latter description. The powers of the legislature are defined and limited; and that those limits may not be mistaken, or forgotten, the constitution is written. To what purpose are powers limited, and to what purpose is that limitation committed to writing, if these limits may at, any time, be passed by those intended to be restrained? The distinction between a government with limited and unlimited powers is abolished, if those limits do not confine the persons on whom they are imposed, and if acts prohibited and acts allowed, are of equal obligation. It is a proposition too plain to be contested, that the constitution controls any legislative act repugnant to it; or, that the legislature may alter the constitution by an ordinary act.

Between these alternatives there is no middle ground. The constitution is either a superior paramount law, unchangeable by ordinary means, or it is on a level with ordinary legislative acts, and, like other acts, is alterable when the legislature shall please to alter it.

If the former part of the alternative be true, then a legislative act contrary to the constitution is not law: if the latter part be true, then written constitutions are absurd attempts, on the part of the people, to limit a power in its own nature illimitable.

Certainly all those who have framed written constitutions contemplate them as forming the fundamental and paramount law of the nation, and, consequently, the theory of every such government must be, that an act of the legislature, repugnant to the constitution, is void. . . .

It is emphatically the province and duty of the judicial department to say what the law is. Those who apply the rule to particular cases, must of necessity expound and interpret that rule. If two laws conflict with each other, the courts must decide on the operation of each.

So if a law be in opposition to the constitution; if both the law and the constitution apply to a particular case, so that the court must either decide that case comfortably to the law, disregarding the constitution; or conformably to the constitution, disregarding the law; the court must determine which of these conflicting rules governs the case. This is of the very essence of judicial duty.

If, then, the courts are to regard the constitution, and the constitution is superior to any ordinary act of the legislature, the constitution, and not such ordinary act, must govern the case to which they both apply.

Those, then, who controvert the principle that the constitution is to be considered, in court, as a paramount law, are reduced to the necessity of maintaining that courts must close their eyes on the constitution, and see only the law.

This doctrine would subvert the very foundation of all written constitutions. It would declare that an act which, according to the principles and theory of our government, is entirely void, is yet, in practice, completely obligatory. It would declare that if the legislature shall do what is expressly forbidden, such act, notwithstanding the express prohibition, is in reality effectual. It would be given to the legislature a practical and real omnipotence, with the same breath which professes to restrict their powers within narrow limits.

That it thus reduces to nothing what we have deemed the greatest improvement on political institutions, a written constitution, would of itself be sufficient, in America, where written constitutions have been viewed with so much reverence, for rejecting the construction. But the peculiar expressions of the constitution of the United States furnish additional arguments in favour of its rejection.

The judicial power of the United States is extended to all cases arising under the constitution.

Could it be the intention of those who gave this power, to say that in using it the constitution should not be looked into? That a case arising under the constitution should be decided without examining the instrument under which it arises?

This is too extravagant to be maintained.

In some cases, then, the constitution must be looked into by the judges. And if they can open it at all, what part of it are they forbidden to read or to obey?

There are many parts of the constitution which serve to illustrate this subject.

It is declared that "no tax or duty shall be laid on articles exported from any state." Suppose a duty on the export of cotton, of tobacco, or of flour; and a suit instituted to recover it. Ought judgment to be rendered in such a case? ought the judges to close their eyes on the constitution, and only see the law?

The constitution declares "that no bill of attainder or ex post facto law shall be passed."

If, however, such a bill should be passed, and a person should be prosecuted under it; must the court condemn to death those victims whom the constitution endeavors to preserve?

"No person," says the constitution, "shall be convicted of treason unless on the testimony of two witnesses to the same overt act, or on confession in open court."

Here the language of the constitution is addressed especially to the courts. It prescribes, directly for them, a rule of evidence not to be departed from. If the legislature should change that rule, and declare one witness, or a confession out of court, sufficient for conviction, must the constitutional principle yield to the legislative act?

From these, and many other selections which might be made, it is apparent, that the framers of the constitution contemplated that instrument as a rule for the government of courts, as well as of the legislature.

Why otherwise does it direct the judges to take an oath to support it? This oath certainly applies in an especial manner, to their conduct in their official character. How immoral to impose it on them, if they were to be used as the instruments, and the knowing instruments, for violating what they swear to support!

The oath of office, too, imposed by the legislature, is completely demonstrative of the legislative opinion on this subject. It is in these words:

"I do solemnly swear that I will administer justice without respect to persons, and do equal right to the poor and to the rich; and that I will faithfully and impartially discharge all the duties incumbent on me as _____, according to the best of my abilities and understanding agreeably to the constitution and laws of the United States."

Why does a judge swear to discharge his duties agreeably to the constitution of the United States, if that constitution forms no rule for his government? if it is closed upon him, and cannot be inspected by him? If such be the real state of things, this is worse than solemn mockery. To prescribe, or to take this oath, becomes equally a crime.

It is also not entirely unworthy of observation, that in declaring what shall be the supreme law of the land, the constitution itself is first mentioned; and not the laws of the United States generally, but those only which shall be made in pursuance of the constitution, have that rank.

Thus, the particular phraseology of the constitution of the United States confirms and strengthens the principle, supposed to be essential to all written constitutions, that a law repugnant to the constitution is void; and that courts, as well as other departments, are bound by that instrument.

The rule must be discharged.

18.2. AN ARGUMENT AGAINST JUDICIAL SUPREMACY

In response to John Marshall's assertions of judicial supremacy, Thomas Jefferson argued in a series of letters that each branch of the government is the arbiter of constitutionality in matters normally falling within its own sphere. Vesting supremacy in a federal judiciary seemed to him an undemocratic limitations on the constitutional principle of checks and balance.

. . . I OBSERVE that the case of Marbury v. Madison has been cited, and I think it material to stop at the threshold the citing that case as authority, and to have it denied to be law. 1. Because the judges, in the outset, disclaimed all cognizance of the case, altho' they then went on to say what would have been their opinion, had they had cognizance of it. This, then, was confessedly an extrajudicial opinion, and, as such, of no authority. 2. Because, had it been judicially pronounced, it would have been against law; for to a commission, a deed, a bond, *delivery* is essential to give validity. Until, therefore, the commission is delivered out of the hands of the Executive & his agents, it is not his deed. He may withhold or cancel it at pleasure, as he might his private deed in the same situation. The Constitution intended that the three great branches of the government should be co-ordinate, & independent of each other. As to acts, therefore, which are to be done by either, it has given no controul to another branch. A

From *The Writings of Thomas Jefferson*, ed. by P. L. Ford (New York: G. P. Putnam's Sons, 1897), Vol. IX, pp. 53–54, 517–519; Vol. X, 140–143.

judge, I presume, cannot sit on a bench without a commission, or a record of a commission; & the Constitution having given to the judiciary branch no means of compelling the executive either to *deliver* a commission, or to make a record of it, shews it did not intend to give the judiciary that controul over the executive, but that it should remain in the power of the latter to do it or not. Where different branches have to act in their respective lines, finally & without appeal, under any law, they may give to it different and opposite constructions. . . .

On this construction I have hitherto acted; on this I shall ever act, and maintain it with the powers of the government against any control which may be attempted by the judges, in subversion of the independence of the executive & Senate within their peculiar department. I presume, therefore, that in a case where our decision is by the Constitution the supreme one, & that which can be carried into effect, it is the constitutionally authoritative one, and that that by the judges was *coram non judice*, & unauthoritative, because it cannot be carried into effect. I have long wished for a proper occasion to have the gratuitous opinion in Marbury *v.* Madison brought before the public, & denounced as not law; & I think the present a fortunate one, because it occupies such a place in the public attention. I should be glad, therefore, if, in noticing that case, you could take occasion to express the determination of the executive, that the doctrines of that case were given extrajudicially & against law, and that their reverse will be the rule of action with the executive. If this opinion should not be your own, I would wish it to be expressed merely as that of the executive. If it is your own also, you would of course give to the arguments such a development as a case, incidental only, might render proper. I salute you with friendship and respect.

[To W. H. Torrance (June 11, 1815)] . . . The . . . question, whether the judges are invested with exclusive authority to decide on the constitutionality of a law, has been heretofore a subject of consideration with me in the exercise of official duties. Certainly there is not a word in the constitution which has given that power to them more than to the executive or legislative branches. Questions of property, of character and of crime being ascribed to the judges, through a definite course of legal proceeding, laws involving such questions belong, of course, to them; and as they decide on them ultimately and without appeal, they of course decide *for themselves*. The constitutional validity of the law again prescribing executive action, and to be administered by that branch ultimately and without appeal, the executive must decide *for themselves* also, whether, under the constitution, they are valid or not. So also as to laws governing the proceedings of the legislature, that body must judge *for itself* the constitutionality of the law, and equally without appeal or control from its co-ordinate branches. And, in general, that branch which is to act ultimately and without appeal, on any law, is the rightful expositor of the validity of the law, uncontrolled by the opinions of the other coordinate authorities. It may be said that contradictory decisions may arise in such case, and produce inconvenience. This is possible, and is a necessary failing in all human proceedings. Yet the prudence of the public functionaries, and authority of public opinion, will generally produce accommodation. . . . But there is another opinion entertained by some men of such judgment and information as to lessen my confidence in my own. That is, that the legislature alone is the exclusive expounder of the sense of the constitution, in every part of it whatever. And they allege in its support, that this branch has authority to impeach and punish a member of either of the others acting contrary to its declaration of the sense of the constitution. It may indeed be answered, that an act may still be valid although the party is punished for it, right or wrong. However, this opinion which ascribes exclusive exposition to the legislature, merits respect for its safety, there being in the body of the nation a control over them, which, if expressed by rejection on the subsequent exercise of their elective franchise, enlists public opinion against their exposition, and encourages a judge or executive on a future occasion to adhere to their former opinion. Between these two doctrines, every one has a right to choose, and I know of no third meriting any respect. . . .

[To Judge Spencer Roane (September 6, 1819)] I had read in the Enquirer, and with great approbation, the pieces signed Hampden, and have read them again with redoubled approbation, in the copies you have been so kind as to send me. I subscribe to every tittle of them. They contain the true principles of the revolution of 1800, for that was as real a revolution in the principles of our government at that of 1776 was in its form; not effected indeed by the sword, as that, but by the rational and peaceable instrument of reform, the suffrage of the people. The nation declared its will by dismissing functionaries of one principle, and electing those of another, in the two branches, executive and legislative, submitted to their election. Over the judiciary department, the constitution had deprived them of their control. That, therefore, has continued the reprobated system, and although new matter has been occasionally incorporated into the old, yet the leaven of the old mass seems to assimilate to itself the new, and after twenty years' confirmation of the federal system by the voice of the nation, declared through the medium of elections, we find the judiciary on every occason, still driving us into consolidation.

In denying the right they usurp of exclusively explaining the constitution, I go further than you do, if I understand rightly your quotation from the Federalist, of an opinion that "the judiciary is the last resort in relation *to the other departments* of the government, but not in relation to the rights of the parties to the compact under which the judiciary is derived." If this opinion be sound, then indeed is our constitution a complete *felo de se*. For intending to establish three departments, co-ordinate and independent, that they might check and balance one another, it has given, according to this opinion, to one of them alone, the right to prescribe rules for the government of the others, and to that one too, which is unelected by, and independent of the nation. . . . The constitution, on this hypothesis, is a mere thing of wax in the hands of the judiciary, which they may twist and shape into any form they please. . . . My construction of the constitution is very different from that you quote. It is that each department is truly independent of the others, and has an equal right to decide for itself what is the meaning of the constitution in the cases submitted to its action; and especially, where it is to act ultimately and without appeal. . . .

18.3. JUDICIAL REVIEW: A JUDICIAL DISSENT

In Marbury v. Madison, *John Marshall brilliantly proclaimed that it is within the power of the Supreme Court to pass upon the constitutionality of acts of legislation. This claim has been challenged many times by politicians and laymen, but rarely has it been denied by a learned judge. The following selection is unique in that, although Judge Gibson's is a dissenting opinion in a State Supreme Court, it states what may be called a legal rebuttal to Marshall by a judicial contemporary of that great Chief Justice.*

GIBSON, J. *dissenting:* . . . I am aware that a right (of the courts) to declare all unconstitutional acts void . . . is generally held as a professional dogma; but, I apprehend, rather as a matter of faith than of reason. I admit that I once embraced the same doctrine, but without examination, and I shall therefore state the arguments that impelled me to abandon it, with great respect for those by whom it is still maintained. . . .

. . . Our judiciary is construed on the principles of the common law, which enters so essentially into the composition of our social institutions as to be inseparable from them and to be, in fact, the basis of our whole scheme of civil and political liberty. In adopting any organ or instrument of the common law, we take with just such powers and capacities as were incident to it at the common law, except where these are expressly, or by necessary implication, abridged or enlarged in the act of adoption; and that such act is a written instrument cannot vary its consequences or construction. . . . Now what are the powers of the judiciary at the common law? They are those that necessarily arise out of its immediate business; and they are therefore commensurate only with

From *Eakin et al.* v. *Raub* [1825] (Pennsylvania Supreme Court).

the judicial execution of the municipal law, or in other words, with the administration of distributive justice, without extending to anything of a political cast whatever.

. . . With us, although the legislature be the depository of only so much of the sovereignty as the people have thought fit to impart, it is nonetheless sovereign within the limits of its powers and may relatively claim the same pre-eminence here that it may claim elsewhere. It will be conceded, then, that the powers of the judiciary do not extend to the annulling of an act of the legislature. . . . it can exercise no power of supervision over the legislature without producing a direct authority for it in the constitution, either in terms or by irresistible implication from the nature of the government; without which the power must be considered as reserved, along with the other ungranted portions of the sovereignty, for the immediate use of the people.

The Constitution and the *right* of the legislature to pass the act may be in collision. But is that a legitimate subject for judicial determination? If it be, the judiciary must be a peculiar organ, to revise the proceedings of the legislature and to correct its mistake; and in what part of the Constitution are we to look for this proud pre-eminence? Viewing the matter in the opposite direction, what would be thought of an act of assembly in which it should be declared that the Supreme Court had, in a particular case, put a wrong construction on the Constitution of the United States and the judgment should therefore be reversed? It would doubtless be thought a usurpation of legislative power. It is an act of sovereignty; and sovereignty and legislative power are said by Sir William Blackstone to be convertible terms. It is the business of the judiciary to interpret the laws, not scan the authority of the law-giver; . . .

But it has been said to be emphatically the business of the judiciary, to ascertain and pronounce what the law is; and this necessarily involves a consideration of the Constitution. It does so: but how far? If the judiciary will inquire into anything besides the form of enactment, where shall it stop? There must be some point of limitation to such an inquiry; for no one will pretend that a judge would be justifiable in calling for the election returns, or scrutinizing the qualifications of those who composed the legislature. . . .

. . . Repugnance to the constitution is not always self-evident; for questions involving the consideration of its existence require for their solution the higher faculties of the mind, and the conflicts will be inevitable, if any branch is to apply the Constitution after its own fashion to the acts of all other. I take it, then, the legislature is entitled to all the deference that is due the judiciary; that its acts are in no case to be treated as *ipso facto* void, except where they would produce a revolution in the government; and that, to avoid them requires the act of some competent tribunal under the Constitution (if any such there be) to pass on their validity. All that remains, therefore, is to inquire whether the judiciary or the people are that tribunal.

Now, as the judiciary is not expressly constituted for that purpose, it must derive whatever authority it may possess from the reasonableness and fitness of the thing. But, in theory, all the organs of the government are of equal capacity; or, if not equal, each must be supposed to have superior capacity only for those things which peculiarly belong to it; and as legislation peculiarly involves the consideration of those limitations which are put on the law-making power, and the interpretation of the laws, when made, involves only the constructon of the laws themselves, it follows that the construction of the constitution in this particular belongs to the legislature, which ought therefore to be taken to have superior capacity to judge of the constitutionality of its own acts. But suppose all to be of equal capacity in every respect, why should one exercise a controlling power over the rest? That the judiciary is of superior rank has never been pretended, although it has been said to be co-ordinate. It is not easy, however, to comprehend how the power which gives law to all the rest can be of no more than equal rank with one which receives it and is answerable to the former for the observance of its statutes. Legislation is essentially an act of sovereign power; but the execution of the laws by instruments that are governed by prescribed rules and exercise no power of volition is essentially otherwise. The very definition of law, which is said to be "a rule of civil conduct prescribed by the *supreme* power in the state," shows the intrinsic superiority of the legislature. It may be said, the power of the legislature, also, is limited by prescribed rules. It is so. But it is, nevertheless, the power of the people, and sovereign as far as it extends. It cannot be said that the judiciary is co-ordinate merely because it is established by the constitution. . . . Inequality of rank arises, not from the manner in which the organ has been constituted, but from its essence and the nature of its function; and the legislative organ is superior to every other, inasmuch as the power to will and to command is essentially superior to the power to act and to obey. . . .

Every one knows how seldom men think exactly alike on ordinary subjects; and a government constructed on the principle of assent by all its parts would be inadequate to the most simple operations.

The notion of a complication of counter checks has been carried to an extent in theory, of which the framers of the constitution never dreamed. When the entire sovereignty was separated into its elementary parts, and distributed to the appropriate branches, all things incident to the exercise of its powers were committed to each branch exclusively. The negative which each part of the legislature may exercise, in regard to the acts of the other, was thought sufficient to prevent material infractions of the restraints which were put on the power of the whole; for, had it been intended to interpose the judiciary as an additional barrier, the matter would surely not have been left in doubt. The judges would not have been left to stand on the insecure and ever-shifting ground of public opinion as to constructive powers; they would have been placed on the impregnable ground of an express grant. . . .

But the judges are sworn to support the Constitution, and are they not bound by it as the law of the land? In some respects they are. In the very few cases in which the judiciary, and not the legislature, is the immediate organ to execute its provisions, they are bound by it in preference to any act of assembly to the contrary. In such cases, the constitution is a rule to the courts. But what I have in view in this inquiry is the supposed right of the judiciary to interfere in cases where the constitution is to be carried into effect through the instrumentality of the legislature, and where that organ must necessarily first decide on the constitutionality of its own act. The oath to support the constitution is not peculiar to the judges but is taken indiscriminately by every officer of the government and is designed rather as a test of the political principles of the man, than to bind the officer in the discharge of his duty: . . .

But do not the judges do a positive act in violation of the Constitution when they give effect to an unconstitutional law? Not if the law has been passed according to the forms established in the Constitution. The fallacy of the question is in supposing that the judiciary adopts the acts of the legislature as its own; whereas the enactment of a law and the interpretation of it are not concurrent acts, and as the judiciary is not required to concur in the enactment, neither is it in the branch of the Constitution which may be the consequence of the enactment. The fault is imputable to the legislature, and on it the responsibility exclusively rests. . . .

But it has been said that this construction would deprive the citizens of the advantages which are peculiar to a written constitution by at once declaring the power of the legislature, in practice, to be illimitable. I ask, what are these advantages? The principles of a written constitution are more fixed and certain, and more apparent to the apprehension of the people, than principles which depend on tradition and the vague comprehension of the individuals who compose the nation, and who cannot all be expected to receive the same impressions or entertain the same notion on any given subject. But there is no magic or inherent power in parchment and ink to command respect and protect principles from violation. . . . for, after all, there is no effectual guard against legislative usurpation but public opinion, the force of which, in this country, is inconceivably great. Happily, this is proved, by experience, to be a sufficient guard against palpable infractions. . . .

For these reasons, I am of opinion that it rests with the people, in whom full and absolute sovereign power resides, to correct abuses in legislation, by instructing their representatives to repeal the obnoxious act. What is wanting to plenary power in the government is reserved by the people for their own immediate use; and to redress an infringement of their rights in this respect would seem to be an accessory of the power thus reserved. It might, perhaps, have been better to vest the power in the judiciary; as it might be expected that its habits of deliberation, and the aid derived from the arguments of counsel, would more frequently lead to accurate conclusions. On the other hand, the judiciary is not infallible; and an error by it would admit of no remedy but a more distinct expression of the public will, through the extraordinary medium of a convention; whereas, an error by the legislature admits of a remedy by an exertion of the same will, in the ordinary exercise of the right of suffrage,—a mode better calculated to attain the end, without popular excitement. It may be said, the people would probably not notice an error of their representatives. But they would as probably do so as notice an error of the judiciary; and beside, it is a *postulate* in the theory of our government, and the very basis of the superstructure, that the people are wise, virtuous, and competent to manage their own affairs; if they are not so, in fact, still every question of this sort must be determined according to the principles of the Constitution, as it came from the hands of its framers, and the existence of a defect which was not foreseen would not justify those who administer the government in applying a corrective in practice which can be provided only by a convention.

18.4. PRELUDE TO CONFLICT OVER THE JUDICIAL ROLE

The alleged duty of the Supreme Court to strike down congressional legislation deemed unconstitutional is stressed in the Adkins *case. Justice George Sutherland, a strong proponent of economic conservativism, held invalid a 1918 law establishing minimum wages for women in the District of Columbia.*

MR. JUSTICE GEORGE SUTHERLAND delivered the opinion of the Court. . . .

The judicial duty of passing upon the constitutionality of an act of Congress is one of great gravity and delicacy. The statute here in question has successfully borne the scrutiny of the legislative branch of the government, which, by enacting it, has affirmed its validity; and that determination must be given great weight. This Court, by an unbroken line of decisions from Chief Justice Marshall to the present day, has steadily

From *Adkins* v. *Children's Hospital*, 261 U.S. 525 (1923).

adhered to the rule that every possible presumption is in favor of the validity of an act of Congress until overcome beyond rational doubt. But if by clear and indubitable demonstration a statute be opposed to the Constitution we have no choice but to say so. The Constitution, by its own terms, is the supreme law of the land, emanating from the people, the repository of the ultimate sovereignty under our form of government. A congressional statute, on the other hand, is the act of an agency of this sovereign authority and if it conflict with the Constitution must fall; for that which is not supreme must yield to that which is. To hold it invalid (if it be invalid) is a plain exercise of the judicial power— that power vested in courts to enable them to administer justice according to law. From the authority to ascertain and determine the law in a given case, there necessarily results, in case of conflict, the duty to declare and enforce the rule of the supreme law and reject that of an inferior act of legislation which, transcending the Constitution, is of no effect and binding on no one. This is not the exercise of a substantive power to review and nullify acts of Congress, for no such substantive power exists. It is simply a necessary concomitant of the power to hear and dispose of a case or controversy properly before the court, to the determination of which must be brought the test and measure of the law.

18.5. ROOSEVELT'S PROPOSAL TO "REFORM" THE COURT

The early legislative program of Franklin Roosevelt's New Deal was repeatedly thwarted by decisions of the Supreme Court ruling the statutes unconstitutional. President Roosevelt turned to Congress to increase the number of justices in the hope of gaining "new blood" and judicial support for his program. The "court-packing" controversy of 1937 was ignited in this famous fireside chat.

THE AMERICAN PEOPLE have learned from the depression. For in the last three national elections an overwhelming majority of them voted a mandate that the Congress and the President begin the task of providing that protection—not after long years of debate, but now.

The courts, however, have cast doubts on the ability of the elected Congress to protect us against catastrophe by meeting squarely our modern social and economic conditions.

From "Address on Court Reform, March 9, 1937," by President Franklin D. Roosevelt.

We are at a crisis in our ability to proceed with that protection. It is a quiet crisis. There are no lines of depositors outside closed banks. But to the farsighted it is far-reaching in its possibilities of injury to America.

I want to talk with you very simply about the need for present action in this crisis—the need to meet the unanswered challenge of one-third of a nation ill-nourished, ill-clad, ill-housed.

Last Thursday I described the American form of government as a three-horse team provided by the Constitution to the American people so that their field might be plowed. The three horses are, of course, the three branches of government—the Congress, the executive, and the courts. Two of the horses are pulling in unison today; the third is not. Those who have intimated that the President of the United States is trying to drive that team overlook the simple fact that the President, as Chief Executive, is himself one of the three horses.

It is the American people themselves who are in the driver's seat.

It is the American people themselves who want the furrow plowed.

It is the American people themselves who expect the third horse to pull in unison with the other two. . . .

Since the rise of the modern movement for social and economic progress through legislation, the Court has more and more often and more and more boldly asserted a power to veto laws passed by the Congress and State legislatures. . .

In the last 4 years the sound rule of giving statutes the benefit of all reasonable doubt has been cast aside. The Court has been acting not as a judicial body, but as a policy-making body.

When the Congress has sought to stabilize national agriculture, to improve the conditions of labor, to safeguard business against unfair competition, to protect our national resources, and in many other ways to serve our clearly national need, the majority of the Court has been assuming the power to pass on the wisdom of these acts of the Congress—and to approve or disapprove the public policy written into these laws.

That is not only my accusation. It is the accusation of most distinguished Justices of the present Supreme Court. I have not the time to quote to you all the language used by dissenting Justices in many of these cases. But in the case holding the Railroad Retirement Act unconstitutional, for instance, Chief Justice Hughes said in a dissenting opinion that the majority opinion was "a departure from sound principles," and placed "an unwarranted limitation upon the commerce clause." And three other Justices agreed with him.

In the case holding the A.A.A. unconstitutional, Justice Stone said of the majority opinion that it was a "tortured construction of the Constitution." And two other Justices agreed with him.

In the case holding the New York Minimum Wage Law unconstitutional, Justice Stone said that the majority were actually reading into the Constitution their own "personal economic predilections," and that if the legislative power is not left free to choose the methods of solving the problems of poverty, subsistence, and health of large numbers in the community, then "government is to be rendered impotent." And two other Justices agreed with him.

In the face of these dissenting opinions, there is no basis for the claim made by some members of the Court that something in the Constitution has compelled them regretfully to thwart the will of the people. . . .

We have, therefore, reached the point as a Nation where we must take action to save the Constitution from the Court and the Court from itself. We must find a way to take an appeal from the Supreme Court to the Constitution itself. We want a Supreme Court which will do justice under the Constitution—not over it. In our courts we want a government of laws and not of men.

I want—as all Americans want—an independent judiciary as proposed by the framers of the Constitution. That means a Supreme Court that will enforce the Constitution as written—that will refuse to amend the Constitution by the arbitrary exercise of judicial power—amendment by judicial say-so. It does not mean a judiciary so independent that it can deny the existence of facts universally recognized. . . .

When I commenced to review the situation with the problem squarely before me, I came by a process of elimination to the conclusion that short of amendments the only method which was clearly constitutional, and would at the same time carry out other much-needed reforms, was to infuse new blood into all our courts. We must have men worthy and equipped to carry out impartial justice. But at the same time we must have judges who will bring to the courts a present-day sense of the Constitution—judges who will retain in the courts the judicial functions of a court and reject the legislative powers which the courts have today assumed.

In 45 out of the 48 States of the Union, judges are chosen not for life but for a period of years. In many States judges must retire at the age of 70. Congress has provided financial security by offering life pensions at full pay for Federal judges on all courts who are willing to retire at 70. In the cases of Supreme Court Justices, that pension is $20,000 a year. But all Federal judges, once appointed, can, if they choose, hold office for life no matter how old they may get to be.

What is my proposal? It is simply this: Whenever a judge or justice of any Federal court has reached the age of 70 and does not avail himself of the opportunity to retire on a pension, a new member shall be appointed by the President then in office, with the approval, as required by the Constitution, of the Senate of the United States.

That plan has two chief purposes: By bringing into the judicial system a steady and continuing stream of new and younger blood, I hope, first, to make the administration of all Federal justice speedier and therefore less costly; secondly, to bring to the decision of social and economic problems younger men who have had personal experience and contact with modern facts and circumstances under which average men have to live and work. This plan will save our National Constitution from hardening of the judicial arteries.

The number of judges to be appointed would depend wholly on the decision of present judges now over 70 or those who would subsequently reach the age of 70. . . .

Those opposing this plan have sought to arouse prejudice and fear by crying that I am seeking to "pack" the Supreme Court and that a baneful precedent will be established.

What do they mean by the words "packing the Court"?

Let me answer this question with a bluntness that will end all honest misunderstanding of my purposes.

If by that phrase "packing the Court" it is charged that I wish to place on the bench spineless puppets who would disregard the law and would decide specific cases as I wished them to be decided, I make this answer: That no President fit for his office would appoint, and no Senate of honorable men fit for their office would confirm, that kind of appointees to the Supreme Court.

But if by that phrase the charge is made that I would appoint and the Senate would confirm Justices worthy to sit beside present members of the Court who understand those modern conditions; that I will appoint Justices who will not undertake to override the judgment of the Congress on legislative policy; that I will appoint Justices who will act as Justices and not legislators—if the appointment of such Justices can be called "packing the Courts"—then I say that I, and with me the vast majority of the American people, favor doing just that thing—now.

Is it a dangerous precedent for the Congress to change the number of the Justices? The Congress has always had, and will have, that power. The number of Justices has been changed several times before—in the administrations of John Adams and Thomas Jefferson, both signers of the Declaration of Independence, Andrew Jackson, Abraham Lincoln, and Ulysses S. Grant. . . .

Like all lawyers, like all Americans, I regret the necessity of this controversy. But the welfare of the United States, and indeed of the Constitution itself, is what we all must think about first. Our difficulty with the Court today rises not from the Court as an institution but from human beings within it. But we cannot yield our constitutional destiny to the personal judgment of a few men who, being fearful of the future, would deny us the necessary means of dealing with the present.

This plan of mine is no attack on the Court; it seeks to restore the Court to its rightful and historic place in our system of constitutional government and to have it resume its high task of building anew on the Constitution "a system of living law." . . .

I am in favor of action through legislation—

First, because I believe that it can be passed at this session of Congress.

Second, because it will provide a reinvigorated, liberal-minded judiciary necessary to furnish quicker and cheaper justice from bottom to top.

Third, because it will provide a series of Federal courts willing to enforce the Constitution as written, and unwilling to assert legislative powers by writing into it their own political and economic policies.

During the past half century the balance of power between the three great branches of the Federal Government has been tipped out of balance by the courts in direct contradiction of the high purposes of the framers of the Constitution. It is my purpose to restore that balance. You who know me will accept my solemn assurance that in a world in which democracy is under attack I seek to make American democracy succeed.

18.6. FAILURE OF FDR'S COURT PLANS

The Senate Judiciary Committee refused to recommend FDR's rejuvenation program for the Supreme Court. In this selection, the Committee excoriates Roosevelt's attempt to alter the independent judiciary, but offers the hope that the passage of time will cure the underlying problem. Decline of the conservative group through retirement, resignation, and death subsequently enabled the President to place "liberals" of his own choosing on the bench.

THE COMMITTEE on the Judiciary, to whom was referred the bill to reorganize the judicial branch of the Government, after full consideration, having unanimously amended the measure, hereby report the bill adversely with the recommendation that it do not pass. . . .

The committee recommends that the measure be rejected for the following primary reasons:

I. The bill does not accomplish any one of the objectives for which it was originally offered.

From U.S. Senate, *Report of the Committee on the Judiciary*, June 7, 1937.

II. It applies force to the judiciary and in its initial and ultimate effect would undermine the independence of the courts.

III. It violates all precedents in the history of our Government and would in itself be a dangerous precedent for the future.

IV. The theory of the bill is in direct violation of the spirit of the American Constitution and its employment would permit alteration of the Constitution without the people's consent or approval; it undermines the protection our constitutional system gives to minorities and is subversive of the rights of individuals.

V. It tends to centralize the Federal district judiciary by the power of assigning judges from one district to another at will.

VI. It tends to expand political control over the judicial department by adding to the powers of the legislative and executive departments respecting the judiciary. . . .

Let us, for the purpose of the argument, grant that the Court has been wrong, wrong not only in that it has rendered mistaken opinions but wrong in the far more serious sense that it has substituted its will for the congressional will in the matter of legislation. May we nevertheless safely punish the Court?

Today it may be the Court which is charged with forgetting its constitutional duties. Tomorrow it may be the Congress. The next day it may be the Executive. If we yield to temptation now to lay the lash upon the Court, we are only teaching others how to apply it to ourselves and to the people when the occasion seems to warrant. Manifestly, if we may force the hand of the Court to secure our interpretation of the Constitution, then some succeeding Congress may repeat the process to secure another and a different interpretation and one which may not sound so pleasant in our ears as that for which we now contend.

There is a remedy for usurpation or other judicial wrongdoing. If this bill be supported by the toilers of this country upon the ground that they want a Court which will sustain legislation limiting hours and providing minimum wages, they must remember that the procedure employed in the bill could be used in another administration to lengthen hours and to decrease wages. If farmers want agricultural relief and favor this bill upon the ground that it gives them a Court which will sustain legislation in their favor, they must remember that the procedure employed might some day be used to deprive them of every vestige of a farm relief.

When members of the Court usurp legislative powers or attempt to exercise political power, they lay themselves open to the charge of having lapsed from that "good behavior" which determines the period of their official life. But, if you say, the process of impeachment is difficult and uncertain, the answer is, the people made it so when they framed the Constitution. It is not for us, the servants of the people, the instruments of the Constitution, to find a more easy way to do that which our masters made difficult.

But, if the fault of the judges is not so grievous as to warrant impeachment, if their offense is merely that they have grown old, and we feel, therefore, that there should be a "constant infusion of new blood," then obviously the way to achieve that result is by constitutional amendment fixing definite terms for the members of the judiciary or making mandatory their retirement at a given age. Such a provision would indeed provide for the constant infusion of new blood, not only now but at all times in the future. The plan before us is but a temporary expedient which operates once and then never again, leaving the Court as permanently expanded to become once more a court of old men, gradually year by year falling behind the times. . . .

Shall we now, after 150 years of loyalty to the constitutional ideal of an untrammeled judiciary, duty bound to protect the constitutional rights of the humblest citizen even against the Government itself, create the vicious precedent which must necessarily undermine our system? The only argument for the increase which survives analysis is that Congress should enlarge the Court so as to make the policies of this administration effective.

We are told that a reactionary oligarchy defies the will of the majority, that this is a bill to "unpack" the Court and give effect to the desires of the majority; that is to say, a bill to increase the number of Justices for the express purpose of neutralizing the views of some of the present members. In justification we are told, but without authority, by those who would rationalize this program, that Congress was given the power to determine the size of the Court so that the legislative branch would be able to impose its will upon the judiciary. This amounts to nothing more than the declaration that when the Court stands in the way of a legislative enactment, the Congress may reverse the ruling by enlarging the Court. When such a principle is adopted, our constitutional system is overthrown! . . .

This is the first time in the history of our country that a proposal to alter the decisions of the court by enlarging its personnel has been so boldly made. Let us meet it. Let us now set a salutary precedent that will never be violated. Let us, of the Seventy-fifth Congress, in words that will never be disregarded by any succeeding Congress, declare that we would rather have an independent Court, a fearless Court, a Court that will dare to announce its honest opinions in what it believes to be the defense of the liberties of the people, than a Court that, out of fear or sense of obligation to the appointing power, or factional passion, approves any measure we may enact. We are not the judges of the judges. We are not above the Constitution.

Even if every charge brought against the so-called "reactionary" members of this Court be true, it is far better that we await orderly but inevitable change of personnel than that we impatiently overwhelm them with new members. Exhibiting this restraint, thus demonstrating our faith in the American system, we shall set an example that will protect the independent American judiciary from attack as long as this Government stands.

It is essential to the continuance of our constitutional democracy that the judiciary be completely independent of both the executive and legislative branches of the Government, and we assert that independent courts are the last safeguard of the citizen, where his rights, reserved to him by the express and implied provisions of the Constitution, come in conflict with the power of governmental agencies. . . .

Courts and the judges thereof should be free from a subservient attitude of mind, and this must be true whether a question of constitutional construction or one of popular activity is involved. If the court of last resort is to be made to respond to a prevalent sentiment of a current hour, politically imposed, that Court must ultimately become subservient to the pressure of public opinion of the hour, which might at the moment embrace mob passion abhorrent to a more calm, lasting consideration. . . .

Inconvenience and even delay in the enactment of legislation is not a heavy price to pay for our system. Constitutional democracy moves forward with certainty rather than with speed. The safety and the permanence of the progressive march of our civilization are far more important to us and to those who are to come after us than the enactment now of any particular law. The Constitution of the United States provides ample opportunity for the expression of popular will to bring about such reforms and changes as the people may deem essential to their present and future welfare. It is the people's charter of the powers granted those who govern them. . . .

It stands now before the country, acknowleged by its proponents as a plan to force judicial interpretation of the Constitution, a proposal that violates every sacred tradition of American democracy.

Under the form of the Constitution it seeks to do that which is unconstitutional.

Its ultimate operation would be to make this Government one of men rather than one of law, and its practical operation would be to make the Constitution what the executive or legislative branches of the Government choose to say it is—an interpretation to be changed with each change of administration.

It is a measure which should be so emphatically rejected that its parallel will never again be presented to the free representatives of the free people of America.

18.7. A PROPOSAL TO LIMIT
THE COURT'S POWER

*A political device for checking the Supreme Court's power is the pro-
vision in Article III of the Constitution that Congress may determine
those cases which the Court may hear on appeal. Dissatisfaction with
recent decisions involving congressional investigations, the internal control of Communism, and states' rights resulted in Senate Bill 2646 in
1958, which would have removed some cases from the appellate jurisdiction of the Supreme Court. The Bill was defeated.*

PRO BY WILLIAM E. JENNER

The Supreme Court has dealt a succession of blows at key points
of the legislative structure erected by the Congress for the protection of
the internal security of the United States against the world Communist
conspiracy.

Time after time, Congress has acted to shore up these legislative
bulwarks; and time after time, the Supreme Court has knocked the props
out from under the structure which Congress has built.

There was a time when the Supreme Court conceived its function to be the interpretation of the law. For some time now, the Supreme
Court has been making law—substituting its judgment for the judgment
of the legislative branch.

Laymen and lawyers, the legislative branch and the executive
branch of Government, have come to recognize the predilection of the
Supreme Court for making new law. Even the lower courts have come to
expect it, with the result that it has become commonplace for decisions
to be held up in lower courts waiting for the Supreme Court to make
some new law that will apply to the case.

By some of these decisions, antisubversive laws and regulations
have been rendered ineffective. States have been denied the right to fight
subversion, and have been denied the right to bar Communists from prac-
ticing law. Violators of Federal antisubversive laws have been turned loose

---

From Senator William E. Jenner, "Pro—Should Congress Limit the U.S.
Supreme Court's Area of Appellate Jurisdiction?" and Senator Thomas C.
Hennings, Jr., "Con—. . ." in *The Congressional Digest,* May, 1958, pp. 142–
147.

on flimsy technicalities. Confidential files of the FBI and of other investigative and law-enforcement agencies have been opened up to fishing expeditions by defendants and their counsel. The Court has challenged the authority of Congress to decide upon the scope of its own investigations and the right of a congressional committee to make up its own mind about what questions to ask its witnesses.

Many pending cases may be affected, and an undetermined number of cases already settled may be reopened, as a result of recent decisions of the Supreme Court, regardless of what Congress may find it possible to do toward curing the situation, because while Congress cannot make a new law that will affect a case already tried, the Supreme Court can, and does. The Supreme Court can change overnight a rule of law 100 years old, and can make the new rule apply to all cases underway, and provide a basis for reopening cases already tried which involved the point covered by the new rule.

There is no way for Congress to invalidate or repeal a decision of the Supreme Court of the United States, even when that decision is legislative and policy-making in nature. Congress can in some cases strike down judge-made law by enacting new law, or by correcting the Court's error, respecting the intent of Congress, by a new declaration of intent. This power of the Congress should be exercised to the maximum of course, but it will not fully meet the situation. The Court has become for all practical purposes a legislative arm of the Government, and many of its feats are subject to no review. . . .

Reasonable men may err. If the Court had erred only once or twice in these decisions involving the greatest threat to human freedom which history ever had to look upon, reasonable men could find excuses for it. But what shall we say of this parade of decisions that came down from our highest bench on Red Monday after Red Monday? . . .

The objective of my bill S. 2646 is to check judicial legislation in certain fields where it has been damaging the internal security of the United States.

Utilization by the Congress, as this bill proposes, of the power conferred by paragraph 2 of section 2 of article III of the Constitution to regulate the appellate jurisdiction of the Supreme Court is the only effective way to reply to the Supreme Court's usurpation of legislative power in these fields.

This authority did not get into the Constitution by chance. It was specifically inserted, as a part of the system of checks and balances which distinguishes the Constitution of the United States. The purpose of this provision could only have been to put the Congress in a position to divest the Supreme Court of its appellate jurisdiction when, in the discretion of the Congress, circumstances required such action. In fact, under the interpretation of this clause which has been uniform since 1796, the

Congress can withhold appellate jurisdiction from the Supreme Court simply by not in terms granting it. Thus, all the appellate jurisdiction the Supreme Court has, it holds by virtue of congressional act; and of course, what the Congress has granted, the Congress may take away.

. . . we must consider the nature of the cases in which my bill would take from the Court its appellate jurisdiction. With respect to the investigatory power of the Congress, the Court never should have such appellate powers. As Mr. Justice Clark said in his dissenting opinion in the Watkins case: "So long as the object of a legislative inquiry is legitimate and the questions propounded are pertinent thereto, it is not for the courts to interfere with the committee system of inquiry. To hold otherwise would be an infringement on the power given the Congress to inform itself, and thus a trespass upon the fundamental American principle of separation of powers." Mr. Justice Clark declared that the majority "has substituted the judiciary as the grand inquisitor and supervisor of congressional investigations," and asserted "it has never been so."

Substantial portions of my bill have to do with areas involving States' rights, and the performance by States of functions which are primarily of concern to the States. So it is with the matter of home rule in the administration of schools and so it is with respect to actions by State legislatures to combat subversion within the boundaries of their respective States; and so it is with respect to the powers of States to control the practice of law within their boundaries. There is no need for any national uniformity with respect to these matters. They are things for each State to decide for itself. Leaving the decisions in each State to the highest court of that State, and taking from the Supreme Court of the United States any power to step in and impose an arbitrary rule, can only be a salutary thing, a step away from regimentation and back toward freedom of the individual. . . .

The Founding Fathers understood that if any one branch of the Government got complete ascendency, we would not have a Government of checks and balances but an oligarchy which would lead unquestionably and irresistibly to tyranny.

The genius of the Constitution is that it does not provide for a final arbiter; it does provide for checks and balances which may be used by the different branches of the Government, one against the other, to guard against or to repel encroachments.

It is this very system of uneasy balances which gives the citizen his best guarantee that his rights will continue to be observed. For once all power is put in a single place, so, surely as "power corrupts and absolute power corrupts absolutely," the individual rights of citizens are doomed from that day on. . . .

CON BY THOMAS C. HENNINGS, JR.

I have complete confidence in the ability and common sense of the nine men who occupy the highest bench in the land, the Supreme Court of the United States.

All of the nine Justices have been confirmed by the United States Senate. If one man sits on that bench who does not understand the nature of the Communist conspiracy, then the appointing President and the Senate have been utterly remiss in the performance of their duty.

I do not believe that either had acted with such irresponsibility.

The Communist conspiracy, as we all know, is an ever-present danger to our Government. It seeks to destroy our traditional democratic processes. It is absolutely necessary that we have laws which will protect our nation against such destruction. But I believe in establishing barriers against the destruction of our system; let us not ourselves destroy one of the great bulwarks of our country.

For over 170 years the Supreme Court has been the court of last resort respecting the meaning of the Constitution. This, of course, is our traditional legal system which is part of our democratic processes. And even though Congress has had the power to limit the Supreme Court's appellate jurisdiction, it has always given to the Court broad appellate jurisdiction over cases where the Constitution is involved. Only once has the Congress limited the Court's appellate jurisdiction. Only once has this power of jurisdiction been limited and this limitation went only to the Court's power to review denials of writs of habeas corpus. It did not cut out the Court's review power over a complete area of law.

S. 2646, if enacted, would result in the Constitution meaning one thing in one place and something else in another.

The ultimate effect of the bill would be to destroy a significant part of our legal system, a part of our democratic processes. Therefore, to meet the threat against our system of government posed by the Communist conspiracy, this bill proposes that the Congress destroy an integral part of the traditional system itself.

I most emphatically do not believe it is necessary to take from the Supreme Court a part of its jurisdiction to meet the threats of the Communist conspiracy. Furthermore, and to the contrary, such a step would belittle our system of government in the eyes of the rest of the world.

The Court does not dwell upon any high plateau of infallibility. Under our system, the Court is open to criticism and the Court should, like all of us, be subject to criticism by men of good will and learned in the law and who are informed on these matters. . . .

S. 2646, . . . would completely destroy the privilege to appeal to the Supreme Court in the five areas of the law. If a person claimed that his constitutional rights had been violated in any of these areas, he could not go to the Supreme Court with his grievance. The final determination of his claim would be made by a State supreme court or a Federal circuit court of appeals.

So, then, the decision would depend upon which court had the last say. There would no longer be conformity as to the meaning of the Constitution. The constitutional issue involved in almost every case in these areas is the due-process clause of the 5th or 14th amendment.

Now, Congress was given the power to limit the Supreme Court's appellate jurisdiction by article III, section 2 of the Constitution. This power of the Congress became effective upon the ratification of the Constitution. The people of our nation in 1789 had certain misgivings as to the power which they had bestowed upon the Government, as we all know from reading the debates of the Constitutional Convention. They quickly engrossed upon the Constitution what we now know as the Bill of Rights. The Bill of Rights limits the powers given to the Government by the original Constitution. Therefore, the power of Congress to limit the appellate jurisdiction of the Supreme Court is subject to the restrictions, several restrictions of the Bill of Rights. . . .

A proposal such as we have here will destroy the philosophy of equal justice under law which is basic to our system of jurisprudence, Anglo-Saxon jurisprudence.

A bill which will result in the Constitution requiring certain safeguards in one part of the nation and not requiring the same safeguards in another would be repugnant to the due-process clause. Therefore, it might well be declared void on that ground. Congress must always keep in mind that the amendments to the Constitution restrict the powers originally given to it by the Constitution.

This bill would establish a very dangerous precedent and would be a first step toward the destruction of our present judicial system.

By S. 2646, we would take from the Supreme Court its appellate jurisdiction in certain areas because of disagreement with its decisions in these respective areas. The next step might be to take from the Supreme Court its jurisdiction in other areas where there is disagreement with its decisions.

Furthermore, if the Supreme Court's jurisdiction is limited, I can also visualize an attempt to limit the jurisdiction of the United States circuit courts, if they should reach decisions which are contrary to the views of the proponents of this bill.

And this sequence logically could easily lead to the piecemeal destruction of our independent judiciary. Our courts would possess only limited power, and the guaranties of the Constitution, from a practical point of view, I think would become meaningless. . . .

Mere disagreement with a decision of the Supreme Court is not grounds for withdrawing jurisdiction. The powers of the State are limited by the Constitution, and the Supreme Court has traditionally been the final authority on the construction of the Constitution. Violence will be done to the spirit of the U. S. Constitution even by this limited withdrawal of jurisdiction and a dangerous precedent will be established. . . .

19

Equal Justice Under Law

19.1. JUDGES AS LAWMAKERS

On what standards do judges rely in reaching their decisions? President Theodore Roosevelt points out the danger of relying on the courts to strike down technically slipshod legislation, and the equal danger of the courts nullifying legislation simply because they consider it unwise or improper.

THE CHIEF LAWMAKERS in our country may be, and often are, the judges, because they are the final seat of authority. Every time they interpret contract, property, vested rights, due process of law, liberty, they necessarily enact into law parts of a system of social philosophy; and as such interpretation is fundamental, they give direction to all law-making. The decisions of the courts on economic and social questions depend upon their economic and social philosophy; and for the peaceful progress of our people during the twentieth century we shall owe most to those judges who hold to a twentieth century economic and social philosophy and not to a long outgrown philosophy, which was itself the product of primitive economic conditions. Of course a judge's views on progressive social philosophy are entirely second in importance to his possession of a high and fine character; which means the possession of such elementary virtues as honesty, courage, and fairmindedness. The judge who owes his election to pandering to demagogic sentiments or class hatreds and prejudices, and the judge who owes either his election or his appointment to the money

From President Theodore Roosevelt, "Message to Congress," December 8, 1908.

or the favor of a great corporation, are alike unworthy to sit on the bench, are alike traitors to the people; and no profundity of legal learning, or correctness of abstract conviction on questions of public policy, can serve as an offset to such shortcomings. But it is also true that judges, like executives and legislators, should hold sound views on the questions of public policy which are of vital interest to the people.

The legislators and executives are chosen to represent the people in enacting and administering the laws. The judges are not chosen to represent the people in this sense. Their function is to interpret the laws. The legislators are responsible for the laws; the judges for the spirit in which they interpret and enforce the laws. We stand aloof from the reckless agitators who would make the judges mere pliant tools of popular prejudice and passion; and we stand aloof from those equally unwise partisans of reaction and privilege who deny the proposition that, inasmuch as judges are chosen to serve the interests of the whole people, they should strive to find out what those interests are, and, so far as they conscientiously can, should strive to give effect to popular conviction when deliberately and duly expressed by the lawmaking body. The courts are to be highly commended and staunchly upheld when they set their faces against wrongdoing or tyranny by a majority; but they are to be blamed when they fail to recognize under a government like ours the deliberate judgment of the majority as to a matter of legitimate policy, when duly expressed by the legislature. Such lawfully expressed and deliberate judgment should be given effect by the courts, save in the extreme and exceptional cases where there has been a clear violation of a constitutional provision. Anything like frivolity or wantonness in upsetting such clearly taken governmental action is a grave offense against the Republic. To protest against tyranny, to protect minorities from oppression, to nullify an act committed in a spasm of popular fury, is to render a service to the Republic. But for the courts to arrogate to themselves functions which properly belong to the legislative bodies is all wrong, and in the end works mischief. The people should not be permitted to pardon evil and slipshod legislation on the theory that the court will set it right; they should be taught that the right way to get rid of a bad law is to have the legislature repeal it, and not to have the courts by ingenious hair-splitting nullify it. A law may be unwise and improper; but it should not for these reasons be declared unconstitutional by a strained interpretation, for the result of such action is to take away from the people at large their sense of responsibility and ultimately to destroy their capacity for orderly self restraint and self government. Under such a popular government as ours, founded on the theory that in the long run the will of the people is supreme, the ultimate safety of the Nation can only rest in training and guiding the people so that what they will shall be right, and not in devising means to defeat their will by the technicalities of strained construction.

19.2. THE FEDERAL COURT SYSTEM

Article III of the Constitution provides the authority for our Federal court system. The organization of the so-called inferior courts is determined by Congress. The following congressional document describes the functions of the Federal judiciary.

THE CONSTITUTION assures the equality and independence of the Judicial Branch from the Legislative and Executive Branches. Although Federal judges are appointed by the President of the United States with the advice and consent of the Senate, and although funds for the operation of the courts are appropriated by Congress, the independence of the United States courts is provided for in three respects:

First, under the Constitution these courts can be called upon to exercise only judicial powers and to perform only judicial work. Judicial power and judicial work involve essentially the application and interpretation of the law in the decision of real differences, that is, in the language of the Constitution, the decision of "Cases" and "Controversies." The courts cannot be called upon to make laws—the function of the Legislative Department—nor to enforce and execute laws—the function of the Executive Department.

Secondly, Federal judges "hold their Offices during good Behavior," that is, as long as they desire to be judges and perform their work. They can be removed from office against their will only by impeachment.

Third, the Constitution provides that the "Compensation" of Federal judges "shall not be diminished during their continuance in office." Neither the President nor Congress can reduce the salary of a Federal judge.

These three provisions—for judicial work only, for holding office during good behavior, and for undiminished compensation—are designed to assure judges of independence from outside influence so that their decisions may be completely impartial.

Throughout the United States there are two sets of judicial systems. One set is that of the State and local courts established in each State under the authority of the State governments. The other is that of the United States courts set up under the authority of the Constitution by the Congress of the United States.

The State courts have general, unlimited power to decide almost every type of case, subject only to the limitations of State law. They are

From *The United States Courts,* House Document No. 233, 86th Congress, 1st Session (Washington, D.C., 1959), pp. 1–3, 10–11.

located in every town and county and are the tribunals with which citizens most often have contact. The great bulk of legal business concerning divorce and the probate of estates and all other matters except those assigned to the United States courts is handled by these State courts.

The United States courts, on the other hand, have power to decide only those cases in which the Constitution gives them authority. They are located principally in the larger cities. Only the controversies in a few carefully selected types of cases set forth in the Constitution can be heard in the United States courts.

The controversies which can be decided in the United States courts are set forth in section 2 of article III of the United States Constitution. These are first of all "Controversies to which the United States shall be a party," that is, cases in which the United States Government itself or one of its officers is either suing someone else or is being sued by another party. . . .

Secondly, the . . . Federal judicial power extends "to Controversies between two or more States; between a State and Citizens of another State; between Citizens of different States; between Citizens of the same State claiming Lands under Grants of different States, . . ." If the State of Missouri sues the State of Illinois for pollution of the Mississippi River, the courts of either Missouri or Illinois would be inappropriate and perhaps not impartial forums. . . . It has seemed better to avoid any suspicion of favoritism by vesting power to decide these controversies in the United States courts.

State courts are also inappropriate in "Cases affecting Ambassadors, other public Ministers and Consuls" and in cases "between a State, or the Citizens thereof, and foreign States, Citizens, or Subjects." The United States Government has responsibility for our relations with other nations, and cases involving their representatives or their citizens may affect our foreign relations so that such cases should be decided in the United States courts.

And, thirdly, the Constitution provides that the judicial powers extends "to all Cases, in Law and Equity, arising under this Constitution, the Laws of the United States, and Treaties made, or which shall be made, under their Authority" and "to all Cases of admiralty and maritime jurisdiction." Under these provisions the United States courts decide cases involving the Constitution, laws of Congress, treaties, or laws relating to navigable waters.

The Constitution declares what cases may be decided in the United States courts. Congress can and has determined that some of these cases may also be tried in State courts and that others may be tried only in the United States courts. Thus Congress has provided that, with some exceptions, cases arising under the Constitution or laws of the United States or between citizens of different States may be tried in the United

States courts only if the amount involved exceeds $10,000 and even then may be tried in either the State or the United States courts. Congress has also provided that maritime cases and suits against consuls can be tried only in the United States courts. When a State court decides a case involving Federal law, it in a sense acts as a United States court, and its decision on Federal law may be reviewed by the United States Supreme Court.

In any event this discussion should make it clear that the United States courts cannot decide every case which arises, but only those which the Constitution and the laws of Congress allot to them. And as you may suspect from the length of this discussion, whether a case is one which may be decided by the United States courts is an extremely technical and complicated matter which lawyers and judges frequently spend a great deal of time resolving.

The United States courts to which decision of the types of cases just discussed has been entrusted have varied a great deal throughout the history of our country. The Constitution merely provides: "The judicial Power of the United States, shall be vested in one supreme Court, and in such inferior Courts as the Congress may from time to time ordain and establish." Thus, the only indispensable court is the Supreme Court, and Congress has from time to time established and abolished various other United States courts.

At the present time the United States court system may be likened to a pyramid. At the apex of the pyramid stands the Supreme Court of the United States, the highest court in the land. On the next level stand the United States court of appeals, 11 in all. On the next level stand the United States district courts, 87 in all, the United States District Court for the District of Columbia and the district courts in the Canal Zone, Guam and the Virgin Islands. In a sense certain administrative agencies may be included here because the review of their decisions may be directly in the courts of appeals. Some agency reviews, however, are handled by the district courts.

A person involved in a suit in the United States courts may thus proceed through three levels of decision. His case will be heard and decided by one of the courts or agencies on the lower level. If either party is dissatisfied with the decision rendered, he may usually have review of right in one of the courts of appeals. Then, if he is still dissatisfied, but usually only if his case involves matters of great national importance, he may obtain review in the Supreme Court of the United States.

This pyramidal organization of the courts serves two purposes. First, the Supreme Court and the courts of appeals can correct errors which have been made in the decisions below. Secondly, these higher courts can assure uniformity of decision by reviewing cases where two or more lower courts have reached different results. . . .

[The] whole rather complex problem of the various cases that may be tried in the United States courts may be illustrated for you by the story of an automobile collision. Bill Smith from Chicago driving his car on an Illinois road has a collision with another vehicle. Ordinarily no suit arising out of that accident could be tried in a United States court; it would be heard and decided in a State court. But if the other vehicle were an army truck driven by a soldier, Bill Smith may want to sue the United States, or the United States may decide to sue Bill Smith. In either event Bill Smith or the United States may commence a suit in the United States district court in Illinois.

If the other vehicle belonged to a private person who lived in Illinois, Bill Smith or the other owner may sue only in the State court, unless under certain circumstances the suit involved some provision of the Federal statutes or the Federal Constitution. If, on the other hand, the other vehicle belonged to John Jones who lived in St. Louis, Mo., then either John Jones or Bill Smith may sue in a United States district court because they were from different States.

These possible suits have been civil cases brought to compensate the parties for damage done, and it is unlikely that a criminal case brought by the Government would arise. Yet, if either Bill Smith or the other driver had been handling his car so recklessly as to warrant a criminal prosecution for reckless driving, manslaughter, etc., the suit would be brought by the State of Illinois in the State court. Let us suppose, however, that the other driver was in a car which he had stolen in Indiana and had driven into Illinois. Then that driver might be prosecuted by the United States Government in the United States district court under Federal law for transporting a stolen automobile from one State into another.

If either Bill Smith or his adversary is dissatisfied with the decision of the United States district court, he may appeal to a United States court of appeals, and if still dissatisfied after a decision by that court, he may seek review in the United States Supreme Court on questions of Federal law which arose in the proceedings. So you can see how an accident usually gives rise to suits which can be tried in State courts only, but which under special circumstances may be tried or reviewed in the United States courts.

The work of the United States district courts is partly reflected in the statistics on the types of cases which are filed every year. In the fiscal year ending June 30, 1959, exactly 57,800 civil cases were filed in these courts. Of these over 20,000 involved the United States either as a party plaintiff or party defendant. The United States as plaintiff commenced about 1,150 cases under the food and drug laws, 5,400 cases to collect money due on promissory notes, and about 8,450 other cases. The United States was a defendant in about 675 habeas corpus cases and 500 cases involving motions to vacate criminal sentences, 1,300 Tort Claims

Act cases, 1,250 tax cases and many others. These figures show the important role the district courts play in enforcing Federal statutes and in achieving justice even when the United States Government is involved in a lawsuit.

Private parties brought into the district courts during the fiscal year 1959 about 37,500 cases of which 9,000 involved questions arising under Federal laws. The largest category of these cases (over 3,000) was that involving the Jones Act which permits lawsuits for personal injuries to seamen. About 25,700 cases came into the district courts in suits between private persons from different States. Of this number about 9,600 were concerned with personal injuries arising out of motor vehicle accidents. In addition to these cases, private parties brought into the district courts during the fiscal year about 2,800 suits arising in admiralty controversies. An additional 8,200 civil cases of a local nature were brought in the District Court for the District of Columbia and in the territorial courts.

Of the 28,729 criminal cases filed in the district courts during the year ending June 30, 1959, about 9,150 involved fraud and other thefts, 2,300 involved the immigration laws, 3,900 were for the illegal transportation of stolen motor vehicles, 4,200 were for the violation of the liquor tax laws, 1,460 involved narcotics, and the remainder were for violations of a host of other laws. In these criminal cases the United States courts share with the officers of the law and the United States attorneys the enforcement of criminal laws for the protection of all citizens.

During the fiscal year 1959, probation officers attached to the United States district courts had under supervision over 34,000 persons and thus relieved the Federal prisons of an expensive burden and afforded these persons a greater chance of "going straight" away from the contaminating prison influences. During this same fiscal year the referees in bankruptcy attached to the district courts undertook the administration of the property of about 100,000 persons unable to pay their debts, for the purpose of enabling creditors to receive a proper share of the money due to them.

In its work of enforcing the Federal laws, deciding controversies between citizens, sentencing convicted criminal defendants, distributing the estates of debtors and rehabilitating violators of the law, the United States courts perform an essential and vital function in the American pattern of democratic government.

19.3. THE ESSENTIALS OF JUDICIAL REFORM

An effective system of justice can be undermined by unduly complex court procedures, poor personnel, political influence on judges, incom-

petent juries, and unqualified lawyers. The late Chief Justice of the New Jersey Supreme Court, Arthur Vanderbilt, proposes some key planks in a program of judicial reform.

AS A RESULT of our experience, I hazard a guess that real judicial reform will not come in any large jurisdiction by any other method than direct appeal to the people. What happened in England and, much more recently, in New Jersey, proves it. The stage is now set in New York for such a campaign. I can well understand the discouragement today of the members of the Temporary Commission, but I venture to repeat what I said after the years of battling in New Jersey: "Manifestly judicial reform is no sport for the short-winded or for lawyers who are afraid of temporary defeat." It will not be necessary to walk around Jericho seven times and blow the trumpets; all that is neded to tumble down the walls of the present inadequate court system is to let the people know how really simple judicial reform actually is.

It is so simple that any high school student can understand its essential elements. The first requirement is an integrated set of courts. The second requirement is the best possible judges, lawyers, and juries. The third is an effective businesslike organization of the courts, with responsible leadership. The fourth is a flexible system of rules of procedure promulgated, not by the legislature—which is already overburdened and which cannot be expected to be expert in these matters—but by the judges of the court of last resort, with the aid of a Judicial Conference. This conference would be made up of the ablest and most unselfish judges and lawyers as well as some lay members who, I have found, are adept in asking embarrassing questions which very much need to be answered if we desire to have a judicial establishment geared to the demands of the times.

It is characteristic of an immature system of law that it is beset by a multiplicity of courts. Lord Coke in his classic "Fourth Institute" describes over 100 different courts; Holsworth, in the first volume of his monumental "History of English Law," even more. All the courts that any American state really needs, however, are three:

(1) A general trial court with state-wide jurisdiction over every kind of case. This court may and should have a considerable degree of specialization within it, with specialized judges in law and equity, probate and divorce matters. However, every judge of the court should be authorized when occasion requires to try every other kind of case. There should be no jurisdictional conflicts among courts.

(2) There should also be a local court for the trial of minor cases, civil and criminal, and for the holding of defendants for action by the

From Arthur T. Vanderbilt, "Brief for a Better Court System," in *The New York Times Magazine,* May 5, 1957, pp. 9, 67–69; © 1957 by The New York Times Company. Reprinted by permission.

grand jury. In some states it has been found advisable to divide this local court into two, one civil and the other criminal.

(3) There must, of course, be an appellate tribunal to review questions of law from the trial courts and from the administrative tribunals. In the larger states there must be an intermediate court or court of appeals, the number depending upon the volume of appellate business in the particular jurisdiction.

Very few of our states have achieved this ideal of the three-court system. The degree to which they have progressed in this direction is one measure of their judicial civilization. New York State now has twenty-one kinds of courts. Such a system is needlessly complicated; I defy most lawyers and most judges, for that matter, to define the jurisdiction of so many courts.

Such a multiplicity of courts creates confusion that frequently results in cases being determined on the basis of jurisdictional technicalities rather than on their merits. Unnecessary compartmentalization reduces the flexibility of the judicial system and its ability to adapt itself to the constantly changing nature and volume of litigation. Inevitably the more different kinds of courts, each with its own clerical staff, the greater the cost of operating the courts. A simple integrated court structure eliminates jurisdictional conflicts, permits the most efficient use of the available judicial manpower, and reduces the administrative overhead necessary for the proper operation of the system.

We are primarily concerned with the caliber of judges, jurors and lawyers—though all other court personnel are also important to the operation of a sound judicial system.

What constitutes a good judge? If I may quote myself:

We need judges learned in the law, not merely the law in books but, something far more difficult to acquire, the law as applied in action in the courtroom; judges deeply versed in the mysteries of human nature and adept in the discovery of the truth in the discordant testimony of fallible human beings; judges beholden to no man, independent and honest and—equally important—believed by all men to be independent and honest; judges, above all, fired with consuming zeal to mete out justice according to law to every man, woman, and child that may come before them and to preserve individual freedom against any aggression of government; judges with the humility born of wisdom, patient and untiring in the search for truth and keenly conscious of the evils arising in a workaday world from any unnecessary delay.

Judges with all of these attributes are not easy to find, but which of these traits dare we eliminate if we are to hope for evenhanded justice? Good judges can after a fashion make even an inadequate system of substantive law achieve justice. On the other hand, judges who lack these qualifications will defeat the best system of substantive and procedural law imaginable.

The method of selecting judges is crucial. It may come as a surprise to many people that the popular election of judges is unknown anywhere in the world outside of several of the American states, such as New York, and in Soviet Russia and its satellites.

This issue is basic. Not a year goes by but that *The New York Times,* for example, editorially decries the farce of popular elections of judges. Former Governor Alfred E. Smith, who was generally conceded to be one of the ablest students of government this country has ever produced, disposes of the issue in a single sentence:

In the long run [the elective system] means the selection of judges by political leaders and the ratification of their selection by an electorate who are not really in a position to pass upon the legal and other abilities of the individual.

Such a master politican as Edward J. Flynn, formerly chairman of the Democratic National Committee as well as chairman of the Democratic State Committee in New York and for many years Democratic leader of the Bronx, frankly admits the effects of the popular election of judges. Not long before his death he wrote a book entitled, rather ironically, "You're the Boss." His description of the sinister contacts between the political leaders and "his" judiciary is shocking, and the more so because he confesses to a realization of its iniquity. He wrote:

Political leaders have always maintained, not only in New York but throughout the entire United States, that they have the right to speak on behalf of a client to a judge on the bench. Ethically it is wrong; but practically the custom has always existed and it would be difficult to eradicate.

Nor are the conditions any better in the rural areas. Only recently Judge Harvey Uhlenhopp addressed the Iowa State Bar Foundation in this frank language:

The situation is even worse in the country. The lawyers control the nomination of the judges, and in many rural counties one of the lawyers is politically prominent who holds the delegation in his hand. You ought to sit in this spot: on one side of the table in a close case is a political nobody. On the other side is a man who controls your job. It is a farce to call this a system of justice where the employer of the judge is on one side of the table. That is your rural system.

If the people of a state are not ready to consider the appointive system, especially where appointees are chosen on a bipartisan basis as in New Jersey, they should at least have the American Bar, or California, or Missouri Plan—as it is variously called—submitted to them. Under this system the influences of partisan politics are kept at a minimum since the candidates for judicial office are first chosen by a nomination commission, composed not of party representatives but of representatives of the bench and the bar. Then, after a brief trial period the judges run on their own record without any opponent, with the public voting upon the simple question: "Shall Judge A be continued in office on his record?"

In cases where juries are used, they are, within their sphere, quite as important as the judges themselves. What will it avail a litigant to have the best possible judge and the ablest lawyers in his case, if there are dishonest or unintelligent jurors in the box?

Strangely, there are those who carry their notions of "democracy" and equality to the extreme of asserting that every one has a right to be a juror, and that a litigant or an accused has the right to have a jury chosen at random from the populace. But if we look at the administration of justice as a practical matter vitally concerned with affairs touching intimately the welfare both of private citizens and the state, can we possibly say that there is a place on the jury for convicts, the illiterate, or persons mentally or physically unfit? Obviously not, if justice is to be done.

To be effective, a jury must constitute a cross-secton of the honest and intelligent citizens of the county and be imbued with a sense of the solemnity of their function and determined to perform it.

Jury panels should always be selected by the judges (provided, of course, the system of judicial selection in use insures judges free from politics) or by commissions selected for this purpose by the judges, and such jury commissioners should be chosen on a bipartisan basis and should be entirely divorced from politics. It is shocking to learn that the jury in at least twenty-four states are still made up by political officers, which means that in such states there is always the danger and generally the reality that the jury panel will be selected with political considerations in mind.

I remember the reply of a United States senator to my plea to him years ago for his support of a bill authorizing the courts to appoint jury commissioners to select the jury panels; he had no objection to such a method of selection in civil cases, but he would tolerate no change in the political selection of jurors in criminal matters—one could never tell when one would need help!

The ability, conscientiousness, and integrity of the jury commissioners in any state is measured by the competence and suitability of the persons whom they select for jury service. As the word "selection" indicates, the process of choosing jurors is not an arbitrary or mechanical function, but a task requiring the exercise of judgment, discretion, and good faith on the part of those in whom the responsibility for selection is vested. In New Jersey our Supreme Court has instructed its jury commissioners that their selection should be controlled by the following considerations:

(1) All names should not be selected from the same source (such as a tax roll, election list, or directory); (2) sources should be so coordinated as together to include all wards and municipalities in the county; (3) sources should be included which are likely to produce the names of persons possessed of intelligence, morality, integrity and common sense; (4) economic and social status, including race and color, should be considered only to the extent necessary to assure that there is no discrimination on account of them; (5) political affiliations should be completely ignored; and (6) unsolicited requests of persons who seek to have their names placed upon the jury lists and unsolicited recommendations of names should be accepted with extreme caution.

To obtain real justice, we must have lawyers who are competent, industrious and courageous, always mindful of their professional obligations, as epitomized in the Canons of Professional Ethics, to present the facts to the court and jury and to argue the law to the court—for the law in operation is necessarily the joint product of judge, jury, and counsel.

Raising the standards of the bar in any state is something which cannot be accomplished merely by the passing of a statute or the enactment of a rule of court. It requires that law schools throughout the country continue to increase their educational standards and to devise ways and means of inculcating in their students a deep sense of professional responsibility, it calls for the fixing by the court of last resort in the state of high standards for admission to practice and for continued vigilance both on the part of the courts and bar associations to see that those few lawyers who ignore their professional obligations are dealt with in the interest of protecting the public. . . .

19.4. RECENT CHANGE IN THE LAW OF CRIMINAL PROCEDURE

The Fourth Amendment prevents the use of illegally obtained evidence against a defendant in the Federal courts. Not until June, 1961, was this exclusionary rule adopted by the Supreme Court to prevent the use of illegal evidence in State court prosecutions. The following case sets forth the judges' reasons for expanding the protection of the Fourth Amendment.

MR. JUSTICE CLARK delivered the opinion of the Court. . . .

. . . our holding that the exclusionary rule is an essential part of both the Fourth and Fourteenth Amendments is not only the logical dictate

From *Mapp v. Ohio,* 367 U.S. 643 (1961).

of prior cases, but it also makes very good sense. There is no war between the Constitution and common sense. Presently, a federal prosecutor may make no use of evidence illegally seized, but a State's attorney across the street may, although he supposedly is operating under the enforceable prohibitions of the same Amendment. Thus the State, by admitting evidence unlawfully seized, serves to encourage disobedience to the Federal Constitution which it is bound to uphold. . . . In nonexclusionary States, federal officers, being human, were by it invited to and did, as our cases indicate; step across the street to the State's attorney with their unconstitutionally seized evidence. Prosecution on the basis of that evidence was then had in a state court in utter disregard of the enforceable Fourth Amendment. If the fruits of an unconstitutional search had been inadmissible in both state and federal courts, this inducement to evasion would have been sooner eliminated. . . .

The ignoble shortcut to conviction left open to the State tends to destroy the entire system of constitutional restraints on which the liberties of the people rest. Having once recognized that the right to privacy embodied in the Fourth Amendment is enforceable against the States, and that the right to be secure again rude invasions of privacy by state officers is, therefore, constitutional in origin, we can no longer permit that right to remain an empty promise. Because it is enforceable in the same manner and to like effect as other basic rights secured by the Due Process Clause, we can no longer permit it to be revocable at the whim of any police officer who, in the name of law enforcement itself, chooses to suspend its enjoyment. . . .

The judgment of the Supreme Court of Ohio is reversed and the cause remanded for further proceedings not inconsistent with this opinion. *Reversed and remanded.*

· · · · · ·

Mr. Justice Douglas, concurring.

Though I have joined the opinion of the Court, I add a few words. This criminal proceeding started with a lawless search and seizure. The police entered a home forcefully, and seized documents that were later used to convict the occupant of a crime.

She lives alone with her fifteen-year-old daughter in the second floor flat of a duplex in Cleveland. At about 1:30 in the afternoon of May 23, 1957, three policemen arrived at this house. They rang the bell, and the appellant, appearing at her window, asked them what they wanted. According to their later testimony, the policemen had come to the house on information from "a confidential source that there was a person hiding out in the home, who was wanted for questioning in connection with a recent bombing."[1] To the appellant's question, however, they replied only

---

[1] This "confidential source" told the police, in the same breath, that "there was a large amount of policy paraphernalia being hidden in the home".

that they wanted to question her and would not state the subject about which they wanted to talk.

The appellant, who had retained an attorney in connection with a pending civil matter, told the police she would call him to ask if she should let them in. On her attorney's advice, she told them she would let them in only when they produced a valid search warrant. For the next two and a half hours, the police laid siege to the house. At four o'clock, their number was increased to at least seven. Appellant's lawyer appeared on the scene; and one of the policemen told him that they now had a search warrant, but the officer refused to show it. Instead, going to the back door, the officer first tried to kick it in and, when that proved unsuccessful, he broke the glass in the door and opened it from the inside.

The appellant, who was on the steps going up to her flat, demanded to see the search warrant; but the officer refused to let her see it although he waved a paper in front of her face. She grabbed it and thrust it down the front of her dress. The policemen seized her, took the paper from her, and had her handcuffed to another officer. She was taken upstairs, thus bound, and into the larger of the two bedrooms in the apartment; there she was forced to sit on the bed. Meanwhile, the officers entered the house and made a complete search of the four rooms of her flat and of the basement of the house.

The testimony concerning the search is largely nonconflicting. The approach of the officers; their long wait outside the home, watching all its doors; the arrival of reinforcements armed with a paper; breaking into the house; putting their hands on appellant and handcuffing her; numerous officers ransacking through every room and piece of furniture, while the appellant sat, a prisoner in her own bedroom. There is direct conflict in the testimony, however, as to where the evidence which is the basis of this case was found. To understand the meaning of that conflict, one must understand that this case is based on the knowing possession of four little pamphlets, a couple of photographs and a little pencil doodle —all of which are alleged to be pornographic.

According to the police officers who participated in the search, these articles were found, some in appellant's dressers and some in a suitcase found by her bed. According to appellant, most of the articles were found in a cardboard box in the basement; one in the suitcase beside her bed. All of this material, appellant—and a friend of hers— said were odds and ends belonging to a recent boarder, a man who had left suddenly for New York and had been detained there. As the Supreme Court of Ohio read the statute under which appellant is charged, she is guilty of the crime whichever story is true.

The Ohio Supreme Court sustained the conviction even though it was based on the documents obtained in the lawless search. For in

Ohio evidence obtained by an unlawful search and seizure is admissible in a criminal prosecution at least where it was not taken from the "defendant's person by the use of brutal or offensive force against defendant." *State* v. *Mapp,* 170 Ohio St. 427, syllabus 2; *State* v. *Lindway,* 131 Ohio St. 166. This evidence would have been inadmissible in a federal prosecution. *Weeks* v. *United States,* 232 U. S. 383; *Elkins* v. *United States,* 364 U. S. 206. For, as stated in the former decision, "The effect of the Fourth Amendment is to put the courts of the United States and Federal officials, in the exercise of their power and authority, under limitations and restraints. . . ." *Id.,* 391–392. It was therefore held that evidence obtained (which in that case was documents and correspondence) from a home without any warrant was not admisssible in a federal prosecution.

We held in *Wolf* v. *Colorado,* 338 U. S. 25, that the Fourth Amendment was applicable to the States by reason of the Due Process Clause of the Fourteenth Amendment. But a majority held that the exclusionary rule of the *Weeks* case was not required of the States, that they could apply such sanctions as they chose. That position had the necessary votes to carry the day. But with all respect it was not the voice of reason or principle.

As stated in the *Weeks* case, if evidence seized in violation of the Fourth Amendment can be used against an accused "his right to be secure against such searches and seizures is of no value, and . . . might as well be stricken from the Constitution." 232 U. S., at 393.

When we allowed States to give constitutional sanction to the "shabby business" of unlawful entry into a home (to use an expression of Mr. Justice Murphy, *Wolf* v. *Colorado,* at 46), we did indeed rob the Fourth Amendment of much meaningful force. There are, of course, other theoretical remedies. One is disciplinary action within the hierarchy of the police system, including prosecution of the police officer for a crime. But as Mr. Justice Murphy said in *Wolf* v. *Colorado,* at 42, "Self-scrutiny is a lofty ideal but its exaltation reaches new heights if we expect a District Attorney to prosecute himself or his associates for well-meaning violations of the search and seizure clause during a raid the District Attorney or his associates have ordered."

The only remaining remedy, if exclusion of the evidence is not required, is an action of trespass by the homeowner against the offending officer. Mr. Justice Murphy showed how onerous and difficult it would be for the citizen to maintain that action and how meagre the relief even if the citizen prevails. 338 U. S. 42–44. The truth is that trespass actions against officers who make unlawful searches and seizures are mainly illusory remedies.

Without judicial action making the exclusionary rule applicable to the States, *Wolf* v. *Colorado* in practical effect reduced the guarantee against unreasonable searches and seizures to "a dead letter," as Mr. Justice Rutledge said in his dissent. See 338 U. S., at 47.

Wolf v. *Colorado, supra,* was decided in 1949. The immediate result was a storm of constitutional controversy which only today finds its end. I believe that this is an appropriate case in which to put an end to the asymmetry which *Wolf* imported into the law. . . . It is an appropriate case because the facts it presents show—as would few other cases— the casual arrogance of those who have the untrammelled power to invade one's home and to seize one's person. . . .

Moreover, continuance of *Wolf* v. *Colorado* in its full vigor breeds the unseemly shopping around of the kind revealed in *Wilson* v. *Schnettler,* 365 U. S. 381. Once evidence, inadmissible in a federal court, is admissible in a state court a "double standard" exists which, as the Court points out, leads to "working arrangements" that undercut federal policy and reduce some aspects of law enforcement to shabby business. The rule that supports that practice does not have the force of reason behind it.

19.5. THE RIGHT OF COUNSEL

The Sixth Amendment provides that "in all criminal prosecutions, the accused shall enjoy the right to have the assistance of counsel for his defense." The Supreme Court has held that this guarantee applies to all criminal prosecutions in Federal courts and to trials of capital crimes in State courts. But in many states the right to counsel in criminal trials of less than capital crimes was not recognized. In the case of Betts *v.* Brady, *the Supreme Court upheld the lower court's decision that the right to counsel was not a "fundamental" right guaranteed by the Sixth Amendment in State criminal trials. But in March, 1963, in the case reported here,* Betts *v.* Brady *was reversed. The case is a landmark in the expansion of the liberties guaranteed in the Bill of Rights.*

MR. JUSTICE BLACK delivered the Opinion of the Court:

Petitioner was charged in a Florida state court with having broken and entered a poolroom with intent to commit a misdemeanor. This offense is a felony under Florida law. Appearing in court without funds and without a lawyer, petitioner asked the court to appoint counsel for him, whereupon the following colloquy took place:

The court: "Mr. Gideon, I am sorry, but I cannot appoint counsel to

From *Gideon* v. *Wainwright* as reported in *The New York Times,* March 19, 1963.

represent you in this case. Under the laws of the State of Florida, the only time the court can appoint counsel to represent a defendant is when that person is charged with a capital offense. I am sorry, but I will have to deny your request to appoint counsel to defend you in this case."

The defendant: "The United States Supreme Court says I am entitled to be represented by counsel!"

Put to trial before a jury, Gideon conducted his defense about as well as could be expected from a layman. He made an opening statement to the jury, cross-examined the state's witnesses, presented witnesses in his own defense, declined to testify himself, and made a short argument "emphasizing his innocence to the charge contained in the information filed in this case." The jury returned a verdict of guilty, and petitioner was sentenced to serve five years in the state prison. Later, petitioner filed in the Florida Supreme Court this habeas corpus petition attacking his conviction and sentence on the ground that the trial court's refusal to appoint counsel for him denied him rights "guaranteed by the Constitution and the Bill of Rights by the United States Government." Treating the petition for habeas corpus as properly before it, the Supreme Court, "upon consideration thereof" but without an opinion, denied all relief. Since 1942, when Betts v. Brady, 316 U.S. 455, was decided by a divided court, the problem of a defendant's Federal constitutional right to counsel in a state court has been a continuing source of controversy and litigation in both state and Federal courts. To give this problem another review here, we granted certiorari. Since Gideon was proceeding forma pauperis, we appointed counsel to represent him and requested both sides to discuss in their briefs and oral arguments the following: "Should this court's holding in Betts v. Brady, 316 U.S. 455, be reconsidered?"

I

The facts upon which Betts claimed that he had been unconstitutionally denied the right to have counsel appointed to assist him are strikingly like the facts upon which Gideon here bases his Federal constitution claim. . . . Betts was denied any relief, and on review this court affirmed. It was held that a refusal to appoint counsel of an indigent defendant charged with a felony did not necessarily violate the due process clause of the 14th Amendment, which for reasons given, the court deemed to be the only applicable Federal constitutional provision. . . .

Treating due process as "a concept less rigid and more fluid than those envisaged in other specific and particular provisions of the Bill of Rights," the court held that refusal to appoint counsel under the particular facts and circumstances in the Betts case was not so "offensive to the common and fundamental ideas of fairness" as to amount to a denial of due process. Since the facts and circumstances of the two cases are so nearly indistinguishable, we think the Betts v. Brady holding if left standing would require us to reject Gideon's claim that the Constitution guarantees him the assistance of counsel. Upon full reconsideration we conclude that *Betts* v. *Brady*, should be overruled.

II

The Sixth Amendment provides, "in all criminal prosecutions, the accused shall enjoy the right to have the assistance of counsel for his defense." . . . The Betts court refused to accept the contention that the Sixth Amendment's guarantee of counsel for indigent Federal defendants was extended to or, in the words of that court, "made obligatory upon the states by the 14th Amendment." Plainly, had the court concluded that appointment of counsel for an indigent criminal defendant was "a fundamental right, essential to a fair trial," it would have held that the 14th Amendment requires appointment of counsel in a state court, just as the sixth Amendment requires in a Federal court.

We think the court in Betts had ample precedent for acknowledging that those guarantees of the Bill of Rights which are fundamental safeguards of liberty immune from Federal abridgement are equally protected against state invasion by the due process clause of the 14th Amendment. This same principle was recognized, explained, and applied in *Powell* v. *Alabama*, 287 U.S. 45 (1932), a case upholding the right of counsel. In our adversary system of criminal justice, any person haled into court, who is too poor to hire a lawyer, cannot be assured a fair trial unless counsel is provided for him. The right of one charged with crime to counsel may not be deemed fundamental and essential to fair trials in some countries, but it is in ours. . . .

The court in *Betts* v. *Brady* departed from the sound wisdom upon which the court's holding in *Powell* v. *Alabama* rested. Florida, supported by two other states, has asked that *Betts* v. *Brady* be left intact. Twenty-two states, as friends of the court, argue that *Betts* was "an anachronism when handed down," and that it should now be overruled. We agree.

The judgment is reversed and the cause is remanded to the Supreme Court of Florida for further action not inconsistent with this opinion.

19.6. THE NEED TO ELIMINATE JUDICIAL DELAY

Delay in our court system can work great hardship on litigants. Chief Justice Warren here states the problem of delay and the case for enlarging the Federal judiciary. The problem has been somewhat relieved by passage of the Omnibus Judgeship Bill of 1961.

WE MUST NOT FORGET that the role of the courts is not merely to define the light. It is also to administer the remedy. Unless the remedy is actually applied to persons and things, the right is a mere pious idea.

With these thoughts in mind, I must report that the delay and the choking congestion in the federal courts today have created a crucial problem for constitutional government in the United States. It is so chronically prevalent that it is compromising the quantity and quality of justice available to the individual citizen and, in so doing, it is leaving vulnerable throughout the world the reputation of the United States for protecting and securing these rights and remedies.

We have made some progress, but the truth is that for every inch we gain, the normal healthy economic and population growth of our country extends a yard—leaving in its wake a whole new volume of litigation for the courts. . . . [In one year] the backlog in civil actions alone, in United States district courts, has increased by more than 5,000 new cases. The federal judiciary is simply unable—as long as it lacks a sufficient number of judges, improved administrative and procedural techniques, and ample supporting staff—to keep pace with the dynamic growth of our country.

The business of the district courts is the best evidence of this. If we go back to the pre-war year 1941—the first year that complete statistics were compiled in the Administrative Office—we can trace a veritable upward surge in the volume of litigation in our federal trial courts.

You know, of course, that I am not referring to the criminal business of the courts because, despite its importance, it takes only a minor portion of the court time. Criminal business has priority and is promptly disposed of.

It is, rather, the civil business of the courts which has sky-rocketed since 1941. In that year, 38,000 civil cases were filed, and an equal number of cases were disposed of. The pending caseload at the end of the year was 29,000. The time interval—vital issue-to-trial period —during which time the case is entirely in the control of the court, was only five months for the average or median case. In that year, 1941, we had approximately 200 trial judges.

Today—sixteen years later—the number of cases filed annually has increased to 62,000, and the pending backlog of business totals some 66,000 cases. We have, in our federal trial courts, 250 judges.

In other words, the number of cases filed annually in federal district courts has increased more than 60 percent since 1941. The backlog of cases has risen more than 125 percent. But, in contrast, there has been but a 25 percent increase in the number of judges to handle

From Chief Justice Earl Warren, Address before the Annual Meeting of the American Law Institute, Washington, D.C., May 21, 1958.

the increased volume of business. This also applies generally to supporting personnel.

The inevitable result has been a most discouraging increase in the length of time for getting a case heard. From five months in 1941, the interval from issue-to-trial for the median case has risen to nine months. At the present time, over 38 percent of all civil cases in the federal courts are subject to undue delay—that is, delay from one to four years between the date of filing and the time of trial. . . .

The *type* of case is important, too. For example, during the war and shortly thereafter we had on our dockets a large number of government price and rent control cases, which took a minimum amount of time. Studies that we have made show that on the average, cases between private individuals, the majority of them under the diversity of citizenship jurisdiction, take three times as much time to handle as government cases. These private cases, therefore, are the most important factor in the caseload. And it is this group which has increased most rapidly. Between 1941 and 1957, private civil cases based upon diversity of citizenship jurisdiction increased from some 7,000 per year to over 23,000. The backlog has increased 150 percent.

Bankruptcy matters, while usually handled by the referees, are also an important part of federal court business. The number of bankruptcy cases has not increased significantly excepting cases involving wage earners. . . .

These statistics are a record of delay piled upon delay in the federal courts. But, serious as they may be, they are no accurate measure of the extent to which our administrative weaknesses have caused injustice. They do not reflect the hardship and suffering caused to unfortunate victims of such delays, not the inadequate settlements which individuals are frequently forced to accept on that account. Neither do these figures include what are probably the worst and most numerous cases of all: those instances in which citizens with causes that cry for justice under law have turned from our court system in despair and have sought ways of working out their problems without resort to the courts at all.

It is evident that if this condition is not remedied it will seriously undermine what we have described as "the keystone of America's strength," and will dilute what we have proclaimed as "our main claim to moral leadership in the world community." Certainly we must be gravely concerned when our judicial machinery is facing an outlook of this kind. . . .

20

The Blessings of Liberty

20.1. THE DEFENSE OF FREEDOM OF SPEECH AND PRESS

The classic statement in behalf of freedom of speech is Milton's Areopagitica. *This work expresses a deep faith in the idea that truth will overwhelm falsehood. Formal censorship of publications acts as a barrier to the testing of ideas and the triumph of truth.*

I DENY NOT, but that it is of greatest concernment in the church and commonwealth, to have a vigilant eye how books demean themselves, as well as men; and thereafter to confine, imprison, and do sharpest justice on them as malefactors; for books are not absolutely dead things, but do contain a potency of life in them to be as active as that soul was whose progeny their are; nay, they do preserve as in a vial the purest efficacy and extraction of that living intellect that bred them. I know they are as lively, and as vigorously productive, as those fabulous dragon's teeth: and being sown up and down, may chance to spring up armed men. And yet, on the other hand, unless wariness be used, as good almost kill a man as kill a good book: who kills a man kills a reasonable creature, God's image; but he who destroys a good book, kills reason itself, kills the image of God, as it were, in the eye. Many a man lives a burden to the earth; but a good book is the precious life-blood of a master-spirit, embalmed and treasured up on purpose to a life beyond life. It is true, no age can restore a life, whereof, perhaps, there is no great loss; and revolutions of ages do not oft recover

From John Milton, *Areopagitica* (1644).

the loss of a rejected truth, for the want of which whole nations fare the worse. We should be wary, therefore, what persecution we raise against the living labours of public men, how we spill that seasoned life of man preserved and stored up in books; since we see a kind of homicide may be thus committed, sometimes a martydom; and if it extend to the whole impression, a kind of massacre, whereof the execution ends not in the slaying of an elemental life, but strikes at that ethereal and fifth essence, the breath of reason itself; slays an immortality rather than a life. . . .

Give me the liberty to know, to utter, and to argue freely according to conscience, above all liberties. . . .

. . . And though all the winds of doctrine were let loose to play upon the earth, so Truth be in the field, we do injuriously by licensing and prohibiting to misdoubt her strength. Let her and Falsehood grapple; who ever knew Truth put to the worse, in a free and open encounter? Her confuting is the best and surest suppressing. . . . When a man hath been labouring the hardest labour in the deep mines of knowledge, hath furnished out his findings in all their equipage, drawn forth his reasons as it were a battle ranged, scattered and defeated all objections in his way, calls out his adversary into the plain, offers him the advantage of wind and sun, if he please, only that he may try the matter by dint of argument, for his opponents then to skulk, to lay ambushments, to keep a narrow bridge of licensing where the challenger should pass, though it be valour enough in soldiership, is but weakness and cowardice in the wars of Truth. For who knows not that Truth is strong, next to the Almighty; she needs no policies, nor stratagems, nor licensings to make her victorious, those are the shifts and the defences that error uses against her power: give her but room, and do not bind her when she sleeps, for then she speaks not true. . . .

And as for regulating the press, let no man think to have the honour of advising ye better than yourselves have done in that order published next before this: "That no book be printed, unless the printer's and the author's name, or at least the printer's be registered." Those which otherwise come forth, if they be found mischievous and libellous, the fire and the executioner will be the timeliest and the most effectual remedy that man's prevention can use.

20.2. FREEDOM AND THE DEVELOPMENT OF THE INDIVIDUAL

Among the benefits to society of freedom of speech is the enrichment of knowledge stemming from the exchange and development of ideas. The individual profits also from freedom of speech, according to John Stuart

Mill, through the enhancement of his moral and intellectual capacities.

THE OBJECT OF THIS ESSAY is to assert one very simple principle, as entitled to govern absolutely the dealings of society with the individual in the way of compulsion and control, whether the means used by physical force in the form of legal penalties, or the moral coercion of public opinion. That principle is, that the sole end for which mankind are warranted, individually or collectively, in interfering with the liberty of action of any of their number, is self-protection. That the only purpose for which power can be rightfully exercised over any member of a civilised community, against his will, is to prevent harm to others. His own good, either physical or moral, is not a sufficient warrant. He cannot rightfully be compelled to do or forbear because it will be better for him to do so, because it will make him happier, because, in the opinions of others, to do so would be wise, or even right. These are good reasons for remonstrating with him, or reasoning with him, or persuading him, or entreating him, but not for compelling him, or visiting him with any evil in case he do otherwise. To justify that, the conduct from which it is desired to deter him must be calculated to produce evil to some one else. The only part of the conduct of any one, for which he is amenable to society, is that which concerns others. In the part which merely concerns himself, his independence is, of right, absolute. Over himself, over his own body and mind, the individual is sovereign. . . .

But there is a sphere of action in which society, as distinguished from the individual, has, if any, only an indirect interest; comprehending all that portion of a person's life and conduct which affects only himself, or if it also affects others, only with their free, voluntary, and undeceived consent and participation. When I say only himself, I mean directly, and in the first instance; for whatever affects himself, may affect others through himself; and the objection which may be grounded on this contingency, will receive consideration in the sequel. This, then, is the appropriate region of human liberty. It comprises, first, the inward domain of consciousness; demanding liberty of conscience in the most comprehensive sense; liberty of thought and feeling; absolute freedom of opinion and sentiment on all subjects, practical or speculative, scientific, moral, or theological. The liberty of expressing and publishing opinions may seem to fall under a different principle, since it belongs to that part of the conduct of an individual which concerns other people; but, being almost of as much importance as the liberty of thought itself, and resting in great part on the same reasons, is practically inseparable from it. Secondly, the principle requires liberty of tastes and pursuits; of framing the plan of our life to suit our own character; of doing as we like, subject to such

From John Stuart Mill, essay "On Liberty" (1859).

consequences as may follow: without impediment from our fellow-creatures, so long as what we do does not harm them, even though they should think our conduct foolish, perverse, or wrong. Thirdly, from this liberty of each individual, follows the liberty, within the same limits, of combination among individuals; freedom to unite, for any purpose not involving harm to others: the persons combining being supposed to be of full age, and not forced or deceived.

No society in which these liberties are not, on the whole, respected, is free, whatever may be its form of government; and none is completely free in which they do not exist absolute and unqualified. . . .

Apart from the peculiar tenets of individual thinkers, there is also in the world at large an increasing inclination to stretch unduly the powers of society over the individual, both by the force of opinion and even by that of legislation; and as the tendency of all the changes taking place in the world is to strengthen society, and diminish the power of the individual, this encroachment is not one of the evils which tend spontaneously to disappear, but, on the contrary, to grow more and more formidable. The disposition of mankind, whether as rulers or as fellow-citizens, to impose their own opinions and inclinations as a rule of conduct on others, is so energetically supported by some of the best and by some of the worst feelings incident to human nature, that it is hardly ever kept under restraint by anything but want of power; and as the power is not declining, but growing, unless a strong barrier of moral conviction can be raised against the mischief, we must expect, in the present circumstances of the world, to see it increase. . . .

The time, it is to be hoped, is gone by, when any defence would be necessary of the "liberty of the press" as one of the securities against corrupt or tyrannical government. . . . Let us suppose, therefore, that the government is entirely at one with the people, and never thinks of exerting any power of coercion unless in agreement with what it conceives to be their voice. But I deny the right of the people to exercise such coercion, either by themselves or by their government. The power itself is illegitimate. The best government has no more title to it than the worst. It is as noxious, or more noxious, when exerted in accordance with public opinion, than when in opposition to it. If all mankind minus one were of one opinion, and only one person were of the contrary opinion, mankind would be no more justified in silencing that one person, than he, if he had the power, would be justified in silencing mankind. . . . But the peculiar evil of silencing the expression of an opinion is, that it is robbing the human race; posterity as well as the existing generation; those who dissent from the opinion, still more than those who hold it. If the opinion is right, they are deprived of the opportunity of exchanging error for truth: if wrong, they lose, what is almost as great a benefit, the clearer perception and livelier impression of truth, produced by its collision with error.

20.3. THE COURTS AS PROTECTORS OF LIBERTIES

A basic function of the courts, as noted earlier, is the protection of fundamental liberties from invasion by the Federal and State governments. Justice Benjamin N. Cardozo in his incisive and perceptive study of the legal process calls on the courts to protect the ideals of the Constitution and to exercise judicial power with due regard for changing social values.

SOME CRITICS of our public law insist that the power of the courts to fix the limits of permissible encroachment by statute upon the liberty of the individual is one that ought to be withdrawn. It means, they say, either too much or too little. If it is freely exercised, if it is made an excuse for imposing the individual beliefs and philosophies of the judges upon other branches of the government, if it stereotypes legislation within the forms and limits that were expedient in the nineteenth or perhaps the eighteenth century, it shackles progress, and breeds distrust and suspicion of the courts. If, on the other hand, it is interpreted in the broad and variable sense which I believe to be the true one, if statutes are to be sustained unless they are so plainly arbitrary and oppressive that right-minded men and women could not reasonably regard them otherwise, the right of supervision, it is said, is not worth the danger of abuse. "There no doubt comes a time when a statute is so obviously oppressive and absurd that it can have no justification in any sane polity." Such times may indeed come, yet only seldom. The occasions must be few when legislatures will enact a statute that will merit condemnation upon the application of a test so liberal; and if carelessness or haste or momentary passion may at rare intervals bring such statutes into being with hardship to individuals or classes, we may trust to succeeding legislatures for the undoing of the wrong. That is the argument of the critics of the existing system.

My own belief is that it lays too little stress on the value of the "imponderables." The utility of an external power restraining the legislative judgment is not to be measured by counting the occasions of its exercise. The great ideals of liberty and equality are preserved against the assaults of opportunism, the expediency of the passing hour, the erosion of small encroachments, the scorn and derision of those who have

From Benjamin N. Cardozo, *The Nature of the Judicial Process* (New Haven, Conn.: Yale University Press, 1921), pp. 91–94.

no patience with general principles, by enshrining them in constitutions, and consecrating to the task of their protection a body of defenders. By conscious or subconscious influence, the presence of this restraining power, aloof in the background, but none the less always in reserve, tends to stabilize and rationalize the legislative judgment, to infuse it with the glow of principle, to hold the standard aloft and visible for those who must run the race and keep the faith. I do not mean to deny that there have been times when the possibility of judicial review has worked the other way.

Legislatures have sometimes disregarded their own responsibility and passed it on to the courts. Such dangers must be balanced against those of independence from all restraint, independence on the part of public officers elected for brief terms, without the guiding force of a continuous tradition. On the whole, I believe the latter dangers to be the more formidable of the two. Great maxims, if they may be violated with impunity, are honored often with lip-service, which passes easily into irreverence. The restraining power of the judiciary does not manifest its chief worth in the few cases in which the legislature has gone beyond the lines that mark the limits of discretion. Rather shall we find its chief worth in making vocal and audible the ideals that might otherwise be silenced, in giving them continuity of life and of expression, in guiding and directing choice within the limits where choice ranges. This function should preserve to the courts the power that now belongs to them, if only the power is exercised with insight into social values, and with suppleness of adaptation to changing social needs.

20.4. LIMITS UPON FREEDOM OF SPEECH

The First Amendment forbids interference with freedom of speech by the federal government. But the exercise of speech is not an absolute right. In cases of subversion, for example, the Supreme Court permits limitations on speech, through application of standards like the "clear and present danger" test first enunciated in the Schenck *decision.*

MR. JUSTICE HOLMES delivered the opinion of the court.

The document in question upon its first printed side recited the first section of the Thirteenth Amendment, said that the idea embodied in it was violated by the Conscription Act and that a conscript is little better than a convict. In impassioned language it intimated that conscription was despotism in its worst form and a monstrous wrong against

From *Schenck* v. *United States,* 249 U.S. 47 (1919).

humanity in the interest of Wall Street's chosen few. It said, "Do not submit to intimidation," but in form at least confined itself to peaceful measures such as a petition for the repeal of the act. The other and later printed side of the sheet was headed "Assert Your Rights." It stated reasons for alleging that any one violated the Constitution when he refused to recognize "your right to assert your opposition to the draft," and went on "If you do not assert and support your rights, you are helping to deny or disparage rights which it is the solemn duty of all citizens and residents of the United States to retain." It described the arguments on the other side as coming from cunning politicians and a mercenary capitalist press, and even silent consent to the conscription law as helping to support an infamous conspiracy. It denied the power to send our citizens away to foreign shores to shoot up the people of other lands, and added that words could not express the condemnation such cold-blooded ruthlessness deserves, &c., &c., winding up "You must do your share to maintain, support and uphold the rights of the people of this country." Of course the document would not have been sent unless it had been intended to have some effect, and we do not see what effect it could be expected to have upon persons subject to the draft except to influence them to obstruct the carrying of it out. The defendants do not deny that the jury might find against them on this point.

But it is said, suppose that that was the tendency of this circular, it is protected by the First Amendment to the Constitution. . . . We admit that in many places and in ordinary times the defendants in saying all that was said in the circular would have been within their constitutional rights. But the character of every act depends upon the circumstances in which it is done. The most stringent protection of free speech would not protect a man in falsely shouting fire in a theatre and causing a panic. It does not even protect a man from an injunction against uttering words that may have all the effect of force. The question in every case is whether the words used are used in such circumstances and are of such a nature as to create a clear and present danger that they will bring about the substantive evils that Congress has a right to prevent. It is a question of proximity and degree. When a nation is at war many things that might be said in time of peace are such a hindrance to its effort that their utterance will not be endured so long as men fight and that no Court could regard them as protected by any constitutional right. It seems to be admitted that if an actual obstruction of the recruiting service were proved, liability for words that produced that effect might be enforced. The statute of 1917 in sec. 4 punishes conspiracies to obstruct as well as actual obstruction. If the act, its tendency and the intent with which it is done are the same, we perceive no ground for saying that success alone warrants making the act a crime. . . . Judgments affirmed.

20.5. THE CONTROL OF SUBVERSIVE MOVEMENTS

Freedom of speech and association may be limited when used for illegal purposes. The Dennis and Yates cases involving the conviction of members of the Communist Party for conspiracy to teach or advocate overthrow of the Government by force helped to define the meaning of the Smith Act and to clarify the essentials of subversive activity. Dennis also marks the end of the "clear and present danger" doctrine as a guide.

[IN THE DENNIS CASE,] Mr. Justice Vinson announced the judgment of the Court. . . .

We granted certiorari, 340 U.S. 863, limited to the following two questions: (1) Whether either Sec. 2 or Sec. 3 of the Smith Act, inherently or as construed and applied in the instant case, violates the First Amendment and other provisions of the Bill of Rights; (2) whether either Sec. 2 or Sec. 3 of the Act, inherently or as construed and applied in the instant case, violates the First and Fifth Amendments because of indefiniteness. . . .

The obvious purpose of the statute is to protect existing Government, not from change by peaceable, lawful and constitutional means, but from change by violence, revolution and terrorism. That it is within the *power* of the Congress to protect the Government of the United States from armed rebellion is a proposition which requires little discussion. Whatever theoretical merit there may be to the argument that there is a "right" to rebellion against dictatorial governments is without force where the existing structure of the government provides for peaceful and orderly change. We reject any principle of governmental helplessness in the face of preparation for revolution, which principle, carried to its logical conclusion, must lead to anarchy. No one could conceive that it is not within the power of Congress to prohibit acts intended to overthrow the Government by force and violence. The question with which we are concerned here is not whether Congress has such *power*, but whether the *means* which it has employed conflict with the First and Fifth Amendments to the Constitution.

One of the bases for the contention that the means which Congress has employed are invalid takes the form of an attack on the face of the statute on the grounds that by its terms it prohibits academic

From *Dennis et al.* v. *United States,* 341 U.S. 494 (1951); *Yates* v. *United States,* 354 U.S. 298 (1957).

discussion of the merits of Marxism-Leninism, that it stifles ideas and is contrary to all concepts of a free speech and a free press. Although we do not agree that the language itself has that significance, we must bear in mind that it is the duty of the federal courts to interpret federal legislation in a manner not inconsistent with the demands of the Constitution. . . .

The very language of the Smith Act negates the interpretation which petitioners would have us impose on that Act. It is directed at advocacy, not discussion. . . . Congress did not intend to eradicate the free discussion of political theories, to destroy the traditional rights of Americans to discuss and evaluate ideas without fear of governmental sanction. Rather Congress was concerned with the very kind of activity in which the evidence showed these petitioners engaged.

But although the statute is not directed at the hypothetical cases which petitioners have conjured, its application in this case has resulted in convictions for the teaching and advocacy of the overthrow of the Government by force and violence, which, even though coupled with the intent to accomplish that overthrow, contains an element of speech. For this reason, we must pay special heed to the demands of the First Amendment marking out the boundaries of speech.

We pointed out in *Douds* that the basis of the First Amendment is the hypothesis that speech can rebut speech, propaganda will answer propaganda, free debate of ideas will result in the wisest governmental policies. It is for this reason that this Court has recognized the inherent value of free discourse. An analysis of the leading cases in this Court which have involved direct limitations on speech, however, will demonstrate that both the majority of the Court and the dissenters in particular cases have recognized that this is not an unlimited, unqualified right, but that the societal value of speech must, on occasion, be subordinated to other values and considerations.

No important case involving free speech was decided by this Court prior to *Schenck* v. *United States,* 249 U.S. 49 (1919). . . .

Where an offense is specified by a statute in nonspeech or nonpress terms, a conviction relying upon speech or press as evidence of violation may be sustained only when the speech or publication created a "clear and present danger" of attempting or accomplishing the prohibited crime. . . .

Speech is not an absolute, above and beyond control by the legislature when its judgment, subject to review here, is that certain kinds of speech are so undesirable as to warrant criminal sanction. Nothing is more certain in modern society than the principle that there are no absolutes, that a name, a phrase, a standard has meaning only when associated with the considerations which gave birth to the nomenclature. See *Douds,* 339 U.S. at 397. To those who would paralyze our

Government in the face of impending threat by encasing it in a semantic straitjacket we must reply that all concepts are relative.

In this case we are squarely presented with the application of the "clear and present danger" test, and must decide what that phrase imports. We first note that many of the cases in which this Court has reversed convictions by use of this or similar tests have been based on the fact that the interest which the State was attempting to protect was itself too insubstantial to warrant restriction of speech. . . . Overthrow of the Government by force and violence is certainly a substantial enough interest for the Government to limit speech. Indeed, this is the ultimate value of any society, for if a society cannot protect its very structure from armed internal attack, it must follow that no subordinate value can be protected. If, then, this interest may be protected, the literal problem which is presented is what has been meant by the use of the phrase "clear and present danger" of the utterances bringing about the evil within the power of Congress to punish.

Obviously, the words cannot mean that before the Government may act, it must wait until the *putsch* is about to be executed, the plans have been laid and the signal is awaited. If Government is aware that a group aiming at its overthrow is attempting to indoctrinate its members and to commit them to a course whereby they will strike when the leaders feel the circumstances permit, action by the Government is required. The argument that there is no need for Government to concern itself, for Government is strong, it possesses ample powers to put down a rebellion, it may defeat the revolution with ease needs no answer. For that is not the question. Certainly an attempt to overthrow the Government by force, even though doomed from the outset because of inadequate numbers or power of the revolutionists, is a sufficient evil for Congress to prevent. The damage which such attempts create both physically and politically to a nation makes it impossible to measure the validity in terms of the probability of success, or the immediacy of a successful attempt. In the instant case the trial judge charged the jury that they could not convict unless they found that petitioners intended to overthrow the Government "as speedily as circumstances would permit." This does not mean, and could not properly mean, that they would not strike until there was certainty of success. What was meant was that the revolutionists would strike when they thought the time was ripe. We must therefore reject the contention that success or probability of success is the criterion. . . .

Chief Judge Learned Hand, writing for the majority below, interpreted the phrase as follows: "In each case [courts] must ask whether the gravity of the 'evil,' discounted by its improbability, justifies such invasion of free speech as is necessary to avoid the danger." 183 F.2d at 212. We adopt this statement of the rule. As articulated by Chief Judge Hand, it is as succinct and inclusive as any other we might devise at this time. It takes into consideration those factors which we deem relevant, and relates their significances. More we cannot expect from words.

Likewise, we are in accord with the court below, which affirmed the trial court's finding that the requisite danger existed. . . .

We hold that sections 2 (a) (1), 2 (a) (3) and 3 of the Smith Act, do not inherently, or as construed or applied in the instant case, violate the First Amendment and other provisions of the Bill of Rights, or the First and Fifth Amendments because of indefiniteness. Petitioners intended to overthrow the Government of the United States as speedily as the circumstances would permit. Their conspiracy to organize the Communist Party and to teach and advocate the overthrow of the Government of the United States by force and violence created a "clear and present danger" of an attempt to overthrow the Government by force and violence. They were properly and constitutionally convicted for violation of the Smith Act. The judgments of conviction are *Affirmed.* . . .

Mr. Justice Douglas, dissenting.

If this were a case where those who claimed protection under the First Amendment were teaching the techniques of sabotage, the assassination of the President, the filching of documents from public files, the planting of bombs, the art of street warfare, and the like, I would have no doubts. The freedom to speak is not absolute; the teaching of methods of terror and other seditious conduct should be beyond the pale along with obscenity and immorality. This case was argued as if those were the facts. The argument imported much seditious conduct into the record. That is easy and it has popular appeal, for the activities of Communists in plotting and scheming against the free world are common knowledge. But the fact is that no such evidence was introduced at the trial. There is a statute which makes a seditious conspiracy unlawful. Petitioners, however, were not charged with a "conspiracy to overthrow" the Government. They were charged with a conspiracy to form a party and groups and assemblies of people who teach and advocate the overthrow of our Government by force or violence and with a conspiracy to advocate and teach its overthrow by force and violence. It may well be that indoctrination in the techniques of terror to destroy the Government would be indictable under either statute. But the teaching which is condemned here is of a different character.

So far as the present record is concerned, what petitioners did was to organize people to teach and themselves teach the Marxist-Leninist doctrine contained chiefly in four books: Foundations of Leninism by Stalin (1924), The Communist Manifesto by Marx and Engels (1848), State and Revolution by Lenin (1917), History of the Communist Party of the Soviet Union (B) (1939). . . .

The opinion of the Court does not outlaw these texts nor condemn them to the fire, as the Communists do literature offensive to their creed. But if the books themselves are not outlawed, if they can lawfully remain on library shelves, by what reasoning does their use in a classroom become a crime? It would not be a crime under the Act to introduce these books to a class, though that would be teaching what the creed of violent overthrow of the government is. The Act, as construed, requires the element of intent—that those who teach the creed believe in it. The crime then depends not on what is taught but on who the teacher is. That is to make freedom of speech turn not on *what is said,* but on the *intent* with which it is said. Once we start down that road we enter territory dangerous to the liberties of every citizen. . . .

There comes a time when even speech loses its constitutional immunity. Speech innocuous one year may at another time fan such destructive flames that it must be halted in the interests of the safety of the Republic. That is the meaning of the clear and present danger test. When conditions are so critical that there will be no time to avoid the evil that the speech threatens, it is time to call a halt. Otherwise, free speech which is the strength of the Nation will be the cause of its destruction.

Yet free speech is the rule, not the exception. The restraint to be constitutional must be based on more than fear, on more than passionate opposition against the speech, on more than a revolted dislike for its contents. There must be some immediate injury to society that is likely if speech is allowed. . . .

. . . Free speech—the glory of our system of government—should not be sacrificed on anything less than plain and objective proof of danger that the evil advocated is imminent. On this record no one can say that petitioners and their converts are in such a strategic position as to have even the slightest chance of achieving their aims. . . .

[IN THE YATES CASE,] Mr. Justice Harlan delivered the opinion of the Court. . . .

We brought these cases here to consider certain questions arising under the Smith Act which have not heretofore been passed upon by this Court, and otherwise to review the convictions of these petitioners for conspiracy to violate that Act. Among other things, the convictions are claimed to rest upon an application of the Smith Act which is hostile to the principles upon which its constitutionality was upheld in *Dennis* v. *United States,* 341 U.S. 494. . . .

Instructions to the Jury

Petitioners contend that the instructions to the jury were fatally defective in that the trial court refused to charge that, in order to convict, the jury must find that the advocacy which the defendants conspired to promote was of a kind calculated to "incite" persons to action for the forcible overthrow of the Government. It is argued that advocacy of forcible overthrow as mere *abstract doctrine* is within the free speech protection of the First Amendment; that the Smith Act, consistently with that constitutional provision, must be taken as proscribing only the sort of advocacy which incites to illegal *action*; and that the trial court's charge, by permitting conviction for mere advocacy, unrelated to its tendency to produce forcible action, resulted in an unconstitutional application of the Smith Act. The Government, which at the trial also requested the court to charge in terms of "incitement," now takes the position, however, that the true constitutional dividing line is not between inciting and abstract advocacy of forcible overthrow, but rather between advocacy as such, irrespective of its inciting qualities, and the mere discussion or exposition of violent overthrow as an abstract theory. . . .

We are thus faced with the question whether the Smith Act prohibits advocacy and teaching of forcible overthrow as an abstract principle, divorced from any effort to instigate action to that end, so long as such advocacy or teaching is engaged in with evil intent. We hold that it does not.

The distinction between advocacy of abstract doctrine and advocacy directed at promoting unlawful action is one that has been consistently recognized in the opinions of this Court, beginning with *Fox* v. *Washington*, 236 U. S. 273, and *Schenck* v. *United States*, 249 U. S. 47. This distinction was heavily underscored in *Gitlow* v. *New York*, 268 U. S. 652, . . .

We need not, however, decide the issue before us in terms of constitutional compulsion, for our first duty is to construe this stature. In doing so we should not assume that Congress chose to disregard a constitutional danger zone so clearly marked, or that it used the words "advocate" and "teach" in their ordinary dictionary meanings when they had already been construed as terms of art carrying a special and limited connotation. . . . The legislative history of the Smith Act and related bills shows beyond all question that Congress was aware of the distinction between the advocacy or teaching of abstract doctrine and the advocacy or teaching of abstract doctrine and the advocacy or teaching of action, and that it did not intend to disregard it. The statute was aimed at the advocacy and teaching of concrete action for the forcible overthrow of the Government, and not of principles divorced from action.

The Government's reliance on this Court's decision in *Dennis* is misplaced. The jury instructions which were refused here were given there, and were referred to by this Court as requiring "the jury to find the facts *essential* to establish the substantive crime." 341 U.S. at 512 (emphasis added). It is true that at one point in the late Chief Justice's opinion it is stated that the Smith Act "is directed at advocacy, not discussion," but it is clear that the reference was to advocacy of action, not ideas, for in the very next sentence the opinion emphasizes that the jury was properly instructed that there could be no conviction for "advocacy in the realm of ideas." . . .

In failing to distinguish between advocacy of forcible overthrow as an abstract doctrine and advocacy of action to that end, the District Court appears to have been led astray by the holding in *Dennis* that advocacy of violent action to be taken at some future time was enough. It seems to have considered that, since "inciting" speech is usually thought of as calculated to induce immediate action, and since *Dennis* held advocacy of action for future overthrow sufficient, this meant that advocacy, irrespective of its tendency to generate action, is punishable, provided only that it is uttered with a specific intent to accomplish overthrow. In other words, the District Court apparently thought that *Dennis* obliterated the traditional dividing line between advocacy of abstract doctrine and advocacy of action. . . .

. . . The essence of the *Dennis* holding was that indoctrination of a group in preparation for future violent action, as well as exhortation to immediate action, by advocacy found to be directed to "action for the accomplishment" of forcible overthrow, to violence "as a rule or principle of action," and employing "language of incitement," is not constitutionally protected when the group is of sufficient size and cohesiveness, is sufficiently oriented towards action, and other circumstances are such as reasonably to justify apprehension that action will occur. This is quite a different thing from the view of the District Court here that mere doctrinal justification of forcible overthrow, if engaged in with the intent to accomplish overthrow, is punishable per se under the Smith Act. That sort of advocacy, even though uttered with the hope that it may ultimately lead to violent revolution, is too remote from concrete action to be regarded as the kind of indoctrination preparatory to action which was condemned in *Dennis*.

20.6. RECENT VIEWS OF THE COMMUNIST THREAT

In June, 1961, the Supreme Court again made significant determinations in the area of subversive activities. In the Communist Party *case the Court upheld the Smith Act requirement that Communist-action organizations dominated by a foreign power register with the Federal government. In the* Noto *case the judges reiterated the standards applied earlier in the*

Yates *case and acquitted the defendant because of lack of sufficient evidence of present advocacy of violence.*

[IN COMMUNIST PARTY V. CONTROL BOARD,] Mr. Justice Frankfurter delivered the opinion of the Court. . . .

This is a proceeding pursuant to § 14 (a) of the Subversive Activities Control Act of 1950 to review an order of the Subversive Activities Control Board requiring the Communist Party of the United States to register as a Communist-action organization under § 7 of the Act. . . .

The constitutional contentions raised by the Party with respect to the registration requirement of § 7 are (A) that that requirement, in the context of the Act, in effect "outlaws" the Party and is in the nature of a bill of attainder; (B) that compelling organizations to register and to list their members on a showing merely that they are foreign-dominated and operate primarily to advance the objectives of the world Communist movement constitutes a restraint on freedom of expression and association in violation of the First Amendment; (C) that requiring Party officers to file registration statements for the Party subjects them to self-incrimination forbidden by the Fifth Amendment; (D) that the Act violates due process by legislative predetermination of facts essential to bring the Communist Party within the definition of a Communist-action organization, and that the evidentiary elements prescribed for consideration by the Board bear no rational relation to that definition; (E) that in several aspects the Act is unconstitutionally vague; and (F) that the Subversive Activities Control Board is so necessarily biased against the Communist Party as to deprive it of a fair hearing.

A. *"Outlawry" and Attainder.* Our determination that in the present proceeding all questions are premature which regard only the constitutionality of the various particular consequences of a registration order to a registered organization and its members, does not foreclose the Party from arguing—and it does argue—that in light of the cumulative effect of those consequences the registration provisions of § 7 are not what they seem, but represent a legislative attempt, by devious means, to "outlaw" the Party. The registration requirement, the Party contends, was designed not with the purpose of having Communist-action organizations register, but with a purpose to make it impossible to register, because of the onerous consequences of registration, and thus to establish a pretext for criminal prosecution of the organization and its members. The Act is said to be aimed particularly at the Communist Party as an identifiable

From *Communist Party* v. *Control Board,* 367 U.S. 1 (1961); *Noto* v. *United States,* 367 U.S. 290 (1961).

entity, intending to punish it, and in this aspect to constitute a bill of attainder prohibited by Art. I, § 9, cl. 3 of the Constitution. . . .

The Act is not a bill of attainder. It attaches not to specified organizations but to described activities in which an organization may or may not engage. The singling out of an individual for legislatively prescribed punishment constitutes an attainder whether the individual is called by name or described in terms of conduct which, because it is past conduct, operates only as a designation of particular persons. The Subversive Activities Control Act . . . requires the registration only of organizations which, after the date of the Act, are found to be under the direction, domination, or control of certain foreign powers and to operate primarily to advance certain objectives. This finding must be made after full administrative hearing, subject to judicial review which opens the record for the reviewing court's determination whether the administrative findings as to fact are supported by the preponderance of the evidence. Present activity constitutes an operative element to which the statute attaches legal consequences, not merely a point of reference for the ascertainment of particular persons ineluctably designated by the legislature. . . .

Nor is the statute made an act of "outlawry" or of attainder by the fact that the conduct which it regulates is described with such particularity that, in probability, few organizations will come within the statutory terms . . . whatever the source from which the legislative experience and instruction derived, the Act applies to a class of activity only, not to the Communist Party as such. Nothing in this offends the constitutional prohibition of attainder.

B. *The Freedoms of Expression and Association Protected by the First Amendment.* The Communist Party would have us hold that the First Amendment prohibits Congress from requiring the registration and filing of information, including membership lists, by organizations substantially dominated or controlled by the foreign powers controlling the world Communist movement and which operate primarily to advance the objectives of that movement: the overthrow of existing government by any means necessary and the establishment in its place of a Communist totalitarian dictatorship (§§ 3 (3), 2 (1) and (6)). We cannot find such a prohibition in the First Amendment. So to find would make a travesty of that Amendment and the great ends for the well-being of our democracy that it serves. . . .

On the basis of its detailed investigations Congress has found that there exists a world Communist movement, foreign-controlled, whose purpose it is by whatever means necessary to establish Communist totalitarian dictatorship in the countries throughout the world, and which has already succeeded in supplanting governments in other countries. Congress has found that in furthering these purposes, the foreign government controlling the world Communist movement establishes in various countries action organizations which, dominated from abroad, endeavor to bring about the overthrow of existing governments, by force if need be, and to establish totalitarian dictatorships subservient to that foreign government. And Congress has found that these action organizations employ methods of infiltration and secretive and coercive tactics; that by operating in concealment and through Communist-front organizations they are able to obtain the support of persons who would not extend such support knowing of their true nature; that a Communist network exists in the United States; and that the agents of communism have devised methods of sabotage and espionage carried out in successful evasion of existing law. The purpose of the Subversive Activities Control Act is said to be to prevent the world-wide Communist conspiracy from accomplishing its purpose in this country.

It is not for the courts to re-examine the validity of these legislative findings and reject them. . . . They are the product of extensive investigation by Committees of Congress over more than a decade and a half. . . . We certainly cannot dismiss them as unfounded or irrational imaginings. . . . And if we accept them, as we must, as a not unentertainable appraisal by Congress of the threat which Communist organizations pose not only to existing government in the United States, but to the United States as a sovereign, independent nation—if we accept as not wholly unsupportable the conclusion that those organizations "are not free and independent organizations, but are sections of a world-wide Communist organization and are controlled, directed, and subject to the discipline of the Communist dictatorship of [a] . . . foreign country," § 2 (5)—we must recognize that the power of Congress to regulate Communist organizations of this nature is extensive. . . .

Of course, congressional power in this sphere, as in all spheres, is limited by the First Amendment. Individual liberties fundamental to American institutions are not to be destroyed under pretext of preserving those institutions, even from the gravest external dangers. But where the problems of accommodating the exigencies of self-preservation and the values of liberty are as complex and intricate as they are in the situation described in the findings of § 2 of the Subversive Activities Control Act —when existing government is menaced by a world-wide integrated movement which employs every combination of possible means, peaceful and violent, domestic and foreign, overt and clandestine, to destroy the government itself—the legislative judgment as to how that threat may best be met consistently with the safeguarding of personal freedom is not to be set aside merely because the judgment of judges would, in the first instance, have chosen other methods. Especially where Congress, in seeking to reconcile competing and urgently demanding values within our social institutions, legislates not to prohibit individuals from organizing for the effectuation of ends found to be menacing to the very existence of those institutions, but only to prescribe the conditions under which such organization is permitted, the legislative determination must be respected. . . .

[IN NOTO V. UNITED STATES,] Mr. Justice Harlan delivered the opinion of the Court. . . .

The only one of petitioner's points we need consider is his attack on the sufficiency of the evidence. . . .

In considering that challenge we start from the premise that Smith Act offenses require rigorous standards of proof. We find that the record in this case, which was tried before our opinion issued in *Yates* v. *United States,* 354 U. S. 298, bears much of the infirmity that we found in the *Yates* record, and requires us to conclude that the evidence of illegal Party advocacy was insufficient to support this conviction. . . .

We must consider this evidence in the light most favorable to the Government to see whether it would support the conclusion that the Party engaged in the advocacy "not of . . . mere abstract doctrine of forcible overthrow, but of action to that end, by the use of language reasonably and ordinarily calculated to incite persons to . . . action" immediately or in the future. *Yates* v. *United States, supra,* at 316. . . .

We held in *Yates,* and we reiterate now, that the mere abstract teaching of Communist theory, including the teaching of the moral propriety or even moral necessity for a resort to force and violence, is not the same as preparing a group for violent action and steeling it to such action. There must be some substantial direct or circumstancial evidence of a call to violence now or in the future which is both sufficiently strong and sufficiently pervasive to lend color to the otherwise ambiguous theoretical material regarding Communist Party teaching, and to justify the inference that such a call to violence may fairly be imputed to the Party as a whole, and not merely to some narrow segment of it. . . .

. . . But in examining that evidence it appears to us that, in the context of this record, this too fails to establish that the Communist Party was an organization which presently advocated violent overthrow of the Government now or in the future, for that is what must be proven. The most that can be said is that the evidence as to that program might justify an inference that the leadership of the Party was preparing the way for a situation in which future acts of sabotage might be facilitated, but there is no evidence that such acts of sabotage were presently advocated; and it is *present* advocacy, and not an intent to advocate in the future or a conspiracy to advocate in the future once a groundwork has been laid, which is an element of the crime under the membership clause. To permit an inference of present advocacy from evidence showing at best only a purpose or conspiracy to advocate in the future would be to allow the jury to blur the lines of distinction between the various offenses punishable under the Smith Act.

The kind of evidence which we found in *Scales* sufficient to support the jury's verdict of present illegal Party advocacy is lacking here in any adequately substantial degree. It need hardly be said that it is upon the particular evidence in a particular record that a particular defendant must be judged, and not upon the evidence in some other record or upon what may be supposed to be the tenets of the Communist Party.

21

Nationalization of the Bill of Rights

21.1. AN EARLY VIEW OF STATE ABUSE OF THE BILL OF RIGHTS

The question of whether the fundamental guarantees of the Bill of Rights apply to the States arose in the Barron *case in 1833. Barron sought to invoke the due process clause of the Fifth Amendment against the city of Baltimore as a result of damage to his wharf property by city employees. Justice Marshall ruled that the Bill of Rights limits the national government only.*

MR. CHIEF JUSTICE MARSHALL delivered the opinion of the court: . . .

The plaintiff in error contends that [this case] comes within the clause in the fifth amendment to the Constitution which inhibits the taking of private property for public use without just compensation. He insists that this amendment, being in favor of the liberty of the citizens, ought to be so construed as to restrain the legislative power of a State, as well as that of the United States. If this proposition be untrue, the court can take no jurisdiction of the cause.

The question thus presented is, we think, of great importance, but not of much difficulty.

The Constitution was ordained and established by the people of the United States for themselves, for their own government, and not for the government of the individual States. Each State established a constitution for itself, and in that constitution provided such limitations and restrictions on the powers of its particular government as its judgment dictated. The people of the United States framed such a government for

---

From *Barron* v. *Mayor and City Council of Baltimore,* 7 Peters 243 (1833).

the United States as they supposed best adapted to their situation, and best calculated to promote their interests. The powers they conferred on this government were to be exercised by itself; and the limitations on power, if expressed in general terms, are naturally, and, we think, necessarily applicable to the government created by the instrument. They are limitations of power granted in the instrument itself; not of distinct governments, framed by different persons and for different purposes.

If these propositions be correct, the fifth amendment must be understood as restraining the power of the general government, not as applicable to the States. In their several constitutions they have imposed such restrictions on their respective governments as their own wisdom suggested; such as they deemed most proper for themselves. It is a subject on which they judge exclusively, and with which others interfere no farther than they are supposed to have a common interest.

The counsel for the plaintiff in error insists that the Constitution was intended to secure the people of the several States against the undue exercise of power by their respective State governments; as well as against that which might be attempted by their general government. In support of this argument he relies on the inhibitions contained in the tenth section of the first article.

We think that section affords a strong if not a conclusive argument in support of the opinion already indicated by the court.

The preceding section contains restrictions which are obviously intended for the exclusive purpose of restraining the exercise of power by the departments of the general government. Some of them use language applicable only to Congress, others are expressed in general terms. The third clause, or example, declares that "no bill of attainder or ex post facto law shall be passed." No language can be more general; yet the demonstration is complete that it applies solely to the government of the United States. In addition to the general arguments furnished by the instrument itself, some of which have been already suggested, the succeeding section, the avowed purpose of which is to restrain State legislation, contains in terms the very prohibition. It declares that "no State shall pass any bill of attainder or ex post facto law." This provision, then, of the ninth section, however comprehensive its language, contains no restriction on State legislation.

The ninth section having enumerated, in the nature of a bill of rights, the limitations intended to be imposed on the powers of the general government, the tenth proceeds to enumerate those which were to operate on the State legislatures. These restrictions are brought together in the same section, and are by express words applied to the States. "No State shall enter into any treaty," etc. Perceiving that in a Constitution framed by the people of the United States for the government of all, no limitation of the action of government on the people would apply to the State government unless expressed in terms; the restrictions contained in the tenth section are in direct words so applied to the States. . . .

If the original Constitution, in the ninth and tenth sections of the first article, draws this plain and marked line of discrimination between the limitations it imposes on the powers of the general government and on those of the States; if in every inhibition intended to act on State power, words are employed which directly express that intent, some strong reason must be assigned for departing from this safe and judicious course in framing the amendments, before that departure can be assumed.

We search in vain for that reason.

. . . Had the framers of these amendments intended them to be limitations on the powers of the State governments they would have imitated the framers of the original Constitution, and have expressed that intention. Had Congress engaged in the extraordinary occupation of improving the constitutions of the several States by affording the people additional protection from the exercise of power by their own governments in matters which concerned themselves alone, they would have declared this purpose in plain and intelligible language.

21.2 INCORPORATION OF FREEDOM OF SPEECH INTO THE FOURTEENTH AMENDMENT

Under the Barron *rule, the First Amendment restricted only the Federal government. Protection of free speech from State interference has evolved, however, through the interpretation of "liberty" under the Fourteenth Amendment adopted in 1868. Although it upheld the constitutionality of the New York Criminal Anarchy statute, the* Gitlow *case is famous as the first decision to nationalize part of the Bill of Rights.*

MR. JUSTICE SANFORD delivered the opinion of the Court.

Benjamin Gitlow was indicted in the Supreme Court of New York, with three others, for the statutory crime of criminal anarchy. He was separately tried, convicted, and sentenced to imprisonment. The judgment was affirmed by the Appellate Division and by the Court of Appeals. The case is here on writ of error to the Supreme Court, to which the record was remitted.

From *Gitlow* v. *New York*, 268 U.S. 652 (1925).

The contention here is that the statute, by its terms and as applied in this case, is repugnant to the due process clause of the Fourteenth Amendment. Its material provisions are:

§ 160. *Criminal anarchy defined.* Criminal anarchy is the doctrine that organized government should be overthrown by force or violence, or by assassination of the executive head or of any of the executive officials of government, or by any unlawful means. The advocacy of such doctrine either by word of mouth or writing is a felony.

§ 161. *Advocacy of criminal anarchy.* Any person who:

1. By word of mouth or writing advocates, advises or teaches the duty, necessity or propriety of overthrowing or overturning organized government by force or violence, or by assassination of the executive head or of any of the executive officials of government, or by any unlawful means; or,

2. Prints, publishes, edits, issues or knowingly circulates, sells, distributes or publicly displays any book, paper, document, or written or printed matter in any form, containing or advocating, advising or teaching the doctrine that organized government should be overthrown by force, violence or any unlawful means . . .

Is guilty of a felony and punishable by imprisonment or fine or both.

The indictment was in two counts. The first charged that the defendant had advocated, advised and taught the duty, necessity and propriety of overthrowing and overturning organized government by force, violence and unlawful means, by certain writings therein set forth entitled "The Left Wing Manifesto"; the second that he had printed, published and knowingly circulated and distributed a certain paper called "The Revolutionary Age," containing the writings set forth in the first count advocating, advising and teaching the doctrine that organized government should be overthrown by force, violence and unlawful means. . . .

There was no evidence of any effect resulting from the publication and circulation of the Manifesto. . . .

The Court of Appeals held that the Manifesto "advocated the overthrow of this government by violence, or by unlawful means." In one of the opinions representing the views of a majority of the court, it was said: "It will be seen . . . that this defendant through the manifesto . . . advocated the destruction of the state and the establishment of the dictatorship of the proletariat. . . . To advocate . . . the commission of this conspiracy or action by mass strike whereby government is crippled, the administration of justice paralyzed, and the health, morals and welfare of a community endangered, and this for the purpose of bringing about a revolution in the state, is to advocate the overthrow of organized government by unlawful means." . . .

The sole contention here is, essentially, that as there was no evidence of any concrete result flowing from the publication of the

Manifesto or of circumstances showing the likelihood of such result, the statute as construed and applied by the trial court penalizes the mere utterance, as such, of "doctrine" having no quality of incitement, without regard either to the circumstances of its utterance or to the likelihood of unlawful sequences; and that, as the exercise of the right of free expression with relation to government is only punishable "in circumstances involving likelihood of substantive evil," the statute contravenes the due process clause of the Fourteenth Amendment. The argument in support of this contention rests primarily upon the following propositions: 1st, That the "liberty" protected by the Fourteenth Amendment includes the liberty of speech and of the press; and 2nd, That while liberty of expression "is not absolute," it may be restrained "only in circumstances where its exercise bears a causal relation with some substantive evil, consummated, attempted or likely," and as the statute "takes no account of circumstances," it unduly restrains this liberty and is therefore unconstitutional.

The precise question presented, and the only question which we can consider under this writ of error, then is, whether the statute, as construed and applied in this case by the state courts, deprived the defendant of his liberty of expression in violation of the due process clause of the Fourteenth Amendment.

The statute does not penalize the utterance or publication of abstract "doctrine" or academic discussion having no quality of incitement to any concrete action. It is not aimed against mere historical or philosophical essays. It does not restrain the advocacy of changes in the form of government by constitutional and lawful means. What it prohibits is language advocating, advising or teaching the overthrow of organized government by unlawful means. . . .

For present purposes we may and do assume that freedom of speech and of the press—which are protected by the First Amendment from abridgment by Congress—are among the fundamental personal rights and "liberties" protected by the due process clause of the Fourteenth Amendment from impairment by the States. . . .

It is a fundamental principle, long established, that the freedom of speech and of the press which is secured by the Constitution, does not confer an absolute right to speak or publish, without responsibility, whatever one may choose, or an unrestricted and unbridled license that gives immunity for every possible use of language and prevents the punishment of those who abuse this freedom. . . .

That a State in the exercise of its police power may punish those who abuse this freedom by utterances inimical to the public welfare, tending to corrupt public morals, incite to crime, or disturb the public peace, is not open to question. . . .

And, for yet more imperative reasons, a State may punish utterances endangering the foundations of organized government and threatening its overthrow by unlawful means. These imperil its own existence as a constitutional State. . . .

It does not protect publications or teachings which tend to subvert or imperil the government or to impede or hinder it in the performance of its governmental duties. . . . It does not protect publications prompting the overthrow of government by force; the punishment of those who publish articles which tend to destroy organized society being essential to the security of freedom and the stability of the State. . . . And a State may penalize utterances which openly advocate the overthrow of the representative and constitutional form of government of the United States and the several States, by violence or other unlawful means. . . . In short this freedom does not deprive a State of the primary and essential right of self preservation; which, so long as human governments endure, they cannot be denied. . . .

Mr. Justice Holmes, dissenting.

Mr. Justice Brandeis and I are of opinion that this judgment should be reversed. The general principle of free speech, it seems to me, must be taken to be included in the Fourteenth Amendment, in view of the scope that has been given to the word "liberty" as there used, although perhaps it may be accepted with a somewhat larger latitude of interpretation than is allowed to Congress by the sweeping language that governs or ought to govern the laws of the United States. If I am right, then I think that the criterion sanctioned by the full Court in *Schenck* v. *United States,* 249 U.S. 47–52, applies. "The question in every case is whether the words used are used in such circumstances and are of such a nature as to create a clear and present danger that they will bring about the substantive evils that [the State] has a right to prevent." . . . If what I think the correct test is applied, it is manifest that there was no present danger of an attempt to overthrow the government by force on the part of the admittedly small minority who shared the defendant's views. It is said that this manifesto was more than a theory, that it was an incitement. Every idea is an incitement. It offers itself for belief and if believed it is acted on unless some other belief outweighs it or some failure of energy stifles the movement at its birth. The only difference between the expression of an opinion and an incitement in the narrower sense is the speaker's enthusiasm for the result. Eloquence may set fire to reason. But whatever may be thought of the redundant discourse before us it had no chance of starting a present conflagration. If in the long run the beliefs expressed in proletarian dictatorship are destined to be accepted by the dominant forces of the community, the only meaning of free speech is that they should be given their chance and have their way.

If the publication of this document had been laid as an attempt to induce an uprising against government at once and not at some indefinite time in the future it would have presented a different question. The object would have been one with which the law might deal, subject to the doubt whether there was any danger that the publication could produce any result, or in other words, whether it was not futile and too remote from possible consequences. But the indictment alleges the publication and nothing more.

21.3. FREEDOM OF THE PRESS AND THE FOURTEENTH AMENDMENT

In a free society the normal remedy for the publication of untruthful or malicious matter is a libel suit. Thirty years ago the State of Minnesota attempted an additional sanction—a "gag" law closing down newspapers found to be malicious, scandalous, and defamatory. In this landmark case Chief Justice Hughes ruled the State law unconstitutional.

MR. CHIEF JUSTICE HUGHES delivered the opinion of the Court.

Chapter 285 of the Session Laws of Minnesota for the year 1925 provides for the abatement, as a public nuisance of a "malicious, scandalous and defamatory newspaper, magazine or other periodical." Section one of the Act is as follows:

Section 1. Any person who, as an individual, or as a member or employee of a firm, or association or organization, or as an officer, director, member or employee of a corporation, shall be engaged in the business of regularly or customarily producing, publishing or circulating, having in possession, selling or giving away

(a) an obscene, lewd and lascivious newspaper, magazine, or other periodical, or

(b) a malicious, scandalous and defamatory newspaper, magazine or other periodical, is guilty of a nuisance, and all persons guilty of such nuisance may be enjoined, as hereinafter provided.

Participation in such business shall constitute a commission of such nuisance and render the participant liable and subject to the proceedings, orders and judgments provided for in this Act. Ownership, in whole or in part, directly or indirectly, of any such periodical, or of any stock or interest in any corporation or organization which owns the same in whole or in part, or which publishes the same, shall constitute such participation.

In actions brought under (b) above, there shall be available the defense that the truth was published with good motives and for justifiable ends and in such actions the plaintiff shall not have the right to report

From *Near* v. *Minnesota*, 283 U.S. 697 (1931).

(sic) to issues or editions of periodicals taking place more than three months before the commencement of the action.

Section two provides that whenever any such nuisance is committed or exists, the County Attorney of any country where any such periodical is published or circulated, or, in case of his failure or refusal to proceed upon written request in good faith of a reputable citizen, the Attorney General, or upon like failure or refusal of the latter, any citizen of the county, may maintain an action in the district court of the county in the name of the State to enjoin perpetually the persons committing or maintaining any such nuisance from further committing or maintaining it. Upon such evidence as the court shall deem sufficient, a temporary injunction may be granted. The defendants have the right to plead by demurrer or answer, and the plaintiff may demur or reply as in other cases.

The action, by section three, is to be "governed by the practice and procedure applicable to civil actions for injunctions," and after trial the court may enter judgment permanently enjoining the defendants found guilty of violating the Act from continuing the violation and, "in and by such judgment, such nuisance may be wholly abated." The court is empowered, as in other cases of contempt, to punish disobedience to a temporary or permanent injunction by fine of not more than $1,000 or by imprisonment in the county jail for not more than twelve months.

Under this statute, clause (b), the County Attorney of Hennepin County brought this action to enjoin the publication of what was described as a "malicious, scandalous and defamatory newspaper, magazine and periodical," known as The Saturday Press, published by the defendants in the city of Minneapolis. . . .

Without attempting to summarize the contents of the voluminous exhibits attached to the complaint, we deem it sufficient to say that the articles charged in substance that a Jewish gangster was in control of gambling, bootlegging and racketeering in Minneapolis, and that law enforcing officers and agencies were not energetically performing their duties. Most of the charges were directed against the Chief of Police; he was charged with gross neglect of duty, illicit relations with gangsters, and with participation in graft. The County Attorney was charged with knowing the existing conditions and with failure to take adequate measures to remedy them. The Mayor was accused of inefficiency and dereliction. One member of the grand jury was stated to be in sympathy with the gangsters. A special grand jury and a special prosecutor were demanded to deal with the situation in general, and, in particular, to investigate an attempt to assassinate one Guilford, one of the original defendants, who, it appears from the articles, was shot by gangsters after the first issue of the periodical had been published. There is no question but that the articles made serious accusations against the public officers named and others in connection with the prevalence of crimes and the failure to expose and punish them.

At the beginning of the action, on November 22, 1927, and upon the verified complaint, an order was made directing the defendants to show cause why a temporary injunction should not issue and meanwhile forbidding the defendants to publish, circulate or have in their possession any editions of the periodical from September 24, 1927, to November 19, 1927, inclusive, and from publishing, circulating, or having in their possession, "any future editions of said The Saturday Press" and "any publication, known by any other name whatsoever containing malicious, scandalous and defamatory matter of the kind alleged in plaintiff's complaint herein or otherwise."

(The constitutionality of the statute was upheld by the Supreme Court of Minnesota. Subsequently a permanent injunction "padlocking" the newspaper was also sustained by that Court.)

From the judgment as thus affirmed, the defendant Near appeals to this Court.

This statute, for the suppression as a public nuisance of a newspaper or periodical, is unusual, if not unique, and raises questions of grave importance transcending the local interests involved in the particular action. It is no longer open to doubt that the liberty of press, and of speech, is within the liberty safeguarded by the due process clause of the Fourteenth Amendment from invasion by state action. It was found impossible to conclude that this essential personal liberty of the citizen was left unprotected by the general guaranty of fundamental rights of person and property. *Gitlow* v. *New York*, 268 U.S. 652, 666. . . . In maintaining this guaranty, the authority of the State to enact laws to promote the health, safety, morals and general welfare of its people is necessarily admitted. The limits of this sovereign power must always be determined with appropriate regard to the particular subject of its exercise. . . . Liberty of speech, and of the press, is also not an absolute right, and the State may punish its abuse. . . . Liberty, in each of its phases, has its history and connotation and, in the present instance, the inquiry is as to the historic conception of the liberty of the press and whether the statute under review violates the essential attributes of that liberty.

. . . It is thus important to note precisely the purpose and effect of the statute as the state court has construed it.

First. The statute is not aimed at the redress of individual or private wrongs. Remedies for libel remain available and unaffected. . . .

Second. The statute is directed not simply at the circulation of scandalous and defamatory statements with regard to private citizens, but at the continued publication by newspapers and periodicals of charges against public officers of corruption, malfeasance in office, or serious neglect of duty. Such charges by their very nature create a public scandal. They are scandalous and defamatory within the meaning of the statute, which has its normal operation in relation to publications dealing prominently and chiefly with the alleged derelictions of public officers.

Third. The object of the statute is not punishment, in the ordinary sense, but suppression of the offending newspaper or periodical. . . .

This suppression is accomplished by enjoining publication and that restraint is the object and effect of the statute.

Fourth. The statute not only operates to suppress the offending newspaper or periodical but to put the publisher under an effective censorship. . . .

The statute in question cannot be justified by reason of the fact that the publisher is permitted to show, before injunction issues, that the matter published is true and is published with good motives and for justifiable ends. If such a statute, authorizing suppression and injunction on such a basis, is constitutionally valid, it would be equally permissible for the legislature to provide that at any time the publisher of any newspaper could be brought before a court, or even an administrative officer (as the constitutional protection may not be regarded as resting on mere procedural details) and required to produce proof of the truth of his publication, or of what he intended to publish, and of his motives, or stand enjoined. If this can be done, the legislature may provide machinery for determining in the complete exercise of its discretion what are justifiable ends and restrain publication accordingly. And it would be but a step to a complete system of censorship. The recognition of authority to impose previous restraint upon publication in order to protect the community against the circulation of charges of misconduct, and especially of official misconduct, necessarily would carry with it the admission of the authority of the censor against which the constitutional barrier was erected. The preliminary freedom, by virtue of the very reason for its existence, does not depend, as this Court has said, on proof of truth. . . .

Equally unavailing is the insistence that the statute is designed to prevent the circulation of scandal which tends to disturb the public peace and to provoke assaults and the commission of crime. Charges of reprehensible conduct, and in particular of official malfeasance, unquestionably create a public scandal, but the theory of the constitutional guaranty is that even a more serious public evil would be caused by authority to prevent publication. . . . There is nothing new in the fact that charges of reprehensible conduct may create resentment and the disposition to resort to violent means of redress, but this well-understood tendency did not alter the determination to protect the press against censorship and restraint upon publication. . . .

The danger of violent reactions becomes greater with effective

organization of defiant groups resenting exposure, and if this consideration warranted legislative interference with the initial freedom of publication, the constitutional protection would be reduced to a mere form
of words.

For these reasons we hold the statute, so far as it authorized
the proceedings in this action under clause (b) of section one, to be an
infringement of the liberty of the press guaranteed by the Fourteenth
Amendment. We should add that this decision rests upon the operation
and effect of the statute, without regard to the question of the truth of
the charges contained in the particular periodical. The fact that the
public officers named in this case, and those associated with the charges
of official dereliction, may be deemed to be impeccable, cannot affect
the conclusion that the statute imposes an unconstitutional restraint upon
publication.

Judgment reversed.

21.4. SEPARATION OF CHURCH AND STATE

*To what extent may a State give indirect help to religion without violating
the Fourteenth Amendment? The* Zorach *decision examines the meaning
of separation of church and State and concludes that New York's "released
time" program does not violate the Constitution.*

MR. JUSTICE DOUGLAS delivered the opinion of the Court.

New York City has a program which permits its public schools
to release students during the school day so that they may leave the
school buildings and school grounds and go to religious centers for religious instruction or devotional exercises. A student is released on written
request of his parents. Those not released stay in the classrooms. The
churches make weekly reports to the schools, sending a list of children
who have been released from public school but who have not reported
for religious instruction.

This "released time" program involves neither religious instruction in public school classroom nor the expenditure of public funds. All
costs, including the application blanks, are paid by the religious organizations. The case is therefore unlike McCollum v. Board of Education,
which involved a "released time" program from Illinois. In that case the
classrooms were turned over to religious instructors. We accordingly held
that the program violated the First Amendment which (by reason of the
Fourteenth Amendment) prohibits the states from establishing religion
or prohibiting its free exercise.

From *Zorach* v. *Clauson,* 343 U.S. 306 (1952).

Appellants, who are taxpayers and residents of New York City and whose children attend its public schools, challenge the present law, contending it is in essence no different from the one involved in the McCollum case. Their argument, stated elaborately in various ways, reduces itself to this: the weight and influence of the school is put behind a program for religious instruction; public school teachers police it, keeping tab on students who are released; the classroom activities come to a halt while the students who are released for religious instruction are on leave; the school is a crutch on which the churches are leaning for support in their religious training; without the cooperation of the schools this "released time" program, like the one in the McCollum case, would be futile and ineffective. . . .

The briefs and arguments are replete with data bearing on the merits of this type of "released time" program. Views pro and con are expressed, based on practical experience with these programs and with their implication. We do not stop to summarize these materials nor to burden the opinion with an analysis of them. For they involve considerations not germane to the narrow constitutional issue presented. They largely concern the wisdom of the system, its efficiency from an educational point of view, and the political considerations which have motivated its adoption or rejection in some communities. Those matters are of no concern here, since our problem reduces itself to whether New York by this system has either prohibited the "free exercise" of religion or has made a law "respecting an establishment of religion" within the meaning of the First Amendment.

It takes obtuse reasoning to inject any issue of the "free exercise" of religion into the present case. No one is forced to go to the religious classroom and no religious exercise or instruction is brought to the classrooms of the public schools. A student need not take religious instruction. He is left to his own desires as to the manner or time of his religious devotions, if any. . . .

There cannot be the slightest doubt that the First Amendment reflects the philosophy that Church and State should be separated. And so far as interference with the "free exercise" of religion and an "establishment" of religion are concerned, the separation must be complete and unequivocal. The First Amendment within the scope of its coverage permits no exception; the prohibition is absolute. The First Amendment, however, does not say that in every and all respects there shall be a separation of Church and State. Rather, it studiously defines the manner, the specific ways, in which there shall be no concert or union or dependency one on the other. That is the common sense of the matter. Otherwise the state and religion would be aliens to each other—hostile, suspicious, and even unfriendly. Churches could not be required to pay even property taxes. Municipalities would not be permitted to render police or fire protection to religious groups. Policeman who helped parishioners into their places of worship would violate the Constitution. Prayers in our legislative halls; the appeals to the Almighty in the messages of the Chief Executive; the proclamations making Thanksgiving Day a holiday; "so help me God" in our courtroom oaths—these and all other references to the Almighty that run through our laws, our public rituals, our ceremonies would be flouting the First Amendment. A fastidious atheist or agnostic could even object to the supplication with which the Court opens each session: "God save the United States and this Honorable Court."

We would have to press the concept of separation of Church and State to these extremes to condemn the present law on constitutional grounds. The nullification of this law would have wide and profound effects. A Catholic student applies to his teacher for permission to leave the school during hours on a Holy Day of Obligation to attend mass. A Jewish student asks his teacher for permission to be excused for Yom Kippur. A Protestant wants the afternoon off for a family baptismal ceremony. In each case the teacher requires parental consent in writing. In each case the teacher, in order to make sure the student is not a truant, goes further and requires a report from the priest, the rabbi, or the minister. The teacher in other words cooperates in a religious program to the extent of making it possible for her students to participate in it. Whether she does it occasionally for a few students, regularly for one, or pursuant to a systemized program designed to further the religious needs of all the students does not alter the character of the act.

We are a religious people whose institutions presuppose a Supreme Being. We guarantee the freedoms to worship as one chooses. We make room for as wide a variety of beliefs and creeds as the spiritual needs of man deem necessary. We sponsor an attitude on the part of government that shows no partiality to any one group and that lets each flourish according to the zeal of its adherents and the appeal of its dogma. When the state encourages religious instruction or cooperates with religious authorities by adjusting the schedule of public events to sectarian needs, it follows the best of our traditions. . . .

Mr. Justice Jackson dissenting:
This released time program is founded upon a use of State's power of coercion, which, for me, determines its unconstitutionality. Stripped to its essentials, the plan has two stages, first, that the State compel each student to yield a large part of his time for public secular education and, second, that some of it be "released" to him on condition that he devote it to sectarian religious purposes. . . .

The day that this country ceases to be free for irreligion it will cease to be free for religion—except for the sect that can win political power. The same epithetical jurisprudence used by the Court today to beat down those who oppose pressuring children into some religion can devise as good epithets tomorrow against those who object to pressuring them into a favored religion. And, after all, if we concede to the State power and wisdom to single out "duly constituted religious" bodies as exclusive alternatives for compulsory secular instruction, it would be logical to also uphold the power and wisdom to choose the true faith among those "duly constituted." We start down a rough road when we begin to mix compulsory public education with compulsory godliness. . . .

21.5. THE PRAYER CASES

Among the most controversial issues to reach the Supreme Court under the First Amendment are those in which state and local authorities have sought to encourage, support, or in some official way endorse religious practices of some kind. In the following case, the Court deals with the problem of an officially prescribed, nonsectarian prayer in the public schools. This case in 1962 was followed by other cases in June, 1963 in which the prescribed prayers were taken directly from the Bible, not composed, as here, by public officials. The result, however, was the same in all cases—an officially prescribed prayer, whether especially composed for the purpose or taken from the Bible, is held to be a violation of the First Amendment.

MR. JUSTICE BLACK delivered the opinion of the Court, saying in part:

    The respondent Board of Education of Union Free School District No. 9, New Hyde Park, New York, acting in its official capacity under state law, directed the School District's principal to cause the following prayer to be said aloud by each class in the presence of a teacher at the beginning of each school day:

    Almighty God, we acknowledge our dependence upon Thee, and we beg Thy blessings upon us, our parents, our teachers, and our country.

This daily procedure was adopted on the recommendation of the State Board of Regents, a governmental agency created by the State Constitution to which the New York Legislature has granted broad supervisory, executive, and legislative powers over the State's public school system. These state officials composed the prayer which they recommended and published as a part of their "Statement on Moral and Spiritual Training in the Schools," saying: "We believe that this Statement will be subscribed to by all men and women of good will, and we call upon all of them to aid in giving life to our program."

From *Engel* v. *Vitale,* 370 U.S. 421 (1962).

Shortly after the practice of reciting the Regents' prayer was adopted by the School District, the parents of ten pupils brought this action in a New York State Court insisting that use of this official prayer in the public schools was contrary to the beliefs, religions, or religious practices of both themselves and their children. Among other things, these parents challenged the constitutionality of both the state law authorizing the School District to direct the use of prayer in public schools and the School District's regulation ordering recitation of this particular prayer on the ground that these actions of official governmental agencies violate that part of the First Amendment of the Federal Constitution which commands that "Congress shall make no law respecting an establishment of religion"—a command which was "made applicable to the State of New York by the Fourteenth Amendment of the said Constitution." The New York Court of Appeals . . . upheld the power of New York to use the Regents; prayer so long as the schools did not compel any pupil to join in the prayer over his or his parents' objection . . .

We think that by using its public school system to encourage recitation of the Regents' prayer, the State of New York has adopted a practice wholly inconsistent with the Establishment Clause. There can, of course, be no doubt that New York's program of daily classroom invocation of God's blessings as prescribed in the Regents' prayer is a religious activity . . .

The petitioners contend among other things that the state laws requiring or permitting use of the Regents' prayer must be struck down as a violation of the Establishment Clause because that prayer was composed by governmental officials as part of a governmental program to futher religious beliefs. For this reason, petitioners argue, the State's use of the Regents' prayer in its public school system breaches the constitutional wall of separation between Church and State. We agree with this contention since we think that the constitutional prohibition against laws respecting an establishment of religion must at least mean that in this country it is no part of the business of government to compose official prayers for any group of the American people to recite as a part of a religious program carried on by government . . .

It is a matter of history that this very practice of establishing governmentally composed prayers for religious services was one of the reasons which caused many of our early colonists to leave England and seek religious freedom in America. The Book of Common Prayer, which was created under governmental direction and which was approved by Acts of Parliament in 1548 and 1549, set out in minute detail the accepted form and content of prayer and other religious ceremonies to be used in the established, tax-supported Church of England . . .

It is an unfortunate fact of history that when some of the very groups which had most strenuously opposed the established Church of England found themselves sufficiently in control of colonial governments in this country to write their own prayers into law, they passed laws making their own religion the official religion of their respective colonies. . . . But the successful Revolution against English political domination was shortly followed by intense opposition to the practice of establishing religion by law. This opposition crystallized rapidly into an effective political force in Virginia, where the minority religious groups such as Presbyterians, Lutherans, Quakers, and Baptists had gained such strength that the adherents to the established Episcopal Church were actually a minority themselves. In 1785–1786, those opposed to the established Church, led by James Madison and Thomas Jefferson, who though themselves not members of any of these dissenting religious groups, opposed all religious establishments by law on grounds of principle, obtained the enactment of the famous "Virginia Bill for Religious Liberty" by which all religious groups were placed on an equal footing so far as the State was concerned. Similar though less far-reaching legislation was being considered and passed in other states.

By the time of the adoption of the Constitution, our history shows that there was a widespread awareness among many Americans of the dangers of a union of Church and State . . . The First Amendment was added to the Constitution to stand as a guarantee that neither the power nor the prestige of the Federal Government would be used to control, support or influence the kinds of prayer the American people can say . . . Under that Amendment's prohibition against governmental establishment of religion, as reinforced by the provisions of the Fourteenth Amendment, government in this country, be it state or federal, is without power to prescribe by law any particular form of prayer which is to be used as an official prayer in carrying on any program of governmentally sponsored religious activity.

There can be no doubt that New York's state prayer program officially establishes the religious beliefs embodied in the Regents' prayer. . . . Neither the fact that the prayer may be denominationally neutral, nor the fact that its observance on the part of the students is voluntary can serve to free it from the limitations of the Establishment Clause, as it might from the Free Exercise Clause, of the First Amendment, both of which are operative against the States by virtue of the Fourteenth Amendment. Although these two clauses may in certain instances overlap, they forbid two quite different kinds of governmental encroachment upon religious freedom. The Establishment Clause, unlike the Free Exercise Clause, does not depend upon any showing of direct governmental compulsion and is violated by the enactment of laws which establish an official religion whether those laws operate directly to coerce nonobserving individuals or not . . . When the power, prestige and financial support of government is placed behind a particular religious belief, the indirect coercive pressure upon religious minorities to conform to the prevailing officially approved religion is plain. But the purposes underlying the Establishment Clause go much further than that. Its first and most immediate purpose rested on the belief that a union of government and religion tends to destroy government and to degrade religion. The history of governmentally established religion, both in England and in this country, showed that whenever government had allied itself with one particular form of religion, the inevitable result had been that it had incurred the hatred, disrespect and even contempt of those who held contrary beliefs. That same history showed that many people had lost their respect for any religion that had relied upon the support of government to spread its faith. The Establishment Clause thus stands as an expression of principle on the part of the Founders of our Constitution that religion is too personal, too sacred, too holy, to permit its "unhallowed perversion" by a civil magistrate. . . . The New York laws officially prescribing the Regents' prayer are inconsistent with both the purposes of the Establishment Clause and with the Establishment Clause itself.

It has been argued that to apply the Constitution in such a way as to prohibit state laws respecting an establishment of religious services in public schools is to indicate a hostility toward religion or toward prayer. Nothing, of course, could be more wrong. The history of man is inseparable from the history of religion . . . It is neither sacrilegious nor antireligious to say that each separate government in this country should stay out of the business of writing or sanctioning official prayers and leave that purely religious function to the people themselves and to those the people choose to look to for religious guidance.

. . . To those who may subscribe to the view that because the Regents' official prayer is so brief and general there can be no danger to religious freedom in its governmental establishment, however, it may be appropriate to say in the words of James Madison, the author of the First Amendment:

[I]t is proper to take alarm at the first experiment on our liberties . . . Who does not see that the same authority which can establish Christianity, in exclusion of all other Religions, may establish with the same ease any particular sect of Christians, in exclusion of all other Sects? That the same authority which can force a citizen to contribute three pence only of his property for the support of any one establishment, may force him to conform to any other establishment in all cases whatsoever?

The judgment of the Court of Appeals of New York is reversed and the cause remanded for further proceedings not inconsistent with this opinion.

Reversed and remanded.

Mr. Justice Frankfurter took no part in the decision of this case.

Mr. Justice White took no part in the consideration or decision of this case.

Mr. Justice Douglas, concurring, said in part:
. . . The point for decision is whether the Government can constitutionally finance a religious exercise. Our system at the federal and state levels is presently honeycombed with such financing. Nevertheless, I think it is an unconstitutional undertaking whatever form it takes . . .

The question presented by this case is . . . an extremely narrow one. It is whether New York oversteps the bounds when it finances a religious exercise.

What New York does on the opening of its public school is what we do when we open court. Our Marshal has from the beginning announced the convening of the Court and then added "God save the Uited States and this honorable court." That utterance is a supplication, a prayer in which we, the judges, are free to join, but which we need not recite any more than the students need recite the New York prayer.

What New York does on the opening of its public schools is what each House of Congress does at the opening of each day's busines . . .

In New York the teacher who leads in prayer is on the public payroll; and the time she takes seems miniscule as compared with the salaries appropriated by state legislatures and Congress for chaplains to conduct prayers in the legislative halls. Only a bare fraction of the teacher's time is given to reciting this short 22-word prayer, about the same amount of time that our Marshal spends announcing the opening of our sessions and offering a prayer for this Court. Yet for me the principle is the same, no matter how briefly the prayer is said, for in each of the instances given the person praying is a public official on the public payroll, performing a religious exercise in a governmental institution. It is said that the element of coercion is inherent in the giving of this prayer. If that is true here, it is also true of the prayer with which this Court is convened, and with those that open the Congress. Few adults, let alone children, would leave our courtroom or the Senate or the House while those prayers are being given. Every such audience is in a sense a "captive" audience.

At the same time I cannot say that to authorize this prayer is to establish a religion in the strictly historic meaning of those words . . . Yet once government finances a religious exercise it inserts a divisive influence into our communities . . .

. . . The First Amendment leaves the government in a position not of hostility to religion but of neutrality. The philosophy is that the atheist or agnostic—the non-believer—is entitled to go his own way. The philosophy is that if government interferes in matters spiritual, it will be a divisive force. The First Amendment teaches that a government neutral in the field of religion better serves all religious interests.

. . . . . .

Mr. Justice Stewart, dissenting, said in part:

. . . The Court today decides that in permitting this brief non-denominational prayer the school board has violated the Constitution of the United States. I think this decision is wrong.

The Court does not hold, nor could it, that New York has interfered with the free exercise of anybody's religion. For the state courts have made clear that those who object to reciting the prayer must be entirely free of any compulsion to do so, including any "embarrassments and pressures." But the Court says that in permitting school children to say this simple prayer, the New York authorities have established "an official religion."

With all respect, I think the Court has misapplied a great constitutional principle. I cannot see how an "official religion" is established by letting those who want to say a prayer say it. On the contrary, I think that to deny the wish of these school children to join in reciting this prayer is to deny them the opportunity of sharing in the spiritual heritage of our Nation . . .

21.6. LIMITS TO NATIONALIZATION OF THE BILL OF RIGHTS

Despite the incorporation of freedom of speech, press, and religion into the Fourteenth Amendment through judicial construction, not every section of the Bill of Rights applies to the States. Justice Cardozo's decision in the Palko *case points out that only those parts of the Bill of Rights which are "of the very essence of a scheme of ordered liberty" limit State action.*

MR. JUSTICE CARDOZO delivered the opinion of the Court.

A statute of Connecticut permitting appeals in criminal cases to be taken by the state is challenged by appellant as an infringement of the Fourteenth Amendment of the Constitution of the United States. Whether the challenge should be upheld is now to be determined.

Appellant was indicted in Fairfield County, Connecticut, for the crime of murder in the first degree. A jury found him guilty of murder

From *Palko* v. *Connecticut,* 302 U.S. 319 (1937).

in the second degree, and he was sentenced to confinement in the state prison for life. Thereafter the State of Connecticut, with the permission of the judge presiding at the trial, gave notice of appeal to the Supreme Court of Errors. . . . Upon such appeal, the Supreme Court of Errors reversed the judgment and ordered a new trial. . . . It found that there had been error of law to the prejudice of the state (1) in excluding testimony as to a confession by defendant; (2) in excluding testimony upon cross-examination of defendant to impeach his credibility; and (3) in the instructions to the jury as to the difference between first and second degree murder.

Pursuant to the mandate of the Supreme Court of Errors, defendant was brought to trial again. Before a jury was impaneled, and also at later stages of the case, he made the objection that the effect of the new trial was to place him twice in jeopardy for the same offense, and in so doing to violate the Fourteenth Amendment of the Constitution of the United States. Upon the overruling of the objection the trial proceeded. The jury returned a verdict of murder in the first degree, and the court sentenced the defendant to the punishment of death. The Supreme Court of Errors, affirmed the judgment of conviction. . . .

The execution of the sentence will not deprive appellant of his life without the process of law assured to him by the Fourteenth Amendment of the Federal Constitution.

The argument for appellant is that whatever is forbidden by the Fifth Amendment is forbidden by the Fourteenth also. The Fifth Amendment, which is not directed to the states, but solely to the federal government, creates immunity from double jeopardy. No person shall be "subject for the same offense to be twice put in jeopardy of life or limb." The Fourteenth Amendment ordains, "nor shall any State deprive any person of life, liberty, or property, without due process of law." To retry a defendant, though under one indictment and only one, subjects him, it is said, to double jeopardy in violation of the Fifth Amendment, if the prosecution is one on behalf of the United States. From this the consequence is said to follow that there is a denial of life or liberty without due process of law, if the prosecution is one on behalf of the People of a State. . . .

We have said that in appellant's view the Fourteenth Amendment is to be taken as embodying the prohibitions of the Fifth. His thesis is even broader. Whatever would be a violation of the original Bill of Rights (Amendments 1 to 8) if done by the federal government is now equally unlawful by force of the Fourteenth Amendment if done by a state. There is no such general rule. . . .

The Fifth Amendment provides, among other things, that no person shall be held to answer for a capital or otherwise infamous crime unless on presentment or indictment of a grand jury. This court has held that, in prosecutions by a state, presentment or indictment by a grand jury may give way to informations at the instance of a public officer. . . . The Fifth Amendment provides also that no person shall be compelled in any criminal case to be a witness against himself. This court has said that, in prosecutions by a state, the exemption will fail if the state elects to end it. . . . The Sixth Amendment calls for a jury trial in criminal cases and the Seventh for a jury trial in civil cases at common law where the value in controversy shall exceed twenty dollars. This court has ruled that consistently with those amendments trial by jury may be modified by a state or abolished altogether. . . .

On the other hand, the due process clause of the Fourteenth Amendment may make it unlawful for a state to abridge by its statutes the freedom of speech which the First Amendment safeguards against encroachment by the Congress . . . or the like freedom of the press. . . . or the free exercise of religion. . . . or the right of peaceable assembly, without which speech would be unduly trammeled. . . . or the right of one accused of crime to the benefit of counsel. . . . In these and other situations immunities that are valid as against the federal government by force of the specific pledge of particular amendments have been found to be implicit in the concept of ordered liberty, and thus, through the Fourteenth Amendment, become valid as against the states.

The line of division may seem to be wavering and broken if there is a hasty catalogue of the cases on the one side and the other. Reflection and analysis will induce a different view. There emerges the perception of a rationalizing principle which gives to discrete instances a proper order and coherence. The right to trial by jury and the immunity from prosecution except as the result of an indictment may have value and importance. Even so, they are not of the very essence of a scheme of ordered liberty. To abolish them is not to violate a "principle of justice so rooted in the traditions and conscience of our people as to be ranked as fundamental." . . . Few would be so narrow or provincial as to maintain that a fair and enlightened system of justice would be impossible without them. What is true of jury trials and indictments is true also, as the cases show, of the immunity from compulsory self-incrimination. . . . This too might be lost, and justice still be done. Indeed, today as in the past there are students of our penal system who look upon the immunity as a mischief rather than a benefit, and would limit its scope, or destroy it altogether. No doubt there would remain the need to give protection against torture, physical or mental. . . . Justice, however, would not perish if the accused were subject to a duty to respond to orderly inquiry. The exclusion of these immunities and privileges from the privileges and immunities protected against the action of the states has not been arbitrary or casual. It has been dictated by a study and appreciation of the meaning, the essential implications, of liberty itself.

We reach a different plane of social and moral values when we pass to the privileges and immunities that have been taken over from the earlier articles of the federal bill of rights and brought within the Fourteenth Amendment by a process of absorption. These in their origin were effective against the federal government alone. If the Fourteenth Amendment has absorbed them, the process of absorption has had its source in the belief that neither liberty nor justice would exist if they were sacrificed. . . . This is true, for illustration, of freedom of thought and speech. Of that freedom one may say that it is the matrix, the indispensable condition, of nearly every other form of freedom. With rare aberrations a pervasive recognition of that truth can be traced in our history, political and legal. So it has come about that the domain of liberty, withdrawn by the Fourteenth Amendment from encroachment by the states, has been enlarged by latter-day judgments to include liberty of the mind as well as liberty of action. . . .

Our survey of the cases serves, we think, to justify the statement that the dividing line between them, if not unfaltering throughout its course, has been true for the most part to a unifying principle. On which side of the line the case made out by the appellant has appropriate location must be the next inquiry and the final one. Is that kind of double jeopardy to which the statute has subjected him a hardship so acute and shocking that our polity will not endure it? Does it violate those "fundamental principles of liberty and justice which lie at the base of all our civil and political institutions"? The answer surely must be "no." . . . If the trial had been infected with error adverse to the accused, there might have been review at his instance, and, as often as necessary to purge the vicious taint. A reciprocal privilege, subject at all times to the discretion of the presiding judge . . . has now been granted to the state. There is here no seismic innovation. The edifice of justice stands, its symmetry, to many, greater than before. . . .

22

Due Process and Equal Protection

22.1. THE DUE PROCESS CLAUSE AS A LIMITATION ON STATE POWER

What constitutes deprivation of life, liberty, or property without due process of law? This 1905 Supreme Court decision invalidates as an interference with freedom of contract under the due process clause of the Constitution an early effort by New York State to limit the work week in bakeries and confectioneries to sixty hours.

MR. JUSTICE PECKMAN delivered the opinion of the Court. . . .

The indictment, it will be seen, charges that the plaintiff in error violated the 110th section of article 8, chapter 415, of the Laws of 1897, known as the labor law of the state of New York, in that he wrongfully required and permitted an employee working for him to work more than sixty hours in one week. There is nothing in any of the opinions delivered in this case, either in the supreme court or the court of appeals of the state, which construes the section, in using the word "required," as referring to any physical force being used to obtain the labor of an employee. It is assumed that the word means nothing more than the requirement arising from voluntary contract for such labor in excess of the number of hours specified in the statute. There is no pretense in any of the opinions that the statute was intended to meet a case of involuntary labor in any form. All the opinions assume that there is no real distinction, so far as this question is concerned, between the words "required" and "permitted." The mandate of the statute, that "no employee shall be required or permitted to work," is the substantial equivalent of an enactment that "no employee shall contract or agree to

From *Lochner* v. *New York*, 198 U.S. 45 (1905).

work," more than ten hours per day; and, as there is no provision for special emergencies, the statute is mandatory in all cases. It is not an act merely fixing the number of hours which shall constitute a legal day's work, but an absolute prohibition upon the employer permitting, under any circumstances, more than ten hours' work to be done in his establishment. The employee may desire to earn the extra money which would arise from his working more than the prescribed time, but this statute forbids the employer from permitting the employee to earn it.

The statute necessarily interferes with the right of contract between the employer and employees, concerning the number of hours in which the latter may labor in the bakery of the employer. The general right to make a contract in relation to his business is part of the liberty of the individual protected by the 14th Amendment of the Federal Constitution. . . . Under that provision no state can deprive any person of life, liberty, or property without due process of law. The right to purchase or to sell labor is part of the liberty protected by this amendment, unless there are circumstances which exclude the right. There are, however, certain powers, existing in the sovereignty of each state in the Union, somewhat vaguely termed police powers, the exact description and limitation of which have not been attempted by the courts. Those powers, broadly stated, and without, at present, any attempt at a more specific limitation, relate to the safety, health, morals, and general welfare of the public. Both property and liberty are held on such reasonable conditions as may be imposed by the governing power of the state in the exercise of those powers, and with such conditions the 14th Amendment was not designed to interfere. . . .

The state, therefore, has power to prevent the individual from making certain kinds of contracts, and in regard to them the Federal Constitution offers no protection. If the contract be one which the state, in the legitimate exercise of its police power, has the right to prohibit, it is not prevented from prohibiting it by the 14th Amendment. Contracts in violation of a statute, either of the Federal or state government, or a contract to let one's property for immoral purposes, or to do any other unlawful act, could obtain no protection from the Federal Constitution, as coming under the liberty of person or of free contract. Therefore, when the state, by its legislature, in the assumed exercise of its police powers, has passed an act which seriously limits the right to labor or the right of contract in regard to their means of livelihood between persons who are *sui juris* (both employer and employee), it becomes of great importance to determine which shall prevail,—the right of the individual to labor for such time as he may choose, or the right of the state to prevent the individual from laboring, or from entering into any contract to labor, beyond a certain time prescribed by the state.

It is manifest to us that the limitation of the hours of labor as provided for in this section of the statute under which the indictment was found, and the plaintiff in error convicted, has no such direct relation to, and no such substantial effect upon, the health of the employee, as to justify us in regarding the section as really a health law. It seems to us that the real object and purpose were simply to regulate the hours of labor between the master and his employees in a private business, not dangerous in any degree to morals, or in any real and substantial degree to the health of the employees. Under such circumstances the freedom of master and employee to contract with each other in relation to their employment, and in defining the same, cannot be prohibited or interfered with, without violating the Federal Constitution.

Mr. Justice Holmes dissenting:

I regret sincerely that I am unable to agree with the judgment in this case, and that I think it my duty to express my dissent.

This case is decided upon an economic theory which a large part of the country does not entertain. If it were a question whether I agreed with that theory, I should desire to study it further and long before making up my mind. But I do not conceive that to be my duty, because I strongly believe that my agreement or disagreement has nothing to do with the right of a majority to embody their opinions in law. It is settled by various decisions of this court that state constitutions and state laws may regulate life in many ways which we as legislators might think as injudicious, or if you like as tyrannical, as this, and which, equally with this, interfere with the liberty to contract. Sunday laws and usury laws are ancient examples. A more modern one is the prohibition of lotteries. The liberty of the citizen to do as he likes so long as he does not interfere with the liberty of others to do the same, which has been a shibboleth for some well-known writers, is interfered with by school laws, by the Postoffice, by every state or municipal institution which takes his money for purposes thought desirable, whether he likes it or not. The 14th Amendment does not enact Mr. Herbert Spencer's Social Statics. The other day we sustained the Massachusetts vaccination law. . . . United States and state statutes and decisions cutting down the liberty to contract by law of combination are familiar to this court. . . . Two years ago we upheld the prohibition of sales of stock on margins, or for future delivery, in the Constitution of California. . . . The decision sustaining an eight-hour law for miners is still recent. . . . Some of these laws embody convictions or prejudices which judges are likely to share. Some may not. But a Constitution is not intended to embody a particular economic theory, whether of paternalism and the organic relation of the citizen to the state or of *laissez faire*. It is made for people of fundamentally differing views, and the accident of our finding certain opinions natural and familiar, or novel, and even shocking, ought not to conclude our judgment upon the question whether statutes embodying them conflict with the Constitution of the United States. . . .

22.2. NARROWING THE SUBSTANTIVE LIMITS OF DUE PROCESS

The vigorous dissent by Justice Holmes in the Lochner *case has become the prevailing view of the courts in construing the due process clause in recent years. Justice Roberts' decision in the* Nebbia *case illustrates the reluctance of the courts to invoke the due process clause to strike down economic or social regulations of the states.*

MR. JUSTICE ROBERTS delivered the opinion of the Court.

The Legislature of New York established by chapter 158 of the Laws of 1933, a Milk Control Board with power, among other things to "fix minimum and maximum . . . retail prices to the charged by . . . stores to consumers for consumption off the premises where sold." . . . The board fixed nine cents as the price to be charged by a store for a quart of milk. Nebbia, the proprietor of a grocery store in Rochester, sold two quarts and a 5-cent loaf of bread for 18 cents; and was convicted for violating the board's order. At his trial he asserted the statute and order contravene the equal protection clause and the due process clause of the Fourteenth Amendment, and renewed the contention in successive appeals to the county court and the Court of Appeals. Both overruled his claim and affirmed the conviction.

The question for decision is whether the Federal Constitution prohibits a state from so fixing the selling price of milk. . . .

The appellant urges that the order of the Milk Control Board denies him the equal protection of the laws. It is shown that the order requires him, if he purchases his supply from a dealer, to pay 8 cents per quart and 5 cents per pint, and to resell at not less than 9 and 6, whereas the same dealer may buy his supply from a farmer at lower prices and deliver milk to consumers at 10 cents the quart and 6 cents the pint. We think the contention that the discrimination deprives the appellant of equal protection is not well founded. For aught that appears, the appellant purchased his supply of milk from a farmer as do distributors, or could have procured it from a farmer if he so desired. There is therefore no

From *Nebbia* v. *New York,* 291 U.S. 502 (1934).

showing that the order placed him at a disadvantage, or in fact affected him adversely, and this alone is fatal to the claim of denial of equal protection. But, if it were shown that the appellant is compelled to buy from a distributor, the difference in the retail price he is required to charge his customers, from that prescribed for sales by distributors is not on its face arbitrary or unreasonable, for there are obvious distinctions between the two sorts of merchants which may well justify a difference of treatment, if the Legislature possesses the power to control the prices to be charged for fluid milk. . . .

The more serious question is whether, in the light of the conditions disclosed, the enforcement of section 312(e) denied the appellant the due process secured to him by the Fourteenth Amendment. . . .

Under our form of government the use of property and the making of contracts are normally matters of private and not of public concern. The general rule is that both shall be free of governmental interference. But neither property rights nor contract rights are absolute; for government cannot exist if the citizen may at will use his property to the detriment of his fellows, or exercise his freedom of contract to work them harm. Equally fundamental with the private right is that of the public to regulate it in the common interest. . . .

The Fifth Amendment, in the field of federal activity, and the Fourteenth, as respects state action, do not prohibit governmental regulation for the public welfare. They merely condition the exertion of the admitted power, by securing that the end shall be accomplished by methods consistent with due process. And the guaranty of due process, as has often been held, demands only that the law shall not be unreasonable, arbitrary, or capricious, and that the means selected shall have a real and substantial relation to the object sought to be attained. It results that a regulation valid for one sort of business, or in given circumstances, may be invalid for another sort, or for the same business under other circumstances, because the reasonableness of each regulation depends upon the relevant facts. . . .

The court has repeatedly sustained curtailment of enjoyment of private property, in the public interest. The owner's rights may be subordinated to the needs of other private owners whose pursuits are vital to the paramount interests of the community. The state may control the use of property in various ways; may prohibit advertising bill boards except of a prescribed size and location, or their use for certain kinds of advertising; may in certain circumstances authorize encroachments by party walls in cities; may fix the height of buildings, the character of materials, and methods of construction, the adjoining area which must be left open, and may exclude from residential sections offensive trades, industries and structures likely injuriously to affect the public health or safety; or may establish zones within which certain types of buildings or businesses are permitted and other excluded. And although the Fourteenth Amendment extends protection to aliens as well as citizens, a state may for adequate reasons of policy exclude aliens altogether from the use and occupancy of land.

Laws passed for the suppression of immorality, in the interest of health, to secure fair trade practices, and to safeguard the interests of depositors in banks, have been found consistent with due process. These measures not only affected the use of private property, but also interfered with the right of private contract. Other instances are numerous where valid regulation has restricted the right of contract, while less directly affecting property rights.

The Constitution does not guarantee the unrestricted privilege to engage in a business or to conduct it as one pleases. Certain kinds of business may be prohibited; and the right to conduct a business, or to pursue a calling, may be conditioned. Regulation of a business to prevent waste of the state's resources may be justified. And statutes prescribing the terms upon which those conducting certain businesses may contract, or imposing terms if they do enter into agreements, are within the state's competency. . . .

But we are told that because the law essays to control prices it denies due process. Notwithstanding the admitted power to correct existing economic ills by appropriate regulation of business, even though an indirect result may be a restriction of the freedom of contract or a modification of charges for services or the price of commodities, the appellant urges that direct fixation of prices is a type of regulation absolutely forbidden. His position is that the Fourteenth Amendment requires us to hold the challenged statute void for this reason alone. The argument runs that the public control of rates or prices is per se unreasonable and unconstitutional, save as applied to businesses affected with a public interest; that a business so affected is one in which property is devoted to an enterprise of a sort which the public itself might appropriately undertake, or one whose owner relies on a public grant or franchise for the right to conduct the business, or in which he is bound to serve all who apply; in short, such as is commonly called a public utility; or a business in its nature a monopoly. The milk industry, it is said, possesses none of these characteristics, and therefore, not being affected with a public interest, its charges may not be controlled by the state. Upon the soundness of this contention the appellant's case against the statute depends.

We may as well say at once that the dairy industry is not, in the accepted sense of the phrase, a public utility. We think the appellant is also right in asserting that there is in this case no suggestion of any monopolistic practice. It goes without saying that those engaged in the business are in no way dependent upon public grants or franchises for the privilege of conducting their activities. But if, as must be conceded, the industry is subject to regulation in the public interest, what constitutional principle bars the state from correcting existing maladjustments by legislation touching prices? We think there is no such principle. The due process clause makes no mention of sales or of prices any more than it speaks of business or contracts or buildings or other incidents of property. The thought seems nevertheless to have persisted that there is something peculiarly sacrosanct about the price one may charge for what he makes or sells, and that, however able to regulate other elements of manufacture or trade, with incidental effect upon price, the state is incapable of directly controlling the price itself. This view was negatived many years ago. . . .

It is clear that there is no closed class or category of businesses affected with a public interest, and the function of courts in the application of the Fifth and Fourteenth Amendments is to determine in each whether circumstances vindicate the challenged regulation as a reasonable exertion of governmental authority or condemn it as arbitrary or discriminatory. . . . The phrase "affected with a public interest" can, in the nature of things, mean no more than that an industry, for adequate reason, is subject to control for the public good. In several of the decisions of this court wherein the expressions "affected with a public interest," and "clothed with a public use," have been brought forward as the criteria of the validity of price control, it has been admitted that they are not susceptible of definition and form an unsatisfactory test of the constitutionality of legislation directed at business practices or prices. These decisions must rest, finally, upon the basis that the requirements of due process were not met because the laws were found arbitrary in their operation and effect. But there can be no doubt that upon proper occasion and by appropriate measures the state may regulate a business in any of its aspects, including the prices to be charged for the products or commodities it sells.

So far as the requirement of due process is concerned, and in the absence of other constitutional restriction, a state is free to adopt whatever economic policy may reasonably be deemed to promote public welfare, and to enforce that policy by legislation adapted to its purpose. The courts are without authority either to declare such policy, or, when it is declared by the legislature, to override it. If the laws passed are seen to have a reasonable relation to a proper legislative purpose, and are neither arbitrary nor discriminatory, the requirements of due process are satisfied, and judicial determination to that effect renders a court functus officio. . . . With the wisdom of the policy adopted, with the adequacy or practicability of the law enacted to forward it, the courts are both incompetent and unauthorized to deal. . . .

22.3. A JUSTIFICATION OF RACIAL SEGREGATION

The "seperate but equal" doctrine as a justification for racial segregation was first enunciated by the Supreme Court in 1896. In this excerpt, the judges uphold the validity of a Louisiana statute of 1890 requiring racial segregation on railroads operating within the state.

MR. JUSTICE BROWN . . . delivered the opinion of the Court: . . .

By the Fourteenth Amendment, all persons born or naturalized in the United States, and subject to the jurisdiction thereof, are made citizens of the United States and of the state wherein they reside; and the states are forbidden from making or enforcing any law which shall abridge the privileges or immunities of citizens of the United States, or shall deprive any person of life, liberty or property without due process of law, or deny to any person within their jurisdiction the equal protection of the laws. . . .

The object of the amendment was undoubtedly to enforce the absolute equality of the two races before the law, but in the nature of things it could not have been intended to abolish distinctions based upon color, or to enforce social, as distinguished from political, equality, or a commingling of the two races upon terms unsatisfactory to either. Laws permitting, and even requiring, their separation in places where they are liable to be brought into contact do not necessarily imply the inferiority of either race to the other, and have been generally, if not universally, recognized as within the competency of the state legislatures in the exercise of their police power. The most common instance of this is connected with the establishment of separate schools for white and colored children, which has been held to be a valid exercise of the legislative power even by courts of states where the political rights of the colored race have been longest and most earnestly enforced.

One of the earliest of these cases is that of Roberts *v.* City of Boston, 5 Cush. 198 (1849), in which the Supreme Judicial Court of Massachusetts held that the general school committee of Boston had power to make provision for the instruction of colored children in separate schools established exclusively for them, and to prohibit their attendance

From *Plessy* v. *Ferguson,* 163 U.S. 537 (1896).

upon the other schools. . . . It was held that the powers of the committee extended to the establishment of separate schools for children of different ages, sexes and colors, and that they might also establish special schools for poor and neglected children, who have become too old to attend the primary schools, and yet have not acquired the rudiments of learning, to enable them to enter the ordinary schools. Similar laws have been enacted by Congress under its general power of legislation over the District of Columbia . . . as well as by the legislatures of many of the states, and have been generally, if not uniformly, sustained by the courts. . . .

So far, then, as a conflict with the Fourteenth Amendment is concerned, the case reduces itself to the question whether the statute of Louisiana is a reasonable regulation, and with respect to this there must necessarily be a large discretion on the part of the legislature. In determining the question of reasonableness it is at liberty to act with reference to the established usages, customs and traditions of the people, and with a view to the promotion of their comfort, and the preservation of the public peace and good order. Gauged by this standard, we cannot say that a law which authorizes or even requires the separation of the two races in public conveyances is unreasonable or more obnoxious to the Fourteenth Amendment than the acts of Congress requiring separate schools for colored children in the District of Columbia, the constitutionality of which does not seem to have been questioned, or the corresponding acts of state legislatures.

We consider the underlying fallacy of the plaintiff's argument to consist in the assumption that the enforced separation of the two races stamps the colored race with a badge of inferiority. If this be so, it is not by reason of anything found in the act, but solely because the colored race chooses to put that consideration upon it. The argument necessarily assumes that if, as has been more than once the case, and is not unlikely to be so again, the colored race should become the dominant power in the state legislature, and should enact a law in precisely similar terms, it would thereby relegate the white race to an inferior position. We imagine that the white race, at least, would not acquiesce in this assumption. The argument also assumes that social prejudices may be overcome by legislation and that equal rights cannot be secured to the Negro except by an enforced commingling of the two races. We cannot accept this proposition. If the two races are to meet upon terms of social equality, it must be the result of natural affinities, a mutual appreciation of each other's merits, and a voluntary consent of individuals. . . .

Legislation is powerless to eradicate racial instincts or to abolish distinctions based upon physical differences, and the attempt to do so can only result in accentuating the difficulties of the present situation. If the civil and political rights of both races be equal, one cannot be inferior to the other civilly or politically. If one race be inferior to the other socially, the Constitution of the United States cannot put them upon the same plane. . . .

Mr. Justice Harlan, dissenting:

. . . If a white man and a black man choose to occupy the same public conveyance on a public highway, it is their right to do so, and no government, proceeding alone on grounds of race, can prevent it without infringing the personal liberty of each. . . .

The white race deems itself to be the dominant race in this country. And so it is, in prestige, in achievements, in education, in wealth, and in power. So, I doubt not, it will continue to be for all time, if it remains true to its great heritage and holds fast to the principles of constitutional liberty. But in the view of the Constitution, in the eye of the law, there is in this country no superior, dominant, ruling class of citizens. There is no caste here. Our Constitution is color-blind and neither knows nor tolerates classes among citizens. In respect of civil rights, all citizens are equal before the law. The humblest is the peer of the most powerful. The law regards man as man and takes no account of his surroundings or of his color when his civil rights as guaranteed by the supreme law of the land are involved. . . .

The arbitrary separation of citizens, on the basis of race, while they are on a public highway, is a badge of servitude wholly inconsistent with the civil freedom and the equality before the law established by the Constitution. It cannot be justified upon any legal grounds.

22.4. RACIAL SEGREGATION IN SCHOOLS IS OUTLAWED

Between 1896 and 1954 a series of judicial decisions invalidated numerous instances of racial segregation as denials of equal protection under the Fourteenth Amendment. None of these expressly reversed the "separate but equal" doctrine, however. In the historic Brown *case, the Court rules that "separate educational facilities are inherently unequal."*

MR. CHIEF JUSTICE WARREN delivered the opinion of the Court. . . .

The plaintiffs contend that segregated public schools are not "equal" and cannot be made "equal," and that hence they are deprived of the equal protection of the laws. Because of the obvious importance of the

From *Brown* v. *Board of Education*, 347 U.S. 483 (1954).

question presented, the Court took jurisdiction. Argument was heard in the 1952 Term, and reargument was heard this Term on certain questions propounded by the Court.

Reargument was largely devoted to the circumstances surrounding the adoption of the Fourteenth Amendment in 1868. It covered exhaustively consideration of the Amendment in Congress, ratification by the states, then existing practices in racial segregation, and the views of proponents and opponents of the Amendment. This discussion and our own investigation convince us that, although these sources cast some light, it is not enough to resolve the problem with which we are faced. At best, they are inconclusive. The most avid proponents of the post-War Amendments undoubtedly intended them to remove all legal distinctions among "all persons born or naturalized in the United States." Their opponents, just as certainly, were antagonistic to both the letter and the spirit of the Amendments and wished them to have the most limited effect. What others in Congress and the state legislatures had in mind cannot be determined with any degree of certainty.

An additional reason for the inconclusive nature of the Amendment's history, with respect to segregated schools, is the status of public education at that time. In the South, the movement toward free common schools, supported by general taxation, had not yet taken hold. Education of Negroes was almost nonexistent, and practically all of the race were illiterate. In fact, any education of Negroes was forbidden by law in some states. Today, in contrast, many Negroes have achieved outstanding success in the arts and sciences as well as in the business and professional world. It is true that public school education had advanced further in the North, but the effect of the Amendment on Northern States was generally ignored in the congressional debates. Even in the North, the conditions of public education did not approximate those existing today. The curriculum was usually rudimentary; ungraded schools were common in rural areas; the school term was but three months a year in many states; and compulsory school attendance was virtually unknown. As a consequence, it is not surprising that there should be so little in the history of the Fourteenth Amendment relating to its intended effect on public education.

In the first cases in this Court construing the Fourteenth Amendment, decided shortly after its adoption, the Court interpreted it as proscribing all state-imposed discriminations against the Negro race. The doctrine of "separate but equal" did not make its appearance in this Court until 1896 in the case of Plessy v. Ferguson, . . . involving not education but transportation. American courts have since labored with the doctrine for over half a century. In this Court, there have been six cases involving the "separate but equal" doctrine in the field of public education. . . . In none of these cases was it necessary to reexamine the doctrine to grant relief to the Negro plaintiff. And in Sweatt *v.* Painter, . . . the Court expressly reserved decision on the question whether Plessy *v.* Ferguson should be held inapplicable to public education.

In the instant cases, that question is directly presented. Here, unlike Sweatt *v.* Painter, there are findings below that the Negro and white schools involved have been equalized, or are being equalized, with respect to buildings, curricula, qualifications and salaries of teachers, and other "tangible" factors. Our decision, therefore, cannot turn on merely a comparison of these tangible factors in the Negro and white schools involved in each of the cases. We must look instead to the effect of segregation itself on public education.

In approaching this problem, we cannot turn the clock back to 1868 when the Amendment was adopted, or even to 1896 when Plessy *v.* Ferguson was written. We must consider public education in the light of its full development and its present place in American life throughout the Nation. Only in this way can it be determined if segregation in public schools deprives these plaintiffs of the equal protection of the laws.

Today, education is perhaps the most important function of state and local governments. Compulsory school attendance laws and the great expenditures for education both demonstrate our recognition of the importance of education to our democratic society. It is required in the performance of our most basic public responsibilities, even service in the armed forces. It is the very foundation of good citizenship. Today it is a principal instrument in awakening the child to cultural values, in preparing him for later professional training, and in helping him to adjust normally to his environment. In these days, it is doubtful that any child may reasonably be expected to succeed in life if he is denied the opportunity of an education. Such an opportunity, where the state has undertaken to provide it, is a right which must be made available to all on equal terms.

We come then to the question presented: Does segregation of children in public schools solely on the basis of race, even though the physical facilities and other "tangible" factors may be equal, deprive the children of the minority group of equal educational opportunities? We believe that it does.

In Sweatt *v.* Painter, . . . in finding that a segregated law school for Negroes could not provide them equal educational opportunities, this Court relied in large part on "those qualities which are incapable of objective measurement but which make for greatness in a law school." In McLaurin *v.* Oklahoma State Regents, . . . the Court, in requiring that a Negro admitted to a white graduate school be treated like all other students, again resorted to intangible considerations: ". . . his ability to study, to engage in discussions and exchange views with other students, and, in general, to learn his profession." Such considerations apply with added force to children in grade and high schools. To separate them from others of similar age and qualifications solely because of their race generates a feeling of inferiority as to their status in the community that may affect their hearts and minds in a way unlikely ever to be undone. The effect of this separation on their educational opportunities was well stated by a finding in the Kansas case by a court which nevertheless felt compelled to rule against the Negro plaintiffs:

> Segregation of white and colored children in public schools has a detrimental effect upon the colored children. The impact is greater when it has the sanction of the law; for the policy of separating the races is usually interpreted as denoting the inferiority of the Negro group. A sense of inferiority affects the motivation of a child to learn. Segregation with the sanction of law, therefore, has a tendency to retard the educational and mental development of Negro children and to deprive them of some of the benefits they would receive in a racially integrated school system.

Whatever may have been the extent of psychological knowledge at the time of Plessy v. Ferguson, this finding is amply supported by modern authority. Any language in Plessy v. Ferguson contrary to this finding is rejected.

We conclude that in the field of public education the doctrine of "separate but equal" has no place. Separate educational facilities are inherently unequal. Therefore, we hold that the plaintiffs and others similarly situated for whom the actions have been brought are, by reason of the segregation complained of, deprived of the equal protection of the laws guaranteed by the Fourteenth Amendment. This disposition makes unnecessary any discussion whether such segregation also violates the Due Process Clause of the Fourteenth Amendment. . . .

22.5 THE JUDGES FACE A CHALLENGE

When the Little Rock, Arkansas, School Board attempted to comply with the judicial desegregation order, state officials, led by the Governor, opposed the plan to allow Negro students to enter Little Rock High School. Following outbreaks of violence, the School Board ordered suspension of the plan. The justices of the Supreme Court here reiterate unanimously the view that constitutional rights do not yield to violence and disorder.

OPINION OF THE COURT by the Chief Justice, Mr. Justice Black, Mr. Justice

From *Cooper* v. *Aaron*, 358 U.S. 1 (1958).

Frankfurter, Mr. Justice Douglas, Mr. Justice Burton, Mr. Justice Clark, Mr. Justice Harlan, Mr. Justice Brennan, and Mr. Justice Whittaker.

As this case reaches us it raises questions of the highest importance to the maintenance of our federal system of govenment. It necessarily involves a claim by the Governor and Legislature of a State that there is no duty on state officials to obey federal court orders resting on this Court's considered interpretation of the United States Constitution. Specifically it involves actions by the Governor and Legislature of Arkansas upon the premise that they are not bound by our holding in Brown v. Board of Education, 347 U.S. 483. That holding was that the Fourteenth Amendment forbids States to use their governmental powers to bar children on racial grounds from attending schools where there is state participation through any arrangement, management, funds or property. We are urged to uphold a suspension of the Little Rock School Board's plan to do away with segregated public schools in Little Rock until state laws and efforts to upset and nullify our holding in Brown v. Board of Education have been further challenged and tested in the courts. We reject these contentions. . . .

One may well sympathize with the position of the Board in the face of the frustrating conditions which have confronted it, but, regardless of the Board's good faith, the actions of the other state agencies responsible for those conditions compel us to reject the Board's legal position. Had Central High School been under the direct management of the State itself, it could hardly be suggested that those immediately in charge of the school should be heard to assert their own good faith as a legal excuse for delay in implementing the constitutional rights of these respondents, when vindication of those rights was rendered difficult or impossible by the actions of other state officials. The situation here is in no different posture because the members of the School Board and the Superintendent of Schools are local officials; from the point of view of the Fourteenth Amendment, they stand in this litigation as the agents of the State.

The constitutional rights of respondents are not to be sacrificed or yielded to the violence and disorder which have followed upon the actions of the Governor and Legislature. As this Court said some 41 years ago in a unanimous opinion in a case involving another aspect of racial segregation: "It is urged that this proposed segregation will promote the public peace by preventing race conflicts. Desirable as this is, and important as is the preservation of the public peace, this aim cannot be accomplished by laws or ordinances which deny rights created or protected by the Federal Constitution." Buchanan v. Warley, 245 U.S. 60, 81. Thus law and order are not here to be preserved by depriving the Negro children of their constitutional rights. The record before us clearly establishes that the growth of the Board's difficulties to a magnitude beyond its unaided power to control is the product of state action. Those difficulties, as counsel for the Board forthrightly conceded on the oral argument in this Court, can also be brought under control by state action.

The controlling legal principles are plain. The command of the Fourteenth Amendment is that no "State" shall deny to any person within its jurisdiction the equal protection of the laws. . . . In short, the constitutional rights of children not to be discriminated against in school admission on grounds of race or color declared by this Court in the Brown case can neither be nullified openly and directly by state legislators or state executive or judicial officers, nor nullified indirectly by them through evasive schemes for segregation whether attempted "ingeniously or ingenuously." Smith v. Texas, 311 U.S. 128, 132.

What has been said, in the light of the facts developed, is enough to dispose of the case. However, we should answer the premise of the actions of the Governor and Legislature that they are not bound by our holding in the Brown case. It is necessary only to recall some basic constitutional propositions which are settled doctrine.

Article VI of the Constitution makes the Constitution the "supreme Law of the Land." . . . the federal judiciary is supreme in the exposition of the law of the Constitution, and that principle has ever since been respected by this Court and the Country as a permanent and indispensable feature of our constitutional system. It follows that the interpretation of the Fourteenth Amendment enunciated by this Court in the Brown case is the supreme law of the land, and Art. VI of the Constitution makes it of binding effect on the States "any Thing in the Constitution or Laws of any State to the Contrary notwithstanding." Every state legislator and executive and judicial officer is solemnly committed by oath taken pursuant to Art. VI, ¶3 "to support this Constitution." Chief Justice Taney, speaking for a unanimous Court in 1859, said that this requirement reflected the framers' "anxiety to preserve it [the Constitution] in full force, in all its powers, and to guard against resistance to or evasion of its authority, on the part of a State. . . ." Ableman v. Booth, 21 How. 506, 524.

No state legislator executive or judicial officer can war against the Constitution without violating his undertaking to support it. Chief Justice Marshall spoke for a unanimous Court in saying that: "If the legislatures of the several states may, at will annul the judgments of the courts of the United States, and destroy the rights acquired under those judgments, the constitution itself becomes a solemn mockery . . ." United States v. Peters, 5 Cranch 115, 136. A Governor who asserts a power to nullify a federal court order is similarly restrained. If he had such power, said Chief Justice Hughes, in 1932, also for a unanimous Court, "it is manifest that the fiat of a state Governor, and not the Constitution of the United States, would be the supreme law of the land; that the restrictions of the Federal

Constitution upon the exercise of state power would be but impotent phrases . . ." Sterling v. Constantin, 287 U.S. 378, 397–398.

It is, of course, quite true that the responsibility for public education is primarily the concern of the States, but it is equally true that such responsibilities, like all other state activity, must be exercised consistently with federal constitutional requirements as they apply to state action. The Constitution created a government dedicated to equal justice under law. The Fourteenth Amendment embodied and emphasized that ideal. State support of segregated schools through any arrangement, management, funds, or property cannot be squared with the Amendment's command that no State shall deny to any person within its jurisdiction the equal protection of the laws. The right of a student not to be segregated on racial grounds in schools so maintained is indeed so fundamental and pervasive that it is embraced in the concept of due process of law. . . . The basic decision in Brown was unanimously reached by this Court only after the case had been briefed and twice argued and the issues had been given the most serious consideration. Since the first Brown opinion three new Justices have come to the Court. They are at one with the Justices still on the Court who participated in that basic decision as to its correctness, and that decision is now unanimously reaffirmed. The principles announced in that decision and the obedience of the States to them, according to the command of the Constitution, are indispensable for the protection of the freedoms guaranteed by our fundamental charter for all of us. Our constitutional ideal of equal justice under law is thus made a living truth.

22.6. SCHOOL SEGREGATION OUTSIDE THE SOUTH

The problems stemming from racial segregation in the public schools are national, rather than purely regional, in scope. In this excerpt, the Civil Rights Commission examines the incidence of racial discrimination in schools of the northern and western States.

ALTHOUGH ATTENTION has been focused on school segregation in the South, it would be both unrealistic and unfair not to note the presence of discrimination in Northern and Western school systems. . . .

The trend of Negro migration to the nation's largest metropolitan areas is bringing about new patterns of segregation of residential areas.

From U.S. Commission on Civil Rights, *Report, 1959* (Washington, D.C.: U.S. Government Printing Office, 1959), pp. 245–260.

Increasingly serious social and economic problems are accompanying these patterns. One result, of course, is *de facto* segregation of many schools.

The residential areas, and the one-race schools that result, arise without the force of any legal compulsion. These cities have no laws requiring segregated schools, no laws designating segregated housing along racial or ethnic lines. Neither are the school attendance zones necessarily gerrymandered to produce *de facto* segregation in schools.

Especially where language is a problem, minority groups often prefer to live among others having the same background, All-Puerto Rican, or all-Latin American communities have grown up without overt discrimination, but the citizens in these one-race communities have often found that discrimination in employment limits their income and thus their ability to choose suitable homes. If prosperity comes to them, they may find that social factors restrict them, as when the whites in a community refuse to accept a family of another race as their neighbors.

School officials in these one-race communities are faced with difficult problems they did not create. Chicago has had very severe difficulties of this kind. In 1958, 72 white students boycotted their assigned school because it was predominantly colored, and racial battles between white and Negro students have also occurred recently in that city. The Illinois House of Representatives recently passed a bill designed to avoid alleged racial segregation in the Chicago schools. The charges of segregation were denied, but a Chicago Representative, when queried, said Negro schools were on crowded double-shift classes, while neighboring districts contained schools with empty classrooms.

Reports to this Commission from its State Advisory Committee of Minnesota indicate that this type of *de facto* segregation exists within that State. Although the public education system had no inherent or deliberate discriminatory practices in any of its school districts, discriminatory attitudes existed and there were pockets of all-Negro enrollment. The Committee concluded that discrimination by residential pattern, occupational role, and community attitude created serious problems, which, however, could be helped by sustained emphasis on better human relations. Other state committees have reported similarly.

New York City has been particularly concerned with this problem of *de facto* segregation ever since the Supreme Court's decision. In December, 1954, the city's Board of Education passed a resolution appointing a Commission on Integration to examine the matter. The Commission submitted its report in June of 1958, stating at the outset that the existing residential segregation created inequality on the following basis:

Increasingly, the schools in the colored neighborhoods of Greater New York, have tended to be older, less well equipped and more crowded than the schools in the white neighborhoods; the quality of teaching provided in these predominantly colored schools has also suffered.

The problem in New York City was considered one of "integration" as opposed to "desegregation." Under law, segregation was illegal. But in order to alleviate the situation arising from *de facto* residential segregation, some method of integration was sought. The Commission recommended that this might be achieved: (1) through substantial re-zoning, to be undertaken by a new bureau with the specific objective of integration; (2) through "strategic building in the fringe areas" to "anticipate and in some degree . . . prevent the growth of future school and residential segregation"; and (3) through reassignment of school personnel "to reduce and eventually overcome the present *de facto* discrimination against minority groups."

These recommendations were unanimously approved by the Board of Education. A central zoning unit has been set up to work out long-range zoning patterns. But implementation of the program will not be an overnight job, and there still is doubt on the part of some that full implementation will ever be accomplished. . . .

22.7. A COMPREHENSIVE PROGRAM TO ELIMINATE SEGREGATION

Segregation by race in schools and colleges, restaurants, buses, hotels, and other public facilities has long been a feature of American life in many parts of the Union. Discrimination against minority groups has been widely practiced in respect to voting registration, employment, and housing. Segregation and discrimination have been maintained by legislation and judicial decisions, and by informal pressures of public opinion fortified by long-standing custom. In recent years the entire pattern has come under heavy attack. By 1963 the demand for racial integration and equal rights for all people regardless of race had reached a point where it was termed a "Negro Revolt." In June President Kennedy proposed that Congress enact a "Civil Rights Act of 1963." Three months later the United States Commission on Civil Rights unanimously recommended a number of steps to reduce or alleviate many aspects of racial discrimination.

I AM PROPOSING that the Congress stay in session this year until it has enacted—preferably as a single omnibus bill—the most responsible,

From the President's Message to Congress on Civil Rights, as reported in *The Wall Street Journal,* June 20, 1963, and from the Third Biennial Report of the United States Commission on Civil Rights (Washington, D.C.: U.S. Government Printing Office, 1963) as reported in *The New York Times,* October 1, 1963.

reasonable and urgently needed solutions to this problem, solutions which should be acceptable to all fair-minded men. This bill would be known as the "Civil Rights Act of 1963." . . .

EQUAL ACCOMMODATIONS IN PUBLIC FACILITIES

Events of recent weeks have again underlined how deeply our Negro citizens resent the injustice of being arbitrarily denied equal access to those facilities and accommodations which are otherwise open to the general public. That is a daily insult which has no place in a country proud of its heritage—the heritage of the melting-pot, of equal rights, of one nation and one people. No one has been barred on account of his race from fighting or dying for America—there are no "white" or "colored" signs on the foxholes or graveyards of battle. Surely, in 1963, 100 years after Emancipation, it should not be necessary for any American citizen to demonstrate in the streets for the opportunity to stop at a hotel, or to eat at a lunch counter in the very department store in which he is shopping, or to enter a motion picture house, on the same terms as any other customer.

. . . It is clear that further Federal action is needed now to secure the right of all citizens to the full enjoyment of all facilities which are open to the general public.

Such legislation is clearly consistent with the Constitution and with our concepts of both human rights and property rights. The argument that such measures constitute an unconstitutional interference with property rights has consistently been rejected by the courts in upholding laws on zoning, collective bargaining, minimum wages, smoke control and countless other measures designed to make certain that the use of private property is consistent with the public interest.

Laws Already Enacted

Some 30 states, the District of Columbia and numerous cities—covering some two-thirds of this country and well over two-thirds of its people—have already enacted laws of varying effectiveness against discrimination in places of public accommodation, many of them in response to the recommendation of President Truman's Committee on Civil Rights in 1947. . . . the failure of more states to take effective action makes it clear that Federal legislation is necessary.

Clearly the Federal Government has both the power and the obligation to eliminate these discriminatory practices: first, because they adversely affect the national economy and the flow of interstate commerce; and secondly, because Congress has been specifically empowered under the Fourteenth Amendment to enact legislation making certain that no state law permits or sanctions the unequal protection or treatment of any of its citizens.

For these reason, I am today proposing, as part of the Civil Rights Act of 1963, a provision to guarantee all citizens equal access to the services and facilities of hotels, restaurants, places of amusement and retail establishments.

SUMMARY OF RECOMMENDATIONS OF THE UNITED STATES COMMISSION ON CIVIL RIGHTS

Voting

1. Limit state voter disqualifications to age, length of residence, legal confinement, judicially determined mental disability, conviction of a felony, and failure to complete six grades of formal education or its equivalent.

2. Authorize the President to order investigation into any political subdivision where 10 or more persons file sworn affidavits alleging discrimination in registration. If investigation warrants action, the President would be authorized to appoint a then-existing Federal official in that state to act as a temporary registrar.

3. In event the first two recommendations proved ineffective, Congress would be expected to enforce Section 2 of the 14th Amendment by reducing representation in the United States House proportionately by number of qualified citizens not allowed to vote.

Education

1. Require every school board maintaining schools to which pupils were assigned on basis of race to adopt a desegregation plan within 90 days. If the board failed to do so, the Attorney General would be authorized to institute legal action.

2. Authorize Civil Rights Commission to provide technical and financial assistance to school districts seeking help on problems resulting from school segregation or desegregation.

3. Suggest that the President call a White House conference of experts to discuss how the Federal Government can assist in solving the problem of giving all children an equal opportunity in education.

4. Amend the Urban Renewal Law so that it not impede local efforts aimed at eliminating or reducing racial imbalance in schools in or near the renewal area.

Employment

1. Establish a right to equal opportunity in employment that is assisted by Federal Government or which affects interstate commerce,

with authority to institute action vested in administrator in Department of Labor.

2. Require that Federally assisted vocational programs be non-segregated.

3. Enforce nondiscrimination in selection and referral of trainees for training classes.

4. Establish vocational programs for persons who lack educational prerequisites needed to qualify for technician and other courses, and provide manpower funds to permit training in functional literacy and basic work skills.

5. Permit the Federal Government to make arrangements for manpower, literacy and work skill training with education agencies other than state vocational agencies which cannot provide such training on a nonsegregated basis.

6. Direct that affirmative steps be taken to ensure that employment directly or indirectly generated by Federal loan, grant or aid programs be open to qualified persons regardless of race, creed, color, or national origin.

Housing

No recommendations.

Justice

1. Empower the Attorney General to intervene in or initiate civil proceedings to prevent denials to persons of any rights, privileges or immunities guaranteed by law or the Constitution.

2. Enact a program of grants-in-aid to help states and local governments, upon their request, to increase the professional and quality of their police forces.

3. Make local governmental units employing officers who deprive persons of their rights jointly liable with the officers.

4. Permit removal by a defendant of a state civil action or criminal prosecution to a district Federal court in cases where the defendant cannot, in state court, secure civil rights because of state laws or acts of individuals administering the laws.

Health Facilities and Services

1. Refuse approval of applications for grants under the separate-but-equal provision of the Hospital Survey and Construction Act of 1946.

2. Refuse approval of applications for Federal funds under the Hospital Survey and Construction Act of 1946 when plans call for duplicate facilities to be used on a racially segregated basis.

3. Assure that grant recipients comply with the nondiscrimination requirements of the Hospital Survey and Construction Act of 1946.

Urban Areas

1. That the President encourage resolution of civil rights problems at local level, possibly through the form of Presidential awards of merit given annually to persons and organizations.

Armed Forces

1. That the President direct that corrective action be undertaken by the Navy to assure equality of opportunity for Negroes to serve as officers and enlisted men and to broaden their occupational assignments and promotional opportunities.

2. That the President direct the Secretary of Defense to reappraise testing procedures used in procurement of enlisted and officer personnel.

3. That the President request the Secretary of Defense to undertake periodic reviews of recruitment, selection, assignment and promotion policies and develop programs to utilize fully both Negro and white manpower resources.

4. That the President request the Secretary of Defense to discontinue R.O.T.C. programs at any college or university which does not accept all students without regard to race or color.

5. That the Department of Defense seek to remove all vestiges of racial discrimination from military installations and insure that in dealings with local communities the policy of the armed forces of equality of treatment prevails.

6. That the granting of funds for construction and operation of schools under the impacted area program be conditioned upon assurances that all children in the district be assigned without regard to race.

23

Federalism: Theory and Practice

23.1. WHO DECIDES WHAT IS "NECESSARY AND PROPER"?

In McCulloch *v.* Maryland *in 1819, the Supreme Court upheld the power of the Federal Government to establish the Bank of the United States and in so doing first enunciated the doctrine of implied powers. President Jackson's veto in 1832 of the bill to continue the Bank asserts the right of the President and Congress to decide, independently of the Court, whether particular actions of the national government are necessary and proper.*

TO THE SENATE: The bill "to modify and continue" the act entitled "An act to incorporate the subscribers to the Bank of the United States" was presented to me on the 4th July instant. Having considered it with that solemn regard to the principles of the Constitution which the day was calculated to inspire, and come to the conclusion that it ought not to become a law, I herewith return it to the Senate, in which it originated, with my objections.

A bank of the United States is in many respects convenient for the Government and useful to the people. Entertaining this opinion, and deeply impressed with the belief that some of the powers and privileges possessed by the existing bank are unauthorized by the Constitution, subversive of the rights of the States, and dangerous to the liberties of the people, I felt it my duty at an early period of my Administration to call the attention of Congress to the practicability of organizing an institution

From President Andrew Jackson's "Veto Message of 1832 Bill to Continue the Bank of the United States," July 10, 1832.

combining all its advantages and obviating these objections. I sincerely regret that in the act before me I can perceive none of those modifications of the bank charter which are necessary, in my opinion, to make it compatible with justice, with sound policy, or with the Constitution of our country.

The present corporate body, denominated the president, directors, and company of the Bank of the United States, will have existed at the time this act is intended to take effect twenty years. It enjoys an exclusive privilege of banking under the authority of the General Government, a monopoly of its favor and support, and, as a necessary consequence, almost a monopoly of the foreign and domestic exchange. The powers, privileges, and favors bestowed upon it in the original charter, by increasing the value of the stock far above its par value, operated as a gratuity of many millions to the stockholders. . . .

It is maintained by the advocates of the bank that its constitutionality in all its features ought to be considered as settled by precedent and by the decision of the Supreme Court. To this conclusion I can not assent. Mere precedent is a dangerous source of authority, and should not be regarded as deciding questions of constitutional power except where the acquiescence of the people and the States can be considered as well settled. . . .

If the opinion of the Supreme Court covered the whole ground of this act, it ought not to control the coordinate authorities of this Government. The Congress, the Executive, and the Court must each for itself be guided by its own opinion of the Constitution. Each public officer who takes an oath to support the Constitution swears that he will support it as he understands it, and not as it is understood by others. It is as much the duty of the House of Representatives, of the Senate, and of the President to decide upon the constitutionality of any bill or resolution which may be presented to them for passage or approval as it is of the supreme judges when it may be brought before them for judicial decision. The opinion of the judges has no more authority over Congress than the opinion of Congress has over the judges, and on that point the President is independent of both. The authority of the Supreme Court must not, therefore, be permitted to control the Congress or the Executive when acting in their legislative capacities, but to have only such influence as the force of their reasoning may deserve.

But in the case relied upon the Supreme Court have not decided that all the features of this corporation are compatible with the Constitution. It is true that the court have said that the law incorporating the bank is a constitutional exercise of power by Congress; but taking into view the whole opinion of the court and the reasoning by which they have come to that conclusion, I understand them to have decided that inasmuch as a bank is an appropriate means for carrying into effect the enumerated powers of the General Government, therefore the law incorporating it is in accordance with that provision of the Constitution which declares that Congress shall have power "to make all laws which shall be necessary and proper for carrying those powers into execution." Having satisfied themselves that the word *"necessary"* in the Constitution means *"needful," "requisite," "essential," "conducive to,"* and that "a bank" is a convenient, a useful, and essential instrument in the prosecution of the Government's "fiscal operations," they conclude that to "use one must be within the discretion of Congress" and that "the act to incorporate the Bank of the United States is a law made in pursuance of the Constitution;" "but," they say, *"where the law is not prohibited and is really calculated to effect any of the objects intrusted to the Government, to undertake here to inquire into the degree of its necessity would be to pass the line which circumscribes the judicial department and to tread on legislative ground."*

The principle here affirmed is that the "degree of its necessity," involving all the details of a banking institution, is a question exclusively for legislative consideration. A bank is constitutional, but it is the province of the Legislature to determine whether this or that particular power, privilege, or exemption is "necessary and proper" to enable the bank to discharge its duties to the Government, and from their decision there is no appeal to the courts of justice. Under the decision of the Supreme Court, therefore, it is the exclusive province of Congress and the President to decide whether the particular features of this act are *necessary* and *proper* in order to enable the bank to perform conveniently and efficiently the public duties assigned to it as a fiscal agent, and therefore constitutional, or *unnecessary* and *improper,* and therefore unconstitutional. . . .

23.2. POPULAR SOVEREIGNTY AND STATES' RIGHTS

A basic component of our governmental system is the concept of popular sovereignty. We believe that all governmental powers are derived from the people. Jefferson Davis maintains in this selection that the term "people" means "people of respective states," not people of the United States as a whole. This would make the States the final arbiters of the Federal system.

LOOKING BACK for a moment at the ground over which we have gone, I

From Jefferson Davis, *Rise and Fall of the Confederacy* (1881), Vol. I, pp. 157–158.

think it may be fairly asserted that the following propositions have been clearly and fully established:

1. That the States of which the American Union was formed, from the moment when they emerged from their colonial or provincial condition, became severally sovereign, free, and independent States—not one State, or nation.

2. That the union formed under the Articles of Confederation was a compact between the States, in which these attributes of "sovereignty, freedom, and independence," were expressly asserted and guaranteed.

3. That, in forming the "more perfect union" of the Constitution, afterward adopted, the same contracting powers formed an *amended compact,* without any surrender of these attributes of sovereignty, freedom, and independence, either expressed or implied: on the contrary, that, by the tenth amendment to the Constitution, limiting the power of the Government to its express grants, they distinctly guarded against the presumption of a surrender of anything by implication.

4. That political sovereignty resides, neither in individual citizens, nor in unorganized masses, nor in fractional subdivisions of a community, but in the people of an organized political body.

5. That no "republican form of government," in the sense in which that expression is used in the Constitution, and was generally understood by the founders of the Union—whether it be the government of a State or of a confederation of States—is possessed of any sovereignty whatever, but merely exercises certain powers delegated by the sovereign authority of the people, and subject to recall and reassumption by the same authority that conferred them.

6. That the "people" who organized the first confederation, the people who dissolved it, the people who ordained and established the Constitution which succeeded it, the only people, in fine, known or referred to in the phraseology of that period—whether the term was used collectively or distributively—were the people of the respective States, each acting separately and with absolute independence of the others.

7. That, in forming and adopting the Constitution, the States, or the people of the States—terms which, when used with reference to acts performed in a sovereign capacity, are precisely equivalent to each other—formed a new *Government,* but no new *people;* and that, consequently, no new sovereignty was created—for sovereignty in an American republic can belong only to a people, never to a government—and that the Federal Government is entitled to exercise only the powers delegated to it by the people of the respective States.

8. That the term "people," in the preamble to the Constitution and in the tenth amendment, is used distributively; that the only "people of the United States" known to the Constitution are the people of each State in the Union; that no such political community or corporate unit as

one people of the United States then existed, has ever been organized, or yet exists; and that no political action by the people of the United States in the aggregate has ever taken place, or ever can take place, under the Constitution.

The fictitious idea of *one* people of the United States, contradicted in the last paragraph, has been so impressed upon the popular minds by false teaching, by careless and vicious phraseology, and by the ever-present spectacle of a great Government, with its army and navy, its custom-houses and post-offices, its multitude of office-holders, and the splendid prizes which it offers to political ambition, that the tearing away of these illusions and presentation of the original fabric, which they have overgrown and hidden from view, have no doubt been unwelcome, distasteful, and even repellent to some of my readers. The artificial splendor which makes the deception attractive is even employed as an argument to prove its reality.

23.3. A COMMENTARY ON DIVIDED POWER

The division of power between the Federal Government and the States has never been precisely determined. During the era of dual federalism from the middle of the nineteenth century until the late 1930s, the Supreme Court contended that each level was supreme in its own limited sphere and that neither could use its power to encroach upon the domain of the other. The following excerpt from Justice Waite in 1876 offers a typical expression of that view.

JUSTICE WAITE delivered the opinion of the Court. . . .

We have in our political system a Government of the United States and a government of each of the several states. Each one of these governments is distinct from the others, and each has citizens of its own who owe it allegiance, and whose rights, within its jurisdiction, it must protect. The same person may be at the same time a citizen of the United States and a citizen of a state,—but his rights of citizenship under one of these governments will be different from those he has under the other.

Citizens are the members of the political community to which they belong. They are the people who compose the community, and who, in their associated capacity, have established or submitted themselves to the dominion of a government for the protection of their individual as well as their collective rights. In the formation of a government, the people may confer upon it such powers as they choose. The government when so formed, may, and when called upon should, exercise all the powers it has

From *United States* v. *Cruikshank,* 92 U.S. 542 (1876).

for the protection of the rights of its citizens and the people within its jurisdiction; but it can exercise no other. The duty of a government to afford protection is limited always by the power it possesses for that purpose.

Experience made the fact known to the people of the United States, that they required a national government for national purposes. The separate governments of the separate states, bound together by the Articles of Confederation alone, were not sufficient for the promotion of the general welfare of the people in respect to foreign nations, or for their complete protection as citizens of the confederated states. For this reason, the people of the United States . . . ordained and established the Government of the United States, and defined its powers by a Constitution, which they adopted as its fundamental law, and made its rule of action.

The government thus established and defined is to some extent a government of the states in their political capacity. It is, also, for certain purposes, a government of the people. Its powers are limited in number, but not in degree. Within the scope of its powers, as enumerated and defined, it is supreme and above the states; but beyond, it has no existence. It was erected for special purposes and endowed with all the powers necessary for its own preservation and the accomplishment of the ends its people had in view. It can neither grant nor secure to its citizens any right or privilege not expressly or by implication placed under its jurisdiction.

The people of the United States resident within any State are subject to two governments: one State and the other National; but there need be no conflict between the two. The powers which one possesses, the other does not. They are established for different purposes, and have separate jurisdictions. Together they make one whole, and furnish the people of the United States with a complete government, ample for the protection of all their rights at home and abroad. True, it may sometimes happen that a person is amenable to both jurisdictions for one and the same act. Thus, if a Marshal of the United States is unlawfully resisted while executing the process of the courts within a state, and the resistance is accompanied by an assault on the officer, the sovereignty of the United States is violated by the resistance, and that of the State by the breach of the peace, in the assault. So too, if one passes counterfeited coin of the United States within a state, it may be an offense against the United States and the State: the United States because it discredits the coin; and the State, because of the fraud upon him to whom it is passed. This does not, however, necessarily imply that the two governments possess powers in common, or bring them into conflict with each other. It is the natural consequences of a citizenship which owes allegiance to two sovereignties, and claims protection from both. The citizen cannot complain, because he has voluntarily submitted himself to such a form of government. He owes allegiance to the two departments, so to speak, and within their respective spheres must pay the penalties which each exacts for disobedience of its laws. In return, he can demand protection from each within its own jurisdiction.

The Government of the United States is one of delegated powers alone. Its authority is defined and limited by the Constitution. All powers not granted to it by that instrument are reserved to the States or to the people.

23.4. THE MEANING OF FEDERALISM TODAY

In practice the division of powers between the Federal Government and the States gives substantial authority to each level of government and allows the relationship between these levels to change in accord with the needs of the times. The Report of the Commission on Intergovernmental Relations traces the changing contours of the Federal system and examines current limits on Federal and State power.

THE PROPER DIVISION of labor and authority between the Nation and the States is the key to maintaining the federal nature of our system of government. The lines of division are not static. They have been controversial from the beginning of our life as an independent country. They remain so today.

The American federal system began as an experiment. It was the third try for a solution on this continent to the age-old problem of striking a satisfactory balance between the needs for central strength and central regulation on the one hand and the values of local freedom of action on the other. The framers of our Constitution had joined in a revolution that cut them loose from the old British imperial system, because that system imposed unwelcome controls from a remote center. They had also lived under the "league of friendship" established by the Articles of Confederation. They met under the reluctant auspices of the Congress of that Confederation, to seek "a more perfect union," and began their work by discarding the Articles.

The federal system devised by the framers of the Constitution was the product of necessity rather than doctrine. There was no dictionary definition of federal government to apply nor any working model to copy. They found the classical examples from Greece and the medieval unions of European cities too remote in time and circumstance to be suitable. Their experience under the Articles of Confederation had taught them what to

From the Commission on Intergovernmental Relations, *A Report to the President,* 1955, pp. 9–12, 28–33.

strive for and what to avoid. They were content to keep the States substantially as they knew them, but they deplored certain economic and fiscal tendencies in some States. Chiefly, they felt a very practical need for a central government of much greater strength and potentialities than the Articles provided.

MIDDLE COURSE CHOSEN

Characteristically, they took a middle course to meet that need —in retrospect probably the only course that was both "adequate to the exigencies of government and the preservation of the union" and capable of winning majority support. They rejected summarily the advice of those few, like Hamilton, who sought to build a unitary authority, to abolish the States as autonomous units, and to provide for the appointment of governors from the National Capital. They also overruled decisively the considerably greater number who wanted to keep the union a mere confederation, with a few strengthening amendments to the Articles. Instead, they adopted in substance the Virginia Plan.

The Virginia Plan left the States unchanged so far as their domestic institutions were concerned, though the new Constitution expressly forbade some practices the framers thought would be undesirable —State taxes on exports and imports, the issuance of State currency, the impairment of contract obligations, separate agreements with foreign nations or with each other unless with National consent, and other matters now mainly of historical interest. But the Virginia Plan envisaged and the Constitution erected a new National Government, deriving its powers also from the people, capable of dealing with the people directly rather than exclusively through the State governments, and fitted out with a full complement of executive, legislative, and judicial institutions, with powers delegated by the terms of the Constitution. By implication the States were excluded from regulating interstate and foreign commerce and other subjects thus committed to National control. The framers spelled out a list of enumerated powers, including the "necessary and proper" clause, in order to give the National Government what the Virginia Plan had broadly described as:

power to legislate in all cases to which the separate States are incompetent or in which the harmony of the United States may be interrupted by the exercise of individual legislation.

In a secondary series of decisions the framers modified the Virginia Plan somewhat to compromise, in the composition of the two Houses of Congress, the rival claims of the large States and the small. They also hit upon a device, the electoral college, for extending that compromise while notably increasing the strength and independence of the executive. By means of the "supreme law of the land" clause they introduced a National judicial control over unconstitutional State action. But in leaving the States to define the voting franchise, to conduct National elections along with their own, to choose Senators, and to pass on constitutional amendments, they guaranteed the indispensability of the States to the National Government. And in leaving to the States all powers not delegated to the National Government or otherwise prohibited to them, the Constitution recognized their vital role in the domestic affairs of government.

. . . The federal system they devised was one of the great innovations in the art of representative government. In building a nation out of diverse elements, the urgent need in the formative stages is to create a viable measure of union where unity is impossible. The dangers of overcentralization may be foreseen and feared, but they do not materialize until later stages of national development. It was the invaluable merit of the proposed federal system that it promised a means of reconciling the need and the fear.

This system has characteristically been very flexible, leaving a great deal of room for argument and adjustment. The division of powers between the Nation and the States leaves substantial authority with each, but the use and relative importance of powers may shift. The Constitution cannot be formally amended by either level of government without the participation of the other, but interpretation and usage may expand or contract the powers at either level. The National Government deals with the people directly, but it may also utilize the States to reach them indirectly. The States can write and change their own constitutions, but they must meet minimum requirements of the National Constitution. The States are equal in legal status, but not in size, wealth, and influence. In all these essentials the federal relationship is adjustable, within limits. It is affected by controversies over what any government in the system should do, as well as by concepts of what no government should do. Historically, the invocation of States rights has sometimes been as much a sign of opposition to a specific National policy as of attachment to local action as such.

THE HANDIWORK OF MILLIONS

As we know it today, the federal system is no longer solely the work of the original framers, or indeed the result of any single act or authority. It is rather the product of thousands of decisions in which millions of people have taken part over the years, facing and resolving concrete problems as they deemed best at the time. Each participant, according to his lights and his influence, has been a latter-day framer of the Constitution.

The initial success of our federal system brought high prestige to the work of the original framers, and the flattery of imitation elsewhere in the world. Yet of necessity many questions of principle and detail either could not be foreseen or were deliberately left unanswered by the framers. Even in the country of its origin, our federal system may still be regarded as an experiment, although we have the oldest representative republic in the world.

Age and success develop a tendency toward conservatism. In a time of relative peace and prosperity, readjustments in intergovernmental relations are likely to be modest in scope and moderate in tempo. This Commission is especially concerned with the marginal area of policy where changes in direction are practicable. For perspective in reappraisal, it is instructive to look first to the past to identify the dynamic forces that have shaped our constitutional development, to recognize settled doctrine, and to discern emerging trends. . . .

Two related premises regarding the federal system underlay the judicial interpretation of National and State power for a full half century after 1880. One was that workably clear and distinct boundaries between their respective realms of activity could be drawn in terms of constitutional powers. The other was that the Supreme Court was the final arbiter of the system. Experience showed both assumptions to be illusory. So many judicial precedents of contrary tendency accumulated that the boundary lines became unpredictable and, indeed, a zone of governmental no man's land sometimes appeared to lie between them. On the major issues of National and State power, the Supreme Court during the early 1900s often had a free choice in decision. Having such a choice, the Court was exposed again, as it had been on some earlier notable occasions, to a crossfire of political criticism. The clash culminated in 1937 when the Court began a series of sweeping reversals or modifications of former decisions.

Since 1937, judicial doctrine has recognized the emergence of a new concept of National-State relations, sometimes labelled "cooperative federalism" in contrast with the separatism of the previous era. The concept rests constitutionally on a broad view of National authority, on the abandonment of the due process clause as a source of substantive restraints on State regulation of economic affairs, and on the Court's refusal to entertain taxpayers' suits challenging exercises of the spending power. Coming full circle after 125 years by the route of implied powers, the Supreme Court now gives to the list of powers delegated to Congress in Article I, Section 8, of the Constitution approximately the same broad sweep of meaning conveyed by the Virginia Plan. . . . At the same time, the Court has generally refused to invoke the prerogative of review over economic policy that it exercised for 40 years prior to 1937. State and

National laws touching economic affairs are no longer held to be deprivations of due process because they conflict with natural rights of property or
liberty of contract. The Court has accepted a reading of the general welfare clause that places no discernible judicial limits on the amounts or
purposes of Federal spending, although it does not follow that the power
to spend carries with it unlimited power to regulate. The potentialities of
the spending power were only dimly apprehended before the income tax
and the Federal Reserve System opened up new reservoirs of Federal
revenues and credit. Grants-in-aid are only one characteristic use of the
power, along with many other direct spending and lending programs.
Finally, the Court has directed the lower Federal courts to follow State law
in handling litigation based on diversity of citizenship, so as to minimize
conflicts in the applicable rules of decision.

THE SITUATION TODAY

Under judicial doctrine since 1937 the Supreme Court has largely
removed itself as a practical factor in determining the economic policies
of the States and the Nation. It has not, however, eliminated the historic
role of judicial review in our federal system. Two remaining functions
are noteworthy here, apart from its task of promoting uniformity of interpretation and filling in the gaps in Federal law. One is the duty of
judging when the States have overstepped and encroached on whatever
area should be the exclusive domain of Federal regulation, if any, or have
actually legislated in conflict with Federal law. The exercise of this
function is as old as the Court itself and as recent as the 1955 decision
that only the Interstate Commerce Commission, and not a State, can
revoke the license of an interstate trucking concern to use the highways.

The other function is very recent in its present-day significance,
dating only from 1925, though its roots go back to the Fourteenth Amendment. This is the guardianship of civil liberties. In the face of its withdrawal from supervision over economic policies, the Court during the
past 30 years has become noticeably more stern in construing State responsibilities under the Fourteenth Amendment to protect civil and
political rights. Beginning in 1925, earlier doctrine has in effect been
reversed, and the guarantees of freedom of speech, press, and religion, as
well as some (but not all) of the procedural safeguards in criminal cases
written in the Bill of Rights against the National Government, have been
read also into the due process clause of the Fourteenth Amendment against
the States. More recently, racial discriminations have been brought further
under the ban of the equal protection clause of the same amendment. In
this whole area, in contrast to the field of economic affairs, the Congress
has moved slowly, and the Supreme Court has become the principal instrument of Federal surveillance. There is a surface paradox in this extension

of National judicial power at the very time the Court is emphasizing its deference to State legislative policy. But the paradox disappears in a view of the purposes of our federal system which puts the strengthening and preservation of basic personal freedoms among the first objects of the Union.

What then, is the present position of constitutional doctrine as it bears on National-State relations? Reviewing current Supreme Court interpretations in the light of their historical development, the following generalizations appear to be warranted:

First, the constitutional restrictions now applicable to any government in the United States are chiefly procedural, are quite similar in their admonitions to the Nation and to the States, and consequently under the philosophy of these decisions exert no major thrust on the working division of labor and authoriy between them one way or the other.

These restrictions are found chiefly in the Bill of Rights and the Fourteenth Amendment. They put important limits on the permissible ways of using the coercive powers of government, and on some policies related to the provision of certain services and to the conduct of elections. In the main they have been left to the judiciary to enforce. In the sense that they subject State policies and procedures to a National judicial review, they are a significant feature of our federal system. Court enforcement of them may cut across time-honored policies and deeply felt beliefs. But they do not have the effect of transferring activities from one governmental level to another. Nor do they prevent either level from pursuing substantive programs of any kind likely to be adopted in this country. The federal blance might be different if there were major disparities in the procedural restraints applied at one level in contrast with the other; or if the Congress showed any disposition to make full use of powers conferred on it by the Fourteenth Amendment.

Second, the prohibitions on the States, express and implied, that keep them from actions deemed to encroach on powers delegated to the National Government have only a minimal effect on the capacity of the States to discharge their functions.

These prohibitions set the lower limits of the zone of National responsibility for governmental action. So far as they have a nationalizing tendency, it comes chiefly from the judiciary in the form of Court review of State action. In general, these limitations keep the States out of interstate commerce, admiralty, bankruptcy, and currency matters, and prevent them from imposing burdens on Federal instrumentalities. It does not follow that these prohibitions on the States automatically or necessarily compel the Congress to act in these fields; this depends on the will of Congress. They do, of course, present some borderline problems that have nevertheless proved manageable. For one thing, the trend of recent judicial opinion outside the civil liberties field has on the whole been tolerant and accommodating to State policy: the States, for instance, can tax some interstate commerce, or set up quarantine inspections at their borders, or fix weight limits for trucks, or enforce highway traffic regulations, provided they do not discriminate against interstate commerce or burden it "unduly." Moreover, congressional waivers or administrative cessions of a National jurisdiction staked out by the Court can make flexible room for State action; this is the pattern made familiar by the Twenty-first (Repeal) Amendment. It is also illustrated in the Tidelands Act, and in the refusal of the National Labor Relations Board to hear some local cases. Even where action by the States is precluded by virtue of positive congressional action, as in some aspects of labor relations, the boundary adjustments are within congressional control. Broadly speaking, the working division of duties is not determined by rigid constitutional limits on the States.

Third, the range of activities that lie primarily within the power of the States by reason of the lack of any coercive authority in Congress to deal with them, is substantial. While the National Government has extensive authority to regulate, especially under its tax and interstate commerce powers, there is still a broad field of regulatory activity beyond its reach. The limits of the delegated and implied National powers fix the maximum range of National action. The existence of such constitutional bounds is probably more important than their exact location for the purpose of maintaining the federal nature of our governmental system. It is important that National powers be adequate to all truly national needs; it is also important that they do not jeopardize the proper functioning of the States. The former object is a matter of power and hence of constitutional law; the latter is primarily a matter of policy. It is improbable that judicial action would be needed to prevent the National military or taxing power, for example, from being used directly on the State governments to destroy or cripple them. The more likely danger is that the National Government will dissipate its energies and prestige, or discourage the States from developing their talents, by taking on matters that lie in the field of concurrent powers and that the States can handle acceptably.

Fourth, the possibility of a significant constitutional no man's land in our federal system has been disposed of by judicial reinterpretations. The early child labor cases, and the decisions invalidating the Municipal Bankruptcy Act and the Bituminous Coal Act during the depression, pointed for a time to subjects beyond the reach of any legislation. But apparently there are no longer any areas of economic policy barred to Congress for want of delegated power, on the one hand, and impractical or unconstitutional for the States to enter, on the other. The States are accorded more latitude now, and National powers are broadly available for all the great exigencies of government for which the Union was created. . . .

Fifth, it follows that the basic problems of maintaining our federal system today lie in those areas of National and State power where both Congress and the States have real choices to make, and where many alternative courses of action are open. It is in these areas that practical issues arise and tensions between interested groups and organizations are felt. Legislatures and administrative agencies within their assigned jurisdictions provide the appropriate forums for settling these issues.

Under our federal system, the division of responsibilities between the National Government and the States was once thought to be settled mainly in terms of power: either one level, or both, or neither, had the authority to move; and that was enough to settle their functions. Such a decision was usually one for the judiciary. Under current judicial doctrine, there are still limits on the coercive powers at both levels, but the National powers are broad and the possibilities by means of spending are still broader. The crucial questions now are questions of policy: Which level ought to move? Or should both? Or neither? What are the prudent and proper divisions of labor and responsibility between them? These are questions mainly for legislative judgment, and the criteria are chiefly political, economic, and administrative, rather than legal. The emphasis is on mutual and complementary undertakings in furtherance of common aims. . . .

SUMMARY

Our federal system is a unique phenomenon, without an earlier model and bearing only a general resemblance to later federal systems established elsewhere. It is the product of human purpose, partly of unconscious adaptation to the circumstances and the felt needs of our people. It has survived the vicissitudes of over a century and a half of our history to become now the oldest federal system. It has met the test of civil war. It has accommodated vast territorial expansion to the significant principle that the new States shall enjoy constitutional equality with the old. It has furnished a governmental environment compatible with unparalleled economic growth and social advances. It has shouldered an increased degree of responsibility for social security and welfare. It has enabled the mustering of resources for waging two world wars and developing atomic energy.

At the same time, it has preserved a degree of local autonomy unmatched among the world's other great powers. The States make their own constitutions, and the laws that govern elections, crimes, property, contracts, torts, domestic relations, and the like. Most States in their turn have tended in practice to establish a virtually federal division of powers and responsibilities between themselves, their counties, and municipalities. This autonomy has kept under local controls most of the schools, the police, the ordinary administration of criminal and civil justice, the local taxes, and the provision of most municipal services. It has kept in local hands also the machinery of elections and with it, in the main, the control of the party system. It has enabled local option to prevail on a wide range of domestic concerns. It has furnished local bases of power and refuge for political leaders, parties, and policies in opposition to those for the time being dominant in Washington. It has made possible a large degree of popular participation and consent. . . .

23.5. POLITICAL PARTIES AND THE FEDERAL SYSTEM

Contrary to expectations, political parties in the United States generally encourage decentralization of government because of their lack of uniform organization and discipline. Professor Grodzins reviews the attributes of our party system that contribute to the diffusion of political power.

MANY CAUSES contribute to dispersed power in the federal system. One is the simple historical fact that the states existed before the nation. A second is in the form of creed, the traditional opinion of Americans that expresses distrust of centralized power and places great value in the strength and vitality of local units of government. Another is pride in locality and state, nurtured by the nation's size and by variations of regional and state history. Still a fourth cause of decentralization is the sheer wealth of the nation. It allows all groups, including state and local governments, to partake of the central government's largesse, supplies room for experimentation and even waste, and makes unnecessary the tight organization of political power that must follow when the support of one program necessarily means the deprivation of another. . . .

The nation's politics reflect these decentralizing causes and adds some of their own. The political parties of the United States are unique. They seldom perform the function that parties traditionally perform in other countries, the function of gathering together diverse strands of power and welding them into one. Except during the period of nominating and electing a president and for the essential but non-substantive business of organizing the houses of Congress, the American parties rarely coalesce power at all. Characteristically they do the reverse, serving as a canopy under which special and local interests are represented with little regard for anything that can be called a party program. National leaders are

From Morton Grodzins, "The Federal System," in The Report of the President's Commission on National Goals, *Goals for Americans,* by The American Assembly, pp. 271–276. © 1960. By permission of Prentice-Hall, Inc., Englewood Cliffs, N.J.

elected on a party ticket, but in Congress they must seek cross-party support if their leadership is to be effective. It is a rare president during rare periods who can produce legislation without facing the defection of substantial numbers of his own party. (Wilson could do this in the first session of the sixty-third Congress; but Franklin D. Roosevelt could not, even during the famous hundred days of 1933.) Presidents whose parties form the majority of the congressional houses must still count heavily on support from the other party.

The parties provide the pivot on which the entire governmental system swings. Party operations, first of all, produce in legislation the basic division of functions between the federal government, on the one hand, and state and local governments, on the other. The Supreme Court's permissiveness with respect to the expansion of national powers has not in fact produced any considerable extension of exclusive federal functions. The body of federal law in all fields has remained, in the words of Henry M. Hart, Jr. and Herbert Wechsler, "interstitial in its nature," limited in objective and resting upon the principal body of legal relationships defined by state law. It is difficult to find any area of federal legislation that is not significantly affected by state law.

In areas of new or enlarged federal activity, legislation characteristically provides important roles for state and local governments. This is as true of Democratic as of Republican administrations and true even of functions for which arguments of efficiency would produce exclusive federal responsibility. Thus the unemployment compensation program of the New Deal and the airport program of President Truman's administration both provided important responsibilities for state governments. In both cases attempts to eliminate state participation were defeated by a cross-party coalition of pro-state votes and influence. A large fraction of the Senate is usually made up of ex-governors, and the membership of both houses is composed of men who know that their re-election depends less upon national leaders or national party organization than upon support from their home constituencies. State and local officials are key members of these constituencies, often central figures in selecting candidates and in turning out the vote. Under such circumstances, national legislation taking state and local views heavily into account is inevitable.

Second, the undisciplined parties affect the character of the federal system as a result of senatorial and congressional interference in federal administrative programs on behalf of local interests. Many aspects of the legislative involvement in administrative affairs are formalized. The Legislative Reorganization Act of 1946, to take only one example, provided that each of the standing committees "shall exercise continuous watchfulness" over administration of laws within its jurisdiction. But the formal system of controls, extensive as it is, does not compare in importance with the informal and extralegal network of relationships in producing continuous legislative involvement in administrative affairs.

Senators and congressmen spend a major fraction of their time representing problems of their constituents before administrative agencies. An even larger fraction of congressional staff time is devoted to the same task. The total magnitude of such "case work" operations is great. . . . In 1958, to take only one example, the Department of Agriculture estimated (and underestimated) that it received an average of 159 congressional letters per working day. Special congressional liaison staffs have been created to service this mass of business, though all higher officials meet it in one form or another. The Air Force in 1958 had, under the command of a major general, 137 people (55 officers and 82 civilians) working in its liaison office.

The widespread, consistent, and in many ways unpredictable character of legislative interference in administrative affairs has many consequences for the tone and character of American administrative behavior. . . . the important consequence is the comprehensive, day-to-day, even hour-by-hour, impact of local views on national programs. No point of substance or procedure is immune from congressional scrutiny. A substantial portion of the entire weight of this impact is on behalf of the state and local governments. It is a weight that can alter procedures for screening immigration applications, divert the course of a national highway, change the tone of an international negotiation, and amend a social security law to accommodate local practices or fulfill local desires.

The party system compels administrators to take a political role. This is a third way in which the parties function to decentralize the American system. The administrator must play politics for the same reason that the politician is able to play in administration: the parties are without program and without discipline.

In response to the unprotected position in which the party situation places him, the administrator is forced to seek support where he can find it. One ever-present task is to nurse the Congress of the United States, that crucial constituency which ultimately controls his agency's budget and program. From the administrator's view, a sympathetic consideration of congressional requests (if not downright submission to them) is the surest way to build the political support without which the administrative job could not continue. Even the completely task-oriented administrator must be sensitive to the need for congressional support and to the relationship between case work requests, on one side, and budgetary and legislative support, on the other. "You do a good job handling the personal problems and requests of a Congressman," a White House officer said, "and you have an easier time convincing him to back your program." Thus there is an important link between the nursing of congressional requests, requests that largely concern local matters, and the most comprehensive national programs. The administrator must accommodate to the former as a price of gaining support for the latter.

. . . The politics of administration is a process of making peace with legislators who for the most part consider themselves the guardians of local interests. The political role of administrators therefore contribute to the power of states and localities in national programs.

Finally, the way the party system operates gives American politics their over-all distinctive tone. The lack of party discipline produces an openness in the system that allows individuals, groups, and institutions (including state and local governments) to attempt to influence national policy at every step of the legislative-administrative process. This is the "multiple-crack" attribute of the American government. "Crack" has two meanings. It means not only many fissures or access points; it also means, less statically, opportunities for wallops or smacks at government.

If the parties were more disciplined, the result would not be a cessation of the process by which individuals and groups impinge themselves upon the central government. But the present state of the parties clearly allows for a far greater operation of the multiple crack than would be possible under the conditions of centralized party control. American interest groups exploit literally uncountable access points in the legislative-administrative process. If legislative lobbying, from committee stages to the conference committee, does not produce results, a cabinet secretary is called. His immediate associates are petitioned. Bureau chiefs and their aides are hit. Field officers are put under pressure. Campaigns are instituted by which friends of the agency apply a secondary influence on behalf of the interested party. A conference with the President may be urged.

. . . If a conference in a senator's office will expedite matters, someone on the local scene can be found to make such a conference possible and effective. If technical information is needed, technicians will supply it. State or national professional organizations of local officials, individual congressmen and senators, and not infrequently whole state delegations will make the local cause their own. Federal field officers, who service localities, often assume local views. So may elected and appointed state officers. Friendships are exploited, and political mortgages called due. Under these circumstances, national policies are molded by local action.

In summary, then, the party system functions to devolve power. The American parties, unlike any other, are highly responsive when directives move from the bottom to the top, highly unresponsive from top to bottom. Congressmen and senators can rarely ignore concerted demands from their home constituencies; but no party leader can expect the same kind of response from those below, whether he be a President asking for congressional support or a congressman seeking aid from local or state leaders.

Any tightening of the party apparatus would have the effect of strengthening the central government. The four characteristics of the system, discussed above, would become less important. If control from the top were strictly applied, these hallmarks of American decentralization might entirely disappear. To be specific, if disciplined and program-oriented parties were achieved: (1) It would make far less likely legislation that takes heavily into account the desires and prejudices of the highly decentralized power groups and institutions of the country, including the state and local governments. (2) It would to a large extent prevent legislators, individually and collectively, from intruding themselves on behalf of non-national interests in national administrative programs. (3) It would put an end to the administrator's search for his own political support, a search that often results in fostering state, local, and other non-national powers. (4) It would dampen the process by which individuals and groups, including state and local political leaders, take advantage of multiple cracks to steer national legislation and administration in ways congenial to them and the institutions they represent.

Alterations of this sort could only accompany basic changes in the organization and style of politics which, in turn, presuppose fundamental changes at the parties' social base. The sharing of functions is, in fact, the sharing of power. To end this sharing process would mean the destruction of whatever measure of decentralization exists in the United States today.

24

Federalism in Transition

24.1. DEBATE OVER FEDERAL-STATE RELATIONS

At the 1959 Governors' Conference, George C. S. Benson, President of Claremont Men's College, and Professor William G. Carleton of the University of Florida debated on the theme, "The States and the Nation." In this excerpt, Carleton points out why we may be closer to another great spurt in federal expansion than many of us realize, while Benson urges further decentralization of government.

WILLIAM G. CARLETON:
. . . The adoption of the Constitution in 1789 was the biggest step in our history in the direction of centralization. In opposing adopting of the Constitution such leaders as George Mason and Patrick Henry declared that the Constitution contained within itself the seeds of an indefinite federal expansion. They were, of course, correct.

Over a century later, Woodrow Wilson gave this same idea a little different slant when he observed that the American people, through judicial review, had made of their Constitution not a strait jacket but a vehicle of life.

Since 1789 all units of government in the United States have taken on more powers and functions. As society has grown more complex, so also have all units of government.

During the twentieth century the powers of the state govern-

From W. G. Carleton and George C. S. Benson, "The States and the Nation," *Proceedings of the Governors' Conference* (Chicago, Ill.: The Governors' Conference, 1959), pp. 104–120.

ment have grown. Some of these powers were taken from the counties, and some of them represent new powers never before exercised by any government in the United States. At the same time, the powers of the federal government have grown. Some of these powers were taken from the states, and some of them represent new powers never before exercised by any government in the United States. But the powers of the federal government have grown at a more rapid rate than those of the state. In short, while the powers of the states have grown absolutely, they have declined relatively.

Even if the federal government of today operated only in the areas it operated in during the time of George Washington's administration, such operation would represent a stupendous expansion of federal power because of the wide-ranging and ramifying undertakings required by foreign policy and national defense.

But the federal government today operates in many more areas than it did formerly. Today it is charged with nothing less than the smooth functioning of the American economy, keeping it on an even keel. Constitutional theory and practice now allow this, and the American people overwhelmingly demand it. . . .

However, the federal government is now moving into a new area. There is a shift in the centralization-decentralization controversy from the national *economy* to the national *society*. The federal government is now concerning itself more and more with roads, welfare, housing, slum clearance, urban renewal, rural community development, health, and education. Traditionally, where touched by government at all, these have been matters for the states and the localities. For the past several decades the federal government has increasingly been entering some of these fields either directly, or indirectly through grants-in-aid.

Now from all sides come demands for new and enlarged government services. . . .

These demands are coming out of conditions. What are some of these conditions? Increasing population. Continuing and accelerating shift of population to the cities. The phenomenal expansion of the private sector of the economy, and as the private sector of the economy expands, so also must the public sector of the economy—otherwise we face grave imbalances. The growing realization that goods and services produced by the public sector are not just luxuries, not just consumer goods, that they, too, are wealth, that they are productive wealth, that they are used to produce more and better goods and services. Better educated and trained citizens are better workers, managers, scientists, technicians, technologists. The sky-rocketing of medical, hospital, and education costs, making it more and more difficult for the individual to bear these costs. The feeling that we must keep ahead of the Soviet Union in national and individual well-being. The urgent feeling, too, that we must keep ahead of the Soviet

Union in industrial and military technology. Crisis is the health of centralization, and we are in a continuing crisis.

A new rationale is developing to justify a new spurt of federal expansion. Increasingly it is being said that our *society* is national, that it is more and more interrelated and interdependent, that our population is more mobile than ever before, that health and education in one state affect health and education in every other state and in the nation.

At the turn of the century it would have taken a bold man to assert that because our *economy* is national, therefore the government most concerned with that economy must be the national government and not the state. Today this is a commonplace. Now it is increasingly being said that because our American *society* is national, therefore the government most concerned with that society must be the national government and not the state. Today this is an advanced position, but tomorrow it may well be a commonplace.

Will the states do their part adequately to meet these growing national expectations? Leonard D. White of the University of Chicago, one of the most distinguished scholars in the field of public administration, was moderately optimistic that they will. . . . Professor White assumed that the federal government will relinquish some of its tax sources to the states and that the states will explore creatively new sources of revenue. Professor White further believed that the states will revitalize themselves by pursuing three avenues of action. First, that they will relinquish some of the federal grants-in-aid, that they themselves will assume independently some of the services now rendered jointly with the federal government. Second, that the states will make a much greater use of the interstate compact. And third, that the states will make a much fuller use of their own powers, that in their traditional services they will adapt to the great advances made in criminology, penology, mental health, and education; and that they will resume their old role as laboratories of experimentation and boldly assume new services such as adult education and training, government aid to superior students, government health insurance, even perhaps disability insurance. . . .

But I am afraid I must disagree, for I see little evidence that the states are doing any of these things.

Now, there is no doubt that some progress is being made in all the states. . . . But what is the record of most of the state legislators that have met during this past year? The record is largely that of economy, retrenchment, the slashing of budgets submitted by the executives. The truth is that most states are barely able to keep their old services abreast of increasing population and the shifts to the cities, and some states are failing in that.

Are the states relinquishing any of the federal grants-in-aid? Not at all. Not a single grant-in-aid has been relinquished. The states do not want to lose that federal revenue. The story of a federal grant-in-aid runs something like this: the grant-in-aid is used to get a necessary service started and to soften opposition to it in the state; then the service becomes a going concern, vested interests are created, the controversial becomes customary, and the opposition vanishes. . . .

Are the states making significantly greater use of the interstate compact? . . . The truth seems to be that the interstate compact works fairly well in the noncontroversial, that is, the less important, areas such as regional educational councils, the return of parolees, and so forth. But in the controversial areas, that is, the more important areas—such as electric power, water pollution, tapping water supplies, conservation of soil and other resources—they are much less successful. . . .

And finally, are the states making an adequately fuller use of their own powers? I think not, emphatically not. One reason for this, and the most important, is the matter of realistic group politics. The groups demanding expanded and new government services exist in all of the states. But there are more of them and they are better organized on the national level. There are fewer of these groups and they are less organized and less articulate in the states, particularly in the less industrial states. In spite of their intrinsic numerical strength, the groups demanding action would have a difficult time in the states, particularly in the less industrial states, in the face of the opposition of the older, better organized, and more prestigeful groups in those states. But they are fatally handicapped by certain structural and mechanical arrangements in the states. . . .

Malapportionment of our state legislatures is now an old and familiar story: how the rural areas are over-represented and the urban areas under-represented; how thirty or twenty-five or even twenty per cent or less of the population frequently controls a majority in the legislature; how one vote in a rural area may equal one hundred or two hundred or even three hundred votes in an urban area. . . .

And the implications of all this are even less known. Over-representative of the rural areas means not so much the rule of the rural folk as it does the rule of the rural politicians, who largely reflect the values and interests of the county rings, the large landowners, the small-scale and local-minded businessmen of the county-seat towns, and certain corporate businesses, themselves located in the cities, which would rather deal with a small oligarchy than a widely representative and democratic legislature.

Domination of legislatures by rural politicians becomes even more ominous in the one-party states, where these politicians are even more in-bred and often form a ruling clique unchecked by even a rival party clique. . . .

All of this results in decisive road blocks to positive action by the states. It results in road blocks to revision of horse-and-buggy constitutions, road blocks to genuine reapportionment, road blocks to exploring new sources of taxation, road blocks to adequate civil service and merit systems in the states, road blocks to the ability of the states to compete with the federal government and private enterprise for trained administrative personnel, road blocks to expanding the old state services, road blocks to the assumption of new state services. . . .

All of this adds up to "too little and too late." In the meantime, the federal government will step in with new and expanded services—directly, and indirectly with more grants-in-aid.

We may be much closer to another great spurt in federal expansion than many of us realize. Indeed, the present Congress would greatly expand federal activities, and it is held in check only by Mr. Veto in the White House. After January, 1961, a Mr. Veto may no longer be in the White House. . . .

GEORGE C. S. BENSON:

. . . Shall we first summarize the three main advantages of decentralized government?

First: Decentralization—or the federal system—avoids undue concentration of power in one bureaucracy or in one administration. De Tocqueville, a thoughtful French observer of America in the 1830s, considered that our dispersion of power was a potent factor in preventing despotism. I need hardly remind you that, forty years earlier, Madison and Hamilton in *The Federalist* had made the same point at the very beginning of our national existence. Nor need I remind you that the first Congress passed the first ten amendments, the Bill of Rights, to reassure those patriotic citizens who wanted an energetic central government but who feared a top-heavy system.

Today, in order to secure our defense and to insure our internal welfare, we are using approximately one-third of our total national income in governmental services. The question naturally arises as to whether *one* group, *one* policy-making organ, should have complete control both over our economic activities and over our ultimate goals. Thus far, safeguards to liberty have been reasonably adequate. The Supreme Court has been reasonably judicious. The Congress has been reasonably diversified. But there is always a danger—evidenced in other countries—that a central legislature and a central court may be swept by a "trend" of public opinion. If localism has had its dangers—and we all recall examples—it is also true that enlightened localism in the best sense has sometimes sounded a needed warning against national policies which disregarded local exigencies. It would be very hard to establish a dictatorship in the United States so long as there are fifty state Governors, with state police working for them, in fifty state capitols. . . .

The second great reason for maintaining decentralization of government is that decentralized government gives an opportunity to develop the citizenry of a democracy for political self-government. . . .

It certainly is true that adequate popular education, a well-established system of courts, economic freedom, separation of Church and State, and a long-time cultural appreciation of freedom are other environmental elements which help to sustain democratic institutions. But I suspect that decentralization of government is as important as any of these. . . .

Decentralization is important for development of the citizenry simply because the individual citizen can be a more important person in a smaller unit. The City Manager of Claremont listens respectfully to my opinion; the Governor of California nods to me; but the President of the United States never heard of me, and the last time I was in the White House there was no recognition that I had been there before. Yet I have worked much longer and harder for the President than for the other gentlemen. The reason is simply that an unimportant individual becomes more important in smaller units. If we want our people to be self-respecting, to have some sense of doing things themselves, should we not try to keep some aspects of important policy-making in their local and state governments? . . .

Critics of pure decentralization may reasonably say that centralization of government like the one which the United States is currently going through in the grants-in-aid process tends to increase state and local government activities and thus increases the opportunity for citizens to participate in their government and to develop the sense of social responsibility which is important for democracy. The answer to this question revolves around the issue of whether citizens are better developed by assuming minor roles in a federally directed grants-in-aid enterprise or by assuming complete responsibility for certain functions themselves. My own feeling is that complete responsibility is more likely to develop good citizens.

I must admit the force of the counter-argument that where states and localities do not administer their enterprises well, the citizens may secure practice in bad government from working with such bad government. However, I do not rate state and local administration as low in comparison with federal administration as do some of my political science colleagues. . . .

The third great reason for maintaining decentralization of government is that decentralized governmental units can adapt their policies to the needs of particular areas. The United States is a vast country even if one can fly across it in a few hours. People in different sections of the country have different psychological outlooks.

While a few activities of the national government, such as defense, interstate commerce, and currency have imperative reasons for uniformity of governmental policy throughout the nation, a much larger number of governmental activities would be benefited by opportunities for experimentation and adaptation which a decentralized government furnishes. . . .

Closely related to the argument that decentralized governmental units can best adapt their policies to local needs is the argument that decentralization gives healthy scope for experimentation in government. I have recently talked to an Oxford professor who has been making a study of the source of innovations in science and technology. He tells me that there is impressive evidence, and in fact it has proven true, that individual inventors and men working with small outfits have made a very high proportion of the striking new discoveries. Do we want to lose that opportunity? If this is true in business, why should it not also be true in government?

The total grants to states and localities is about $7,000,000,000 counting the so-called highway trust fund. There are almost eighty separate major appropriation heads.

I need not tell you that grants imply matching funds. But perhaps you are not all aware that, according to the reports of the Kestnbaum Commisison, the grants and required matching funds averaged about one quarter of state and local expenditures. To the wealthy states this does not make too much difference. In certain low per-capita income states the proportion reached 40 percent. It is a hardy executive or legislature which turns down the grant-in-aid, but acceptance means that the allocation of one-fourth to one-third of the state revenue is predetermined by federal policy. . . .

Let me make it quite clear that I am *not* criticizing the federal agencies. It is quite natural and proper if one appropriates money for a particular purpose to require guarantees that the money be used for that purpose. It isn't only natural and proper—it is, in a sense, essential to fiscal responsibility. But the fact remains that too much is spent on public assistance in Louisiana and Colorado, too little on general education in Mississippi. This is not the "fault" of the federal agencies; it is not the "fault" of the state administrations. It is the "fault" of a system which increasingly makes policy in one central place, and which by matching provisions ties up a substantial portion of local revenue. . . .

The big thing we are losing through grants-in-aid centralization is the responsiblity of state and local governments for determining their own destinies, working out their own patterns of government, and coordinating their own governmental programs to meet the needs of their own areas. . . .

I submit, quite modestly, a few suggestions:

First, see that your state government is run efficiently and economically. . . .

Second, work for top-quality state administrators and civil servants. Many a time sheer technical competence on the national level has embarrassed—and subordinated—state officials.

Third, for the greatest defect of our state and local machinery, currently, look to your local governmental systems. In American constitutional laws, states are responsible for localities. That means, responsible to help them. The state should try to work out a pattern of grants to localities—taking equalization into account—but using a minimum of coercive measures. The states should use reason and imagination in the formation or authorization of local units for meeting metropolitan problems—encouraging the formation of large "metropolitan" areas where traffic, health, safety, education indicate the need, but respecting deeply felt "unity" in smaller areas. . . .

My fourth modest suggestion is that you support wholeheartedly a system of consolidated—or, as the British say, "block"—grants, from the federal government to the states. Since, in the early 1920s, the Supreme Court in effect opened up practically all avenues of taxation to the federal government, it is obvious that Washington will be the major repository of tax money. . . . A system of consolidated grants to states could be worked out in the United States. Such consolidated grants would avoid a series of specific controls over specific expenditures. A state, receiving its overall grant, would be free to work out a program which seemed locally desirable. . . .

With the support of these few things, better state government, better local government, and consolidated grants, there is no reason why our tradition of decentralized government cannot continue to be a basic feature of American tradition—a means of keeping power broken up, or developing a responsible citizenry, and of adapting policy to the needs of areas.

24.2. LEADERSHIP FROM THE STATES

Many problems which can be handled at the State level are turned over to the Federal Government for resolution as a result of State inaction or lethargy. Here, the Chairman of the Intergovernmental Relations Subcommittee of the House of Representatives points out that the States "have not done all that they might" and urges a resurgence of State leadership in governmental affairs.

FEDERAL-STATE RELATIONS

(Address by Congressman L. H. Fountain, Democrat, of North Carolina, at the 52d annual meeting of the Governors' conference, Glacier National Park, Mont., June 28, 1960.)

. . . More than a century ago that wise and penetrating foreign observer, de Tocqueville, sensed the importance of the American Federal system to the vitality of our democratic political institutions.

In his classic, "Democracy in America," published in 1835, de Tocqueville wrote:

The Federal system was created with the intention of combining the different advantages which result from the greater and the lesser extent of nations; and a single glance over the United States of America suffices to discover the advantages which they have derived from its adoption.

In great centralized nations the legislator is obliged to impart a character of uniformity to the laws which does not always suit the diversity of customs and of districts; as he takes no cognizance of special cases, he can only proceed upon general principles; and the population is obliged to conform to the exigencies of the legislation, since the legislation cannot adapt itself to the exigencies and the customs of the population, which is the cause of endless trouble and misery. This disadvantage does not exist in confederations. Congress regulates the principal measures of the National Government, and all the details of the administration are reserved to the provincial legislatures. It is impossible to imagine how much this division of sovereignty contributes to the well-being of each of the States which compose the Union. In these small communities, which are never agitated by the desire of aggrandizement or the cares of self-defense, all public authority and private energy is employed in internal amelioration. . . . It is generally believed in America that the existence and the permanence of the republican form of government in the New World depend upon the existence and the permanence of the Federal system.

This commentary, I submit, is as valid today in its general principles as in de Tocqueville's day. In the Federal principle we have an admirable political concept well suited to the conditions of a country as large and diverse as ours. This extraordinary political invention of the Founding Fathers has weathered the tests of time and adaptability to changing conditions.

The clear-cut division of functions between the States and the National Government, while appropriate in the early days of the Republic, in time gave way to a sharing of certain responsibilities in response to the advent of new economic and social conditions. Various methods of intergovernmental cooperation, like the grant-in-aid and the tax credit device, were found to assure the continued workability of our Federal structure. The challenge is now ours to discover practical methods for further strengthening the Federal system to better serve contemporary America and future generations.

Political inventiveness is sorely needed if we are to deal success-

From Representative L. H. Fountain, Address before the 1960 Governors' Conference (Washington, D.C., *The Congressional Record*, August, 1960), pp. 18947–18948.

fully with the newer problems of government, such as those associated with the growth of metropolitan complexes. We can no longer safely rely exclusively on existing methods of intergovernmental cooperation. Here State government has a major responsibility—and a great opportunity— to contribute to the solution of metropolitan area problems. Effective State leadership in meeting this challenge would constitute incontrovertible evidence of the vitality of State government.

It has been said that the extension of Federal legislation into program areas traditionally a State responsibility has come about because of inactivity on the part of the States. While true in part, this is far too simple an explanation for a very complex situation. Unquestionably, the States can and must be more responsive to public needs if they are to occupy the position of equality which is rightfully theirs in the Federal structure.

It is not merely a question of shoring up the States to preserve in actuality as well as in theory the division of powers. The Federal Government needs help. With the demands of national defense, international relations, and space exploration increasingly requiring more of the Federal Government's energies, it is only logical that the States should equip themselves more responsibility for domestic programs.

Even in the traditional service areas, the numerous tasks confronting the States and their local governments are tremendously important and demanding today. Permit me to cite but one example—education.

In Jefferson's words: "If a nation expects to be ignorant and free in a state of civilization, it expects what never was and never will be." With great international and domestic problems confronting the Nation today, education is more than ever before the key to world peace and our very survival.

History offers ample evidence that democracy cannot flourish where a people are uneducated, politically inactive, or fail to understand their binding common interests.

What, then, are the necessary conditions for a satisfactory educational system?

It is not necessary, or probably desirable, that all teachers be paid the same salary scales throughout the country—so long as the salaries paid teachers are adequate to attract the best qualified persons to this extremely important profession. It is not necessary that all schoolbuildings be built according to the same specifications—so long as these buildings are safe and efficient and we have adequate school facilities to accommodate the student population. It is not necessary that the curriculum from one school district to the next be as alike as the products of an automated assembly line—so long as our schools are providing the essentials for active participation in a highly industrialized democratic society, and beyond that, seek to challenge our children to develop their minds to the fullest extent of their potential.

No, centralization and uniformity are neither essential for nor will they necessarily produce the excellence which our Nation must attain in education and other public programs. But a centralized program sometimes becomes a necessary expedient for satisfying public needs when those who have the primary responsibility wait too long to take effective action. It is axiomatic that the less we solve public problems at the State and local levels, the more such problems will be dealt with at the national level. Whether we like it or not (and I am one of those who doesn't), the consequence will almost surely be a further concentration of power in the Federal Government if the States and localities neglect their responsibilities. Let us never forget that the Members of Congress and the President are elected by the same people who elect State and local officials. If the needs on the local and State levels are not met, most assuredly these same people will call upon the President and especially the Congress for action.

While it is true that some States have pioneered in recent years with imaginative programs for dealing with matters such as broadening employment opportunities, special housing needs, and temporary disability insurance for workers, the States have not done all that they might for meeting public problems falling within their competence. It is most encouraging that the council of State governments annually takes stock of many of the matters requiring the attention of the State governments in its program of "Suggested State Legislation." State accomplishment in response to those suggestions, however, is not equally encouraging.

I am reminded in this connection of several outstanding examples of State legislative leadership demonstrated earlier in the century.

We are all aware that workmen's compensation laws were enacted by all of the States on their own initiative and, significantly, this remains a field in which there is no apparent pressure for Federal participation. (However, it might be noted parenthetically that some of these State programs are badly out of date and in need of considerable improvement.) The State of Wisconsin in 1932 led the way with an unemployment compensation plan which served largely as the model for Federal legislation 3 years later. And a number of States contributed to the development of the public assistance programs upon which our Federal grant legislation was patterned.

Unfortunately, the notion is still widely held that Government services are of a fixed kind and amount which remain constant as our economy grows. Many Government activities, on the contrary, are intimately related to economic growth and technological progress, both as a consequence and a stimulant.

Witness, for example, the new regulatory problems created by the use of atomic energy and the use of powerful chemical pesticides which contribute so mightily to agricultural productivity. Such advances in technology increase our consumable private income but are not without their social costs. So, too, the growth and concentration of population in metropolitan centers necessitates proportionately larger Government expenditures to cope with the resulting problems of water supply, air and water pollution, traffic congestion, and commuter transportation.

When difficult problems arise, the solution is not to turn back the clock to some romanticized golden age of the past. Nor is there so easy a solution as sending these problems to Washington on the grounds that the Federal Government has access to the more productive tax sources. The need, rather, is for all units in our Federal system to go forward with imagination, initiative, and determination in dealing with the complex problems of our time.

Much remains to be done, not only in anticipating and planning for emerging governmental responsibilities, but also in dealing effectively with older problems. Certainly, the States have before them a tremendous opportunity to strengthen themselves through constitutional revision and appropriate legislation aimed at facilitating effective and responsible government at the local level. As a very minimum, the States should enlarge the home rule powers of local governments to an extent commensurate with their administrative capabilities and their fiscal needs and capacities.

It is my firm conviction that we must have strong local self-government in this country if we are to preserve our Federal system. Monopoly is no more desirable in government than it is in science or industry. The free competition of ideas and a broad base of participation in the political affairs of the Nation are indispensable ingredients of democracy.

Throughout our history, we Americans have demonstrated a genius for adapting our political institutions to new conditions and new problems, although the time lags have sometimes given cause for concern. Unencumbered by slavish adherence to rigid political dogmas, while steadfastly devoted to the heritage of our democratic ideals, we have been a Nation of political pragmatists. This national trait is pointedly reflected in Grover Cleveland's famous remark: "It is a condition and not a theory which confronts us."

With the active support of your organization, the Federal Government last year created a permanent Advisory Commission on Intergovernmental Relations. In view of the fact that the President has entrusted the leadership of the Commission to a very able gentleman who needs no introduction to this conference, I am all the more hopeful that the Commission will become an important and constructive force in helping to plot a sound and orderly course for the future development of intergovernmental activities.

I believe deeply in our Federal form of Government and in the desirability of preserving and strengthening this remarkable political institution; but there are no easy solutions or automatic mechanisms for doing so. Constant vigilance and hard work are the price we must pay for democratic institutions.

24.3. A RECENT EXPRESSION OF THE STATES' RIGHTS VIEWPOINT

Representative Smith, as Chairman of the Rules Committee of the House of Representatives, has consistently believed in and applied the concept that the powers of the Federal Government are narrow and limited. In his keynote address to the Democratic Party of Virginia in 1960, he calls for a restoration to the States of "their just rights."

MY FELLOW DEMOCRATS, you are assembled here today as the chosen representatives of the Democrats of Virginia, the home State of Jefferson, the founder of the Democratic Party. The party that has survived the vicissitudes of political warfare throughout a century and a half. The party that could only survive because of the basic principles of government upon which it was founded.

Broadly speaking, those principles are that the best governed people are the least governed, that the closer the local self-government is to the people, the better. That the centralization of power in the Federal Government is an evil that will eventually strangle the sovereignty of the States and destroy the carefully preserved concept of free, sovereign, and independent States. Sovereign States with every right, duty, and power save only those specifically granted to the Central Government by the Constitution.

This was the univerally accepted concept on which the Constitution was ratified by the States. Without that concept written into the Constiution and reemphasized in the Bill of Rights, the compact would never have been ratified by the States.

In other words, under the Constitution as written and adopted, the Federal Government has no power whatsoever outside of those specifically granted by the Constitution. All other powers of government are specifically reserved to the States, and when we speak of States rights it embraces every right of the sovereign government, with the exception of the limited powers granted to the Federal Government. The complaint so

From Representative Howard W. Smith, Keynote Address at the 1960 Convention of the Democratic Party of Virginia (Washington, D.C., *The Congressional Record,* May, 1960), pp. 10891–10892.

persistently and loudly voiced by those of us who believe in a strict interpretation of the limitations imposed by the Constitution which every Federal officer (legislative, executive, and judicial) is solemnly sworn to uphold.

Perhaps we have drifted away so far from the moorings that bound us to our forefathers' conception of our system of government that it is too late to return. Perhaps we have drifted so far into that conception of socialistic government that presently infests the whole world that we can never return. There are, however, those of us who will maintain until we die that the course we are now pursuing will lead this Nation, the greatest the world has ever known, into pitfalls of disintegration, deterioration, and ultimate disaster. We see in Washington today in the Congress a reckless disregard of fiscal responsibility and extravagant expenditures on almost every fanciful, do-good scheme that the mind of man can conceive to drain from the people of the States the taxes to feed the hungry maws'of Federal expenditures. While, in spite of this unbearable burden of taxation, Congress passes—and the President approves—expenditures which over the past 20 years, have resulted in unbalanced budgets that have required annual and continuous increases in the Federal debt to meet deficiencies in Federal revenues. In these transgressions against financial responsibility, there is little difference between the Democratic and Republican National Parties. . . .

While we meet here today the Congress is considering new schemes, new bills, new plans, for the new and additional extravagance that will further burden the American taxpayer and further increase the national debt, further increase the interest rates, and further burden the American taxpayer, and further reduce the value of the dollar.

If the things which I here decry lie outside of the proper and constitutional functions of the Federal Government, both of the great national parties are equally guilty. . . .

Fundamentally, all of the things of which I speak arise from a disregard for the limitations of power placed upon the Federal Government under the Constitution. Nor can we confine these transgressions to any one of the three divisions of Government created by the Constitution. The executive department, the legislative department, and the judicial department all have contributed to the grasp for powers that they do not rightly possess under our system. All from time to time have sought to deprive the States of the Union of their sovereign rights guaranteed us by our charter of government devised by our forefathers out of bitter years of experience with misrule and oppression, and imitated throughout the world by peoples seeking new freedom.

We have seen the Chief Executive invade a sovereign State with the Armed Forces to impose the will of the Central Government on the people of that State in open and flagrant violation of the specific prohibition contained in the Constitution, unless done at the request of the legislature or the Governor of such State.

We have seen the legislative department of the Federal Government, the Congress, recklessly assume power to govern, control and rule in the exercise of the local functions of the government reserved to the people of the sovereign States.

Saddest of all have been the decisions of the U.S. Supreme Court, that vital and final bulwark against the encroachment of the Federal Government on the rights of the sovereign States and the individual liberties of our people.

Time permits only the mention of a few instances where that Court, guided by its own sociological ideals, has reversed previous decisions of that Court that have stood as the law of the land for generations.

By its decision in the school segregation case it changed the constitutional rights of the States to operate their public school systems and reversed decisions of the former courts that had stood the test of time and had been the law of the land for a hundred years. Basing its decision, not upon the law of the land, but upon the writings of a socialist Swedish author.

In the Girard College case where Stephen Girard a hundred years ago had established a fund of his own money in trust to the city of Philadelphia for the education of poor white children, and though it had been operated for a century under the conditions laid down by the donor, the Supreme Court substituted its own will for the will of Stephen Girard and held that Negro children must also be permitted to share the bounty of this benefactor against his will.

In the case where the Health Department of the State of Alabama under State law undertook to inspect unwholesome foods, the Supreme Court by its decision deprived the State of Alabama of its inherent right to protect the health of its citizens against impure food because of the mere fact that Congress had enacted a pure food law.

In New Mexico where State law prohibits license to practice law except to persons of good character, authorities of the State of New Mexico decided that a person with a record of subversive and treasonable activities was not of the good character that the State desired to license, the Supreme Court substituted its judgment of good character for the judgment of the sovereign State of New Mexico in dealing with a purely local problem.

In the city of New York where the State legislature, in enacting a city charter, provided that any schoolteacher who in any procedure took advantage of the fifth amendment automatically severed his employment with the city, and where the city authorities discharged a schoolteacher for violation of its charter provision as being a person not desirable as a teacher of the youth of that community, the Supreme Court substituted its judgment as to whom New York should hire for the education of their youth, for the judgment of the State legislature of that State.

In the famous Steve Nelson case where a known and active working Communist seeking to overthrow the Government by force was convicted under the law of Pennsylvania, the Supreme Court denied to the sovereign State of Pennsylvania, and all other States having similar laws, the inherent right to protect itself against subversive criminals seeking to overthrow the Government by force.

What we do here today, what we say here today, may be, I fear, an exercise in futility. A call for return to constitutional government as designed by the framers of this government; a call for a fiscal policy to restore the solvency of the government and relieve our people of the burden of taxation for improvident expenditures; a call to restore to the States their just rights of local self-government; a call for a Supreme Court that would confine its present exercise of unlimited powers to the functions prescribed in the Constitution; these calls may be a voice calling in the wilderness at the National Convention of the Democratic Party which will shortly assemble in Los Angeles. Such a call would be equally futile if addressed to the Republican Convention.

But we can at least voice to our friends and fellow Democrats who will assemble and assume to speak for the Democratic Party, our hopes, our desires, and our pleas for a moderate and sympathetic consideration of the hopes and aspirations of that great body of loyal and conservative Democrats throughout the Nation who view with the gravest apprehension the political motivations that have brought about the division in the great party of Jefferson. . . .

There are those among us who feel that we should divorce ourselves from the National Democratic Party. There are others of equal patriotism and equal apprehension as to the course of the party who feel we can be more effective in our efforts by remaining within the party. Certainly the National Republican Party offers no haven of refuge for unhappy Democrats. . . . No, my friends, there is no haven of refuge in the Republican Party for the beleaguered southern Democrats.

On the other hand, we have under Virginia law the power to reconvene this convention after the national convention if the Butlers, the Hoffas, and the Reuthers, and others fix upon us a situation that is intolerable.

It is my hope that this convention may proceed to its work in harmony and friendly understanding. Certainly the objectives of all gathered here are in accord. It is my hope that we endorse to the national convention a candidate of demonstrated ability and fundamental belief of our system of constitutional government, and with the courage to lead us in turning the tide of socialism back into the quiet channels of responsible constitutional government and fiscal sanity.

24.4. THE FEDERAL GOVERNMENT'S ROLE IN HOUSING

Disputes continue over the role of the Federal Government in solving such problems as housing, education, and social welfare. Are these problems the concern of the States and private industry, or does the national government have responsibility for affirmative action? President Eisenhower's veto of the housing bill expresses fundamental doubts about the need for Federal participation. Senator Sparkman criticizes the Eisenhower view as "miserly." In 1961, Congress again passed a comprehensive housing bill, and President Kennedy signed it.

TO THE SENATE OF THE UNITED STATES:

I am returning herewith, without my approval, S. 57, "An act to extend and amend laws relating to the provision and improvement of housing and the renewal of urban communities, and for other purposes."

For many months I have been looking forward to approving a sound and constructive housing bill. New homes are now being built at near record rates. I have hoped to receive from the Congress legislation that would further advance the cause of better housing for Americans within the limits of fiscal responsibility.

To my disappointment, the Congress has instead presented me with a bill so excessive in the spending it proposes, and so defective in other respects, that it would do far more damage than good.

First, the bill is extravagant and much of the spending it authorizes is unnecessary. Its spending authorizations total a minimum of $2.2 billion—all of which would be available for commitment without further congressional or Presidential action. The comparable budget recommendations of the administration totaled $810 million.

Its authorizations of $900 million for urban renewal—telescoped into 2 years—are excessive.

Even though we have over 100,000 previously authorized public housing units as yet unbuilt, the bill would authorize 190,000 more.

A new program of direct Federal lending is authorized for housing for elderly persons when needs in this area can be adequately met by private funds invested under the protection of Federal insurance. The

---

From President Dwight D. Eisenhower, Veto Message on the Housing Bill, in *The Congressional Record*, July, 1959, pp. 11689–11690, and Senator John Sparkman's Answer to the Veto Message, in *The Congressional Record*, July, 1959, pp. 11695–11698.

college housing loan program would be continued with increased author- izations at interest rates below the cost of money to the Treasury and a new program for college classrooms and related academic facilities at the same subsidy interest rates would be started. Although the amounts initially authorized for the latter program would be relatively small, the eventual demand for these loans would reach staggering proportions. To the extent that these and other programs merely displace private financing they lead to Federal spending that is entirely unnecessary.

Second, the bill is inflationary. The spending authorizations of S. 57, taken together with other seriously objectionable provisions would be inflationary and therefore an obstacle to constructive progress toward better housing for Americans. One of the most damaging effects of in- flation is that it dries up the sources of long term credit. There is perhaps no industry in the Nation more heavily dependent for its operations on long-term funds borrowed at reasonable rates of interest than the housing industry. We have made good progress in the fight against inflation but we cannot win that fight if we add one spending program to another, without thought of how they are going to be paid for, and invite deficts in times of general prosperity. No one can gain from a fiscal policy of this inflationary type—least of all, the housing industry.

Third, the bill would tend to substitute Federal spending for private investment. Many provisions of the bill, instead of stimulating private investment, would drive private credit from areas where it is urgently needed. . . .

In view of these defects I have withheld my approval from this bill. . . .

MR. SPARKMAN. Mr. President, with regard to public housing, the ad- ministration should make up its mind whether it intends to have a public housing program continued or intends to drop it completely. We simply had no recommendation from the administration, although the testimony which the representatives of the administration gave before the committee was that public housing is needed in order to take care of those who are displaced from housing by government action under urban renewal, slum clearance, interstate highway construction, and various other government activities. The representatives of the administration admitted that housing had to be provided for those purposes.

The President has stated that more than 100,000 public housing units have previously been authorized. As a matter of fact, throughout the veto message are statements which do not tell the whole story. The President should have said that 100,000 units have not yet been con- structed and occupied. The testimony before our committee was that prior to June 30, 1958, every authorized unit of public housing would be allocated; and I understand all of them have been allocated, and none remains to be allocated. It does not matter so much whether each one is constructed at this time. After all, if a town or city wishes to engage in an urban renewal project for the benefit of its people, but if all available units have been allocated, no further units can be allocated, and that city or town simply will be unable to have such a project. . . .

In the veto message the President said the bill which went to him for his signature was inflationary. Mr. President, I submit that the staff of our Housing Subcommittee is very capable and knows about housing. When the conference report was being debated, the staff gave us figures which were placed in the Record at that time, and upon which I relied; and they show that the total impact upon the 1960 budget would have been about $24 million more than what the President himself had recommended to Congress. So the argument along that line in the veto message simply does not stand up.

The President stated in the message that he favors an urban renewal program, but stated that the amount the Congress voted was entirely too large. I wonder whether the housing agency officials or those who advised the President told him that there are now pending $510 million worth of applications from cities that are ready to proceed with the cleaning up of slums. Slums constitute a terrible problem against which the President cried out several years ago, at which time he said it would take about 200 years, at the rate we were then going, to clear out the slums.

But since that time the President has advocated a program which, if adopted, would result in even less progress than that formerly made. In fact, last year and this year there was none at all; and goodness knows whether we shall have a slum clearance program next year. Certainly we are not making headway on the 200-year problem to which the President referred, nor shall we make headway on it if we have to rely on the miserly amounts the President wants in connection with the cleaning up of the slums. . . .

25

The State Governments

25.1. A COMMENTARY ON FEDERAL-STATE RELATIONS

In this section the former Executive Director of the Council on State Governments examines the changes in relationships between the State and Federal Governments wrought by time and changing circumstances. He reviews the progress and problems of the States in government organization, service, and finance.

PRIOR TO 1900, the question of federal-state relations was largely a legal constitutional problem. Hamilton and Madison fought about it. Calhoun and Webster wrote their names large in American history by their exposition of fundamental disagreements concerning it.

But over the past several decades federal-state relations have become largely—almost entirely—a question of public functions and services on the one hand and of taxes and revenue on the other. It is not necessary here to detail this development. We have already done so at the direction of the Board in two reports, one on "Federal Grants-in-Aid," the other the previously mentioned report for the "Hoover Commission." Suffice it to say that the major questions involved are: Who shall do what and how? And who shall finance the doing thereof, and in what manner? These questions apply to many of the major functions of government; they also apply to the broad problems of taxation and revenue. . . .

What can and should be done relative to the functions, and what can and should be done relative to finances? That, is a double-barreled question. The two parts are the two sides of the same coin; they must be considered together. . . .

The national government makes a number of grants to the states in the field of education, notably for vocational education, vocational re-

---

From Frank Bane, "Progress and Opportunities of the States," *State Government,* Vol. 27 (January, 1954).

habilitation, and the school lunch program. Two of these grant programs, vocational education and vocational rehabilitation, were started many years ago—as demonstrations—to encourage and assist the states in providing for needs that were nation-wide in character. The school lunch grant program was established as a depression measure, designed largely to provide an outlet for surplus agricultural commodities.

All three of these programs are going concerns. The demonstrations have been made, and they have been successful. All of the states have such programs, and almost four-fifths of their total cost is being borne by the states and agencies within the states. And so it might be pertinent to ask whether it is still necessary for the national government further to demonstrate and further to subsidize these activities.

The highway systems in the United States are the marvel of the world. It can be said that in deed and in fact we have paved America within the last generation. The highways have been constructed, maintained and operated by the states. The establishment of the Bureau of Public Roads in 1916 and federal grants for roads stimulated this program. They developed standards and contributed greatly to the planning and operation of the gigantic enterprise. No governmental agency that I have known has done a better job than the federal Bureau of Public Roads. . . .

In 1952 state expenditures for highways were more than $2.9 billion. Most of this revenue comes from state gasoline taxes. The national government is levying a two-cent tax on gasoline on top of the state tax. From this two-cent gasoline tax, the national government collects something over $800 million, while it grants to the states approximately $450 million for highway construction. If the national two-cent gasoline tax were repealed, states would have access to that revenue source, and the total of money available for highways could rise accordingly. . . .

The Social Security Act established two programs to deal with problems of the aged: first, an old age assistance program; second, an old age and survivors insurance program. The old age assistance program was designed to provide immediate relief for aged persons in need; the insurance program was designed to enable persons during their working years to build up annuities to provide for their old age.

It was the general hope and belief at the outset that the old age insurance program, in a reasonable period of time, would make larger and larger grants for old age assistance unnecessary. It hasn't worked that way—primarily because the old age insurance program never has been adequate. The result has been that the largest grants from the federal government to the states—more than $800 million annually—are for old age assistance. . . .

We who work in state government do not suffer from lack of advice. "The states should assume more responsibilities." "The states should do more of their own jobs." "The way to govern is to govern." These statements we hear on every hand. True—quite true! One hard, cold fact, however, stands out in bold relief. We should not and cannot expect the states to assume broad, additional, large-scale responsibilities unless and until additional sources of revenue are made available to them to raise the funds necessary to provide the services involved. To a very considerable extent that means the abandonment by the national government of certain tax resource areas which it is now using and using extensively, and it means the reduction of national rates in some other areas. . . .

The states are now hard pressed for funds to do their jobs. They are using the tax resources available to them. Most of the states have sales taxes, many of them have income taxes, many have both; most of the states are taxing almost everything else in sight. But there is a limit to which any given tax source can stand levies by the federal and state governments at the same time. If the states are to assume additional responsibilities, which I hope and believe they will, they need larger financial resources—not additional help in the nature of grants, but provisions that will enable them to find the sources from which to raise the revenue themselves, to do their own jobs. . . .

The major task of all state organizations and agencies—in fact of all state officials and legislators—is to improve and perfect state government so that it can perform its full role in providing necessary public services and in maintaining our essential freedoms.

What are the criticisms that have been made?

First, most state constitutions, it is contended, were written long before the development of our urban industrial society, and the states, therefore, are not capable of meeting present-day social and economic problems adequately—in fact are prohibited by their constitutions from doing so. A number of states have recognized the constitutional problem and have taken action accordingly. New Jersey, New York, Georgia, Missouri, Tennessee and others have done so, and many other states are considering the problem. The Council of State Governments has made its facilities and resources available to all states interested in constitutional revision and, subject to your approval, it plans to expand this service. . . .

Again and again, the General Assembly of the States and organizations affiliated with the Council of State Governments have discussed and developed suggestions and recommendations pointing to more extensive home rule for municipalities. Municipalities contend, with some justification, that they suffer from many of the same handicaps as those of which the states complain with reference to the federal government. If so-called home rule for municipalities were expanded, could we not relieve state legislators from the consideration of hundreds of bills purely local in character? And could we not also expect municipalities to raise through their own efforts a larger proportion of the revenue they need for their own services? . . .

The last few years have witnessed extensive re-examination of the organization and operation of the executive branches of state government. Since 1949 thirty-five states have established commissions to study this subject. Great progress has been made, and the progress is continuing. Three specific problems may be cited as examples of those that are receiving much additional consideration in many of the states:

In many states, an acute question has to do with the earmarking of funds. In some states, about 75 percent of total revenue is earmarked by constitutional provision or by legislative enactment. This practice, it is contended, seriously limits the discretion of state legislatures and hampers effective, economical operation of state government.

Many of the states still elect their Governors for a two-year term. At the turn of the century the Governor, although an important political leader with large prestige, had responsibilties incomparably smaller than those of a Governor today. Today the Governor is the effective head of an enormous operation in which his political leadership, his policy making, his organization of public programs, and his administration of them are fundamental. Should Governors of states, accordingly, be elected for four-year terms?

And third, in many of the states are we electing directly too many administrative officials? Would effective operation be served better by a shorter ballot?

Again and again the question will be asked of the recently appointed national Commission on Intergovernmental Relations: "What can the states do?" During the coming year we plan, subject to your approval, to give much attention to this question, and to report to you on it at your next annual meeting.

It is not our idea—nor that of any other organization familiar with our country and our governmental scheme of things—that there should be uniformity among all of the states. We wish to maintain the right, the privilege and the pleasure of being different. But it *is* our idea that state governments should be the most efficient and effective governmental agencies that they can be.

Nowhere have the states made more measurable progress in affecting the lives and well-being of their citizens in the past few years than in the field of mental health. At no time has so much thought and energy been given to this subject among the states. By the end of the 1952 fiscal year, the states were spending more than $560 million annually for the care and treatment of the mentally ill. It has been increasingly apparent, however, that care and treatment are not enough; that if our mental hospitals are not to continue to be crowded with too many patients who don't get well, the states must expand their activities in the realm of research and training: research into the nature, prevention and effective treatment of mental illness; training of the personnel at all levels who work in our mental health programs. . . .

One of the dramatic developments in state government has been the increasing use of interstate compacts. In recent years the interstate compact method has revealed a versatility and flexibility that have allowed groups of states to pool their resources and experiences in many different fields. New and expanded applications have ranged from conservation and development of natural resources to civil defense, higher education, harbor development and law enforcement.

Probably the most spectacular development in the highway field in recent years has been the rapid trend in a number of states to build or plan toll roads. States now have realized that these wide, through highways must "hook up" if our transportation problems are to be met effectively, and they are, therefore, considering the creation of interstate agreements and compacts on toll roads.

25.2. A CALL TO ACTION

How to make our State governments more vigorous and effective has long been a concern of scholars and statesmen. President Eisenhower appointed a Commission to probe this vital question during his first term in office, and the Commission's Report contains a wide range of suggestions including better representation for urban areas, stronger governors, and modernized legislative practices.

EARLY IN ITS STUDY, the Commission was confronted with the fact that many State constitutions restrict the scope, effectiveness, and adaptability of State and local action. These self-imposed constitutional limitations make it difficult for many States to perform all of the services their citizens require, and consequently have frequently been the underlying cause of State and municipal pleas for Federal assistance.

It is significant that the Constitution prepared by the Founding Fathers, with its broad grants of authority and avoidance of legislative detail, has withstood the test of time far better than the constitutions later adopted by the States. A due regard for the need for stabiliy in government requires adherence to basic constitutional principles until strong and persistent public policy requires a change. A dynamic society requires a constant review of legislative detail to meet changing conditions and circumstances. . . .

From the U.S. Commission on Intergovernmental Relations, *A Report to the President* (June, 1955).

In the early history of our country, State legislatures were the most powerful and influential instruments of government in the Nation. It was to them that the average citizen looked primarily for initiative and wisdom in the formulation of public policy on domestic issues. They overshadowed the other branches of State government. In power and influence they are no longer as dominant as they were, partly because of the ascendancy of the National Government, partly because of the increased influence of the State executive, but primarily because they have not found effective solutions to problems that become more chronic and more difficult to cope with in a rapidly changing society.

One of these problems is to maintain an equitable system of representation. In a majoriy of States, city dwellers outnumber the citizens of rural areas. Yet in most States the rural voters are overwhelmingly in control of one legislative house, and overweighted if not dominant in the other. . . .

The constitutions of 43 States call for some reapportionment in at least one house as often as every 10 years. In nearly half of these States, reapportionment lags behind schedule. Ten States provide for reapportionment of one or both houses by some agency other than the legislature, either initially or in case the legislature fails to act. In these States, some reapportionment takes place on schedule—a fact worthy of study by States whose legislatures have been reluctant to obey the constitutional mandate to reapportion themselves. . . .

The problem of reapportionment is important in the area of study of this Commission because legislative neglect of urban communities has led more and more people to look to Washington for more and more of the services and controls they desire. One of the study reports prepared for the Commission makes this very clear:

If states do not give cities their rightful allocation of seats in the legislature, the tendency will be toward direct Federal-municipal dealings. These began in earnest in the early days of the depression. There is only one way to avoid this in the future. It is for the states to take an interest in urban problems, in metropolitan government, in city needs. If they do not do this, the cities will find a path to Washington as they did before, and this time it may be permanent, with the ultimate result that there may be a new government arrangement that will break down the constitutional pattern which has worked so well up to now.

One result of State neglect of the reapportionment problem is that urban governments have bypassed the States and made direct cooperative arrangements with the National Government in such fields as housing and urban development, airports, and defense community facilities. Although necessary in some cases, the multiplication of National-local relationships tends to weaken the State's proper control over its own policies and its authority over its own political subdivisions.

Paradoxically enough, the interests of urban areas are often more effectively represented in the National legislature than in their own State legislatures. Originally there was no substantial difference between the representativeness of Congress and of State legislatures, but history and population shifts have affected these bodies differently. Reapportionment in the House of Representatives has occurred after nearly every census; since 1929 it has been automatic. The same shift of population which has resulted in State legislatures becoming less representative of urban areas has had the effect of making the United States Senate more representative of these areas, because Senators, elected at large, must depend heavily upon urban voters, even in predominantly rural States. . . .

. . . A few States have recently provided for annual sessions, at least for action on the budget. More than two-thirds of the legislatures have equipped themselves with legislative councils to develop objective information as a basis for policy decisions. A smaller number of States have reorganized their committee systems and revised their rules. Legislative pay is improving, though slowly and moderately.

Perhaps the chief obstacles to legislative flexibility are those created by over-detailed provisions of State constitutions, designed to correct specific actions of past legislative sessions. Some of these provisions rigidly prohibit certain forms of legislative action; others contain elaborate restrictions and prescriptions of an essentially statutory nature. Some of them attempt to regulate in detail such rapidly changing or technical matters as the powers of corporations, the routes of the State highway system, and the conduct of State and county administration. Some interfere with the full use of modern tools of budgeting, accounting, auditing, and personnel administration. . . .

Today, few States have an adequate executive branch headed by a governor who can be held generally accountable for executing and administering the laws of the State. State constitutions provide in principle for three equal branches of government, but most of these constitutions and numerous laws based on them include provisions that tend to undermine this principle. Early fears of royal governors and the natural preference for the legislative bodies that had spoken for the colonies in their contests with the crown have left their mark on the development of the State executive. The growth of State functions in the last half century and the increasing importance of National-State cooperative relations have created the need for a governor who is in a position to provide executive direction to the State's business, and to see to it that grant-aided programs dovetail with other State programs and operate under State supervision.

Typically, though not universally, the governor is the nominal chief of a sprawling State administration consisting of scores of separate departments, commissions, and agencies. Department heads, many of them boards or commissions, are often selected or appointed for long or overlapping terms. This enables them to be more or less independent of normal executive controls. Still other agency heads may be separately elected, or may be appointed by the legislature or by someone other than the governor. In most States, the governor's removal power over many of his "subordinates" is so restricted that it is of little value as a tool of administrative control. Few governors have been supplied with modern staff agencies and tools of management adequate to the administrative responsibility presumed to be vested in them. Furthermore, constitutional limitations on tenure frequently weaken their leadership in policy and administration. More than one-third of our governors still have only 2-year terms, while of the 4-year governors, more than one-half may not succeed themselves.

The separate election of other State administrative officers deserves special attention. In 40 States, the people elect from 5 to 12 administrative officials or agency heads, in addition to the governor. Since the agencies are in some cases headed by boards, the actual number of persons elected my run even higher, being over 20 in 4 States. This arrangement seriously divides or hides responsibility and makes difficult the achievement of unity of command and consistency of action within a State administration.

Experience in the administration of Federal grants-in-aid emphasizes the need for effective gubernatorial supervision of State administration and for effective review by both governor and legislature of policies carried out by all State agencies. In the absence of such supervision and review, there is a tendency for groups of professional administrators in a single, specialized field, working at National, State, and local levels, to become a more or less independent government of their own, organized vertically and substantially independent of other State agencies. Programs may be agreed upon, State as well as Federal money may be committed, and important public projects may be carried out without even a review by the governor's office to determine how they relate to other State activities or requirements. On the other hand, States with fairly strong governors served by active budget and other staff aids have reported relatively little difficulty of this sort. . . .

While there is no unanimous agreement on a precise pattern of administrative organization applicable to all States, there is substantial agreement on certain arrangements which, if generally applied, would greatly strengthen State administration. The following statement reflects the consensus of some 20 State reorganization commissions:

. . . In general it was felt that reorganization movements should result in strengthening the office of the governor; reducing the independent agencies and administrative boards and commissions and grouping them into major departments; extending the gubernatorial power over appointment and removal of department heads; and strengthening executive controls over budgeting, accounting, purchasing, state property, etc. At the same time, it was pointed out, it is of the utmost necessity to revise legislative procedures in the direction of greater efficiency, and to provide the legislature with more effective reporting and auditing controls—in order that the executive may be held to proper accountability. . . .

Many good citizens and well-intentioned groups that respond readily to an appeal to improve the efficiency of the National Government have not shown an equal interest in similar proposals for improving and strengthening State government. Citizens who fail to understand the essential conditions of effective government in their home States may unintentionally promote the centralization they deplore. More attention should be given to the education of citizens with respect to their responsibilities as citizens of their own States. The federal system and decentralization in government cannot be improved and strengthened without special effort to maintain adequate sources of information, channels of communication, and forums for discussion of State and local issues.

25.3. THE TWENTIETH CENTURY STATE LEGISLATURE

From this experience as a member of both the Oregon legislature and the national Senate, the late Senator Neuberger contrasts the functions and procedures of the two institutions. He advocates that education, administration of justice, and the regulation of intrastate commerce are among the primary tasks for the States to fulfill. To do this, adequate resources of information, time, and revenue must be made available to state legislators.

. . . THE GREAT MAJORITY of citizens of the United States, although they are equally citizens of the several states, have comparatively little confidence in the ability of their state governments to tackle and solve the great problems of economic and social policy that concern them most. In matters such as protection against want in retirement or disability, promotion of decent working standards and fair labor relations, slum clearance and housing development, even the control of smog and of crime, individuals and groups turn to the federal government to a degree unheard of a generation ago. Natural resources entrusted to the care of state government are often regarded as practically lost beyond recovery.

From an Address by Senator Richard L. Neuberger, "Twentieth Century Legislatures for Twentieth Century Problems," *Streamlining State Legislatures,* prepared by Stanley Scott, Bureau of Public Administration (Berkeley: University of California, 1956), *passim,* pp. 63–72.

To some extent, obviously, the development of federal functions at the expense of the states has inevitably accompanied the development of our integrated national economy. This economic growth has continued steadily since the Civil War with the building of the railroads and the great industrial empires that were frequently richer than many states combined. To some extent, the contrast has been sharpened by the immense progress which the federal government made with explosive suddenness, under the forced draft of depression and war, as an instrument for translating public demand into policy and action. Only in recent years, as this modern federal government is apparently going into a period of acceptance and stability, has attention again turned to state government, which only participated to a minor degree in the crises of the past quarter-century. . . .

We still need good state government. As the economic and social values over which government has control grow in magnitude, we increasingly need honest and competent government at the state and local levels, quite as much as at the federal level.

It is true that the increasing network of interstate commerce and the insatiable demands of national defense have brought many important phases of the national economy under federal control. But when we stop to consider the governmental functions which are still the responsibility of the states, and which will remain their responsibility as long as our present federal system lasts, we find they include many functions which are essential to the life of any society. Let me identify only a few.

The most essential single state function, of course, is the formulation and administration of the civil and criminal laws. People sometimes forget that the "common" law is state law, and that its administration by state courts is the sanction of almost all our civil and commercial relations, our property and its transfer from one generation to another. Unfortunately, this part of state government is too often left to the lawyers. Many states have found how much progress is needed to make this vital sector of state government an efficient instrument, and some have found the means to do something about it.

The second most important responsibility of local government is education. The federal and state governments agree in their determination that this shall remain a state function, free from any suggestion of federal direction or control. But there is now widespread recognition of the fact that the fiscal resources of many states cannot cope with the educational needs of the largest single generation of children in our history. . . .

The states still have exclusive power to regulate large sections of purely intrastate business, and such regulation continues to expand in such fields as labor relations, working conditions, price fixing, professional standards, methods of competition, sanitary regulations and a host of others. The states also build roads, and they render a variety of social services, from unemployment compensation and old-age assistance to child-welfare programs.

Thus, attention to the manner and the shortcomings of the states' performance of these functions is overdue.

Why does the performance of most state governments fall so far short of their powers and responsibilities that people expect really constructive action only from the national capital? The governments of our states are not equipped to do their job, and they often decline the responsibility to prepare and equip themselves to do it. Let me only summarize some of the structural deficiencies—I am sure they are familiar to you—which in my experience have seemed the most damaging.

The marvelous Constitution of the United States defines in about 7,500 words the basic form of a national government that has functioned highly effectively for a century and a half. The document entitled the Constitution of California contains perhaps ten times as many words.

Even before its amendments, the traditional state constitution is less a charter of government than a legal code jealously guarding particular interests from the action of official bodies, which have carefully been made as impotent as possible. The Constitution of Oregon, for instance, restricts the location of all new state institutions, such as colleges and hospitals, to a single county. Subsequent amendments then "improve" the basic charter by giving new special interests a measure of permanence. I seem to recall that, a few years ago, the sovereign people of California wrote into their constitution the name and address of the lady who should direct an elaborate new constitutional welfare scheme that had failed to win the favor of the normal legislative authorities. Legislative limitations written into state constitutions cannot be changed even in an emergency in less than two years' time, and often longer. Thus, the more agile and flexible federal government must often step into the breach.

Besides writing too much special legislation into fundamental law, state constitutions generally diffuse authority and responsibility so that no man is clearly accountable at the ballot box.

Our 165,000,000 Americans elect one Chief Executive, and the success or failure of every member of his cabinet, his generals and admirals, and the lowliest collector of internal revenue is reflected in the success or failure of his administration and his party at the polls in the next election. But 1,650,000 citizens of Oregon elect a governor, a secretary of state, a state treasurer, an attorney general, a labor commissioner and a superintendent of public instruction, for over-lapping terms, and the first three of these must make executive decisions jointly as a "board of control." If the notion is that three men of political ambition, who may even belong to opposing parties, will control one another, surely no better device could be invented to forestall the vigorous and effective pursuit of a program of government. No wonder that the pattern is then elaborated further turning over much important regulatory responsibility to a proliferation of special boards and commissions, mostly drawn from or responsive to the interests supposed to be regulated. Our state has about 75 such boards, which actually represent the interests supposedly regulated, rather than the general public which is supposed to be protected.

It seems to me every state should consider adoption of the cabinet form of government, which has served the nation so well since we won our freedom from George III. Under this arrangement, the President is responsible for the acts of his aides and appointees. But, in so many state governments, free-lancing by separately-elected departmental heads leads inevitably to absurd divisions of authority. I would suggest the election only of the governor and perhaps one other watch-dog official, either an attorney general or state auditor, let us say. Then, if the state has a corrupt treasurer or inefficient secretary, the public will know where to place the blame—in the governorship.

If the present-day state executive suffers from being underpaid, understaffed, and from divided authority, the present-day legislature suffers even more from those and a host of other crippling deficiencies. First, it is an old, familiar story that state legislatures are many times hopelessly unrepresentative. Reapportionment has been the core of reform as long as there have been state legislatures, and it has recently been urged again by the Kestnbaum Commission. I shall not take your time to cite once more the horrible examples of the disenfranchisement of urban populations. But clearly the fact that state legislatures, heavily dominated by remote constituencies, simply will not recognize and face up to urban needs has driven the cities to seek direct assistance from Washington, D.C. . . .

Second, most legislatures, such as Oregon's, meet only every other year, and rarely for more than three months. Many are limited by state constitutions to a specific maximum term, and the closing days of every session are a pandemonium as bills get gaveled through to passage without debate or even explanation. Contrary to the popular attitude towards Congressmen, who are expected to be on the job fourteen hours a day, every day—and often are—service in the state legislature is firmly kept down to the level of a part-time job, if not actually a hobby. The characteristics of the legislature bespeak a deepseated suspicion of professional, full-time government on the part of the framers of some state constitutions.

This also is demonstrated by the third of the conditions which together almost assure that the state legislature cannot and will not effectively represent the public interest. This is the low pay of state legislators. In Oregon annual legislative pay is $600. This does not even meet hotel bills. State legislators are part-time officials whose basic incomes, therefore, must come from other sources. They are rarely paid enough by their constituents to cover even the expenses of leaving their private affairs for the biennial three months in the state capital. Can we expect the lawyer, the accountant or the insurance agent turned legislator for three months to forget the client whose fees house and feed his family between sessions? This is "conflict of interests" with a vengeance! . . .

Because I am so recently "sprung" from a state legislature, people invariably ask me about the difference between service in the U.S. Senate and a typical state senate. If there is any one dividing characteristic, it is in the vastly superior information and assistance which are available to a United States Senator. State senators are on their own. United States Senators have the advantage of extensive and well-trained committee staffs, of the reference facilities of the Library of Congress, of the vigilant majority and minority conferences of their respective political parties.

When I first entered the Senate, I was shocked to see bills gaveled to passage like pickets flashing past on a fence. "Without objection, the bill is passed," intoned the presiding officer with monotonous regularity. Then I began to realize that all such bills had been carefully screened prior to reaching the unanimous-consent calendar. This was the result of elaborate staff work. It probably could not be risked in a state legislature, with so relatively few aides and researchers. . . .

In addition to staff work, one of the great differences between the Congress and the typical staff legislature is the completeness and wide public distribution of the records made at committee hearings and during floor debate, and of committee reports. The committees of the state legislature of Oregon, the one with which I am most familiar, for instance cannot begin to fill the public role in the legislative process which congressional committees play on the national level. True, they hold hearings and do preliminary work on legislation pending before them. But the testimony developed at these hearings is not published and made available to other members of the Senate or House and to the public at large before voting, nor are committee reports. And the committees do not engage in investigations comparable to those of congressional committees, with the power to compel truthful testimony.

Finally, no verbatim record is kept of statements in floor debate itself. In the Congress, hearing transcripts, committee reports and the *Congressional Record* permit a legislator to study an issue upon which he will have to vote and to base the reasons for his action upon the public record. Under the conditions prevailing in state legislatures, on the other hand, important votes must often be cast in ignorance of any considerations except those brought out in floor debate, and perhaps in reliance upon actual—but unrecorded—misstatements of fact. . . .

In a way, money is the proverbial root of all evil in state government. I have already mentioned that not enough money is spent on executive and legislative salaries and on the research and clerical machinery of the legislature. But in a far more substantive way, the lack of financial resources as compared with those of the federal government is at the bottom of the present low standing of state government. The fact has become widely recognized that the dangerous debility of the states in our modern federal system reflects the fiscal strains created by the heavy revenue demands of necessary national expenditures.

In part, this condition merely reinforces the ever-present resistance to increased state taxes. In addition, in using their powers to reach their still substantial remaining sources of revenues, the individual states often are inhibited by the necessity—real or not—of competing with their neighbors in offering attractive conditions to the investment of capital and the expansion of business within their borders.

Thus, for example, Oregon, nestled among states which rely upon substantial sales taxes for a major portion of their annual revenue, is one of the tiny fraction of states which has so far eschewed this regressive form of taxation. Oregon, instead, has one of the heaviest progressive state income taxes in the nation. Standing by itself, Oregon's tax structure is unquestionably more desirable than that of the great majority of states. In the actual geographical context, however, our relatively progressive tax system gives rise to continual apprehension about the effect it is having on the economic expansion of the state and, thus, indirectly on the burden of the average taxpayer himself.

There is no doubt that it can lead to some unusual results. Wealthy men who play an important role in Oregon business or industry can avoid paying our state income tax on their earnings and profits by maintaining their offices in downtown Portland but living and voting across the Columbia River in the State of Washington. Needless to say, they can avoid almost all of Washington's sales tax by buying their groceries, their clothes, their jewelry, even their refrigerators and washing machines, tax free in Portland. I might add that this comfortable arrangement does not prevent some of these financial leaders from playing very important roles in shaping the government and politics of our state.

25.4. APPORTIONMENT IN THE LEGISLATURES

Congress and the legislatures of the several States are above all representative assemblies. Indeed, among the unique features of the American Republic as conceived by the Founding Fathers was this representative principle. For in it they developed a formula for providing both responsible and rational government over an extensive territory. Although each

State was to have equal representation in the Senate, the House of Repre-
sentatives was to be apportioned according to population after each census.
This apportionment, however, along with the apportionment of represen-
tation in their own legislatures, was left to the States. The result has been
not only a variety in systems of apportionment but glaring inequalities
in the size and population of representative districts. Do these inequalities
amount in extreme cases to a denial of equal protection of laws? Do they
present merely a political issue to be resolved only by political means, or
a justiciable issue for which a judicial remedy may be sought? These are
the two major questions to which the Supreme Court addressed itself in
the case of Baker *v.* Carr.

MR. JUSTICE BRENNAN delivered the opinion of the Court.

This civil action was brought under 42 U.S.C. §§ 1983 and 1988
to redress the alleged deprivation of federal constitutional rights. The
complaint, alleging that by means of a 1901 statute of Tennessee appor-
tioning the members of the General Assembly among the State's 95 counties, "these plaintiffs and others similarly situated, are denied the equal
protection of the laws accorded them by the Fourteenth Amendment to
the Constitution of the United States by virtue of the debasement of their
votes," was dismissed by a three-judge court convened under 28 U.S.C.
§ 2281 in the Middle District of Tennessee. The court held that it lacked
jurisdiction of the subject matter and also that no claim was stated upon
which relief could be granted. . . . We hold that the dismissal was error,
and remand the cause to the District Court for trial and further proceedings consistent with this opinion.

The General Assembly of Tennessee consists of the Senate with
33 members and the House of Representatives with 99 members.

. . . . . .

. . . Tennessee's standard for allocating legislative representation among her counties is the total number of qualified voters resident
in the respective counties, subject only to minor qualifications. Decennial
reapportionment in compliance with the constitutional scheme was effected by the General Assembly each decade from 1871 to 1901. . . . In
the more than 60 years since that action (1901), all proposals in both
Houses of the General Assembly for reapportionment have failed to pass.

Between 1901 and 1961, Tennessee has experienced substantial
growth and redistribution of her population. . . . The relative standings
of the counties in terms of qualified voters have changed significantly. It
is primarily the continued application of the 1901 Apportionment Act

---

From *Baker* v. *Carr,* 369 U.S. 186 (1962).

to this shifted and enlarged voting population which gives rise to the present controversy.

Indeed, the complaint alleges that the 1901 statute, even as of the time of its passage, "made no apportionment of Representatives and Senators in accordance with the constitutional formula . . . , but instead arbitrarily and capriciously apportioned representatives in the Senate and House without reference . . . to any logical or reasonable formula whatever." It is further alleged that "because of the population changes since 1900, and the failure of the Legislature to reapportion itself since 1901," the 1901 statute became "unconstitutional and obsolete." . . . The complaint concludes that "these plaintiffs and others similarly situated, are denied the equal protection of the laws accorded them by the Fourteenth Amendment to the Constitution of the United States by virtue of the debasement of their votes." They seek a declaration that the 1901 statute is unconstitutional and an injunction restraining the appellees from acting to conduct any further elections under it. They also pray that unless and until the General Assembly enacts a valid reapportionment, the District Court should either decree a reapportionment by mathematical application of the Tennessee consitutional formulae to the most recent Federal Census figures, or direct the appellees to conduct legislative elections, primary and general, at large. They also pray for such other and further relief as may be appropriate.

THE DISTRICT COURT'S OPINION
AND ORDER OF DISMISSAL

Because we deal with this case on appeal from an order of dismissal granted on appellees' motions, precise identification of the issues presently confronting us demands clear exposition of the grounds upon which the District Court rested in dismissing the case. The dismissal order recited that the court sustained the appellees' grounds "(1) that the Court lacks jurisdiction of the subject matter, and (2) that the complaint fails to state a claim upon which relief can be granted. . . ."

The court went on to express doubts as to the feasibility of the various possible remedies sought by the plaintiffs. Then it made clear that its dismissal reflected a view not of doubt that violation of constitutional rights was alleged, but of a court's impotence to correct that violation:

With the plaintiffs' argument that the legislature of Tennessee is guilty of a clear violation of the state constitution and of the rights of the plaintiffs the Court entirely agrees. It also agrees that the evil is a serious one which should be corrected without further delay. But even so the remedy in this situation clearly does not lie with the courts. It has long been recognized and is accepted doctrine that there are indeed some rights guaranteed by the Constitution for the violation of which the courts cannot give redress.

In light of the District Court's treatment of the case, we hold today only (a) that the court possessed jurisdiction of the subject matter; (b) that a justiciable cause of action is stated upon which appellants would be entitled to appropriate relief; and (c) because appellees raise the issue before this Court, that the appellants have standing to challenge the Tennessee apportionment statutes. Beyond noting that we have no cause at this stage to doubt the District Court will be able to fashion relief if violations of constitutional rights are found, it is improper now to consider what remedy would be most appropriate if appellants prevail at the trial.

. . . . . .

An unbroken line of our precedents sustains the federal courts' jurisdiction of the subject matter of federal constitutional claims of this nature.

. . . . . .

The appellees refer to *Colegrove* v. *Green,* 328 U.S. 549, as authority that the District Court lacked jurisdiction of the subject matter. Appellees misconceive the holding of that case. The holding was precisely contrary to their reading of it. Seven members of the Court participated in the decision. Unlike many other cases in this field which have assumed without discussion that there was jurisdiction, all three opinions filed in *Colegrove* discussed the question. Two of the opinions expressing the views of four of the Justices, a majority, flatly held that there was jurisdiction of the subject matter. . . . Indeed, it is even questionable that the opinion of Mr. Justice Frankfurter, joined by Justices Reed and Burton, doubted jurisdiction of the subject matter. . . .

Several subsequent cases similar to *Colegrove* have been decided by the Court in summary *per curiam* statements. None was dismissed for want of jurisdiction of the subject matter. . . .

We hold that the District Court has jurisdiction of the subject matter of the federal constitutional claim asserted in the complaint. . . .

We hold that the appellants do have standing to maintain this suit. Our decisions plainly support this conclusion. Many of the cases have assumed rather than articulated the premise in deciding the merits of similar claims. And *Colegrove* v. *Green, supra,* squarely held that voters who allege facts showing disadvantages to themselves as individuals have standing to sue. A number of cases decided after *Colegrove* recognized the standing of the voters there involved to bring those actions.

These appellants seek relief in order to protect or vindicate an interest of their own, and of those similarly situated. Their constitutional claim is, in substance, that the 1901 statute constitutes arbitrary and capricious state action, offensive to the Fourteenth Amendment in its irrational disregard of the standard of apportionment prescribed by the State's Constitution or of any standard, effecting a gross disproportion of representation to voting population. . . .

It would not be necessary to decide whether appellants' allegations of impairment of their votes by the 1901 apportionment will, ultimately, entitle them to any relief, in order to hold that they have standing to seek it. . . . They are entitled to a hearing and to the District Court's decision on their claims. . . .

JUSTICIABILITY

In holding that the subject matter of this suit was not justiciable, the District Court relied on *Colegrove* v. *Green, supra,* and subsequent *per curiam* cases. . . . We understand the District Court to have read the cited cases as compelling the conclusion that since the appellants sought to have a legislative apportionment held unconstitutional, their suit presented a "political question" and was therefore nonjusticiable. We hold that this challenge to an apportionment presents no nonjusticiable "political question." The cited cases do not hold the contrary.

Of course the mere fact that the suit seeks protection of a political right does not mean it presents a political question. Such an objection "is little more than a play upon words." . . .

. . . . . .

We come, finally, to the ultimate inquiry whether our precedents as to what constitutes a nonjusticiable "political question" bring the case before us under the umbrella of that doctrine. . . . The question here is the consistency of state action with the Federal Constitution. . . .

When challenges to state action respecting matters of "the administration of the affairs of the State and the officers through whom they are conducted" have rested on claims of constitutional deprivation which are amenable to judicial correction, this Court has acted upon its view of the merit of the claim. . . . And only last Term, in *Gomillion* v. *Lightfoot,* 364 U.S. 339, we applied the Fifteenth Amendment to strike down a redrafting of municipal boundaries which effected a discriminatory impairment of voting rights, in the face of what a majority of the Court of Appeals thought to be a sweeping commitment to state legislatures of the power to draw and redraw such boundaries. . . .

This Court's answer to the argument that States enjoyed unrestricted control over municipal boundaries was:

Legislative control of municipalities, no less than other state power, lies within the scope of relevant limitations imposed by the United States Constitution. . . . The opposite conclusion, urged upon us by respondents, would sanction the achievement by a State of any impairment of voting rights whatever so long as it was cloaked in the garb of the realignment of political subdivisions. "It is inconceivable that guaranties embedded in the Constitution of the United States may thus be manipulated out of existence." 364 U.S., at 344–345.

To a second argument, that *Colegrove* v. *Green, supra,* was a barrier to hearing the merits of the case, the Court responded that *Gomillion* was lifted "out of the so-called 'political' arena and into the conventional sphere of constitutional litigation" because here was discriminatory treatment of a racial minority violating the Fifteenth Amendment.

. . . . . .

We conclude that the complaint's allegations of a denial of equal protection present a justiciable constitutional cause of action upon which appellants are entitled to a trial and a decision. The right asserted is within the reach of judicial protection under the Fourteenth Amendment. . . .

Reversed and remanded.

Mr. Justice Whittaker did not participate in the decision of this case.

Mr. Justice Douglas, concurring.

While I join the opinion of the Court and, like the Court, do not reach the merits, a word of explanation is necessary. I put to one side the problems of "political" questions involving the distribution of power between this Court, the Congress, and the Chief Executive. We have here a phase of the recurring problem of the relation of the federal courts to state agencies. More particularly, the question is the extent to which a State may weight one person's vote more heavily than it does another's.

. . . . . .

It is said that any decision in cases of this kind is beyond the competence of courts. Some make the same point as regards the problem of equal protection in cases involving racial segregation. Yet the legality of claims and conduct is a traditional subject for judicial determination. . . .

. . . . . .

There is no doubt that the federal courts have jurisdiction of controversies concerning voting rights. . . .

With the exceptions of *Colegrove* v. *Green,* 328 U.S. 549; *MacDougall* v. *Green,* 335 U.S. 281; *South* v. *Peters,* 339 U.S. 276, and the decisions they spawned, the Court has never thought that protection of voting rights was beyond judicial cognizance. Today's treatment of those cases removes the only impediment to judicial cognizance of the claims stated in the present complaint.

. . . . . .

Although I find the Tennessee apportionment statute offends the Equal Protection Clause, I would not consider intervention by this Court into so delicate a field if there were any other relief available to the people of Tennessee. But the majority of the people of Tennessee have no "practical opportunities for exerting their political weight at the polls" to correct the existing "invidious discrimination." Tennessee has no initiative and referendum. I have searched diligently for other "practical opportunities" present under the law. I find none other than through the federal courts. The majority of the voters have been caught up in a legislative strait jacket. . . . The people have been rebuffed at the hands of the Assembly; they have tried the constitutional convention route, but since the call must originate in the Assembly it, too, has been fruitless. They have tried Tennessee courts with the same result, and Governors have fought the tide only to flounder. It is said that there is recourse in Congress and perhaps that may be, but from a practical standpoint this is without substance. To date Congress has never undertaken such a task in any State. We therefore must conclude that the people of Tennessee are stymied and without judicial intervention will be saddled with the present discrimination in the affairs of their state government.

. . . . . .

Mr. Justice Stewart, concurring.

The separate writings of my dissenting and concurring Brothers stray so far from the subject of today's decision as to convey, I think, a distressingly inaccurate impression of what the Court decides. For that reason, I think it appropriate, in joining the opinion of the Court, to emphasize in a few words what the opinion does and does not say.

The Court today decides three things and no more: (a) that the court possessed jurisdiction of the subject matter; (b) that a justiciable cause of action is stated upon which appellants would be entitled to appropriate relief; and (c) . . . that the appellants have standing to challenge the Tennessee apportionment statutes." . . .

The Court does not say or imply that there is anything in the Federal Constitution "to prevent a State, acting not irrationally, from choosing any electoral legislative structure it thinks best suited to the interests, temper, and customs of its people." And contrary to the suggestion of my Brother Douglas, the Court most assuredly does not decide the question, "may a State weight the vote of one county or one district more heavily than it weights the vote in another?"

. . . . . .

. . . My Brother Clark has made a convincing prima facie showing that Tennessee's system of apportionment is in fact utterly arbitrary— without any possible justification in rationality. My Brother Harlan has, with imagination and ingenuity, hypothesized possibly rational bases for Tennessee's system. But the merits of this case are not before us now. The defendants have not yet had an opportunity to be heard in defense of the State's system of apportionment; indeed, they have not yet even filed an answer to the complaint. As in other cases, the proper place for the trial is in the trial court, not here.

Mr. Justice Frankfurter, whom Mr. Justice Harlan joins, dissenting.

The Court today reverses a uniform course of decision established by a dozen cases, including one by which the very claim now sustained was unanimously rejected only five years ago.

. . . . . .

This is the latest in the series of cases in which the Equal Protection and Due Process Clauses of the Fourteenth Amendment have been invoked in federal courts as restrictions upon the power of the States to allocate electoral weight among the voting populations of their various geographical subdivisions.

. . . . . .

In sustaining appellants' claim, based on the Fourteenth Amendment, that the District Court may entertain this suit, this Court's uniform course of decision over the years is overruled or disregarded. Explicitly it begins with *Colegrove* v. *Green, supra,* decided in 1946, but its roots run deep in the Court's historic adjudicatory process.

Colegrove held that a federal court should not entertain an action for declaratory and injunctive relief to adjudicate the constitutionality, under the Equal Protection Clause and other federal constitutional and statutory provisions, of a state statute establishing the respective disricts for the State's election of Representatives to the Congress.

. . . . . .

The *Colegrove* doctrine, in the form in which repeated decisions have settled it, was not an innovation. It represents long judicial thought and experience. From its earliest opinions this Court has consistently recognized a class of controversies which do not lend themselves to judicial standards and judicial remedies. . . .

. . . The Court has been particularly unwilling to intervene in matters concerning the structure and organization of the political institutions of the States. . . .

. . . . . .

. . . The Court has refused to exercise its jurisdiction to pass on "abstract questions of political power, of sovereignty, of government." . . . The "political question" doctrine, in this aspect, reflects the policies underlying the requirement of "standing": that the litigant who would challenge official action must claim infringement of an interest particular and personal to himself, as distinguished from a cause of dissatisfaction with the general frame and functioning of government—a complaint that the political institutions are awry. . . . What renders cases of this kind non-justiciable is not necessarily the nature of the parties to them, for the Court has resolved other issues between similar parties; nor is it the nature of the legal question involved, for the same type of question has been adjudicated when presented in other forms of controversy. The crux of the matter is that courts are not fit instruments of decision where what is essentially at stake is the composition of those large contests of policy traditionally fought out in non-judicial forms, by which governments and the actions of governments are made and unmade.

. . . At first blush, this charge of discrimination based on legislative under-representation is given the appearance of a more private, less impersonal claim, than the assertion that the frame of government is askew. Appellants appear as representatives of a class that is prejudiced as a class, in contradistinction to the polity in its entirety. However, the discrimination relied on is the deprivation of what appellants conceive to be their proportionate share of political influence. This, of course, is the practical effect of any allocation of power within the institutions of government. Hardly any distribution of political authority that could be assailed as rendering government non-republican would fail similarly to operate to the prejudice of some groups, and to the advantage of others, within the body politic. It would be ingenuous not to see, or consciously blind to deny, that the real battle over the initiative and referendum, or over a delegation of power to local rather than state-wide authority, is the battle between forces whose influence is disparate among the various organs of government to whom power may be given. No shift of power but works a corresponding shift in political influence among the groups composing a society.

What, then, is this queston of legislative apportionment? Appellants invoke the right to vote and to have their votes counted. They go to the polls, they cast their ballots, they send their representatives to the state councils. Their complaint is simply that the representatives are not sufficiently numerous or powerful—in short, that Tennessee has adopted a basis of representation with which they are dissatisfied. Talk of "debasement" or "dilution" is circular talk. One cannot speak of "debasement" or "dilution" of the value of a vote until there is first defined a standard of reference as to what a vote should be worth. What is actually asked of the Court in this case is to choose among competing bases of representation—ultimately, really, among competing theories of political philosophy—in order to establish an appropriate frame of government for the State of Tennessee and thereby for all the States of the Union.

In such a matter, abstract analogies which ignore the facts of history deal in unrealities; they betray reason. This is not a case in which a State has, through a device however oblique and sophisticated, denied Negroes or Jews or redheaded persons a vote, or given them only a third or a sixth of a vote. . . . What Tennessee illustrates is an old and still widespread method of representation—representation by local geographical division, only in part respective of population—in preference to others, others, forsooth, more appealing. Appellants contest this choice and seek to make this Court the arbiter of the disagreement. They would make the Equal Protection Clause the charter of adjudication, asserting that the equality which it guarantees comports, if not the assurance of equal weight to every voter's vote, at least the basic conception that representation ought to be proportionate to population, a standard by reference to which the reasonableness of apportionment plans may be judged.

To find such a political conception legally enforceable in the broad and unspecific guarantee of equal protection is to rewrite the Constitution. . . .

The notion that representation proportioned to the geographic spread of population is so universally accepted as a necessary element of equality between man and man that it must be taken to be the standard of a political equality preserved by the Fourteenth Amendment—that it is, in appellants' words, "the basic principle of representative government"—is, to put it bluntly, not true. However desirable and however desired by some among the great political thinkers and framers of our government, it has never been generally practiced, today or in the past. It was not the English system, it was not the colonial system, it was not the system chosen for the national government by the Constitution, it was not the system exclusively or even predominantly practiced by the States at the time of adoption of the Fourteenth Amendment, it is not predominantly practiced by the States today. . . .

. . . . . .

The several state conventions throughout the first half of the nineteenth century were the scenes of fierce sectional and party strifes respecting the geographic allocation of representation. Their product was a wide variety of apportionment methods which recognized the element of population in differing ways and degrees. Particularly pertinent to appraisal of the contention that the Fourteenth Amendment embodied a standard limiting the freedom of the States with regard to the principles and bases of local legislative apportionment is an examination of the apportionment provisions of the thirty-three states which ratified the Amendment between 1866 and 1870, at their respective times of ratification. . . . All thirty-three are significant, because they demonstrate how unfounded is the assumption that the ratifying States could have agreed on a standard apportionment theory or practice, and how baseless the suggestion that by voting for the Equal Protection Clause they sought to establish a test mold for apportionment which—if appellants' argument is sound, struck down *sub silentio* not a few of their own state constitutional provisions.

. . . . . .

The constitutions of the thirteen States which Congress admitted to the Union after the ratification of the Fourteenth Amendment showed a similar pattern. . . .

Detailed recent studies are available to describe the present-day constitutional and statutory status of apportionment in the fifty States. They demonstrate a decided twentieth-century trend away from population as the exclusive base of representation. Today, only a dozen state constitutions provide for periodic legislative reapportionment of both houses by a substantially unqualified application of the population standard, and only about a dozen more prescribe such reapportionment for even a single chamber. . . .

.   .   .   .   .   .

The stark fact is that if among the numerous widely varying principles and practices that control state legislative apportionment today there is any generally prevailing feature, that feature is geographic inequality in relation to the population standard. . . .

.   .   .   .   .   .

. . . Apportionment, by its character, is a subject of extraordinary complexity, involving—even after the fundamental theoretical issues concerning what is to be represented in a representative legislature have been fought out or compromised—considerations of geography, demography, electoral convenience, economic and social cohesions or divergencies among particular local groups, communications, the practical effects of political institutions like the lobby and the city machine, ancient traditions and ties of settled usage, respect for proven incumbents of long experience and senior status, mathematical mechanics, censuses compiling relevent data, and a host of others. Legislative responses through the country to the reapportionment demands of the 1960 Census have glaringly confirmed that these are not factors that lend themselves to evaluations of a nature that are the staple of judicial determinations or for which judges are equipped to adjudicate by legal training or experience or native wit. And this is the more so true because in every strand of this complicated, intricate web of values meet the contending forces of partisan politics. The practical significance of apportionment is that the next election results may differ because of it. Apportionment battles are overwhelmingly party or intra-party contests. It will add a virulent source of friction and tension in federal-state relations to embroil the federal judiciary in them. . . .

.   .   .   .   .   .

Although the District Court had jurisdiction in the very restricted sense of power to determine whether it could adjudicate the claim, the case is of that class of political controversy which, by the nature of its subject, is unfit for federal judicial action. The judgment of the District Court, in dismissing the complaint for failure to state a claim on which relief can be granted, should therefore be affirmed.

Dissenting opinion of Mr. Justice Harlan, whom Mr. Justice Frankfurter joins.

The dissenting opinion of Mr. Justice Frankfurter, in which I join, demonstrates the abrupt departure the majority makes from judicial history by putting the federal courts into this area of state concerns—an area which, in this instance, the Tennessee state courts themselves have refused to enter.

. . . . . .

I can find nothing in the Equal Protection Clause or elsewhere in the Federal Constitution which expressly or impliedly supports the view that state legislatures must be so structured as to reflect with approximate equality the voice of every voter. Not only is that proposition refuted by history, as shown by my Brother Frankfurter, but it strikes deep into the heart of our federal system. Its acceptance would require us to turn our backs on the regard which this Court has always shown for the judgment of state legislatures and courts on matters of basically local concern.

. . . . . .

In short, there is nothing in the Federal Constitution to prevent a State, acting not irrationally from choosing any electoral legislative structure is thinks best suited to the interests, temper, and customs of its people. . . .

In conclusion, it is appropriate to say that one need not agree, as a citizen, with what Tennessee has done or failed to do, in order to deprecate, as a judge, what the majority is doing today. Those observers of the Court who see it primarily as the last refuge for the correction of all inequality or injustice, no matter what its nature or source, will no doubt applaud this decision and its break with the past. Those who consider that continuing national respect for the Court's authority depends in large measure upon its wise exercise of self-restraint and discipline in constitutional adjudication, will view the decision with deep concern.

I would affirm.

26

The Urban Drift

26.1. CRIME AND THE CITIES

In this famous book, a distinguished journalist of the "muck-raking" era examines the corruption in seven major American cities at the turn of the nineteenth century. His study of Minneapolis leads him to ask, "Can a city be governed without any alliance with crime?"

. . . IN MINNEAPOLIS "Doc" Ames was the man.

Minneapolis is a New England town on the upper Mississippi. The metropolis of the Northwest, it is the metropolis also of Norway and Sweden in America. Indeed, it is the second largest Scandinavian city in the world. But Yankees, straight from Down East, settled the town, and their New England spirit predominates. They had Bayard Taylor lecture there in the early days of the settlement; they made it the seat of the University of Minneosta. Yet even now, when the town has grown to a population of more than 200,000, you feel that there is something Western about it too—a Yankee with a round Puritan head, an open prairie heart, and a great, big Scandinavian body. The "Roundhead" takes the "Square-head" out into the woods, and they cut lumber by forests, or they go out on the prairies and raise wheat and mill it into fleet-cargoes of flour. They work hard, they make money, they are sober, satisfied, busy with their own affairs. There isn't much time for public business. Taken together, Miles, Hans, and Ole are very American. Miles insists upon strict laws, Ole and Hans want one or two Scandinavians on their ticket. These things granted, they go off on raft or reaper, leaving whoso will to enforce the laws and run the city. . . .

. . . The people had just secured the passage of a new primary law to establish direct popular government. There were to be no more nominations by convention. The voters were to ballot for their party

From Lincoln Steffens, *The Shame of the Cities* (New York: Hill and Wang, 1960; originally: 1904).

candidates. By a slip of some sort, the laws did not specify that Republicans only should vote for Republican candidates, and only Democrats for Democratic candidates. Any voter could vote at either primary. Ames, in disrepute with his own party, the Democratic, bade his followers vote for his nomination for mayor on the Republican ticket. They all voted; not all the Republicans did. He was nominated. Nomination is far from election, and you would say that the trick would not help him. But that was a Presidential year, so the people of Minneapolis had to vote for Ames, the Republican candidate for mayor. Besides, Ames said he was going to reform; that he was getting old, and wanted to close his career with a good administration. The effective argument, however, was that, since McKinley had to be elected to save the country, Ames must be supported for mayor of Minneapolis. Why? The great American people cannot be trusted to scratch a ticket.

Well, Minneapolis got its old mayor back, and he was indeed "reformed." Up to this time Ames had not been very venal personally. He was a "spender," not a "grafter," and he was guilty of corruption chiefly by proxy; he took the honors and left the spoils to his followers. His administrations were no worse than the worst. Now, however, he set out upon a career of corruption which for deliberateness, invention, and avarice has never been equaled. It was as if he had made up his mind that he had been careless long enough, and meant to enrich his last years. He began promptly.

Immediately upon his election, before he took office (on January 7, 1901), he organized a cabinet and laid plans to turn the city over to outlaws who were to work under police direction for the profit of his administration. He chose for chief his brother, Colonel Fred W. Ames, who had recently returned under a cloud from service in the Philippines. But he was a weak vessel for chief of police, and the mayor picked for chief of detectives an abler man, who was to direct more difficult operations. This was Norman W. King, a former gambler, who knew the criminals needed in the business ahead. King was to invite to Minneapolis thieves, confidence men, pickpockets and gamblers, and release some that were in the local jail. They were to be organized into groups, according to their profession, and detectives were assigned to assist and direct them. The head of the gambling syndicate was to have charge of the gambling, making the terms and collecting the "graft," just as King and a Captain Hill were to collect from the thieves. The collector for women of the town was to be Irwin A. Gardner, a medical student in the Doctor's office, who was made a special policeman for the purpose. These men looked over the force, selected those men who could be trusted, charged them a price for their retention, and marked for dismissal 107 men out of 225, the 107 being the best policemen in the department from the point of view of the citizens who afterward reorganized the force. John Fitchette, better known as "Coffee John," a Virginian (who served on the Jefferson Davis jury), the keeper of a notorious coffee-house, was to be a captain of police, with no duties except to sell places on the police force.

And they did these things that they planned—all and more. The administration opened with the revolution on the police force. The thieves in the local jail were liberated, and it was made known to the Under World generally that "things were doing" in Minneapolis. The incoming swindlers reported to King or his staff for instructions, and went to work, turning the "swag" over to the detectives in charge. Gambling went on openly, and disorderly houses multiplied under the fostering care of Gardner, the medical student. But all this was not enough. Ames dared to break openly into the municipal system of vice protection.

. . . The novel feature of this scheme was that disorderly houses were practically licensed by the city, the women appearing before the clerk of the Municipal Court each month to pay a "fine" of $100. Unable at first to get this "graft," Ames's man Gardner persuaded women to start houses, apartments, and, of all things, candy stores, which sold sweets to children and tobacco to the "lumber Jacks" in front, while a nefarious traffic was carried on in the rear. But they paid Ames, not the city, and that was all this "reform" administration cared about. . . .

It was . . . in April, 1902, that the grand jury for the summer term was drawn. An ordinary body of unselected citizens, it received no special instructions from the bench; the county prosecutor offered it only routine work to do. But there was a man among them who was a fighter—the foreman, Hovey C. Clarke. He was of an old New England family. Coming to Minneapolis when a young man, seventeen years before, he had fought for employment, fought with his employers for position, fought with his employees, the lumber Jacks, for command, fought for his company against competitors; and he had won always, till now he had the habit of command, the impatient, imperious manner of the master, and the assurance of success which begets it. He did not want to be a grand juryman, he did not want to be foreman; but since he was both, he wanted to accomplish something. . . .

. . . He hired a lot of local detectives who, he knew, would talk about what they were doing, and thus would be watched by the police. Having thus thrown a false scent, he hired some other detectives whom nobody knew about. This was expensive; so were many of the other things he did; but he was bound to win, so he paid the price, drawing freely on his own and his colleagues' pockets. (The total cost to the county for a long summer's work by this grand jury was $259.) With his detectives out, he himself went to the jail to get tips from the inside, from criminals who, being there, must have grievances. He made the acquaintance of the jailer, Captain Alexander, and Alexander was a friend of Sheriff Mergaarden. . . .

Nothing stopped this jury, however. They had courage. They indicted Gardner, Norbeck, Fred Ames, and many lesser persons. But the gang had courage, too, and raised a defense fund to fight Clarke. Mayor Ames was defiant. Once, when Mr. Clarke called at the City Hall, the mayor met and challenged him. The mayor's heelers were all about him, but Clarke faced him.

"Yes, Doc Ames, I'm after you," he said. "I've been in this town for seventeen years, and all that time you've been a moral leper. I hear you were rotten during the ten years before that. Now I'm going to put you where all contagious things are put—where you cannot contaminate anybody else." . . .

All men were now on the side of law and order. The panic among the "grafters" was laughable, in spite of its hideous significance. Two heads of departments against whom nothing had been shown suddenly ran away, and thus suggested to the grand jury an inquiry which revealed another source of "graft," in the sale of supplies to public institutions and the diversion of great quantities of provisions to the private residences of the mayor and other officials. Mayor Ames, under indictment and heavy bonds for extortion, conspiracy, and bribe-offering, left the State on a night train; a gentleman who knew him by sight saw him sitting up at eleven o'clock in the smoking-room of the sleeping-car, an unlighted cigar in his mouth, his face ashen and drawn, and at six o'clock the next morning he still was sitting there, his cigar still unlighted. . . .

But the town was not yet easy. The grand jury, which was the actual head of the government, was about to be discharged, and, besides, their work was destructive. A constructive force was now needed, and Alderman Jones was pelted with telegrams form home bidding him hurry back. He did hurry, and when he arrived, the situation was instantly in control. The grand jury prepared to report, for the city had a mind and a will of its own once more. The criminals found it out last.

Percy Jones, as his friends call him, is of the second generation of his family in Minneapolis. His father started him well-to-do, and he went on from where he was started. College graduate and business man, he has a conscience which, however, he has brains enough to question. He is not the fighter, but the slow, sure executive. As an alderman he is the result of a movement begun several years ago by some young men who were convinced by an exposure of a corrupt municipal council that they should go into politics. A few did go in; Jones was one of these few.

The acting mayor was confronted at once with all the hardest problems of municipal government. Vice rose right up to tempt or to fight him. He studied the situation deliberately, and by and by began to settle it point by point, slowly but finally, against all sorts of opposition. One of his first acts was to remove all the proved rascals on the force, putting in their places men who had been removed by Mayor Ames.

Another important step was the appointment of a church deacon and personal friend to be chief of police, this on the theory that he wanted at the head of his police a man who could have no sympathy with crime, a man whom he could implicitly trust. Disorderly houses, forbidden by law, were permitted, but only within certain patrol lines, and they were to pay nothing, in either blackmail or "fines." The number and the standing and the point of view of the "good people" who opposed this order was a lesson to Mr. Jones in practical government. One very prominent citizen and church member threatened him for driving women out of two flats owned by him; the rent was the surest means of "support for his wife and children." Mr. Jones enforced his order. . . .

When the gamblers called again, they found the acting mayor ready to give his decision on their propositions. It was this: There should be no gambling, with police connivance, in the city of Minneapolis during his term of office.

Mr. Jones told me that if he had before him a long term, he certainly would reconsider this answer. He believed he would decide again as he had already, but he would at least give studious reflection to the question—Can a city be governed without any alliance with crime?

26.2. THE HOPE FOR GOOD GOVERNMENT

In this selection Steffens focuses on New York City during the Tammany Hall period of domination. He is not at all convinced that the American people really want honest government for the cities.

DO WE AMERICANS really want good government? Do we know it when we see it? Are we capable of that sustained good citizenship which alone can make democracy a success? Or, to save our pride, one other: Is the New York way the right road to permanent reform?

For New York has good government, or, to be more precise, it has a good administration. It is not a question there of turning the rascals out and putting the honest men into their places. The honest men are in, and this election is to decide whether they are to be kept in, which is a very different matter. Any people is capable of rising in wrath to overthrow bad rulers. Philadelphia has done that in its day. New York has done it several times. With fresh and present outrages to avenge, particular villains to punish, and the mob sense of common anger to excite, it is an emotional gratification to go out with the crowd and "smash something." This is nothing but revolt, and even monarchies have uprisings to the

From Lincoln Steffens, *The Shame of the Cities* (New York: Hill and Wang, 1960; originally: 1904).

credit of their subjects. But revolt is not reform, and one revolutionary administration is not good government. That we free Americans are capable of such assertions of our sovereign power, we have proven; our lynchers are demonstrating it every day. That we can go forth singly also, and, without passion, with nothing but mild approval and dull duty to impel us, vote intelligently to sustain a fairly good municipal government, remains to be shown. And that is what New York has the chance to show; New York, the leading exponent of the great American anti-bad government movement for good government. . . .

But again I say, also, that the New York way is on trial, for New York has what the whole country has been looking for in all municipal crises—the nonpolitical ruler. Mr. Low's very faults, which I have emphasized for the purpose, emphasize the point. They make it impossible for him to be a politician even if he should wish to be. As for his selfishness, his lack of tact, his coldness—these are of no consequence. He has done his duty all the better for them. Admit that he is uninteresting; what does that matter? He has served the city. Will the city not vote for him because it does not like the way he smiles? Absurd as it sounds, that is what all I have heard against Low amounts to. But to reduce the situation to a further absurdity, let us eliminate altogether the personality of Mr. Low. Let us suppose he has no smile, no courtesy, no dignity, no efficiency, no personality at all; suppose he were an It and had not given New York a good administration, but had only honestly tried. What then?

Tammany Hall? That is the alternative. The Tammany politicians see it just as clear as that, and they are not in the habit of deceiving themselves. They say "it is a Tammany year," "Tammany's turn." They say it and they believe it. They study the people, and they know it is all a matter of citizenship; they admit that they cannot win unless a goodly part of the independent vote goes to them; and still they say they can beat Mr. Low or any other man the anti-Tammany forces may nominate. So we are safe in eliminating Mr. Low and reducing the issue to plain Tammany.

Tammany is bad government; not inefficient, but dishonest; not a party, not a delusion and a snare, hardly known by its party name—Democracy; having little standing in the national councils of the party and caring little for influence outside of the city. Tammany is Tammany, the embodiment of corruption. All the world knows and all the world may know what it is and what it is after. For hypocrisy is not a Tammany vice. Tammany is for Tammany, and the Tammany men say so. Other rings proclaim lies and make pretensions; other rogues talk about the tariff and imperialism. Tammany is honestly dishonest. Time and time again, in private and in public, the leaders, big and little, have said they are out for themselves and their own; not for the public, but for "me and my friends"; not for New York, but for Tammany. Richard Croker said under oath once that he worked for his own pockets all the time, and Tom Grady, the Tammany orator, has brought his crowds to their feet cheering sentiments as primitive, stated with candor as brutal. . . .

Tammany's democratic corruption rests upon the corruption of the people, the plain people, and there lies its great significance; its grafting system is one in which more individuals share than any I have studied. The people themselves get very little; they come cheap, but they are interested. Divided into districts, the organization subdivides them into precincts or neighborhoods, and their sovereign power, in the form of votes, is bought up by kindness and petty privileges. They are forced to a surrender, when necessary, by intimidation, but the leader and his captains have their hold because they take care of their own. They speak pleasant words, smile friendly smiles, notice the baby, give picnics up the River or the Sound, or a slap on the back; find jobs, most of them at the city's expense, but they have also newsstands, peddling privileges, railroad and other business places to dispense; they permit violations of the law, and, if a man has broken the law without permission, see him through the court. Though a blow in the face is as readily given as a shake of the hand, Tammany kindness is real kindness, and will go far, remember long, and take infinite trouble for a friend.

The power that is gathered up thus cheaply, like garbage, in the districts is concentrated in the district leader, who in turn passes it on through a general committee to the boss. This is a form of living government, extra-legal, but very actual, and, though the beginnings of it are purely democratic, it develops at each stage into an autocracy. . . .

. . . New York has gone on fighting, advancing and retreating, for thirty years, till now it has achieved the beginnings, under Mayor Low, of a government for the people. Do the New Yorkers know it? Do they care? They are Americans, mixed and typical; do we Americans really want good government? Or, as I said at starting, have they worked for thirty years along the wrong road—crowded with unhappy American cities—the road to . . . despair?

Post Scriptum: Mayor Low was nominated on the Fusion ticket. Tammany nominated George B. McClellan. The local corporations contributed heavily to the Tammany campaign fund and the people of New York elected the Tammany ticket by a decisive majority of 62,696. The vote was: McClellan, 314,782; Low, 252,086.

26.3. PROBLEMS FACING THE CITY

This classic report was prepared twenty-five years ago. The major problems it identifies—such as transportion, health, housing, crime, and public finance—have become crucial ones for our cities in the intervening years.

THIS REPORT, made for the President, following the request of a number of national organizations, is the first major national study of cities in the United States. The Country Life Commission reporting to President Theodore Roosevelt in 1909 explored the problems of rural living for the first time in systematic fashion, but until now there has been no similar examination of urban conditions. There have been many special studies in particular cities, but none of the place of cities in our national scheme of things. . . .

The modern nation finds in its cities the focal point of much that is threatening and much that is promising in the life of its people. Scanning the troubled horizons of the past few years for these symptoms of national strength and national strain, we find first of all that the city has become not only one of the fundamental supports but also one of the primary problems of the Nation's economy.

As America pitches back and forth between alernate depression and recurrent prosperity, it is in the Nation's cities that the shadow of economic insecurity is darkest. For in the city will be found the workshop of our industrial society and the nerve center of our vast and delicate commercial mechanism. In 1935 one-fifth of all the employable persons on relief in the country were to be found in our 10 largest cities. Subject to continuing unemployment, lacking the rural reserves of shelter and subsistence, the city worker is seriously handicapped in the struggle for existence.

In time of national stress the task of relief and recovery falls not merely upon a single community or segment of the Nation, but upon the Nation as a whole. It is the Federal Government that has had to assume the major burdens of providing emergency relief for the city as well as the farm, of stimulating public works in the Nation's urban centers, and even of reviving insolvent municipal finances. . . .

It is important to look at some of the emerging problems of urban communities and to consider such forms of guidance and support as may seem feasible and appropriate under all the circumstances.

1. The most drastic inequalities of income and wealth are found within the urban community. Relatively to their rich fellow citizens, the poor are poorer in the city than they are elsewhere despite an increasing standard of living for the city worker. Widespread poverty and cyclical unemployment and insecurity threaten purchasing power, and without continuous mass purchasing power our urban industry and mass-production economy cannot continue to function properly.

2. One of our specific economic problems is the lack of articulation among the various industries within our urban communities. Fre-

From the Report of the Urbanism Committee of the U.S. National Resources Committee, *Our Cities* (Washinton, D.C.: U.S. Government Printing Office, 1937).

quently the decision to locate an industry in one city or another is based upon the immediate opportunities of a particular enterprise or the desire of a community to increase the total amount of industrial activity, regardless of its effect upon the local industrial structure. Localities, by means of subsidies, tax exemption, and free sites, have indiscriminately attracted enterprises which did not mesh with the rest of the community's industries and which sooner or later helped to throw the entire industrial pattern out of gear. Under such unbalanced conditions, it is impossible to achieve a maximum employment for the available labor supply and a minimum of seasonal and cyclical fluctuations in the total pay roll of the community. Instead, the results may be migrant labor, increased unemployment load, lower wages, shruken purchasing power, loss of business, high cost of relief, untenanted property, tax arrears, and curtailed municipal services.

3. Rapid obsolescence of physical plan and plant is another problem which the American city has had to face. Villages, in all too short a period of time, have become towns, towns have become cities, and cities have turned into metropolitan centers, where brick houses replaced frame, apartment hotels succeeded residences, office buildings replaced shops and lofts, inns became grand hotels, and the early skyscrapers were converted into colossal cloud-scratchers. Some cities on the other hand have become deserted mill sites and dreary ghosts towns. America was growing, but it was also wasting away, and traces of this deterioration are with us today in the form of many blighted neighborhoods.

4. Competing forms of transportation have left their disrupting imprint upon the national urban pattern. Located originally on natural waterways, American cities found their sister towns rising up during the canal era on new water routes. With the coming of the railroads these canal cities met in their turn a similarly disastrous fate. Then came competing railroads, and cities again began to rival one another with excessive subsidies and cut-throat competition for rate reduction. Nor have we yet reached the end of this process. The motor truck and the passenger bus have long since entered the field of competition, and now the airplane begins to affect the national distribution of our urban centers and even the local pattern and the plan of our cities.

5. The unparalleled growth of cities has been accompanied by uncontrolled subdivision and speculative practices and by the most fantastic real estate booms which have meant dramatic profits to a few, but tragic personal losses to others and burdensome delinquent properties to the community; and this on a scale affecting the economic situation of the entire Nation. The history of the recent industrial depression cannot be written without an account of the role of unsound financing and of speculation in real estate which at times became mere gambling. We are now faced with the problem of arriving at a rational urban land policy

which, while affording private owners and developers adequate opportunity for wise and profitable land uses, will curb the forms of speculation that prove calamitous to the investing and the tax-paying public.

6. Urban housing is one of the most burdensome problems the country now has to face and it calls for the Nation's most serious consideration. A real property inventory of 64 cities made in 1934 by the Department of Commerce and the Civil Works Administration showed that more than one-sixth of 1,500,000 residential dwellings were substandard, about four-fifths of the dwelling units are made of wood, about one-third are over 30 years old, a large proportion are in a state of serious disrepair. Even at their most reasonable figures rentals are so high that they exclude vast blocs of urban families from housing facilities of minimum standard.

7. Urban public health is endangered particularly in blighted areas and among low income groups. Morbidity and mortality rates in infants' diseases and tuberculosis are higher here than elsewhere, in spite of an admirable development of urban public health services. Dirt, smoke, waste, soot, grime, and the reckless pollution of water are still among the noxious enemies of city life despite valiant official attempts to regulate these evils.

8. The city with its diversity of ethnic, religious, and cultural strains is the haven par excellence of many widely varying types of personalities whose names loom large in the history of America, but in this heterogeneity the city also finds some of its weightiest problems. The various parts and participants of the urban economy are very highly specialized and the urban way of life is often socially disconnected though economically interdependent. Allegiances may become group, class, or sectional rather than community or city-wide. How to prevent these strains of separation from disrupting the whole city or its civic groups or even its families, how to weave these vivid and variegated cultures into a positive civic program of intercommunication and co-operation is one of the challenging problems of the coming decades.

9. While free primary and secondary education is now widely available in urban areas, city youths in all too many cases are still barred from higher educational opportunities they might well utilize because they must all too frequently supplement the family income by going to work. Vocational education and adaptation still limp and lag behind their possibilities although much work has already been started. Adult education after so many years of enthusiasm for this form of civic enlightenment in cities is an inadequately supported service and is still an experiment instead of an accepted responsibility of the community. Much has been accomplished through Federal aid, but much more needs to be done.

10. Juvenile delinquency, organized crime, and commercial rackets are among the vexations of the city. None of our reforms in the

field of criminal justice has successfully come to grips with these persistent urban problems.

11. Urban public finance is another emerging problem of vast proportions. In the recent depression, urban areas pouring millions into the national treasury were forced to pass the hat, begging for financial support. The anomaly of the situation is the fact that the 48 State governments which determine the local system of taxation are from the standpoint of total expenditures only one-half as important as all the local governments they must control. Our largest cities alone, New York, Chicago, Boston, and Detroit, have larger budgets than the States which contain them. The problem of municipal finance is becoming even more complicated with the extension of Federal and State taxation to support the newer services of government such as social security and extensive public works.

12. Another of the city's . . . tasks is the adjustment of the traditional scope of urban powers. In spite of its vital and growing significance as the principal instrument of public service and community control, the American city is still the legal creature of higher authorities, subject to their fiat for the most minor of powers and procedures, reaching down in one State to legislation to permit the peddling of peanuts on a municipal pier. The city is in many ways the ward of a guardian who refuses to function.

13. Our overlapping medley of independent governmental units was intended for a rural and a manorial society but never for the sprawling metropolitan regions of America and the satellite suburbs. The concrete facts of our urban and administrative life frequently defy State lines and local control. Twenty-two of our 96 metropolitan districts containing 26,000,000 or one-fifth of all our inhabitants, straddle State lines and call for a larger measure of interstate, and Federal cooperation in certain fields that is now found.

14. We have made striking technical advances in municipal government and for years now we have developed, contrary to opinions widely held, skill and talent and expert knowledge among our municipal career officers, but we are still faced in some cities with systematic evasions of civil service laws, irresponsible political leadership, and official tolerance of discriminatory or questionable administrative practices.

26.4. PROBLEMS OF THE
EXPANDING METROPOLIS

This report by the Council on State Governments to the Governors'
Conference traces the causes and implications of the movement of rural

dwellers to the cities and of city dwellers to the suburbs. The need for coordination of control of governmental districts and the problems of variation between service needs and financial resources are emphasized.

THE EXTENSIVE development of metropolitan areas results from many factors. Agricultural improvements forced many former farm workers to go to urban locations to earn a livelihood. The development of power-machine industry, especially in the form of electrical energy which could be transmitted and applied long distances from its source, made possible a wider distribution of people, industry and commerce. Continued advances in medicine and sanitation substantially lowered the death rate. All of these factors facilitated the metropolitan movement, but the immediate causes that brought on the highly intensified growth of metropolitan areas were in the field of transportation. Widespread use of the internal combustion engine, the establishment of modern roads, and improvements in rapid mass transit all were basic. Private automobiles, in particular, provided increased flexibility and individuality in transportation. Together with truck transport and high-speed interurban trains, they greatly increased the freedom of movement of people and goods over a widening area, whose parts thus became increasingly interrelated.

Technological changes had to be supported by human wishes to make large-scale metropolitan development a reality. In many instances, although people wanted to be near the central city for work and social opportunities, they established their homes outside its limits in the hope of acquiring more pleasant living conditions. New or improved transportation facilities gave city dwellers the opportunity to move from the city, upon which they continued to have various types of economic or social dependence. Similar opportunities were available to business and other organizations. Thus, numerous people, industries, manufacturing plants and trade establishments settled in the outlying sections. Some relocated from sites within the city, and others tranferred from locations outside of the metropolitan area.

New communities developed, and new governments were created to provide services and regulation. The relatively detached economic and social position of older, established cities situated within ten to twenty miles of the central city disappeared. The comparative self-sufficiency of many urban localities gave way to greater interdependence in a metropolitan area. Numerous old and new settlements alike therefore becoming parts of a metropolitan whole, and a heavy volume of travel and contact, both for work and social purposes, became common between the central city and other sections.

From *The States and the Metropolitan Problem* (Chicago: Council of State Governments, 1956).

The factors that have permitted and expedited the development of metropolitan areas are still present and active. Some have had appreciably stronger effect in recent years than before. Widespread use of private automobiles and continued improvements in roads are examples. No major counter factor, such as dispersion to lessen the potential effects of atomic war, has yet taken hold. Consequently there are no current indications that the metropolitan trend—already of enormous proportions—has reached its peak. Obviously, therefore, the problems resulting from the rise and expansion of metropolitan areas will not be solved merely by passage of time. Instead, the difficulties must be expected to become more aggravated unless remedial actions are taken. . . .

Metropolitan areas are large in total number and they represent a nationwide rather than a regional development. There are 172 such areas in the continental United States, comprising territory in forty-two states and in the District of Columbia. The only states that do not currently contain at least part of an area defined by the Census Bureau as metropolitan are Idaho, Montana, Nevada, North Dakota, Vermont and Wyoming, and in some of them certain sections are approaching this status. . . .

Within the metropolitan trend a large-scale decentralization has materialized. Consequently, approximately one-fourth of the central cities do not contain a majority of the people of the metropolitan areas in which they are located. Such population distribution is present in at least one metropolitan area in each of nineteen states and exists in most metropolitan sectors of California and Pennsylvania. Numerous new metropolitan residents have settled in the outlying portions, and some people have moved to them from the central cities. Increasing numbers of people are residing in incorporated localities that are beyond the service and regulatory jurisdictions of the central cities. . . .

According to the sample survey, in the five-year period that ended in April, 1955, the increase in metropolitan areas was approximately 11,500,000 and that of the remainder of the country was only 300,000. With a total population of more than 95,000,000, metropolitan areas have 59 percent of the population of the nation as compared to 56 percent in 1950. The population in the portions of metropolitan areas outside central cities grew seven times as fast as that of the central cities. Approximately 46 percent of all metropolitan residents now live in the non-central city sections. Moreover, the total number of people of the non-central city portions classified as rural by the Census Bureau in 1950, and located in large part at the outer borders of metropolitan areas, enlarged almost three and one-half times as fast as the entire metropolitan population. On the basis of the latest data, it thus is evident that the population growth of metropolitan areas and the decentralization of population within them are not slowing down but are proceeding at a very rapid pace.

Most metropolitan areas—almost seven of every ten—contain the territory of a single county, but a significant number are intercounty. Furthermore, many that are intercounty are also interstate. Of thirty metropolitan areas that are intercounty and entirely within one state, nineteen involve two counties. Consisting of three counties each are six metropolitan areas whose central cities are Albany-Schenectady-Troy, New York; Atlanta, Georgia; Brockton, Massachusetts; Detroit, Michigan; Knoxville, Tennessee; and New Orleans, Louisiana. Three metropolitan areas—Denver, Colorado; Minneapolis-St. Paul, Minnesota; and Pittsburgh, Pennsylvania—include four counties each. One (Boston) involves five counties and another (San Francisco-Oakland) has six. . . .

The greatest significance of intercounty metropolitan areas, however, is not their size. Many of them are larger territorially than those within a single county, but this is not universally the case; areas of counties vary considerably on a state-by-state basis and in some instances appreciably within a single state. The real importance of the intercounty status is that the metropolitan territory is not within the limits of any one general unit of local government. This is a matter that requires close consideration in the formulation of metropolitan reorganization proposals. . . .

Metropolitan areas in general represent a concern of many state governments because a large proportion of the total state population resides in them and because they characteristically involve intergovernmental problems. Interstate metropolitan areas in particular need state-level attention. About two of every five metropolitan inhabitants live in interstate metropolitan areas, and certain activities in such areas require cooperation between at least two state governments. In addition to twenty-four interstate metropolitan areas, twenty-nine others currently border state lines. These twenty-nine contain approximately 12 percent of the total metropolitan population of the country, and population trends indicate that some of them soon will become interstate. Thus the interstate problem seems about to become more extensive. More than a fourth of the nation's people reside in metropolitan areas that are either currently or potentially interstate. . . . ◆

The common pattern of governments functioning in metropolitan areas is complex and confusing. The number of local governmental units is large, averaging ninety-six in each metropolitan area. Moreover, several types of local governments are in operation, and they generally differ as to functions and the means of financing granted to them. The variations are still more pronounced in numerous interstate metropolitan areas. Comparable units, situated on opposite sides of a state boundary, operate under different state constitutions, different state laws and may differ in functional and financial authority. Usually metropolitan areas contain one or more classes of municipalities, one or more counties, and a variety of special districts. In certain regions, towns or townships also are present. Many or all of these local governments individually occupy only portions of the metropolitan area.

As metropolitan areas have become more populous and extensive, local governments in them ordinarily have increased in number. This is apparent among incorporated places and in particularly noticeable among non-school special districts. The only numerical reduction in recent years has been that of school districts, and their decrease in metropolitan areas generally has been much less than in rural portions of some states.

The government of metropolitan areas, already complicated in the early decades of the century, have become more complex. Fourteen percent of all local governments in the United States are located in metropolitan areas. For each 1,000 square miles in metropolitan areas there are slightly more than seventy-five local governments—more than double the number for 1,000 square miles of non-metropolitan territory.

Individually, the more populous metropolitan areas are generally the most complex governmentally. For example, the three largest contain the most governmental units and are interstate. The New York metropolitan area has 1,071 governmental units, the Chicago area, 960, and the area centering on Philadelphia, 702. There are important exceptions to this pattern, the most striking of which is the Madison, Wisconsin, metropolitan area. Ranking 102nd in population in 1950, it stood eleventh in number of local governmental units, with 292. . . .

Local governments in metropolitan areas present a bewildering pattern both because of their extreme numbers and their frequent territorial overlapping. Most of their boundaries are not coterminous with one another. In some states, for example, a city, a county, and a township occupy part of the same territory and therefore overlie portions of one another's jurisdiction. In many instances special districts increase the overlapping maze. Unlike other classes of governments, special districts may generally function in an area regardless of what other governments exist there. As a result, several types of special districts, of which school districts are simply one kind, occupy portions or all of the area of one another, as well as territory of other local governments. Thus layer upon layer of government exists in many sections of metropolitan areas. . . .

Prominent in the series of problems is the inadequacy of governmental organization. Current metropolitan needs have outmoded substantial parts of the local governmental system, which was largely conceived in the eighteenth century. "The basic structure of local government, by and large," notes a recent commentator, "fails miserably to reflect the best that is known concerning governmental structure. . . . We cannot overlook the fact that our failure to devise improved local and metropolitan structures of government results in the less efficient use of the supply [of public money]." Adjustments have taken place in some types of local governments, such as certain cities and counties, but the alterations have not been sufficient to handle the mounting difficulties. The rapid rise of large and small special district governments in metropolitan areas is indicative of the insufficiency of the general, traditional local units. . . .

Service and control deficiencies are another part of the series of problems. These deficiencies are numerous because the many governments involved operate in only limited portions of the metropolitan areas and provide varying levels of services and regulation. Although some of their policies affect metropolitan developments, they often are made on the basis of what is advantageous for the restricted segment of the area each government occupies. As a result, services and regulation are uneven, and area-wide approaches in attacking common difficulties are lacking or slow in materializing. . . .

Financial inequalities and shortcomings are also part of the series of problems. There are wide variances in different sections of metropolitan areas between service needs and financial resources. The policy of providing city-wide services on the basis of need rather than the fiscal resources of each block, precinct or ward is not extended in the great majority of instances to metropolitan areas. Instead, the individual governmental unit relies upon a small amount of territory for its local financial resources. Thus some units are wealthy but have relatively few needs; others are extremely poor and have extensive needs. Such disparity between needs and resources is particularly apparent in the central cities, which must furnish services to many non-residents but cannot tap the financial resources of the localities in which these people reside. The broad variations between needs and resources make for gross inequalities in financial burdens. . . .

Not least important in the financial situation of metropolitan areas is the matter of grants-in-aid for the state and national governments. In some instances such grants have fostered improved governmental organization in metropolitan areas. In others they have had the effect of bolstering uneconomic and inefficient governmental units. Grants-in-aid are a powerful implement that can have substantial impact in supporting or hindering metropolitan reorganization.

Finally, popular control of government is a crucial part of "the metropolitan problem." Citizen control over metropolitan areas is inadequate and ineffective. People living within many sections of a metropolitan area reside in numerous governmental jurisdictions and are confronted with an extremely large number of issues and personalities on which they are to form judgments. Conscientious citizens probably are able to stay sufficiently well informed about the activities of the national government, the state government, and one or two local governments, but the proliferation of local units has made the total task impossible. The scattering of public authority and responsibility and resulting complexity overburden local residents. The existing demands in many segments of metropolitan areas greatly exceed the span of attention that citizens can be expected to maintain. . . .

Citizen control in metropolitan areas is inadequate and ineffective in another important way. Even if residents were able to fulfill the herculean role of observing and controlling the numerous governments in whose jurisdiction they live, this would be insufficient. Residents can make a decision at elections about such functions as transportation or sewage disposal, for example—but it is usually binding on only a limited amount of the metropolitan territory. Generally there is no method of metropolitan-wide electoral participation in matters of metropolitan scope. Without it, no adequate citizen control of metropolitan areas can exist. . . .

The complex of difficulties that make up the metropolitan problem can be substantially overcome. But to do so requires establishment of general governmental jurisdictions of metropolitan scope—jurisdictions that are representative of the people directly affected and are accountable and responsive to them.

27

Government and the Economy

27.1. GOVERNMENT AS REGULATOR, COORDINATOR, AND SPENDER

Under the Employment Act of 1946 the President is required to submit to the Congress an annual report on the economic state of the Union, to make such recommendations as he deems appropriate to insure full employment, economic stability, and a healthy rate of economic growth. In the following excerpt from his Economic Report to Congress, January 21, 1963, President Kennedy outlines some of the measures needed to accomplish these goals.

THE STATE OF THE ECONOMY poses a perplexing challenge to the American people. Expansion continued throughout 1962, raising total wages, profits, consumption, and production to new heights. This belied the fears of those who predicted that we were about to add another link to the ominous chain of recessions which were more and more frequently interrupting our economic expansion—1953–54, after 45 months of expansion, in 1957–58 after 35 months, in 1960–61 after 25 months. Indeed, 22 months of steady recovery have already broken this melancholy sequence, and the prospects are for further expansion in 1963.

Yet if the performance of our economy is high the aspirations of the American people are higher still—and rightly so. For all its advances the nation is still falling substantially short of its economic potential—a potential we must fulfill both to raise our standards of well-being at home and to serve the cause of freedom abroad.

From President John F. Kennedy, *Annual Economic Report to Congress* (*The New York Times*, January 21, 1963).

When in spite of a sizable drop in the unemployment rate (seasonally adjusted) from 6.7 percent as 1961 began to 5.6 percent as 1962 ended the unemployment rate has fallen below 5 percent in but 1 month in the past five years and there are still 4 million people unemployed today;

When in spite of a gratifying recovery which raised gross national product (GNP) from an annual rate of $501,000,000,000 as 1961 began to $562,000,000,000 as 1962 ended, $30,000,000,000–$40,000,000,000 of usable productive capacity lies idle for lack of sufficient markets and incentives;

When, in spite of a recovery growth rate of 3.6 percent yearly from 1960 to 1962, our realized growth trend since 1955 has averaged only 2.7 percent annually as against Western European growth rates of 4, 5, and 6 percent and our own earlier postwar growth rate of 4½ percent;

When, in spite of achieving record corporate profits befores taxes of $51,000,000,000 in 1962, against a previous high of $47,000,000,000 in 1959, our economy could readily generate another $7,000,000,000–$8,000,000,000 of profits at more normal rates of capacity use;

When, in spite of a rise of $28,000,000,000 in wages and salaries since the trough of the recession in 1961—with next-to-no-erosion by rising prices—the levels of labor income could easily be $18,000,000,000–$20,000,000,000 higher at reasonably full employment.

We cannot now reclaim the opportunities we lost in the past. But we can move forward to seize the even greater possibilities of the future. . . . What we require is a coherent national determination to lift our economy to a new plane of productivity and initiative. It is in this context that we examine the record of progress in the past two years and consider the means for achieving the goals of the Employment Act of 1946. . . .

. . . The outlook for continued moderate expansion in 1963 is now favorable:

1. Business investment, responding in part to the stimulus of last year's depreciation reform and investment tax credit and to the prospect of early tax reduction and reform is expected to rise at least modestly for 1963 as a whole.

2. Home construction should continue at about its 1962 level.

3. Government purchases—Federal, state, and local combined—are expected to rise at a rate of $2,000,000,000 a quarter.

4. Consumer purchases should rise in line with gains in business and government activity.

These prospects, taking into account the proposed tax reduction, lead to the projection of a gross national product for 1963 of $578,000,-000,000 understood as the midpoint of a $10,000,000,000 range.

I do not expect a fifth post-war recession to interrupt our progress in 1963. It is not the fear of recession but the fact of five years of excessive unemployment, unused capacity, and slack profits—and the consequent hobbling of our growth rate—that constitutes the urgent case for tax reduction and reform. An economic expansion in 1963, at any reasonably predictable pace, will leave the economy well below the Employment Act's high standard of maximum employment, production and purchasing power. . . .

. . . The main block to full employment is an unrealistically heavy burden of taxation. The time has come to remove it.

. . . Early action on the tax program outlined in my State of the Union message—and shortly to be presented in detail in my tax message—will be our best investment in a prosperous future and our best insurance against recession.

. . . . . .

Our need today, then, is:

To provide markets to bring back into production under-utilized plants and equipment;

To provide incentives to invest, in the form both of wider markets and larger profits—investment that will expand and modernize, innovate, cut costs;

Most important, by means of stronger markets and enlarged investment, to provide jobs for the unemployed and for the new workers streaming into the labor force during the sixties—and closing the circle, the new jobholders will generate still larger markets and further investments. . . .

. . . In order to enlarge markets for consumer goods and services and translate these into new jobs, fuller work schedules, higher profits, and rising farm incomes, I am proposing a major reduction in individual income tax rates. . . .

These revisions would directly increase the annual rate of disposable after-tax incomes of American households by about $6,000,000,-000 in the second half of 1963, and some $8,000,000,000 when the program is in full effect, with account taken of both tax reductions and tax reform. Taxpayers in all brackets would benefit, with those in the lower brackets getting the largest proportional reductions.

A reduction of corporate taxes would provide a further increment to the flow of household incomes as dividends are enlarged; and this, too would directly swell the consumer spending stream.

The direct effects, large as they are, would be only the beginning. Rising output and employment to meet the new demands for consumer goods will generate new income—wages, salaries, and profits. Spending from this extra income flow would create more jobs, more production, and more incomes. The ultimate increases in the continuing flow of incomes, production, and consumption will greatly exceed the initial amount of tax reduction.

. . . . . .

As a first step, we have already provided important new tax incentives for productive investment. Last year the Congress enacted a 7 percent tax credit for business expenditures on major kinds of equipment. And the Treasury, at my direction, revised its depreciation rules to reflect today's conditions. Together, these measures are saving business over $2,000,000,000 a year in taxes and significantly increasing the net rate of return on capital investments.

The second step in my program to lift investment incentives is to reduce the corporate tax rate from 52 percent to 47 percent, thus restoring the pre-Korean rate. Particularly to aid small business, I am recommending that effective January 1, 1963, the rate on the first $25,000 of corporate income be dropped from 30 to 22 percent while the 52 percent rate on corporate income over $25,000 is retained. In later stages, the 52 percent rate would drop to 47 percent. These changes will cut corporate liabilities by over $2,500,000,000 before structural changes.

The resulting increase in profitability will encourage risk-taking and enlarge the flow of internal funds which typically finance a major share of corporate investment. . . . As the total impact of the tax program takes hold and generate pressures on existing capacity, more and more companies will find the lower taxes a welcome source of finance for plant expansion.

. . . . . .

. . . Side-by-side with tax measures, I am confident that the Federal Reserve and the Treasury will continue to maintain, consistent with their responsibilities for the external defense of the dollar, monetary and credit conditions favorable to the flow of savings into long-term investment in the productive strength of the country.

. . . . . .

IMPACT ON THE DEBT

Given the deficit now in prospect, action to raise the existing legal on the public debt will be required.

The ability of the Nation to service the Federal debt rests on the income of citizens whose taxes must pay the interest . . .

. . . . . .

Clearly we would prefer smaller debts than we have today. But this does not settle the issue. The central requirement is that debt be incurred only for constructive purposes and at time and in ways that serve to strengthen the position of the debtor. In the case of the Federal Government, where the nation is the debtor, the key test is whether the increases serve to strengthen or weaken our economy. In terms of jobs and output generated without threat to price stability—and in terms of the resulting higher revenue—the debt increases foreseen under my tax program clearly pass this test.

. . . . . .

IMPACT ON PRICES AND THE BALANCE OF PAYMENTS

The Administration tax program for 1963 can strengthen our economy within a continuing framework of price stability and an extension of our hard-won gains in the United States balance of payments position.

. . . . . .

We are determined to maintain this stability and to avoid the risk of either an inflationary excess of demand in our markets or a renewed price-wage spiral.

. . . . . .

Price stability has extra importance today because of our need to eliminate the continuing deficit in the international balance of payments. During the past two years we have cut the overall deficit from nearly $4,000,000,000 in 1960 to about $2,000,000,000 in 1962. But we cannot relax our efforts to reduce the payments deficit still further. One important force working strongly in our favor is our excellent record of price stability. Since 1959, while United States wholesale prices have been unchanged, those in every major competing country (except Canada) have risen appreciably. Our ability to compete in foreign markets—and in our own—has accordingly improved . . .

The area in which our greatest effort must now be concentrated is one in which Government can provide only leadership and opportunity; private business must produce the results. Our commercial trade surplus —the excess of our exports of goods and services over imports—must rise substantially to assure that we will reach balance of payments equilibrium within a reasonable period . . .

. . . . . .

. . . As the Organization for Economic Cooperation and Development has emphatically stated in recent months, a prosperous American economy and a sound balance of payments position are not alternatives between which we must choose; rather, expansionary action to bolster our domestic growth—with due vigilance against inflation—will solidify confidence in the dollar.

IMPACT ON STATE AND LOCAL GOVERNMENTS

The Federal budget is hard pressed by urgent responsibilities for free world defense and by vital tasks at home. But the fiscal requirements laid upon our states, cities, school districts, and other units of local government are even more pressing. It is here that the first impacts fall—of rapidly expanding populations, especially at both ends of the age distribution; of mushrooming cities; of continuing shift to new modes of transportation; of demands for more and better education; of problems of crime and delinquency; of new opportunities to combat ancient problems of physical and mental health; of the recreational and cultural needs of an urban society.

To meet these responsibilities, the total of state and local Government expenditures has expanded 243 percent since 1948—in contrast to 166 percent for the Federal Government; their debts by 334 percent—in contrast to 18 percent for the Federal Government.

The Federal budget has helped to ease the burdens on our states and local governments by an expanding program of grants for a multitude of purposes, and inevitably it must continue to do so. The Federal tax reductions I propose will also ease these fiscal burdens, chiefly because greater prosperity and faster growth will automatically increase state and local tax revenues at existing rates . . .

POLICIES FOR FASTER GROWTH

. . . No one doubts that the foundations of America's economic greatness lie in the education, skill, and adaptability of our population and in our advanced and advancing industrial technology . . .

. . . The Federal Government is already the main source of financial support for research and development in the United States. Most funds now spent on research are channeled to private contractors through the Department of Defense, the National Aeronautics and Space Administration, and the Atomic Energy Commission. The space and atomic energy activities of the country absorb two-thirds of the trained people available for exploring our scientiffc and technical frontiers. These activities also assert a strong influence on their direction and substance of scientific and engineering education. In many fields, they have transformed our understanding of nature and our ability to control it. But in the course of meeting specific challenges so brilliantly, we have paid a price by sharply limiting the scarce scientific and engineering resources available to the civilian sectors of the American economy.

The Government has for many years recognized its obligation to support research in fields other than defense. Federal support of medical and agricultural research has been and continues to be particularly important. My proposal for adding to our current efforts new support of science and technology that directly affect industries serving civilian markets represents a rounding out of Federal programs across the full spectrum of science.

Since rising productivity is a major source of economic growth, and research and development are essential sources of productivity growth, I believe that the Federal Government must now begin to redress the balance in the use of scientific skills. To this end I shall propose a number of measures to encourage civilian research and development and to make the byproducts of military and space research easily accessible to civilian industry. These measures will include:

1. Development of a Federal-state engineering extension service;

2. New means of facilitating the use by civilian industry of the results of Government-financed research;

3. Selected support of industrial research and development and technical information services;

4. Support of industry research associations;

5. Adjustment of the income tax laws to give business firms an additional stimulus to invest in research equipment;

6. Stimulus of university training of industrial research personnel.

Together, these measures would encourage a growing number of scientists and engineers to work more intensively to improve the technology of civilian industry, and a growing number of firms and industries to take greater advantage of modern technology. For Americans as a whole, the returns will be better products and services at lower prices. A National research and development effort focused to meet our urgent needs can do much to improve the quality of our lives . . .

CONCLUSION

Stepping up the United States growth rate will not be easy. We no longer have a large agricultural population to transfer to industry. We do not have the opportunity to capitalize on a generation's worth of advanced technology developed elsewhere. The only easy growth available to us is the growth that will flow from success in ending the period of sluggishness dating back to 1957. That we must have if only because it is inexcusable to have the American economy operating in low gear in a time of crisis.

27.2. THE GOVERNMENT AS CUSTOMER

The national Government buys and sells more goods and services than any other part of our economy. To what extent has economic stability of the nation come to depend upon the activities of the Government? What factors should determine how much the Government should spend and on what? In this selection, these perennial questions are examined from the economist's point of view.

AT THE START OF THIS STUDY of the interconnections between Federal spending and economic growth, it seems a fair presumption that each will have an effect on the other. Thus, there are two separate questions to be considered, which may be phrased as follows:

(1) *How are the level and nature of Federal expenditures likely to affect our prospects for economic growth in the coming decades?* Under this heading we will want to decide whether it can be said that one size or kind of Federal budget will promote growth and another size and kind will impede it.

(2) *Assuming an environment of economic growth, how should this affect our decisions as to the proper amounts and objects of Federal spending?* In other words we will want to see how economic growth will affect our need for, and our ability to afford, the various types of Federal spending.

Question 1 will be taken up first. . . .

The analyst looking for a connection between Federal spending and economic growth must very quickly develop a feeling of frustration. Growth has occurred under so wide a variety of spending levels that one must wonder whether there is any connection whatever between the two.

During the first 140 years of our existence as an independent nation—surely, a period of economic growth—Federal expenditures (except during brief war periods) were at levels which must be considered purely nominal compared with the levels we have become accustomed to in recent decades. Yet the past two decades apparently have also been a period of growth. . . .

This contrast between recent and historical levels of Federal spending suggests that economic growth may be affected very little by the level of government spending. The same conclusion is indicated by a more detailed examination of the recent years.

Compared with historical precedents, Federal expenditures have remained high since 1941. Yet there has been considerable variation in spending levels within that period. These variations do not seem to be

From George G. Hagedorn, "Federal Expenditures and Economic Growth," *Federal Expenditure Policy for Economic Growth and Stability,* Papers submitted by panelists appearing before the Subcommittee on Fiscal Policy, Joint Economic Committee, 85th Congress, 1st Session (Washington, D.C.: U.S. Government Printing Office, 1957), pp. 292–298.

closely related to economic growth, which proceeded throughout the period with only short and minor interruptions.

During World War II, Federal spending amounted to almost 50 percent of our gross national product. After the war spending was reduced to about 13 percent of gross national product. Contrary to some predictions, this reduction caused no cessation of economic growth. During the Korean war, expenditures rose again, reaching 21 percent of gross product in 1953. Since that year there has been some decline and the figure for 1956 was 17 percent.

This factual record gives no support to glib assertions that there is a determinable minimum level of Federal expenditures necessary for the support of economic growth. Equally, the record does not encourage the assumption that there is a clearly definable upper limit such that when expenditures rise above it they become destructive of prospects for growth. One is tempted to conclude that government spending has very little to do with the process of growth, either positively or negatively.

Yet common sense forbids us to dismiss the subject with this negative conclusion. There must be limits—both minimal and maximal—to the levels of Federal spending which can make economic growth possible, whether or not we can define those limits precisely. The subject is worth pursuing further, provided we recognize the futility of attempting to set up precise operating rules on this basis.

Although the present discussion is oriented toward the spending side of the budget, we should not forget that the effects of spending in discouraging or encouraging growth depend to an important degree on the methods used in obtaining the necessary funds. A badly designed tax system might be destructive of growth potentials even if the total revenue it provided was moderate in amount. A well-designed tax system might protect growth possibilities to a point much higher in the spending scale, but certainly there are limits to this protection. . . .

A thought which underlies some discussion of the proper level of Federal expenditures, is that the Government is an important customer for our national output of goods and services. Approximately 11 percent of our total output was sold to the Federal Government in 1956.

Every businessman recognizes the customer as a most essential element in the conduct of his business. He cannot grow—in the sense of expanding his output and his employment—unless the can find new customers or persuade existing customers to take more of his output.

These are indisputable facts of business life. From like considerations many people conclude that the Federal Government, by increasing its expenditures (i.e., by becoming a better customer), can provide an essential support for economic growth. They further conclude that as our productive capacity expands it will be more and more necessary for the Government to take a substantial part of the product off the market, in order that men and machines may not be left idle through lack of sufficient demand for their expanding output.

The train of reasoning described above is not customarily expressed explicitly. The view seems to be going out of fashion that we can predict statistically the gap between demand and potential output and adjust Federal spending to fill it.

But emphasis on the importance of the Government as a customer is still implicit in much of the argument over Federal spending. For example, we hear fears that a reduction of defense spending might have a depressing effect on our economy. With economic growth and expanded productivity there might seem to be even greater difficulty in finding sufficient non-governmental demand to keep us going.

The customary answer to this argument, and the one which will be given here, is that there is no limit to the growth of private demand, since human wants are insatiable.

This thesis has a stale, trite sound—more like a copybook maxim than a realistic basis for economic confidence. Yet in our lifetime we have seen it vindicated to an extent which should astonish even those who have been most sure of it. In 1929 we thought we were prosperous enough, but since that time per capita expenditures on consumption, in real terms, have increased by more than 50 percent. The average person consumes half again as much, in the way of goods and services, as he did a generation ago, and with no visible signs of satiety. Surely the burden of proof is on those who would claim that this process has come to an end, and that we shall henceforth be unable to generate sufficient demand to keep an expanded economy growing.

That is not to say that there is no conceivable danger of depressed markets in the future. Goods are produced not simply because people want them but because they can be sold at a price which will repay their costs and yield some profit. Unworkable relationships between cost levels and the state of demand might make it impossible to keep our resources at a high level of employment.

But these are problems which ought to be dealt with on their own terms. They should be solved by preserving the flexibility of our economy in adjusting cost and price levels to changing conditions. Merely to offset such difficulties by increasing government spending is to risk converting the temporary maladjustment into a chronic one.

Of course it can be argued that we will not have to worry about these difficult problems if we simply resolve to keep government demand at a high enough level to keep everyone employed, no matter what maladjustments occur. But this is the fallacy of regarding production, rather than the enjoyment of the product, as the ultimate aim of economic activity. Government spending which is motivated solely by the desire to increase total demand is not a support to economic growth but a dissipation of the benefits of growth.

All this is not to say that there is no minimum below which Federal expenditures may not fall without injury to economic growth. The Government has functions to perform which are essential to the well-being of the Nation generally, and therefore to economic growth. These functions cost money and unless the budget provides adequately for them, economic growth might be seriously impeded. But the basic function of the Government is to govern, and not to provide a market for the Nation's output. This still leaves a broad area of controversy as to the proper level of government expenditures, but it is helpful at least in clarifying the objective.

One other point which it may be well to clarify is that there is nothing wrong in principle with a government timing its purchases with some regard for the possibility of getting lower prices by waiting. Every prudent buyer will seek to time his purchases, whenever possible, so as to make them in the most favorable markets. But no prudent buyer ever buys something he does not need or want, simply because the market for that product is depressed. . . .

We have examined the impact of spending on growth, and the next question is the impact of growth on spending—question 2, as posed at the beginning of this paper. This may be approached either from the point of view of needs for Government services or from the point of view of ability to afford Government services.

First, what will be the effect of economic expansion on our need for Federal services? At first blush it might seem that our needs in this respect might be expected to expand roughly in proportion to the expansion of the economy. However, an examination of the specific objects of current Government spending indicates a quite contrary conclusion:

Federal Expenditures, Calendar 1956 (billions of dollars)

Purchases of goods and services:	
National defense	40.4
Other national security	2.0
Other	5.2
Transfer Payments	13.5
Grants-in-aid to State and local governments	3.2
Net interest paid	5.2
Subsidies less current surplus of Government enterprises	2.8
Total	72.3

SOURCE: *U.S. Department of Commerce.*

National defense is the largest item. What our future needs for this purpose will be is unpredictable but there is no reason to suppose that these needs will grow pari passu with the growth of the economy. Economic growth will neither increase nor decrease our need for defense, which depends on other factors.

The same is true of Federal interest payments, which are determined by the size of the debt and the average rate of interest on it —factors which are only indirectly (if at all) related to economic growth.

The $5.2 billion of outlays for goods and services, other than national defense or national security, may contain some items which would have to grow along with economic growth. These, however, must be an extremely small part of total expenditures.

The $13.5 billion of transfer payments consists mainly of payments from social insurance funds (which are outside the regular budget) and veterans benefits. The social insurance benefits will probably increase, but this will be the result of maturing of contractual obligations rather than of economic growth per se. Unfortunately the increase will occur whether or not the economic growth is realized.

Government expenditures of the type which are intended to relieve individual distress might be expected to decline with economic growth. As general economic well-being improves there is less need for such Federal aid. Although this principle may be of little help with respect to future benefits already contracted for, it might be kept in mind when questions arise of expanding such obligations or assuming new ones.

Similarly, there is reason to hope that grants-in-aid can be reduced as economic growth progresses. With improving economic conditions the States and localities should become better able to take care of their own needs, and the need for Federal assistance will decline.

Welfare expenditures generally are a process of taking money from one group of citizens and paying it to, or spending it for the benefit of another group. Whatever humanitarian reasons may be advanced to justify such a process, the need for it must become less cogent as economic growth makes us more prosperous.

Thus the Federal budget is a mixture of various kinds of expenditure. In some cases (covering the larger part of the budget) the needs which the expenditure is intended to satisfy will be unaffected by economic growth. In other cases the need will decline as the economy grows. A comparatively small part of total expenditures are for needs which will increase along with growth. . . .

The propriety, or impropriety, of any proposed item of Federal expenditures is only partly a subject for economic analysis. In an ultimate sense it is simply a question of what people want from their government and what they are willing to pay for. When they have made their choice it is not for the economist to say that what they want is wrong. . . .

27.3. THE FARMER'S SHARE IN PROSPERITY

Chronic recession and overproduction have impaired the prosperity of the American farmer. This proposal for "a full prosperity budget for agriculture" is highly critical of efforts to solve the farm problem through the free market principle of supply and demand. A "new approach" to the farm problem is urged so as to subject agriculture to the same regulatory philosophy and practices as other sectors of the economy.

OUR NATIONAL FARM POLICIES have become bankrupt. The urgent task now is to commence their liquidation. This action should not be negative. It should take the positive form of an entirely new national farm program.

The new need is to restore moral justice and economic soundness to agriculture. In addition, the prolonged farm income depression is hurting our entire economy sorely. The slow erosion of our farm plant jeopardizes our future food and fiber needs. The mounting farm surpluses and their public cost are but one vivid aspect of failure throughout our whole economy to translate our tremendous technological progress into wise utilization for the benefit of all. Today, in other key sectors of our economy, surpluses of productive power over use—represented by idle men and plants—are much bigger than the farm surpluses. While we need constant shifts in the composition of production and employment, the total adjustments must result in full production and full employment for the whole economy.

The new farm program proposed in this study is geared to these broader objectives. It urges a short-range and long-range *Full Prosperity Budget For Agriculture.* This involves coordinated goals for: expanded domestic and overseas consumption of American farm products, farm production and employment adjusted to consumption, and farm purchasing power rising toward income parity with others. It would seek to achieve, these farm objectives consistently with maximum production, employment, and purchasing power for the economy as a whole. It would thus, for the first time, apply to agriculture the purposes and approaches of the Employment Act of 1946. . . .

First and foremost, since World War II—and mostly after 1951 —there has been a vast deflation of farm income. Since 1947, the farmer's income from all sources has been pushed downward 23 percent in real terms, while incomes of the nonfarm population have moved upward

From "Toward a New Farm Program," *A Conference on Economic Progress,* 1958, pp. 1–6.

48 percent in real terms. After a brief upward flurry in 1958, farm incomes and prices are again moving downward. Our farm families now have only about 50 percent of income parity with other groups. Morally, in a great Nation capable of economic justice for all, this is unconscionable.

Second, the farm plant is being eroded by this income deflation. Farm families—the vital human element in agriculture—are being driven off the land, without opportunity for full employment at good incomes elsewhere. The "factory in the field" is supplanting the family type farm. And this change, instead of lifting farm living standards, is accentuating the impoverishment of farm families. The land care and machinery needed to conserve and prepare agriculture for the growing needs of a growing population are being neglected. To achieve good diets for all American families, and to add fairly to the food and fiber supply of the free world, would require nearly one-fourth more U.S. farm production by 1964 than in 1957.

Third, the accumulated farm surpluses, and the public costs of an irrational farm program, are mounting by leaps and bounds. Since the middle of 1952, accumulated wheat stocks have become 6 times as large, and cotton stocks have risen from approximately zero to about a million bales. The government investment in farm surpluses is now about 5 times (in constant dollars about 4 times) as high as it was in mid-1952, and the funds in the Federal Budget devoted to agriculture are now more than 6 times (in constant dollars about 5 times) as high as in fiscal 1952. The net losses to the Government on the farm program, during the past five years, have averaged almost 5½ times as high annually as during the preceding seven-year period.

These farm surpluses and public costs would be undesirable but not intolerable, if they represented programs contributing to the prosperity of more than twenty million farm people and to general prosperity. But these surpluses and public costs *are* intolerable, when they have resulted from the same national farm policies which have thrown farm families into an enduring depression and hurt the whole economy. . . .

The overwhelming flaw in our recent approaches to the farm problem can be stated simply. The prevalent theory has been that organized protection of farm prices or income was the reason why farmers were "producing too much;" that this "overproduction" was depressing farm prices and incomes despite this "expensive" protection; and that systematic and continuous removal of this farm price or income protection would lead 5 million uncoordinated farmers—guided by "free market" prices without other regulation of production—to a neat adjustment of supply to demand. And this adjustment, according to the theory, would soon make agriculture prosperous and everybody else happy. In short, the effort has been to solve the farm problem by a steadfast backward movement toward letting farmers get whatever prices and incomes they could while producing whatever they would.

To put this in another way, we have sought to solve the farm problem by asking agriculture to return to the *laissez-faire* economics of the 19th or early 20th Centuries. This is an approach which all the rest of our economy—and all the rest of the thinking world—has abandoned since the Great Depression of the Nineteen Thirties, and abandoned still further in the face of the great problems of today. In our economic life and national policies generally, we have—while maintaining the essential initiative and freedom of our enterprise system—substituted conscious organized efforts for *laissez-faire*. In many major sectors of our economy except agriculture, production is regularized or rationalized, and prices and other incomes are deliberately fixed or administered. Usually this is done through private action, where the particular group concerned is able to take such action. Frequently it is done through public action, or a mixture of private and public action.

These profound changes have not been without some defects. Certainly, the power of huge industries to administer prices needs to be tempered by much more private restraint and public scrutiny. Nonetheless, the substitution of order for chaos has brought great improvements in our economic structure during the past quarter-century, and nobody now wants to cancel out these gains. These changes have liberated the American economy in general from the periodic ravages of depression. Under these circumstances, to thrust agriculture backward toward a complete *laissez-faire* position which has not worked, while others are moving forward toward purposeful coordination, condemns agriculture by decree of national policy to an exploited position in American life. The farmer is being forced to sell for whatever he can get, and to buy for what others asks.

The new approach to the farm problem herein proposed is that agriculture, instead of being dispossessed from our general economy, should be incorporated into the main stream of our general economic efforts. The farm sector of our economy should be brought under the influence of the same philosophy and practices which have been helpful to many other sectors.

Toward this end, the Employment Act of 1946 should now be applied in a practical way to the farm problem. This Act calls for the periodic establishment of goals for maximum employment, production, and purchasing power, and for an integrated set of private and public economic policies directed toward the achievement of these goals. The Employment Act is not now being sufficiently used. But its utility and soundness are now without serious challenge.

Specifically, the application of the Employment Act to agriculture would mean this: The President, with the aid of the appropriate

Executive Departments, would be required to submit to the Congress at least once a year *A Full Prosperity Budget For Agriculture*. This would contain short-range and long-range goals for expansion of the consumption of farm products, taking into account both our growing domestic needs and our fair world responsibilities. It would equate these consumption goals with goals for the short-run and long-run readjustment of farm production and farm plant, taking account also of new farm technology. It would favor the family type farm, as an economically efficient and socially desirable unit of production. It would facilitate the movement of some farmers to full employment at full pay in other parts of the economy. It would employ credit tools, income protection tools, and other inducements, toward the achievement of all these adjustments through the voluntary cooperation of farmers.

And of highest priority, it would embody income goals for farm families, designed to reward appropriate production adjustments with a level of farm income and living standards moving gradually toward parity with that of other Americans. The public costs of the new farm program, which would form a part of this *Prosperity Budget For Agriculture,* would be rationalized and reduced, because the public costs of a bad farm program have already been proved far higher than were these costs under a better though insufficiently good farm program.

And finally, through this operation under the Employment Act, full prosperity for agriculture would be meshed with full prosperity goals for the whole American economy. This would help to maintain better balance between the agricultural and the industrial sectors, not only with respect to production, but also with respect to employment and incomes. In view of the very rapid pace of agricultural technology, even fully expanded consumption may not forestall some further contraction of acreage and total farm employment. But we must make sure that any transition is sensible rather than brutal; and that those moving from agriculture are absorbed by full employment and maximum growth for the economy as a whole.

This fundamentally new approach should precede continuance of debate on the details of price support formulae, production payments, and production adjustments. For this kind of debate, without the needed reorientation, has long been flying in the dark. It has resulted in one crash landing after another.

The argument that this new approach would substitute a "managed" agriculture for a "free" agriculture has no more merit than the same argument when raised unsuccessfully against vast improvements in other sectors of our economy. The new approach would merely substitute a voluntary but intelligently coordinated farm effort for a hodgepodge of errors, a prosperous agriculture for a depressed agriculture. I would make full use of our abundant capabilities for the benefit of people, and move forthrightly against the dire economic threat to our enterprise system which our current failure to deal with the farm problem thrusts upon our whole economy. . . .

27.4. PROPOSALS TO SOLVE
THE FARM PROBLEM

One of the most persistent and troublesome problems of the American political economy is the so-called "farm problem." The hard core of the problem is in what may be called the "paradox of plenty." Improved methods of production in agriculture have resulted in a spectacular increase in output. Uncontrolled, these "surpluses" would depress farm prices beyond tolerable limits. To meet the problem, the Federal Government has tried many things, from the Federal Farm Board of the Hoover Administration to the present system of production control and parity prices. The following is an objective diagnosis and prescription for the "farm problem" by the well-known Committee for Economic Development.

ROOTS OF THE AMERICAN FARM PROBLEM are to be found in a combination of . . . conditions, no one of which, alone, would have caused it.

SWIFTLY RISING PRODUCTIVITY

1. Total productivity has been growing very rapidly in agriculture. The total amount of resources—land, labor and capital combined—required in agriculture to produce a given quantity of agricultural products has been falling rapidly. . . . This resulted from large public and private outlays for research and education affecting agricultural equipment, materials and management, and quick adaptation of American farming to these improvements.

2. It has become efficient to use less labor, and more capital, in farming. The amount of farm labor required to produce a given amount of agricultural product has declined relatively more than the total amount of resources required. . . . While total resources used in agriculture per unit of agricultural output declined 20 percent from 1950 to 1960, farm labor used per unit of output declined 45 percent. . . .

3. The total demand for agricultural products has grown slowly, and this is typical. In the aggregate, the quantity of agricultural products that can be sold at unchanged prices does not rise much from year to

From the Research and Policy Committee, *An Adaptive Program for Agriculture* (New York: Committee for Economic Development, 1962).

year. The American people are at a level of diet where they wish to spend only a very small percentage of any increase in their per capita incomes on increasing their food consumption. . . . Thus, although there are differences from one product to another, aggregate consumer expenditure for agricultural products grows only a little more rapidly than population. Foreign markets are also important for agriculture, but contribute little to the rate of growth of demand, for two main reasons. One, in the underdeveloped countries dietary levels are low and population is growing rapidly, but these countries can spare little of their income for buying imported food. Two, the countries of Western Europe have rising incomes but also rising productivity in their own agriculture and most of them have tight restrictions on imports of farm goods.

4. A relatively large decline in prices of our farm products brings about only a small increase in consumption of them. Foods are not close substitutes for other objects of consumer expenditures, so that a decline in the price of foods does not cause people to shift from buying other things to buying foods. . . . Numerous studies show that to induce an increase in consumption of farm products as a whole by 1 percent, other things being equal, requires a price decline of about 5 percent, although consumption of particular farm products is more responsive to changes in their prices. . . .

5. Resources, most importantly labor, do not flow freely out of agriculture at the rate necessary to avoid falling incomes.

· · · · · ·

Although the exodus from agriculture in the past decade or longer has been large by almost any standards, it has not been large enough. . . .

A PROGRAM FOR AGRICULTURAL ADJUSTMENT

First and fundamentally, we propose a set of measures designed to bring about a condition in which:

1. A much smaller total quantity of resources will be used in agricultural production;
2. This smaller total of resources . . . be composed of a much smaller amount of labor, and, possibly, somewhat less capital;
3. Production per unit of resources used in agriculture will be higher;
4. Earnings per unit of resources used in agriculture will be higher, on the average, and these earnings will be obtained through sale of farm products without government subsidy or support.

Adjustment of farming to this condition is basic to solution of the farm problem.

Second, we propose a set of temporary, transitional measures designed to:

1. Prevent a sharp decline in farm incomes, and
2. Avoid further additions to stocks of farm goods, while the basic adjustment to the condition sketched above is being brought about.

It is an essential characteristic of these transitional programs that they should cushion the adjustment, but should do so in ways that do not prevent or retard the adjustment.

Attracting Excess Resources from Use in Farm Production

This is the heart of the matter in agricultural adjustment. Excess resources in use in the production of farm goods *is* the farm problem. . . .

An Improved Labor Market

. . . . . .

1. High Employment

The maintenance of employment opportunities in non-agricultural industry and services is an essential condition for the most satisfactory agricultural adjustment.

. . . . . .

2. Education

. . . Forty-four percent of the farm population is presently below the age of 20. Here, in our opinion, is a main key to agricultural adjustment: we have an opportunity to secure long-lasting relief from the overburden of people pressing upon farm income by getting a large number of people out of agriculture before they are committed to it as a career.

. . . . . .

The United States as a whole derives 4.3 percent of its personal income from farming, and no state derives more than 26.1 percent; yet the nation devotes 44.5 percent of its vocational education funds, exclusive of funds for home economics training, to training for agriculture. . . .

This means that in many states where farming is strongest vocational education tends to perpetuate the farm problem of too many people in agriculture by holding out extraordinary opportunities to train for farming as a vocation. . . .

3. Mobility

. . . . . .

We are glad to see the problem of the excess use of resources *in farming*, particularly excess commitment of people, integrated with the *general* problem of the nation's manpower requirements, and the national, general need for policies to help the nation adapt to the ever changing skill requirements of the economy.

4. Retraining and Movement

The retraining of farm workers leaving farming should be considered one of the principal objectives. . . . We recommend that retrained farm workers leaving farming should be assisted in moving to nonfarm work sites, by a program of loans to cover the cost of moving themselves and their families.

Cushioning the Process of Adjusting the Resources Used in Farm Production

A Cropland Adjustment Program. What we are recommending with respect to land use is a program designed to turn land being misused in agriculture to better agricultural use. It is not a program to take land out of farming where there is no non-agricultural alternative use, since that would be wasteful. . . .

It is recommended that a Cropland Adjustment Program be instituted, to induce the reconversion of at least 20 million acres of Western Plains and Mountain Region land from crop use to grass, as rapidly as possible. . . .

A Temporary Income Protection Program. If price supports for wheat, rice, and cotton were reduced immediately to the level at which adjustment of resources would begin to take place, the income of the producers of these crops would decline sharply in the absence of any compensatory public policy. While such a quick and sharp decline in income might conceivably increase the rate at which needed adjustments took place, it would exact a high cost in terms of suffering of the farm people displaced. Therefore:

We suggest that a *Temporary Income Protection Program be inaugurated,* to prevent the major impact of the required price adjustments from bearing excessively upon the farm community.

We recommend Temporary Income Protection payments only

for wheat, rice and cotton because the price drop in other crops would be much less than for these three.

The Temporary Income Protection Program would . . .

1. Make payments . . . only to farmers who now have acreage allotments for wheat, rice and cotton. . . .
2. The program would continue only five years.

· · · · · ·

A Temporary Soil Bank. The third measure for cushioning adjustment should be a Temporary Soil Bank, to prevent feed grain production from exceeding demand in the next few years.

It is recommended that a Temporary Soil Bank should be established, to last not more than five years, and to hold feed grain output, during that time, to not over 150–155 million tons a year. The Temporary Soil Bank would extend, under conditions set forth below, the existing Soil Bank.

The Export Market

The fact that the United States is a low cost producer of goods and natural fibers should give us more advantage in foreign trade than we are realizing.

· · · · · ·

Our past price-support programs have interfered with United States efforts to achieve reduction of European barriers to imports of farm products. Our sales of farm commodities in world markets below our domestic prices, and our application of import quotas to protect our domestic prices, have been used by importing countries as justification for their own restrictions on trade. . . . The program we recommend here would eliminate the differential between domestic and world prices. This should strengthen the effectiveness of U. S. efforts to achieve a liberalization of world agricultural trade.

Liberalization of agricultural trade, now blocked chiefly by the use of restrictive quotas in Europe, should be a cardinal point of United States trade policy. There is a danger that the agriculture policy of the European Economic Community (the Common Market) will be such as to promote agricultural self-sufficiency in Europe. This would be a mistake from the point of view of the efficiency of the entire free world. Europe should accept, as a fundamental decision in the course of its current economic integration, the idea that there is an advantage to Europe in the increased use of American farm goods, and the decreased use of high cost European farm products.

Limiting Seasonal Price Swings

Under the program recommended here farm price supports would be terminated at the end of five years and the trend of farm prices would be·governed by free market forces. It would, however, be desirable to take certain limited government actions tending to moderate seasonal fluctuations of prices after the five year transition period.

. . . The stability of farm life and the efficiency of agricultural production would be improved if the government were prepared to moderate the effects of this problem by making non-recourse loans based on some fraction, say 80 percent, of the expected average prices for the year.

Agricultural Research

We have stressed that the solution of the farm problem lies in eliminating the excess resources now being applied to the production of farm goods.

We want to lay equally strong stress upon our view that while we bring agricultural supply and demand into balance by reducing the resources employed in producing farm products, *we should not slack off the search for ways to produce more farm goods with fewer resources,* . . . On the other hand, decisions to incur the costs of research for agriculture, as for other industries, should be guided by the criterion of the relation between prospective benefits and costs.

. . . . . .

The programs we are suggesting for the better use of our resources in agriculture would, vigorously prosecuted, bring production and use into balance at a level of prices that would enable the people and land in farming after a reasonable period to receive higher incomes without extensive government controls or subsidy.

28

To Promote the General Welfare

28.1. RESPONSIBILITY OF THE FEDERAL GOVERNMENT FOR EDUCATION

Advocates of Federal aid to education, like Congressman Moulder, stress that the need for improvement of our educational facilities calls for financial support that only the Federal Government can provide. Opponents, such as Representative Weaver, fear that financial support of schools by the Federal Government would soon be followed by Federal control of the schools. President Kennedy proposes a three-year program of Federal assistance for construction of public school classrooms and for teachers' salaries.

MR. MOULDER. . . . Mr. Speaker, State and local school districts cannot alone bear the financial burden required to provide the expanding educational needs of today. The financial support of the education of the children and young people of the United States is a joint responsibility of all divisions of our Government—Federal, State, and local. . . .

Mr. Speaker, the people of America understand and we can justify the major part of our expenditure of $38 billion to $40 billion each year on military programs, including sputniks, rockets, guided missiles, and other worthy Federal defense and domestic programs. But the people do not understand why their Federal Government continues to neglect the vital and extremely important responsibility of assistance to education.

We all know the United States gives billions of dollars to foreign

From "Remarks of Representatives Morgan Moulder and Phil Weaver on Federal School Subsidies," *The Congressional Record,* August, 1960, pp. 18836, A6687; and President John F. Kennedy's "Message to the Congress on Education," March, 1961.

518

countries each year. I have opposed and voted against these wasteful expenditures. But most of the people do not know that last year our Federal Government agreed to pay $237,000 to improve teaching in Philippine schools; $1.18 million for better schools and vocational training in Thailand or Siam; and $2.1 million for educational facilities in Korea. In varying amounts, every year our Government has spent millions for aid to education in Burma, Cambodia, Free China, India, Indonesia, Laos, Vietnam, Afghanistan, Ceylan, and a host of other countries in Asia, Europe, Africa, and South America. Yes, and even Yugoslavia, a Communist country. Some of this may be good for our international policy. But what about our educational problems right here at home?

Mr. Speaker, the effort of Missouri school districts to provide needed school buildings is reflected by the issuance of $328,651,805 in bonds during the last 10 years. The outstanding bonds of school districts increased from $33,527,473 on June 30, 1949, to $277,146,002 on June 30, 1959—an increase of 726 percent.

Despite heroic efforts, many Missouri school districts are losing in their battle to provide classrooms for their increasing enrollments. One hundred and thirty-nine districts are bonded to 80 percent or more of their bonding capacity. Eighty-five of the one hundred and thirty districts are bonded to 90 percent or more of bonding capacity.

A total of 3,958 additional classrooms were needed last year in all school districts in the State. The estimated costs of these classrooms and other needed building facilities was $129,949,713.

The bonds that may be issued by school districts are limited by the State constitution to 10 percent of their assessed valuations. This was increased from 5 percent to 10 percent by a constitutional amendment adopted in 1952. This gave all school districts additional leeway in issuing bonds. Districts experiencing substantial enrollment increases for the most part have now issued the maximum bonds and can vote additional bonds only as present bonds are paid.

We must recognize and appreciate the limitations of local tax revenues. It is unrealistic to assume and expect State and local sources of revenue to be sufficient to provide the educational facilities so vital to our national security and future of the United States.

The need for expansion and improvement of our educational facilities demands the breadth, strength, and flexibility of a financial structure that only the Federal Government can provide. The benefits from education transcend all State and local lines. It is a national problem and the Federal Government must share in the financial responsibility. If we are to prevail as a free and prosperous Nation, we must become as interested in launching educated men and women as we are in launching satellites.

Great education comes from dedicated teachers and dedicated

teachers are entitled to salaries commensurate with the importance and responsibilities of their position as teachers. State laws properly set up high standards and qualifications for schoolteachers, requiring many years of education and special training, but the expense to the person seeking to so qualify for a teaching career and the inadequacy of teachers' salaries have created a critical shortage of teachers.

Mr. Speaker, I have supported and voted for all Federal aid to education bills presented in Congress. If reelected, I shall do so again at the next session of Congress. The Federal Government can no longer afford to neglect the necessity of providing financial assistance to our schools.

I cannot help feeling—and I hope others will realize it—that our teachers are our first line of defense. In fact, they always have been, but we have never talked about it enough. Our schoolteachers, who are so grossly underpaid, are the quiet force in this country that molds our most precious resource—our children. The full impact of the valuable service teachers give to the people of this country and its future, in a sense, will ultimately guide the destiny of the world. We must find a way should control their own future and that a Government subsidy means Government control.

I believe the school aid bill as proposed this year was a bad one. The measure would have taken away control of school construction and handed it over to the Department of Health, Education, and Welfare in the name of a national emergency which does not actually exist.

Mr. Speaker, I will concede that there are areas in this country where there is a shortage of classrooms and teachers. However, these areas are relatively few in number and the problems can be solved at the local—or at worst, the State—level. I say at worst advisedly because I do not think schools should be controlled at the State capital any more than I think they should be controlled in Washington. Education is a problem for the people themselves to handle and one which they alone are capable of handling in a truly democratic manner and with the best interests of everybody kept uppermost in mind.

As far as Nebraska is concerned, I would like to point out that the Federal aid program would have, in actuality, placed us deeper in to provide for our school systems the additional financial support which they so urgently need.

MR. WEAVER. Mr. Speaker, one of the most insidious proposals made during the 86th Congress was the attempt to steal from the American people their right to control their own educational facilities and turn it over to a high-priced bureaucracy in Washington. Fortunately for the American people this bit of chicanery was blocked by the men and women in this Congress who still believe as I do that the people themselves the hole. The program was designed—or so it was claimed—to help those States which have small populations and small tax bases. Actually, Nebraska would have gotten a couple of million dollars out of the program while New York was getting some $26 million. By comparison Nebraska would have been further and further behind New York.

This type of legislation involves what is known as matching funds. In other words, to take part we have to put up half the money and supposedly "get as a gift" half of the money from Uncle Sam. The truth is that we put up all the money, both the local contribution and the national contribution. The trouble is that instead of dealing through an elected school board at the local level we have to add the costs of support-ing a massive Federal bureaucracy.

All in all, for the people of Nebraska, this is bad legislation. No matter how you cut it, it still comes out a trifle ripe and unsavory.

For these reasons I have opposed this legislation from the very beginning and I still oppose it.

HIGHLIGHTS OF THE KENNEDY MESSAGE ON EDUCATION

OUR PROGRESS as a nation can be no swifter than our progress in edu-cation. Our requirements for world leadership, our hopes for economic growth, and the demands of citizenship itself in an era such as this all require the maximum development of every young American's capacity.

The human mind is our fundamental resource. A balanced Fed-eral program must go well beyond incentives for investment in plant and equipment. It must include equally determined measures to invest in human beings—both in their basic education and training and in their more advanced preparation for professional work.

Education must remain a matter of state and local control, and higher education a matter of individual choice. But education is increas-ingly expensive. Too many state and local governments lack the resources to assure an adequate education for every child. Too many classrooms are overcrowded. Too many teachers are under-paid. Too many talented individuals cannot afford the cost of, or find room for, the growing numbers of students seeking admission in the Sixties.

Our twin goals must be: A new standard of excellence in educa-tion—and the availability of such excellence to all who are willing and able to pursue it.

We cannot obtain more and better teachers—and our children should have the best—unless steps are taken to increase teachers' salaries. At present salary levels, the classroom cannot compete in financial rewards with other professional work that requires similar academic background.

It is equally clear that we do not have enough classrooms. In order to meet current needs and accommodate increasing enrollments, if every child is to have the opportunity of a full-day education in an adequate classroom, a total of 600,000 classrooms must be constructed during the next ten years.

These problems are common to all states. They are particularly severe in those states which lack the financial resources to provide a better education, regardless of their own efforts. Additional difficulties, too often overlooked, are encountered in areas of special educational need, where economic or social circumstances impose special burdens and opportunities on the public school.

These areas of special educational need include our depressed areas of chronic unemployment and the slum neighborhoods of our larger cities, where underprivileged children are overcrowded into substandard housing.

I recommend to the Congress a three-year program of general Federal assistance for public elementary and secondary classroom construction and teachers' salaries.

. . . this program would assure every state of no less than $15 for every public school student in average daily attendance, with the total amount appropriated ($666,000,000 being authorized in the first year, rising to $866,000,000 over a three-year period) distributed according to the equalization formula contained in the last year's Senate bill, and already familiar to the Congress by virtue of its similarity to the formulas contained in the Hill-Burton hospital construction and other acts. Ten per cent of the funds allocated to each state in the first year, and an equal amount thereafter, is to be used to help meet the unique problems of each state's "areas of special educational need"—depressed areas, slum neighborhoods and others.

This is a modest program with ambitious goals. The sums involved are relatively small when we think in terms of more than 36,000,000 public school children, and the billions of dollars necessary to educate them properly. Nevertheless, a limited beginning now—consistent with our obligations in other areas of responsibility—will encourage all states to expand their facilities to meet the increasing demand and enrich the quality of education offered, and gradually assist our relatively low-income states in the elevation of their educational standards to a national level.

In accordance with the clear prohibition of the Constitution, no elementary or secondary school funds are allocated for constructing church schools or paying church school teachers' salaries; and thus nonpublic school children are rightfully not counted in determining the funds each state will receive for its public schools.

Each state will be expected to maintain its own effort or contribution; and every state whose effort is below the national average will be expected to increase that proportion of its income which is devoted to public elementary and secondary education. . . .

These stimulatory measures represent an essential though modest contribution which the Federal Government must make to American education at every level. One-sided aid is not enough. . . .

We do not undertake to meet our growing educational problems merely to compare our achievements with those of our adversaries. These measures are justified on their own merits—in times of peace as well as peril, to educate better citizens as well as better scientists and soldiers. The Federal Government's responsibility in this area has been established since the earliest days of the Republic—it is time now to act decisively to fulfill that responsibility for the Sixties.

28.2. PRIVATE VS. PUBLIC ASSISTANCE

In spite of wide agreement that problems about welfare exist, there is disagreement about whether private or public agencies should handle them. Mr. Barkin holds the view that there is no special value to a rigid distinction between public and private action in the welfare field. We are free to use the State to achieve different ends as different times require; the need is not to avoid government action, but to use it wisely.

CONCEPTS OF THE PROPER FUNCTIONS OF GOVERNMENT have been profoundly changed during the last few decades. Older shibboleths, which hailed the best government as the one which governed least, are now of little use in evaluating the propriety of new functions. They reflect the rear-guard defenses of dogmatists opposed to the Government's assuming any new functions no matter what the national need for such action.

Adam Smith defined the duties of government as being defense, internal justice, and the erection and maintenance of public institutions and public works, including roads and education. They long served as guides for the students of government. . . . But we have now gone far beyond this level of thinking. The major issues now center about the question of which positive functions the Government shall assume. Which gaps in our social and economic system and failings in our present operations should be met by assigning them to Government? . . .

Recent developments have added new complexities to this problem of distinguishing public from private functions. When the government assumes direct responsibilities in a given area, it no longer automatically

From Solomon Barkin, "Expansion of Governmental Responsibilities," in *Federal Expenditure Policy for Economic Growth and Stability* (Washington, D.C.: U.S. Government Printing Office, 1957), pp. 87–95.

means direct operations therein. There is no necessary inference that an operating institution will be erected or that an army of employees will be necessary for the particular function. Governmental policy and interest may be implemented in the above traditional way, or it may be reflected through its program of purchase of goods and services, by the use of its credit position, the transfer of payments, or regulation and control of particular private operations. Many significant recent extensions in government interest in the operation of our private economy have required few additional employees. Moreover, the implementation of our monetary policy has called for little direct use of Federal funds. The assurance of proper minimum wages and working conditions has necessitated few employees or governmental expenses other than those required in the direct administration of the law itself. Economic policy directives are being used to implement government purposes. . . .

The essential characteristic of a governmental organization is that it is a community institution whose functions are prescribed and funds allotted to it by a governmental body. It is controlled through the budget. The alternatives in our private economy and society have some similarities. True, the market more or less determines these operations. But we are no longer faced with the simple choice of large government versus the single individual. The latter has found it desirable to organize into voluntary groups which require no governmental authority or support, or to secure sanction from the government for forming such groups. The business corporation, the philanthropic foundation, and many trusts and membership organizations are creatures of the government administered by private authority.

The important fact for our present purpose is that the individual assigns some of his power over personal expenditures to these groups. They spend it for him. For example, instead of granting charitable aid himself, he is likely to give his money to a philanthropic institution. Incidentally, some of these organizations, like the community chest, collect funds on such a wide basis that it is tantamount to a voluntary levy upon the local citizens. Similarly, members pay dues to their unions, and in union shops all must pay, or to membership organizations for the realization of common purposes. Many of these groups operate on the budget rather than the market principle.

If the previous discussion highlights how much less appropriate is the use of the old dichotomy between the public and private economies, so the older contrasts may not be employed for the study of collective versus private expenditure. The latter is now significantly controlled and affected by governmental influences so it is more an instrument of public purpose than a completely independent agent. Personal expenditures are at all times a function of prevailing social patterns; new governmental controls have been developed to further restrict private choices of expenditures.

Besides the basic protective legislation related to cleanliness, pure goods and drugs, labeling, and other similar controls, and taxes on items such as alcoholic beverages, we have seen two major developments affecting private expenditures. The first is represented by the growth of welfare programs. Funds are transferred to people who would otherwise not have been able to purchase specific goods and services or proper amounts of them. Matching this so-called welfare state, which slogan became an issue of national concern some 5 years ago, is the relatively less-trumpeted development, the incentive state. Not only are governmental funds transferred to certain private business in the form of subsidies, and generous sales of government surpluses or properties, but the government has used various financial inducements to stimulate businessmen to engage in specific functions such as housing, construction, research activities, expansion of capacity for the production of vital war materials, and general industrial production. Even the individual has been provided incentives to spend his funds in governmentally approved ways. The Federal income-tax system allows generous exemptions to philanthropic contributions, which have led to the creations of thousands of foundations for the organized expenditure of funds for these purposes. These exemptions, in effect, allow the private administration of publicly taxable funds.

A review of this twofold development involving, on the one hand, the multiplication of the forms of government influence ranging from governmental enterprises to a positive system of economic policy implementation and the appearance of many collective institutions for the spending of private funds, and, on the other hand, the striking growth in incentives guiding private expenditures and the transfer of purchasing power among private citizens, clearly unfolds the fact that any determination respecting a governmental function and responsibility does not automatically carry with it a decision on the form of governmental intervention in a particular area. The decision as to whether the influence is to be exerted through direction, operation as a public enterprise, or some less direct or completely indirect form of influence, is a moot question. Similarly, the fact that the forms of governmental operation and influence are most diverse, permits it more easily to extend its concern and to condition the behavior of individuals in a wider area of our private society and economy. Since the choice is not merely between governmental and private enterprise, various means can be devised to achieve public purposes. Where particular gaps or failings are recognized in our economic or social structure and performance, the government can intervene or influence the situation without necessarily establishing a public enterprise. The issue as to what is a public function must, therefore, be defined in terms of this concept of the wide range of choice of methods of exerting influence available to governmental authorities. . . .

The basic challenge is, therefore, not to distinguish between public and private goods but to determine the effectiveness of the operation of the private society and economy and to seek methods of correcting whatever the shortcomings may be, whether they be omissions or imperfections.

28.3. GOVERNMENTAL ACTION IN MEETING HUMAN NEEDS

Another view of the desirability of governmental action in the welfare field is expressed by Dr. Dixon. In his view, when individual needs cannot be met by private voluntary agencies, it is in the national interest and in keeping with our belief in a rational society to provide effective national leadership for such problems as mental health, juvenile delinquency, and dependent children.

WE ARE a compassionate people. We have a strong desire to help persons in need. We believe that the individual is central to our society, that the principal asset of human society is human life itself, and that society must therefore help to protect the lives and interests of every individual.

We know too that the spread of juvenile delinquency, or an increase in the desertion of fathers, or widespread loss of income due to involuntary unemployment, creates a hazard for the whole community. Individuals cease to contribute to the community, and become dependent on it.

At the same time, deep conviction that the individual and his productivity are basic to our free society makes us reluctant to meet human needs in a fashion which might reduce individual initiative and self-reliance. In the planning, design, and execution of programs to improve the human condition, there is a constant dilemma: interference with individual freedom and self-reliance must be balanced against the need to maintain social justice and security for the group as a whole. Many decisions of the past and discussions of the present hinge on variations in perception of this moral judgment.

Most people handle most of their needs by themselves or with

From James P. Dixon, "Meeting Human Needs," in The Report of the President's Commissions on National Goals, *Goals for Americans,* by The American Assembly, pp. 249–260. © 1960. By permission of Prentice-Hall, Inc., Englewood Cliffs, N.J.

the help of family and friends. Society as a whole has two functions. It can develop ways by which people can meet their own needs more readily and fruitfully, and it can develop ways by which society as a whole can meet needs that would otherwise be unmet. These are individuals who will not meet their own needs, and others who cannot.

These two functions of society are performed through organized social institutions. A substantial number of these are privately run and supported. Private support is a distinctive characteristic of our general hospitals, as well as of many agencies which serve the needs of families and children. These institutions are of particular importance, for while they cannot extend their services to everyone, they have a major responsibility for setting standards of service. They provide a tremendous volume of services. They perform experimental and pilot functions. They are legitimate extensions of our economic system into the field of social service.

Another principal social institution involved in maintaining minimum standards of human health and decency is government. The role which government may play in devising and implementing new goals for human welfare depends conspicuously upon people's feelings about it, the responsibility we are prepared to vest in it, and our views concerning the effectiveness of voluntary efforts to meet human needs with or without government assistance.

Government's role should not be determined by the application of pious general principles. In modern society it is not possible to escape into the jungle and choose the threat of the lions as a substitute for the annoyances of bureaucracy. The tests should be these. In the particular case, will the use of government yield advantages unobtainable through voluntary efforts? Will it, in the specific instance, damage essential qualities of health or welfare service so that standards of performance will be impaired? Will it interfere unduly with the personal and economic freedoms and responsibilities of either the provider or the recipient of the services? . . .

Three areas of human need call for specific attention in the decade ahead. These are improved health, the remaining unfinished business in our effort to lessen poverty through income security, and the reduction of juvenile delinquency, family breakdown and other instances of social disorganization. The reasons are manifest. Good health is necessary to the full functioning of the individual, poverty is destructive to the individual and to family organization, and social disorganization is destructive to our entire society. . . .

Prevention of illness is ʰa particular responsibility of public health departments. New environmental hazards, such as exposure to

X-rays, increased water pollution and increased use of agricultural pesticides raise additional problems for these departments in this decade.

Community health departments are becoming increasingly involved in the planning of medical services. No other existing agency has the capacity to identify a community's needs for medical care and to evaluate continuously the quality of its health practices and the adequacy of its health facilities and manpower.

The responsibility of a community health department to provide direct medical services to persons who would not otherwise be served should be equally clear. There is a myth which has it that only the very rich and the very poor receive high-quality medical care; the very rich because they can afford to purchase the best services available, the very poor because the community sees to it that the very best is provided for them. The fact, however, is that the seven million persons on public relief, and other low-income families, have more than their share of illness and receive by ordinary standards inadequate health care. . . .

There is widespread agreement that a third desirable health goal is to provide more adequate services to older people. The number of older persons is increasing. This is in part due to the victories of medicine and public health over the infectious diseases, especially of childhood. In part it is due to a rising standard of living. Older age involves a wearing out of the human body, and a consequent increase in demand for health services. There is disagreement as to how this demand should be met. . . .

If we are to attain minimum standards of health service for older people throughout the nation, there must be national action. In the author's opinion, the logical choice is an extension of the present federal social security system. Such an extension would reflect the principle of contribution, during working years, of funds identified to provide as much health service as possible in old age. . . .

Mental illness is one of the most anguishing and exasperating health problems in our time. It has received great attention within the health professions, by community organizations, and by state and federal governments. It is an important cause of disability and an expensive part of our health service. Indeed, the cost to state governments alone is in excess of $1 billion. Some 17 million persons are estimated to be suffering from it in our country. The present state of our knowledge does not provide adequate means for its prevention and cure. . . .

Many of the services now provided for the mentally ill, particularly in institutions, are more for the custody of the ill person than for the treatment of his illness. These services are financed and operated by state governments. There is clear evidence that this custodial function would not require the isolation of many of the mentally ill in remote institutions, if there were proper community services permitting them to enjoy a family and home life.

State and federal governments should together undertake to fashion programs of coordinated community service that would permit a sensible relationship between the services of the community clinic, the community hospital, the home, and the specialized mental hospitals and clinics. State governments should at least elevate standards of service in their own mental institutions to the levels which they demand of homes and hospitals over which they have regulatory authority.

Voluntary health insurance has generally provided extensive coverage for mental illness. There are encouraging experiments to enlarge such coverage. It is particularly important that voluntary insurance endeavor to cover forms of treatment which can be carried out over short periods of time in community or specialized hospitals. . . .

In the United States, as in other western cultures, we have attacked poverty by significant use of devices to provide income security. While we have not devised a system of family allowances, such as is common in many countries, we have made extensive use of social insurance against the involuntary interruption of income. Social insurance in general involves contributions by the earner, so that when earnings are interrupted by death, injury, disability, unemployment, or old age, an amount related to earnings will be paid to him or his dependents. Social insurance is created by legislative action. Ours is not a tidy single system, but was established by such legislation as the federal Social Security Act of 1935, and workmen's compensation and federal-state unemployment insurance acts in all of the states. Social insurance is complemented extensively by private pension plans.

This system has evolved slowly, and it is quite natural that it should still contain some defects in its coverage. In addition to the need to extend social insurance to provide medical service to older persons, there are two other types of coverage which call for prompt strengthening. These are protection against income loss due to unemployment or disability. . . .

The programs we have just described for income security and assistance to the needy have as their premise that the way to meet human needs arising from poverty is to supplement incomes. This is a valuable premise, when those who are in need will use the added income constructively, for it results in the least interference with freedom and independence of the individual. But what should society do to meet the needs of children who do not have parents to care for them, or whose parents cannot be counted on to use financial help constructively, or who appear to fail to respond to their parents and society alike?

The question is acutely presented by the category of public assistance which is supported by federal aid to states and is known as Aid to Dependent Children. This program makes financial assistance available for the protection and care of 2,300,000 homeless, dependent, and neglected children, and children in danger of becoming delinquent. These children are found not only where a parent is dead or physically incapacitated, but also in families where there is desertion, divorce, or, indeed, where there was no marriage. For the most part, the assistance is paid to the parent with whom the children are living.

This program is now subject to widespread attack on the ground that it subsidizes immorality and desertion. It is no doubt true that the funds are spent in families where there is extensive family breakdown; that is precisely the reason the funds are needed. But there is little logic to the notion, which has its ardent supporters, that rates of illegitimacy will be reduced by withdrawal of assistance from families where the mother has borne two illegitimate children.

It is more likely that the relationships between the prevention and cure of family breakdown are akin to the relationships between preventive and curative medicine. Financial support or welfare services are forms of treatment directed to the needs of each child who is affected. They will not materially increase the extent of family breakdown, nor will they much reduce it. But our knowledge of how to prevent such breakdown is pitifully inadequate, and such services are the only way we know to offset the disadvantages a youngster may incur from his inability to choose his parents or from the social circumstances of his birth. . . .

Of all the symptoms of social disorganization, there is none more perplexing than juvenile delinquency. It has some of the characteristics of a contagious disease, for its presence constitutes a threat not only to the young person involved, but also to the life and property of citizens at large, who have not been directly involved in the development of the juvenile's delinquent behavior.

Like a contagious disease, juvenile delinquency spreads geographically. Its heaviest incidence is in areas in American cities which have long had high rates. It is increasing in suburban areas adjacent to the city, and the rate of increase there is higher than in the central city. The present rate of increase in the number of cases coming before juvenile courts is about five times the increase in the number of young people aged ten to seventeen. If the present trend continues unabated, it has been estimated that by 1970 one boy in every five will be involved in at lease one court delinquency during his adolescence. . . .

We are a rational society and must believe that juvenile delinquency and other forms of social maladjustment have specific causes. We must also believe that patient research will lead us ever closer to a clear understanding of those causes, and we must continue to hope that the clearer our knowledge becomes about cause, the more effective will be our techniques of treatment and our options for prevention. Whether we shall decide to exercise these options is a matter for decision in the future, for it is not necessarily true that society will apply knowledge in hand. In the end, we may discover that to reduce juvenile delinquency to the full extent our knowledge permits would require that we control human behavior more rigidly than we are willing to do.

We have no reason to be satisfied with the present state of our endeavors. Substantial new leadership for research, demonstration and training is needed. And substantial financial support will be necessary.

28.4. THE DANGERS OF THE QUEST FOR ECONOMIC SECURITY

Senator Goldwater presents a case against government welfare programs. He believes that the quest for economic security may well destroy our traditional values of individual responsibility and liberty. When the government assumes responsibility, we run the unintentional danger of falling into the horrors of the totalitarian systems of Nazi Germany or the Soviet Union.

MR. PRESIDENT, I shall not detain the Senate long at this late hour. By a peculiar coincidence, I prepared this speech some months ago. It comes in quite handy today, only a few days after the vote was taken on the medical care for the aged bill, against which I voted. Naturally, a number of people have asked me: Why? I think if they will read what I have to say about the whole subject of the welfare state, they will understand why I oppose such measures.

A candidate for the Democratic nomination for President recently startled the country by charging that "17 million Americans go to bed hungry every night." I say "startled" advisedly because while most of us are aware that some Americans, because of unemployment and other factors, do not enjoy a diet on par with those gainfully employed, the figure "17 million hungry Americans" does sound a bit padded. It is also, of course, a well-worked Soviet propaganda stereotype that most Americans suffer from malnutrition and that thousands drop dead in the streets of America every day of hunger.

I am inclined to be charitable and I attribute this particular exaggeration to youthful exuberance and perhaps a bit of overstriving for political effect. What does disturb me is that the claim of so many millions of Americans as being ill fed, ill housed, and ill clothed is not unique or recent. Ever since the early days of the unlamented New Deal, we have been fed a regular and overfull diet of statistics along the same

From Senator Barry Goldwater, "What Price Social Welfare?" in *The Congressional Record,* Vol. 106 (August 25, 1960), pp. 17650–17653.

general line. The Soviets merely pick up and rebroadcast our own lamentations as proof of the truth of their charges.

Then the socialized medicine boys got into the act and we were given a liberal dosage of figures and statistics tending to show that despite the highest income level in the world we still had X number million people or X percent of our population suffering from below par medical care—or what was represented to be absolute par in dental and medical care. Then came the Forand bill to take care of the problems of the elderly and retired, and the President's own medical care for the aged plan which was hastily put together as an answer to the Forand bill—all of which prompted me to do a little bit of research to see if it was possible to arrive at some rough figure of what all forms of social welfare have cost the American taxpayer since 1933 or 1934. In other words, "What price social welfare?"

In 1913, all public expenditures for social welfare amounted to a shadow over three percent of the gross national product. By 1929, with mounting relief costs, public welfare expenditures had increased only one percent to a trifle over 4 percent of the gross national product. Six years later, in 1935, or 2 years after the beginning of the New Deal, the percentage of welfare expenditure in relation to our gross national product had jumped or tripled to 12 percent. We were well on the way to the welfare state.

In December 1951, the Chamber of Commerce of the United States released a special report showing that some 300 Federal, State, and local welfare plans had cost $23 billion or 34.2 percent of money expanded by Federal, State, and local agencies. The Federal Security Agency itself was quoted as authority for the figures. This meant a tax burden of $575 in 1950 for every American taxpaying family. The FSA included $6.5 billion spent by State and local authorities on education, so even if we deduct this figure it still leaves a total of over $16 billion or one-quarter of all tax money spent at all levels by the Federal Government and State and local agencies.

It is admittedly difficult, if not impossible, for even conservatives to agree on just what may properly be defined as "welfare." Communist propaganda, New Deal semantics, and word twisting by the liberals into new shapes and forms have raised hob with old-line, accepted definitions. To those who object that expenditures included in the above totals for education, some veterans' benefits, and other forms of disbursement of questionable social welfare classification should not have been added, I repeat that extensive statistical analysis and research, which would take months, would no doubt uncover an equal or even larger sum total definitely classifiable as welfare, but sandwiched in other disbursements, including gray or borderline categories. . . .

We do have some rough breakdowns since 1939 in the Federal

budget for "Labor and welfare." Since 1939, the Federal Government has spent a total of $52 billion in 22 fiscal years. The Social Security Bulletin for October 1955 had an extended table showing local and State expenditures on social welfare from fiscal 1934 to fiscal 1954 as totaling $170.344 billion. As State and local social welfare payments since 1954 have jumped to well over $20 billion per year, we can add another $100 billion for the past 5 years, making a grand total of at least $322 billion.

If, as it is claimed, we still have 17 million hungry people after spending $322 billion in 25 years, then it is obvious we must do one of two things. One, raise taxes still higher a la the New Deal dictum "tax and tax; spend and spend," boost the national debt still higher, and give the spiral of inflation another whirl. Or, two, try something else. That is, spend less, tax less, give away less abroad, balance the budget, and let people keep more of their earned income to prime the economic pump by old and tried economic laws which seemed to have worked pretty well until we started monkeying with them. . . .

While welfarism is as old as the first primitive social organizations lost in the mist of pre-Sumerian culture, the concept certainly was well developed and historically established at least in rudimentary forms in the early Greek and Etruscan city-states.

It remained, however, for the iron chancellor, Prince Bismarck, to give the stamp of bureaucratic authority to social welfarism as a state monopoly. Authorities tell us that all present forms of social security and other forms of welfarism can be traced directly to the Prussian chancellor. We are all familiar with Bismarck's difficulties with the socialists in control of the German unions and the liberals who were powerful in the Reichstag. In converting the newly created German Empire into a militaristic state, Bismarck was faced with enormous difficulties and problems.

German socialism was pacifist to the core and bitterly anti-militarist. German industry and commerce, which were in competition with France, joined Great Britain in looking askance at heavy military budgets. In order, as he said, to "steal the thunder away from the Socialists," Bismarck was forced to adopt "nationalistic socialism to end international socialism." German employers as a class, as well as liberals, were of the same mind that social insurance should properly be a private matter taken care of by the workers themselves through their unions or through religious and other organizations already in existence for that purpose.

Bismarck also had revenue troubles. His universal military training program, a revolutionary innovation in European military history, required enormous sums of money which the Reichstag granted with increasing reluctance. The new German Reich, like our own infant

Republic, had almost no important source of revenue other than the excise taxes and import duties. Involved parliamentary bickering produced some revenues as contributions from the various once-independent states absorbed into the Reich. By setting up a comprehensive social security program under federal control, Bismarck assured himself of a substantial source of revenue beyond the control of the Reichstag. The German example was quickly followed by neighboring European states and modern day social security collected and administered by a vast and all-pervasive bureaucracy was on its way. Like the proverbial camel's nose under the tent, it was now merely a matter of gradual and imperceptible extension before the whole camel of paternalistic and bureaucratic state welfarism ousted the liberal concept of individual freedom and social responsibility.

It is very significant and interesting to note that before Hitler maneuvered himself into power, he was violently opposed to the social insurance system of Germany. He ranted that it weakened and demoralized sturdy German concepts of thrift and self-reliance. His real opposition, of course, was due to the fact that he considered social welfare insurance as a powerful weapon of his main political enemy, the Social Democrats of the Weimar Republic.

Nazi propagandists made a great deal of political capital out of charges that there was considerable corruption and waste of money in the compulsory medical care program. This naturally won them considerable support among doctors, businessmen, and conservative middle class elements. The Bruening government was forced, into 1931, to make a number of reforms tending to eliminate the worst abuses. The Nazis naturally reaped the credit.

However, when Hitler took power in 1933, he soon changed his tune. With its heavy emphasis on racial superiority and physical fitness, the Nazi ideology perforce had to concentrate on social welfare as an important state function. A high birth rate and maximum physical fitness were obviously very important to a totalitarian state planning military aggression against its neighbors. Hitler heavily financed all manner of social welfare programs, not for humanitarian reasons but because German human resources had to be mobilized and strengthened for the enormous strains and sacrifices which Hitler knew he would have to impose upon the German people in order to consummate his grandiose plans.

Lenin was a great admirer of Bismarck. The rigid Prussian bureaucratic system of social control struck the father of bolshevism as just the ticket, with some modifications, for huge and chaotic Russia exhausted by World War I blood losses. It is true that there was a basic philosophical difference between Lenin and Bismarck in their concern with bureaucratic control of social welfare for their subjects. Bismarck professed to be actuated by Christian precepts and morality. Lenin, as an atheistic materialist, was concerned only with insuring the health, docility, and productivity of the Russian masses as the solid underpinning of the Bolshevist form of Socialist state which he announced "we shall now proceed to create," in November 1917.

It was years before the last vestiges of private ownership and free enterprise were eradicated in Soviet Russia. Social welfarism, or what passed for it under the iron heel of the Bolshevists, was one of the first monopolies set up by the victorious Bolsheviks in 1917, almost simultaneously with the creation of the Cheka or secret police charged with the extirpation of all opposition and even minor and harmless dissent. It has now been long forgotten with the passage of the years, but the abolition by formal decree of all private social insurance, relief, and charity, whether by the church, trade unions, cooperatives, or other established organizations followed the Bolshevik consolidation of power in a matter of months.

I do not mean to infer from this belief historical analysis of social welfarism under various forms of despotism that totalitarianism and social welfarism go hand in hand, or that one leads inevitably to the other. There have been a few exceptions, notably in smaller countries in northeastern Europe with long histories of limited government, where some degree of individual freedom has been maintained. Note that I say "some degree" advisedly, because nowhere else is the old maxim "Something gained; something lost" more true than in the field of welfarism. The supposed tangible gains and material advantages are usually far outweighed by the longrun, intangible values of human freedom and dignity.

The examples I have cited, and others—although the lack of time prohibits study and examination of the latter group—do leave the ineluctable conclusion that social welfarism, in its most advanced form, has always been an inseparable part of all totalitarian systems, ancient and modern, Fascist and Communist, openly as brutalitarian or heavily disguised as benevolent despotisms.

I have already pointed out that socialism—that is to say, the expropriation of private property, for exploitation by the state, for the theoretical maximum benefit of all—has been a dead issue in this country for lo these many years. The Socialists were smart enough to disguise themselves as New Dealers, and have openly boasted of the success of their strategem. We have learned that socialism can be sneaked over, against the wishes of the majority, through the simple device of expropriation by taxation and the creation of an all-embracing welfare program which effectively robs the individual of all control over his more basic and fundamental human freedoms and the right to regulate his own personal affairs as he may see fit.

Nationalization has acquired a sinister connotation, particularly after Great Britain's disastrous experience with disguised socialism. But welfarism has a disarming universal appeal. Who, except an embittered and confirmed misanthrope, could possibly be opposed to human welfare? Those who fish for the souls and minds of men have learned, through long experience, to be exceedingly cunning in their weaving of gossamer-fine nets and simply irresistible lures and bait. Time and again, I *have* tried to show that no one is opposed to human welfare per se. We conservatives are merely opposed to the establishment of a government bureaucratic monopoly to deal with basic human problems traditionally handled and best solved, first, through religious and private organizations and, second, through the lowest form of political organization closest to the individual or individuals concerned.

In their search for votes in this presidential election year, the Democrats seem to feel that they have staked out a real Klondike strike in our aged. The Forand bill is the sluiceway which is expected to wash out solid gold nuggets of bloc votes in every State. The estimated cost of the Forand bill—$1.1 billion the first year, and nearly $6 billion over a 5-year period—is, to me, not the main consideration, bad enough as it is. The Forand bill and all other measures promising "more" or the most to 17 million of our citizens over 65 are merely continuations of a welfare state trend which has become a matter of increasing concern to the economist, the believer in a free enterprise system, and the Constitutionalist.

One of the charges leveled against Marxism is that it envisions and strenuously works for the elimination of the family and the transfer of many of the family's functions to the state. Communist China, in her fanatic drive toward the commune system, has gone further in this direction than has her older brother, Russia. The Marxists correctly, from their viewpoint, regard the family as a serious hindrance to the setting up of the Communist Utopia. As far back as we have any historical evidence, the family, as a unit, cared for its own elderly people. One of the first steps taken by the Bolsheviks in Russia, after they seized power, was to abolish all charitable and welfare work of the Orthodox church. The Soviet state was to be the sole protector and guardian of the aged, the ill, and the disabled. The Soviet state was a jealous state, and would not permit any other agency to stand between it and its enslaved masses, even in the fields of welfare, social insurance, relief, and charity.

Mankind passed from a state of savagery to one of semicivilization when men began to care for their ill and aged, instead of dispatching them as a hindrance, or turning them adrift, to starve, as a costly nuisance. Many savages, even until recent times, practiced geronticide, because the rigors of nature and chronic semistarvation made care for the aged and crippled an intolerable burden on the tribe or social unit.

As men became semicivilized and as the influence of religion spread over the world, greater and greater concern was devoted to the aged, the helpless, and the disabled. Hospitals and shelters for the indigent aged were first set up by the church. Each family, rich or poor, took care of its own elderly members. Only elderly and helpless poor who had no living relatives found their way to the poorhouse or a religious-supported home or shelter. In all countries the family—regardless of religion or race—took care of its own elderly people. It was a matter of fierce pride that even the very poorest took care of their own.

All this has now changed, at least in this country, thanks to social security. It is now considered shameful for older people to be taken care of in their declining years by their children whom they nourished and spent small fortunes on bringing up. Sending one's parents to the poorhouse, so that one can buy a new house or a new and flashier auto, would, of course, be considered a bit raw; but the same individual sees nothing shameful in turning his parents adrift to shift for themselves on a meager social security pittance. They earned this social security themselves; and any deficits which have to be made up come out of the public treasury—that is, somebody else's pocket.

The impersonal arm of a vast bureaucracy centered in Washington can never transmit to the individual recipient the warmth and personal feeling provided by a family which shelters and protects its own. Even religious, charitable, or fraternal assistance at the local level, because it has been, and remains, in direct personal contact with the recipient, is bound to be a warmer and more sympathetic bond than that of a mere statistical figure in a bureaucratic budget. And I believe it has been amply demonstrated that Federal collection, administration, and distribution of welfare funds are bound to cost more, because of higher administrative overhead than the same process when carried on within the community and administered by the community or by private organizations.

Mr. President, we went through all this years ago. I am sorry to bring it up again; but I still do not understand why it is shameful and humiliating to expect support from one's children, but why it is ruggedly independent and dignified to accept from the public exchequer a thinly disguised dole in the form of a monthly security check.

Nor has anyone pointed out the fundamental immorality of taxing those who already take care of their own aged relatives, in addition to helping support others, whose children pass their own obligations on to the State. Then there are many spinsters and bachelors who devoted their lives to caring for their parents until they died and, as a result of discharging such an obligation, never married. They are now taxed at the higher rates for single persons, to help pay the enormous annual cost of caring for those whose own children refuse to do so. One of the most shameful situations presently plaguing welfare agencies in this country is the subsidization by the State of wholesale bastardy practiced by women who have made illegitimacy a profession, or at least a source of easy and steady income.

It should have been plain years ago to even the most obtuse that once we open the Pandora's box of the welfare state, we cannot stop at any particular point or draw the line against any particular segment of the population. Bismarck tried it in Germany 80 years ago, only to learn that the Socialists would invariably raise the ante every time he threw in a new concession.

All of us—left, right, and center—make numerous speeches and declamations against the evils of communism. We affect great horror and deep moral indignation over the brutal methods used by the Chinese Reds in setting up the commune system and their calculated destruction of the ages-old Chinese family system. We lose sight of the fact that it is just as easy to slip unintentionally into a hole on a dark night as it is to jump down into it deliberately in the daytime.

The gradual and imperceptible erosion of the family, through ill-advised and misguided welfare schemes over a period of years, may bring us in the not too distant future to a commune system of social organization, with cradle-to-grave welfarism. Goldsmith's often quoted couplet might well be paraphrased and brought up to date:

> Ill fares the land to hastening ills a prey,
> Where welfarism· is accelerated and the fam-
>   ily is permitted to decay.

28.5. THE WELFARE STATE

The scope and purpose of Federal-State welfare policies and expenditures have engendered intense political controversy. This has been particularly true since the adoption of the so-called Social Security System ushered in what its critics and protagonists alike often call the "Welfare State." In chapter 12 of his recent book, The American Economic Republic, *the distinguished lawyer-economist-statesman Adolf Berle offers a dispassionate analysis of the Welfare State.*

IN EVERY ECONOMIC STATE there is a stratum of individuals temporarily or permanently unable to pay for their current needs with current work or previously accumulated wealth. Neither the economic republic nor Communist societies can avoid this.

Some individuals in this group are defeated. There are those who have refused or been unable to accept social obligations and social discipline, who prefer to be (or at any event act as) vagrants, criminals, or irresponsibles. A larger group may be defeated by addiction to alcohol, narcotics, or other habits rendering them unable to work and pull their weight in the social and economic boat. Still others are defeated by injury, physical ailment, or bad health, putting them out of the running. . . .

There is a second group defeated by age and the passing of years. Defeat by time comes inevitably to all who live beyond a certain span of years. In the nineteenth- and early twentieth-century free-market economies an enormous majority of the population in all countries proved unable to accumulate wealth sufficient to meet this period of life. Classical economists begged the question, and merely accepted the thesis that failure to acquire sufficient wealth for this period was presumptively a defect or fault of the individual. This, I think, was error. Under a fully competitive system, a workman could indeed acquire enough if (a) he went through life in good health, (b) was continuously employed, and (c) competently invested his savings. Included in "competence" was capacity to anticipate and hedge against inflation. Few men could, or even now can, expect a lifetime of perfect health, uninterrupted employment, and sure-fire skill in investment. Aside from a tiny class possessing comfortable wealth, the aged wound up living as state-supported paupers, or, more often, on the charity of their relatives. The agricultural system of family farms made a kind of human adjustment to this. The industrial system did not.

And always there were children. Infants are wholly dependent. Growing children can contribute a trifle. Youth somewhat more. Full participation means being an adult. Meanwhile, they must be fed, educated, equipped with tools to work and launched in adult life. Responsibility is placed on the family to take care of this. If the families cannot do this from their own resources, then help has to be provided.

Finally, there is unemployment, sporadic or permanent, not caused by irresponsibility, addiction or bad health. The individual is willing to the extent of his capacity, but the opportunity is not there.

Obviously, the combined total of these individuals falls into two groups. Some are defeated primarily by the operations of the social-economic system itself. These include the wealthless, the aging, the unsupported children, and the unemployed. Some are defeated by themselves, or, more accurately, by the combination of their lack of

From *The American Economic Republic* © 1963 by Adolf A. Berle, pp. 176–183. Reprinted by permission of Harcourt, Brace & World, Inc. Also, by permission of Sidgwick & Jackson Ltd., London.

moral or intellectual strength and a set of circumstances with which they are unable to cope.

The economic republic considers that it has three responsibilities. The first is to the victims of the system. . . . The second is to the irresponsibles, the addicts, and the sick. . . . For the third responsibility, the political state must arrange relief and assistance for those who (for these and any other reasons) lie outside the areas in which wealth is distributed through salaries, wages, or otherwise by the economic system.

The American economic republic recognizes all these responsibilities. This combination has been christened "The Welfare State." There is no foreseeable likelihood of its discontinuance. . . . The political state, represented by local agencies (towns and cities, countries; to some extent, state government), has traditionally dealt with some part of these problems for centuries. . . . Organizing the responsibility as an expression of national function by the federal government has been very recent.

Crisis conditions compelled the federal government to intervene in 1933. Before that year it had not done so . . . In the breakdown of that national economy no state government (let alone local government units) could possibly cope with the cumulative tide of unemployment and resulting destitution. . . . A series of emergency measures, which will always be associated with the name of Harry Hopkins, evolved at length into the present organized instrumentalities.

These proceeded on two theories. Individuals displaced from time to time by the economic system, or defeated eventually by old age, needed wealth sufficient to meet their necessities when they no longer had wages or pay checks. Accordingly, the political state undertook the task of collecting from time to time from them, or from the system, enough wealth to be held for their account, and paid out in time of need. In effect, it forced savings by them in conjunction with their employers . . . Second, the federal government could provide, or assist local governments in providing, direct relief in areas where wealth could not be accumulated by or on behalf of the individual himself. . . .

By 1961, total federal expenditures for all these groups amounted to $37 billion. Of this amount, $22 billion represented, not taxation, but forced savings, collected through the Social Security system from employing enterprises and from workers as payment for social insurance. These were in effect deferred wages. . . .

Slightly over $15 billion was collected by the federal government through taxation and applied directly for assistance or "relief," usually supplementing funds raised by local government. Taking all items together, between 7 percent and 9 percent of the gross national product of the United States is annually directed by way of forced saving or through taxation to the Welfare State for distribution.

It cannot be said that the economic republic has allowed its less fortunate stratum to go without food or shelter. Actually, an unemployed workman drawing insurance pay is better supplied with goods and services than a fully employed and paid workman in the Soviet Union or Czechoslovakia. The lowest "reliefer" is economically placed far above the level of the "Proletarian" classes in most parts of the world. The republic is still not satisfied, nor will it be satisfied until its "lower stratum" has shrunk to its irreducible minimum of irresponsibles and incapables, and perhaps not then.

The Welfare State reached its present form of organization with the advent of the Department of Health, Education, and Welfare under President Dwight D. Eisenhower's administration in 1956. The new department, with the Treasury as administrative partner to handle social-insurance funds, inherited general jurisdiction over two great instruments. The best known is the Social Security Act of 1935, subsequently amended. This provides for forced savings—insurance premiums collected from employers and employees—to be accumulated and paid in pension form to individuals attaining retirement age (presently 65 for men) and, within limits, to wives, widows, and children, with particular privileges for parents caring for children. Payments from this fund should not accurately be included in "state" assistance. The funds have been collected by levy on employers and employees. They really amount to delayed payment of wages or salaries earned during the individual's working years and paid to him in his old age. About $12 billion was paid out under this scheme in 1961.

The other instrument is the so-called Unemployment Compensation Act, also passed in 1935, and now administered under the Social Security Act. The arrangement undertakes to pay an involuntarily unemployed individual a stated portion of his average monthly wage for a period of six months of unemployment. In case of a major economic depression, the period probably would be extended. In addition, facilities (not too effective) are provided to help find the unemployed individual a new job. Not quite $4 billion was expended for these purposes in 1961. Obviously, the amount of payments varies with the extent of unemployment.

In less defensible addition, nearly $5 billion was expended for pensions and compensation to veterans of past wars. . . .

More than $4 billion was paid for "public assistance," . . . In this field need does exist. There are uninsured aged, there are dependent children, there are mentally and physically disabled, and and there are blind. Usually through grants to the several states, arrangements are made for this relief, and the several states themselves pick up an added part of the load.

The remaining expenditures (nearly $5 billion) deal chiefly with hospital and medical care, medical facilities, medical research, maternal and child-health services, and public health. There is a current proposal for a comprehensive medical care, forced-savings, and insurance program. It is at present under debate, exciting violent opposition—and no less forceful protagonists, including the President of the United States.

Classical economics included an assumption that every man will be as lazy as he dares be. Quite possibly this was a valid point. Especially in weaker and less-educated sectors of the population, there has always been a propensity to be supported in idleness if it can conveniently be arranged. . . . When a man is out of a job, it is not always easy to determine whether it was his fault or desire, or his employer's fault, or the result of the ups and downs of the free market. When an individual is sick, it is not always certain that he is not malingering. Even when an individual is old, it is not certain at what point years take from him his capacity to contribute. . . .

The welfare frontier of the economic republic will be in conflict as long as human nature maintains its present form. One current of public opinion, more nearly classic in its idea, asserts that the cost of the Welfare State is already too great, that the workers carry too much of a load to provide for too many drones, and that these burdens retard the country's work and production. Another, taking a more generous view of human nature, believes that alleviations of the free-market casualties by the welfare route should be carried much further—as evidenced by the support of the new and somewhat expensive program for medical care to be paid for by additional forced savings collected in the form of Social Security insurance.

An economic analyst . . . introduces a different thought. Thirty-seven billion dollars taken annually from the prosperous of the country and spent among the less prosperous increases and tends to make continuous the market for goods and services. Capacity to produce these exists. The Welfare State puts purchasing power in the hands of individuals who otherwise would not have it. Consequently, the item is sometimes referred to by business (who are always anxious to sell) as a "built-in stabilizer"—the maintenance of effective demand and therefore of a market sector which will continue more or less irrespective of those economic ups and downs euphemistically called "booms" and "recessions." About 8 percent of income paid to individuals has been "socialized" and applied to "welfare" needs. To that extent the erratic distribution of income by the free-market system has been, if not tamed, at least kept in some bounds of humanity. At all events, a large proportion of the former casualties has been better taken care of than by poorhouses or private giving, and one effect is to maintain a current of private consumption.

Moral arguments, of course, enter a different field. Does the economic republic become too soft, too flabby, too lazy if it fails to apply the ruthless law that those who do not or cannot work shall live in acute misery? Is a hardy race maintained in greater vigor by the severity of individual economic struggle, with attendant individual fear of the ghastly consequences of defeat? I do not know. The American conscience never considered acceptable the results of such struggles as one finds them described in Dickens' *Bleak House* or *Oliver Twist,* or in Upton Sinclair's *The Jungle* (which was not a great exaggeration of Chicago in 1900). Neither does it morally accept the right of a drone or parasite to exist. Probably, therefore, the conflict will go on, continuously endeavoring to separate the malingerer from the weak, and the drone from the unfortunate, dealing harshly with the first and generously with the second, and having some difficulty in making the distinction.

.   .   .   .   .   .

29

Foreign Policy and Foreign Aid

29.1. PROTECTION THROUGH NON-ENTANGLEMENT

Fearful of the machinations of European colonial powers, President Washington deemed it wise at the outset of our life as a nation to avoid foreign entanglements. In his "Farewell Address" of 1796 he admonishes his fellow citizens to preserve "our detached and distant situation" and to avoid implicating ourselves in the "ordinary vicissitudes" of European politics.

. . . THE GREAT RULE of conduct for us in regard to foreign nations is, in extending our commercial relations to have with them as little political connection as possible. So far as we have already formed engagements let them be fulfilled with perfect good faith. Here let us stop.

Europe has a set of primary interests which to us have none or a very remote relation. Hence she must be engaged in frequent controversies, the causes of which are essentially foreign to our concerns. Hence, therefore, it must be unwise in us to implicate ourselves by artificial ties in the ordinary vicissitudes of her politics or the ordinary combinations and collisions of her friendships or enmities.

Our detached and distant situation invites and enables us to pursue a different course. If we remain one people, under an efficient gov-

From George Washington, "Farewell Address," in *Messages and Papers of the Presidents,* comp. by James D. Richardson (New York: Bureau of National Literature and Art, 1903), Vol. I, pp. 222–223.

ernment, the period is not far off when we may defy material injury from external annoyance; when we may take such an attitude as will cause the neutrality we may at any time resolve upon to be scrupulously respected; when belligerent nations, under the impossibility of making acquisitions upon us, will not lightly hazard the giving us provocation; when we may choose peace or war, as our interest, guided by justice, shall counsel.

Why forego the advantages of so peculiar a situation? Why quit our own to stand upon foreign ground? Why, by interweaving our destiny with that of any part of Europe, entangle our peace and prosperity in the toils of European ambition, rivalship, interest, humor, or caprice?

It is our true policy to steer clear of permanent alliances with any portion of the foreign world, so far, I mean, as we are now at liberty to do it; for let me not be understood as capable of patronizing infidelity to existing engagements. I hold the maxim no less applicable to public than to private affairs that honesty is always the best policy. I repeat, therefore, let those engagements be observed in their genuine sense. But in my opinion it is unnecessary and would be unwise to extend them.

Taking care always to keep ourselves by suitable establishments on a respectable defensive posture, we may safely trust to temporary alliances for extraordinary emergencies. . . .

29.2. FOREIGN POLICY AND THE HOME FRONT

In a striking speech at the close of his administration, President Eisenhower warned the nation of the potentially harmful effects our foreign and military commitments could have on our institutions at home. He cautions us to avoid domination of the nation's scholars by the Federal Government and to keep public policy from becoming the captive of a "scientific-technological elite."

OUR MILITARY ORGANIZATION today bears little relation to that known by any of my predecessors in peacetime, or indeed by the fighting men of World War II or Korea.

Until the latest of our world conflicts, the United States had no armaments industry. American makers of plowshares could, with time and as required, make swords as well. But now we can no longer risk emergency improvisation of national defense; we have been compelled to create

From President Dwight D. Eisenhower, "A Farewell Message," January 17, 1961.

a permanent armaments industry of vast proportions. Added to this, three and a half million men and women are directly engaged in the defense establishment. We annually spend on military security more than the net income of all United States corporations.

This conjunction of an immense military establishment and a large arms industry is new in the American experience. The total influence —economic, political, even spiritual—is felt in every city, every State house, every office of the Federal government. We recognize the imperative need for this development. Yet we must not fail to comprehend its grave implications. Our toil, resources and livelihood are all involved; so is the very structure of our society.

In the councils of government, we must guard against the acquisition of unwarranted influence, whether sought or unsought, by the military-industrial complex. The potential for the disastrous rise of misplaced power exists and will persist.

We must never let the weight of this combination endanger our liberties or democratic processes. We should take nothing for granted. Only an alert and knowledgeable citizenry can compel the proper meshing of the huge industrial and military machinery of defense with our peaceful methods and goals, so that security and liberty may prosper together.

Akin to, and largely responsible for the sweeping changes in our industrial-military posture, has been the technological revolution during recent decades.

In this revolution, research has become central; it also becomes more formalized, complex, and costly. A steadily increasing share is conducted for, by, or at the direction of, the Federal Government.

Today, the solitary inventor, tinkering in his shop, has been overshadowed by task forces of scientists in laboratories and testing fields. In the same fashion, the free university, historically the fountainhead of free ideas and scientific discovery, has experienced a revolution in the conduct of research. Partly because of the huge costs involved, a government contract becomes virtually a substitute for intellectual curiosity. For every old blackboard there are now hundreds of new electronic computers.

The prospect of domination of the nation's scholars by federal employment, project allocations, and the power of money is ever present— and is gravely to be regarded.

Yet, in holding scientific research and discovery in respect, as we should, we must also be alert to the equal and opposite danger that public policy could itself become the captive of a scientific-technological elite.

It is the task of statesmanship to mold, to balance, and to integrate these and other forces, new and old, within the principles of our democratic system—ever aiming toward the supreme goals of our free society.

29.3. THE PRESIDENT VIEWS OUR FOREIGN POLICY

In his inaugural address, President Kennedy stated eloquently the foreign policy his administration would pursue. He pledged his opposition to all forms of colonial control and urged the establishment of a new world of law "where the strong are just and the weak are secure."

TO THOSE OLD ALLIES whose cultural and spiritual origins we share, we pledge the loyalty of faithful friends, United, there is little we cannot do in a host of cooperative ventures. Divided, there is little we can do—for we dare not meet a powerful challenge at odds and split asunder.

To those new States whom we welcome to the ranks of the free, we pledge our word that one form of colonial control shall not have passed away merely to be replaced by a far greater iron tyranny. We shall not always expect to find them supporting our view. But we shall always hope to find them strongly supporting their own freedom—and to remember that, in the past, those who foolishly sought power by riding the back of the tiger ended up inside.

To those peoples in the huts and villages across the globe struggling to break the bonds of mass misery, we pledge our best efforts to help them help themselves, for whatever period is required—not because the Communists may be doing it, not because we seek their votes, but because it is right. If a free society cannot help the many who are poor, it cannot save the few who are rich.

To our sister republics south of our border, we offer a special pledge—to convert our good words into deeds, in a new alliance for progress, to assist free men and free governments in casting off the chains of poverty. But this peaceful revolution of hope cannot become the prey of hostile powers. Let all our neighbors know that we shall join them to oppose aggression or subversion anywhere in the Americas. And let every other power know that this hemisphere intends to remain the master of its own house.

To that world assembly of sovereign states, the United Nations, our last best hope in an age where the instruments of war have far outpaced the instruments of peace, we renew our pledge of support—to prevent it from becoming merely a forum for invective—to strengthen its shield of the new and the weak—and to enlarge the area in which its writ may run.

From President John F. Kennedy, Inaugural Address, January 20, 1961.

Finally, to those nations who would make themselves our adversary, we offer not a pledge but a request: that both sides begin anew the quest for peace, before the dark powers of destruction unleashed by science engulf all humanity in planned or accidental self-destruction.

We dare not tempt them with weakness. For only when our arms are sufficient beyond doubt can we be certain beyond doubt that they will never be employed.

But neither can two great and powerful groups of nations take comfort from our present course—both sides overburdened by the cost of modern weapons, both rightly alarmed by the steady spread of the deadly atom, yet both racing to alter that uncertain balance of terror that stays the hand of mankind's final war.

So let us begin anew—remembering on both sides that civility is not a sign of weakness, and sincerity is always subject to proof. Let us never negotiate out of fear. But let us never fear to negotiate.

Let both sides explore what problems unite us instead of laboring those problems which divide us.

Let both sides, for the first time, formulate serious and precise proposals for the inspection and control of arms—and bring the absolute power to destroy other nations under the absolute control of all nations.

Let both sides seek to invoke the wonders of science instead of its terrors. Together let us explore the stars, conquer the deserts, eradicate disease, tap the ocean depths, and encourage the arts and commerce.

Let both sides unite to heed in all corners of the earth the command of Isaiah—to "undo the heavy burdens and to let the oppressed go free."

And if a beachhead of cooperation may push back the jungle of suspicion, let both sides join in creating a new endeavor, not a new balance of power, but a new world of law, where the strong are just and the weak secure and the peace preserved.

29.4. THE ECONOMICS OF FOREIGN POLICY

American leadership in world affairs has been marked by the use of foreign assistance to help stabilize the economies and raise the living standards of countries facing economic and political crises. In this selection, Charles Bohlen, as special assistant to the Secretary of State, examines the history, current status, and long-range objectives of our foreign assistance programs.

. . . IN DISCUSSING the history of assistance to foreign countries and its

From Charles E. Bohlen, "Economic Assistance in U.S. Foreign Policy," in the *Department of State Bulletin*, March 28, 1960, pp. 495–501.

development as an integral part of our relations with friendly countries abroad, it should be emphasized that this is a comparatively new venture in relations between nations. Prior to World War II, with the exception of wartime loans, certain emergencies, and a modest amount of foreign lending by the Export-Import Bank established in 1934, government-to-government assistance was virtually unknown. To grasp what has happened to the United States position in the world in the last generation, I might mention that, at the time I joined the Foreign Service in 1929, the budget of the State Department for that year was $14.5 million. This appropriation was not only for the administrative expenses of the Department of State, including salaries of its employees in Washington and abroad, but also included the U.S. contribution to existing international organizations such as the U.S.-Mexican boundary committee, the Pan American Union, and the International Fisheries Commission. The State Department budget thus represented, together with some small additional appropriations from other Government departments, the total cost to the U.S. taxpayer of conducting our foreign relations.

Now what is the comparable cost of United States foreign relations today, 30 years later?

For the 1961 fiscal year the Department of State budget is $247 million, 17 times greater than in 1929. But this does not include the cost of our foreign military and economic assistance, which is embodied in the Mutual Security Program. On February 16 the President transmitted to Congress the administration's request for the Mutual Security Program in the 1961 fiscal year of $4.175 billion. There can be no more dramatic indication of the changed role of the United States in the world today than in the comparison with the figure I gave you earlier for 1929—$14 million—and approximately $5 billion. And this of course does not take into account that portion of national defense which supports our military establishments overseas. . . .

The beginning of the conceptions which underlie our policies of assistance to foreign countries may in part be found in a specific measure adopted by the United States before it was a belligerent in World War II. I refer, of course, to lend-lease. Although we were not militarily involved in the war, lend-lease was nonetheless a clear expression of the recognition of the United States Government at that time that our interests were vitally and indissolubly bound up with the fate of the Western democracies engaged in a struggle with the Axis powers. Lend-lease was the forerunner of our future aid programs in that it recognized that U.S. contributions to the common cause of national survival could not be treated merely as commercial transactions.

We had learned after World War I that the attempt to collect, on a bookkeeping basis, loans advanced for the prosecution of a war in a common cause was not only morally questionable but also economically and politically undesirable. The idea of lend-lease, which was subsequently carried over into the time when we were an active belligerent in both the European and Far Eastern theaters of war, was predicated on the recognition of these simple facts. We have never, therefore, sought to collect from any of our former allies repayment for the military supplies and equipment, and indeed for any supplies consumed, during the course of the war itself. Lend-lease settlements dealt merely with what is known as civilian inventory with due allowance for depreciation of such items of lend-lease supply as had a continuing and real value to the economy of the recipient country. Although entirely related to the prosecution of the war, nevertheless lend-lease itself indicated a keen awareness on the part of the United States of the role that it might be called upon to play in the postwar world in the field of foreign assistance.

The second phase of this developing program of assistance was found in our contribution to take care of the immediate human needs of the people who had suffered so heavily during the war. For the Allied and friendly countries this took the form of UNRRA [United Nations Relief and Rehabilitation Administration]. For former enemy countries this assistance went under the name of GARIOA [Government and Relief in Occupied Areas]. It was obvious that the first great task of the postwar period of reconstruction and recovery would be to take care of the simple human wants of the peoples most afflicted by the ravages of the war. This was the essential purpose of UNRRA and GARIOA. However, it soon became apparent that the mere alleviation of human suffering was not sufficient to restore economic health and political stability. Measures of a longer term and more coordinated nature were clearly necessary. . . .

I might go back here a bit into history and describe to you a single event which had a very important impact on the thinking of General Marshall, then Secretary of State, and therefore on the development of this concept of American foreign assistance. In Moscow in 1947, toward the close of the Council of Foreign Ministers meeting, General Marshall paid a courtesy call upon Stalin. I accompanied him as his interpreter. We were about to terminate almost 6 frustrating weeks of discussion of the central problems of the postwar settlement in Europe, particularly that of German reunification. We had encountered during this time Foreign Minister Molotov's unquestionable skill in obstruction, diversion, and delaying tactics. The conference, as you all know, made no progress whatsoever in the task of postwar European solutions. During this interview Stalin seemed to view with complete equanimity, and even satisfaction, the prospect of a Europe continuing to flounder in economic disorder and hopelessness. He saw no reason for any urgency in the solution of the problems put to him by the Western foreign ministers. In fact, he very clearly left General Marshall with the impression that he welcomed rather than deplored the prospect of a steady deterioration in the European situation. It was clear that he looked on an enfeebled Europe as nothing but an asset to Soviet ambitions.

Stalin's cynical attitude toward the problem of European recovery made a deep imprint upon the mind of General Marshall. I have always believed that this meeting in the Kremlin convinced General Marshall that some program would have to be devised with the utmost urgency if Europe were to recover and not to drop like a ripe plum into Soviet hands.

Time does not permit me to outline in any detail the various steps which led to the congressional adoption of the Marshall plan in 1948. The speech of General Marshall at Harvard University on June 5, 1947, while very short, nevertheless set forth most succinctly and clearly the concept of this great venture in foreign assistance.

It is this philosophy of self-help and mutual assistance expressed in this speech which has remained at the heart of all our foreign aid programs, whether administered bilaterally or under U.N. aegis. . . .

Before proceeding to a description of our current aid policies and programs, I should like to say a few words concerning the Soviet entry into this field. Up to 1954 the Soviet Union had no programs of assistance to any parts of the non-Soviet world. Her efforts in this direction were directed solely toward her economic relations with the satellites in Eastern Europe and subsequent to 1949 to Communist China. In 1954, however, the Soviet Union entered the field of economic assistance to countries outside of her immediate area of control and influence. If, as the popular saying goes, imitation is the sincerest form of flattery, surely there is no better tribute to the efficacy and value of the assistance programs of the United States than the fact that the Soviet Union, once it was economically able to do so, has emulated our policies in this field. Their effort has not been inconsiderable and shows every prospect of growing. In the period from 1954 to 1959 the Soviets committed themselves to a total amount of assistance, both economic and military, of some $3.2 billions, of which $2,450 million were in economic assistance alone. . . .

Assistance programs of one form or another and in varying degrees of magnitude have now become an organic part of our international relations. What has been the effect of this major new development on the conduct of our foreign policy? One of the first results has been to involve Congress more directly and intimately in the operation of our foreign affairs. At the time I entered the Foreign Service some 31 years ago, as I have already pointed out, the cost to the U.S. Government of its relations abroad was minute. Congressional interest, therefore, was confined merely to the budget of the State Department and, as far as the Senate in particular was concerned, to the treaties concluded by the executive branch. As a matter of fact it was extremely difficult in those days to generate any interest in Congress, particularly in the House of Representatives, in our foreign relations.

This has radically changed. Now Congress is called upon annually to appropriate vast sums of money for the implementation of the assistance part of our foreign policy. Its Members quite properly have an acute and profound interest in the purposes for which these moneys are to be appropriated and the manner in which they are to be spent for their achievement. No program therefore of foreign assistance can have any hope of coming into being unless it can engage the support of the Congress as representatives of the people. As a result, during the period when these programs are being presented to Congress, hardly a day goes by in Washington that a senior official of either the Defense or State Department does not appear to testify before one of these committees. The very fact of increased congressional responsibility and involvement in the conduct of our foreign affairs has greatly increased congressional interest in the entire subject and has radically affected the relationships between the executive and legislative branches in the entire field of our foreign affairs. . . .

To bring this question now more up to date, I would like to mention briefly how we envisage the application of U.S. aid at the present time. The Mutual Security Act for fiscal 1961 asks for a total of $4.175 billion divided into $2 billion military assistance and the balance for economic aid. Under the heading of economic aid is included $724 million in defense support, $268 million in special assistance, $206 million in technical assistance, and $700 million for the Development Loan Fund. In addition the United States continues to be the chief contributor and supporter of assistance through the international bodies such as the World Bank, the International Monetary Fund, and, of particular interest to this audience, the U.N.

Initially the U.S. Government decided that the bulk of its aid, military and economic, would be handled on a bilateral basis. But we have never at any time neglected our obligations or support of the U.N. or any of its specialized agencies. Since its founding in 1945 the United States has contributed to the U.N., its specialized agencies, and voluntary programs $2.6 billion, of which $280 million has gone to the organization in which you are particularly interested, UNICEF [United Nations Children's Fund]. We have also contributed $225 million to the Expanded Technical Assistance Program, $106 million to the World Health Organization, and $376 million to the United Nations Relief and Works Agency for Palestine Refugees in the Near East.

During the period when the United States was not only the major contributor to foreign aid in the free world but virtually the sole source of such assistance, it was understandable that the Congress and the Government of the United States would find it necessary to exercise a degree of purely American control and supervision over the aid thus rendered. This was devised not for the purpose of promoting a specific American business or other interest but rather for the purpose of assuring that the money contributed by the American taxpayer would be expended for the purposes indicated and would not be frittered away or diverted to other ends. . . .

I am well aware of the criticisms which from time to time have been directed against these foreign aid programs. I should like to say here that I feel the popular term "foreign aid" is unfortunate in that it carries with it the connotation that only the foreign recipient benefits. This is not true. While the benefits to the United States, certainly in those portions of the program which would involve grant aid, cannot be calculated in dollars and cents, nevertheless their value in intangibles of security and well-being far transcend the cost to us all. Had the United States recoiled from the challenge and responsibility that its position in the world has placed upon us and at the end of the war had refrained from this aspect of our foreign policy, we would be confronting unimaginable dangers and increased cost to our taxpayers for our national defense and our economic well-being. These added costs would many times transcend the cost of the programs themselves. Even in terms of the actual outlay, they do not represent an unduly severe burden on the American economy. The present Mutual Security Act, plus the contributions to the U.N. and its specialized agencies, accounts for hardly 5 percent of the total Federal budget and, with a gross national product estimated to reach $500 billion in 1960, less than 1 percent of our national income.

I might also add that, contrary to popular belief, the economic advancement of less developed countries will in the long run be a benefit to the type of economy such as ours. In its initial stages substantial expenditures on our part may be involved, but in the end, if these programs are successful and if some of the countries assisted reach a self-sustaining posture, they will be much more flexible partners for trade with the United States, both as sources of supply for basic raw materials and as markets for U.S. goods. This consideration nonetheless remains secondary compared to the harmful effect on world stability and security which failure to assist them would produce.

I would, therefore, like to terminate this very brief account of some aspects of our foreign assistance programs by stating to you that a country placed by history in a position of responsibility cannot fail to meet its destiny without dire consequences to itself. We are entering a period of sustained struggle to determine what kind of world the second half of the 20th century will see. To sacrifice now for the sake of the future is surely one of the hallmarks of a country's greatness. . . .

29.5. SUMMARY OF FOREIGN AID

To review the nation's program of foreign aid and to make recommenda-
tions for its improvement, President Kennedy appointed a special Advisory
Committee under General Lucius D. Clay. Anticipating the Committee's
report in March 1963, The New York Times *published the following brief*
summary of the foreign aid record from July 1, 1945, through mid-1962.

THE TOTAL of United States foreign aid since World War II will pass
$100,000,000,000 this year. . . .

Figures provided by the Agency for International Development,
which administers United States aid, list $97,700,000,000 worth of mili-
tary and economic help to 111 countries and foreign groups from July 1,
1945, through mid-1962. . . .

Ranking first in total receipts of United States aid since the war
is France, with $9,400,000,000. Britain is second with $8,700,000,000.

The Western allies got the bulk of their financial help from the
United States in the early postwar years when the Marshall Plan focused
on European recovery. This plan was named for the late General of the
Army George C. Marshall, then President Truman's Secretary of State.

Today, the aid pattern is different. With Europeans now prosper-
ing and some of them dispensing aid themselves, United States assistance
is now focused on underdeveloped countries and poorer lands being
pressed by the Communists.

Thus, far more assistance has gone to nations like India, Korea,
South Vietnam and Turkey since the end of the Marshall Plan in 1952
than to West European countries.

In 1962, India was the biggest recipient of United States aid,
with $838,000,000. This brought her over-all total to nearly $4,000,000,-
000. Pakistan was next highest in 1962 with $439,000,000, for a total of
$1,900,000,000. Turkey got $356,000,000, for a $3,900,000,000 total and
Korea $345,000,000 for a total of $5,400,000,000.

France, with $51,000,000, and Britain, with $25,000,000, are
still listed as aid receivers in 1962—but this was all in arms and assistance
connected with the North Atlantic defense effort.

United States aid has undergone other changes, too. In the
Marshall Plan years of 1949–52 all but $3,000,000,000 of the $19,000,-
000,000 in United States overeas economic help went out as grants, or
gifts. By 1962 the emphasis had changed to easy term loans aimed at
stimulating economic development.

Of the $5,200,000,000 in economic aid dispensed in 1962, a total of $2,900,000,000 was in loans and $2,300,000,000 in grants. The $1,500,000,00 in arms aid, however, was almost entirely in grants, as before.

Of the $97,700,000,000 cumulative total, $66,600,000,000 has been in economic aid, and of this $42,700,000,000 was in grants. Military assistance totaled $31,000,000,000, all except $279,000,000 in grants.

The United States aid program also has used a wider variety of measures in recent years, ranging from food-for-peace disposals of farm surpluses to the Peace Corps.

The biggest of the new programs is food-for-peace. Accounting for only a negligible portion of the aid total during the Marshall Plan years, the food-for-peace outlay in 1962 was listed at $1,600,000,000. The 1962 spending for the Peace Corps, a Kennedy Administration innovation, was reported at $29,600,000.

29.6. FOREIGN AID IN THE FUTURE

One of the most dramatic and effective aspects of American foreign policy has been the economic and military assistance we have extended to other countries. Beginning with the Marshall Plan in postwar Europe, the so-called Truman Doctrine in Greece and Turkey, the Point Four program of aid to underdeveloped countries, American foreign aid has continued to be a major force in the economic development and security of the Free World. In the following excerpt from his address to Congress, April 2, 1963, President Kennedy reviews this program and outlines its future course.

THE UNITED STATES today is spending over 10 percent of its gross national product on programs primarily aimed at improving our national security. Somewhat less than 1/20th of this amount, and less than .07 percent of our GNP [gross national product] goes into the mutual assistance program: roughly half for economic development, and half for military and other short-term assistance. The contribution of this program to our national interest clearly outweighs its cost. The richest nation in the world would surely be justified in spending less than 1 percent of its national income on assistance to its less fortunate sister nations solely as a matter of international responsibility; but inasmuch as these programs are not merely the right things to do, but clearly in our national self-

From President John F. Kennedy, Message to Congress on the Foreign Aid Program (*The New York Times*, April 2, 1963).

interest, all criticisms should be placed in that perspective. That our aid programs can be improved is not a matter of debate. But that our aid programs serve both our national traditions and our national interest is beyond all reasonable doubt.

History records that our aid programs to Turkey and Greece were the crucial element that enabled Turkey to stand up against heavy-handed Soviet pressures, Greece to put down Communist aggression and both to re-create stable societies and to move forward in the direction of economic and social growth.

History records that the Marshall Plan made it possible for the nations of Western Europe, including the United Kingdom, to recover from the devastation of the world's most destructive war, to rebuild military strength, to withstand the expansionist thrust of Stalinist Russia, and to embark on an economic renaissance which has made Western Europe the second greatest and richest industrial complex in the world today—a vital center of free world strength, itself now contributing to the growth and strength of less developed countries.

History records that our military and economic assistance to nations on the frontiers of the Communist world—such as Iran, Pakistan, India, Vietnam and Free China—has enabled threatened peoples to stay free and independent, when they otherwise would have either been overrun by aggressive Communist power or fallen victim of utter chaos, poverty and despair.

History records that our contributions to international aid have been the critical factor in the growth of a whole family of international financial institutions and agencies, playing an even more important role in the ceaseless war against want and the struggle for growth and freedom.

And, finally, history will record that today our technical assistance and development loans are giving hope where hope was lacking, sparking action where life was static, and stimulating progress around the earth—simultaneously supporting the military security of the free world, helping to erect barriers against the growth of communism where those barriers count the most, helping to build the kind of world community of independent, self-supporting nations in which we want to live, and helping to serve the deep American urge to extend a generous hand to those working toward a better life for themselves and their children.

Despite noisy opposition from the very first days—despite dire predictions that foreign aid would "bankrupt" the republic—despite warnings that the Marshall Plan and successor programs were "throwing our money down a rat-hole"—despite great practical difficulties and some mistakes and disappointments—the fact is that our aid programs generally and consistently have done what they were expected to do.

. . . . . .

The question now is: What about the future? In the perspective of these past gains, what is the dimension of present needs, what are our opportunities, and what chances do we face at this juncture in world history? . . .

. . . . . .

In a changing world, our programs of mutual defense and assistance must be kept under constant review. My recommendations herein reflect the work of the Clay committee, the scrutiny undertaken by the new administrator of the Agency for International Development, and the experience gained in our first full year of administering the new and improved program enacted by the Congress in 1961. There is fundamental agreement throughout these reviews: that these assistance programs are of great value to our deepest national interest. . . .

In addition, there is fundamental agreement in all these reviews regarding six key recommendations for the future.

Objective No. 1: To apply stricter standards to selectivity and self-help in aiding developing countries. . . . The proportion of development loans, as contrasted with outright grants, has increased from 10 percent to 60 percent. We have placed all our development lending on a dollar repayable basis; and this year we are increasing our efforts, as the Clay committee recommended, to tailor our loan terms so that interest rates and maturities will reflect to a greater extent the differences in the ability of different countries to service debt.

. . . . . .

Objective No. 2: To achieve a reduction and ultimate elimination of U.S. assistance by enabling nations to stand on their own as rapidly as possible. . . .

The record clearly shows that foreign aid is not an endless or unchanging process. Fifteen years ago our assistance went almost entirely to the advanced countries of Europe and Japan—today it is directed almost entirely to the developing world. Ten years ago most of our assistance was given to shoring up military forces and unstable economies—today this kind of aid has been cut in half, and our assistance goes increasingly toward economic development. . . .

Objective No. 3: To secure the increased participation of other industrialized nations in sharing the cost of international development assistance. The United States is no longer alone in aiding the developing countries, and its proportionate share of the burden is diminishing. The flow of funds from other industrialized countries—now totaling on the order of $2,000,000,000 a year—is expected to continue; and we expect to work more closely with these other countries in order to make the most effective use of our joint efforts. . . .

Objective No. 4: To lighten any adverse impact of the aid

program on our own balance of payments and economy. A few years ago, more than half of U.S. economic aid funds were spent abroad, contributing to the drain on our dollars and gold. Of our current commitments, over 80 percent will be spent in the United States, contributing to the growth of our economy and employment opportunities. . . .

Our economy is also being helped by the expansion of commercial exports to countries whose present growth and prosperity were spurred by U.S. economic assistance in earlier years.

. . . . . .

The relative burden of our assistance programs has been steadily reduced—from some 2 percent of our national product at the beginning of the Marshall Plan to seven-tenths of 1 percent today—from 11.5 percent of the Federal budget in 1949 to 4 percent today.

. . . . . .

Objective No. 5: To continue to assist in the defense of countries under threat of external and internal Communist attack. Our military assistance program has been an essential element in keeping the boundary of Soviet and Chinese military power relatively stable for over a decade. . . . "Dollar for dollar," said the Clay committee with particular reference to the border areas, "these programs contribute more to the security of the free world than corresponding expenditures in our defense appropriations . . . these countries are providing more than two million armed men ready, for the most part, for any emergency." Clearly, if this program did not exist, our defense budget would undoubtedly have to be increased substantially to provide an equivalent contribution to the free world's defense.

Objective No. 6: To increase the role of private investment and other non-Federal resources in assisting developing nations. . . .

The primary new initiative in this year's program relates to our increased efforts to encourage the investment of private capital in the under-developed countries. . . .

I believe much more should be done, however, both administratively through more vigorous action by the Agency for International Development, and legislatively by the Congress. . . .

Legislatively, I am recommending the following:

(a) An amendment to the Internal Revenue Code for a trial period to grant U.S. taxpayers a tax credit for new investments in developing countries, which should also apply to some extent to reinvestments of their earnings in those countries.

. . . . . .

(b) Amendments in the investment guaranty provisions of the foreign assistance act designed to enlarge and clarify the guaranty program.

Economic and social growth cannot be accomplished by governments alone. The effective participation of an enlightened United States businessman, especially in partnership with private interests in the developing country, brings not only his investment but his technological and management skills into the process of development. His successful participation in turn helps create that climate of confidence which is so critical in attracting and holding vital external and internal capital. . . .

In a special sense, the achievements of the Alliance for Progress in the coming years will be the measure of our determination, our ideals, and our wisdom. Here in this hemisphere, in this last year, our resourcefulness as a people was challenged in the clearest terms. We moved at once to resist the threat of aggressive nuclear weapons in Cuba, and we found the nations of Latin America at our side. They, like ourselves, were brought to a new awareness of the danger of permitting the poverty and despair of a whole people to continue long anywhere in this continent.

Had the needs of the people of Cuba been met in the pre-Castro period—their need for food, for housing, for education, for jobs, above all, for a democratic responsibility in the fulfillment of their own hopes—there would have been no Castro, no missiles in Cuba, and no need for Cuba's neighbors to incur the immense risks of resistance to threatened aggression from that island.

There is but one way to avoid being faced with similar dilemmas in the future. It is to bring about in all the countries of Latin America the conditions of hope, in which the peoples of this continent will know that they can shape a better future for themselves, not through obeying the inhuman commands of an alien and cynical ideology, but through personal self-expression, individual judgment, and the acts of responsible citizenship.

. . . . . .

At this point in history we can look back to many successes in the struggle to preserve freedom. Our nation is still daily winning unseen victories in the fight against Communist subversion in the slums and hamlets, in the hospitals and schools, and in the offices of Governments across a world bent on lifting itself. Two centuries of pioneering and growth must be telescoped into decades and even years. This is a field of action for which our history has prepared us, to which our aspirations have drawn us, and into which our national interests move us.

Around the world cracks in the monolithic apparatus of our adversary are there for all to see. This, for the American people, is a time for vision, for patience, for work and for wisdom. For better or worse, we are the pace-setters. Freedom's leader cannot flag or falter, or another runner will set the pace.

We have dared to label the sixties the decade of development. But it is not the eloquence of our slogans, but the quality of our endurance, which will determine whether this generation of Americans deserves the leadership which history has thrust upon us.

30

International Organization, Peace, and Disarmament

30.1. THE IMPORTANCE OF BEING SOVEREIGN

More than 165 years after Washington's Farewell Address, there is still no certain consensus on the degree to which we should or must become involved in world affairs. In the opinion of Representative Clare E. Hoffman of Michigan, participation by the United States in the work of the United Nations imposes dangerous limits on our national sovereignty. The following excerpts are from three of Representative Hoffman's speeches.

. . . TODAY, there was handed to me a statement showing that we had contributed to Latin nations somewhere between $800 and $900 million since 1946.

How much we have spent in attempting to carry out foreign policy no one is able to accurately state. We do know that our expenditures and obligations are running close to $100 billion.

Let me repeat—what are our advantages? What have we won? We are told that we have avoided war. True, we have not as yet engaged in a shooting war. Whether war would have come had we not followed this policy is problematical. The answer is not certain. . . .

Instead of being free from fear, instead of being secure both as a nation and as individuals, instead of being free to govern ourselves, we find that we are so far committed to cooperation with other nations that those in authority in Cuba, just off our shores, are able to defy us.

From Representative Clare E. Hoffman, "Speech to the House of Representatives," *The Congressional Record*, Vol. 106, pp. 17490–17492, August 24, 1960).

We find we can take no action to protect either our citizens or their property in that island until we have secured the consent of other members of the agreement into which we have entered, it is said, for national defense and security.

And what do the papers of today tell us? Is there peace throughout the world? Almost everywhere there is trouble, one nation at the throat of another. Nation after nation, no matter how small, threatening to involve us in another world war which the advocates of this measure seem to think can only be avoided by the creation of another advisory body and the expenditure of additional funds. F.D.R. told us we had nothing to fear but fear itself. Fear is with us all the time, forcing us each day into unsound action.

Just a few days ago a native of the Congo, reportedly without funds to even pay for his own transportation to this country, defied the United Nations and told it to get out of that country.

True, a few days later, realizing his impudence, his total lack of power, he withdrew his threat. But there is still with us the prospect of another world war. In an early August issue of *Life* my attention was drawn to a picture of a young American fleeing pursuit by natives of the Congo who carried spears. What was he doing in the Congo? He was an officer—a pilot—in charge of a helicopter, likewise shown in the picture, sent in by the United States to rescue a missionary. . . .

The incident shows that we cannot with safety delegate to other nations the solution of the problems which affect us, which are brought upon us by our vain attempt to, by law, confer liberty and independence upon people who do not know their meaning, or endow others with the benefits of the civilization which we now enjoy and have earned through years of hardship and effort.

The chosen representative of the Congo who has so recently assumed to tell the United Nations what it should or should not do; the ruler of Cuba, just outside our door, who defies us when we attempt to protect our citizens, as well as others, are emboldened, encouraged in their unjustifiable assumptions by the fact that we can no longer exercise our own authority for our own protection and the protection of our people without the consent of other nations. We have lost our independence.

We seem to have forgotten that a Teddy Roosevelt ever existed. We seem to have surrendered everything we won at the Boston Tea Party, by the War of Independence. And there seems to be nothing that a minority of us can do to prevent the repeated creation of a new commission a new agency, a new department, a new appropriation running into billions of dollars.

As long ago as January 27, and again on January 30, 1942, it was my privilege to call to the attention of the Members of Congress what

I considered to be the unsoundness of the move then on foot to create a one-world organization, the United Nations, to which we now turn as does an alcoholic to his bottle. . . .

(January 27, 1942): Mr. Chairman, on the assumption that, following the Declaration of Independence, guided by the principles enunciated in the Constitution, our people have established here a nation where the average man enjoys a greater degree of material prosperity, intellectual advancement, and religious freedom than in any other part of the world, the people of these United States of America are fighting a war, so it is said, to carry those blessings to all other people.

That war, the cost of which no man can estimate and which, if carried on according to present plans, will take the lives of millions of American men, the President and his supporters tell us, is being fought to bring to other peoples the same right of independence and self-government which we have enjoyed.

The hypocrisy of those who claim that to be the purpose of our present involvement in this war is clearly demonstrated when we receive from them a petition to repudiate our own independence, surrender our existence as an independent nation, and become a part of a United States of the World.

It is quite true that, under our Constitution, men have the right of a free press and free speech; that, under the provisions of that Constituition and the security granted by it, they may advocate its repudiation. Therefore, the man Streit and all those who join with him in asking us to surrender our independence and become a part of a world nation are within their legal rights.

However, Hitler, Mussolini, Hirohito are, it is said, also seeking to destroy our independence and make us a part of a world group. Streit and his associates seek to accomplish the same end—the destruction of our independence—by a more subtle and a peaceful method, and they say for a different purpose. . . .

It is said that we are the richest nation in the world. It is undenied that the average citizen of these United States of America enjoys more of everything that goes to make man contented and happy than the people of any other land or nation. And yet these men, like Judas, who betrayed his Master, would, before we are fairly in this war, betray our people; surrender our independence; connive to destroy our liberty and our freedom. They would surrender that for which the war is being fought—our national existence—before the war is fairly begun.

Let them be stripped of their hypocrisy. Let us expose them for what they are—enemies of the Republic, boring from within. They seek to take advantage of our involvement in this war and while the attention of the people is directed to the winning of the war. They would do what the armies of the Confederacy could not accomplish—destroy us as a nation, one and indivisible; make us a part of the United States of the World, where the communistic Russian, who denies the existence of God, where the Chinese, the Hottentot, and the people of India would have equal voice in curtailing the liberties, spending the tax money, of American workers, farmers and businessmen—a United States of the World where all the peoples of the world would be glorified participants in a WPA, a PWA, a Federal housing program, the triple A—a program to rebuild after the war all the cities, towns, and villages which may be destroyed in that war—and all at the expense of the American taxpayer. . . .

If the administration wants to win this war, let it put aside the ambition of the President's advisers to make him or one of themselves a president of the world. Let this administration get rid of the more than a thousand Communists on the Federal payroll—bloodsuckers seeking to destroy our national existence. . . .

(January 30, 1942): Mr. Speaker, inasmuch as it is the President's birthday, it may not be out of place to call attention to the fact that a birthday gift has been requested of Congress for the Chief Executive.

The 4th day of July 1776 was the day when our Declaration of Independence was adopted. Here is an organization which undoubtedly has expended considerable sums, which now proposes to celebrate the President's birthday by having Congress adopt a resolution doing away with the Declaration of Independence. I do not know; I have not been able to learn, whether any Member of the House has introduced such a resolution. . . .

This movement to surrender our independence and become a part of a world supergovernment has the support of Cabinet Member Ickes, Justice Roberts of the Supreme Court, Federal Union, Inc., Red Christian Fronters, and Communists. . . .

Using the false plea that we can win the war and after it is over establish permanent peace throughout the world—a desirable objective—Federal Union, Inc., headed by Clarence K. Streit, by the expenditure of thousands of dollars, is carrying on a campaign of propaganda, the purpose of which is, while our attention is distracted by the war, to cause us to surrender our independence and our national existence and become the economic slaves of other world powers.

That organization would inveigle our citizens into a united states of the world where their property, their incomes, would be at the mercy of Old World politicians.

. . . . . .

Federal Union, Inc., and World Fellowship, Inc., which has a similar objective, would make the American taxpayer the Santa Claus of the world; the peoples of Europe, Asia, and Africa glorified members of a would WPA. We Americans—workers, farmers, merchants, industrialists, professional men and women, all of us—would furnish the money for the boondoggling and the warring of princes, dukes, kings, and dictators.

We would, in addition, furnish the cannon fodder for the war games which they might play when they grew tired of boondoggling.

Is the foregoing but a creature of the imagination? In full-page ads in newspapers of the East the campaign to do the things just mentioned is being carried on.

Yesterday, January 29, to me, as a Congressman, and no doubt to every other Congressman and to every Senator, from World Fellowship, Inc., came propaganda asking that, as a Member of the House of Representatives, I support a joint resolution which this organization asks be passed on the President's birthday, January 30, 1942, as, I quote, "a present to him, to us, to the world." The word "him" is capitalized. A proposal for a birthday gift which the President should lose no time in condemning.

That resolution proposes, as step 1, among other things:

That the Congress of the United States of America does hereby solemnly declare that all peoples of the earth should now be united in a commonwealth of nations to be known as the United Nations of the World, and to that end it hereby gives to the President of the United States of America all the needed authority and powers of every kind and description without limitations of any kind that are necessary in his sole and absolute discretion to set up and create the Federation of the World, a world peace government under the title of the United Nations of the World, including its constitution and personnel and all other matters needed or appertaining thereto to the end that all nations of the world may by voluntary action become a part thereof under the same terms and conditions.

If you are an American citizen, willing to make the needed sacrifices to win this war, if you believe in the independence of our Nation, what do you think of this proposed grant of authority to the President of the United States to set up a United Nations of the World? Why should Congress grant to the President of the United States power to create a new world government, United Nations of the World, of which we would be a part? . . .

30.2. THE UNITED STATES AND THE UNITED NATIONS

In Ambassador Stevenson's analysis, the United Nations is the principal instrument capable of achieving order in the world. The United Nations must cope with the political pressures wielded by East and West, colonial and noncolonial, while attempting to achieve a strong, legal basis for lasting peace. It is in our best interest, he states, to support the institution that enshrines "the great dialog of humanity."

. . . THERE ARE CRITICS who are beginning strongly to question whether the United Nations, constituted as it is and behaving as it now does, can really fulfill its peacemaking function. There are, I believe, two main lines of attack, and both converge on the same point—the fact that again and again any solution of crises through the machinery of the United Nations depends upon a two-thirds vote in a world assembly now made up of 99 members and likely to pass the hundred mark at any moment. These nations represent an unbelievable variety of history, interests, experience, and maturity. Their ability to agree on any course of action is inherently limited by the immense differences in their angles of vision. Regional differences, historical differences, barriers of race and culture cross and recross the more prosaic frontiers of self-interest and national concern.

For this reason it is exceedingly difficult to secure a consensus on most issues, and the severer critics argue that to submit to such procedures not only produces incoherence in the United Nations; it exports the incoherence to the scene of operations and makes the confusion worse than might otherwise have been the case.

Nor is incoherence the gravest charge. In the last year or so it has become increasingly obvious, say the critics, that a profoundly anti-Western bias has crept into the United Nations debates. The majority of the new nations have emerged to independence out of one form or other of Western colonial control. Many of them have an instinctive bias against their ex-masters. All of them respond compulsively to anything that suggests a Western relapse into colonialism. For historical reasons they do not react with the same concern against aggressive acts by Russia or China. The Africans urge sanctions against South Africa, but no one suggests they should be applied to Russia over its East European tyranny. Even so respected a world statesman as Mr. Nehru was slow to condemn Russian oppression in Hungary. But he was quick to denounce America's backing for the anti-Castro landings in Cuba.

How then can the Western Powers use and respect an institution whose inherent bias seems to be against them and whose members appear to apply two quite different standards of judgment—one of excuse or indifference toward ill doings of the Communist great powers, one of loud condemnation and hostility toward the West? This surely, so the argument

---

From Adlai E. Stevenson, "The United Nations, First Step Toward a World under Law," in the *Department of State Bulletin,* July 10, 1961, pp. 69–71.

runs, cannot lead to peace. The United Nations is becoming a forum for a further steady undermining of the Western World, a further whittling away of any effective balance of world power.

What are we to say to these criticisms? I believe that the charge of incoherence is not borne out by the record. The United Nations has continued to evolve and maintain a policy for minimal security in the Middle East—even after the debacle at Suez. It did act in the Korean crisis. Its mediators, its control commissions, its on-the-spot investigations have held before the eyes of the world the fundamental obligation not to settle issues by force. Even the interventions which have been most resented—the bringing of Algeria before the United Nations or the discussion of the responsibilities of the colonial powers to hasten independence —may have somewhat strengthened the forces making for negotiation and away from violence.

Similarly the accusation of bias is not so straightforward as it appears. The United Nations is not responsible for the fact that most of the new nations are ex-colonial. Their anti-imperialist inclinations are simply a fact of contemporary life. The United Nations is not responsible for the fact that Russia does not seem to most peoples in Asia, Africa, or Latin America to be imperialist. This view simply reflects that fact that in Africa and Latin America Russia was not the colonial master. In Asia the spread of Russian power has been on a slow continental scale—like the spread of American power to the Pacific—and the local peoples, unlike the Bantu of South Africa or the fellahs of Algeria, have been brought very fully into the educational and economic expansion of the Soviet Union.

It may be illogical to exclude Khazaks and Uzbeks and Armenians from the ranks of people deserving self-determination, but the United Nations did not create the distinction. It is there in the minds of the current leaders of the new nations.

But if the bias is there, why submit disputes to the United Nations at all? It is here we have to ask the crucial question: What is the alternative? Do not forget the historical background of our day. Empires are collapsing. New power systems backed by a fanatic faith seek to take their place. Most of the disputes that come to the United Nations concern this crumbling background of pressure and counterpressure. The Congo crisis, which has brought so many of these criticisms to a head, is preeminently such a crisis. The Belgian withdrawal was followed by anarchy with which on the one hand the Belgians stepped back and on the other the Russians began to step in. In these circumstances any direct intervention by the West would have been interpreted as an attempt to reimpose colonialism. Local opinion would have swung over to support the Communists, and the West would have been left in the impossible position of fighting a guerrilla war against a background of implacable local hostility. . . .

The result is that in situations such as the Congo the Western World would be almost powerless if there were no United Nations force available to restore order, check a takeover by an outside power—Eastern or Western—and gradually build up the preconditions of genuine independence. Direct Western action would only hasten a Communist takeover. By putting the whole task of restoring order onto an international basis, favoring neither East nor West, there is at least a chance of avoiding first a Western defeat and secondly the risk of spiraling war. In short, while nations cannot intervene in the internal affairs of other nations, the United Nations can.

It is surely significant that it is since the United Nations frustrated the Communists' plans of rapid infiltration in the Congo that Mr. Khrushchev has been trying to extend his veto to the whole Organization and make sure that neither the Secretary-General nor any other organ of the United Nations shall be free to act or intervene. We by the same token must support and back with all our influence the only instrument by which the end of the Western system of colonialism can be prevented from opening the doors to the new imperialism of the East.

And this is not, I hasten to add, only a Western interest. It is above all the new nations themselves that need an impartial instrument with which to keep themselves out of the perils of great power rivalry. As President Nkrumah [of Ghana] has reminded Africa: "When the bull elephants fight, the grass is trampled down." The ability of the new nations to interpose the United Nations between their own quarrels and the great powers' struggles is their best hope of safeguarding the independence they have so urgently wanted and so recently received. Never before have emergent nations had such an instrument for their defense. Never before has the attempt been made to overcome the perils of post-imperial transition by purposive international action. All the rivalries, all the dangers, all the threats are as old as empire itself. Only the United Nations is new. It alone therefore offers the hope that this time the ending of empire will not lead to general war. . . .

. . . The United Nations remains and must remain the arena in which the great dialog of humanity is carried on. That dialog is too vital for us to depreciate the institution which enshrines it.

30.3. THE QUEST FOR PEACE

So complex has the issue of arms control become that the layman is increasingly tempted to be satisfied with a comforting word rather than an explanation. In this selection Professor Brennan endeavors to explain some of the most technical and perplexing aspects of armament policy.

IT IS DESIRABLE at the outset to review some fundamental facts. Most of us do not regard either war or the means of war as ends in themselves. We regard military force as means to other, nonmilitary goals. This simply means that there is a consensus among a large number of people that military action is not one of the ends of life.

What, then, are the goals that armament is intended to serve? The first answer to this question is seemingly easy: it is simply survival—national survival at the level of the nation, personal survival at the level of the individual. But it is possible to distinguish different kinds of survival—physical survival, political survival, of a standard of living. The significance of such distinctions is that different armament policies would support some kinds of survival without necessarily supporting others. For example, some people believe that a policy of complete unilateral disarmament and nonresistance would possibly support sheer physical survival. Even if true, this policy would surely be unlikely to support political survival, and still less likely to support the survival of our standard of living. (I am here speaking of the possibility of another nation making large demands on our economic output or other resources, and not about the problem of internal adjustments to disarmament.) On the other hand, modern weapons are so impressive that a strong "Fortress America" armament policy would probably support national survival in all three senses, but might fail to support other national goals and purposes. . . .

Several critics have maintained that we do not, in fact *have* an adequate sense of national purpose, and that this problem infects the formulation of foreign policy and, consequently, the formulation of politico-military strategies to support such policy. On the other hand, there are many who have more or less explicit ideas about the fundamental ends of what has been called "the affluent society." But it is not my present purpose to enter this debate *per se*. It is sufficient here to point out that there *is* a debate—which, perhaps, may be intrinsic to a pluralistic society. While we have a consensus that military action is not among the ends of life, and that survival *is* among the ends of life, we have no similarly complete consensus concerning the basic national purpose (beyond survival) of the United States.

At the bottom, therefore, armament policy is one of many

Donald G. Brennan, "Setting and Goals of Arms Control," reprinted from *Arms Control, Disarmament, and National Security,* ed. by Donald G. Brennan; © George Braziller, Inc., 1961, and © 1960, 1961, by the American Academy of Arts and Sciences in whose Journal, *Daedalus,* this article first appeared; book pp. 19–26, 29–30, 32, 33, 37–39, and Journal p. 704.

aspects of the general problem of achieving a world to our liking; but we seem to lack a clear collective sense of just what that world should or could be like in the long term. . . .

The most significant aspect of our foreign policy of the present and the recent past is perhaps best characterized as a holding operation. This is the main virtue of the doctrine of containment; whether or not we have good collective ideas of what we are ultimately holding *for,* we certainly have good ideas of what we are holding *against.* This agreement, while minimal, is important. The aggression in Korea is too fresh in our minds, and the possible loss of Western Europe to other Communist aggression seems too great a potential catastrophe to permit us to contemplate the philosophical basis of our foreign policy while the world around us burns. At least, to the extent that it does not directly conflict with national survival, and possibly to the extent of considerable risk that it may eventually do so, most of us feel obliged to support and defend the non-Communist world in general and our allies in particular. This obligation has heavily dominated our armament policy of the last decade.

The phrase "national security" is one that receives much use but little analysis. Various views of security are possible, and a brief indication of the range of possibilities is useful. . . .

The most basic view of national security commonly held is the protection of national survival, in all three senses discussed above. This is usually the minimal demand on "national security." Beyond this, the concept quite generally extends to the military and politico-military support of national goals in general and foreign-policy objectives in particular. Improvement of relative military capabilities to support such goals may be obtained at the expense, sooner or later, of impaired national security with respect to national survival. This can and does happen because of economic or political limitations on the armament that can be bought; because of the armament obtained in response by hostile power; because of a basically defective strategy or armament policy; or because of any combination of these factors. In spite of this conflict, the common consensus of national security is that it relates to the protection of national survival and the support of foreign-policy goals, in some mixture of the two. The character of the mixture and the extent of the interaction and conflict between the two objectives is at best dimly understood, and sometimes not perceived at all. . . .

The essence of a deterrent is a threat to carry out some punitive measure in the event that the action against which the threat is aimed does transpire. Deterrence is therefore a basically defensive phenomenon, and, as such, has always been present in military strategy to the extent that the strategy was defensively oriented. However, as the first three examples above illustrate, and as the fourth tends to suggest, deterrence can fail. The consequence of a failure of military deterrence is at least the increased likelihood of military action, and perhaps war itself, unless the deterrent threat involved proves to be an empty bluff. In the past, a failure of military deterrence has undoubtedly been painful for the participants involved, but not intolerably painful for Western society as a whole; in particular, it has not been catastrophic for the United States. The deterrent aspect of defensive military forces was formerly taken for granted.

But, today, the doctrine of deterrence has assumed paramount and explicit importance in contemporary strategic thinking. The consequence of a failure of strategic nuclear deterrence could be a general nuclear war and a resultant catastrophe for Western society of a magnitude unparalleled in the whole of human history. This possibility has focused attention on the problem of keeping a nuclear war from happening—that is, of deterring it. . . .

It is useful to analyze some of the strategic requirements a national security policy must meet in terms of the different kinds of deterrent functions that must be provided. Many different breakdowns are possible; a widely known classification introduced by Herman Kahn is as follows.

> *Type I:* Deterrence of direct nuclear attack on the United States.
> *Type II:* Deterrence of extreme provocations. These include major attacks on United States forces, on our NATO and SEATO allies, and on other important areas of the non-Communist world.
> *Type III:* Deterrence of moderate provocations. These range from the shelling of Quemoy and cutting submarine cables, through shutting off access to Berlin, up to aggressions on the scale of Korea. . . .

In a general context such as the present discussion, however, the specific breakdown given above can be improved by distinguishing between extreme *nuclear* provocations and extreme *nonnuclear* provocations. The lack of this distinction (a lack probably traceable to people who place primary reliance on "massive retaliation") can be rectified by a breakdown of deterrent functions such as the following.

> *Type A:* Deterrence of direct nuclear attack.
> *Type B:* Deterrence of extreme nuclear provocations.
> *Type C:* Deterrence of extreme nonnuclear provocations.
> *Type D:* Deterrence of moderate provocations.

The distinctions between these four are worth brief comment. It has occasionally been held that each of Types A, B, and C deterrence could be adequately implemented with a single type of threat capability, namely, the capability of delivering a major nuclear strike on the homeland of the aggressor. The use of this threat to implement Type C deterrence could be, and was, questioned trenchantly on moral grounds alone (among others), even in the days when we had an essential monopoly of nuclear weapons. To any reasonable person, the growth of Soviet nuclear capabilities has since placed this policy nearly or entirely beyond the realm of credibility, on several counts. To name only three: first, a Soviet retaliatory strike on the United States could be extremely painful —with perhaps 10 to 70 million people dead, with grave hazards to the health, to political survival, and to the standard of living of the survivors. Second, there is only slight likelihood that our strategic nuclear response to a failure of Type C deterrence would in fact secure the protection of the original object of the provocation. Third, and perhaps most important, there could be an alternative response that could be at once much less painful and much more successful: the use of conventional (HE) forces. We could, if necessary, mobilize and equip a 15-million-man army that would probably be able to defeat the aggressive conventional forces of any nation in the world, not excepting China, which could mobilize the men, but could not adequately equip, train, or transport them. An army of this size need not be in existence on the first day of the provocation, and probably would never need to be that large.

For such reasons, there should no longer be any serious intention of responding to a failure of Type C deterrence with a major nuclear strike. For example, Secretary of State Christian Herter said in the United States Senate on the occasion of the hearing on his nomination: "I *cannot conceive* of any President involving us in an all-out nuclear war unless the facts showed clearly we are in danger of all-out devastation ourselves." . . . Apart from a few people who would probably be quick to change their minds about the issue in a crisis, the policy of responding to a conventional-force attack with a strategic nuclear strike seems to be an essentially dead issue. . . .

As the foregoing survey might suggest, that part of our national security that is measured by our ability to guarantee national survival in all its various senses has undergone a precipitous decline in recent years. At the close of World War II, no nation had the capability of inflicting any damage worthy of the name on the United States. At the present time, the Soviet Union could mount an attack that would kill tens of millions of citizens and leave the standard of living of the survivors very seriously depressed. Every projection based on this trend points to an increasingly serious capability; by the late 1960s, the USSR might be able to launch a strike that would extinguish 90 percent of our populace.

This is sometimes taken to mean that the national security of the Soviet Union, relative to ours, has been improving. Perhaps it has, perhaps not; it depends on what is understood by the term and on when the comparisons are made. In the mid-1950s, for example, we had a very nearly one-sided capability to obliterate the Soviet Union, so that their relative position has improved since then—*they* can now threaten "massive retaliation" to deter provocations. On the other hand, our capability of this type was all but negligible in 1946, so that their relative security has not improved from 1946 to 1960.

But talk of relative security is somewhat beside the point, in any event. The central fact is that the absolute national security (measured in the same sense of their ability to guarantee national survival) of the Soviet Union has also undergone a precipitous decline since 1946. The Soviets cannot be sure that our forces will never be used, whether because of accident, misunderstanding, or our response to a crisis. Neither can we be sure that the Soviet capability will never be used. It is possible to feel moderately relaxed about these facts at the present time, but anyone who feels completely relaxed about them either does not understand the situation or is not acting in a manner that is rational with respect to the goals of society.

For it would seem that each side is likely to be able to inflict more damage on the other in a general war than either would find at all justified by the original objectives of the conflict, whichever side suffered the greater absolute damage. And the possibility of a general war occurring is a real one. The chance of a general war within the next year is not zero, and, assuming the present course of events continues, the likelihood of a general war within the next ten or fifteen years appears very disturbing. Again, assuming the present course of events continues, the possibility of a general war involving China as a participant in the era of 1975 and beyond must appear a very disturbing one indeed—both to the Soviet Union and to the United States. . . .

. . . Seven years after the Hiroshima and Nagasaki bombs, the first thermonuclear device was tested. The Soviets tested their first the following year. Today there exist thermonuclear weapons with an energy yield approximately one thousand times as great as the Nagasaki bomb, a yield measured in millions of tons, or "megatons," of equivalent TNT. It is often said that a single high-yield thermonuclear weapon can release more energy than all the high explosive used in the whole of World War II—perhaps more than was used in all past wars altogether. Most people have not yet really assimilated this development. . . .

There is another side to this problem. Nuclear weapons very much smaller than the Nagasaki bomb are possible. For example, weapons having a yield as low as 55 tons (0.055 kilotons) have been tested. Weapons having a yield of 10 tons or less could presumably be developed, and much of the motivation on the part of weapon scientists to continue the development of nuclear weapons stems from the possible development of weapons in this range. . . . And they probably would be militarily advantageous for the United States, *provided that they did not lead to the use of much larger weapons.* The difficulty, of course, is that as soon as one side achieved an advantage by the use of 10-ton weapons, the other side could promptly neutralize it (and possibly much more besides) by introducing 10-kiloton weapons.

[A] high-yield thermonuclear weapon can reduce a standard frame house to absolute rubble as far as 12 miles from the point of explosion, and leave one very seriously damaged as much as 20 miles away. This implies an area of blast destruction of several hundred square miles. The radioactive fallout from a single such weapon can kill unprotected people throughout an area of several thousand square miles.

The cumulative effects of a large attack involving many such weapons are much more difficult to estimate. As of 1959, a hypothetical attack on the United States analyzed for the Holifield hearings involved 263 bombs with a total yield of 1,446 megatons. It was estimated that this attack would produce 50 million deaths, 20 million serious casualties, would destroy or damage 50 percent of all homes, and leave the remainder radioactive from two weeks to a year. . . .

Broadly speaking, approaches to arms control are of two kinds. The first is to examine current and projected armament policies, to isolate their major unnecessary hazards, and to attempt to reduce or eliminate these, one at a time, leaving the basic armament policies largely unchanged. This is the realm of *limited* arms-control measures. The second approach is to attempt a survey of the basic requirements for armament to implement the various types of deterrence that must be provided for the participating nations, and to adjust all types of armament to fit these basic needs in such a way as to give maximum net security. This is the realm of *comprehensive* arms-control systems. In both cases, of course, the analysis must consider both unilateral and reciprocal points of view and must take into account the performance obtained under both calm and stressed conditions, the possible consequences of clandestine or overt evasion or other failures in cooperation, the possible failure of various types of deterrence, and the irritations introduced.

Comprehensive arms-control programs seem much more attractive on several counts than do limited measures. The goals of such programs may be better matched to basic needs, they seem generally safer, they may provide economic savings through substantial disarmament, and they may actually require less inspection than a small collection of independent limited measures. . . .

Comprehensive controls, however, have not proved to be at all easy to negotiate, and are not likely to be so in the future. Some of the reasons for this difficulty operate with little or no force in certain limited measures of arms control which may prove to be more negotiable. (This "may" is very weak; they well may not.)

Although the goals of such measures are limited in scope, they are not necessarily trivial. The major hazards stem, not from the armament *per se* in the possession of the major powers, but from the fact that it might be used. Several measures are aimed at inhibiting such use. For example, two of the hazards to our security are the "catalytic war" (i.e., the initiation of a major nuclear war by one of the smaller powers) and the "escalation" problems; the major goals of a nuclear weapon test ban are to eliminate the problem of catalytic war altogether (by preventing the spread of weapons to other nations) and to eliminate those escalation problems that might result from a limited nuclear war initiated by one or more of the smaller powers. Most of the various types of accidental war depend for their initiation on misinformation about what the other party is doing in a crisis; Schelling has proposed the use of special surveillance forces whose primary goal would be to minimize such misinformation. Many other potential limited measures may have considerable merit. . . .

It is possible, and sometimes useful, to view arms-control measures of practically any type as intended to provide warning. In some cases, this objective is explicit, as with measures designed to monitor strategic forces and provide immediate warning when an attack is launched. Many of the measures proposed by the Western delegation to the Surprise Attack Conference were of this type. However, even a very comprehensive arms-control program that provides a substantial reduction of military forces can be regarded as a measure to provide warning, but in this case the warning given would be a long-term strategic warning of hostile intentions. As long as such an agreement was functioning satisfactorily, it would provide some evidence that the participants did not intend to launch an overwhelming attack—they would not have the capability. Any observed failure of cooperation in the carrying out of the provisions of the agreement, such as the repudiation of the treaty, would then provide a warning of aggressive intentions. The amount of time this warning would provide might range from a few months to a few years, depending on the extent to which disarmament had gone and on the scale of the aggression contemplated by the violator. Intermediate types of measures would provide intermediate degrees of warning; for example, certain deployment restrictions, such as a disengagement of Soviet and United States forces in Europe, would provide a warning of from several hours to a few days. In general, the more severe the restrictions in force levels or deployment, the longer the warning time provided by the corresponding arms-control measures. . . . [I]n order that inspection should not appear entirely as "institutionalized distrust," it is desirable, when feasible, to have an inspectorate perform constructive functions of direct utility to the host nation. This would provide experience in the cooperative operation of constructive international services and might tend to reduce national hostilities. It would also provide the host country with a minor vested interest in the successful operation of the inspectorate beyond that provided by the successful implementation of the arms-control measure itself. Better personnel would be attracted to the inspectorate. It is possible to find examples in which the addition of relatively small increments of men and money to an inspectorate may provide relatively large gains in its constructive utility. Such examples include: (1) the use of a network for detecting bomb tests so as to provide a permanent continuation of the International Geophysical Year; (2) the use of radar monitoring systems for missile-control purposes in connection with the peaceful exploration of space; (3) the use of inspectors of nuclear production to do radiation monitoring as a public health measure; (4) the use of inspectors of industrial production to provide industrial census information and production statistics. I do not know whether all these examples are feasible, and they are obviously insubstantial, but they suggest an approach that should be useful.

30.4. THE ECONOMICS OF DISARMAMENT

One of the most difficult questions of our time is the relationship between the health of the economy and the level of military expenditures. Critics have suggested that the threat of war is sometimes invoked to bolster a flagging economy through armament production. Professor Boulding believes that our economy is strong enough to absorb and replace the loss of billions of dollars of defense production through increased consumer purchases, business investment, and government spending for civilian purposes.

. . . THE PROSPERITY of the 1940s and 1950s, by contrast with the misery of the 1930s, is associated, whether the association is justified or not, in the minds of many people with the high level of war and defense expenditures in the former periods, and with the low level in the latter. The memories of the Great Depression are still strong in the minds of the middle-aged and the powerful, and the fear of another such experience, though by now driven down into the unconscious, is an active determinant

Kenneth E. Boulding, "Economic Implications of Arms Control," reprinted from *Arms Control, Disarmament, and National Security,* ed. by Donald G. Brennan; © George Braziller, Inc., 1961, and © 1960, 1961, by the American Academy of Arts and Sciences in whose Journal, *Daedalus,* this article first appeared; book pp. 154–156, 158, 164.

of our value system. Nobody wants to suggest that the United States would deliberately sabotage an attempt at arms control because of this fear of depression; the frivolity and hypocrisy with which the subject of disarmament was treated in official circles in the pre-sputnik era was due almost entirely to an emotional and intellectual commitment to unilateral national defense, not to any fear of economic consequences.

There are, then, three major domestic economic problems which arms control may represent, summarized as *conversion, stabilization,* and *growth*. These are all general problems of the economy and are not peculiar to arms control. Conversion is the problem of how to adjust the structure of production in the economy—that is, the commodity mix of total output—to shifts in the structure of total demand, public and private. Stabilization is the problem of how to control the vicious dynamic processes of deflation, depression, and unemployment, on the one hand, or inflation on the other, which may be initiated by these shifts in the structure of total demand. Growth is the problem of achieving a structure of total demand which will give the society an optimum rate of economic growth; the latter might be defined as the maximum rate of growth which is subject to the constraints of its basic value system. . . .

To come closer to the immediate topic, the United States has suffered enormous fluctuations in the proportion of the gross national product allotted to national security (defense) in the past twenty years; at present, the latter is a little less than 10 percent of the gross national product, and the recent trend is illustrated in Table 1.

The rise in national security expenditures from the almost negligible levels of the 1930s to the heights of the mid-1940s (World War II) was, of course, accompanied by a sharp rise in GNP and a dramatic fall in the percentage of unemployment. Here we have the origin of the myth of defense-inspired prosperity. It is a myth which derives its power from the fact that it is not wholly untrue and is rooted in the personal experiences of millions of people. Nevertheless, it *is* basically only a half truth. The outstanding fact is the remarkable stability and success of the American economy under the impact of the massive armament and disarmament of the 1940s, when, for instance, in one year (1945-1946) we transferred an absolute amount of manpower and resources from war to civilian employments, more than twice as much as would be involved (in real terms) in total and complete disarmament at present. The post-Korean disarmament was less well managed: unemployment rose to a disquieting 5 percent in 1954, but subsided again in later years in the face of a continued fall in the real defense burden. . . .

I am not arguing, of course, that conversion is costless, painless, and creates no problems, and least of all am I arguing that there should be no national policy about it and no organization to deal with it. I would argue indeed that this is a perennial problem, that even though the Amer-

TABLE 1. United States Gross National Product (GNP) and National Security Expenditures (NSE) in real terms (billions of dollars) at 1959 prices, selected years

Year	GNP	NSE[a]	NSE/GNP (Percent)	Unemployment as Percent of Labor Force[b]
1939	211.5	3.2	1.5	17.2
1944	366.3	164.7	45.0	1.2
1945	359.4	139.8	39.1	1.9
1946	316.0	26.7	8.4	3.9
1947	315.7	15.3	4.8	3.6 (3.9)
1953	417.1	60.1	14.4	2.5 (2.9)
1954	408.8	49.5	12.2	5.0 (5.6)
1959	478.8	45.5	9.5	(5.5)

[a] NSE figures are net of government sales, hence may be a little too small. There has been a substantial revision of these figures in recent years.
[b] The figures in parentheses are according to the new definition.
SOURCE: *Economic Report of the President,* 1960.

ican economy is remarkably flexible and deals fairly well with this problem even in the absence of any governmental organization, there is a strong case for more positive social organization to deal with depressed areas and industries, whether these result from tariff changes, exhaustion of natural or human resources, shifts in technology or tastes, or changes in the defense industry. I argue also, however, that this is a manageable problem, and that it can be solved well within the limits of toleration which our value system imposes. . . .

Suppose then, we look at a model of an American economy in, say, 1959, in which the national security budget has been virtually eliminated. The total government budget is still about 10 percent of the GNP. This is a situation suprisingly similar to that of 1929, as is shown in the table on the next page.

It may come as a shock to many people to learn that apart from national defense, the proportion of real product actually absorbed by government in the late 1950s was almost exactly the same as in the late 1920s, in spite of a more than doubled real GNP. Creeping socialism

TABLE 2.   United States Nonmilitary Government Expenditure in Real Terms (in billions of 1959 dollars)

	Total		As Percent of GNP	
	1929	1959	1929	1959
Federal nonmilitary expenditure	3.4[a]	8.1	1.8[a]	1.7
State and local government expenditure	17.4	44.3	8.9	9.2
Total nonmilitary government expenditure	20.8	52.4	10.7	10.9
GNP	203.6	478.8		

[a] This figure is for total Federal expenditure, as military expenditure is not available separately. It would be of the order of 1.0 billion.
SOURCE: *Economic Report of the President*, 1960.

does not seem to have crept very far, outside the Pentagon, which is in terms of GNP the world's third largest nonmarket economy, with only Russia and possibly China exceeding it. There may even be something in Galbraith's thesis that the public economy needs to expand, arms control or no arms control. The question needs to be raised, therefore, as to whether a nonmilitary American economy in 1960 would be any safer from depression than in 1929 without the introduction of organizational machinery which we do not now possess. No definite answer could be given to this question without a good deal more study. There are many important differences between now and 1929. The national debt is larger. We have pay-as-you-go taxes, which are a great stabilizer (before this, income taxes were paid on the previous year's income and so went up as a percentage of income when incomes were falling). We have social security, and also agricultural price supports, which for all their vices are also built-in stabilizers. Nevertheless, it is a moot question whether these devices are quantitatively adequate to deal with a sharp deflation. We may not expect anything like 1929-1932, but something like 1937-1938 would not be beyond the bounds of possibility. . . .

The important thing is that there are many ways of stabilizing (within limits of tolerance) the gross national product. There is an important unsolved problem regarding the extent to which this can be done without long-run inflation, and how the answer to this question is related to noncompetitive labor, capital, and commodity markets, but this, in a sense, is a secondary problem. To put the matter in a rather crude form: if we take 40 billion dollars of defense production out of the gross national product, where can we find another 40 billion dollars' worth of goods and services which can be absorbed without causing deflation? The answer is partly in increased household purchases as a result of tax decreases, partly in increased investment by businesses, partly by increased government expenditure in civilian uses, and partly by an export surplus created by foreign investment or foreign aid. . . .

. . . The Pentagon and Hollywood seem to be the only two places in our society where extravagance is cultivated as a virtue. Therefore, when research is hitched to the military rocket, it proceeds at a pace far beyond that of the civilian and merely peripatetic philosopher. I am quite willing to deplore this fact, but I am forced to acknowledge it. Perhaps the biggest social invention of the mid-twentieth century was the RAND Corporation, which perpetually makes obsolete the institution that fathered it.

Here again the economic problem is almost trivial. If we spent as much on research and training for human welfare as we spend for defense, it is hard to believe that the results would not be even more dramatic. If all science could be pursued without the smell of brimstone, and if all secrecy were abolished, how much more quickly, and joyfully, would knowledge grow. The problem is essentially one of the political consciousness: can we organize, through both private and public organization, the same kind of effort, or an even greater effort, for pure knowledge, useful skill, and human betterment than we can for the road to doomsday? If we cannot, it can only be because of a failure of the imagination, of a lack of clear purpose, and a poverty of symbols. But if we lack these things, we do not deserve anything better than doomsday.

In spite of the fact that the main theme of this paper is the domestic implications, we should take a brief glance abroad, for several reasons. One is that the domestic implications of arms control for other countries may be different from what they are in the United States. In Russia, for instance, though exact information is not available, the proportion of the gross national product going into national security is considerably larger than in the United States—though in an economy that is substantially poorer. National security is correspondingly a much greater economic burden. In the United States the marginal significance of the arms dollar is in the realm of a little more or a little less luxury; in Russia it is much closer to basic comfort, and in India it is close to sheer necessity. The Russians correspondingly have a greater incentive than we do toward "cheap" arms control, and this may explain something of their (and our) attitudes. In really poor countries like India, Pakistan, and China, arms expenditure literally snatches life from the starving: there is an enormous economic interest in cheap security. . . .

Another reason for looking at the world economic scene is that one of the domestic implications of arms control (at least, of "cheap" arms control) for the United States may be a release of resources for investment and development abroad. This has implications for the reduction, or increase, of world tensions which may be relevant to the success or failure of arms control itself. It is important, too, in the moral mythology of disarmament: the plea that disarmament would release large resources for economic development and for raising standards of life in the poor countries is a powerful part of the motivation which drives ordinary decent people toward it, even if it does not have much appeal for political realists and those who direct the destinies of states.

Like other myths, this also embodies an important half truth. It is true that disarmament (or cheap arms control) would release resources which could indeed be used for this purpose. They do not have to be used for this purpose, however, and there is no guarantee that they would be. If we assume that no method of domestic stabilization is acceptable, other than manipulating the export surplus, then of course the stabilization program which followed cheap arms control would involve extensive gifts and investments abroad. It is perfectly possible, however, to draw up a domestic stabilization plan which involves no increase in the export surplus and no contribution to the development of the rest of the world. The plain fact is that, beyond a certain point of profitable investment abroad, the increase in the American export surplus involves a real cost to Americans, in terms of consumption foregone, or what may be more serious, domestic growth impaired. . . .

We are, however, totally unprepared for peace. We have never had peace, and it may be forced upon us before we really want it. One can only, in the spirit of Newton's *Opticks,* raise some queries. What, for instance, can hold society together in the absence of an external threat? What are the institutions which can embody "conflict control"—that general social system of which arms control is only a special case? How do we catch the disintegrating dynamic processes in society—the epidemics of hatred, the infectious images of falsehood, the powerful symbols which lead to destruction—and stop them, by education, by quarantine, by counter-eloquence, before they spread too far? How do we give the individual an image of self-respect, of identification with some larger group, without permitting the development of images of hatred and intolerance? How do we preserve the richness and variety of cultural differences in a world of rapid communication and peace—how, in other words, do we preserve the very real virtues of nationalism in a warless world? How do we prevent the great latent social processes (population growth, emotional hysteria, charismatic leadership, mistaken images of social fact) from carrying societies to poverty, factionalism, and decay? More difficult perhaps, how do we prevent boredom, how do we preserve danger, excitement, and a sense of high purpose? How do we deal with sadism and masculinism, masochism and femininism, the strut and the swagger, the cringe and the death wish? How do we release people from the crippling "binds" of ambivalence, and release their creative potential? How do we raise children in a warless world? What kind of ethic do we inculcate, and what are our defenses against its corruption? What rituals shall we have, and what heroes? How can we prevent the corrupting influence of wealth, luxury, and the treacherous ability to satisfy the flesh? Peace, it is clear, insinuates her soft fingers into every nerve of life. We have dreamed of utopia, and secretly been thankful that it is only a dream. Now we are going to be compelled to think about it, and think hard and long, for we may be forced into it by the absence of any alternative but doomsday.

30.5. THE NUCLEAR TEST BAN TREATY

Among the agonizing consequences of the nuclear age in which we live has been the pollution of the world's air space by atmospheric testing of nuclear weapons. Since Adlai Stevenson's proposed suspension of these tests in 1952, negotiators have sought to translate this suggestion into policy. Finally, in 1963, a Treaty was signed by representatives of the United States, the United Kingdom, and the USSR, in which the three original parties agreed to an indefinite suspension of atmospheric testing of nuclear weapons.

[A] TREATY banning nuclear weapon tests in the atmosphere, in outer space and underwater.

The Governments of the United States of America, the United Kingdom of Great Britain and Northern Ireland, and the Union of Soviet Socialist Republics, hereinafter referred to as the "Original Parties",

Proclaiming as their principal aim the speediest possible achievement of an agreement on general and complete disarmament under strict international control in accordance with the objectives of the United Nations which would put an end to the armaments race and eliminate the incentive to the production and testing of all kinds of weapons, including nuclear weapons,

Seeking to achieve the discontinuance of all test explosions of nuclear weapons for all time, determined to continue negotiations to this end, and desiring to put an end to the contamination of man's environment by radioactive substances,

---

From the *Department of State Bulletin* August 12, 1963, pp. 239–240.

Have agreed as follows:

ARTICLE I

1. Each of the Parties to this Treaty undertakes to prohibit, to prevent, and not to carry out any nuclear weapon test explosion, or any other nuclear explosion, at any place under its jurisdiction or control:

(a) in the atmosphere; beyond its limits, including outer space; or underwater, including territorial waters or high seas; or

(b) in any other environment if such explosion causes radioactive debris to be present outside the territorial limits of the State under whose jurisdiction or control such explosion is conducted. It is understood in this connection that the provisions of this subparagraph are without prejudice to the conclusion of a treaty resulting in the permanent banning of all nuclear test explosions, including all such explosions underground, the conclusion of which, as the Parties have stated in the Preamble to this Treaty, they seek to achieve.

2. Each of the Parties to this Treaty undertakes furthermore to refrain from causing, encouraging, or in any way participating in, the carrying out of any nuclear weapon test explosion, or any other nuclear explosion, anywhere which would take place in any of the environments described, or have the effect referred to, in paragraph 1 of this Article.

ARTICLE II

1. Any Party may propose amendments to this Treaty. The text of any proposed amendment shall be submitted to the Depositary Governments which shall circulate it to all Parties to this Treaty. Thereafter, if requested to do so by one-third or more of the Parties, the Depositary Governments shall convene a conference, to which they shall invite all the Parties, to consider such amendment.

2. Any amendment to this Treaty must be approved by a majority of the votes of all the Parties to this Treaty, including the votes of all of the Original Parties. The amendment shall enter into force for all Parties upon the deposit of instruments of ratification by a majority of all the Parties, including the instruments of ratification of all the Original Parties.

ARTICLE III

1. This Treaty shall be open to all States for signature. Any State which does not sign this Treaty before its entry into force in accordance with paragraph 3 of this Article may accede to it at any time.

2. This Treaty shall be subject to ratification by signatory States.

Instruments of ratification and instruments of accession shall be deposited with the Governments of the Original Parties—the United States of America, the United Kingdom of Great Britain and Northern Ireland, and the Union of Soviet Socialist Republics—which are hereby designated the Depositary Governments.

3. This Treaty shall enter into force after its ratification by all the Original Parties and the deposit of their instruments of ratification.

4. For States whose instruments of ratification or accession are deposited subsequent to the entry into force of this Treaty, it shall enter into force on the date of the deposit of their instruments of ratification or accession.

5. The Depositary Governments shall promptly inform all signatory and acceding States of the date of each signature, the date of deposit of each instrument of ratification of and accession to this Treaty, the date of its entry into force, and the date of receipt of any requests for conferences or other notices.

6. This Treaty shall be registered by the Depositary Governments pursuant to Article 102 of the Charter of the United Nations.

ARTICLE IV

This Treaty shall be of unlimited duration.

Each Party shall in exercising its national sovereignty have the right to withdraw from the Treaty if it decides that extraordinary events, related to the subject matter of this Treaty, have jeopardized the supreme interests of its country. It shall give notice of such withdrawal to all other Parties to the Treaty three months in advance.

ARTICLE V

This Treaty, of which the English and Russian texts are equally authentic, shall be deposited in the archives of the Depositary Governments. Duly certified copies of this Treaty shall be transmitted by the Depositary Governments to the Governments of the signatory and acceding States.

IN WITNESS WHEREOF the undersigned, duly authorized, have signed this Treaty.

DONE in triplicate at the city of Moscow the 5th day of August, one thousand nine hundred and sixty-three.

For the Government of the United States of America
For the Government of the United Kingdom of Great Britain and
   Northern Ireland
For the Government of the Union of Soviet Socialist Republics

31

Taxation and Fiscal Policy

31.1. PRESIDENTIAL PLANNING OF THE BUDGET

Prior to the beginning of every fiscal year, the President must estimate the government's revenues and expenses for the coming year. Here, outgoing President Eisenhower presents the budgetary proposals of his administration for the 1962 fiscal year. Needless to say, the incoming Kennedy administration was not bound by the Eisenhower estimates.

TO THE CONGRESS OF THE UNITED STATES:

For the fiscal year 1962 I send you budget and legislative proposals which will meet the essential domestic needs of the Nation, provide for the national defense, and at the same time preserve the integrity and strength of our Federal Government's finances.

With this budget, I leave to the new administration and the Congress a progressive and workable financial plan which recognizes national priorities and which reflects my confidence in the strength of our economy now and in the years to come. . . .

In total and in its parts, this budget embodies a sensible and forward-looking plan of action for the Government. In brief, it provides for:

1. Increasing our own military capabilities and promoting increased strength in other free world forces;

2. Advancing activities important to economic growth and domestic welfare;

From the 1962 Budget Message presented by President Dwight D. Eisenhower, January, 1961, in *Federal Budget in Brief* (Washington, D.C.: U.S. Government Printing Office), pp. 8–9, 14–20.

3. Continuing assistance to the less-developed nations of the world whose peoples are striving to improve their standards of living;

4. Increasing support for scientific activities in outer space;

5. Achieving savings by making desirable modification in existing programs and by charging users the costs of special benefits received by them; and

6. Continuing present tax rates to maintain the revenues needed for a sound fiscal plan.

The policies and proposals in this budget will enable us to meet fully our national and international responsibilities and to promote real and sustainable national progress. . . .

Current estimates indicate a close balance in the 1961 budget. On the newly adopted basis of excluding interfund transactions, expenditures are estimated at $78.9 billion and receipts at $79.0 billion, resulting in a budget surplus of $0.1 billion.

The revenue estimate reflects a justifiably optimistic view as to the course of our economy, based on circumstances described in my Economic Report.

Last January, I proposed a budget for 1961 that showed a surplus of $4.2 billion. The enactment by the Congress of unrecommended expenditures and the unwillingness of the Congress to increase postal rates reduced this prospect by approximately $2 billion. In the meantime, lower corporate profits have materially reduced our expectation of tax collections from this source.

The small surplus of $79 million currently estimated for 1961 takes into account an assumption that postal rates will be increased not later than April 1, 1961.

Despite the congressional increases in the budget last year, the present estimate of $78.9 billion for 1961 expenditures is about $900 million less than the figure of $79.8 billion which appeared in the budget a year ago. The apparent reduction results from (1) the elimination, as announced in last year's budget, of certain interfund transactions totaling $0.7 billion from the current estimate of expenditures and (2) the shift of employment security grants of $0.3 billion to trust fund financing as provided by law. As explained elsewhere in this budget, these changes affect receipts as well as expenditures and do not affect the surplus.

Apart from these accounting adjustments, the increases and decreases from last year's estimate of 1961 expenditures are approximately offsetting.

Major increases from the original budget include $766 million for Federal employee pay raises; $554 million in losses of the postal service because rates were not increased as proposed; $269 million for defense programs; $118 million for health, education, and welfare activities; and $164 million for civil space activities.

Major decreases from the original estimates include $600 million for interest on the public debt; $496 million for the activities of the Commodity Credit Corporation; $311 million for veterans compensation, pensions, and readjustment benefits; $93 million for the Export-Import Bank; and $50 million for military assistance. In addition, a reduction of $160 million is estimated under the proposal to reduce the postal deficit in 1961 by increasing postal rates effective April 1. Other reductions, including a normal downward revision in the allowance for contingencies, total $210 million.

For the fiscal year 1962, my recommendations provide for $82.3 billion in budget receipts and $80.9 billion in budget expenditures. The resulting budgetary surplus of $1.5 billion will permit another modest payment on the public debt.

The estimate of receipts in 1962 is $3.3 billion higher than the current estimate for 1961, and $4.6 billion more than the receipts actually collected in 1960. Expenditures are also increasing, from a total of $76.5 billion in 1960 to $78.9 billion currently estimated for 1961 and $80.9 billion proposed for 1962.

The increase of $1.9 billion in estimated expenditures between 1961 and 1962 reflects several factors which are worthy of special note.

First, outlays for our Nation's defenses are estimated to rise by $1.4 billion in 1962 to a total of $42.9 billion. Much of this increase reflects continued emphasis on certain expanding defense programs, such as Polaris submarines, the Minuteman missile, the B–70 long-range bomber, a strengthened airborne alert capability, airlift modernization, and modernization of Army equipment. These improvements are for the purpose of keeping our military might the strongest in the world.

Second, the budget provides for substantial continuing efforts to support the cause of freedom through the mutual security program. Expenditures for this program in 1962 are estimated at $3.6 billion, an increase of $250 million over 1961.

Third, civil space vehicles and space exploration will require $965 million in 1962, up $195 million from 1961, and $564 million more than in 1960. In total, the recommendations in this budget provide for $9.4 billion in expenditures in 1962 for carrying forward research and development efforts, of which $7.4 billion is for major national security purposes. The total represents an increase of $770 million over 1961. As part of the overall research and development effort, increasing Federal support for basic research is being provided. This budget includes $1 billion for the conduct and support of basic research in universities, industrial establishments, Government laboratories, and other centers of research.

Fourth, increases in expenditures are proposed for certain activities important to domestic well-being and to the future development of our Nation. These include, among others, broadening medical care for the aged; making major improvements in transportation programs; continuing development of our natural resources at a new record level of expenditures; improving our health and welfare programs; providing assistance for construction of elementary and secondary schools and college facilities; assisting areas of substantial and persistent unemployment; and fostering rural development. Expenditures in 1962 for labor, education, health, welfare, community development, transportation aids and services, and conservation of natural resources are estimated to total $8.6 billion, an increase of $627 million over 1961. . . .

Estimated budget receipts of $82.3 billion in 1962 are based on an outlook for higher production, employment, and income as the calendar year 1961 progresses.

It is necessary to extend for another year the present tax rates on corporation income and the excise taxes which are scheduled for reduction or termination on July 1, 1961. The excise tax rates scheduled for reduction include those on distilled spirits, beer, wines, cigarettes, passenger automobiles, automobile parts and accessories, and transportation of persons; the 10 percent tax on general telephone service is scheduled to expire. Unless these tax rates are extended, the Federal Government will lose an estimated $2.6 billion in revenues in 1962, and $3.7 billion on a full annual basis.

In the conduct of certain of its activities, the Government provides special services, sells products, and leases federally owned resources, which convey to the recipients benefits above and beyond those which accrue to the public at large. In fairness to the general taxpayer, the cost of these services or the fair market value of the products and resources which are transferred to private use should be recovered, wherever feasible, through adequate fees and charges. To this end, the Congress was requested last year to provide increased fees and charges for a number of special benefits. With the one exception of fees for noncompetitive oil and gas leases no final action was taken. The Congress is again requested to raise postal rates to eliminate the postal deficit and to act favorably on the proposals for increased highway and aviation fuel taxes and for a number of other fees or charges.

The present highway fuel tax rate should be increased by one-half cent per gallon and the resulting rate of 4½ cents should be continued through 1972. This step is necessary to permit timely completion of the Interstate System. It will also make possible the repeal of the unwise diversion from the general fund to the trust fund of excise tax receipts amounting to 5 percent of the manufacturers' price of passenger automobiles and automobile parts and accessories; this diversion is presently scheduled by law to begin July 1, 1961, and to continue for the fiscal years 1962 through 1964. The Congress should also raise the excise tax rate on aviation gasoline from 2 to 4½ cents per gallon; impose the same excise tax rate on jet fuels, now untaxed; and retain the receipts from these taxes in the general fund to help pay the cost of the Federal airways system.

Achievement of the proposed budget surplus for 1962 will enable the Federal Government to make another modest reduction in the public debt. It is estimated that the public debt, which stood at $286.3 billion on June 30, 1960, will decline to $284.9 billion by the end of fiscal year 1961 and to $283.4 billion on June 30, 1962.

If the Congress accepts the proposals in this budget, and the proposed budget surplus for fiscal year 1962 is achieved, at the end of that year the Government will have some operating leeway within the permanent debt limit of $285 billion. Due to the seasonal pattern of tax collections, however, it will again be necessary for the Congress to provide a temporary increase in the debt limit during 1962. The present temporary debt limit of 293 billion expires June 30, 1961.

The Congress is again urged to remove the 4¼ percent statutory limitation on new issues of Treasury bonds, which remains a serious obstacle to efficient long-run management of the public debt. The marketable debt is still too heavily concentrated in securities of relatively short maturity, with almost 80 percent of the total coming due within 5 years. Although interest rates have declined in recent months, the continued existence of the interest rate ceiling limits the flexibility of debt operations by the Treasury. It effectively prevents the Treasury under certain circumstances from lengthening the debt by offering longer term securities or exchanges at maturity and, more importantly, it reduces considerably the possible use of the advance refunding technique, which offers the greatest promise for lengthening the average maturity of the debt.

31.2. PROBLEMS OF AN EQUITABLE TAX SYSTEM

The ability of the government to appropriate and spend money depends in large measure on the scope and efficiency of the taxation system. In these excerpts from his first tax message, President Kennedy examines the problems of inequities in tax burdens and outlines proposals for checking on tax evaders.

A STRONG AND SOUND FEDERAL TAX SYSTEM is essential to America's future. Without such a system, we cannot maintain our defenses and give leadership to the free world. Without such a system, we cannot render the public services necessary for enriching the lives of our people and furthering the growth of our economy.

The tax system must be adequate to meet our public needs. It must meet them fairly, calling on each of us to contribute his proper share to the cost of government. It must encourage efficient use of our resources. It must promote economic stability and stimulate economic growth. Economic expansion in turn creates a growing tax base, thus increasing revenue and thereby enabling us to meet more readily our public needs, as well as our needs as private individuals.

This message recognizes the basic soundness of our tax structure. But it also recognizes the changing needs and standards of our economic and international position, and the constructive reform needs to keep our system up to date and to maintain its equity. Previous messages have emphasized the need for prompt congressional and executive action to alleviate the deficit in our international balance of payments—to increase the modernization, productivity, and competitive status of American industry—to stimulate the expansion and growth of our economy—to eliminate to the extent possible economic injustice within our own society—and to maintain the level of revenues requested in my predecessor's budget. In each of these endeavors, tax policy has an important role to play and necessary tax changes are herein proposed. . . .

Changing economic conditions at home and abroad, the desire to achieve greater equity in taxation, and the strains which have developed in our balance of payments position in the last few years, compel us to examine critically certain features of our tax system which, in conjunction with the tax system of other countries, consistently favor U.S. private investment abroad compared with investment in our own economy.

Profits earned abroad by American firms operating through foreign subsidiaries are, under present tax laws, subject to U.S. tax only when they are returned to the parent company in the form of dividends. In some cases, this tax deferral has made possible indefinite postponement of the U.S. tax; and, in those countries where income taxes are lower than in the United States, the ability to defer the payment of U.S. tax by retaining income in the subsidiary companies provides a tax advantage for companies operating through oversea subsidiaries that is not available to companies operating solely in the United States. Many American investors properly made use of this deferral in the conduct of their foreign investment. Though changing conditions now make continuance of the privilege undesirable, such change of policy implies no criticism of the investors who so utilize this privilege.

From President John F. Kennedy, *Our Federal Tax System*, House of Representatives Document No. 140, 87th Congress, 1st Session, May 3, 1961.

The undesirability of continuing deferral is underscored where deferral has served as a shelter for tax escape through the unjustifiable use of tax havens such as Switzerland. Recently more and more enterprises organized abroad by American firms have arranged their corporate structures—aided by artificial arrangements between parent and subsidiary regarding intercompany pricing, the transfer of patent licensing rights, the shifting of management fees, and similar practices which maximize the accumulation of profits in the tax haven—so as to exploit the multiplicity of foreign tax systems and international agreements in order to reduce sharply or eliminate completely their tax liabilities both at home and abroad.

To the extent that these tax havens and other tax deferral privileges result in U.S. firms investing or locating abroad largely for tax reasons, the efficient allocation of international resources is upset, the initial drain on our already adverse balance of payments is never fully compensated, and profits are retained and reinvested abroad which would otherwise be invested in the United States. Certainly since the postwar reconstruction of Europe and Japan has been completed, there are no longer foreign policy reasons for providing tax incentives for foreign investment in the economically advanced countries. . . .

At the same time, I recommend that tax deferral be continued for income from investment in the developing economies. The free world has a strong obligation to assist in the development of these economies, and private investment has an important contribution to make. Continued income tax deferral for these areas will be helpful in this respect. In addition, the proposed elimination of income tax deferral on U.S. earnings in industrialized countries should enhance the relative attraction of investment in the less developed countries. . . .

Our system of combined withholding and voluntary reporting on wages and salaries under the individual income tax has served us well. Introduced during the war when the income tax was extended to millions of new taxpayers, the wage-withholding system has been one of the most important and successful advances in our tax system in recent times. Initial difficulties were quickly overcome, and the new system helped the taxpayer no less than the tax collector.

It is the more unfortunate, therefore, that the application of the withholding principle has remained incomplete. Withholding does not apply to dividends and interest, with the result that substantial amounts of such income, particularly interest, improperly escape taxation. It is estimated that about $3 billion of taxable interest and dividends are unreported each year. This is patently unfair to those who must as a result bear a larger share of the tax burden. Recipients of dividends and interest should pay their tax no less than those who receive wage and salary income, and the tax should be paid just as promptly. Large continued avoidance of tax on the part of some has a steadily demoralizing effect on the compliance of others.

This gap in reporting has not been appreciably lessened by educational programs. Nor can it be effectively closed by intensified enforcement measures, except by the expenditure of inordinate amounts of time and money. Withholding on corporate dividends and on investment-type interest, such as interest paid on taxable government and corporate securities and saving accounts, is both necessary and practicable. . . .

One of the major characteristics of our tax system, and one in which we can take a great deal of pride, is that it operates primarily through individual self-assessment. The integrity of such a system depends upon the continued willingness of the people honestly and accurately to discharge this annual price of citizenship. To the extent that some people are dishonest or careless in their dealings with the Government, the majority is forced to carry a heavier tax burden.

For voluntary self-assessment to be both meaningful and productive of revenues, the citizens must not only have confidence in the fairness of the tax laws, but also in their uniform and vigorous enforcement of these laws. If noncompliance by the few continues unchecked, the confidence of the many in our self-assessment system will be shaken and one of the cornerstones of our Government weakened. . . .

The Internal Revenue Service has begun the installation of automatic data processing equipment to improve administration of the growing job of tax collection and enforcement. A system of identifying taxpayer account numbers, which would make possible the bringing together of all tax data for any one particular taxpayer, is an essential part of such an improved collection and enforcement program.

For this purpose, social security numbers would be used by taxpayers already having them. The small minority currently without such numbers would be assigned numbers which these persons could later use as well for social security purposes if needed. The numbers would be entered on tax returns, information returns, and related documents.

I recommend that legislation be enacted to authorize the use of taxpayer account numbers beginning January 1, 1962, to identify taxpayer accounts throughout the processing and recordkeeping operations of the Internal Revenue Service.

The examination of tax returns is the essence of the enforcement process. The number of examining personnel of the Internal Revenue Service, however, has been consistently inadequate to cope with the audit workload. Consequently, it has been unable to audit carefully many of the returns which should be so examined. Anticipated growth in our population will, of course, increase this enforcement problem.

Related to broadened tax audit is the criminal enforcement program of the Revenue Service. Here, the guiding principle is the creation of a deterrent to tax evasion and to maintain or, if possible, increase voluntary compliance with all taxing statutes. This means placing an appropriate degree of investigative emphasis on all types of tax violations, in all geographical areas, and identifying violations of substance in all income brackets regardless of occupation, business, or profession.

Within this framework of a balanced enforcement effort, the Service is placing special investigative emphasis on returns filed by persons receiving income from illegal sources. I have directed all Federal law enforcement agencies to cooperate fully with the Attorney General in a drive against organized crime, and to utilize their resources to the maximum extent in conducting investigations of individuals engaged in criminal activity on a major scale. With the foregoing in mind, I have directed the Secretary of the Treasury to provide through the Internal Revenue Service a maximum effort in this field.

To fulfill these requirements for improved audits, enforcement and anticrime investigation, it is essential that the Service be provided additional resources which will pay their own cost many times over. In furthering the Service's long-range plans, the prior administration asked additional appropriations of $27.4 million to hire about 3,500 additional personnel during fiscal 1962, including provisions for the necessary increases in space and modern equipment vital to the efficient operation of the Service. To meet the commitments described above, this administration reviewed these proposals and recommended that they be increased by another $7 million and 765 additional personnel to expedite the expansion and criminal enforcement programs. The pending alternative of only 1,995 additional personnel, or less than one-half of the number requested, this administration would constitute little more than the additional employees needed each year during the 1960s just to keep up with the estimated growth in number and complexity of returns filed. Thus I must again strongly urge the Congress to give its full support to my original request. These increases will safeguard the long-term adequacy of the Nation's traditional voluntary compliance system and, at the same time, return the added appropriations several times over in added revenue. . . .

31.3. PROGRAM FOR TAX REDUCTION AND REFORM

The taxing power of Congress is critically important not only to provide the revenues necessary for financing the government but to do so in a way best calculated to contribute to the nation's economic growth and stability. How important tax policy can be as an instrument for national economic planning is well illustrated in the following excerpt from the President's Special Message on Tax Reduction and Reform of January 24, 1963.

THE MOST URGENT TASK FACING OUR NATION at home today is to end the tragic waste of unemployment and unused resources—to step up the growth and vigor of our national economy—to increase job and investment opportunities—to improve our productivity—and thereby to strenghten our nation's ability to meet its worldwide commitments for the defense and growth of freedom. The revision of our federal tax system on an equitable basis is crucial to the achievement of these goals.

. . . It has become increasingly clear—particularly in the last five years—that the largest single barrier to full employment of our manpower and resources and to a higher rate of economic growth is the unrealistically heavy drag of federal income taxes on private purchasing power, initiative and incentive. Our economy is checkreined today by a war-born tax system at a time when it is far more in need of the spur than the bit.

. . . The chief problem confronting our economy in 1963 is its unrealized potential—slow growth, under-investment, unused capacity, persistent unemployment.

. . . . . .

Despite the improvements resulting from last year's depreciation reform and investment credit—which I pledged two years ago would be only a first step—our tax system still siphons out of the private economy too large a share of personal and business purchasing power and reduces the incentive for risk, investment and effort—thereby aborting our recovery and stifling our national growth rate.

In addition, the present tax code contains special preferences and provisions, all of which the narrow tax base (thus requiring higher rates), artificially distort the use of resources, inhibit the mobility and formation of capital, add complexities and inequities which undermine the morale of the taxpayer, and make tax avoidance rather than market factors a prime consideration in too many economic decisions.

I am therefore proposing the following:

1. Reduction in income tax rates from their present levels of 20 to 91 percent, to a range of 14 to 65 percent. . . .

2. Reduction in the rate of the corporate income tax from 52 to 47 percent;

3. Reversal of the corporate normal and surtax rates, so that the tax rate applicable to the first $25,000 of corporate income could

From President John F. Kennedy, Message to Congress on Tax Reduction and Reform (*The New York Times*, January 24, 1963).

drop from 30 to 22 percent, so as to give particular encouragement to small business;

4. Acceleration of tax payments by corporations with anticipated annual liabilities of more than $100,000, to bring the corporate payment schedule to a current basis of a five-year transition period;

5. Revision of the tax treatment of capital gains, designed to provide a freer and fuller flow of capital funds and to achieve a greater equity;

6. Removal of certain inequities and handicaps [hardships] in our present tax structure;

7. Broadening of the base of the individual and corporate income taxes, to remove unwarranted special privileges, correct defects in the tax law, and provide more equal treatment of taxpayers—thereby permitting a larger reduction in tax rates than would otherwise be possible and making possible my proposals to alleviate hardships and inequities.

. . . The tax program I am recommending . . . provides a cut in tax liabilities of $13.6 billion—$11 billion for individuals and $2.6 billion for corporations. Other adjustments, some of which lose and some of which gain revenue, would, on balance, produce a revenue gain of $3.4 billion, leaving a net reduction of $10.2 billion. Accelerating tax payment of large corporations to a correct basis over a five-year transition period would reduce the effect on tax receipts to $8.7 billion. These figures do not include off-setting revenue gains which would result from the stimulating effect of the program on the economy as a whole and on the level of taxable income, profits and sales—gains which may be expected to increase as the economy recaptures its vigor, and to lead to higher total tax receipts than would otherwise be realized.

. . . Enactment of this program will help strengthen every segment of the American economy and bring us closer to every basic objective of American economic policy.

Total output and economic growth will be stepped up by an amount several times as great as the tax cut itself . . . Additional dollars spent by consumers or invested by producers will lead to more jobs, more plant capacity, more markets, and thus still more dollars for consumption and investment. Idle manpower and plant capacity make this possible without inflation; and strong and healthy economic activity is the best insurance against future recessions.

Unemployment will be reduced, as firms throughout the country hire new workers to meet the new demands released by tax reduction . . .

. . . . . .

Our balance of payments should be improved by the fiscal policies reflected in this program. Its enactment—which will make investment in America more profitable, and which will increase the efficiency of American plants, thus cutting costs and improving our competitive position in world trade—will provide the strongest possible economic backing for the dollar . . . Moreover, a nation operating closer to capacity will be freer to use monetary tools to protect its international accounts, should events so require.

. . . Consumers will convert a major percentage of their personal income tax savings into a higher standard of living, benefiting their own families while generating stronger markets for producers. . . .

Investment will be expanded, as the rate of return on capital formation is increased, and as growing consumer markets create a need for new capacity . . . Reducing the corporate tax from 52 percent to 47 percent will mean not only greater incentives to invest but more internal funds available for investment. Reducing the maximum individual income tax rate from 91 percent to 65 percent makes more meaningful the concept of additional reward and incentive for additional initiative, effort, and risk-taking. A rising level of consumer demand will enable the more than $2 billion worth of investment incentives provided by last year's tax actions (the depreciation reform and investment credit) to achieve their full effect. . . .

State and local governments, hard-pressed by a considerably faster rise in expenditures and indebtedness than that experienced at the federal level, will also gain additional revenues without increasing their own taxes as national income and production expand.

· · · · · ·

A balanced Federal budget in a growing full-employment economy will be most rapidly and certainly achieved by a substantial expansion in national income carrying with it the needed federal revenues—the kind of expansion the proposed tax revision is designed to bring about. With (sic) a few years of the enactment of this program, Federal revenues will be larger than if present tax rates continue to prevail. Full employment, moreover, will make possible the reduction of certain government expenditures caused by unemployment. As the economy climbs toward full employment, a substantial part of the increased tax revenue thereby generated will be applied toward a reduction in the Federal deficit.

· · · · · ·

It would be a grave mistake to require that any tax reduction today be offset by a corresponding cut in expenditures. In my judgment, I have proposed the minimum level of Federal expenditures needed for the security of the nation, for meeting the challenge facing us in space and for the well-being of our people . . .

On the other hand, I do not favor raising demand by a massive increase in Government expenditures. In today's circumstances, it is desirable to seek expansion through our free market processes—to place increased spending power in the hands of private consumers and investors and offer more encouragement to private initiative. The most effective policy, therefore, is to expand demand and unleash incentives through a program of tax reduction and reform, coupled with the most prudent possible policy of public expenditures.

. . . The public debt as a proportion of our gross national product will fall to 53 percent, compared to 57 percent when this Administration took office. Last year the total increase in the Federal debt was only 2 percent—compared to an 8 percent increase in the gross debt of state and local governments.

. . . Taking a longer view, the Federal debt today is only 13 percent higher than it was in 1945—while state and local debt increased over 360 percent and private debt by 300 percent In fact, if it were not for Federal financial assistance to state and local government, the Federal cash budget would actually show a surplus. Federal civilian employment, for example, is actually lower today than it was in 1952, while state and local government employment over the same period has increased 67 percent. This Administration is pledged to enforce economy and efficiency in a strict control of expenditures.

In short, this tax program will increase our wealth far more than it increases our public debt. The actual burden of that debt—as measured in relation to our total output—will decline. To continue to increase our debt as the result of inadequate earnings is a sign of weakness. But to borrow prudently in order to invest in a tax revision that will greatly increase our earning power can be a source of strength.

. . . . . .

. . . Too small a tax cut would be a waste, gaining us little but further deficits. It could not cope with the task of closing a $30 to $40 billion gap in our economic performance. But the next tax cut of over $10 billion envisioned by this program can lead the way to strong economic expansion and a larger revenue yield.

. . . . . .

Tax reduction and structural reform should be considered and enacted as a single integrated program. My recommendations for rate reductions of $13.6 billion are made in the expectation that selected structural changes and reforms will be adopted, adding on balance $3,4 billion in revenue and resulting in a net reduction of tax liabilities of no more than $10.2 billion. . . .

On the other hand, an attempt to solve all tax problems at once by the inclusion of even more sweeping reforms might impair the effect of rate reduction. This program is designed to achieve broad acceptance and prompt enactment.

. . . . . .

The resistance to tax reform should be less when it is coupled with more-than-offsetting tax reductions benefiting all brackets—and the support for tax reform should be greater when it is a necessary condition for greater tax reduction. Reform, as mentioned earlier, includes top-to-bottom rate reduction as well as structural change—and the two are inseparable prerequisites to the achievement of our economic and equity objectives. . . .

. . . . . .

The changes listed below are an integral part of a single tax program which should be enacted this year . . .

These reforms may be divided into three categories:

A) Relief of hardship and encouragement of growth;

B) Base broadening and equity; and

C) Revision of capital gains taxation for growth and equity.

. . . . . .

SUMMARY AND CONCLUSION

The foregoing program of rate reduction and reform provides for a fair and comprehensive net reduction in tax liabilities at all levels of income. . . . The overall savings are proportionately highest at the lower end of the income scale, where for taxpayers with adjusted gross incomes of less than $3,000 the reduction is nearly 40 percent. As we move up the income scale, the percentage reduction in tax liabilities declines to slightly less than 10 percent for taxpayers with incomes in excess of $50,000. For all groups of taxpayers combined, the reduction is approximately 18 percent, but five out of six taxpayers—most of whom have incomes below $10,000 will enjoy a reduction of more than 20 percent.

In addition, the proposed reforms will go a long way toward simplifying the problem of filling out tax returns for the more than 60 million filers each year. Under these proposals more than 6 million people will no longer find necessary the record-keeping and detailed accounting required by itemized deductions. Hundreds of thousands of older people and individuals and families with very low incomes will no longer be required to file any tax returns at all.

Special tax problems of small business, the aged, working mothers and low-income groups are effectively met. Special preferences —for capital gains, natural resources, excessive deductions and other areas outside the tax base—are curbed. Both the mobility and the formation of capital are encouraged. The lower corporate tax rates will encourage and stimulate business enterprise. The reduction of the top 91 percent rate will assist investment and risk-taking. Above all, by expanding consumer demand and investment, this program will raise production and income, provide jobs for the unemployed, and take up the slack in our economy.

31.4. AMBIGUITIES, CONCESSIONS, AND SPECIAL PREFERENCES

The taxpayer is often tempted to seek and to exploit ambiguities and exemptions in the tax laws. Mr. Surrey, a law professor who has since become Assistant Secretary of the Treasury, criticizes the establishment of "loopholes" by Congress favoring special interests. Mr. Martin discusses how concessions and special preferences may discriminate against average citizens and benefit the fortunate few. Although some of the facts in these articles are now dated, they pose serious and basic problems.

STANLEY S. SURREY

The American taxpayer is a lucky man. Given the necessity of paying federal taxes, he pays them in the fairest possible way—on the basis of his income.

Because the policy of relying on income taxes compares so favorably with any other yet devised for the financing of government, we all have a stake in protecting it and keeping it strong.

Yet this policy is being jeopardized by a trend that, unarrested, could ruin it. And ruin would mean that the fairest form of taxation would have to be replaced—by another less fair.

The theory—and the strength—of our income tax is that each man pays in terms of what he makes. If he makes what another man makes, he pays what the other man pays. If he makes more, he pays more.

But recent practice has strayed dangerously far from this theory. The United States Congress is itself creating ways for certain people to escape the very taxes it imposes. So persistent has this practice become that Congress and the country must now awaken to these consequences.

As special favors are granted, the income-tax system becomes unfair, and thus loses respect. As it loses respect, it loses effectiveness, until finally it does not work at all. Here is why:

From personal incomes, the federal government today takes income taxes of $32,000,000,000. No matter what arrangement is made as to who pays how much, the government must get that $32,000,000,000 to pay its present bills. If someone, somehow, escapes his burden, or even a portion of it, someone else must pay up for him. Every time

---

From Stanley S. Surrey, "Do Income-Tax Exemptions Make Sense?" in *Collier's*, March 30, 1956, p. 26; and Harold H. Martin, "What's Wrong with Our Income-Tax Laws," in the *Saturday Evening Post*, July 15, 1961, pp. 25, 54–56; © 1961 by The Curtis Publishing Co.

Congress exempts a special group from the income tax, or a portion of it, the tax load becomes heavier for the rest of us.

Already a number of individuals have been shorn almost completely of their tax burden.

Already this trend is producing a deterioration in our tax morals and a psychology of contempt for our tax laws.

Already groups sophisticated in money matters are beginning to say, "Why pay high taxes when we can go to Washington and have our congressman change the law for us?" As this attitude flourishes, taxpaying becomes a game of lobbying.

When some taxpayers receive favors from Washington, others are going to expect favors, too. Failing as lobbyists, they will seek out experts who, through the adroit use of gimmicks, can ease them into tax shelters created by Congress with other groups in mind. And many an American taxpayer, angered by Congressional favoritism, will indulge in a bit of self-help as he makes out his return each year.

Our income-tax system rests to a great extent on the voluntary compliance of the taxpayers. Without honesty, enforcement becomes a vast impossibility. Without high taxpayer morale, the United States tax system is without value. Yet it is this very morale that is now being threatened.

How did such a system—where the concept of fairness is so basic to success—suddenly find itself becoming unfair, and in danger of failure?

The answer hangs on one fact: Ever since it adopted tax rates rising all the way to 91 percent, Congress has been acting as though possessed by an uneasy conscience. . . .

Arguments for special privilege based on the belief that incentive will be harmed are inconclusive and difficult to weigh. Many a group pressing for a tax break is simply dressing up in high-flown economic terms the dislike for high taxes that we all share. And the need for fairness —for treating equal incomes equally—is so vital under our tax system that if a particular industry is really in need of governmental aid, a direct grant or subsidy, wholly apart from the income tax, is the more appropiate method of furnishing that aid.

Other tax privileges are defended as necessary for relief against hardship, as in the case of the aged. But here also an income-tax concession is not the fair way to relieve hardship. The greatest benefits of such deductions go to people with the most taxable income. But if the hardship is suffered by those whose income is low, the special deduction offers insufficient aid.

The strongest objection to special exemptions, however, is that when Congress grants one favor, it is encouraged to grant another and still another until the basic fabrics of our tax system begins to unravel.

The extent to which taxpayer cynicism has developed as a consequence of special Congressional legislation was illustrated not long ago in a federal courtroom. A woman was being cross-examined in connection with a partnership set up by her husband to include not only herself but their small children as well. Under the law, a partnership group pays a lower over-all tax than a sole proprietorship.

"Now," the prosecutor asked the wife, "do you participate in the management of the business?"

Well, no, the wife replied. She had been too busy recently to participate.

"Too busy doing what?" the prosecutor demanded.

"Producing partners," the wife said. . . .

Apparently Congress has felt that the only way it could justify the high rate for the mass of voters affected by the tax was to preserve at the same time the fantastically high rates in the top brackets. But out of sympathy for people paying those fantastic top-bracket rates, Congress has time and again granted exceptions.

Thus the congressman can be friends with everyone. He can prove to labor that he favors high rates of tax on the wealthy by pointing to the tax tables he has supported with their awesome ceilings of 91 percent. At the same time, he can respond to special pressures by voting for the complex technical jargon that the people don't read but which transforms the 91 percent bracket to 25 percent for this select group or that particular taxpayer.

Compromise is the life of politics, and a congressman must live that life. And compromise he will, so long as he believes that any open, direct reduction of the top income-tax rates would result in political reprisals.

But *would* labor protest strongly against tax reduction for the privileged—thereby making the needed reform impossible? Or would labor realize that these high rates are steadily bringing the entire income tax into disrepute through legislative cynicism, administrative inability to enforce those rates and increasing taxpayer tendency to cut corners? Would not labor understand that the alternative to a hopelessly weakened income-tax system is a federal sales tax on consumer goods that would hurt its own members more than it hurts the wealthy?

In its simplest form—wether labor would agree or not—the argument against the present top rates comes down to this: tax rates are too high if Congress believes they are too high and will not enforce them. And if Congress, instead of enforcing these rates, permits them to be tunneled through, the entire system is menaced. If Congress stops granting privileges, we all someday may be able to enjoy appreciably lower tax rates. If Congress does not, that day may never come. . . .

HAROLD H. MARTIN

The process by which the Federal Government extracts more than $40,000,000,000 in personal income tax from 84,000,000 Americans every year is a miracle and a wonder. Never before, in any country, have so many people parted with so much of their wealth with so little overt protest and so little covert cheating. In all the ages of struggle between taxgatherer and taxpayer no more effective system of collection has been devised than this simple process by which the individual citizen, supervised only by his conscience, sits down to add up his income, assess his own tax, write out his own check and send it to his Government, or permits most, if not all, of his tax to be withheld from his wages or his salary without his ever seeing the money at all.

That he does this with so little grumbling is perhaps as much a measure of his patriotism as of his fear of punishment. It is a measure also of his belief that the tax laws, though sometimes harsh to the point of brutality, are basically equitable and fair.

Once this has been said, it is also necessary to add that anyone who believes that the income-tax laws as they now are applied are simple, logical, or equally fair to all, is naïve to the point of idiocy. The world's most efficient taxing system is actually a fantastic tangle of inequities and special preferences, and every year disenchanted taxpayers in greater numbers are becoming aware that this is so. By any standard which may be applied in determining what makes a tax system good or bad—its fairness, its effect on the economy, the adequacy of the revenue it provides, its ease of administration and compliance—our present taxing process is full of structural faults. . . .

A taxpayer with a wife and two children, with $7000 in income derived exclusively from wages or salary, would pay a tax of $780. A taxpayer in similar circumstances, with $7000 in income derived from dividends, would pay $609.60. A taxpayer with $7000 received from the sale of securities giving him a long-term capital gain would pay a tax of $155. A taxpayer whose $7000 came from interest on state or municipal securities would pay no tax at all.

Here then is an obvious inequity—a tax preference granted mainly to those in the higher brackets, for despite the fact that millions of small taxpayers now own a few shares of stocks, it is mainly the higher-bracket taxpayer who has any appreciable income from dividends or capital gains. And it is almost exclusively the well to do who own tax-exempt state and local bonds.

There are economic reasons for this unequal treatment of equal income, and those who benefit from it can defend their special preference with cogent arguments. The fact that such escape hatches exist, however, reflects a conviction in Congress that the high-bracket rates are far too high, and that special concessions must be made to soften their impact. Even these concessions, though, do not restore fairness to the tax structure. They benefit the man who can spend his time manipulating his money to take advantage of them. They penalize the young doctor, lawyer or business executive who concentrates on his profession or his job and by his dedication, energy and talent pushes his income into upper brackets. . . .

A good tax system should also be simple. The tax laws as they now stand are so complicated that even the tax courts do not agree on what they mean, and 80,000 tax lawyers make a good living trying to interpret them to their clients. They are not always successful. Nor does the system operate with precision. Every year taxpayers pay or have withheld some $4,000,000,000 more than they owe, and thus are entitled to refunds. Internal Revenue audits show that other taxpayers, through carelessness, ignorance or chicanery, have paid in some $600,000,000 less than they owe, and are therefore subject to penalty.

From the above it may be argued that the world's fairest and most effective tax system is neither fair enough nor effective enough, and as more and more taxpayers clamor for, and are granted, special preferences, it is growing less equitable and less effective every year. . . .

The problem, therefore, is to find a plan whereby many billions of dollars now untaxed can be brought into the tax pool, and there taxed at drastically lower rates which still will provide the Government with at least as much revenue as it now receives.

President Kennedy, in his tax message, has taken tentative steps in this direction, and the base-broadening and loophole-closing measures he has recommended have been under bitter debate on Capitol Hill since May. While this battle rages, his tax experts in the Treasury and in his Council of Economic Advisers are working on the even more drastic reforms he will propose for 1962 and thereafter. . . .

. . . It was 1913 before Congress finally acquired the constitutional taxing power in holds today. The provisions of that first law should make today's taxpayers weep. It provided for an exemption of $3000 for a single person, $4000 for a married couple, with an impost of 1 percent on the first $20,000. Above that a surtax was imposed that rose to 6 percent on incomes of $500,000 or more. With these high exemptions, only a handful were affected. Since then the tax has proliferated until today more than one third of the total population is caught in its toils, and personal income taxes provide more than half of the Government's $78,500,000,000 in budget receipts.

In paying this huge tax bill, which in 1960 amounted to $40,700,000,000, the anguished taxpayer naturally feels that all his resources are being taxed away, that no dollar of income has escaped the collector's clutches. The economist knows that this is not true. In 1959, for example, individual Americans had a total personal income of $383,300,000,000. They paid taxes on $167,900,000,000.

What happened to the rest of it—the $215,400,000,000 which bore no tax? How did it escape? And why?

The answer is fairly simple. We not only use our tax laws as a source of revenue, but we temper them to serve certain social and economic ends which we believe to be worth-while. We begin by exempting all Social Security benefits. For humanitarian reasons we exempt unemployment compensation, relief payments, sick pay if it is less than $100 a week, compensation received for illness or accident, life insurance paid after death and the value of the housing allowance furnished to clergymen. For social reasons we exempt payments made to churches and charitable organizations, in the belief that the taxpayer should be encouraged to support such good causes.

Some income is exempted because it would be too hard to identify, evaluate and tax, such as the value of the food and fuel the farmer grows and consumes, and the value of the "imputed" rent that a householder who owns his own home allegedly receives.

Certain exemptions and special deductions are allowed because they are believed to serve national purposes which transcend the mere raising of revenue. The depletion allowance for oil and natural gas was written into the law because it was believed that a business so financially hazardous, and so important to the national defense, was worthy of special protection. The 25 percent applied to capital gains was designed to keep investment money flowing into the economy. The exemption from taxes of interest received from state and municipal bonds has served to encourage local governments to build roads, schools and hospitals out of private money without direct Federal subsidy. . . .

The capital-gains tax, the most complicated of the special tax concessions, was originally conceived as applying to profits made on the sale of property such as stocks or real estate. The law has since been amended to bring under the capital-gains umbrella such diverse activities as the sale of timber, royalties on inventions, livestock held for breeding, draft or dairy purposes, the sale of land with unharvested crops, royalty payments for the production of coal, and lump-sum payments from retirement plans. An asset held until death and passed on to a beneficiary pays no capital-gains tax at all, though the recipient may sell it the next day at its full market value. If it is given away to an approved charity, it is fully deductible. With so many loopholes opening up, the greatest intellectual effort being expended in the United States today, outside the halls of science, is the search for ways to convert ordinary income into capital gains. . . .

Aside from being born rich, or marrying money, the easiest way

to acquire great wealth under the present tax laws it to finance a successful search for oil—an enterprise in which many professional men, such as
doctors and lawyers, invest their spare cash, even though they may
have no more knowledge of oil geology than a baboon. For a man in
the very high brackets there is strong inducement to take a flyer in oil
even though the risks are great. If, for example, a man in the 90-percent
bracket should invest $100,000 in oil exploration and his company drills
a dry hole, his entire loss is deductible from his gross income. The
Government loses the $90,000 that he otherwise would have paid in
income tax. He loses $10,000.

If he hits oil, he is in clover. He is allowed to deduct all the
"intangible expenses" connected with drilling the producing well, and
these expenses, which include such things as geological studies, labor,
and so on, usually come to more than half the cost. In addition he can
keep a "depletion allowance" free of tax, of 27.5 percent of the income
received from the sale of oil, provided this allowance does not exceed
50 percent of net income. . . .

The original depletion laws were designed to protect the small
independent operator, who might become bankrupt after striking a few
dry holes if the tax system did not compensate him for his losses. In
practice it has largely benefited the big company, which presumably is
less in need of this protection. Data compiled by the Internal Revenue
Service in 1958 shows that 71 percent of the $3,100,000,000 in depletion
allowances claimed that year went to companies with more than
$100,000,000 in assets. . . .

The greatest clamor of complaint . . . would rise from many
efforts to change the tax laws from which most taxpayers benefit—and
which cost the Government the greatest loss in revenue. This is the
income-splitting provision which allows a married couple to file a
joint return. A brief example illustrates the value—to the taxpayer
—of this provision. Assuming that the family had a taxable
income of $14,000, all of it earned by the husband: If he should pay
taxes on this as separate income, the tax on the husband would be
$4260, the tax on the wife, nothing. If they file a joint return, each is as-
sumed to have an income of $7000. The tax on $7000 is $1660, or a
total of $3320. . . .

A device called "family income splitting" provides even juicier
benefits. A man operating a business may make all the members of his
family equal partners in the business. The business income is then divided
among the members of the family. It works like this: A man with a wife
and two children with a profit for his business of $50,000 a year would
pay $18,294 in taxes if he filed a simple joint return. By making his
wife and two children partners in the business, he would cut the total
tax by about one third. Here, too, the higher incomes get the greater

benefit. On a $5000 taxable income, under the family income-splitting plan, the tax saving would be twenty dollars. On a taxable income of $320,000, the tax saving would be $40,760. Thus the taxpayer with $320,000 in taxable income saves 2000 times as much on taxes as the man with $5000 taxable income, though his taxable income is only sixty-four times as great.

Last April President Kennedy, as he offered business corporation-tax inducements to expand and modernize, sought to balance off the revenue this plan would cost the Government by certain measures designed to improve collections, eliminate loopholes and broaden the base. These included reductions on expense-account spending, elimination of tax privileges to Americans living or doing business in "developed" countries abroad, elimination of the fifty-dollar deduction and the 4 percent tax credit on dividends, and a withholding tax on interest and dividends, to aid those with faulty memories who each year forget to report some $3,000,000,000 in such funds.

These were merely first steps toward the broad reforms which Mr. Kennedy and his treasury tax expert, Stanley Surrey, the chairman of his Council of Economic Advisers, Walter Heller and Secretary of the Treasury Douglas Dillon have in mind. Still to come are the really tough ones—the fight on the abuses of the capital-gains law, the reappraisal of the depletion allowances, a new look at the tax exemption of local and municipal bonds, and a reconsideration of the exemption on Social Security benefits, if this can be removed without affecting those in the lower brackets. Taken in the aggregate, the escape clauses and the special privileges which Mr. Kennedy has sought to eliminate already, or which he will attack in his tax message next Jaunary, narrow the tax base by nearly $30,000,000,000—and cost the Government nearly $12,000,000,000 in taxes. . . .

31.5. CONTROLLING THE FLOW OF MONEY

In addition to issuing currency, raising revenue, and spending for national defense and the general welfare, the Federal Government exercises control over the economy by regulating credit, debt managment, and interest rates through the Federal Reserve System. The Commission on Money and Credit, established by the Committee for Economic Development, explains these procedures and recommends steps for improving their administration.

THIS REPORT represents the deliberations of a diverse group of American citizens. They were assisted by an able staff of scholars and

From The Commission on Money and Credit, *Money and Credit, A Summary of the Report*, 1961.

by a group of advisers of great competence. The members of the Commission were deliberately selected to provide a group of men with different backgrounds: banking, business, government, labor, and the professions. All members had broad, practical economic experience. It could fairly be said that their conclusions represent a consensus of American philosophy and economic judgment today.

No member of the Commission, whether or not he has written or joined in specific footnotes, endorses personally every specific proposal in its entirety or concurs fully with every statement in the supporting analysis, but all approve the major substance of the report and urge careful consideration of its interrelated recommendations.

The funds for this effort were provided by The Ford Foundation, the Merrill Foundation, and the Committee for Economic Development. None of these organizations exerted the slightest pressure. There were no restrictions as to the scope and method of the work, and certainly no restrictions as to the judgments reached. . . .

The Commission recognizes that our society is based upon the dynamics of the market place. Individual decisions largely determine the direction and growth of our product and its distribution. The greater part of American activity by far is based upon the private sector. What is emphasized is the important and vital complementary role of government in helping a relatively free society to do a better job—and a better job does not envisage economic Utopia.

Although the Commission is vitally concerned with the attainment of our national goals, it recommends no precise and specific formula for this purpose. To do so would be inconsistent with our traditions and practices and probably totally unrealistic.

If we are to be free, some fluctuation in our economic growth pattern is unavoidable. If the Commission's recommendations were to be adopted, one could hope and expect that the degree of fluctuations might be further reduced. They have been reduced in the last decade. . . .

MONETARY POLICY

Control over conditions governing the quantity of money is inevitable in a modern industrial society. As the nation has adopted more positive economic goals, it has become interested in whether monetary control can be used flexibly to influence the behavior of expenditures, output, employment, and prices. Clearly it can, but monetary adjustments alone cannot ensure attainment of these goals. On the other hand, the lack of an appropriate monetary policy can frustrate their accomplishment.

Changes in the degree of restraint or ease in monetary policy have an effect on the total flow of expenditures and in turn on output, employment, and prices. Because the link between the initial actions taken by the Federal Reserve to influence bank reserves and these variables is general, pervasive, and indirect, and because no attempt is made by the monetary authority to allocate credit among specific users, this approach to monetary policy is frequently referred to as general monetary control.

The concept underlying general monetary control is relatively straightforward. Monetary restraint reduces the availability of credit and increases its cost; and these retard the flow of expenditures, employment, income, and output. Monetary ease in general has the opposite effects on credit, and thus encourages an expansion in these flows.

The Federal Reserve System exercises general monetary control through the use of three major instruments. These are: (1) The power to set the level of required reserves that member banks must hold; (2) engagement in open market operations, which alter the volume of actual reserve balances available to banks; and (3) changes in the terms under which banks may replenish a deficiency in required reserves by borrowing from the Federal Reserve banks. All three instruments of policy, and open market operations in particular, directly affect the net reserve position of member banks. They also have direct impacts on other economic variables. . . .

The Federal Reserve autority may attempt to restrain economic activity by engaging in open market sales of Treasury bills. These sales influence at least six distinguishable elements in the economy: net bank reserves are reduced; the money supply falls; the price of government securities tend to decline and yields to rise; the money value of total assets tends to fall; the over-all liquidity of financial portfolios is reduced; and the ability and willingness of banks to lend is reduced.

With interest rates higher, some individuals and businesses reduce their demand deposits on which they earn nothing and purchase securities or shift to interest bearing thrift deposits. The demand deposits are made available to other individuals and businesses who wish to increase their expenditures, or to financial institutions which make loans to individuals and businesses who want to borrow to increase their outlays. Thus, even though the money supply has not expanded, the mobilization of idle balances will finance more expenditures, and the velocity of money is increased. But this does not mean that a restrictive monetary policy is fully offset.

Monetary restraint causes a reduction in the willingness and ability of nearly all institutional lenders to meet all the credit demands made on them. While it is difficult to make any precise assessment of the volume of loans refused during recent tight money episodes, it appears to have been substantial.

Monetary restraint also affects the desire of the public to spend, through the changes it brings about in the rate of interest and in the market value of income-yielding assets, and the liquidity of the public's wealth holdings. . . .

Changes in monetary policy have other less direct effects on the rate of expenditures than through their effect on the cost and availability of credit. The very announcement or recognition of a change in monetary policy may contribute to changes in attitudes and expectations as to the future rate of growth of demand, sales, income, and profits and the future level of prices. These attitude changes may have a substantial effect on investment expenditures since a direct restraint in state and local construction, residential construction, and some categories of business investment will reduce the flow of new orders to a wide range of businesses. Moreover, job uncertainty for employees may also increase, and consumers may become less willing to incur new indebtedness, and curtail consumer durable purchases.

A policy of monetary ease to stimulate an expansion of expenditures operates through the same processes as a restrictive policy but in the reverse direction. An expansive policy would tend to increase the net reserve position of member banks, to increase the prices and reduce the yields on Treasury securities, to improve the liquidity of banks and other lending institutions, to enhance the wealth position of all holders of financial assets, and to increase the money supply. These changes, however, may not be as effective in stimulating economic activity, as the reverse measures can be in restraining it. . . .

CHOICE AND COMBINATION OF INSTRUMENTS

Because they influence our economy in so many important ways, it is essential that federal policies on expenditures, taxation, debt management, and credit terms should be explicitly chosen in such a way as to foster the achievement of sustained high employment, reasonable price stability, and adequate rate of growth. Those goals cannot be achieved by the private enterprise system alone or by the federal government alone, but we are not likely to achieve them unless monetary, fiscal, debt management, and credit policies are chosen with reference to their effect on the achievement of those goals. It is not appropriate to blame the government for every defect in the performance of our economy. But when the economy's performance is not entirely satisfactory, it is appropriate to ask whether changes in government policies can be made to improve its performance.

For economic prescription to be precise, economic diagnosis must be correct. Such diagnosis is likely to be laggard, imperfect and sometimes wrong. In actual practice we shall usually be uncertain as to the character of our economic difficulties. This necessarily limits the effectiveness of the use of single control instrument and of a combination of them. The improvement of diagnosis is vital to the full use of the refinements suggested here. Nevertheless, our policy measures can be combined more effectively than in the past even with the present state of the art of appraising current business conditions. . . .

Several sets of basic decisions by the government are involved. The first is an evaluation of proposals for government expenditure programs against the alternative of either an equivalent amount of private consumption expenditures and/or private investment. These are political decisions and must be made through the democratic process. The Commission said, however, that the decisions on government expenditure and direct lending programs should be made in terms of a high employment budget and on the basis of judgments as to the value of the programs compared with the value of the private consumption or investment. The bulk of the expenditures under such programs should then proceed smoothly without being changed for countercyclical purposes.

The second relates to the normal tax structure. The Commission has stated that there should be a clear separation between the normal tax structure and temporary tax adjustments made for stabilization reasons. It has stated its deep conviction that the basic tax structure should be designed so as to be equitable, and to provide adequate investment and work incentives, and then left unchanged for a time. However, because the tax structure affects the levels and the composition of personal consumption and saving, the level of private investment expenditure, the levels of business saving, and work and investment incentives, the basic tax structure should be related to the strength of the underlying trends in the economy, especially that of private investment demand. It should be designed to influence the level of private investment and the level of consumption so that they together with government expenditures will generate full employment. It should also take into account the stimulus to private investment desired to enhance the growth rate of the economy.

A third decision relates to the magnitude of the money supply. The Commission has urged that the money supply be increased over the long run at a rate commensurate with the productive potential of the economy. Increases in the money supply are, in effect, the portion of current saving that the public chooses to hold as cash balances. The public also chooses to hold additional portions of current saving in the form of highly liquid earning assets, such as savings and time deposits, savings and loan shares, savings bonds, short-term government securities, and other readily marketable short-term securities. The demand for liquid assets in the form of money is not a constant proportion of total output in the economy. The preferences of the public for liquid reserves shifts between money and other liquid assets with changes in their relative yields and their relative availabilities. The monetary authority must allow for these changing preferences in providing the proper amount of money to match the proportion of current saving that the public wishes to hold in this particular form.

It should be noted also that the supply of some other types of liquid assets is under the control of the Treasury. By its debt management activities, the Treasury can increase the portion of its debt which is in the form of short-term bills and savings bonds. As the economy grows, there will be an increased demand for liquid assets of types such as these and the Treasury needs to take this into account in its long-range debt management policies. The Treasury and the monetary authority must work in harmony in the provision of money and short-term securities because, to a degree at least, one form is substitutable for the other.

In almost every recession situation, whatever its cause, there is danger that an initial decline in income will lead to a further decline in expenditures and income and so on in a cumulative downward spiral. The first object of policy, therefore, should be to ensure that such a spiral does not develop. The automatic stabilization resulting from changes in tax and transfer payments has already greatly reduced our vulnerability to downward cumulative processes. Monetary policy can be gradually eased and the debt structure can be shortened to provide downward pressure on interest rates; credit terms for federally insured and guaranteed mortgage loans can be eased. Placing of government orders can be expedited and government expenditures on existing programs can be increased to expand demand.

If action is confined to these policy measures, which can be moved gradually and quickly reversed, the chance that a recession will develop is reduced, while the risk of creating excessive demand is minimized.

If demand resumes its upward course, we can—according to the rapidity of its growth—refrain from further expansive action or reverse the action already taken. If demand fails to increase sufficiently, stronger policy measures to encourage demand can be undertaken gradually.

Ordinarily, temporary tax reductions should not be used before an actual decline in income has occurred. But when income grows slowly for any considerable length of time, and when unemployment and excess capacity have risen to unsatisfactory high levels, the balance between tax revenues and government expenditures should be reassessed to ascertain whether our basic fiscal policy is unduly restrictive. . . .

ORGANIZATION AND COORDINATION

The policy recommendations which the Commission has made in the preceding chapters of this report touch the jurisdictions of many departments and agencies, state as well as national. In order to implement the policy measures advocated by the Commission and to foster the simultaneous achievement of three-fold goals, higher rate of sustainable growth, lower levels of unemployment, and more stable price levels, changes in the organization and structure of some of these agencies and departments are necessary. . . .

Coordination is one of the most difficult and delicate of the organizational demands that can be made upon a governmental system as large and as decentralized as that of the United States. It is also one of the most urgent because the goals of policy are multiple, and success depends on their simultaneous fulfilment; and because the instruments of policy are interdependent and to an important degree interchangeable. If unemployment levels, price level stability, and economic growth hang together on the outcome of a combination of a great many moves, how can the actions be knowledgeably and purposefully concerted?

For present purposes, problems of coordination seem especially acute and critical in four areas: (1) at the top-center of the Administration, the President and his so-called Executive Office, including such staff aids as the Budget Bureau and the Council of Economic Advisers; (2) in the interdepartmental domestic field where monetary, fiscal, and credit policies impinge and where the Treasury, the Federal Reserve and the major agricultural and housing credit agencies operate; (3) in the also inter-departmental foreign field where the balance of payments is an object of concern and State, Treasury, Defense, Agriculture, and the foreign lending agencies pursue their several objectives; and (4) in the interactions between the executive and the Congress. . . .

The simultaneous achievement of the low levels of unemployment, reasonably stable prices, and an adequate rate of growth will require finer adjustments in the use and coordination of the tools of economic policy than our government has so far been able to manage. It is a task for the sixties to do better.

There is a normal presumption that when Congress legislates it will phrase its mandates as specifically as circumstances allow, for our traditions run against unrestricted delegations of power. There is an equally normal presumption that a prudent lawgiver will not tie the hands of the executive where that may defeat the larger ends in view; and statesmen do not seek high office to perform merely ministerial tasks. Commonly, Congress strikes some balance between delegation and speci-fication, even within a single statute. When specifics are frozen into law, they sometimes prove later on to be obstacles to the development of a policy that needs to be based on wider perspectives than were in the minds of the framers of the law.

The Commission believes it is a good rule to state objectives broadly, to fix responsibilities sharply, and to make available in statutory authorizations a variety of means for their discharge. In fuller observance of that rule lie opportunities for better executive coordination and improved cooperation between Congress and the executive for the furtherance of national goals.

Index

615